AF527734

EARLY BUDDHISM AND THE BHAGAVADGĪTĀ

Early Buddhism and The Bhagavadgītā

Kashi Nath Upadhyaya

MOTILAL BANARSIDASS PUBLISHERS
PRIVATE LIMITED • DELHI

Reprint: Delhi, 1983, 1998, 2008
First Edition: Delhi, 1971

ISBN: 978-81-208-0880-5

MOTILAL BANARSIDASS
41 U.A. Bungalow Road, Jawahar Nagar, Delhi 110 007
8 Mahalaxmi Chamber, 22 Bhulabhai Desai Road, Mumbai 400 026
203 Royapettah High Road, Mylapore, Chennai 600 004
236, 9th Main III Block, Jayanagar, Bangalore 560 011
Sanas Plaza, 1302 Baji Rao Road, Pune 411 002
8 Camac Street, Kolkata 700 017
Ashok Rajpath, Patna 800 004
Chowk, Varanasi 221 001

PRINTED IN INDIA

BY JAINENDRA PRAKASH JAIN AT SHRI JAINENDRA PRESS,
A-45 NARAINA, PHASE-I, NEW DELHI 110 028
AND PUBLISHED BY NARENDRA PRAKASH JAIN FOR
MOTILAL BANARSIDASS PUBLISHERS PRIVATE LIMITED,
BUNGALOW ROAD, DELHI 110 007

DEDICATION

Yataḥ pravṛttir bhūtānāṃ yena sarvam idaṃ tatam
svakarmaṇā tam abhyarcya siddhiṃ vindati mānavaḥ

—B. G. XVIII 46

"He from whom all beings arise and by whom all this is pervaded—by worshipping Him through his own work does man attain perfection."

Taṃ cāhaṃ abhivandāmi mahesi santim uttamaṃ
yaṃ viditvā sato caraṃ tare loke visattikaṃ

—Sn. p. 205

"I also bow down to (thee), the unsurpassed Peace, O great sage, by knowing which one dwells on thoughtfully, and overcomes enticement in the world."

PREFACE

Hinduism and Buddhism are, undoubtedly, the two best known philosophical traditions of India. Despite the fact that they seem to hold mutually opposed points of view in relation to some major philosophical questions such as those of God, soul, scriptural authority, etc., they are both held in very high esteem, and are acclaimed for their moral earnestness, spiritual insight and philosophical profundity. A critical and comparative understanding of the fundamental ideas and principles of the two traditions, therefore, is a great desideratum.

Both Hinduism and Buddhism, however, in the long course of their continued growth, have given rise to many schools and sub-schools and their literatures have become so enormously vast and confoundingly diversified, that it is well-nigh an impossibility to attempt a comprehensive, comparative study of the total stock of the two systems of thought,[1] unless one focuses one's attention on some specific phases of their development. Some attempts have been made, for example, to deal comparatively with some branches or aspects of the Mahāyāna school of Buddhism and the Advaita school of the Vedānta.[2] Notwithstanding the merit and value of such comparative studies, one cannot lose sight of the fact that the two schools represent the later phases of the respective traditions, by which time considerable interpenetration of ideas had already taken place, and, hence they had undergone significant changes. It has, therefore, been considered more fruitful for our purpose to attempt a critical and comparative analysis and assessment of the two traditions in their early phases.

The Bhagavadgītā has been looked upon in traditional

1. A small book published under the name, *'Buddhism and Hinduism'* by G. Upadhyaya (Banaras Hindu University Publication) can hardly be regarded as a *comprehensive*, comparative work on the two traditions.

2. Cf. *Dialectic in Buddhism and Vedānta*, and *Bauddha Darshana aur Vedānta* (in Hindi) by Chandradhar Sharma; *Vedānta and Buddhism* by H. Von Glasenapp (Kandy, Ceylon : Wheel Publication, 1958.

Hinduism as containing the quintessence of the Upaniṣads[3], and the latter in turn have been regarded as 'the culmination of the Vedic thought' (vedānta). The Bhagavadgītā, therefore, has rightly been regarded as representing "Hinduism as a whole"[4] and constituting "the philosophical basis"[5] of it. The Pali Canon, particularly the Sutta Piṭaka, on the other hand, represents the earliest collection of the teachings of Buddha. The present work, therefore, seeks to explain and evaluate critically and comparatively the fundamental ideas and doctrines of the Bhagavadgītā and early Buddhism (as embodied in the early stratum of the Pali Canon).

Although there are many books dealing independently with either early Buddhism or the Bhagavadgītā, no attempt has hitherto been made to undertake a systematic and comprehensive study of the two in a critical and comparative manner, except for some casual observations and stray remarks here and there. Naturally, many of the significant ideas which could be brought to focus by viewing the problems in a comparative light have either escaped attention of scholars, or have not been prominently brought out by them. Such a study is particularly relevant in view of the fact that there is a general tendency on the part of scholars to undermine the significant philosophical differences, on the one hand, and to overlook some essential elements of unity, on the other, implying thereby that Buddhism basically is either the reorientation and development of the same traditional thought[6] or is a

3. Sarvopaniṣado gāvo dogdhā gopālanandanaḥ
Pārtho vatsaḥ sudhīr bhoktā dugdhaṃ gītāmṛtaṃ mahat.

4. S. Radhākrishnan, *The Bhagavadgītā* (London : George Allen and Unwin, 1967), p. 12.

5. S. Radhākrishnan, *Indian Philosophy*, vol. I (London : George Allen and Unwin, 1958), p. 521.

6. Cf. S. Radhākrishnan who observes; "Early Buddhism...is only a restatement of the thought of the Upaniṣads from a new standpoint.", *Indian Philosophy*, vol. I (London : George Allen and Unwin, 1958), p. 361. Similarly Chandradhar Sharma remarks : "Buddhism and Vedānta should not be viewed as two opposed systems but only as different stages in the development of the same central thought which starts with the Upaniṣads, ...*Indian Philosophy* (Banaras : Nand Kishore and Bros., 1952) p. 456. Cf. Mrs. Rhys Davids, *Buddhism* (New York, H. Holt and Company, 1912), pp. 83-85; Oldenberg, *Buddha*, tr. by William Hoey (London, Edinburgh : William and Norgate, 1882), p. 53.

protest and revolt against it.[7] At any rate, it has not been considered worthwhile by any scholar to undertake comprehensive, critical, and comparative study of these two important foundational works of the two traditions. The fact that early Buddhism and the Bhagavadgītā are both noted for their intensely practical concerns makes it all the more imperative to bring together their respective points of view for examination and evaluation.

The comparative study of the two works seemed to necessitate a decision with regard to their relative chronology, since the opinions of scholars are widely divided in relation to the question as to whether the Bhagavadgītā is a pre-or post-Buddhistic work. There appear to be certain elements which the Bhagavadgītā has in common with early Buddhism, whereas in some other respects it seems to run counter to the latter. Since many of the doctrines of both the Gītā and early Buddhism can also be traced to the Upaniṣads, the question of borrowing from a common source, as well as that of the one influencing the other, can be decided only through a careful examination of all the available historical data. With this purpose in view, the first two chapters of the book have been devoted to a historical discussion bearing on the chronology and sources of the Gītā and early Buddhism. This discussion is intended to provide historical perspective to the subsequent philosophical discussions of the book, and to lend support to their conclusions. But even if the historical findings are challenged, the results of the comparative philosophical analysis and assessment would remain important and useful in their own right.

The philosophical discussions are contained in the last three chapters of the book. In them, the attempt has been made to cover the whole field of epistemology, metaphysics and ethics in detail and depth. The discussion is based throughout on the original texts, and conclusions are reached by relying on original sources rather than by following the sign posts of other scholars. To make the expositions and

7. Cf. K.N. Jayatilleke, '*Some Aspects of Gītā and Buddhist Ethics*', in U.C.R., vol. XIII, Nos. 2 and 3, pp. 135-151.

criticisms clear and easily intelligible, care has been taken to avoid technical philosophical jargon as far as possible. My desire all through has been to be objective and impartial. Although in dealing with religio-philosophical matters, it is difficult to escape the shadows of one's own approach and the influences of the intellectual atmosphere in which one's mind is nurtured and shaped, yet the genuineness of commitment to truth, it is hoped, will have sufficiently helped me in extending fair and objective treatment to both the systems of thought, and in highlighting the value of their respective approaches. In any case, it is hoped that my effort will arouse interest in the hitherto ignored comparative study of the basic works of the two traditions.

While presenting this book to readers, I am deeply sorry that the late Professor K. N. Jayatilleke, Head of the Department of Philosophy, University of Ceylon, who was most interested in the publication of this work, and who had been a constant source of inspiration to me, is no longer with us to see this work in print. I was waiting for a foreword to the book from him when the shocking news of his sudden and premature death came to me. It is under his guidance that the work was originally submitted for the Ph. D. degree in Philosophy at the University of Ceylon in 1964, although it has been cosiderably changed and revised since then. I am deeply indebted to him, and the references made in the body of the work do not sufficiently indicate the extent of my obligation to him. It is also with a deep sense of gratitude that I remember Dr. G. D. Wijayawardhana, Lecturer in Sinhalese, University of Ceylon, who helped me in many ways during the course of my studies in Ceylon. I would also like to express my thankfulness to Mr. P. D. Premasiri and Mr. N. Abhayawardhana, Lecturers in Pali and Buddhist civilization, University of Ceylon, whose discussions with me on Buddhist Philosophy were quite helpful. (The latter has now assumed the name Śrī Jñānānanda, as a Buddhist monk.) I must also place on record my thankfulness to the Government of Ceylon whose award of Commonwealth Scholarship enabled me to carry on my work at the University of Ceylon.

In this book I am using, with additions and alterations, two of my previously published papers, 'The Impact of Early Buddhism on Hindu Thought (With Special Reference to the Bhagavadgītā)' and 'The Bhagavadgītā on War and Peace.' They appeared in slightly different form in *Philosophy East and West*, vol. 18 (3), July 1968, and vol. 19 (2), April 1969 respectively. They are used by permission of the University of Hawaii Press, for which I am thankful to the Press and the Editor, *Philosophy East and West.* In preparing the Index of the book I have received ungrudging help from Mr. Edward J. Quigley, Graduate Assistant of Philosophy, University of Hawaii, for which I am obliged to him.

I must also thank my publisher, Motilal Banarsidass, who has shown unusual promptness in bringing out the book.

K. N. Upadhyaya
January 21, 1971

ABBREVIATIONS

A.	Aṅguttara Nikāya
AA.	Aṅguttara Nikāya Aṭṭhakathā, i.e. Manorathapūraṇī
A.A.S.	Ānanda Āśrama Series
Ait.	Aitareya Upaniṣad
Ait. Brāh.	Aitareya Brāhmaṇa
B.G.	Bhagavadgītā
B.H.S.	Buddhist Hybrid Sanskrit
Bṛhadā.	Bṛhadāraṇyaka Upaniṣad
B.S.O.S.	Bulletin of the School of Oriental and African Society.
Chānd.	Chāndogya Upaniṣad
D.	Dīgha Nikāya
D.A.	Dīgha Nikāya Aṭṭhakathā, i.e. Sumaṅgalavilāsinī
Dh.	Dhammapada
DhA.	Dhammapada Aṭṭhakathā
H.O.S.	Harvard Oriental Series
I.A.	Indian Antiquary
It.	Itivuttaka
J.A.O.S.	Journal of the American Oriental Society
J B.O.R.S.	Journal of Bihar and Orissa Research Society
J.P.T.S.	Journal of the Pali Text Society
J.R.A.S.	Journal of the Royal Asiatic Society
Kaus.	Kauṣītakī Upaniṣad
M.	Majjhima Nikāya
MB.	Mahābhārata
Muṇḍ.	Muṇḍaka Upaniṣad
O.Z.	Ostasiatische Zeitschrift
P.T.S.	Pali Text Society
P.U.	The Principal Upaniṣads
R.B.G.	Commentary of Rāmānuja on the Bhagavadgītā
S.	Saṃyutta Nikāya

Ś.A.	Saṃyutta Nikāya Aṭṭhakathā, i.e. Sāratthappakāsinī
Śat. Brāh.	Śatapatha Brāhmaṇa
S.B.B.	Sacred Books of the Buddhists
S.B.E.	Sacred Books of the East
S.B.G.	Commentary of Śaṅkara on the Bhagavadagītā
S.B.H.	Sacred Books of the Hindus
Sn.	Suttanipāta
Sn. A.	Suttanipāta Aṭṭhakathā, i.e. Paramatthajotikā II
Śvetā.	Śvetāśvatara Upaniṣad
Tait.	Taittirīya Upaniṣad
Tait. Brāh.	Taittirīya Brāhmaṇa
U.C.R.	University of Ceylon Review
Ud.	Udāna
Up.	Upaniṣad
Vin.	Vinaya Piṭaka
Vm.	Visuddhimagga
Z.D.M.G.	Zeitschrift Deutschen Morganlandischen Gesellschaft.

CONTENTS

SECTION C

CHAPTER II

SECTION A

SECTION B

SECTION C

CHAPTER III

CHAPTER IV

CHAPTER V

Chapter I

Section A

THE CHRONOLOGY OF THE BHAGAVADGĪTĀ

The Divergent Views of Scholars :—

The chronology of the Bhagavadgītā has been widely discussed by scholars both of the East as well as of the West, and widely have they differed in their opinions, so much so that the range of difference covers a period of at least one thousand years.

To mention a few of them, Dr. Lorinser thinks that the Gītā might have been composed after about 500 A.D., for he sees in it influences of the Christian religion.[1] Talboys Wheeler regards it "evidently a product of a Brahmanical age and presumably also a later age."[2] According to Garbe the Original Gītā belongs to 200 B. C. and its present form to 200 A.D.[3] K. T. Telang thinks that "the latest date at which the Gītā can have been composed must be earlier than the 3rd century B.C., though it is altogether impossible to say at present how much earlier."[4] Rudolf Otto feels that "the third century B.C. is perhaps too low a limit for 'The Original Gītā' while the insertion of the individual treatises may have been effected very much later, and was presumably a rather prolonged process."[5] John Davies in his work on the Bhagavadgītā concludes "that the Bhagavadgītā cannot probably be referred to an earlier period than the third century A.C." and with regard to the question of the author's acquaintance with Christian doctrines, he agrees with A. Weber that it "is still subjudice."[6] W. Douglas P. Hill thinks that "this theory (of a

1. Indian Antiquary, Vol. II, 1873, pp. 283 ff.
2. History of India, Vol. I, p. 288.
3. Die Bhagavadgītā, p. 64.
4. S.B.E. Vol. VIII, pp. 21 & 34
5. The Original Gītā, p. 14.
6. Trübner's Oriental Series, 1882, 89; Weber—Hist. of Indian Lit. p. 238, foot note 252a.

Christian influence on the Gītā) is now almost universally discredited" and that "the internal evidence points to the second century B.C. as the period when the Gītā in its present form appeared."[1] R. G. Bhandarkar thinks that the Gītā is at least as old as the fourth century B.C.[2] B. G. Tilak tries to establish through his long-drawn arguments that the Gītā must have been in existence in its present form at least in 500 B.C.[3] According to Radhakrishnan "its date may be assigned to the 5th century B.C., though the text may have received many alterations in subsequent times."[4] Swami Vireswarananda thinks that "the date of the Gītā and the original Mahābhārata, of which the Gītā is a part, can be fixed before the time of Buddha. Both of them are pre-Buddhistic, for they contain no reference to Buddha and Buddhism."[5]

These diverse and mutually conflicting views, it is clear, will prove more a hindrance than a help in deciding the issue, and one is bound to feel bewildered amidst this welter of conflicting opinions.

The Gītā, as we find it today, is a part of the Bhīsma-Parva of the great epic, the Mahābhārata. But here also serious doubts are raised if the Gītā was, from its very beginning, a genuine constituent of the Mahābhārata. A further controversy arises as to whether the present Gītā (irrespective of being a genuine constituent of the Mahābhārata or an independent one) is the single work of one man or it has undergone various additions and alterations in successive ages. On both these issues opinions are again divided, and they contradict and cancel one another.

Mr. Talboys Wheeler, for example, considers the Gītā as an interpolation, "evidently the product of a Brahmanical age."[6] K. T. Telang, on the other hand, is "prepared to adhere to the theory of the genuineness of the Bhagavadgītā as a portion of the original Mahābhārata" and remarks that the ideas of

1. The Bhagavadgītā, p. 276 & p. 18.
2. Vaishnavism, Shaivism and Minor Religious systems. p. 13.
3. Gītā Rahasya—Appendix, p. 579.
4. The Bhagavadgītā, p. 14; see also Ind. Phil., Vol. I, p. 524.
5. Brahma Sūtras, Introduction, p. ix.
6. History of India, Vol. I, p. 288.

Mr. Wheeler "are scarcely appropriate to our old literature."[1] According to Holtzmann the original Mahābhārata was turned into a Dharmaśāstra by the Brāhmans after 900 A.D.[2] Opposite is the view of A.A. Macdonell who says, "In any case, the present state of our knowledge entirely disproves the suggestions put forward by Professor Holtzmann in his work on the Mahābhārata, that the epic was turned into a Dharmaśāstra by the Brāhmans after 900 A.D. and that whole books were added at this late period" and he thinks that "an extension of the original epic must have taken place after 300 B.C. and by the beginning of our era."[3] According to Garbe, the text is a composite work. He believed that the original kernel was a Sāṅkhya treatise, which was later worked over and expanded by an adherent of the later Vedānta philosophy. He thought he could detect and eliminate these later Vedāntic accretions, and he printed them in a type of smaller size in his translation of the Bhagavadgītā.[4] A pupil of Garbe, the late Rudolf Otto, has carried this dissection of the Gītā to a far greater extent. According to him the Original Gītā is "purely and entirely a splendid epic fragment; not the doctrinal literature of any system...., 'doctrinal writ' subsequently became inserted, with the view of securing for it the authority of Krishna's divine Form."[5] Franklin Edgerton, refuting this theory, says: "My own interpretation tacitly assumes the unity of the Gītā."[6] The late Professor Winternitz was one of those who once accepted Garbe's theory, but later in the English version of his History of Indian Literature, he abandoned it, though he was still more inclined to dissect the Gītā than F. Edgerton is.[7] Dahlmann regards not

1. S.B.E. Vol. VIII, pp. 5-6.
2. Das Mahābhārata I. 194.
3. A History of Sanskrit Literature, pp. 286-288.
4. Die Bhagavadgītā, pp. 7, 13-14.
5. The Original Gītā, pp. 10-12.
6. The Bhagavadgītā or Song of the Blessed One, p. 99.
7. "I was formerly in entire agreement with Garbe. However, after repeated readings of the Gītā and the most thorough investigation of the passages cut out by Garbe, I have come to the conclusion that even the Original Poem did not teach pure theism, but theism tinged with pantheism. I do not now believe that we are justified in pronouncing as interpolated all those passages where Kṛṣṇa speaks of himself as immanent in the world."

only the Gītā but also the whole of the Mahābhārata as the work of "one single poetical creative genius."[1] B. G. Tilak also, to a great extent, subscribes to this view.[2] But Professor M. Winternitz attacks this view very vehemently and says that "our present day text of the epic contains not only much that is diverse in content, but also much that is diverse in value. In truth, he who would believe with the orthodox Hindus and the above mentioned Western scholars, that our Mahābhārata, in its present form, is the work of one single man would be forced to the conclusion that this man was at one and the same time, a great poet and a wretched scribbler, a sage and an idiot, a talented artist and a ridiculous pedant..."[3]

The Need for an Analytic Approach :—

In view of all these conflicting and mutually inadjustable views, the entire issue has to be examined *de novo* and with the fullest possible care and caution without letting any bias or prejudice throw its weight on us. The question being a complicated one, we may, for the sake of clarity and precision, divide the entire issue into three parts, and attempt their solution one by one: (a) Is the Gītā a genuine constituent of the Mahābhārata ? (b) Has it undergone any additions and alterations at different times ? and (c) What date can be assigned to it ? The parts are so much interlinked that unless the preceding questions are properly settled, no fruitful investigation with regard to the last can be made.

Is the Gītā a Genuine Constituent of the Mahābhārata ?

The genuineness of the Gītā as a portion of the Mahābhārata is doubted mainly on the ground that it is incongruous and irrelevant to enter into a long moral and spiritual preaching at a critical juncture of the commencement of the war. But a thorough probe into the nature and intent of the great epic can at once expose the incogency of this apparently plausible contention.

However, he continues to think "that the original Bhagavadgītā was much shorter, and the work in its present form contains many interpolations and additions."—A Hist. of Indian Lit, Vol. I, p. 436.

1. Das Mahābhārata als Epos Und Rechtsbuch. p. 302.
2. Gītā Rahasya—Appendix.
3. A History of Indian Literature pp. 460-1.

The Mahābhārata is, evidently, not a bare historical treatise, and so it is too much to expect an exact and accurate account of historical events from its contents. It is, no doubt, based on an historical theme, but the author, highly religious and poetic, as he appears to be, takes full liberty to fashion it out into an enormous epic and Dharma-śāstra. Even a casual survey of the Mahābhārata will at once indicate that the author is uniformly eager to elaborate the principles of dharma whenever and wherever he finds an opportunity to do so. In the 'Karṇa Parva' Kṛṣṇa is found to dissuade Arjuna from killing Yudhiṣṭhira by discussing at some length the problem of truth and untruth, right and wrong.[1] In the 'Vana-Parva' also, trading in meat is defended by the Vyādha in a somewhat similar discourse between him and the Brāhman.[2] Similarly in the 'Tulādhāra-Jājali-dialogue' Tulādhāra justifies the profession of a pedlar by advancing arguments in support of it.[3] These and other such scattered references amply indicate that the author is anxious to bring out, as prominently as possible, his views about the relentless discharge of one's own duty (Svadharma) at all costs and in all situations. It is needless to say that he could have found no better occasion to impart these teachings than this critical juncture of the commencement of the great war when, to add poignancy to the situation, Arjuna is placed against his own friends and relatives, elders and teacher. This, indeed, is a very delicate situation which demands pertinently the determination of the right course of action. It is, thus, quite in keeping with the context that the author undertakes to discuss here at some length the problem of dharma and adharma. By discussing it here with the central theme, viz. the great war of the epic, he has been able to secure a prominent place to his moral and spiritual ideas which, if taught elsewhere, might possibly have been lost sight of. So if the author has worked up a few pointed advices of Kṛṣṇa to Arjuna into a poem of seven hundred verses, it is not at all 'incongruous' or out of context in an enormous work of one lakh of verses, specially if the true nature and the intent of the epic with a

1. Karṇa-Parva, pp. 49-51.
2. Vana-Parva, pp. 206-215.
3. Śānti-Parva, pp. 260-263.

bit of historical imagination of the predominantly religious temperament of the age is taken due note of. E. Senart has rightly pointed out that "the doctrine which is taught there (in the B.G.) with system appears in a more or less developed form in twenty other places of the M.B. and, in fact, it is the system which inspires and dominates the entire epic at least in its definite form."[1]

Besides, there are several references to the Bhagavadgītā in the Mahābhārata itself which clearly indicate that from the time of the composition of the Mahābhārata, the Gītā has been a genuine constituent of it. The first reference to the Bhagavadgītā is found in the very beginning of the Ādi Parva in the course of recounting the contents of its second chapter.[2] Again while enumerating the chapters and verses of the eighteen Parvas, the Gītā is evidently indicated in the course of the description of the Bhīṣma Parva.[3] Similarly in the Ādi Parva Dhṛtarāṣtra, while enumerating the disheartening foreshadows about Duryodhana's victory, makes clear reference to the teachings of the Gītā.[4] Again in the Śānti Parva Vaiśampāyana while narrating the tradition of the Bhāgavata dharma to Janamejaya says that this dharma has directly been revealed by Nārāyaṇa to Nārada and the same has been stated in a nutshell in the 'Hari Gītā' which is but another name for the Bhagavadgītā.[5] Further in another chapter of this very Parva a clear mention of the Gītā is found.[6] Yet another mention of it is found in verse No. 53 of the same chapter.[7] Thereafter in the Aśvamedha Parva when Yudhiṣṭhira has been enthroned and everything is over and Kṛṣṇa expresses his desire to go to Dvārakā, Arjuna requests him to repeat the teachings that the latter had imparted at the time of the com-

---

1. Origines Bouddhiques, trans. by Manoranjan Roy, I.H.Q., Vol. 6, p. 668.
2. Pūrvoktaṃ Bhagavadgītāparva Bhīṣmavadhastataḥ. Ādi. 2. 69.
3. Kaśmalaṃ yatra pārthasya Vāsudevo mahāmatiḥ,
Mohajaṃ nāśayāmāsa hetubhir mokṣadarśibhiḥ. Ādi. 2.247.
4. Yadā śrauṣaṃ kaśmalenābhipanne rathopasthe sīdamāne'rjune vai
Kṛṣṇaṃ lokān darśayānaṃ śarīre tadā nāśaṃse vijayāya sañjaya.
Ādi. 1.179.
5. Kathito Harigītāsu samāsavidhi kalpitaḥ. Śānti. 346. 10.
6. Samupoḍheṣvanīkeṣu Kurupāṇḍavayormṛdhe,
Arjune vimanaske ca gītā Bhagavatā svayam. Śānti. 348. 8.
7. Śānti. 348. 53.

mencement of the war. Kṛṣṇa thereupon indicating difficulties of reproducing it exactly in the same manner, says something in its place which is known as Anugītā, some ideas of which agree closely with the Bhagavadgītā.[1]

These internal references leave little doubt about the fact that the Gītā constitutes an integral part of the Mahābhārata. It would be an excessive and unwarranted scepticism, if one were to doubt the genuineness of all these references scattered over so many Parvas, and to consider them all as deliberate later interpolations.

But even this extreme scepticism will be removed if one undertakes to compare the words, passages, language, versification and ideas of the Gītā and the Mahābhārata. To take a few examples, such words as 'anta' (Gītā II.16), 'bhāṣā' (Gītā II.54), 'Brahma' in the sense of Prakṛti (Gītā XIV.3), 'yoga' in the sense of Karmayoga (Gītā II.39, 50, V.1) and the suffix 'ha' (Gītā II.9)—are not used by later litterateurs like Kālidāsa etc. in the senses in which they have been used in the Gītā. Similarly, the words 'namaskṛtvā' (Gītā XI.35), 'śakya ahaṃ' (Gītā XI.48) and 'senānīnāmahaṃ skandaḥ' (Gītā X.24)—are not in accordance with the grammatical rules of Pāṇini. The Mahābhārata also exhibits similar uses of words and phrases. K. T. Telang and B. G. Tilak, after a long comparison of the Gītā and the Mahābhārata have shown that the two have similar uses of ancient words and combinations, (sandhi) which are not sanctioned by later grammarians like Pāṇini and others and, consequently, not found in later literatures like those of Kālidāsa etc.[2] Not contented with it, B. G. Tilak has given scores of examples of the same or at least similar verses and passages occurring both in the Gītā as well as in the Mahābhārata. These examples of similarities are not restricted to one or two chapters of the Gītā and the Mahābhārata but are taken from almost the entire body of their texts. So it is possible neither for the Gītā to copy out so many verses from different chapters of the enormously extended mass of

1. Aśvamedha-Parva. 16. 9-13.
2. Telang—English Translation of the Bhagavadgītā (Introduction), S.B.E. Vol. VIII. p. 13 ff. Tilak—Gītā-Rahasya (Appendix) pp. 515-6.

the M. B. nor for the huge bulk of the M.B. itself to take out verses from almost every chapter of the Gītā and assimilate them in its various Parvas. This clearly shows that the Gītā is a genuine constituent of the Mahābhārata.

Viewed from the standpoint of their ideas also, they are found to be much in agreement with each other. It is evident from the statement of the Mahābhārata itself (Śānti 346.10) that the Gītā contains the elements of Nārāyaṇīya or Bhāgavata dharma described in the Nārāyaṇīyopākhyāna (Śānti 334-351). Though the Gītā does not accept the idea of Caturvyūha of Bhāgavata dharma and holds fast to ekavyūha, it does not make any material difference. In fact the Bhāgavata dharma of the Mahābhārata and the Gītā hold in common the views that worship of any god goes ultimately to Keśava or Vāsudeva; that the renunciation of the world is not desirable; that everyone should contribute to the revolving wheel of the world-order by performing one's own duty (svadharma) and that there are four kinds of devotees. They have the same account of the transmission of the religious tradition viz. from the Lord to Vivasvān and then to Manu and Ikṣvāku. The philosophical teachings of the Gītā also are quite in consonance with those taught in such parts of the Mahābhārata as Sanatsujātīya, Yājñavalkya-Janaka-dialogue, and Anugītā. Again the view of the Gītā according to which a supreme principle is accepted beyond Puruṣa and Prakṛti comprising twentyfive elements finds a parallel treatment in the dialogue of Vaśiṣṭha and Karāla-Janaka as well as in that of Yājñavalkya and Janaka. Besides these similarities of religious and philosophical ideas, resemblances in other respects also may be found in plenty, for example, the description of the two armies by Duryodhana before Droṇācārya in the first chapter of the Gītā and the same in chapter 51 of the Bhīṣma Parva of the Mahābhārata, the despondency of Arjuna in the latter half of the first chapter in the Gītā and the description of Yudhiṣṭhira in the beginning of the Śānti-Parva of the Mahābhārata. Similarly we can point to the parallel expressions of Arjuna in the Gītā (I.32-37; II.5 & 8) and of Duryodhana in the Mahābhārata (Śalya XXXI. 42-51) about the futility of winning a kingdom after slaying one's own people. Again, the two pathways, buddhiyoga and karmayoga taught in the Gītā find mention in the Mahābhārata (Śānti 334-351; 196 & 320). The ideas of the Gītā (III.8) and (III.10) are well comparable with those of the Mahābhārata (Vana. 32) and (Śānti 267). The description of the factors of creation as mentioned in the seventh and eighth chapters of the Gītā are also found identical with that of the Śānti 231 in the Mahābhārata, and again the yogic postures and practices mentioned in the sixth chapter of the Gītā have their correspondences with those mentioned in the Śānti 239, 300 and Aśvamedha 19 of the Mahābhārata. Again the cosmic form (Viśvarūpa) shown by Kṛṣṇa in the eleventh chapter of the Gītā is at a lesser scale, the same as shown on various occasions by him in the Mahābhārata, e.g. before Duryodhana when he wanted to capture Kṛṣṇa while the latter had been to his court with the proposal of alliance (Udyoga. 130), before Uttaṅka while he was on his way to Dvārakā after the great war of the Mahābhārata (Aśvamedha. 55), before Nārada in the form of Nārāyaṇa (Śānti. 339) and before Paraśurāma in the form of Rāma (Vana. 99). Again the nature and function of the three guṇas discussed in the fourteenth and fifteenth chapters of the Gītā are similar in description to what we find in the Anugītā (Aśva. 36-39) and in other places (Śānti 285 & 300-311) in the Mahābhārata. Just as the month of Mārgaśīrṣa has been said to be the best in the Gītā (X.35), so also it has been given the priority in the Mahābhārata (Anuśāsana. 106 & 109). Many similar ideas are found scattered throughout in the Mahābhārata which are reminiscent of those in the Gītā and this hardly leaves any doubt about the Gītā being regarded as an integral part of the Mahābhārata.

Thus from various explicit references to the Gītā in the Mahābhārata as well as from similarities of words, language, versification and ideas between the two, one is led to the conclusion that the Gītā has been a genuine constituent of the Mahābhārata and has not simply been interpolated into the latter.

Has the Gītā Passed through Successive Stages of Additions and Alterations ?—

The second part of the question is whether the Gītā, right

from its first beginning, has remained as it was or it has undergone some changes, additions and alterations at subsequent periods.

That the Gītā would not have remained strictly the same right from its inception is clearly borne out by the statements of the great epic, the Mahābhārata itself of which the Gītā, as shown above, was an integral part. In the opening chapter of the Mahābhārata it is clearly stated that the work which was previously devoid of subsidiary episodes (upākhyānas) and known as 'the Bhārata' was constituted of only 24,000 verses which Vyāsa enlarged into a colossal poem of 600,000 verses, out of which one lakh has come down to us through Vaiśampāyana.[1] It was also known as 'Jaya', perhaps to indicate the victory of Pāṇḍavas.[2] Further it is mentioned that the Bhārata was taught by Vyāsa to his son Śuka and other disciples.[3] His five disciples, Samantu, Jaimini, Paila, Śuka and Vaiśampāyana wrote five different treatises out of which Vyāsa accepted the Mahābhārata of Vaiśampāyana and only the Aśvamedha Parva of Jaimini's Mahābhārata. By these statements the gradual modifications and additions in the original work are clearly admitted by the Mahābhārata itself. This is further corroborated by the Gṛhya sūtras of Āśvalāyana which clearly mentions the two names, the Bhārata and the Mahābhārata associated with the names of Samantu, Jaimini, Vaiśampāyana and Paila.[4] Now it is but natural to conceive of some such modifications and additions in its constituent, the Gītā as well. It is difficult to agree, therefore, wholly with Dahlmann who speaks of the Mahābhārata as the work of 'one single poetical creative genius.'

Nevertheless, it would be an unsound and hasty judgment, if merely on this ground almost an equal amount of addition and alteration were to be attributed to the Gītā, without caring to look for any other supporting evidence. It must not be forgotten that unlike other predominantly historical and semi-historical portion of the Mahābhārata, the Gītā

1. Ādi. 1. 101-107.
2. Ādi. 62. 20.
3. Ādi. 1. 103.
4. Samantu-Jaimini-Vaiśampāyana-Paila-Sūtra-Bhāṣya-Bhārata-Mahābhārata-Dharmācāryāḥ.—Gṛhya. 3. 4. 4.

was meant to serve a definite didactic purpose. With regard to the former, insertion of so many stories and narratives (Upākhyānas) linked one way or the other with the main theme could be easily possible. But a predominantly didactic work like the Gītā could hardly make room for such insertions. So if insertions and additions are supposed to have been made in the Gītā, they, in all probability, would have been of an elaborative and explicatory nature.

Of course, it is largely a matter of guess and conjecture. Yet it is significant that we do not come across any other version of the Gītā existing at any time which can be considered remarkably different from the present text.[1] From very long time past, there has been the tradition in India of getting the Gītā by heart and so it would not have been easy to make any substantial interpolation in the Gītā portion of the Mahābhārata. Again the authenticity, with which the Gītā is referred to in an old work, namely, the Brahma Sūtra,[2] goes further to suggest that it would have become authoritative and, therefore, unalternable by the time of the composition of the latter. Several Gītās composed in the Purāṇic period on the pattern of the Bhagavadgītā also testify to the fact that by that time the Bhagavadgītā must have acquired that esteem and authenticity as to be considered worthy of imitation. It must have, therefore, been in existence a few centuries before the composition of these imitative Gītās (granting the period of a few centuries for acquiring high esteem and authenticity). The same is supported by the fact that the exponents of the different Vedantic schools, in order to secure authenticity for their own schools, think it necessary to show the conformity of their respective theories to the Bhagavadgītā by writing out commentaries on it suited to their doctrinal purposes.

It, therefore, appears plausible to believe that the Gītā, though not absolutely immune to modifications and additions,

1. A Kashmirian version of the Gītā which has been discovered by Professor F. Otto Schrader, is the only one showing some minor divergences from the Vulgate text here and there. But this hardly affects the basic meaning of even a single stanza, not to speak of the work as a whole. Moreover, it has been proved by F. Edgerton to be of later and secondary origin. (J.A. O.S., Vol. 52, pp. 68-75).

2. Brahma Sūtra I.2.6; I.3.23; II.1.36; II.3.45; III.2.17; III. 2.31; IV.1.10 & IV. 2. 21.

would not have been subjected to such additions and alterations which could vitally affect its original text, and it would have assumed its present form at the time of the extension of the Mahābhārata, and would have continued to remain the same since then.

But this view has been contended rather seriously by various scholars. Finding that the Gītā is not a consistent piece of doctrine, some writers have let loose their conjectures to account for it in different ways. Hopkins supposes that several writers in so many centuries have been at work upon it. He says that "this Divine Song (or Song of the Blessed One) is at present a Kṛṣṇaite version of an older Visnuite form and this in turn was at first an unsectarian work, perhaps a late Upaniṣad."[1] A. Holtzmann also emphasises the necessity of the supposition that the Bhagavadgītā might have been recast, and considers the present Gītā to be "a Visnuite revision of a pantheistic poem".[2] Garbe thinks that the original Gītā was written in the second century B.C. as a theistic tract based on the Sāṅkhyayoga, though, in the second century A.D., it was adapted by the upholders of the Upanisad monism. According to him "the two doctrines—the theistic and the pantheistic—are mixed up with each other and follow each other, sometimes quite unconnected and sometimes loosely connected."[3] He puts his conjecture into practical execution by printing in small types whatever appears interpolated to him. His pupil Rudolf Otto follows his teacher more enthusiastically and in his book, 'The Original Gītā' he clearly dissects what he considers as inserted by people later on "with the view of securing for it the authenticity of Kṛṣṇa's Divine Form."[4] It is, therefore, necessary to examine the worth of such views at some length.

The crux of all these conjectures is that these writers think it impossible for any single work to contain so many mutually incompatible philosophical elements like those of the Sāṅkhya, the yoga and the Vedānta concurrently, as is found to be the

1. The Religions of India, p. 381.

2. Das Mahābhārata ii. pp. 163-165.

3. Garbe's Introduction to the Bhagavadgītā, translated by N.B. Utgikar (I.A. Vol. 47) sup. p. 3.

4. The Original Gītā. p. 12.

case with the Gītā. But one with an historical insight into the nature of early Indian literatures like the Upaniṣads etc., can at once see that the names, Sāṅkhya, Yoga and Vedānta etc., in the senses they occur in the Gītā, may not be mutually incompatible, as they appear to be in the light of the subsequently developed systems after those names. In the Gītā these terms occur in a non-technical and non-rigid sense, unrestricted by the exigencies of any well established philosophical system. It is at a later stage of philosophical progress that system making arises, and then the thoughts which in their initial stage were flexible enough to be combined with others, become too rigid and technical to admit of any adjustment with other thoughts. So the seeming incompatibility of certain ideas of the Gītā should not warrant the conclusion that it is a result of gradual interpolations, but thereby we should only realise the fact that the Gītā is a work of pre-systematizing period.

Leaving other conclusive evidences in support of this view for a later discussion, let us, for the present, refer to a few actual contents of the Gītā where some topics are discussed in common with certain well established systems. Thereby, it would at once be clear that in the Gītā we have only the initial elements of the subsequently well-developed and systematised philosophical thoughts. In the sixth chapter of the Gītā, for example, Arjuna asks Krsna how the mind which is admittedly 'fickle, boisterous, violent and obstinate' is to be brought under control—such control having been declared essential for attaining yoga. Kṛṣṇa straightaway points out that it is possible through practice (Abhyāsa) and non-attachment (Vairāgya) and concludes by saying that to an endeavouring man of self-control, yoga is attainable and to a non-restrained man it is unattainable.[1] Here the subject drops, and no further attempt is made to explain the nature, modification and classification of Abhyāsa and Vairāgya. Now one can see the remarkable difference in the treatment of the same in the systematised 'Yoga Śāstra' of Patañjali. The author there begins in the traditional manner with the sūtra —'Henceforth teaching of yoga begins' (Atha yogānuśāsanam)

1. Gītā VI. 33-36.

and then lays down its well known definition that 'yoga is the restraint of mental operations' (Yogaścitta-vṛtti-nirodhaḥ).[1] The author, then, after its further clarification, gives classifications of these mental operations.[2] Thereafter he says that "their (of mental operations) restraint comes from practice and non-attachment (Abhyāsavairāgyābhyāṁ tannirodhaḥ[3]) —the terms identical with those used in the Gītā. But unlike the Gītā, the author of the Yoga-Śāstra does not drop the subject here but proceeds with further explanation of 'practice' and 'non-attachment' as follows :—"Practice is the effort for steadiness",[4] "And that becomes firmly grounded when resorted to for a long time, without interruption, and with correct conduct."[5] Then the author takes up non-attachment and defines it as follows: "Non-attachment is the controlling consciousness of a person, who has no craving for visible and scriptural enjoyment."[6] He next proceeds to distinguish a higher species of non-attachment, and then goes on to point out the results of that self-restraint which is to be acquired in the mode he has expounded, and thus the topic proceeds on and on.

Similar differences could be discerned with regard to the practical guidance given for yoga by the Gītā on the one hand, and the yoga Śāstra on the other. In Chapter VI, Verse 10 ff, the Gītā gives some specific directions for the practice of yoga, without caring much to be systematic. But Patañjali, while dealing with the subject in his 'Sādhanapāda', systematically and elaborately formulates the well-known theory of eightfold yoga (Aṣṭāṅga-yoga).

These illustrations should make it clear that in the Gītā we have like the Upaniṣads, unarranged, non-systematised, stray thoughts without any attempt at scientific definition, classification, division and subdivision which are the marked

1. Here also one can well contrast the simple, non-technical and commonsense definitions of 'yoga' given by the Gītā II.48 (Samatvaṁ yoga ucyate) and II.50 (Yogaḥ karmasu kauśalaṃ).

2. Yoga sūtras I.3-11.

3. Ibid I.12.

4. Ibid. I. 13.

5. Ibid. I.14.

6. Ibid. I.15.

features of later systematic works. In short, what we have in the Gītā are the germs, the raw materials and not the well-developed, ready made systems of philosophy.

The same is indicated by the loose uses of the various terms in the Gītā which are found to have well-defined technical meanings in the different systems. The term 'yoga' itself has been taken in somewhat varying senses in B. G. II.48.50 and B. G. VI.10ff and again in B. G. X.5 & X.7. To a greater or lesser degree similar variation in the significance of such terms as Ātman, Brahman, Buddhi & Svabhāva etc. can be easily seen. Such non-precision about the uses of words found in the Gītā only corroborates the view set forth above and also explains to a great extent the reason behind the apparent incoherence and incompatibility. Garbe seems to have been mistaken when he explains 'Yogo naṣṭaḥ' of the Gītā IV.2, as indicating the destruction of the Yoga-system of Patañjali and makes it a basis to conclude that the Gītā is a work of post-Yoga-system.[1] Professor Dasgupta is right when he says that the author of the Gītā "was not acquainted with the technical sense of yoga..as used by Patañjali."[2]

As a matter of fact the treatment of the subject matter in the Gītā bears on the face of it very plain marks of the Upaniṣadic character and lends amply to the idea that it is a young member of that very class, as is evidenced by the colophon at the end of each of its chapters. A careful reading of the Gītā with some knowledge of ancient Indian literature will compel one to agree with the views of Professor Fitz-Edward Hall in this regard who observes as follows: "In the Upaniṣads, the Bhagavadgītā and other ancient Hindu books, we encounter, in combination, the doctrines which, after having been subjected to modifications that rendered them as wholes irreconcilable, were distinguished, at an uncertain period, into what have for many ages been styled the Sāṅkhya and the Vedānta.".[3] Professor Dasgupta also voices the same opinion. He says : "The Gītā was probably written at a time when philosophical views had not definitely crystallized into hard-

1. Indian Antiquary, Vol. 47, Suppl. pp. 32-33.
2. A History of Indian Philosophy, Vol. II. p. 443.
3. Sāṅkhya Sāra—Preface p. 7.

and-fast systems of thought, and when the distinguishing philosophical niceties, scholarly disputations, the dictates of argument, had not come into fashion."[1]

Thus with regard to the second part of the question we conclude from the available facts and circumstances that there is a great probability—probability because certainty cannot be claimed without incontrovertible documentary evidence—of the Gītā having been originally composed with the original Bhārata in accordance with the proportion of the original work which, subsequently, would have been enlarged into its present form at the time of the enlargement of the Mahābhārata. It must have passed through a human, undeified period in its initial stage and it is quite possible that during that period some modifications and additions may have been made to it. But it must not be forgotten that after its enlargement as a religious work, it came to acquire extreme sanctity in the eyes of the Hindus (being supposedly the utterances of the Lord himself) which must have enabled it to stand the trials and tribulations of time better than the rest of the Mahābhārata. Even writers like Garbe, Holtzmann and Hopkins etc. who think of subsequent insertions and interpolations in the Gītā, agree that the present Gītā does not belong to the stage of later interpolations of the MB. They also think that "the Gītā even in the revised form in which it lies before us, is regarded rightly as one of the older episodes of the MB."[2] The ancient tradition to get the Gītā by heart as a unit must have protected it to an extraordinary degree from changes and from textual corruptions. So we are inclined to hold the view that the Gītā since its enlargement with the MB. has almost remained free from modifications and interpolations.

The Date of the Gītā :—

(A) *On the Basis of the Date of the Mahābhārata* :—

Now we come to the last part of the question, viz. the date of the Gītā. The Gītā, as is found at present, is a part of the MB. and we have seen that it appears to have always

1. History of Indian Philosophy, Vol. II, p. 534.

2. Translation of Garbe's Introduction to the Bhagavadgītā. I.A., Vol. 47. Suppl. p. 4; cf. Holtzmann—Das Mahābhārata ii. p. 121; Hopkins—Great Epic, p. 205, 402.

remained as such. So by determining the date of the MB. we may very well determine the date of the Gītā. We, therefore, first propose to adduce evidences indicating the date of the MB., and then we may further confirm it by advancing independent evidences in support of the date of the Gītā, so that even if its being a genuine part of the MB. be questioned, the date of the Gītā may remain unaffected.

Evidences for the existence of the MB. after the 1st century A.D. are too numerous and too well known to be recounted here. We may, therefore, begin with the testimony of the works of Aśvaghoṣa, a Mahāyāna Buddhist of the 1st century A.D. In his 'Buddhacarita' as well as 'Saundarananda' he evidently makes use of the episodes of the MB. Again in his 'Bajra Sūci', some verses of the 'Śrāddha Mahātmya' portion of the Harivaṃśa as well of other portions of the MB. are exactly quoted.[1] This indicates that by his time the MB. with its appendix, Harivaṁśa must have been wellknown.

Still earlier references are to be found in the 'Gṛhya-Sūtra' of Āśvalāyana as well as in the Dharma-Sūtra and Grhya-Sūtra of Baudhāyana. Āśvalāyana makes clear mention of the Bhārata as well as the MB. in his Gṛhya-Sūtra III.4.4.[2] In Baudhāyana's Dharma Sūtra II.2.26 a verse occurs which is found in the MB. (Ādi. 78.10). Dr. Buhler, however, thinks that on the ground of this single verse it is "hazardous to assert that the verse proves Baudhāyana's acquaintance with Vyāsa's great epic. It will be safer to wait for further proofs that it was known to the Sūtrakāra, before one bases far going speculations on this hitherto solitary quotation."[3] But to remove the doubt of Dr. Buhler, other references also have been discovered in the Gṛhya Sūtra of Baudhāyana. His Gṛhya Sūtra (I.22.8) clearly mentions the name of the 'Visnu-sahasra-nāma' which is a portion of the MB. and further in Sūtra II.22.9, an important verse of the Gītā (IX.26) is clearly quoted. The date assigned to Baudhāyana by Dr. Buhler himself is not later than 400 B.C.[4]

1. The Mahābhārata—Harivaṃśa 24.20 & 21, Śāntiparva, 261.17.

2. Samantu-Jaimini-Vaiśampāyana-Paila-Sūtra-Bhāṣya-Bhārata-Mahābhārata-Dharmācāryāḥ.

3. S.B.E. Vol. XIV. Introduction p. xli.

4. S.B.E. Vol. II. Introduction. pp. xxii & xliii.

which is universally accepted. By this time the MB. seems to have become popular along with the Gītā, the verses of which are quoted by Baudhāyana with high reverence. Āśvalāyana is supposed to be an early writer of the Sūtra period which means that he belongs to a period not very far removed from the time of the origin of Buddhism. According to Macdonell also both Sāṅkhyāyana and Āśvalāyana, belong to the early time of the Sūtra period which according to him commences from 500 B.C. He clearly says that "the oldest of them seems to go back to about the time when Buddhism came into being. Indeed it is quite possible that the rise of the rival religion gave the first impetus to the composition of systematic manuals of Brahmanic worship."[1]

From the clear mention of the two names, the Bhārata and the Mahābhārata in the Gṛhya Sūtra of Āśvalāyana, it is reasonable to infer that the MB. was developed from the Bhārata, perhaps, not long before Āśvalāyana, for after a considerable lapse of time, the name Bhārata was almost forgotten.

The view that the MB. was composed not long after the time of Buddha is corroborated from the inner evidences of the MB. as well. In the enumeration of the incarnations of Viṣṇu in the Nārāyaṇīyopākhyāna of the MB. (Śānti 339.100), Lord Buddha is not mentioned. Beginning with Haṁsāvatāra as the first, up to Kṛṣṇa, we have nine avatāras, and it is brought to a close by mentioning 'Kalki' as the tenth. But in the course of describing the future state of Kaliyuga in the 'Vana Parva' the line occurs 'Edūka-cihnā pṛthivī na devagṛhabhūsitā, (Vana. 190.68) which means 'in place of temples of gods there would be Buddhist relic mounds on the earth.' 'Eduka' signifies the structure raised upon a spot where a tooth or hair of Buddha lay buried. This, evidently, shows that these portions at least of the MB. were composed after the death of Buddha but prior to the period when he came to be reckoned as an incarnation of Visnu. In the MB. the words 'Buddha' and 'Prati Buddha' occur in many places in the sense of enlightened man,[2] which may reasonably be considered to signify that the author of the MB. knew about Buddha.

---

1. A History of Sanskrit Literature. p. 246.
2. Śānti. 194.58; 307.47; 343.52.

On the basis of these evidences, we think, we are justified in believing that the Bhārata was converted into the Mahā bhārata near about the 5th century B.C. The clear mention of both these names by Āśvalāyana fully testifies to it. But minor additions and modifications would have still continued for a century or two more, as otherwise the mention of Buddhist relic mounds and 'Prati-Buddha' in the MB. could not have been possible. So on the ground of the aforesaid facts, we conclude that the MB., as we have it at present, seems to have been finally fixed by the 3rd century B.C., though it might have been first developed into its major form of the MB. much earlier, perhaps by about the 5th century B.C. As the Gītā is not considered as a later addition of the MB., it is reasonable to believe that it might have been composed sometime between the 5th and the 4th century B.C. We shall, however, further examine this question and see whether this date is confirmed on other independent grounds.

(B) *On the Basis of Independent Evidences* :—

It is needless to go beyond Śaṅkara's time for the evidences of the existence of the present Gītā, for Śaṅkara himself while commenting on it, makes clear mention of its 700 verses, the form in which it is now before us.[1] The date of Śaṅkara, as already mentioned, cannot be later than the 9th century A.D. Śaṅkara in his preface to the Commentary on the Gītā makes reference to various other commentators whose views being unacceptable, he writes out a separate commentary. This indicates that the present Gītā had since long been treated as a work of high esteem upon which several commentaries had been already written.

Earlier than Śaṅkara we have the evidence of Bāṇabhaṭṭa, the writer of Kādambarī who lived in the court of King Harṣavardhana in the middle of the 7th century A.D. Kādambarī alludes to the Gītā along with the MB. through one of its well known equivoques as follows—'Mahābhāratamivānanta-Gītākarṇanānanditanaram.'[2] In it the royal palace has been

---

1. Taṃ dharmaṃ Bhagavatā yathopadiṣṭaṃ vedavyāsaḥ sarvajño bhagavān gītākhyaiḥ saptabhiḥ ślokaśatairupanibabandha.—Preface.

2. Kādambarī (Tārānāth's Ed.). p. 182.

compared to the Mahābhārata and it is said that the people of the palace were delighted by hearing innumerable songs just as Arjuna was delighted at hearing the 'Ananta Gītā'—evidently, another name for the Bhagavadgītā. The high sanctity attached to the MB. and the Gītā by the time of Bāṇabhaṭṭa is further evidenced by the episode of the queen Vilāsavatī who used to go to the temple of Mahākāla where the daily recitation of the MB. was going on. This evidently indicates that the Gītā and the MB. were looked upon as sacred scriptures of very high esteem, but for which their recitation in the temple could not have been narrated by Bāṇabhaṭṭa. This shows that by the time of Bāṇabhaṭṭa, the Gītā must have been several centuries old.

Earlier than Bāṇabhaṭṭa we have the evidence of Kālidāsa who has been referred to by Bānabhatta in his Harṣacarita.[1] In the works of Kālidāsa we have remarkable allusions to the Bhagavadgītā. To mention a few of them, we may first point to 'Raghuvaṃśam' canto X.67, where the gods addressing Viṣṇu say : "There is nothing for you to acquire which has not been acquired. The one motive in your birth and work is the good of the worlds." Now the idea as well as the expression of the first line is strongly reminiscent of the Gītā (III. 22).[2] The words 'birth and work' (Janma & Karma) occurring in the second line are also precisely the same as employed in the Gītā (IV.9) and the idea of the 'good of the worlds', is also identical with the idea expressed in the Gītā (III.20—24). Again the line of 'Kumārsambhavam' canto VI.67 where the seven ṛṣies say to the Himālaya Mountain : "Well hast thou been called Viṣṇu in a firmly fixed form", cannot fail to remind of the Gītā (X.25) where Kṛṣṇa identifies himself with the firmly fixed Himālaya. The term 'firmly fixed' (Sthāvara) is remarkably the same in both the places. The well known commentator of Kālidāsa, namely, Mallinātha also thinks that Kālidāsa, while speaking of the Himālaya in such terms, must have had in his mind the above mentioned line of the Gītā. The date of Kālidāsa is now fairly well established as the middle of the 5th century A.D.[3]

---

1. Vāsavadattā—F.E. Hall. p. 14 footnote.
2. Nānavāptamavāptavyaṃ varta eva ca karmaṇi.
3. Kālidāsa has been referred in a copper-plate inscription of the early

The several other gītās e.g. Avadhūta gītā, Ganeśa gītā, Īśvara gītā, Vyāsa gītā, Brahma gītā, Sūta gītā, Rāma gītā, Yama gītā, Śiva gītā, Haṁsa gītā, Devī gītā etc., composed on the pattern of the Bhagavadgītā, indicate that the latter must have reached a high esteem worthy of imitation, much earlier than the period of the composition of all these imitative gītās. Some of them have been composed independently but others are just abstractions from various Purāṇas. Now the age of the Purāṇas is supposed to begin latest by the 2nd century A.D. So by that time the sanctity and eminence of the Gītā must have been well established.

Bhāsa, who has been referred to by Kālidāsa, takes many themes of his plays from the MB. A remarkable reference to the Gītā also is found in the twelfth verse of his play, namely, Karṇabhāra which reads as follows : '*Hato pi labhate svargaṃ jitvā tu labhate yaśaḥ.*' This verse has a clear echo of the Gītā (II.37).[1] In view of the fact that most of Bhāsa's works derive material from the MB., it is quite reasonable to believe that while writing this passage, he had remembered the said passage of the Gītā. Pt. Gaṇapati Śāstrī, the Compiler of Bhāsa's dramas, has assigned him a date earlier than at least 200 B.C. But some other scholars place him about 200 A.D. Even according to the latter view the Gītā goes earlier than the 2nd century A.D.

Earlier than Bhāsa we have the evidence of Baudhāyana. We have already referred to a quotation of the Gītā (IX.26) made by Baudhāyana in his Gṛhya Sūtra (II.22.9) where he clearly considers the Gītā as an authority, for while making this quotation he uses an honorific reference to the Gītā: 'So

---

part of the 7th century as a poet who had, then, already acquired a high reputation.—(I. A. Vol. V, pp. 68 & 71). K.T. Telang in one of his tracts entitled 'Was the Rāmāyaṇa copied from Homer' (pp. 36-59) has shown that the 'Pañcatantra' which was translated in the beginning of the 6th century A.D. for the Persian King, Nushirvan, quotes one passage from Kālidāsa. On this basis he holds: "Allowing for the time required to raise Kālidāsa to the position of being cited as an authority and for the time required for the spread of the fame of an Indian work to Persia in those early days, I think, the middle of the 5th century is a date to which Kālidāsa cannot well have been subsequent."

1. Hato vā prāpsyasi svargaṃ jitvā vā bhokṣyase mahīm.

the Lord has said'.[1] Again, at the end of the third 'praśna' of the Gṛhya Sūtra, he has referred to the 'Dvādaśākṣara-Mantra' namely, 'Om namo bhagavate Vāsudevāya' by muttering which one acquires the merit of Aśvamedha yajña. So the high sanctity of the Gītā and the practice of 'Vāsudeva-bhakti' seem to have been quite in eminence by the time of Baudhāyana. Another remarkable allusion to the Gītā has been made by him in his 'Pitṛmedha Sūtra' where in the very beginning of the third 'Praśna' a passage occurs as follows:

> "*Jātasya vai manuṣyasya dhruvaṁ maraṇamiti Vijānīyāt tasmāt jāte na prahṛṣyenmṛte ca na viṣīdeta.*"

It can be easily seen that the passage has the echo of the Gītā (II.27).[2] The reference of another quotation from the MB. (I.78.10) in his Dharma Sūtra (II.2.26) has already been made. There, then, remains hardly any doubt with regard to the Gītā having been in existence in the pre-Baudhāyana period. The fairly well settled date of Baudhāyana, as stated earlier, is 400 B.C., and, accordingly, the Gītā which is referred to by Baudhāyana must be placed earlier than this date. Dr. Buhler in his 'Introduction to Āpastamba' has adduced good reasons for holding that Āpastamba, a later Sūtra-Kāra than Baudhāyana, belongs to a period earlier than the 3rd century B.C., and by advancing fairly weighty arguments has concluded that "the distance in years between the first and the last of the three Sūtrakāras (Baudhāyana, Bhāradvāja and Āpastamba) must, therefore, I think, be measured rather by centuries than by decades."[3]

Several references to the Gītā are found in the 'Brahma-Sūtra' under the name 'Smṛti'. The well-known commentators like Śaṅkara, Rāmānuja, Madhva etc. agree in most of the cases that the author of the Brahma Sūtra by the term 'Smrti' refers to the Gītā. We may mention here some of the important Sūtras where, according to Śaṅkara, the Brahma-Sūtra refers to the Gītā :

---

1. Tadāha Bhagavān : Pattraṃ puṣpaṃ phalam toyaṃ yo me bhaktyā prayacchati; Tadahaṃ bhaktyupahṛtamaśnāmi prayatātmanaḥ
2. Jātasya hi dhruvo mṛtyurdhruvaṃ janma mṛtasya ca, Tasmādaparihārye'rthe na tvaṃ śocitumarhasi.
3. S.B.E. Vol. II. Introduction p. xxii.

	Brahmasūtra		Gītā
I.2.6.	Smṛteśca	XVIII.61	Īśvaraḥ sarva-bhūtānām..
I.3.23	Api ca smaryate	XV.6	Na tad bhāsayate sūryaḥ..
II.1.36	Upapadyate cāpy upalabhyate ca	XV.3	Na rūpamasyeha tathopalabhyate
II.3.45	Api ca smaryate	XV.7	Mamaivāṃśo jīva-loke jivabhūtaḥ..
III.2.17	Darśayati cātho api smaryate	XIII.12	Jñeyam yat tat pravakṣyāmi..
III.3.31	Aniyamaḥ sarvāsāma-virodhaḥ śabdānu-mānābhyām	VIII.26	Śukla kṛṣṇa gatī hyete..
IV.1.10	Smaranti ca	VI.11	Śucau deśe prati-ṣṭhāpya..
IV.2.21	Yoginaḥ prati ca smaryate	VIII.23	Yatra kāletvanā-vṛttimāvṛttiṃ caiva yoginaḥ.

We may look to the context of one or two of them and see how unmistakably the references to the Gītā are borne out by them. Let us take, for illustration, Brahma-Sūtra II.3.45 and IV.2.21, where all the four important commentators, namely Śaṅkara, Rāmānuja, Madhva and Vallabha unanimously agree in taking the sūtras as specifically referring to the same verse of the Gītā.

The Sūtra II.3.45 occurs in the context of a discussion regarding the relation between the individual and the supreme soul. Before this Sūtra, it has been stated in the Sūtra II. 3.17 (Nātmā śruternityatvācca tābhyaḥ) that unlike other created objects of the world, the soul is not created by God. Then further it is said in the Sūtra II.3.44 (Amśo nānā vyapadeśāt) that the individual soul is a part of the Supreme and then in the succeeding two Sūtras II.3.44 and II.3.45 ('Mantra varṇācca' & 'Api ca smaryate') reference to the authority of the Śṛuti and Smṛti respectively is made. Now as the context clearly demands the support of the Smṛti for the view that the individual soul is the part of the supreme, the intended reference of the author to the said Gītā's verse (XV.7) conveying exactly the same idea is rather obvious.

Equally obvious is the reference of Sūtra IV.2.21. It is stated in the Sūtra IV.3.4. that the reference to the 'devayāna' and 'pitṛyāna' should not be taken in the sense of the period covered by uttarāyaṇa and dakṣiṇāyana months respectively but should be taken only in the sense of the respective deities presiding during those periods. Now the question arises if the terms uttarāyaṇa and dakṣiṇāyana should never be taken to denote time. Then in this context, the present Sūtra (IV.2.21) says that they may be taken to denote time 'for the yogins, as the Smṛti would have it'. Now the intended sense of the author is clearly set forth in the verse of the Gītā (VIII.23) under reference where Lord Kṛṣṇa describes the effect of the time, having died at which the deceased soul of the yogins returns or does not return to the world. Remarkably here also the four commentators perfectly agree in taking it as a reference to the same Gītā-verse.

Thus the references made by the Brahma-Sūtra to the Gītā are quite obvious and unmistakable. On this evidence most of the scholars place the Gītā prior to the Brahma-Sūtra.

But in that case they have to explain the fact as to how the Gītā itself is found to refer to the Brahma-Sūtra in the verse XIII.4.[1] Śaṅkara interprets the term 'Brahma-Sūtra' occurring in this verse as referring to 'scriptural passages indicating Brahman'[2] and thus he sticks to the greater antiquity of the Gītā which, as shown above, is copiously quoted by the Brahma Sūtra. Various scholars like A. Weber, K.T. Telang and Lassen agree to this solution of Śaṅkara.[3] But this has not been accepted by Rāmānuja, Madhva and even by Ānanda Giri, the well known commentator of Śaṅkara himself. So it may be given a closer examination.

In fact the term 'Brahma-Sūtra' is not found to occur

---

1. Ṛṣibhir bahudhā gītaṃ chandobhir vividhaiḥ pṛthak,
Brahmasūtrapadaiścaiva hetumadbhir viniścitaiḥ.

2. Brahmaṇaḥsūcakāni vākyāni brahmasūtrāṇi. —S.B.G. XIII. 4.

3. A. Weber—History of Indian Literature, p. 242; K.T. Telang—S.B.E. Vol. VIII. Intro. p. 31; Lassen—Preface to his edition of Schlegel's Gītā, p. XXXV.

anywhere in the sense other than the Vedānta-Sūtra of Bādarāyaṇa Vyāsa. Moreover, if the meaning attached to it by Śaṅkara is accepted, the distinctness denoted by the term 'caiva' in the verse, remains unexplained. The verse in question occurs in connection with the discussion of 'Kṣetra' and 'Kṣetrajña', and the author of the Gītā in support of his view seems to refer as authority to (i) that where the same "has been sung by seers in various ways independently in different hymns" and also (caiva) to (ii) that where it has been stated "in well-reasoned and well-ascertained words of the Brahma-Sūtra" (the aphoristic work about Brahman). Now, unless the word 'Brahma-Sūtra' is taken in the sense of a separate work, the distinctness of the two authorities suggested by the word 'caiva' is not explained. So to bring out the contextual as well as the full literal meaning of the verse, it is more reasonable to take the word "Brahma-Sūtra' in the sense of the well-known separate work of Bādarāyaṇa Vyāsa, as Rāmānuja and others understand it, and not in the sense in which Śaṅkara takes it, perhaps with a view to maintain greater antiquity to the Gītā.

But in that case how to account for the mutual references of the Gītā and the Brahma Sūtra ? Only one solution is left, and that is to regard the Gītā as well as the Brahma-Sūtra as the works of the same author. This view is in keeping with the tradition also. The two works are traditionally ascribed to the great sage, Vyāsa.[1] B. G. Tilak also is inclined to accept this view and he has really discovered a good documentary evidence in support of this view. As pointed out by him,[2] in the Southern recension of the MB. published by Krsnā-

---

1. It is, however, difficult to regard Vyāsa as the sole author of the MB. or the Gītā. He appears to be a mere 'arranger' or compiler (as his name, 'Vyāsa' suggests) of the material already found in scattered and unsystematised form. Of course, he might have made many additions and alterations and thereby have given a new form to the work.

It may also be noted in this connection that the term 'Vyāsa' appears as a surname and it is quite possible to think of other individuals bearing this surname separate from one who is the son of Parāśara (Pārāśarya Vyāsa), for the word 'Vyāsa' occurs quite early in the Vedic period as well as at a later period of the Purāṇas. Vyāsa is called Veda-Vyāsa as well as the author of 18 purāṇas.

2. Gītā Rahasya, p. 536, footnote.

cārya, a verse is found which describes the assignment of the composition of various śāstras to different sages. It reads as follows :—

Vedāntaṃ karmayogaṃ ca Vedavid Brahmavid vibhuḥ,
Dvaipāyano nijagrāha śilpaśāstraṃ bhṛguḥ punaḥ.
Śānti 212.34.

In this verse the Vedānta and Karmayoga which are evidently the other names for the Brahma-Sūtra and the Gītā respectively, have been ascribed to Dvaipāyana Vyāsa. Though this verse is not found in other publications of the MB., and so by itself alone it may not be considered as conclusive evidence, still the authenticity of its evidence cannot be simply brushed aside, specially when the view expressed by it is quite in conformity with the tradition, and it also affords a satisfactory explanation of the mutual references of the Gītā and the Brahma-Sūtra. Moreover, Brahma-Sūtra can be shown to be contemporaneous with the Gītā even on independent grounds.

(C) *On the Basis of the Date of the Brahma-Sūtra* :—

Let us look to the independent evidences indicating the date of the Brahma-Sūtra. We may begin with Śabara Svāmī, the well-known commentator of the Mīmāṃsā-Sūtra. His style of the commentary indicates that he must not have flourished much later than Patañjali whose date is well settled as about 140 B.C.[1] Prior to Śabara, there have been so many commentators like Bhartṛmitra,[2] Bhavadāsa,[3] Hari[4] and Upavarsa. Upavarṣa is supposed to be a very old commentator on the Jaimini Sūtra as he is mentioned in the Kathāsarita-sāgara as having Pāṇini, Kātyāyana and Vyāḍi as his pupils. Śabara Svāmi also refers to him with the highly honorific title, 'Bhagavāna', 'the Venerable Upavarṣa'. According to Śaṅkara's statement Upavarṣa appears to have commented also on the Brahma-Sūtra.[5] Now Upavarṣa, who

1. Bühler's Introduction to Āpastamba (S.B.E. Vol. II), p. xxviii; Telang—S.B.E. Vol. viii, p. 32; Radhākṛṣṇana—Ind. Phil. Vol. ii, p. 376.
2. Nyāyaratnākara 10; Kāśikā p. 10.
3. Ślokavārttika I.63.
4. Śāstradīpikā X.2. 59-60.
5. Colebrooke's Essays Vol. I, p. 332.

is the commentator of both the Jaimini-Sūtra and the Brahma-Sūtra and has as his disciples Paṇini, Kātyāyana and Vyāḍi, cannot be later than 400 B.C.,[1] for Paṇini himself is assigned a date not later than 400 B.C. The testimony of Rāmānuja[2] and Mādhava[3] according to which Baudhāyana is recognised as a commentator of the Brahma-Sūtra, also proves the great antiquity of the Brahma-Sūtra. We have already seen that Baudhāyana has referred to the Gītā with authority, and now we see that he has also written a commentary on the Brahma-Sūtra. His date, as already mentioned, is not later than 400 B.C. So the Brahma-Sūtra along with the Gītā has got to be assigned a date some time earlier than Baudhāyana. Thus we see that our view that the Gītā and the Brahmā-Sūtra are contemporaneous works, appears reasonable.

We may also, in this connection, make mention of one Bhikṣu Sūtra of Pārāśarya referred to by Pāṇini (IV.III.110). Now it has to be ascertained whether he means by it the same 'Brahma-Sūtra' of Pārāśarya Vāysa. In fact, we know of no other Pārāśarya than Vyāsa and no other Sūtra-work than the Brahma-Sūtra composed by him. So it is quite plausible to identify this Bhikṣu-Sūtra of Pārāśarya with the Brahma-Sūtra of Pārāśarya Vyāsa. Unfortunately, neither the Mahābhāṣya nor the Kāśikā-vṛtti enlighten us on the point. But a note of Professor Tārānātha Tarka Vācaspati of Calcutta identifies Pārāśarya with Bādarāyaṇa Vyāsa and the Bhikṣu-Sūtra with the Brahma-Sūtra.[4] His views are not only plausible but are supported by the weighty tradition of Bhaṭṭojī-Dīkṣita, Nāgojī Bhaṭṭa and Jñānendra Sarasvatī.[5] It is quite possible that with a view to coin the Buddhist terminology of the time, some might have given it this name of Bhikṣu-Sūtra, though the name is admittedly an unpopular one.

The fact that Pāṇini knew about the Gītā and the devotion of Vāsudeva is well indicated by the mention of his Sūtra IV.3.95 (Bhaktiḥ) and Sūtra IV.3.98 (Vāsudevārjunābhyāṁ vun), which is also corroborated by the commentary of

1. Ibid. p. 321 footnote 1.; cf. Brahma-Sūtras translated by Swami Vīreśvarānanda. Introduction, p. viii.
2. Rāmānuja Bhāṣya—Introduction.
3. Rāmānuja Darśana in Sarvadarśana-Saṅgraha.
4. Siddhānta Kaumudī Vol. I, p. 592; cf. S.B.E. Vol. viii, p. 33.
5. Cf. S.B.E. Vol. viii, p. 33.

Patañjali on the point. So the mention of a contemporaneous work of the Gītā, viz. the Brahma-Sūtra by him under the name 'Bhikṣu-Sūtra' is not ununderstandable.

Thus we see that the date of the Gītā remains unaffected even if we discard Śaṅkara's interpretation of the Gītā-verse XIII.4, and interpret it in its direct and literal sense of referring to the Brahma Sūtra. Now in the light of all these evidences set forth independently, it is reasonable to conclude that the Gītā and the Brahma-Sūtra are both the works of the same author and they seem to have been composed some time between 500 and 400 B.C., when Buddhism had recently emerged as a powerful movement of thought. The use of the term 'Brahma nirvāṇa' or 'Nirvāṇa' in the Gītā remarkably indicates it.[1]

But it may be pertinently asked as to how the Gītā can be placed so close to the Buddha when in its contemporaneous work, viz. the Brahma Sūtra, various later schools of Buddhism like Śūnyavāda and Vijñānavāda have been criticised. Perhaps, in order to escape this very difficulty, some scholars convinced of the great antiquity of the Gītā on other weighty evidences, are inclined to assign a later date to the Brahma-sūtra, and manage to explain away its reference made by the Gītā (XIII.4). But if we intend to arrive at the truth, we must not unduly twist the interpretation but should face the facts squarely and impartially. Now if we try to examine the Brahma-Sūtra (II.2.18-27) dealing with the refutation of the Buddhist views, we can see that the Sūtras, as they stand, do not make any specific reference to the later schools of Buddhism, as the commentators, coming much after the well-developed schools of Buddhism, take them to do. Buddha's anti-metaphysical approach, his disputation of the first cause, viz. Īśvara or Ātman, and the doctrine of constant change, on account of exhibiting bold departure from the prevalent Brahmanical theories, came at once to catch the attention of the Brahmins, and it is these early tenets of Buddhism which are sought to be refuted by the author of the Brahma-Sūtra. There is nothing in the Sūtras themselves to indicate more than that. Of course, by implication, they may be shown to

1. Gītā II.72; V.24-26; VI.15.

refute the well-developed later schools of Buddhism as well, as has actually been done by the later interpreters of the Sūtras. But this should not be considered as a ground to suppose that the author of the Brahma-Sūtra himself knew about all these subsequent developments of the Buddhist schools, and meant to refute them in his text.

It is well known that Buddhism in its full-grown state came to be a very formidable rival of Brahmanism. But had it been so during the days of Bādarāyaṇa Vyāsa, he could have directed his refutation first against Buddhism. But it is significant to note that he takes up Buddhism only after all the major systems of Philosophy have been criticised. Thus it appears that by the time of the composition of the Brahma-Sūtra and the present Gītā, Buddhism as a system of thought had become popular and powerful enough to exert its influence, though its various ramifications were yet to develop.

Conclusion :—

On the basis of the convergence of the above-mentioned independent evidences, we can reasonably conclude that the Bhagavadgītā was composed sometime between the 5th and 4th century B.C. when the growing impact of Buddhism, besides that of the Upaniṣads, had made it essential for the orthodox tradition to resuscitate and vindicate its position by making necessary adjustments and modifications in its thoughts. By combining the various strands of thought, both old and new, the Gītā presents a compromising philosophy, and thereby tries to counteract the growing influence of atheism and renunciation advocated by Buddhism, Jainism and other contemporary currents of thought.

Section B.

THE CHRONOLOGY OF EARLY BUDDHISM

Buddha, as an Historical Person :—

To pass from the chronology of the Bhagavadgītā to that of early Buddhism is to emerge from the dark night to broad daylight where one can see things with greater clarity. The historicity of Gotama, the Buddha, the founder of the great religion, Buddhism cannot be doubted with any seriousness (though there may be some differences regarding the fixation of his exact date). A few Western scholars like E. Senart, A. Barth and R. Otto Franke who have doubted it[1] have only carried their scepticism too far.

The early Buddhist literature, in spite of some exaggerations and discrepancies, gives quite a life-like-picture of Gotama, moving from place to place, preaching his dharma, encountering praise and slander. An epoch-making departure from the tradition with so strong a reaction on the contemporaries would be really passing strange without believing in a great living personality shaping and changing the course of the age. Kapilavastu, otherwise an insignificant place, and its little known Śākya rulers, could not have gained any importance but for a real Buddha. The fact that Kapilavastu, the birth place of Buddha, had become a well-known holy place for Buddhists, at least as early as about 250 B.C. is clearly borne out by the fact that the great Buddhist King, Aśoka visited this place, and recorded his memory on a column which was discovered in 1896 near the Nepalese village of Paderia.

1. R. Otto Franke, following E. Senart and A. Barth, thinks that "Gotama Buddha is not a bit less mythical than his six mythical predecessors..., a form grown nebulous of an ancient conception of the deity." (O.Z. Vol. 4, 1915-16, p. 10; Winternitz—A History of Indian Literature, Vol. II, Appendix, pp. 558-559). According to him "the so called doctrine of Buddha is perhaps only the collection of a bundle of didactic elements from the vast treasury of philosophical thoughts", which came into being in India in the centuries preceding the Christian era. (Z.D.M.G., Vol. 69, 1915, pp. 455ff; Winternitz, op. cit., p. 598). Similarly the reply of E. Senart to the question: 'Has Buddha ever lived ?' has been "an absolute no" (Oldenberg—Buddha, p. 73).

The inscription as translated by Dr. E. Hultzsch reads as follows: "When King Devānāṃpiya Piyadasi had been anointed 20 years, he came himself and worshipped (this spot) because, the Buddha, Śākyamuni was born here."[1]

Another important discovery of inscription was made in 1898 by W. C. Peppe in the vicinity of Kapilavastu near Piprāvā on the Nepalese frontier where a number of reliquaries were found. Round the rim of the lid of one of the stone-reliquaries runs an inscription in characters like those of Aśoka's inscriptions. In spite of divergence in its translation by scholars, they all agree, at least, about that portion of the inscription which means "this is the relic treasury of the Lord Buddha of the Śākyas."[2] Even if it may not establish the authenticity of the relic, it does prove at least the fact that by Aśoka's time (the period to which the inscription belongs) people believed that these were relics of Buddha. Evidently, this belief would not have arisen so early unless a venerable person called Buddha actually lived before that period.

Again the account of Gotama, the Buddha and his contemporaries given by Buddhist tradition has striking similarities with that of the Jaina tradition. Their mutual correlation hardly leaves any doubt regarding, at least, the personalities of these two founders of religion and some major events of their lives.

Thus, not only on the basis of the weighty tradition but also on unmistakable epigraphic evidences and corroborative support by contemporaneous Jaina tradition, we can definitely speak of the established historicity of Gotama, the Buddha, and brush aside the views of Franke and others as baseless barren scepticism.

The Date of Buddha :—

(A) *Non-traditional Views* :

There has been a good deal of controversy regarding the date of Buddha, and let it be made clear at the very outset that it would be simply dogmatic to claim absolute certainty in any case. We may, however, after broadly looking into the

1. Inscriptions of Asoka, Edited by Dr. E. Hultzsch, p. 164.
2. The life of the Buddha. pp. 160-1.—J. Thomas.

whole problem point out as to which view seems to be most reasonable and most probable.

The chief landmark of Buddhist chronology is the year of Buddha's Parinibbāna. Now the general trend of the Western scholars is to favour placing this date somewhere between 487 and 477 B.C.

Cunningham and Max Muller favour 477 B.C. as the date of Buddha's death.[1] J. Charpentier also supports the same view.[2] But this date has now been set aside by modern historians, for it rests on the erroneous premise that the year of Candragupta's accession was 315 B.C.[3]

Another date which found favour was 487 or 486 B.C. V. A. Smith[4] and V. Gopal Aiyer[5] upheld this view. They attached considerable importance to the so-called 'Dotted-Record'[6] which was continued in Canton up to year 489 A.D. It is said that every year was marked with a dot commencing from the date of Buddha's Parinibbāna till the year 489 A.D. The total number of dots accumulated up to that period was 975 which gives 486 B.C. as the year of Buddha's death. But the claim of perfect accuracy to this 'Dotted-Record' is difficult to maintain unless some other supporting evidence from a different source is found. We are inclined to agree with W. Geiger who points out that "it is singularly improbable that in the course of time—it is a question of nearly thousand years !—not a single error or oversight should have occurred."[7]

The third date which we regard, on the basis of the available material, as the most convincing, is 483 B.C. In the Dīpavaṃsa, the oldest source available to us, the year 218 is clearly mentioned as the period which intervened between Buddha's death and Aśoka's consecration :—

---

1. S.B.E. Vol. X, Introduction, pp. xliii-xlvii.

2. Indian Antiquary Vol. 43, 1914, p. 131. He says : "......the death of Buddha, the date of which was first and in my opinion rightly fixed by General Cunningham and Professor Max Muller occurred in 477 B.C."

3. S.B.E. Vol. X. pp. 43ff.

4. The Early History of India, p. 49.

5. The Date of The Buddha : Indian Antiquary, Vol. 37, 1908, pp. 341 ff.

6. Cf. Takakusu, J.R.A.S. 1896, p. 436 ff; J.E. Fleet, J.R.A.S. 1909, p. 9; p. 323 ff; p. 981 ff.

7. Mahāvaṃsa—trans. by Geiger, p. xxvi.

Dve Satāni ca vassāni aṭṭhārasa vassāni ca
Sambuddhe parinibhute abhisitto Piyadassano.

—Dīpavaṃsa VI. 1.

"Piyadassana was consecrated after 218 years of Buddha's Parinibbāna."

The same is confirmed by Mahāvaṃsa which says :—

Jinanibhāṇato pacchā purā tassābhisekato
Saṭṭhārasaṃ vassasatadvayaṃ evaṃ vijānīyaṃ.

—Mahāvaṃsa V.21.

Samantapāsādikā also refers to the same period of 218 years (Tathāgatassa parinibbāṇato dvinnaṃ vassasatānam upari aṭṭhārasame vasse, I.41). Thus this tradition has been uniformly maintained by all the Buddhist works and so gives little room for doubt.

Now, how to determine the date of Aśoka's consecration ? We know that Aśoka was preceded by his father Bindusāra and grandfather Candra Gupta. The former reigned for 28 years according to the Mahāvaṃsa and the latter for 24 years according to both the Mahāvaṃsa and the Dīpavaṃsa.[1] We also know that the consecration of Aśoka was really performed after he had already reigned for four years.[2] This means that his grandfather, Candra Gupta must have ascended the throne 218—(4+28+24)=162 years after Buddha's death. Fortunately the date of Candra Gupta's accession to the throne can be ascertained with a considerable amount of certainty, for it is related with the well-known historical fact of Alexander's invasion to India. Candra Gupta is known to have incurred the displeasure of the Nanda-King and visited Alexander while he was in the Punjab. He, however, offended Alexander due to his boldness of speech, and had to save his life by a speedy flight. It is only after this incident that he gradually organised some force with the help of Cāṇakya or Kauṭilya, and ultimately after the return of Alexander, the Great he acquired the throne of Magadha by overthrowing the existing government of the Nanda-dynasty. It is an established historical fact that Alexander, the Great died on his way back at

---

1. Mahāvaṃsa V. 16-18; Dipavaṃsa V. 100.

2. Dīpavaṃsa VI.21-22; Mahāvaṃsa V.22; Norman (J.R.A.S. 1908, p. 10) is mistaken when he thinks that according to the Mahāvaṃsa accession should be put at the year 218 A.B. and the Abhiṣeka at 222 A.B.

Babylon in 323 B.C.[1] after which Candra Gupta fought against the Nanda-King and ascended the throne. Candra Gupta's accession is, therefore, to be accepted to have taken place in the year 321 B.C. (or allowing margin for mistakes, within two years of this date).[2] So we arrive at the year (321+162)=483 B.C. which seems to be more dependable a date of Buddha's death than any other.

We, of course, do not claim certainty in the strict sense of the term but we do claim that our evidences are good enough to regard this date as the most probable. The data of all our calculations are beyond reasonable doubt. Firstly, the year 218 A.B. for Aśoka's consecration, as indicated above, has the uniform support of the earliest available Buddhist records. It is difficult to regard this exact number as mere fabrication, for there is conceivably no reason for so doing. Besides, if it were pure guess-work, it would have been most likely in the form of some round figure and not in the form of an odd figure. Moreover, it was not too late by that time to make it difficult to remember the years in between the two major events. Secondly, the year 321 B.C. as the date of Candra Gupta's accession, is linked with the event of Greek history whose record is really well-maintained and accepted as reliable by almost all historians. Then, regarding the length of Candra Gupta's and Bindusāra's reign also, our calculation is beyond reasonable doubt. Regarding Candra Gupta's period of reign, the Dīpavaṃsa and the Mahāvaṃsa on the one hand and the Purāṇas on the other, are in perfect agreement, and so it is beyond dispute. Regarding Bindusāra, the Dīpavaṃsa is silent, most probably because there was nothing remarkable about his reign. According to the Mahāvaṃsa he reigned for 28 years; whereas the Purāṇas assign to him 25 years only. Here we have accepted the version of the Mahāvaṃsa in view

1. M' Crindle—Ancient India—Its Invasion by Alexander, the Great, p. 48. J. P. Rapson—The Cambridge History of India. Vol. II. p. 346; H. C. Ray Chaudhury—Ind. Culture. Vol. II, p. 557.

2. V.A. Smith—The Early History of India. pp. 38-9; also J.R.A.S. 1901, pp. 831-4; The Cambridge History of India. Vol. I Edited by Rapson, pp. 424 & 433. H. C. Ray Chaudhury, however, favours 324 B.C. Indian Culture, Vol. II, p. 560. & Political History of Ancient India. p. 324 footnote 3.

of the fact that odd numbers are supposed to be more accurate than the round ones. In any case the difference would be only of three years.

Thus we decide that 483 B.C., at least approximately, is the most reasonable date for Buddha's Parinibbāna.

(B) *Traditional View* :

It would not be proper to close this discussion without saying a few words about the widely accepted tradition of placing Buddha's death in 544 B.C. In most of the Buddhist countries the orthodox Buddhists stick to this date. It is in adherence to this very tradition that in 1956-57 the 2500th anniversary of Buddha's Parinibbāna was celebrated widely in different Buddhist countries.

This tradition, though a widely accepted belief, and coming down from long time past, has hitherto failed to adduce any strong evidence in its support. Buddhist tradition in Ceylon courts the support of some inscriptions, and tries to connect them with some events referred to in the Mahāvaṃsa. According to it "the first coronation of Parākrama Bāhu I took place about the middle of 1153 A.D. or 1696 year after Buddha expired....we get 1046 A.D. or 1589 A.B., as the date of the accession of Parākrama Pāṇḍya."[1] This date is confirmed further by an independent source, viz., the South Indian Manimaṅgalam inscription. All this shows that in the middle of the 12th century A.D., the tradition both in India and Ceylon believed in 544 or 543 B.C. as the date of Buddha's death. M. de Z. Wickremasinghe, however, claims to have established that till the 11th century A.D., the tradition of counting the Buddhist era from 483 B.C. was prevalent both in India as well as in Ceylon.[2] W. Geiger also accepts this view in his translation of the Mahāvaṃsa.[3] But subsequently it has been pointed out by E. Hultzsch[4] that

1. Epigraphia Zeylanica, Vol. I, p. 155 & p. 123; see also Galvihāra Inscription of Polonnaruva II.1-4 (Ed. Muller—Ancient Inscription in Ceylon, pp. 87, 120).

2. Epigraphia Zeylanica, Vol. I, pp. 155ff.

3. The Mahāvaṃsa—translation, pp. xxviii ff.

4. 'Contribution to Sinhalese Chronology' in J.R.A.S. 1913, pp. 517-531.

this view, resting as it does on an erroneous translation by Wijesinha of a passage in the Cūḷavaṃsa (Chap. 53, V.44), is untenable. Wickremasinghe thereupon modifies his views but still insists that even if the continuation of the Buddhist era reckoning with 483 B.C. be doubtful for a period between the 8th to 11th century A.D., its prevalence up to the beginning of the 8th century A.D. is beyond question. But this position also is shown to be equally untenable by Sylvain Levi, since it goes against the Chinese synchronisms according to which the Sinhalese envoys of King Mahānāma were at the Chinese court in 428 A.D.[1] S. Paranavitana also criticises the view of Wickremasinghe at a great length.[2] Geiger realising the great importance of this evidence of the Chinese synchronism concedes in his translation of the Cuḷavaṃsa that the traditional Buddhist era reckoning from 544 B.C. is traceable till the reign of Mahānāma. But recently a new inscriptional evidence has come to light near Anurādhapura in Ceylon which describes the construction of a vihāra and donation of villages and land for the benefit of the Bodhi-shrine by King Upatissa I, the elder brother and predecessor of King Mahānāma.[3] This is the earliest inscription so far found in which a date is given in the Buddhist era reckoning from the Parinibbāna of Buddha along with the regnal year of the King reigning at the time. Professor S. Paranavitana,[4] on the basis of this newly found inscription, has been able to show that the Buddhist era reckoned from 544 B.C. was prevalent in the reign of King Upatissa I (368-410 A.D.).

This, however, only proves a long continuity of the traditional date but not its accuracy. Professor Paranavitana himself accepts that 'the prevalence of the Buddhist era in Ceylon at the close of the fourth century A.C. by no means vouches for the accuracy of the date of the Buddha's Pari-

1. Sylvain Levi in Journal Asiatique, 1900, pp. 297 ff, 401ff; English trans. by John M. Seneviratne of relevant parts of Sylvain Levi's paper in the 'Journal of the Ceylon Branch of the Royal Asiatic Society', Vol. XXIV (No. 68) pp. 82-102.

2. Epigraphia Zeylanica, Vol. V. pp. 88 ff.

3. The entire inscription (text & translation) is given in U.C.R. Vol. XVIII, Nos. 3 & 4, pp. 131 & 132.

4. Ibid. pp. 129-155.

nirvāṇa."[1] He agrees "that the present Buddhist era is in error; for the time of Aśoka....can be ascertained within narrow limits from the references to a number of Greek Kings in his inscriptions."[2] According to him "it is quite possible that the fixing of the starting point of the era (Buddhist era) was based on data which were not accurate. But once the era was fixed, the dates in it would be quite reliable for the period after that."[3]

A suggestion is made by H. C. Raychaudhury in support of the accuracy of the traditional date, viz. 544 B.C. He accepts the authority of the Dipavaṃsa and the Mahāvaṃsa which places the King Piyadassana 218 years after the Parinibbāṇa of Buddha, but he suggests that this epithet, 'Piyadassana' may have been used for Chandra Gupta and not for his grandson Aśoka.[4] In support of this conjecture, he refers to the Mudrārākṣasa, Act iv where this epithet occurs for Chandra Gupta, and remarks that "this surmise can alone reconcile the chronology current in Ceylon with Greek evidence by placing the enthronement of Chandra Gupta in or about (544-218) = 326 B.C."[5]

We consider this suggestion to be untenable, for 326 B.C. as the date of Candra Gupta's accession can hardly be maintained. All historical records clearly bear out this fact that by 326 B.C. Candra Gupta was still a fugitive who, as already stated, had gone to visit Alexander while the latter was camping in the Punjab, where he offended the King by his impertinent speech and had to run back for his life. It is long after this incident that he met Cāṇakya, and under his advice and help he ultimately succeeded in overthrowing the reign of the Nanda-dynasty. H. C. Raychaudhury himself has admitted that it is the date 324 B.C. and not 326 B.C. which "accords with the testimony of Greek writers."[6] Further the Dīpavaṃsa and the Mahāvaṃsa are themselves quite clear in referring the epithet 'Piyadassana' to Aśoka, because

1. U.C.R. Vol. XVIII, Nos. 3 & 4, p. 148.
2. Ibid. pp. 134-135.
3. Ibid. p. 148.
4. Indian Culture, Vol. II, p. 560.
5. Ibid. p. 560.
6. Ibid. p. 560.

besides mentioning the epithet 'Piyadassana' the name 'Aśoka' also is clearly given, and he is mentioned as the son of Bindusāra and grandson of Candra Gupta whose consecration took place after four years of his assuming power.[1] So it is absolutely unlikely that they would confuse Aśoka with Candra Gupta whom they so clearly know to be the grandson of the latter.

A vigorous attempt to prove the correctness of the traditional date, i.e. 544 B.C. was lately made by K. P. Jayaswal and R. D. Banerjee on the basis of a new reading of the Hāthīgumphā inscription of Khārvela.[2] This was enthusiastically received by eminent historian V. A. Smith[3] and reputed Buddhist scholar, G. P. Malalasekara.[4] But all this enthusiasm came to an end when the readings and calculations of the inscription were finally shown to be untenable by R. C. Mazumdar.[5]

Thus the traditional date despite its long continuity is found to be incompatible with the available historical records, and hence we have to accept 483 B.C. as the date of Buddha's Parinibbāna. We must not, however, forget that it has so far remained unaccountable as to why the traditional date started with an inaccuracy of about 60 years, and unless this obscurity is duly clarified, it is better to leave a remote possibility open in favour of the traditional date, not, of course, on account of any dependable support in its favour, but because the case against it is yet to be fully proved.

(C) *Conclusion* :

We thus, conclude that the most probable date of Buddha's Parinibbāna is 483 B.C., and his date of birth, therefore, is 563 B.C.[6] But as stated above, we do not altogether close

---

1. Dīpavaṃsa VI.1-15 and Mahāvaṃsa V. 16-22.

2. J.B.O.R.S., Vol. I, 1915, pp. 67ff; Vol. III, 1917; Vol. IV 1918 pp. 364 ff.

3. J.R.A.S. 1918 pp. 544-547; The Early History of India, pp. 49ff.

4. The Pali Literature of Ceylon, p. 15, footnote 1.

5. Indian Antiquary, Vol. 47, 1918, pp. 223ff; Vol. 48, 1919, p. 187; cf. R. P. Chandra—Indian Antiquary, Vol. 48, 1919, pp. 214ff.; K. G. Śaṅkara Aiyar—Indian Antiquary, Vol. 49, 1920, pp. 43ff.

6. Buddha is supposed to have lived for 80 years. He himself says in the Mahāparinibbāna Sutta (Dīgha 16) before his death, that he is of 80 years. (Asītiko me vayo vattati)—D. II. 100.

the doors against the traditional date in view of the unavailability of any absolutely incontrovertible epigraphic evidence corroborating the date fixed on the evidence of Greek history. It is, however, gratifying that this much debated question[1] of Buddha's death is now tolerably settled, and even when we are granting allowance to the traditional date of 544 B.C., there remain only two rival dates in the field, and the difference between them is only 60 years which is not much in view of the question pertaining to an ancient hoary past.

Where to Look for the Original Tenets of Buddhism :—

Buddha is said to have renounced his home as a young man of 29 years and attained enlightenment after six years of relentless search and arduous struggle. Thus, he discovered the truth at the age of 35, and the remaining 45 years he spent in preaching his 'dhamma' and establishing the 'Saṅgha.' His activity, therefore, falls between 528—483 B.C., which may be looked upon as the date of the origin of, at least, the essential teachings of Buddhism.

But what are these essential teachings ? Where to find them ? Buddha has not left anything written, even as little as Yājñavalkya, Śāṇḍilya or Śaunaka.[2] It is true that in the Pali Tipiṭaka most of the speeches and sayings are put in the mouth of Buddha himself and are shown to be related with the exact place and occasion, the Master delivered those utterances, but the very fact that these collections contain some heterogeneous elements indicates that they are of doubtful origin and uncertain date. Some of the dialogues themselves speak of their origin not from Buddha but from his disciples after his death, e.g. the Mādhuriya Sutta (Majjh. 84), Ghotamukha Sutta (Majjh. 94) etc. Again works like Paṭisambhidāmagga and Niddesa are obviously commentatorial in nature, which must naturally be supposed to have been preceded by some earlier texts. Besides, the descriptions of the supernatural powers of Buddha and his disciples, heaven and hell, gods and demons and other such exaggerations can not conceiv-

1. Fleet—J.RA.S. 1909, pp. 4-5; Marbel Duff—Chronology of India, p. 7. Kern—Manual of Indian Buddhism, p. 107, Note. 6.

2. Winternitz—A History of Indian Literature, Vol. II, p. 2.

ably be looked upon as Buddha's direct sayings. But at the same time it is quite reasonable to suppose that many of his important speeches and utterances must have been faithfully preserved in the memory of his direct disciples and handed down to posterity through them just as the Vedic and the Upaniṣadic passages were faithfully carried on from generation to generation. But the difficult question as the scholars like Mrs. Rhys Davids,[1] M. Winternitz[2], G. C. Pande[3] and others have pertinently pointed out , is how much of this can be really attributed to Buddha and regarded as the original teachings of Buddhism.

It is now wellnigh an impossibility to mark out with any accuracy the original utterance of the Master. Nevertheless, we may legitimately assume that the earliest parts of the Buddhist Canon are likely to represent the original tenets more faithfully than the later ones. So in order to know the original message of Buddhism we must make an inquiry into the chronology of the early Pali Canon known as the Tipiṭaka.

The Chronology of the Pali Canon and the Nature of Buddhist Councils :—

(A) *According to Tradition* :

The belief of the orthodox Buddhists assigns the whole of the existing Canonical books to the period immediately following the death of Buddha, and claims for them the sanction and authority of the immediate disciples of Buddha himself. According to this tradition, soon after the death of Buddha, the first Buddhist Council took place and the whole of the Dhamma and Vinaya were recited in that Council. A later work, Sumaṅgala Vilāsinī further adds that not only the Dhamma and Vinaya but also the Abhidhamma was finally established at this very Council. Thus, if we believe in all this, the whole of the Tipiṭaka, as it is available to us, was finalised at this very stage. Subsequently two other Councils were held, one 100 years and the other 236 years after Buddha's death in which these Canons were recited with a view to keeping them free from foreign elements.

---

1. Sakya or Buddhist origins—Introductory, p. 1.
2. A History of Indian Literature, Vol. II. p. 2.
3. Studies in the Origins of Buddhism. Preface, p. iii.

The description of the first and second Councils is recorded in the Culla vagga XI and XII respectively. According to it, the motive for holding the first Council is suggested in the frivolous utterances of Subhadda who, having learnt of the news of Buddha's death, was telling his profoundly aggrieved fellow-bhikkhus to feel happy about it, for they had thereby got rid of the irksome control of the ruthless Master. Mahā Kassapa took this frivolity as a note of warning against possible degeneration of the Dhamma in future and proposed to hold a Council of the leading bhikkhus in order to make a full collection of the teachings with a view to safeguarding its purity. 500 Arhat-bhikkhus were accordingly nominated including Ānanda who, though not an Arhat at the time of nomination, became so before the actual commencement of the Saṅgīti. The Council was held at Rājagaha where during the first month of Varsā-vāsa they made repairs to the broken and dilapidated parts, and in the middle month the recitation of the whole of the Dhamma and Vinaya was undertaken. Ānanda spoke the Dhamma (Sutta) and Upāli described the Vinaya. Thus the whole of the Sutta and Vinaya is supposed to have been canonised during two months.

100 years after Buddha's death the second Council was necessitated to settle the controversy arising out of the liberty taken by the Vajji monks of Vesāli, regarding the ten rules (dasa vatthūni). The Council was held in Vālukārāma in which seven hundred bhikkhus participated. The matter was decided by bhikkhu Sabbakāmī.

Almost similar accounts of these Councils are found in the Dīpavaṃsa and the Mahāvaṃsa[1], as well as in the historical introduction to Buddhaghoṣa's Samantapāsādikā.[2] In the introduction to his Sumaṅgala Vilāsini, Buddhaghoṣa describes the first Council frequently with the same expressions.[3] The Mahābodhi-Vaṃsa[4] and the Śāsana-Vaṃsa[5] also repeat the same. The account of the first Council given in the Mahā-

1. Geiger –Dīpavaṃsa and Mahāvaṃsa pp. 108 ff. In the Dīpavaṃsa we find double account of each Council.

2. Oldenberg—Vinaya Pitaka III, pp. 283 ff.

3. Edited by Rhys Davids and Carpenter, Vol. I, pp. 2 ff.

4. Edited by Strong, pp. 85 ff.

5. Edited by M. Bode, pp. 3 ff.

vastu[1] also is quite in agreement with it. The same is confirmed by the Tibetan Vinaya of the Sarvāstivādin sect.[2] According to it, besides fixing of the Dhamma by Ānanda and the Vinaya by Upāli, the Mātṛka (Abhidhamma) also was fixed by Mahā Kassapa himself. The two Councils are also confirmed by the accounts of Fā-hian and Hiuen-thsang.[3]

According to these accounts, the first Council took place only three months after Buddha's death, for the Varsā-Vāsa mentioned in Culla vagga XI and supported in subsequent records begins in the month of Āsāḍha in which repairs to the broken and dilapidated parts were made, and the recitation proper of the Dhamma and Vinaya took place in the second month of Varṣā-Vāsa viz. Sāvaṇa which is the third month after the accepted traditional date of Buddha's death, viz. the full-moon-day of Vaisākha.

The date of the second Council, according to the Dīpavaṃsa (iv.44, 47) and the Mahāvaṃsa (iv.8) is assigned as the 11th year of the reign of Kālāśoka which is said to be 100 years after Buddha's death (i.e. 383 or 382 B.C.). Though the Culla vagga does not say anything more than the settlement of the controversy about 10 Vinaya-rules, the Dīpavaṃsa (V.30 ff) speaks of the heretical monks holding a separate Council called Mahāsaṅgīti making out a different redaction of the Canonical scriptures. The Mahāvaṃsa (V.3-4) also seems to support it when it refers to these heretical monks branching off from the Orthodox camp and forming a separate sect under the name 'Mahāsaṅghika'. Regarding almost all other accounts we do not find any important discrepancy among all these records.

About the third Council no mention is found anywhere in the Tipiṭaka. The earliest mention of it is found in the Dīpavaṃsa (VII.34-43; 44-59). Then we have the record of the Samantapāsādikā (p. 306[27]) and the Mahāvaṃsa (V. 228 ff.). All these records agree in saying that this third Council was held in Pāṭaliputra, 236 years after the death of

---

1. Edited by Senart, Vol. I, pp. 69 ff.
2. Rockhill—Life of the Buddha, pp. 148 ff. pp. 171-180.
3. Beal—Buddhist Records, Vol. I, p. liv, lx-lxi; Vol. II, pp. 74-75 & 162-164. cf. Legge—Records of Buddhistic Kingdoms, pp. 75 & 85.

Buddha, in the reign of the great Buddhist King, Aśoka, under the presidentship of his venerable teacher, Moggaliputta Tissa. This Council was necessitated because, owing to Aśoka's kingly patronage and liberal charity different shades of people joined the Buddhist Order and started twisting and distorting the Doctrine in their own ways. They donned the yellow robe with or without proper ordination and styled themselves as bhikkhus enjoying the privilege and honour due to them. This naturally brought in confusion and a deviation from the orthodox Buddhist principles and so the necessity arose for holding a third Council to purge the impure elements. According to both the Dīpavaṃsa and the Mahāvaṃsa, the Council lasted for nine months. The Mahāvaṃsa (V.280) says that it was concluded in the seventeenth year of Aśoka's reign. It is at this Council that the book Kathāvatthu is said to have been compiled by Moggaliputta Tisssa, refuting all prevalent heresies of the time and was incorporated in the Tipiṭaka as its last work.

(B) *Review of the Traditional View* :—

Now we have to see as to how much of this traditional account can be reasonably accepted as an historical fact. The question of the historicity and nature of the first Council has been widely debated for over half a century.[1] All the available sources in Pali, Chinese and Tibetan have been tapped and discussed minutely. Oldenberg regards this first Council as pure fiction. His argument is that the Mahāparinibbāna Sutta though referring to Subhadda's frivolity (the alleged motive for the Council) is conspicuously silent about the Council.[2] Mr. T. W. Rhys Davids also, siding with the views of Oldenberg, observes : "If anywhere, we should certainly have expected to find here (in the Mahāparinibbāna

1. J. P. Minayeff—Recherches Sur le Bouddhisme. pp. 13ff; 25ff. Oldenberg—Introduction to the Vinaya, I, pp. xxv-xxix (P.T.S.):Z.D.M.G. Vol. 52, 1898, pp. 613 ff; Poussin—Indian Antiquary, 1908, pp. 1-18;81-106; R. O. Franke—J.P.T.S. 1908, pp. 1-80; R. C. Majumdar—Buddhistic Studies (Ed. B. C. Law), pp. 26-72; N. Dutt—Early Monastic Buddhism, Vol. I, pp. 324 ff; Rhys Davids—Dialogues of the Buddha, Vol. II. pp. 76-77.

2. Z.D.M.G. Vol. 52, 1918, pp. 613-32.

Sutta) some allusion (to this Council)....This silence is as valuable as the most direct testimony."[1] Rhys Davids, however, is not emphatic like Oldenberg and thinks that "this conclusion....is only almost, and not quite, certain" granting the possibility that this omission might have been deliberately made in view of its unsuitability in the context of the description of the death of Buddha.[2] But R. O. Franke is as emphatic as Oldenberg and thinks that Cullavagga XI and XII, which are the earliest sources of the tradition and upon which all subsequent accounts of the Councils are based, are themselves nothing more than mere concoctions based on the Mahāparinibbāna Sutta.[3] To use his own expression "the two accounts in Cullavagga XI, XII, are but air-bubbles."[4] Jacobi refutes this view and points out that it was not really necessary for the Mahāparinibbāna Sutta to go out of its way to describe the Council. According to him, therefore, this *argumentum e silentio* cannot disprove the historicity of the first Council.[5]

We, however, are inclined to think that Cullavagga XI was originally a part of the Mahāparinibbāna Sutta itself. It can be easily seen that Cullavagga XI unlike other sections of this chapter begins abruptly. It starts with the very same words of the Mahāparinibbāna Sutta. In fact even today a work entitled 'Saṃyukta Vastu', the Vinaya of the Mūlasarvāstivādins, contains the account of both the Parinibbāna and the Councils.[2] It is, thus, quite reasonable to think that Cullavagga XI and the Mahāparinibbāna Sutta (Dīgha. 16) were originally a continuous narrative. Later on, it is possible that in order to shorten its otherwise too lengthy narrative or in view of its unsuitability in the context of the death-narrative, they would have taken out the portion dealing with the first Council and placed it with the account of the second

---

1. General Introduction to the Buddhist Suttas (S.B.E. Vol. xi) p. xiii.

2. Ibid. p. xiv.

3. J.P.T.S. 1908, pp. 1 ff.

4. Ibid. p. 79.

5. Z.D.M.G. Vol. xxxiv, 1880, pp. 184 ff.

6. Saṃyukta-Vastu, p. 1121 Narjio Bunyiu, Catalogue of the Chinese Translation of the Buddhist Tripitaka, Oxford 1883.

Council (Cullavagga XII) with which, evidently, it has the closest affinity. As Cullavagga XII mainly deals with the rules of Discipline (Vinaya), it might have been thought better to add it to the Vinaya Piṭaka, and along with it Cullavagga XI also had to be there. This can be seen also from the fact that the name, Cullavagga has a natural correspondence to the name, Mahāvagga and like the latter, the former also must have originally been designed with only 10 sections.[1] But later on when the account of the first and second Councils were added to it, it came to have two more sections, viz. XI and XII.

Thus, we find it reasonable to endorse the view of M. Winternitz who holds that "sections XI and XII in which the story of the first two Councils of Rājagaha and Vesālī is told are, no doubt, later additions and form a kind of appendix to the Cullavagga."[2] We, however, like to add by way of clarification that by 'later addition' one should not mean their 'later origination'. We, thus, discard the views of those scholars who merely on the basis of the non-mention of the first Council in the present Mahāparinibbāna Sutta try to disprove its historicity. In fact, the episode of Purāṇa in Cullavagga XI, significantly confirms its historicity. Purāṇa refuses to abide by the recitation of the Dhamma and the Vinaya of the Council. This story of his refusal cannot be explained without assuming some sort of prior canonisation of Buddha's teachings which he declines to accept. Nor is it possible to regard this episode as a mere invention, for it hardly serves the interest of enhancing the value of this canonisation; rather it undermines the authority of the theras of the first Council. So the first Council has to be accepted as an historical fact. Indeed, there would not have arisen the tradition about the Council, had not at least one Council been an historical event.[3]

Though we accept the first Council as a fact, we cannot accept everything that is stated in the tradition about its nature. The very fact that the account expects us to believe too much, speaks against its trustworthiness. Scholars have variously

---

1. Cf. Rhys Davids and Oldenberg —S.B.E. Vol. xiii, p. xxi, no. 3.
2. A History of Indian Literature, Vol. II, p. 25.
3. Cf. Copleston—Buddhism, pp. 174 ff. "It (tradition) would hardly have arisen if there had never been any Council at all." Ibid. p. 174

imagined its nature. Professor Poussin is inclined to think that the Council cannot but be regarded as an enlarged Pātimokkha-assembly.[1] According to Minayeff the account of the Council contains two clearly distinguishable parts, of which the one that speaks of the compilation of the Canon must belong to a period posterior to the rise of the sects.[2] N. Dutt is of the view that the purpose of the Council was to determine the less important rules of discipline (Khuddānukhuddakāni Sikkhāpadāni) the abrogation of which was sanctioned by Buddha himself at the time of his Parinibbāna.[3]

It is, indeed, difficult to say definitely as to what exactly could have been done at that Council. It is, however, *prima facie* impossible to think that two huge parts of the Tipiṭaka, viz. the Sutta and the Vinaya were then and there finally composed in that very Council (least to think of the canonisation of the Abhidhamma as spoken of by the Sumaṅgala Vilāsinī). According to Cullavagga xi, during the first month of the Varsāvāsa merely repairs to the broken and dilapidated parts had been made. How then within the remaining two months could the whole of the Sutta and the Vinaya have been recited for which the third Council (of course, along with the Abhidhamma as well) took full nine months according to both the Dīpavaṃsa and the Mahāvaṃsa ?[4] We can only accept this much as the historical kernel that sometime after Buddha's death the elders of the community assembled to agree upon the principal points of the doctrine and of the discipline of the Order. This may have formed the basis of the subsequent growth of the Canon. They must have arranged and brought about some unification in the utterances of the Master delivered on various occasions and at different places. It is suggested by the fact that Purāṇa refused to accept what they had thus decided (by saying that he would prefer to stick to what he had directly learnt from the Master). Evidently, he must have found that what they had agreed upon was not exactly what he had directly heard from Buddha, though in essence and spirit it might have been the same.

1. Cf. Early Monastic Buddhism, Vol. I, p. 339.
2. Recherches Sur le Bouddhisme, pp. 35 36.
3. Early Monastic Buddhism, Vol. I, pp. 339 ff.
4. Dīpavaṁsa vii-37; Mahāvaṁsa v. 280.

Subsequent years of Buddha's death appear to have been marked by increasing growth of this fundamental stock of texts decided in the first Council. Unlike the Vedic and the Upaniṣadic texts, Buddha himself is said to have discouraged the habit of looking upon his words as sacrosanct and to have forbidden their Sanskritization and chanting after the Vedic manner.[1] This must have at once facilitated the interpretative growth of the original doctrines. Theras would have, therefore, acted not only as the transmitters of the tradition but also as commentators—thus quickening the process of scholastic growth.

The first clear evidence of a schism appears a century after Buddha's death which is said to be responsible for holding the second Council. About its historicity the opinion of scholars is almost unanimous. They consider it "more credible".[2] Though, according to Cullavagga xii, the purpose of this Council is indicated as doing away with 10 heresies of the discipline, the Dīpavaṃsa and the Mahāvaṃsa[3] clearly speak of an eight-months' session leading to the revision of the doctrine. It is quite plausible to think that at a time when sectarian controversies were raising heads, the theras might have naturally thought it necessary to bring about rigidity by canonising the whole Dhamma and Vinaya. The ten heresies might have only served as an occasion for it.

Now, the very fact that a learned assembly was summoned to decide debatable points, is a sufficient indication to the fact that there must already have been some authoritative texts which could serve as the criterion for deciding the controversial matters. Besides, we have various internal evidences to support this fact. In fact, from the very early time any utterance whether by individual bhikkhus or by a community of them had had to be examined in the light of the accepted texts, before it could be sanctioned as being really in accord

1. M. III. 234 (Janapadaniruttim nābhiniveseyya, sāmaññaṃ nātidhāveyyāti iti...). See also M. II.240 where Buddha himself has suggested that one should care more for meaning than for mere word.

Cullavagga (V.33). cf. S.B.E. Vol. XX, pp. 150 ff.

2. Winternitz, A History of Indian Literature, Vol. II., p. 5.

3. Dīpavaṃsa. V. 27 ff. Mahāvaṃsa iv. 63-64.

with the teachings of the Master (Satthu Sāsanaṃ).[1] The reference of 9 aṅgas made by early Nikāyas[2] clearly shows that prior to the compilation of the Canon in its present form these diverse forms of the Buddhist literature were already there. Again there are other passages which indicate that there was a great mass of short texts, rules of the Order, speeches, dialogues, versified utterances and even minor collections of the texts which passed as the words of Buddha (Buddha-bacanaṃ), and were memorised and recited by monks.[3] Among the monks some are referred to as Suttantikas (reciters of the Suttantas), some as Dhammakathikas (preachers of the Dhamma), and some as Vinayadharas (experts in the Discipline).[4] Prominent monks are often called as "well-informed, experts of the tradition and well versed in the Dhamma, Vinaya and Mātikas.[5]

Now all these stocks of things developed, it appears, for about a century from Buddha's death, when interpretative divergence made its first appearance, as indicated from the 'dasa vatthūni' of Vajji monks. Now, it is perhaps not too daring to conjecture that the second Council, which was occasioned by this reported 'dasa Vatthūni', took the opportunity to canonise practically the whole of the Dhamma and the Vinaya. It is remarkable that in the concluding line both these Councils are designated as 'Vinaya Saṅgīti'. This clearly indicates that till the second Council the Abhidhamma was not developed. It must have been confined to Mātikas till then.

It is again important to note that the second Council

---

1. D. II. 124; A. II. 168.

2. M. I. 133; A. III. 361-2.

3. e.g. Aṭṭhaka Vagga found in the Sutta Nipāta, which is already mentioned in the Vinaya Piṭaka (Mahāvagga V. 13. 9) and in the Udāna V.6 (p. 59). Cf. Dhammapada 19, 20, 102, 185, 352; Sutta Nipāta 87.

4. Culla Vagga IV.4.4 and in many other passages. cf. N. Dutt, Early History of the Spread of Buddhism, pp. 207 ff. Upāli is mentioned as one of the first Vinayadharas: Cullla Vagga VI.13;IX.5; XI.1, 7 ff.

Cf. S.B.E. Vol. 13, p. xiii.

5. Bahusutta, āgatāgama, dhammadhara, vinayadhara, mātikādhara —Vinaya Pitaka : Mahavagga II.21.2; X.1.2. ; Cullavagga I.11.1; XII. 1.9 ff ; D. II. 125; A.I.117.

is represented as mainly dealing with the rules of discipline, whereas in the first, both Dhamma and Vinaya are clearly said to have been dealt with. From this it appears plausible to infer that the essentials of the Dhamma (Sutta Piṭaka), already determined at the first Council had almost reached their completion by the time of the second Council and in this Council they might have, as a matter of course, been given a finishing touch. But the Vinaya, on the other hand, firstly due to the swelling number of bhikkhus from different walks of life, and secondly due to the reported sanction by Buddha himself for doing away with the 'Khuddānukhuddakāni Sikkhāpadāni' must have passed through a chequered career giving rise ultimately to severe controversy. This explains as to why the second Council devoted itself mainly to the Vinaya, though the Dhamma and Vinaya—both were equally dealt with in the first Council. Thus, though the essentials of the Dhamma and Vinaya both, were determined at the first Council, the former could easily develop and complete itself within a short time, while the latter, on account of the reasons just indicated, had to wait for the tribunal's decision before reaching the final stage. However, with the exceptions of the Parivāra which is an abridged compendium of the rest of the Vinaya Piṭaka (which seems to have been designed later on, most probably for the convenience of general readers and added to the older Vinaya), the entire Vinaya along with the Dhamma (Sutta Piṭaka) appears to have been almost completed on this occasion.

Now, on the whole, the Dhamma comprising of the Nikāyas, on account of its relative uniformity, had to be regarded as the earliest and most authentic. This is not merely a conjecture, but is amply confirmed by the internal evidences. The Nikāyas, in spite of variety, exhibit a general impression of homogeneity.[1] We hardly come across any sectarian controversy in them. At a few places[2], of course, some controversies are referred to, but they are with regard to the meaning or interpretation of the same utterance of the

1. Cf. Keith—Buddhist Philosophy, p. 21.

2. e.g. Wrong interpretation of the Buddha's teachings by Ariṭṭha—(M.I. 130-133).

Master and not with regard to two different sets of independent doctrines. From the Kathāvatthu also which clearly refers to the Nikāyas, it is evident that the difference of the rival parties was not with regard to the scripture but only with regard to its interpretation, which indicates one text for all. The cleavage of Saṅgha (Saṅgha-bheda) is apprehended, but seldom referred to as an actuality.[1] This shows that the Nikāyas go back to a period when the monks were in all doctrinal matters, as yet, one. In fact, without presupposing a more or less developed canon, it is not possible to enter into subtleties of controversy. So, from the standpoint of thought-development also, the sectarian cleavage and diversity must be preceded by the non-sectarian, unified, more or less homogeneous doctrine, which the Nikāyas represent. We can, therefore, legitimately regard the Nikāyas as representing the earliest stage of Buddhist thought, when it was almost a non-controversial common doctrine.

The third Council, which is supposed to have been held under the presidentship of Moggaliputta Tissa, during the reign of the great Buddhist King, Aśoka, has been emphatically denied by some scholars like A. B. Keith[2] and N. Dutt.[3] The main argument of these scholars is the silence of the Tipiṭaka as well as of the hitherto found inscriptions of Aśoka. Keith says: "It is incredible that it ever took place without receiving some mention in the numerous records of Aśoka."[4] According to him "Tissa himself, son of Moggali bears a suspicious aspect,"[5] and so he concludes that "the Council was a figment of the pious or fraudulent imaginings of a sect which desired to secure for its texts and especially for the new Abhidhamma a connexion with the greatest of Buddhist sovereigns."[6]

1. The cutting aloof of a few individuals from the Order like that of Suṇakkhatta Licchavi-Putta (M.I.68) can hardly mean any cleavage in the Saṅgha. Cf. N. Dutt—Early Monastic Buddhism, Vol. 2, pp. 7 ff.

2. Buddhist Philosophy in India and Ceylon, pp. 28-29.

3. Early Monastic Buddhism, Vol. II. pp. 265-6.

4. Buddhist Philosophy in India & Ceylon. p. 18.

5. Ibid, p. 19. cf. Kern—Buddhism II.352; S.B.E. Vol. IV. pp. 198 ff.

6. Ibid, p. 19.

We, however, find it difficult to support Keith's view which tries to make too much merely on the basis of *argumentum e silentio*. It is true that the Council is said to have been held in Aśoka's reign, but even according to the tradition it is not the King himself but his learned teacher, Moggaliputta Tissa who is supposed to have conducted the whole session. So it was not necessary for the King to make mention of this Council in his edicts. Some of his edicts, however, do afford some hints of this Council. In one of the edicts, for example, the King decrees that heretical monks and nuns shall be excommunicated[1] which, according to tradition, was the primary objective of this Council. Dr. D. R. Bhandarkar has quite reasonably shown that some of Aśoka's inscriptions presuppose some such event.[2] The suggestion of G. C. Pande that Aśoka might not have been "as intimately connected with the Council as the Pali tradition would have us believe"[3] is also not to be ruled out.

At any rate, the grounds for the denial of the third Council are not strong enough to permit any serious doubt regarding the tradition of this Council, which is well supported by the later historical facts. It is now a well established historical truth that during Aśoka's reign vigorous attempts were started to take Buddhism beyond the borders of its narrower home, and it is in pursuance of this very campaign that so many missionaries were sent to different countries and Mahinda came to Ceylon. Now it is quite reasonable to believe that before this campaign was started, some concerted efforts must have been made to give a final form to the Buddhist Canons. According to Ceylon chronicles, Mahinda is said to have brought with him the sacred Buddhist texts. Besides, this is, at least, certain that by the time of Aśoka certain confusions had crept in the Order and the Buddhist community was divided into so many sects.[4] So it was quite likely

1. E. Hultzsch—Inscriptions of Aśoka: Corpus Inscriptionum Indicarum, Vol. I. pp. xliii ff; p. 160. No. 5.

2. Aśoka (IInd Edition)—Lectures on Ancient Indian Numismatics, pp. 96-102.

3. Studies in the Origins of Buddhism, p. 15.

4. As many as 18 different schools are mentioned. It is difficult to say whether this number was merely approximate or accurate, for this has

for the leading monks to have assembled once again for the revision and compilation of their Sacred Canons. The occasion was specially suited for such work when a great patron and adherent of Buddhism was the King of the land. However, it must be conceded that it was a sectarian affair, a Council of the Theravādins or Vibhajjavādins, who were supposed to represent the purest form of Buddhism, of which Moggaliputta Tissa was a leading exponent. This alone can explain as to why no mention of it is made by any other sect of Buddhism. So this nine-months' session of Pāṭaliputra may be regarded as a Council of only the Theravāda school.

Now according to the tradition, Tissa is supposed to have compiled the Kathāvatthu, one of the last works of the Abhidhamma on this very occasion in which all the heretical doctrines of the time are refuted. It is, in fact, with this purpose in view that this Council is said to have been summoned.

This traditional belief, however, cannot be fully supported. It can be seen, on closer examination, that the Kathāvatthu, besides referring to the Sutta and the Vinaya, quotes from the Dhammasaṅginī and the Vibhāsā and refers to contents peculiar to the Paṭṭhāna, but no quotation from or reference to either the Dhātukathā, the Puggala-paññatti or the Yamaka is found. So it is quite possible that the first Kathā might have been compiled by Moggaliputta Tissa but was not completed by him. Mrs. Rhys Davids seems to be right when she says that the Kathāvatthu was not composed *en bloc*. It has a "patch-work-quilt-appearance" which can be explained only when we suppose that these Kathās were piled up one after another according as new heresies emerged and their refutations made.[1] This view is supported from some marked linguistic peculiarities also which the first debate of the book, Puggala Kathā, exhibits. We find the use of

been a very favourite number in India, e.g. 18 Purāṇas; 18 Parvas of the Mahābhārata, 18 Chapters of the B.G., 18 aukṣihiṇī army of the Mahābhārata etc.

Besides, the names are not quite the same in various lists, cf. Dīpavaṃsa V. 39-48; Mahāvaṃsa V; Rhys Davids : J.R.A.S. 1891, p. 411. Rockhill—Life of the Buddha, Chapter VI.

1. Points of Controversy: Introduction, p. xxxi.

'ke' for 'ko', 'vattabbe' for 'vattabbo' and 'se' for 'so'.[1] So it seems probable that some parts, at least, of the Kathāvatthu were composed by Tissa during Aśoka's time but the additions went on for some more years. But, as a concerted effort had been already started for the propagation of the religion, the exponents of the doctrine must have tried to finalise the Canons sooner than later. In any case, however, the traditional view about the finalisation of the Abhidhamma at the third Council itself, cannot be accepted.

It is almost an agreed fact that the Abhidhamma gradually emerged out of Mātikās. So its relatively late origin is rather obvious. Till the second Council, we find mention only of the Dhamma and the Vinaya and not of the Abhidhamma. In early Canons, if at all any mention of it is made, it is in the form of Mātikās.[2] Besides, the very fact that the Abhidhamma is found only in two schools, viz. the Theravāda and the Sarvāstivāda, is a sufficient proof of its late origin. It is again remarkable that even these two Abhidhammas teach quite different doctrines,[3] though in contradistinction to it the Sutta and the Vinaya of the two schools have striking similarities. This indicates that their Sutta and the Vinaya have a common origin which is not the case with regard to the later work, the Abhidhamma. After a comparative study of these two Abhidhammas, Takakusu says: "Comparing the two sets of Abhidhamma works, as far as accessible to me, I do not find anything in form or in matter which could lead us to suppose that they were the same, though they treat, as a matter of course, of more or less similar subjects."[4] It is reasonable, therefore, to regard the Abhidhamma as a later development of the doctrines of the Suttas along sectarian lines which might have been completed some time about the end of the 3rd century B.C. We cannot, of course, be very definite here for want of any clear evidence. We can only approximately say that by the time of Aśoka, when Buddhist Missionaries were sent abroad, the whole of the Tipiṭaka with

1. Sakya or Buddhist Origins, p. 359.
2. Dhammadharā, Vinayadharā, Matikādharā.
3. Cf. Farquhar—Outline of the Religious Literature of India, pp. 68ff; Keith—Buddhist Philosophy, p. 22; Poussin—Buddhisme, p. 44.
4. J.R.A.S. 1905, p. 161.

the exception of some portions of the Abhidhamma was completed, and the Pali Canon that has come down to us does, on the whole, correspond to what it was in the 3rd century B.C. Of course, we cannot claim rigidity, for its different versions might have received some editorial retouching, slight addition and alteration, or, to use the words of Professor Winternitz, "the centuries have surely not passed them by without leaving traces."[1]

The inscriptions of Aśoka are clear indications of, at least, the approximate finalisation of the Tipiṭaka, specially of the Sutta and the Vinaya by the 3rd century B.C. Not only some of these edicts represent the general spirit of the Pali Canon but they exhibit even considerable verbal similarities to the texts.[2] It is again remarkable that the inscription of Bairat of the year 249 B.C. reads: "All that the Lord Buddha has said, is well said",[3] and then there is the recommendation of seven scriptures, of which six have been traced in more or less satisfactory manner in the Pali Canon.[4]

Again the inscriptions on the famous stupas of Bharhut and Sāñcī lend full support to this fact.[5] Though there is some controversy about the date of these monuments,[6] the majority of them are written in the same characters as the inscriptions of Aśoka. They contain various sculptures which depict legendary tales of Buddha's life, as found in a few Pali

---

1. A History of Indian Literature, Vol. II. p. 14.

2. F.W. Thomas: J.R.A.S. 1903, pp. 831 ff; Buhler: Z.D.M.G. Vol. 48, pp. 57 ff.; E. Hardy (J.R.A.S. 1901, p. 314) shows verbal similarity between Aśoka's Bhabru Edict: "hevaṃ sa dhammo cilaṭhitiko hāsatīti" and Aṅguttara III. 247, 340 "yena saddhammo ciraṭṭhitiko hotī ti."

3. The dictum of Aṅguttara iv. 164.

4. Rhys David's—Dialogues Vol. I, p. xiii; Oldenburg—Vinaya Piṭaka Vol. I.p. xl; Z.D.M.G. Vol. 52, 1898, p. 634 ff; Winternitz—A History of Indian Literature. Vol. II. pp. 606ff; Keith—Buddhist Philosophy p. 17.

5. The inscriptions have been published and translated by E. Hultzsch, Z.D.M.G. Vol. 40, 1886, pp. 58 ff. Indian Antiquary Vol. 21, 1892, pp. 225ff. & B. M. Barua : Bharhut Inscriptions, Calcutta, 1926.

6. L. A. Waddell—J.R.A.S. 1914, pp. 138ff:
F.C. Maisey—Sāñcī and its Remains, London 1892;
Sir John Marshall—A Guide to Sāñcī, Calcutta, 1918;
V. A. Smith—A History of Fine Art in India & Ceylon, pp. 73 ff.

Suttas, and more specially in later works like the Nidāna Kathā, Lalitavistāra and the Mahāvastu. Some of the reliefs and inscriptions evidently depict Jātakas, most of which have been clearly traced in the Jātaka book of the Tipiṭaka. Besides, these monuments contain some votive inscriptions where we find mention of such epithets as Sutantika (reciter of the Sutta), Pacanekāyika (knower of five nikāyas) Peṭakin (knower of the Piṭakas), Dhammakathika (preacher of the Dhamma) and Bhāṇaka (reciter).[1]

Now, even if we accept the last date assigned by some scholars for these inscriptions i.e. the 2nd and the 1st century B.C., we shall have to leave sufficient margin for the literature to grow and be popular enough to find depiction through sculptures and reliefs. At any rate, they do prove beyond any shadow of doubt that before the 2nd century B.C. there would have existed a collection of Buddhist texts known as Piṭakas as well as the fivefold divisions of the Sutta known as Nikāyas, and the memorising and reciting of the Dhamma must have continued as a long-followed practice. The fact that some of these Suttas as well as Jātakas tally exactly with those contained in the Tipiṭaka afford full confirmation to our conclusion.[2]

The fact that in the whole of the Tipiṭaka, there is no mention of the great Buddhist King, Aśoka, who evidently did for Buddhism more than any other King (whether Bimbisāra, Ajātaśatru or Pasendi who are mentioned at different places in the Pali Canon), goes to show its antiquity as well as its realistic character. The same is confirmed by the absolute absence of any reference to Ceylon which has been one of the strongest footholds of the Theravāda Buddhism right since the religion was brought here by Mahinda. The possibility of treating this silence about Aśoka as a clever attempt by bhikkhus for giving the impression of antiquity to a later work should be ruled out as utter scepticism. Rhys Davids, in this connection, has rightly remarked: "The

1. They can well be compared to similar epithets used in Cullavagga IV.4.4; cf. N. Dutt—Early History of the Spread of Buddhism. pp. 207 ff.

2. Cf. G. C. Pande—Studies in the Origins of Buddhism, pp. 15-16. Winternitz—A History of Indian Literature, Vol. II., pp. 17-18.

Indians have never been such deliberate forgers that, if Aśoka had been mentioned they would have eliminated the references, in order to create the appearance of antiquity."[1] Non-reference to Aśoka even in those portions of the Abhidhamma which are supposed to be compiled during his time or even a little later can be explained by the fact that they were developed in strict fidelity to the older stock and so had no reason to refer to any extraneous matter.

Again, the fact that the larger bulk of the Pali Canon closely resembles the Upaniṣads in language and style, further indicates that it must have come down to us from a time not far removed from Buddha and his immediate disciples.

Conclusion:

By way of conclusion, we may now state that Buddhism originated towards the last quarter of the 6th century B.C., when the Master started his Dhamma-cakka-Pavattana in about 528 B.C. The earliest collection of his teachings is evidently the Sutta-Piṭaka consisting of five Nikāyas which may reasonably be looked upon as constituting the purest form of the Buddhist doctrine. The fact that the Nikāyas take but little notice of the sectarian conflicts, amply indicates that it had practically reached its completion by the time of the second Council i.e. by the 1st century A.B. No other Buddhist literature has come down to us from such an early time. They can, therefore, be regarded as the most trustworthy accounts of the original doctrine of the Buddha. From the point of view of the philosophical importance as well, they alone can be vouched for, because unlike the Vinaya which mostly deals with the rules of discipline and the Abhidhamma which mainly is a later interpretative development of the doctrines of the Sutta, the Nikāyas represent the truest embodiment of the teachings of Buddha's doctrines.

Side by side with the Sutta, the Vinaya also was developing, but as it had to pass through controversial stages, it naturally took relatively more time. But near about the 2nd century A.B., this also seems to have been practically completed, as is evident from its complete silence about the third Council.

---

1. Buddhist India. p. 174.

The Abhidhamma obviously is the latest part of the Canon, but its completion also could not have far succeeded the period of the third Council, as indicated from its silence about Ceylon. The fact that the Sutta, Vinaya, Abhidhamma and Aṭṭhakathā exhibit in an increasing order the elements of exaggeration, supernatural marvels and legendary tales—goes further to support the same chronological order of these works.

Section C

THE CHRONOLOGICAL RELATION BETWEEN THE BHAGAVADGĪTĀ AND THE NIKĀYAS

As shown in the foregoing discussion, it is the Nikāyas of the Pali Canon which constitute the earliest and, therefore, the purest available teachings of Buddha. It would, therefore, be more fruitful and expedient to base ourselves mainly on the Nikāyas, so far as the elements of Early Buddhism are concerned.

Now, we have seen that Buddhism originates in about the last quarter of the 6th century B.C. (528 B.C.), and by the time of the death of Buddha i.e. by the first quarter of the 5th century B.C. (483 B.C.) the religion in all its essential aspects is fully propounded and established,[1] though the canonisation of the Sutta-Piṭaka according to our inquiry and calculation seems to have been completed by the first quarter of the 4th century B.C. i.e. the 1st century A.B. It would not, therefore, be too much to expect the full influence of the fundamental tenets of early Buddhist doctrines by the beginning of the 5th century B.C. None can doubt that Buddhism had emerged as a powerful religious movement in the very life-time of the Buddha who spent all his post-enlightenment days untiringly in preaching and propagating his noble gospel.

We have seen in our discussion about the chronology of the Bhagavadgītā that its composition is post-Buddhistic, of course, not far removed from the time of the rise of Buddhism. Its composition seems to have taken place sometime between the 4th and the 5th century B.C. It would not, therefore, be impossible from this chronological point of view to consider

1. Talk between Buddha and Māra:—"I shall not die, O Evil one, until this pure religion of mine shall have become successful, prosperous, wide-spread and popular in all its full extent— until, in a word, it shall have been well proclaimed among men."

"And now Lord, this pure religion of thine has become all this." D, II. 106.

the Bhagavadgītā as having been composed under the impact of the newly developed thought of Buddhism.

We shall observe in the succeeding chapter, in the course of discussing the ideological sources of the Bhagavadgītā, that this hypothesis is abundantly confirmed. The Bhagavadgītā, though assimilating some elements of Early Buddhism, is found primarily to emerge by way of a counteraction to the growing influence of atheism and renunciation preached by Buddhism.

———

CHAPTER II

Section A

THE SOURCES OF EARLY BUDDHISM

The Need for Inquiry into Pre-Buddhistic Tradition :—

The immediate source of Buddhism, as we know, is the teachings of Buddha, the individual. Yet the germs of some of these teachings are traceable to a much earlier period. Thinkers, like other people, are, in no small measure, the product of their age and cultural traditions. The questions which they try to answer are those their contemporaries are raising; the solutions which they give are relative to the traditions handed down to them. Even when they are propounding theories which are very new, they, at least, use the ideas and concepts of tradition to express the deeper truths towards which they are feeling their way In short, thought does not make any incongruous leap. There is no sudden jump from folly to science and, therefore, it is only by considering Buddhism in relation to its earlier and contemporary Indian thought in the midst of which it arose and grew, that its true nature and significance can be understood in a proper perspective. Oldenberg is right when he says, "Hundreds of years before Buddha's time movements were in progress in Indian thought, which prepared the way for Buddhism and cannot, therefore, be separated from a sketch of the latter."[1]

Attempts made by various scholars to trace the origins of Buddhistic ideas have not, as yet, led them to a definite conclusion. Opinions are widely divided. Jacobi thinks that Buddhism was derived from a corresponding theory of the fore-runners of the Jains.[2] He also speaks of the Sāṅkhya-Yoga influence.[3] A.Weber is inclined to identify Buddha

1. Buddha—trans. by Hoey. p.6.
2. Referred by T. W. Rhys Davids in his 'Origin and Growth of Religion' p. 27.
3. Z. D. M. G. 1898.. p. 1.

with Kapila, and holds the view that the original Sāṅkhya and Buddhism were one and the same. He thinks that his view is well confirmed by the fact that the birth place of Buddha is called Kapilavastu (abode of Kapila).[1] The account of Aśvaghoṣa about Buddha meeting the Sāṅkhyan teacher, Ārāḍa Kālāma is considered a positive proof in support of this view.[2] A.B.Keith, however, though pointing out a number of similarities between Sāṅkhya and Buddhism, says that "the proof of Sāṅkhya influence is obviously indirect and not in itself complete."[3] Oldenberg's view also is somewhat similar. He thinks that Sāṅkhya did not influence Buddhism directly but indirect influence is undeniable.[4] G.C. Pande, on the other hand, altogether denies any distinctive influence of both Jainism and Sāṅkhya. According to him there is "little ground for assuming a direct dependence between early Buddhism and Jainism."[5] He further says: "..as with Jainism Sāṅkhya (also) did not exert any direct or distinctive influence on early Buddhism."[6] Then the influence of Yoga on Buddhism has been asserted more definitely.[7] Besides Yoga, Senart is anxious to prove the influence of Viṣṇu-Kṛṣṇa-cult on Buddhism.[8] Bapat refers to the Vedic and Upaniṣadic influences. He says: "The tenets of these different wandering sects can be traced back to Vedic literature, particularly the literature of the Upaniṣads."[9] According to G.C. Pande, "although direct evidence is lacking, it appears that early Buddhism was fundamentally influenced by the Upaniṣads."[10] T.W. Rhys Davids, however, avers

---

1. History of Indian Literature, p. 284; cf. Radhakrishnan, Indian Philosophy, Vol. I. pp. 472-3.
2. Buddhacarita, XII. X. 16ff.
3. Buddhist philosophy, pp. 140-2.
4. Die Lehre der Upanishaden und die Anfange des Buddhismus, p. 296.
5. Studies in the Origins of Budhism, p. 547.
6. Ibid. p. 551.
7. Keith—Buddhist philosophy, pp. 143ff; Oldenberg—Buddha. pp. 324ff; G. C. Pande—op. cit. pp. 551ff.
8. I. H. Q. Vol 6, pp. 669-673.
9. 2500 years of Buddhism, p. 11.
10. Studies in the Origins of Buddhism, p. 556.

that "it is quite likely that the Buddhist ideas are the originals."[1]

Thus a wide variety of views have been expressed about the origins of Buddhism. It appears that most of the scholars in attempting to answer have been mainly guided by the similarities of ideas, and many of them have tacitly assumed that all thoughts existing before Buddha must necessarily have a Vedic origin. Both these considerations, however, have clear limitations and so, if relied on as an exclusive basis, are bound to misdirect the investigation.

Firstly, the similarity of some ideas is by itself no proof of direct borrowing, for in many cases it may be traceable to a common origin and secondly, the discoveries in the Indus-Valley have proved that a civilised non-Vedic culture once existed in pre-Vedic India which invalidates the common assumption that the foundations of all pre-Buddhistic thought have had to be found in the Vedic culture.

In fact, the Indian thought assumed a composite character at a very early stage. Thoughts, we know, rarely develop in closed rooms. They have to grow in an open atmosphere, meeting and mingling with different ideas around them. Numerous races and religions, communities and cultures have met, struggled and fused into one another in the long history of India and so its process of thought-development cannot be properly viewed without this historical perspective. A perusal of these various thought-currents alone can enable us to understand the social and intellectual atmosphere which occasioned and influenced the emergence of the Buddhist thought. We, therefore, propose to give here a brief survey of the development of pre-Buddhistic thought in India.

The Pre-Vedic Stage :

(A) *Indications from Indus-Valley Excavations*:—

The discovery of Indus civilisation has shown that prior to the arrival of Aryans, a highly organised cultured people already existed in the north-western part of India. The

1. Origin and Growth of Religion, p. 28.

view of L. Sarup[1] about the priority of the Ṛgveda to the Indus-Valley civilisation has been proved to be untenable by Pt. K. Chattopadhyaya.[2] It has been conclusively shown by Sir John Marshall[3] that the Indus civilisation was quite distinct from and earlier than the Vedic civilisation, and R.C. Mazumdar also agrees that this "view is now generally accepted."[4] Some scholars like M. Wheeler[5] and Piggott[6], however, suggest that the Indus civilisation, though pre-Vedic, was thoroughly demolished by the violence of insurgent Aryans and attempts have been made to find references to it in the Ṛgveda. Indra's exploit of releasing the waters has been understood by Piggott in the sense of a description of the Aryan destruction of the bunds built by non-Aryans for the protection of Harappa cities from flood.[7] The fight of Indra with dāsas and dasyus has been interpreted as the fight of the Aryans against non-Aryans.[8] But this also has been ably shown by Pt.K. Chattopadhyaya[9] to be an over-imaginative interpretation. He has rightly pointed out that the tradition always represents Indra as fighting against demons spoken of as dāsas and dasyus whose forts and cities are nothing but a poetic and mythical representation of clouds. We, of course, do not doubt the fact of struggle and conflict which must have taken place between Aryans and non-Aryans on the arrival of the former. But this does not warrant the turning of myth into history. The Ṛgveda is no historical document of Aryan and non-Aryan battles.

In course of time when the nomadic Aryans settled down,

---

1. Indian Culture, Vol. IV, 1937-38, pp. 149ff.
2. Presidential Address in the Vedic section of the Ninth A.I.O.C. (Proceedings. pp. 125ff), Trivandrum.
3. Mohenjodaro and the Indus Civilisation, Vol. I. pp. 110-112; cf. The Vedic Age by R. C. Mazumdar, p. 194.
4. The Vedic Age, p. 194; Mazumdar, however, is inclined to hold that "it represents the synthesis of the Aryan and non-Aryan Cultures." Ibid. p. 195.
5. The Indus Civilisation, p. 90.
6. Pre-historic India, pp. 261-3.
7. Ibid. pp. 261ff.
8. Ibid. pp. 261ff; A.B. Keith—Religion and Philosophy of the Vedas and Upaniṣads (H.O.S. Vol. 31, 1925), p. 234; A.A. Macdonell—Vedic Mythology, p. 157.
9. Dāsa and Dasyu in the Ṛgveda (Proceedings of the Nineteenth International Congress of Orientalists held at Rome), pp. 305-311.

the bitter struggle must have gradually died down, and the non-Aryans must have gradually come in contact with Aryans. We cannot otherwise explain some non-Aryan elements in the later Aryan culture and civilisation. Phallic worship definitely goes back to the pre-Vedic Indus civilisation. The representation of Śiva as Paśupati, Yogī and Naṭarāja, the worship of the Mother-Goddess, of the Pīpal tree, of the bull and other animals as well as the great sanctity attached to water—all are legacies of the Indus civilisation.[1] The most important discovery, for our purpose is that of a figure with a cross-legged posture and the outstretched palms placed on the knees which indicates a yogic posture.[2] Again it has been pointed out by K.A. Nilakanta Śāstrī that "the yogic posture occurs also in a statue of a male figure and in a small faience sealing where a deity in the same attitude is apparently worshipped by a kneeling nāga."[3] Thus the trace of yogic practices as well as of the worship of gods in a personal and iconic form goes back to the pre-Aryan Indus civilisation.[4]

(B) *The Origin of the Buddhist Mendicancy* :—

That the 'munis' and 'yogins' were somewhat alien to the Vedic culture is very clearly indicated from the rare and unfavourable references to them in the early Vedic texts. The first reference to a 'muni' is found in Ṛgveda X. 136 where he is described as a strange long-haired dirty tawny-clad figure walking in the air, behaving like a mad man and inspired.[5] In Aitareya Brāhmaṇa VI. 33 we come across another Aitaśa muni who is regarded as deranged by his own son.[6] The

1. M. Wheeler—The Indus Civilisation, pp. 83-4; Piggott—Prehistoric India, pp. 201-3; Sir John Marshall—Mohenjodaro and the Indus Civilisation, pp. 77-78; E. J. H. Mackay—The Indus Civilisation, pp. 85, 96-97; Proceedings and Transactions of All India Oriental Conference, Patna 1930 'On the Siśnadevas of the Ṛgveda'.

2. Wheeler—The Indus Civilisation, pp. 79 and 83; Marshall—op. cit. I. 70.

3. The Cultural Heritage of India, II.p.22.

4. Vedic Age, pp. 160-1.

5. Vedic Index, Vol. II, p. 167; cf. Early Buddhist Monachism—S.K. Dutt, pp. 51 ff.

6. Vedic Index, Vol. II.p. 167; cf. Early Buddhist Monachism, p. 54; Studies in the Origins of Buddhism, p. 258.

Ṛṣis in the Taittirīya Āraṇyaka[1] also have been called Vātaraśanāḥ (wind-girt) like the muni of Ṛgveda X. 136. The reference is evidently to the naked ascetics. In Ṛgveda VIII. 17.24 Indra is said to be the friend of the munis. This corresponds to the mention of 'Devamuni' (divine muni) in Atharvaveda VII. 74. 1. Then we come across a mystic figure known as 'Vrātya' who appears at one time to be a supernatural being and at another, as a human wanderer in need of food and lodging.[2] From the description it is, indeed, difficult to make out whether he is a non-Aryan or an Aryanised non-Aryan or a degenerate Aryan. But this much is clear that it cannot be a prototype of pure Aryan tradition of the early Vedic time.

These rare and mostly unfavourable references to the munis or ascetics in the early Vedic period only indicate that they were alien to the early Vedic people. Macdonell and Keith are right in observing that it would be unwise "to conclude from the comparative rareness of the mention of the muni in the Vedic texts that he was an infrequent figure in Vedic times ; he was probably not approved by the priests who followed the ritual and whose views were essentially different from the ideals of a muni which were superior to earthly considerations such as the desire for children and dakṣiṇā."[3]

In fact, the whole trend of the Brahmanical literature is antagonistic to the life of mendicancy. Until we come down to the Upaniṣads (by which time the Aryan and non-Aryan culture must have interpenetrated each other), we hardly come across any reverential reference to munis. Even then, it is only a section of the Brahmanical circle and not the entire community which seems to have been favourably influenced by these forest-dwelling wandering ascetics.

We have copious evidences to indicate that these ascetics, sometime styled as 'muni', sometime as 'śramaṇa' and sometime as 'muṇḍaka', were treated with scorn by the

1. Tait. I. 23. 2; 24. 4.; II. 7.I.

2. Griffith's translation of the Atharva-veda, p. 199; cf. Early Buddhist Monachism—S.K. Dutta, p. 55.

3. Vedic Index, Vol. II pp. 167-8. For the Vedic reference to the desire for children and dakṣiṇā see Ṛgveda V. 58. 4.

Brahmins and even during Buddha's time the antagonism had not fully died out. In the Śatapatha Brāhmaṇa, for example, Tura Kāvaṣeya is referred to as a muni.[1] But we know from the Aitareya-Brāhmaṇa that his father Kavaṣa Ailūṣa muni was driven out from a sacrifice with the words "O son of a female slave, you are a rogue and not a Brahmin."[2] In the Pali Nikāyas also Samaṇa-muṇḍakas are frequently delineated in sharp opposition to the Brāhmins. To take just one instance from the Sutta-Nipāta, the Brāhmaṇa, Aggika Bhāradvāja while engaged in his fire worship sees Buddha approaching his house and at once calls out : "Stop there, O shaven-headed, O samaṇaka of a low caste !"[3] Even Patañjali in his Mahābhāṣya has used the compound, 'samaṇa-brāhmaṇa' as an illustration of a rule of Sanskrit Samāsa indicating perpetual enmity (yeṣāñca virodhaḥ śāśvatikaḥ)[4]. It is, perhaps, not without significance that even when asceticism was assimilated later on into Vedic culture it was considered essential for a man taking to the ascetic-life to discard all Brahmanical marks like the scared tuft of hair, the sacred thread, sacrificial rites and the studies of the Vedas.[5]

Again, it is a point of great significance that among the non-Indian branches of the great Aryan stock, although institutions analogous to Indian Brahmanism are found, we do not find any trace of the existence of religious mendicancy in the earliest monuments of their literature.[6] Even as late as Alexander's invasion to India. nothing of the type of mendicancy was known to the Macedonians who were simply wonder-struck at the Indian Gymnosophists.[7] Had they known anything similar in the Hellenic world, they must have,

---

1. Śat. Brāh. II. P. 1041.
2. Ait Brāh. VIII. 1.
3. Tatreva muṇḍaka, tatreva samaṇaka, tatreva vasalaka tiṭṭhāhī ti."-Sn. 21.
4. Patañjali on Pāṇini II. 4. 9.
5. Āruṇeyopaniṣad, I.
6. Early Buddhist Monachism, p. 59.
7. Mc Crindle, Ancient India : Its Invasion by Alexander, the Great, p. 36 . The Cambridge History of India (Ancient India), Vol. I. pp. 321-2.

at least, made a passing reference to it while giving a lengthy account of Indian Gymnosophists.

It is, therefore, reasonable to hold that religious mendicancy was introduced into Indian life by the influence of the pre-Vedic non-Aryan culture and not by the early Aryan settlers whose whole approach to life was worldly or pravṛtti-dharmic. Thus the theory of some eminent Western scholars like Max Muller,[1] Jacobi[2], Buhler[3] and Kern[4] who hold that the Brahmanical asceticism was the archetype for the Buddhist and Jaina mendicancy, is found to be unacceptable both in the light of the Indus-Valley discoveries as well as in view of the Vedic and Brahmanical references to munis and yogins.

It can be easily seen that the ideal of the Jaina and Buddhist mendicancy which enjoins renunciation of family life all and sundry in one's youth or the very heyday of one's life was quite different from the Brahmanical ideal of retirement after the proper fulfilment of all the obligations of family and society. The theory of the fourfold obligations formulated in the Brāhmaṇas[5] had not ceased to have its weight in the Upaniṣadic period and even during the time of Buddha, on at least some sections of society.[6] Yājñavalkya, the leading saint of the Upaniṣadic period is known to have led his full span of a house-holder's life receiving wealth and cows from Janaka, before thinking of retiring to the forest[7], despite the fact that the superiority of the radical renunciation

1. Hibbert Lectures, p. 351.

2. Introduction to the Jaina Sutras (S.B.E. Vol. XXII Part I), pp. xxiv-xxxii.

3. Translation of the Baudhāyana Sūtras (Passim).

4. Manual of Indian Buddhism.

5. Śatapatha Brāh. I. 7. 2. 1.; cf. Tait. Brāh. VI. 3. 10. 7. The Śatapatha Brahmana, clearly states that a man is born wrth fourfold debts of the Ṛsis or sages, the Pitṛs or ancestors, the gods and men. for the fulfilment of which he must study the Vedas, beget a son, offer sacrifices and lead a moral and hospitable life.

6. Frequent references in the Pali Nikāyas are found where people are dissuaded from renunciation in the heyday of their youth. They are advised to acquire virtue while leading a comfortable family-life and not to renounce home while having black hair. cf. Bhavam kho Raṭṭhapālo etarahi daharo yuvā susukālakeso bhadrena yobbanena samannāgato pathamena vayasā...kiṃ bhavaṃ...pabbajito.-M. II.66.

7. Bṛhadā. iv. 5.2.

and mendicancy of the Jaina and Buddhist type was recognised.[1] It is especially the Muṇḍakopaniṣad, which, as its very name suggests, gave the highest rank to such outright renouncers.[2] But if we take the overall picture of things, it appears more reasonable to trace the germs of the Jaina and Buddhist mendicancy in the pre-Aryan non-Brahmanical cult of the 'muni' rather than in the Brahmanical institute of the fourth Āśrama. The latter seems itself to have been partly influenced by the former, though partly it seems to have emerged due to its own inner evolution, as we shall see in the sequel.

Another significant contribution of the pre-Vedic civilization to Indian thought seems to be the theory of transmigration which is traceable neither in the Vedic nor the Brāhmanic conception of the after-life. It appears rather abruptly in the Upaniṣads in a quite developed form which *ipso facto* indicates an *ab extra* source. We shall see this point more clearly in the following accounts of the development of the Vedic and Upaniṣadic thought.

The Vedic and Brahmanical Stage:—

(*A*) *Belief in an After-life*:—

That the Vedas exhibit no trace of it is generally accepted by scholars.[3] The view of Professor P. V. Bapat that "the conception of the transmigration of the souls, that of mortals returning to this world, is as old as the Yamasukta or the Hymn to the Fathers,"[4] is only based on the confusion of reading the transmigration of soul in the mere reference to the future survival after the manner of the life here. We do not deny that some Vedic passages speak of a glorious endless continuance of the future life of sensuous enjoyment[5] and one or two passages indicate the possibility of a departed

1. Ibid. iii. 5. 1 and iv. 4. 22.
2. Muṇḍako. I. 2. 11 & III. 2. 6.
3. cf. T.W. Rhys Davids—Origin and Growth of Religion, p. 73; Keith—Religion and Philosophy of the Veda, pp. 570-1.
4. 2500 years of Buddhism. p. 11.
5. Ṛgveda IX. 113. 7-11; Atharva-veda IV. 34. 2-4; cf. J. Muir's Sanskrit Texts Vol. V. pp. 306ff.

spirit being recalled to life and to ecurity here on earth[1], but there is no idea of a return of the soul to this world either as man, animal, or other species, or of a life before this one.

In the Brāhmaṇas the proper performance of sacrifice is supposed to lead to a blessed life after death. The sacrificer is reborn by virtue of the magical potency of the sacrificial fire[2] and he enjoys a happy life of endless duration in the company of gods.[3] He is supposed to survive solely through the potency of the sacrificial fire and not by virtue of anything inherent in him. Yajña becomes the soul of the yajamāna in the other world.[4] Thrice is one born—of the father, of the mother and of the sacrifice.[5] A suggestion is also made that in some mysterious way, it is this body which is put together (sandhatte) in the form of future existence through the potency of the sacrificial fire.[6] We also find a reference to going to heaven with this body (saśarīra eva svargaṃ lokameti).[7] Difference in the quality of the sacrifice accounts for the difference in the state of the after life[8] and different sacrifices are supposed to lead to the worlds of different gods.[9] Some sacrifices are for the sake of Devaloka and there is a way leading to the gods (devayāna) and another leading to the Fathers (Pitṛyāna)[10]. Some sacrifices are for the sake of Yamaloka.[11] Even the gods are supposed to have gained their immortality through sacrifice[12] and they further stand in need of being fed by the sacrifices of the world.[13] Sometimes, immortality is doubted and fear of death (punarmṛtyu) expressed, for the heaven beyond or within the sun, to be attained through special

1. Ṛgveda X. 58. 1; X. 60. 10; J. Muir.-op. cit. p. 313.
2. Śat. Brāh. II. 1000 and 1383.
3. Ibid. 1208; 1050; Ait. Brāh. I. 197,419, 420.
4. Śat. Brāh. II. 1138-9 and 1141.
5. Śat. Brāh. I. 120; Ait. Āraṇyaka 172-6.
6. Śat. Brāh. I. 528 and 301.
7. Tait. Brāh. III. 1377; cf. Tait. Brāh. I. 453-4; Ibid. III. 1226.
8. Śat. Brāh. I. 250-1.
9. Tait Āraṇyaka I. 156; Tait. Brāh. I. 234-6, 282.
10. Śat. Brāh. I. 143.
11. Ibid. I. 478.
12. Śat. Brāh. II. 1126.
13. Ibid. II. 1138-This notion is still to be seen in the BG. III. 10-12.

ritual alone, is said to be really free from time and death.[1]

Now these references of the Brāhmaṇas can by no means be regarded as indicative of the theory of transmigration. Transmigration presupposes, at least, some sort of continuous conscious principle distinct from the body (call it soul or Vijñāna). But the Brāhmaṇas display a very vague and obscure view about the soul which is often conceived in close relation with the body. They seldom consider it as something distinct and by nature immortal.[2] Regarding karma, they seem to have no idea except that it is regarded as the potency of the sacrificial fire.

So it is difficult to regard the sudden appearnce of the transmigration-theory in a nearly finalised form in the Upaniṣads[3] as a development of the Brahmanical views. Its source, therefore, seems to be that of the munis and śramaṇas outside the Vedic pale. We can, of course, concede that the Brāhmaṇas with their ideas of death as a rebirth, their constant fear of dying, their incessant quest for immortality and with the hope of a timeless world beyond the Sun—must have created a background of receptivity for the adoption and assimilation of this theory. But it is not plausible to accept the views of Oldenberg[4] who thinks that the origin of the idea of transmigration should be seen in the Brahmanical ideas. We find no indication in the Vedas and Brāhmaṇas which may support the theory that the Aryans brought with them the idea of transmigration into India.

(B) *The Ascendancy of Brahmins add Stratification of Society*:—

As is well known, there is no mention of caste in the

---

1. Śat. Brāh. I. 180; II. 1053, 1067, 1097, 1101, 1114-7; The theory that the idea of transmigration arose from the concept of punarmṛtyu has been already refuted by Poussin. (I 'Inde Jusqu' au 300 avant J. C., P. 282-3).

2. Vedic Mythology, p. 166; The Brāhmaṇas even when using Ātman in the sense of Prāṇa, they invariably speak of its dependence on food (Śat. Brāh. II. 948 and Tait. Saṃhita, I. 108). its connection with the length of life (Śat. Brāh. II. 1269) and its location in different parts of body (Tait. Saṃhitā, II. 726).

3. Bṛhadā. Up. III. 2. 13; iv. 4. 5. cf. Religion and Philosophy of the Veda, II. P. 573.

4. Die Religion des Veda (7th Edition) pp. 563ff.

oldest hymns of the Vedas.[1] After the bitter warfare against the non-Aryan died away, the domineering spirit of the Aryan conquerors naturally expressed itself in the pride of class superiority. Some sections of those Aryans who instead of fighting and ruling devoted themselves to religious activities came to be respected by all Aryan people including the rulers and gradually came to be regarded as the highest class, the repository of religion and culture. The development of rituals and sacrifices during the period of the Brāhmaṇas made them indispensable and they became a self-conscious conceited class of people. They then formulated the fourfold classification of society—the Brāhmaṇas, the Rājanyas, the Vaiśyas and the Śūdras—which found expression in the later Vedic hymns[2] and to which all their different offshoots were subsequently traced. Even then the division was into classes, not into castes, as it susequently came to be known.

The relation of the Brahmins with the rulers, whose authority was supreme for the people, can well be understood from the fact that the former occupied the office of Purohita (he who ramains ahead) of the latter. The position of the Brahmin was thus the highest.[3] He did not care to become king. The two classes, viz. the Brahmaṇa and Kṣatriya were regarded as the two deities, viz. Mitra and Varuṇa symbolising intelligence and will, the union of which was essential for the performance of any deed.[4] The Brahmaṇa, however, could do without the king though not *vice versa*. All classes including the Rājanya could offer sacrifice only through the mediation of the Brāhmaṇas. The gods were supposed not to accept the food of a king who was without a Purohita. All people owed respect, security and liberty to the Brāhmaṇas. A natural pride based on the acceptance of class hierarchy, debarring inter-class marriage and a natural tendency to follow the hereditary occupation with the Brahmanical stamp of religious sanctity gradually hardened this class-system. When the occupations began multiplying, this hardened class-

1. In the Ṛgveda no indication of caste-system is found save and except one in the Puruṣa-sūkta which is now accepted as a later interpolation. cf. S. B.E. Vol. XII—Introduction to Śat. Brāh. p. xii.
2. Ṛgveda X. 90. 12; Yajurveda xxxi. 11. and Atharva. XIX. 6.6.
3. Sat. Brāh. II. 4. 4. 5.
4. Ibid. IV. 1. 4. 1-6.

system gradually took the form of a caste-system. The barrier imposed in the beginning against the vanquished class, which the Aryans despised, had now as its natural result, brought in similar barriers within their own circle which bore most bitter fruit later on. By the time of the Upaniṣads, the voice of protest began to be raised against it, and later on Buddha made an open denunciation of it.

(C) *Polytheism Showing Monotheistic and Monistic Trends*:—

A striking feature of the early hymns was their polytheistic character. A great many gods, most of them represening the phenomena of nature were imagined, invoked and worshipped by means of prayer and food-offerings, primarily for the sake of secular welfare. This was the first naturalistic anthropomorphic stage of god-making regarding which Radhakrishnan says: "The process of god-making in the factory of man's mind cannot be seen so clearly anywhere else as in the Ṛgveda".[1] But soon after, this crowding of gods and goddesses proved a weariness to the intellect and a growing tendency to monotheism and monism is discerned which may be roughly regarded as the second and third stages of the development of the Ṛgvedic thought.[2]

An effort to penetrate deeper into the inner nature of things gradually led the Aryans to perceive an unity among them. The fact that from the very beginning gods were attributed the same qualities of might, light, goodness and wisdom, greatly facilitated this tendency. These gods and goddesses playing similar roles and serving the same purpose, of course, in their own ways (e.g. Agni repelling demons by fire and Indra doing the same with his thunderbolt)[3] also contributed to this drive. This unifying trend must have been further eased by the close connection in the nature of elements which these gods represented. All these factors helped the Aryan genius to replace gradually the polytheistic anthropomorphism by monotheistic and monistic spiritualism

1. Indian Philosophy. Vol. I. p. 73.
2. Ibid. p. 72.
3. The Religion and Philosophy of the Veda (H.O.S. 1925), I. p. 88.

treating the various gods and goddesses as aspects of one and the same Supreme.[1] The Nāsadīya Sūkta tracing the origin of the universe refers to the Original One and the monistic idea is clearly mooted in the famous Puruṣa-Sūkta.

(D) *Rituals and Sacrifices Paving Way for Upāsanā and Vidyā* :—

A corresponding development took place in the Vedic practice of rituals. In the beginning, ritual was a simple affair.[2] It consisted in invoking a god by hymns of prayer and making an offering of food to him. But subsequently with the invention of various gods and goddesses, varities of rituals and sacrifices came into practice,[3] entailing the indispensability of priests. It is this period which made the Brahmins a class-conscious priesthood.

Now, some dissatisfaction against the Vedic hymn and ritual persisted from the time of the Ṛgveda itself. The celebrated hymn on Frogs[4], as Max Muller has rightly pointed out[5] has an element of satire at the priestly practice of hymn-chanting. In the Aitareya Āraṇyaka, a school of thinkers known as Kāvaṣeya had raised the objection: "Why should we repeat the Veda or offer this kind of sacrifice?".[6] Mahidāsa is seen to ponder significantly: "People say—'Hymn hymn' (uktha, uktha), but do they know what hymn means?"[7] With the deepening of a philosophic consciousness this tone of protest gained more and more ground and ultimately corresponding to the development of the

---

1. Ṛgveda V.3.1-2; I. 164. 46; X. 114. 5; I. 89. 10; X. 121. 8 (ye deveṣvadhideva eka āsīt).
2. The Religion and Philosophy of the Veda (H. O. S. 1925) I. pp-252-6.
3. The essential nature of sacrifice has been variously interpreted. Some take it as ancestor-worship, others see its motive in gift-offering, still others look upon it as a fertility-rite and some consider it as aiming at the communion with deity itself. Some evidence in support of each view can be found in the Brāhmaṇas which only suggests that by that time several strands of thought were intricately interwoven. The Piṇḍapitryajña has obvious reference to ancestor-worship, the Aśvamedha is indicative of fertility-rite and the practice of Iḍābhakṣaṇa implies the idea of communion with deity. Cf. Religion and Philosophy of the Veda (H.O.S. 1925). I. 257ff.
4. Ṛgveda VI. 163.
5. History of Ancient Sanskrit Literature pp. 494ff.
6. Ait. Āranyaka III. 2. 6. 8.
7. Ibid. II. 12. 1.

monotheistic and monistic conception of the Vedic gods and the recognition of a supreme deity (usually called Prajapati[1] or Indra[2] or Viṣṇu[3] or an impersonal yajña itself), there emerged an important shift in the nature of sacrificial rite. It came to be extolled as a super-divine cosmic principle.[4] It was identified with Prajāpati[5] and Viṣṇu[6]. It was thought to have incalculable potency.[7] It was considered as veritably the nave of the universe.[8] It was essential for creation and the gods depended on it[9] and it is through the help of it alone that the sacrificer was supposed to have safety, longevity, progeny, prosperity, fame in this life[10] and celestial happiness in the life beyond.[11]

This development could be made possible only by giving a symbolic interpretation to the rituals and sacrifices.[12] It was perhaps the only way left to the priests to keep pace with the growing rational approach of people and safeguard their ritualistic tradition. But this could not prove a strong defence, and the weakness of the esoteric interpretation of sacrifices was gradually exposed. If the ritual is really symbolic, is not the 'knowledge' of its underlying significance more important than the actual act? Thus, Vidyā or knowledge came to be recognised as superior to mere Agnicayana. It could secure for man that which nothing else could do.[13] However, this

---

1. Śat. Brāh. I. 3. 30, Tait. Brāh. I. 7. 1. 4. Ait. Brāh. VII. 4.1.
2. Indra or Prajapati spoken as supreme light and various gods imagined as his rays (Śat. Brāh. I. 178, 401 , Prajāpati spoken as father and mother) (Śat. Brāh. I 566, Śat. Brāh. II. 1198-9). cf. Religion and Philosophy of the Veda. II. pp. 442ff.
3. Tait. Samhitā viii. p. 4630; Tait. Brāh. III. p. 1258.
4. Śat. Brāh. I. 656.
5. Ibid. I. 3. 30, Tait. Brāh. I. 7. 4. Ait. Brāh. 4, VII. 1; Tait. Saṃhitā I. 6. 10.
6. Tait. Saṃhitā VIII. 4630; Tait. Brah III. 1258.
7. Śat. Brāh. I. 137 cf. Religion and Philosophy of the Veda II. pp. 454ff.
8. Tait. Saṃhitā VIII p. 4630.
9. Śat. Brāh. I. 32.
10. Ibid. I. 116.
11. Ibid. I. 127; II. 707.
12. Śat. Brāh. I. 654ff; Ibid. I. 648; Ibid. II. 1157ff; 1005; 1043-5; 812-3. Ibid, 865-6, 879 and 909.
13. Sat. Brāh. II 1096; Ibid 1111 ,-"Na haivaṃ taṃ lokam dakṣiṇābhir na tapasā nevaṃ vidaśnuta evaṃ vidāṃ haiva sa lokaḥ. Ibid. 1186 (Svādhyāyāt) prajñā varddhamānā caturo dharmān brāhmaṇamabhiniṣpādayati. Cf. Tait. Brāh. III. 1348-9.

Vidyā could not at once disentangle itself from the long-practised tradition, and symbolic ritualism still persisted as the dominant feature of the Brahmanical period. The symbolic idea was often suggested as a topic fit to be meditated upon and was given the name, 'Upāsanā'.

Thus the early practice of rituals and sacrifices developed into what is known as Upāsanā and an esoteric notion of Vidyā--the further development of which was still to be carried on by the Upaniṣads.

The Upaniṣadic Stage:—

(*A*) *The Fusion of Non-Vedic and Vedic Culture*:—

After the early stages of warfare and the subsequent settling down of the Aryans, the sharp opposition and distinction between the Aryans and the non-Aryans must have gradually narrowed down. The centuries of their living together must have facilitated an intercommunication of ideas. This is well indicated from the remarkable change in the whole trend of the Brahmanical outlook as well as from the sudden appearance of some new ideas in the Upaniṣads, like the theory of karma, the transmigration of the soul and asceticism. All this clearly suggests that by the time of the Upaniṣads Aryan society and thought had reached a stage when it felt the full impact of the pre-Vedic non-Aryan ideals.

(*B*) *The Recognition of Ascetic Ideal and Renunciation*:—

We have already noted that the erstwhile dominating worldly outlook of the Brāhmaṇas began to be superseded by the world-renouncing thought of the Upaniṣads, and the munis and śramaṇas came to gain not only recognition but also superiority over mere fire-worshippers and sacrificers.[1] The Muṇḍakopaniṣad specially, as its very name indicates, championed the case of the shaven headed ascetics (Muṇḍakas) most vociferously and in an unambiguous manner undermined the value of the Vedic rituals and sacrifices.[2]

1. Bhadā. III. 5. 1.; IV. 4.22.
2. Muṇḍaka. I. 2. 7-12.

(C) The Theory of Karma and Transmigration :—

The most important development of this period was the introduction of the theory of karma and transmigration of the soul. We have already seen that it is not found in the Vedas and Brāhmaṇas. In the Bṛhadāraṇyaka it occurs for the first time where Yājñavalkya is found to take unusual care in conveying the idea to Ārtabhāga whom he removes from the public gaze in order to reveal the secret in private.[1] This special precaution in discussing the theory of karma in contradistinction to other discussions of the occasion itself suggests that the idea was new and, on account of its clandestine unpriestly implications, was not likely to be received favourably in the open priestly assembly. The ignorance of the Brahmins about this theory of karma and transmigration is clearly borne out from the dialogue between Yājñavalkya and Śākalya where the former poses this question in the form of a riddle before the entire Brahmanical assembly and none is in a position to solve it.[2] Yājñavalkya himself, however, explains in detail this law of karma and the process of transmigration to King Janaka[3], and this marks the introduction of a new theory within the Brahmanical circles. We then find a number of references to this theory, not only in the Bṛhadāraṇyaka[4] but also in the Chāndogya[5], Aitareya,[6] Kaṭha[7], Īśa[8], Praśna[9], and Muṇḍaka[10]. The sudden appearance of this theory in a full-fledged form is likely to be due, as already pointed out, to an impact of the wandering muni-and-śramaṇa-cult, coming down from the pre-Vedic non-Aryan time.

This theory silently ushered in a veritable revolution in the whole Brahmanical scheme of things. If karma alone is to determine irrevocably the future of a man, shaping the

1. Bṛhadā. III. 2. 13.
2. Bṛhadā. III. 9. 28.
3. Bṛhadā. IV. 4. 1-5.
4. Ibid. IV. 3. 34-38; V. 10. 1; VI. 2. 15-16.
5. Chāndogya. IV. 10; IV. 15.
6. Ait. II. 4; (so asyāyamātmā puṇyebhyaḥ pratidhiyate.)
7. Kaṭh. I. 6; II. 4, III. 7, IV. 10 and V. 7.
8. Iśa. 3 and 9ff;
9. Praśna. I. 9ff; III. 7.
10. Muṇḍaka I.2. 1; I. 2. 9-11.

course of his after-life in one or the other species, then he himself becomes the architect of his fortune. All rituals, sacrifices, priests and gods cease to be indispensable. The divine status of the gods themselves is dependent on their previous karmas, and their potency being exhausted, men and gods alike are bound to fall down from heaven.[1] It is then futile to seek favour from gods by rituals and prayers when they themselves labour under the same law of karma and have no independent power of grace. Again the heavenly bliss of limited duration, the alleged fruit of sacrifices can no longer satisfy the ardent aspirants of immortality.[2]

Thus the implications of the theory began to be reflected on by Upaniṣadic thinkers and were later on brought into fruition by Buddhism.

(D) The Ascendancy of Kṣatriyas and the Slackening of Caste-Rigidity:—

All this had its natural repercussions on the social order. The Brahmins had long remained the exclusive repository of religion and culture, and socially the highest class. But the undermining of ritualism paved the way for diminishing the rigidity of Brahmanical supremacy. The ruling class which comprised the Kṣatriyas and whose hereditary aristocratic status in society was already recognised came to be the leaders of intellectual and religious life as much as the Brahmins. The Upaniṣads introduce many royal philosophers like Ajātaśatru[3] of Kāśī, Aśvapati[4] of Kekaya and Pravāhaṇa Jaivāli[5] of Pañcāla who are found to impart philosophical knowledge to the learned Brahmins. In the Chāndogya the learned sage Nārada is introduced by Sanat Kumara or Skanda[6], the god of war. Janaka, the king of Videha meets Yājñavalkya, the Brahmin on terms of mutual respect. It is significant that Pravāhaṇa Jaivāli, the Kṣatriya king while

---

1. Bṛhadā. I. 4. 5; Kaṭha. II. 10; IV. 2; Muṇḍaka. I.2. 7; I. 2.9 and 12; Chāndo. VIII. 1.6. (yatheha karmajito loko kṣīyate...).
2. Bṛhadā. I. 4. 15; Chāndo. VIII. 1. 6; Kaṭha. IV. I and 2; Muṇḍaka. I. 2. 7; 2. 9-12.
3. Bṛhadā. II. 1; Kauṣītaki IV.
4. Chāndogya. V. 11.
5. Bṛhadā. VI. 2.; Chāndogya V.3.
6. Chāndogya. VII. 26. 2.

imparting knowledge of devayāna and pitṛyāna to Śvetaketu, the Brahmin, remarks : "This knowledge did not go to any Brahmin before but belonged to the Kṣatriya alone".[1] This indicates the occasional claims of superiority by Kṣatriyas over Brāhmins. Even women like Gārgī and Maitreyi are found taking part in philosophical discussions. All this clearly shows that by this time the exclusive monopoly of the Brahmins in religious knowlege had suffered a setback, and the ruling Kṣatriyas had come to acquire an upper hand or at least equality even in matters of religion, and people enjoyed liberty of thought.[2]

It may be noted here that it is this Kṣatriya-led thought-movement which is represented in the Bhagavadgītā, and reflected in the Buddhist philosophy too. The BG., evidently, is taught by Kṛṣṇa, a Kṣatriya to Arjuna, another Kṣatriya and in the course of tracing the tradition (paramparā) of this teaching, only Kṣatriya sages (rajarṣayaḥ) are mentioned.[3] The religion is regarded as 'rāja-vidyā' and 'rāja-guhya'.[4] It contains descriptions of devayāna and pitṛyāna[5] which is referred to as special 'Kṣatriya-Vidyā' in Bṛhadā VI. 2. 8-16 and Chāndogya V. 3. 7-V. 10. 4. Sanat Kumāra or Skanda who is represented in Chāndogya VII. 26. 2 as teaching Narada, is also alluded to in the BG. as war-god along with Nārda.[6] Buddhism also is a religion propounded

1. Bṛhadā. VI. 2. 8,; Chāndogya. V. 3. 7.

2. The important part played by the Kṣatriya kings in the Upaniṣads as well as in the subsequent period, has led some scholars to exaggerated surmises that this indicated a Kṣatriya revolt against Brāhmins. But having no other definite evidence in support of it, the instances cited above can only prove an emergence of a thought-liberation movement in which the Kṣatriyas also participated along with Brāhmins and others. In fact, when the Kṣatriyas are represented in the Upanisads as imparting knowledge to the Brāhmins, they are found to take special care to show respect to the latter, and as against the normal practice of accepting pupils by taking service etc , they accept Brāhmins as pupils merely on their words. They, indeed, embarrassingly say that it is against the normal practice of the Brahmins teaching the Kṣatriyas. cf. Bṛhadā. II. 1. 15; Kauṣītaki IV. 19; Bṛhadā. VI. 2. 7 and 8, and Chāndogya V. 11. 7.

3. B. G. IV. 1 and 2; cf. Buddhist India, p. 257.

4. BG. IX. 2.

5. Ibid. VIII. 24-26.

6. Ibid. X. 24 and 26.

by a teacher belonging to the Kṣatriya caste who denounces the Brahmanical scheme of castes and ritualism. Here also Sanat Kumara frequently appears as an authority speaking of the superiority of Kṣatriyas over others as a caste.[1]

(E) *Gods and Rituals Taking Different Lines of Development* :—

The unification of the gods had already been effected at the pre-Upaniṣadic stage. During the Upaniṣadic period they receded still more to the background. They were now represented as the partial manifestations of the infinite glory of the One Supreme, at times conceived theologically as the highest deity, and at times as an impersonal colourless Absolute. The gods naturally, then, lost their independent power to favour any man. This is well brought out in the Kenopaniṣad where neither the fire-god with all his might could burn a blade of grass nor the wind-god could blow it away when they were bereft of the power from the Supreme.[2] A reconciliation was sought to be made between the theological approach to divinity and the purely rational approach to karma by conceiving some of the gods as executive functionaries for the operation of the law of karma[3] and the Supreme God as the prime-operator of the law of karma (Karmādhyakṣaḥ).[4]

As already pointed out, the rituals and sacrifices of the Brāhmaṇas had passed their spring-time and had started dwindling partly due to their own inner evolution of thought and partly due to the external impact of the ascetic ideals. The symbolic interpretation of sacrifices, therefore, had made its appearance, making room for Upāsanā and Vidyā.

Now, in the Upaniṣadic period when the law of karma also was brought into play, the protest against rituals and sacrifices became all the more effective. The Chāndogya openly declares that ritualism without 'knowledge' may be worse than useless.[5] Pratardana in the Kauṣītaki refers to the

1. D. I. 99; M. I. 358; S. I. 153.
2. Kena. III. 6 and 10.
3. Chāndogya. IV. 15. 5-6.
4. Śvetāśvatara. VI. 11.
5. Chāndogya. I. 10. 11.

knower of the mystery whose practice was other than mere ritualistic.[1] The Vedic knowledge hitherto considered as the highest came to be branded as the 'lower knowledge' (Aparā-Vidyā)[2] by means of which it was not possible to attain the true eternal reality.[3] Now the emphasis was increasingly more on knowledge[4] than on the actual performance of the ritual, more on renunciation than on the pursuit of worldly pleasures. Thus the Upaniṣads introduced a new line of development, viz. knowledge against ritualism; renunciation against worldly pursuits—thus bringing nivṛtti as a parallel rival of pravṛtti.

Under this revolutionising situation, three different tendencies of thought were found in the Upaniṣadic period: (1) The rationalistic group of philosophers, realising the futility of priestly wisdom, completely broke away from the ritualistic and sacrificial tradition. These thinkers naturally looked down upon any earthly or heavenly gain accruing out of rituals, and preferred renunciation for the sake of true immortality.[5] This attitude, however, was only partially expressed in the Upaniṣads. It was only in Buddhism and later, in the Advaita Vedānta that it was taken up in all seriousness. (2) The second line of development was based on a compromise between ritualism and knowledge, between world-living and world-renouncing attitudes.[6] This view known as 'Jñāna-karma-samuccayavāda', a synthesis of pravṛtti and nivṛtti, was favoured by the Bhagavadgītā[7] and with some alterations by the Viśiṣṭādvaita of Rāmānuja. (3) The third alternattive course was the retention of traditional orthodoxy with but slight modifications or adjustments. This school conceded that karma determines the future but argued that the sacri-

---

1. Kauṣītaki. II. 5.
2. Manḍaka. I. 1. 4-5.
3. Kaṭha. I. 2. 10 (na hyadhruvaiḥ prāpyate hi dhruvaṃ tat)
4. Kena. II. 4. (Vidyayā Vindate amṛtam); Kaṭha II. 12; III. 12 and 15; Muṇḍaka I. 1. 3; II. 2. 8; Taittirīya II. 4. 1; Chāndo. VI. 1 and Bṛhadā. III. 5. 11.
5. Chāndogya viii. 1. 6; Śvetā. VI. 4; Kauṣītaki II. 14 and Muṇḍaka I 21. 7ff.
6. Īśa. and 2; Chāndogya II. 23. 1 and Kena. IV. 8.
7. Śaṅkara also has to concede its synthetic character, though he favours the supremacy of knowledge and renunciation. Sāṅkara-Bhāṣya of the BG. Introduction.—"Dvividho hi vidokto dharmaḥ, pravṛttilakṣaṇo nivṛttilakṣaṇaḥ ca...vaidikaṃ hi dharmadvayam Arjunāya...upadideśa..."

ficial acts were the most righteous karmas, the very principle of life[1] and so proper comprehension and right performance of them could lead to an eternally blissful state from which there was no return,[2] and so it was needless to renounce the world. This attitude was upheld and continued later by the Mīmāṃsā school.

(F) *The Nature of the Soul and Salvation*:—

As noted above, the emphasis on knowledge, by and large, became the dominating note of the Upaniṣads. But what was this knowledge about ? This was the knowledge of the soul by knowing which everything was supposed to be known and immortality achieved.[3]

The nature of the soul had not received much serious consideration by the Vedic and Brahmnical priests who only assumed some sort of quasi-physical soul surviving death and were preoccupied with discussion of the various processes of rituals and sacrifices. Roughly speaking, they conceived it sometimes as partly physical (dehātmavāda)[4] and sometimes as the life-beath (prāṇātmavāda)[5] animating the body, though different from it. It is, nevertheless, said to depend on food[6]. This life-breath or vital-air is often conceived as having functional divisions which are supposed to be located in different parts of the body.[7] The chiefest among them, namely, 'prāṇa', at times identified with the golden-person,[8] is said to be located in the heart.[9] When all faculties like mind, senses, etc., cease to function in deep sleep, it is the breathing (prāṇa) alone which remains unimpaired.[10]

1. Chāndogya III. 16-17.
2. Bṛhadā. VII. 2; Chāndogya V. 3-10; Kaṭha. I. 17-18; III. 2.
3. Bṛhadā. II. 4. 3. and 5; IV. 5.6. (Ātmani Khalu are dṛṣṭe śrute mate vijñāte idaṃ sarvaṃ viditam); Chāndogya VI. 1; VI. 8-16; Muṇḍaka I. 1. 3.; II. 2.5. (Tamevaikam jānatha ātmānam anyā vāco vimuñcatha amṛtasyaiṣa setuḥ); Muṇḍaka I. 2. 11 and Māṇḍūkya 7 and 12.
4. Ait. Brah. I. 85; I. 507; Śat. Brāh. II. 845-6; 864, 867, 878 and 905.
5. Vedic Mythology p. 166.
6. Bṛhadā I.3. 17; Śat. Brāh. II. 947, 948; Tait. Saṃhitā I. 198.
7. Tait. Saṁhitā. II. 726.
8. Śat. Brāh. II. 863.
9. Ibid. I. 387.
10. Ibid. II. 1074.

Mostly, it is the prāṇātmavāda which is found to dominate throughout the Brāhmanical period and is met with even in the Upaniṣads. In the Bṛhadāraṇyaka, for example, it is said that prāṇa is the basis of the mind and senses[1] and the Kauṣītaki supports it by pointing out that it is only when the breath functions that the mind and senses can operate.[2] Kauṣītaki, however, identifies this prāṇa with the principle of Intelligence (prajñā).[3] But in the Bṛhadāraṇyaka a distinction is made between prāṇa and Vijñāna, and the latter is recognised to have superiority over the former.[4] This marks a new important development, and occupies prominent place in the Upaniṣads.[5]

Now, this conception of soul as vijñāna was variously understood; some regarding its true nature to be reflected in dream-consciousness[6], some in the state of deep dreamless-sleep[7], while others view it as a mysterious reality undeniable and yet unpredicable.[8] The great predicament of self-consciousness came to be realised and stated. How can one speak of Self-consciousness when consciousness has an inherent duality of subject and object ? How can one know the Knower of all knowledge, the primus of the principle of consciousness ?[9]

This leads to the culmination of the Upaniṣadic conception of the soul. The Ātman cannot but be described negatively,[10] paradoxically[11] and analogically.[12] In it all contradictions are reconciled,[13] it passes beyond all oppositions.[14] It transcends all

---

1. Bṛhadā. I. 3; I. 5. 21.
2. Kauṣitaki. II. 14.
3. Ibid. III. 4.
4. Bṛhadā. II. 1. 17.
5. Ibid. II. 1. 17; IV. 3.7; Kaṭha. IV. 3; Ait. III. 1.4.
6. Chāndogya. VIII. 10.
7. Bṛhadā. IV. 3. 21 and 22; Chāndogya. VIII. 3.; Praśna IV. 6.
8. Kena II. 2-4; Kaṭha VI. 12 and 13; Māṇḍūkya 7 and 12.
9. Bṛhadā. II. 4. 14; IV. 3. 23ff; III. 7. 23; III. 8. 11; Kena. I. 4-8.
10. Bṛhadā. II. 3. 6; IV. 4. 22; Taittirīya II. 7; Kaṭha III. 15.
11. Kena II. 1-3; Kaṭha II. 21; Īśa 4; Śvetāśvatara III. 19.
12. Bṛhadā. IV. 3. 7.
13. Ibid. IV. 3. 22ff; IV. 4. 5; Taittirīya II. 6; Kaṭha II. 20; Īśa. 5.
14. Bṛhadā. III. 8. 8; Kena. I. 3; Kaṭha II. 14; Īsa 10 and 13; Śvetāśvatara IV. 18 and Māṇḍūkya. 7 (nāntaḥ prajñaṃ na bahiṣprajñaṃ nobhayataḥ prajñaṃ...na prajñṃ nāprajñam)

thought and speech, and silence alone is its most eloquent expression.[1]

Though the Upaniṣads do not put forward the various views of the soul in a coherent manner, it is not difficult for a discerning mind to see the gradual development of their thought beginning with Dehātmavāda to Anirvacanīyātmavāda, as has just been shown. A nice hint to this successive development has been given in the Bhṛguvallī of the Taittirīyopaniṣad where in an hierarchical way the realisation of the soul form from its lowest to the highest form has been taught.[2]

Now it is easy to see that the highest point reached in the Upaniṣadic conception of the soul was verging towards what was developed into the Anattā theory in Buddhism. The ineffable Ātman, often described negatively and paradoxically was identified with the universal impersonal Spirit called Brahman. Now the true import of this impersonal Ātman can hardly be brought out in its translation as 'Self', which is usually done for want of a more adequate term or perhaps to retain the terminology of the long tradition. This rendering jars on the ear, for it inevitably suggests something individualistic, personal or selfish; whereas the Ātman has now come to mean the universal, impersonal and the only Reality indeterminable and ineffable, the realisation of which was the attainment of immortality. This immortality was no more a heaven, however fine, but a transcendence of it. It is not the accomplishment of desires, but the abandonment of the same[3]; not an unending continuation of existence, a perpetual afterlife, but the absolute transcendence of empirical existence, the precise negation of this world.[4] It is knowing the true Self and turning back from the world.[5] It needs no clarification that all this was feeling the way towards the Buddhist approach.

---

1. Kena. I.3; Tait. II. 9; Kaṭha II. 8; Muṇḍaka III. 1. 7, Māṇḍūkya 7 (acintyamavyapadeśyam...prapañcopaśamaṃ śāntam).
2. Tait. III. 1-6.
3. Bṛhadā. IV. 4.7; Kaṭha VI. 14 (yadā sarve pramucyante Kāmā ye, sya hṛdi śritāḥ. . . .).
4. Muṇḍaka III. 2. 2; Chāndogya VII. 24 (conception of Bhuman); Kaṭha II. 1-2 (śreya different from preya).
5. Bṛhadā. IV. 4. 14 and 17; Kaṭha VI. 1-2; VI. 14-15; Kena 1.2: II. 4 and Śvetā. VI. 6.

It is again significant to note that in the Bṛhadāraṇyaka[1], Yajñavalkya, while faced with the question as to whether the Puruṣa exists after death when all the different elements are resolved back into their respective physical elements—speaks of nothing other than the karma. At another place in the same Upaniṣad[2], he clearly tells that there remains no 'saṁjñā' after death (na pretya saṁjñā' sti.). This seems to point, at least, vaguely to the Buddhistic theory according to which nothing permanent is there in the individual and the future life is determined by the law of karma.

Thus, the Upaniṣadic views that all the constituent elements of the individual are dissolved after death into the respective physical elements on the one hand, and that the Ātman is an universal, impersonal and ineffable principle on the other—were pointing towards the Buddhist doctrine of Anattā. Buddhism boldly gave a definite and consistent shape to what the Upaniṣads were only vaguely hinting at.

Another significant point which may here be noted is the notion of the Vijñānamaya soul which is regarded as the transmigrating individual self in the Upaniṣads[3], and is met with in the Buddhism too.[4] Of course, in the latter it is not a permanent entity but a changing one.

(*G*) *The Path Prescribed for Salvation*:—

Now, what is the way suggested by the Upaniṣads for the knowledge of Ātman and release from Saṃsāra? Frequently the method suggested is mainly intellectual. Yājñavalkya, after having instructed Janaka, exclaims: "You have reached fearlessness (abhayam)."[5] Śvetaketu requests his father to repeat the instructions till he comprehends

1. Bṛhadā. III. 2. 13-14; cf. R. G. Bhandarkar—A Peep into the Early History of India (J. B. B. R. A. S. Vol. XX) p. 361.
2. Ibid. IV. 5. 13; cf. Bapat—2500 years of Buddhism. p. 12.
3. Bṛhadā IV. 4. 2ff; Muṇḍaka III. 2. 7 also distinguishes Vijñānamaya ātmā from Parāvyaya; and Prasna IV. 9 distinguishes it from Parākṣara. In Taitt. III also it is mentioned as Vijñānamayakoṣa distinct from the highest Ānandamayakoṣa.
4. Viññāṇa is said to be the cause of rebirth, which leaves the dead body :-Viññāṇāhāro āyatiṃ punabbhavābhinibbattiyā paccayo (S. II. 13); cittaṃ . . taṃ uddhagāmi hoti (S. V. 370); Cittamassa Vidhāvati (S.I.37).
5. Bṛhadā IV. 2. 4.

them.[1] After listening to the instructions, reflection and meditation are recommended. Yajñavalkya says to Maitreyī that Ātman should be looked into, listened to, reflected about and meditated upon.[2] But in order to comprehend this highest reality, moral preparedness in the form of faith, control of senses and mind etc. is frequently emphasised.[3] Without these mental and moral prerequisites, scriptures and intellect would be of no avail.[4] The reference to Indra and Virocana undergoing several years of 'brahmacarya' before being imparted higher knowledge, clearly suggests it.[5] 'Brahmacarya' here takes a new meaning signifying moral conduct conducive to the comprehension of Brahman, the highest truth. It is this Upaniṣadic sense of brahmacarya which persists in the pali Nikāyas when bhikkhus are referred to as undergoing brahmacarya under Buddha. We shall see still more towards the close of the discussion in hand that the maturest speculations of the Upaniṣads were preparing the ground for Buddhism in so many other ways.

(H) *Importance of Yoga in Self-Realisation*:—

In the Upaniṣads we also find some passages which stress the need of yoga for self-realisation. The vision of Ātman is said to follow the rapt contemplative gaze of the mind cleansed of its impurities.[6] The Kaṭhopaniṣad calls it 'adhyātma-yoga' (Kaṭha. II. 12). The yoga is defined by Kaṭha as 'the steady control of the senses' (sthirām indriya-dhāraṇām, Katha VI. 11) and reference to the method of yoga (yogavidhi, Kaṭha VI. 18) is made. The Śvetāśvatara (I. 3) speaks of 'dhyāna-yoga'.

The notion of yoga was somewhat vaguely anticipated by the concept of meditative worship (upāsanā). Now in the Upaniṣads the concentration on some symbol specially 'Om' is frequently recommended.[7] There are some implicit

1. Chāndogya. VI. 5.
2. Bṛhadā. II. 4. 5.
3. Muṇḍaka III. 1. 5; Praśna I. 15.
4. Kaṭha II. 23; III. 7.
5. Chāndogya. VIII. 7-11.
6. Katha. VI. 9; Muṇḍaka III. 1.8.
7. Kaṭha. II. 15-17; Muṇḍaka II. 2. 3-4; Chāndogya II. 2; Taitt. I. 8 & Praśna V. 1 5.

references to the control of breath as well.[1] The heart is mentioned with a mystic significance as the abode of the soul[2], connected with various nādīs.[3] Yoga, as found in the Upaniṣads, however, is more often described as something mystical, vague and sporadic where the initiative comes from the Ātman itself[4] and which depends on the grace of God.[5] Here the yogin is rather taken by surprise and, not comprehending the true significance of his experience, regards it as the special grace of god. It is only in a few passages of the Kaṭha and Śvetāśvatara that some systematic and recognisable type of Samādhi-consciousness is met with.[6]

(*I*) *Traces of Sāṅkhya in the Upaniṣads* :—

Besides yoga, we have some passages showing acquaintance with a proto-Sāṅkhya or Sāṅkhya philosophy. Barring the doubtful reference to Pradhāna of Sāṅkhya at Chāndogya VI. 2. 1ff and Muṇḍaka I. 1.6-7, we have the rather definite reference at Kaṭha III. 11-13 and VI. 7-8 to the Sāṅkhya scheme of the tattvas. The Śvetāśvatara (1.8, 10; IV.5, 10) also clearly alludes to the Sāṅkhya conception of Pradhāna, of course, with a theistic bias. We do not here intend to enter into the much vexed controversy whether the Upaniṣadic references to Sāṅkhya are indicative of the first formative stage of the Sāṅkhya system or are an attempt to incorporate and assimilate some of the terms and ideas of an already existing theistic Sāṅkhya system. Our concern is only to show that during this Upaniṣadic period some Sāṅkhya ideas were prevalent, influences of which were seen in some of the contemporaneous thought of Buddha[7] which made the latter react to it by giving a particular shape to his philosophy. We shall, now, briefly see these contemporaneous currents

1. Kaṭha. V. 3; Muṇḍaka III. 1. 9; Śvetā. II. 9.
2. Kaṭha. VI. 14-17; Praśna III. 6.
3. Kaṭha. VI. 16; Praśna III. 6; Chāndogya VIII 6; Bṛhadā IV. 3. 20; Kauṣītaki IV. 19 and Muṇḍaka II. 2. 6.
4. Kaṭha. II. 23; Muṇḍaka III. 2. 3.
5. Kaṭha. II. 20.
6. Kaṭha. III. 13; VI. 7ff; VI. 18 and Śvetā. II. 8-15.
7. The views of Pakudha Kaccāyana and Pūraṇa Kassapa, for example, denying agency to the doer, causing him neither sin nor merit, seems to indicate an influence of the Sāṅkhya theory of indifferent Puruṣa.

of thought which led Buddha to adopt the middle path and avoid extremes.

Religious Condition of Buddha's Time :—

(A) *The Period of Moral and Intellectual Ferment* :—

By the time immediately preceding Buddha, the whole intellectual atmosphere in India seems to be permeated with a diversity of religious and spiritual beliefs. As indicated by the Pali texts and Jaina sources, various religious traditions, speculations and occult teachings were preached and propagated and went by the name of religion. There abounded all kinds of ascetics (tāpasas), hermits (jaṭilas), wandering mendicants (paribbājakas) and numerous other sects (titthiyas). The time was thus ripe for an epoch-making departure from the already dying Brahmanical cult of sacrifices and rituals. It only needed some authoritative lead, a definite and clear direction from a strong-minded convinced and articulate thinker. This was found in Gotama, the Buddha.

In fact, the 6th century B.C. was remarkably a period of spiritual unrest and intellectual ferment all over the ancient world. It produced some epoch-making thinkers in so many countries. In Greece, we have Parmenides and Empedocles; in Iran, Zarathustra; in China, Lao Tzu and in India, Buddha and Mahāvīra. These teachers worked upon their inheritance and taking due note of their contemporary thoughts developed new points of view. The position of Buddha among them proved to be most important and influential.

We are referred to as many as 62 erroneous views in the Brahmajāla-Sutta, and Jaina sources enumerate as many as 363. Scholars have expressed doubt about the actual existence of so many views and consider these lists an indication of a desire to condemn all possible erroneous views rather than the actual existence of them all.[1] As very few schools of that

1. Sir Charles Eliot observes regarding these lists of the Buddhist and Jaina works as follows : "Both catalogues are somewhat artificial, and it is clear that many views are mentioned not because they represent the tenets of real schools but from a desire to condemn all possible errors" Hinduism and Buddhism, I. p. 97.

ancient period have survived and only a few sketchy references to some of them are found, we cannot possibly ascertain the correct position of the time. But from the nature of the arrangement of these views in the respective lists, it is indicated that the list was made exhaustive with a view to cover actual as well as possible erroneous views. There can, however, be no doubt that some of these views mentioned in the Brahmajāla-Sutta were actually held by non-Buddhist thinkers. Professor Jayatilleke who examines in detail the Vedic as well as non-Vedic background of the Buddhist thought (Early Buddhist Theory of Knowledge, pp. 21-168) has tried to show that the majority of the views stated in the Sutta are actually traceable to non-Buddhist sources, though he also does not rule out the possibility of their being hypothetical.[1]

(B) : *Prevalence of Some Theories Subversive to Moral Pursuits*:—

Different views, many of them subversive to moral aspirations, were prevalent. We find reference to a theory known as Kālavāda according to "which Time is the originating and guiding principle of the universe.[2] Then there was Svabhāvavāda according to which all things proceed from their inherent nature—the view indicating perhaps some contact with the Sāṅkhya system. Then there were Niyati-vādins who considered everything as determined by Niyati or Destiny. Yadṛcchāvādins, on the other hand, regarded everything as fortuitous. According to them everything depended on chance, and causation in any form was a fiction. Some were mate-

---

Similarly N. Dutt says "Its main object is to draw up a list of the possible theories about the world and the soul . . . The so called 62 views are really a systematic exposition of the experience of a Buddhist monk and have very little to do with the then existing non-Buddhistic opinions." Early Monastic Buddhism. p. 43, note 4.

1. He says "The possibility that they are hypothetical schools concocted by the author of the Sutta who was anxious to present sixtytwo theories in this Sutta cannot be ruled out especially since there seems to have been a belief at this time that there were 'sixtytwo ways of life' (dvaṭṭhi Paṭipadā, D. I. 54) which means that there would have to be sixtytwo theories on which these were based. On the other hand, since the majority of the views stated here are, in our opinion, traceable to non-Buddhist sources we need not be too sceptical even of this list.— Early Buddhist Theory of Knowledge, pp. 106-7.

2. Atharva-veda XIX. 53 and 54; cf. Gauḍapāda Kārikā 8 : (Kālāt prasūtiṃ bhūtānāṁ manyante Kālacintakāḥ).

rialists and sought to explain everything in terms of physical elements. Some others regarded the soul to be the basic principle, while others attributed the origin of the world to the combination of all these factors. There were some Īśvaravādins as well, according to whom the originating and controlling power was ascribed to Īśvara. These views are well summed up in the Śvetāśvatara.[1]

It may be noted here, that in spite of their different approaches to the problem of origin and operation of the world-process, they all had almost the same moral implication, viz., the futility of human effort and the denial of the freedom of will. So they may broadly be classed under what is known as Akriyāvāda. The Jainas who regarded themselves as champions of the Kriyāvādins, considered these views as pernicious heresies.[2] Nothing but man's own action, according to them, was the cause of joy and suffering, and by right knowledge and good conduct man might secure release from the world of sorrow.

Of the six titthiyas whose views are frequently criticired by Buddha, four of them, namely Makkhali Gosāla, Pūraṇa Kassapa, Pakudha Kaccāyana and Ajitakesakambala may be broadly called Akriyāvādins, for they all denied the value of human efforts. Nigaṇṭhanātaputta, who is no other than the Jaina Tīrthaṇkara, Mahāvīra is alone a Kriyavādin. Sañjaya Belaṭṭhiputta is an agnostic or sceptic who is called by Buddhists a Amarāvikkhepavādin.

(*C*) *Buddha's Unique Approach to the Problem*:—

Buddha, having taken stock of all these various doctrines, directed his analytic method of inquiry (Vibhajja-vāda) to them and showed that they all come under four pairs of extremes (antas) comprising thesis and antithesis. The truth, he pointed out, can be discovered by avoiding the extremes and adopting the middle path (majjhimā paṭipadā). He, thus, tries to solve all problems by holding a balanced

1. Śvetāśvatara I. 2-3.

2. Jainas broadly subsumed the list of 363 views under four heads Kriyāvāda, Akriyāvāda, Ajñānavāda and Vinayavāda and associated themselves with the first. cf. 2500 years of Buddhism, p. 13; Studies in the Origins of Buddhism, p. 341, Note 155.

attitude and thereby reconciling the partial truth of all contending onesided theories (ekānta-diṭṭhis) without jeopardising his own position. The four pairs of extremes[1] are presented in the following way:—

(i) On the one hand there was the view of the eternalists (sassatavādins) that everything exists (sabbaṁ atthi). On the other, the annihilists (ucchedavādins) taught that nothing exists (sabbaṃ natthi). Buddha avoided both these metaphysical extremes by preaching the doctrine of perpetual flux.[2]

(ii) Then we come across the fatalistic theory (niyativāda) according to which everything is predetermined (sabbam pubbekatahetu) which stands in diametrical opposition to the fortuitist theory (yadṛcchāvāda) according to which there is no cause or condition to determine anything, and all events happen by chance, causeless and conditionless (sabbaṃ ahetu-appaccayā). Buddha by his theory of dependent origination (paṭicca samuppāda) avoided both these extremes of complete determination and utter causeless chaotic origination.[3]

(iii) The third pair of opposition was regarding man's moral responsibility and his efforts. According to Kriyāvāda, all pleasures and sufferings were due to one's own actions (sukhadukkhaṃ sayaṃ kataṃ) while according to Akriyāvāda man had no role to play in them, they were due to other factors (sukha-dukkhaṃ parakataṃ). Buddha here also affords a similar solution through his middle path by advocating the theory that the Vedanā depends partly on one elf and partly on other empirical factors.[4]

(iv). The fourth conflict was pertaining to the path of salvation. The extreme ways were suggested for the attainment of this highest goal. The materialists who considered the empirical pleasure as the highest, preached gross sense-indulgence (Kāmesu Kāmasukhallikānuyoga) as the only way to achieve it. Some ascetics like Ājīvakas and Nigaṇṭhas, on

---

1. Barua—A History of Pre-Buddhistic Indian Philosophy, pp. 406-7; Bapat—2500 years of Buddhism, pp. 19-20; Jayatilleke—Early Buddhist Theory of Knowledge, pp. 359-360.

2. S. II. 17; III. 135.

3. A. I. 173.

4. S. II. 19-20; A. III. 440.

the other hand, recommended the way of austere self-mortification (attakilamathānuyoga). Buddha here also avoided the extremes by preaching a moderate self-discipline.[1]

A Resumé of the Development of the Thought-Process:—

We have noted that the germs of asceticism and yoga in some form or other go back to the muni-cult of the pre-Vedic period. With the conquest of the Aryans and consequent ascendency of the Vedic and Brahmanical religion of rituals and sacrifices, the pre-Vedie culture was superseded and receded to the background. But gradually by the time of the Upaniṣads, the Brahmanical religion of polytheistic ritualism by its own inner development was led to a monistic-idealistic position tending to replace the performance of ritual by cultivation of knowledge. By this time Vedic culture appears to have come closer to the non-Vedic and the fusion of the two seems to have silently ushered in a veritable revolution in the whole traditional religion of the Brāhmaṇaṣ.

We have already marked that under the impact of new development, emphasising knowledge and renunciation, the Upaniṣadic thought took three alternative lines:—

(i) A radical departure from the ritualistic tradition which finds full embodiment in Buddhism, and later in Advaita-Vedānta.

(ii) A compromise of the new knowledge with the old tradition which expresses itself in the Bhagavadgītā, and later in the Viśiṣtādvaita, and

(iii) An adherence to the old ritualistic religion with but slight modifications, as later on systematised and followed by the Mīmāṃsā school.

It must not, however, be forgotten that, in spite of the influence of the non-Vedic culture on the Vedic tradition and the absorption of some elements of the former by the latter, all these aforesaid trends of the Upaniṣads remained pre-

1. S. IV. 330; V. 421 :—Dve me bhikkhve antā pabbajitena no sevitabbā Katame dve.
yo cāyam kāmesu kāmasukhallikānuyogo hīno gāmo...anariyo anatthasaṃhito; yo cāyaṃ attakilamathānuyogo dukkho anariyo anatthasaṃhito. Ete kho bhikkhave ubho ante anupagamma majjhimā paṭipadā tathāgatena abhisambuddhā cakkhukaraṇī, ñāṇakaraṇī upasamāya abhiññāya sambodhāya nibbānāya saṃvattati.

dominantly Aryan in spirit and character. It is only in such sects as those of the Ājīvakas and Nigaṇṭhas etc. that the Aryanisation of non-Aryan culture does not seem to have been much effective, and they are found to remain predominantly non-Aryan cults following nudity (like the 'Vātaraśanāḥ' munis of the ancient times) and other practices of extreme self-torture. The Jaina school especially is known to have a very long tradition with the hoary past—most probably linked with the muni-cult of the pre-Aryan days. We are inclined to think that the Sāṅkhya too represents a confluence of the Vedic and non-Vedic traditions which alone can explain the blend of the Vedic and non-Vedic elements in it.[1]

During the late Upaniṣadic period, the two traditions had come so close that the erstwhile despised and neglected samaṇas and muṇḍakas had come to occupy a position equal to the Brāhmaṇas, so much so, that one of the Upaniṣads was called 'Muṇḍakopaniṣad' and the Pali literature placed samaṇas alongside the Brāhmaṇas. In fact, by that time there seems to have evolved some common culture and tradition for all those who aspired after some higher goal. They had to separate themselves from the body of wordly people and follow some special rule of life. Thus, notwithstanding some differences in the details of the various sects, they had some common binding codes of self-restraint and other disciplines which constituted the general pattern of their life. This will explain the similarities often pointed out by scholars between one and the other religions and philosophical schools of the time.

This period, on account of the decay of old traditions and emergence of new ideas, showed a tremendous spiritual unrest and intellectual ferment, and by the time of Buddha the religious atmosphere of India was full of multiple Vedic and non-Vedic sects (though somewhat blurred in their distinctions on account of the confluence of culture). But as the Aryan culture assimilated some elements of the non-Aryan, the latter proved very weak before the former and

1. Sāṅkhya "exhibits both Vedic and non-Vedic elements"—Belvalkar's Sri Gopal Basu Malik Lectures, p. 81; cf. G. C. Pande—Studies in the Origins of Buddhism, pp. 304-5.

ultimately had to lose ground. Though by the time of Buddha, we find mention of so many samaṇas (representing non-Aryan tradition) along with Brāhmaṇas, after the mighty movement of the middle path of Buddha (which is styled as the Āryan path), none except the Jaina could hold any sway.

Couclusion:

In the light of the above discussion, we can now arrive at some conclusions regarding the sources of early Buddhism and can decide with reasonable plausibility if there is any truth in the alleged influence of Jainism, Sāṅkhya, Yoga, Vaiṣṇavism and the upaniṣads on early Buddhism.

(*A*) *The Alleged Influence of Jainism*:—

It is well known that the Jaina Tīrthaṅkara, Mahāvīra was an older contemporary of Buddha, and the two lived and taught for so many years in adjoining regions. This itself must have enabled them to share some common expressions and ideas of the time and place. Thus, many of the similarities between the two schools are nothing but reflections of the general pattern of belief and behaviour prevalent at the time, and some of them are the common (but independent) reactions against the current theories preached by their contemporaries.

But the differences between Jainism and Buddhism are so fundamental that any positive influence of the former on the latter is difficult to entertain. The Jainas, in spite of admitting the obvious psycho-physical changes, continue to adhere to the belief that both Jīva and Ajīva, in essence, are eternal.[1] They maintain that only essential modes (paryāyas) of a substance are subject to change while the substance with its essential quality (guṇa) is unchanging and abiding. Buddhists, on the other hand, altogether deny the substantive view of the world and the soul. They propound the theory of flux which alone holds good in the psycho-physical world. Thus the Buddhist way of avoiding

1. Bhagavatī Viyāhapannatti with Abhayadeva's Commetary IX. 6. 387.

and reconciling the extremes of sassatavāda and ucchedavāda by taking the middle position is quite different from the Jaina way of seeking reconciliation by accepting both at the same time, from different points of view.

Again the Jainas, on account of their view that karma is a quasi-physical element sullying the purity of the soul, lay much emphasis on bodily action and, consequently, prescribe bodily torture with a view to purging off karmic particles. In Buddhism, on the other hand, karma is regarded as a psychological function and so the emphasis is laid on mental action and the control of the mind.[1] The Jainas are, thus, led to preach self-mortification as against self-discipline preached by the Buddhists.

In fact, the Pali Texts frequently direct their polemic against Jaina thought, and we cannot but come to the conclusion that these two schools are mostly independent developments of thought. Though they have some common possessions of the time, and they both react against some prevalent beliefs of their age, they differ fundamentally in their views, and their reactions take quite independent lines. So merely on the basis of certain similarities which are nothing more than the general stamp of the age, one is not justified in speaking of the direct influence of Jainism on Buddhism. We do not find anything unique in the Jaina tradition which may justify the views of Jacobi that Buddhism is derived from the forerunners of the Jainas.[2]

(B) *The Alleged Influence of the Sāṅkhya*:—

As already pointed out, some ideas of Sāṅkhya are clearly traceable in the Upaniṣads.[3] In the Pali Nikāyas, however, we have very scanty references to Sāṅkhya philosophy. In the Brahmajāla-sutta a school of Sassatavādins is referred to which believed the soul (attā) and the world (loka) to be

---

1. Majjhima 56 (Upāli Sutta) clearly brings out the difference between the Jaina and Buddhist emphasis on body and mind respectively.
2. cf. Origin and Growth of Religion, p. 27—T. W. Rhys Davids.
3. cf. Hume—Thirteen Principal Upaniṣads, p. 8; Mrs. Rhys Davids—The Birth Of Indian Philosophy And Its Development In Buddhism, pp. 129-131.

eternal. This is indentified with Sāṅkhya by Garbe.[1] We have already noted that the views of Pakudha Kaccāyana about the ineffectibility of the soul and the eternity of both the soul and the physical elements are reminiscent of the Sāṅkhya thought. Mention of 'sukha and dukkha' as separate from the soul is also suggestive of the same. Pūraṇa Kassapa's theory also has a similar bearing[2]. The teacher of Buddha, Āḷāra Kālāma is identified by Aśvaghoṣa with Arāḍa, an alleged exponent of Sāṅkhya philosophy,[3] though it is difficult to see the source of this assertion.

Evidently, these are not very significant and impressive references. But in view of the Sāṅkhya ideas being found in the Upaniṣads and partially reflected in the contemporaneous thought of Buddha, both of which had an undeniable impact on Buddha, we are inclined to attach some positive value to the above mentioned references to the Sāṅkhyan thought by the Pāli Nikāyas and conclude that, though the Sāṅkhya does not seem to have direct distinctive influence on Buddhism, its indirect influence appears plausible.

(*C*) *The Alleged Influence of the Yoga*:—

With regard to the influence of Yoga on Buddhism, we can be fairly certain. From the internal references of the Pāli Nikāyas themselves, we know that Buddha learnt some impersonal yogic trances (arūpa samāpattis) from his teachers, Āḷāra Kālāma and Uddaka Rāmaputta[4] and some of his other contemporary sects also were conversant with some yogic practices.[5] Before the attainment of enlightenment, in the course of trying different methods, Buddha is found to prac-

---

1. Saṅkhya Philosophie, p. 5, note 1. This is objected to by Rhys Davids (American Lectures on Buddhism, pp. 25ff) on the ground that the heresy in question regards soul and *world* as eternal and not the soul and *Prakṛti*. But S. K. Belvalṛar has rightly pointed out that is is due to the scheme under which the 62 heresies are grouped.

2. It appears. however, that Sassatavāda was not definitely committed to Akriyāvāda, (as the views of the Kaccāyana and Kassapa may give impression to), for in Saṃyutta Nikāya (II. 20) we are clearly referred to a variety of Sassatavāda which believes in action; 'So Karoti, so paṭisamvediyatīti'

3. Buddha Carita XII. X. 16ff.

4. M 163-6 Ariyapariyesanā Sutta.

5. D. I. 180-181.

tise some breath-control (appānakaṃ jhānaṃ) as well.[1] In some later Upanisads too, besides some mystical references to yoga, some references to systematic yoga[2] including breath-control[3] are found. It is, thus, clear that Arūpasamāpatti and Ānāpāna-sati were already known to pre-Buddhistic sages.

When we compare the yoga of Buddhism with the yoga described in the Yoga-Sūtra of Patañjali, the similarities are so striking that they hardly leave any doubt regarding the one being influenced by the other. Not only is Prajñā recognised as the highest faculty in both, but there is perfect identity in the enumeration of the five faculties (Indriyas), viz. saddhā, viriya, sati, samādhi and paññа.[4] Out of the four samādhis mentioned in Yoga-Sūtra I. 17, the first three are in conformity with the first three of the five Jhānas found in the Abhidhamma, and the last stage, viz., the Asamprajñāta-samādhi is just like the eighth Samādhi, when mind is said to be 'Saṃskāraśeṣa' and without any positive basis (ālambana).[5] The attainments of supernormal powers mentioned in the Yoga-Sūtra as well as in the Nikāyas are similar.[6] The definition given by Yoga-Sūtra II. 5 of avidyā is quite close to the Buddhist notion of it. Both mention three duḥkhatās,[7] and the fourfold division of karma as Kṛṣṇa, Śukla etc.[8] Even ātmabhāva of Yoga-Sūtra IV. 25 finds its parallel in the Pali concept of attabhāva. Again like the 'brahmaviharas' of the Buddhists, Yoga-sūtra I. 33 enjoins the practice of maitrī, karuṇā, muditā and upekṣā.

The date of the Yoga-Sūtra is difficult to determine. It would, however, suffice for our purpose to note that Yoga, the germs of which were traceable in pre-Vedic period, had already reached a high stage of development before Buddha, and the latter must have derived (as he himself acknow-

---

1. M. I. 243.
2. Katha. III. 13; VI. 7, 11 and 18 and Švetā. II. 8-15.
3. Śveta II. 6 and 9.
4. S. V. 244-8; Yoga-Sūtra I. 20.
5. Yoga-Sūtra 1. 8; M. I. 400.
6. Yoga-Sūtra III. 45 and D. I. 87.
7. Yoga-Sūtra II. 15; and D. III. 216.
8. Yoga-Sūtra IV. 7. and D. III. 230.

ledges) much from it. We, however, are inclined to think that the systematic formulation of Yoga by Patañjali is later than Buddha and the development of systematic yoga in Buddhism might have contributed to the further systematisation of the Yoga-philosophy of Patañjali.[1]

(*D*). *The Alleged Influence of the Viṣṇuite-Kṛṣṇite Cult*:—

Senart has taken much pains to assert the influence of Viṣṇu-Kṛṣṇa worship on Buddhism. The fact that the same epithet, 'Bhagavat' is assigned both to Kṛṣṇa and Buddha shows according to him that the latter is recast on the model of the former. He refers to the legends of marvels ascribed alike both to Puruṣottama Kṛṣṇa and Mahāpuruṣa Buddha and points out the similarity in the Viṣṇuite concept of Avatāra and the Buddhist tradition of the successive Buddhas descending at intervals from heaven to instruct the people on earth. Besides the alleged borrowal of title, creed and myth, Senart thinks that even the devotionalism of the Viṣṇu-Kṛṣṇa (e. g. B. G. IX. 26) is reflected in the various Buddhist stories in which poor and insufficient offerings to Buddha are said to have resulted into immediate deliverance. He further points out such other common elements of them as jñāna, yoga, samādhi and nirvāṇa ect. and thinks that "Buddhism is undoubtedly the borrower."[2]

Now, none of the similarities pointed out by Senart can be said to be striking peculiarity of only these two schools of thought. The term 'Bhagavat' has for long been a very common epithet used for any venerable person, especially teachers. Very frequent use of it is seen in the Upaniṣads themselves.[3] Likewise the tendencies of weaving myths and legends around great personalities and pushing back the origin of any religion to more ancient times by imagining

1. It is not improbable to identify the Mahābhāṣyakāra and the yoga-Sūtrakāra Patañjali in which case the Yoga-Sūtra will have to be assigned a post-Buddistic date.

2. I.H.Q., Vol. 6, pp. 669-673.

3. Tait. III. 1—5: Right from the lst to 5th anuvādaka, Bhṛgu is saying to Varuṇa :—'Adhīhi *bhagavo* Brahmeti'; Chāndogya. VI.1.7. VI. 5.4; VI.6.5; VI. 8.7 (Bhūya eva ma *bhagavān*, vijñāpayatu). This is repeated till VI. 15. Ibid. VII, 1.3 (So' hom *bhagavaḥ* śocāmi taṁ mā *bhagavān*

various other predecessors to the actual propounder were the common features of that period and almost all religions founded about that time (whether Buddhism, Jainism or Vaiṣṇavism) were found to take these liberties. Similarly great respect, love and adoration for the teacher is a well known Indian institution.[1] But, on this ground it would be wrong to think (as Senart does) that charity and love for Buddha is the same as unqualified surrender to God as prevalent in Vaiṣṇavism. Some other similarities like jñāna, yoga and samādhi etc. are traceable to their common sources, namely, the Upaniṣads and yoga-doctrines. In short, no similarity pointed out by Senart is peculiar only to the Viṣṇu-Kṛṣṇa cult and Buddhism, which cannot be explained either as general characteristic features of the age or as common derivations from earlier traditions.

In fact, it is extremely difficult to conceive of the derivation of an atheistic religion preaching renunciation (as Buddhism does) from a thoroughly theistic religion, highlighting social activism (which Vaiṣṇavism stands for). In the Nikāyas also there is absolutely no mention of Kṛṣṇa, as the supreme deity. The only form of theism which the older portions of Nikāyas seem to be familiar with, is the creator god, Brahmā.[2] Although the name, Kṛṣṇa (Kaṇhā), occurs as the name of a sage[3] or as a pacceka Buddha[4] in the Nikāyas, it hardly bears any resemblance to Kṛṣṇa of Vaiṣṇavism. In fact, the name Kṛṣṇa appears in so many roles right from beginning of the Vedic age[5], but neither in the Vedas nor in the Upaniṣads nor in the Pāli Nikāyas does Kṛṣṇa occur as the supreme deity. The name Viṣṇu (Veṇhu) also does not occur in the Pāli Nikāyas as referring to the Supreme Lord. He is insignificantly mentioned just as thousands of other gods.[6] Thus from the internal evidence of the early Pāli Texts also, hardly any acquaintance with a Viṣṇu-

1. Śvetā. VI. 23.
2. D. I. 18; Majjhima I. 326-7.". . .eso pi bhikkhu brahmā, mahābrahmā abhibhū anabhibhūto aññad atthu-daso vasavattī, issaro, kattā nimmātā seṭṭho sañjitā vasī pitā bhūtabhabyānaṃ".
3. D. I. 96-7.
4. M. II. 71.
5. Ṛgveda VIII. 74; Kauṣītaki Brāhmaṇa XXX. 9; Chāndogya III. 17.
6. S. I. 52.

Kṛṣṇa-cult is indicated. We may, therefore, dismiss this view of Viṣṇuite influence on the early Buddhism as a baseless hypothesis.

(E) *The Alleged Influence of the Upaniṣads* :--

We have already noted that during the Upaniṣadic period the Aryan tradition branched off into three main tendencies of thought, one of which was critical of the ritualistic religion of the tradition. It is this tendency of the Upaniṣads which has been shown to influence Buddhistic thought and the logical culmination of which is to be found in the latter.

It may be noted that in the Pali Canon whenever Buddha is found disputing the Brahmanical religion, his target of attack is invariably the ritualistic religion of the Brahmins—the main topic of refutation being the uncritical acceptance of the Vedic authority, the caste-system, ritualistic rites and sacrifices. Regarding the non-ritualistic side of the tradition his attack is mainly against the substantive concept of the soul. But we have already noted that the highest point reached in the Upaniṣadic conception of the soul was tending to pave the way for Buddha's theory of Anattā (soullessness). Regarding some other matters also, we have already shown that the non-ritualistic tendency of the Upaniṣads was a harbinger of Buddhism, and had prepared the ground for it in so many ways. Buddhism, thus, is an improvement on and not a repudiation of this aspect of the Upaniṣads.

The concept of Vijñāna has pivotal importance both in the Upaniṣads as well as in Buddhism, though the latter often takes it as 'saviśesa' and so ultimately 'anitya'.[1] But there are some infrequent passages where Vijñāna is spoken of as the highest in the same Upaniṣadic fashion.[2] Again, Buddha's conception of Nibbāna can be regarded as somewhat similar to the later Upaniṣadic conception of Mokṣa. The

---

1. cf. Śaṅkara's Commentary on the Brahma-Sūtra II. 2. 28 : (Sākṣiṇovagantuḥ. . . . . .Vijñānasyotpatti pradhvaṃsā' nekatvādi viseṣavattvābhyupagamāt. . .)

2. D.I. 223 (Viññāṇaṃ anidassanaṃ anantaṃ sabbatopabhaṃ. . . .ettha nāmañ ca rupañca asesaṃ uparujjhati); cf. M. I. 229-230.

impermanence and unreality of all names and forms (nāmarūpa) are repeatedly emphasised in the Upaniṣads[1], as is done in Buddhism, notwithstanding the fact that they attach somewhat different meanings to the terms.

Then the influence of the Muṇḍakopaniṣad (literally, the Upaniṣad of the shaven headed) and Māṇḍūkyopaniṣad[2] is of special significance. The Muṇḍaka is the most vociferous in decrying the efficacy of the Vedic rituals, and clearly says that "those fools who consider them as the highest good (śreya) are sure to undergo decay and death again and again".[3] They are compared to the blind led by the blind[4], the same analogy as given by Buddha.[5] Its disapproval of the existing caste-system also is implied in the significant predicate used for Brahman viz. 'agotraṃ', 'avarṇaṃ' i. e. without family and without caste.[6] The fundamental theory of Buddhism that man is born according to his desires in the places appropriate to him is also found stated in the Muṇḍaka.[7] Similalry the ideas of Muṇḍaka III.1. 10 that "whatever world (loka) and whatever pleasure a man of inner purification desires for himself, he attains them"[8] is found well amplified in M. I. 33-36, 289; II. 100-103. Even the rationalistic approach of Buddha and his teaching of the middle path seem to be voiced by the Muṇḍaka when it says "The Ātman is not attainable by the scriptural discourse,

1. Chāndogya. VI. 1; VII. 1; Bṛhadā. I.6.3; Muṇḍaka III. 2.8; Praśna VI. 5.

2. In M. II. 24 we come across one Maṇḍikāputta (son of Maṇḍikā) as a samaṇa. It is not improbable to think of the Māṇḍūkyopaniṣad as representing the views of the same Maṇḍika paribbājaka, the father of Maṇḍikāputta. cf. Barua—A History of Pre-Buddhistic Indian Philosophy. p. 182.

3. Etacchreyo ye'bhinandanti mūḍhāḥ jarā mṛtyuṃ te punarevāpiyānti—Maṇḍaka I.2.7-10.

4. Muṇḍaka I.2.8. (andhenaiva nīyamānā yathāndhāḥ)

5. Seyyathāpi. . . andhaveṇi paramparā saṃsattā—purimo pi na passati majjhimo pi na. . . pacchimo pi na. . . evamevakho. . .andhaveṇūpamaṃ maññe brāhmaṇānam bhāsitaṃ. . . M. II. 170, 200.

6. Muṇḍaka I. 1.6.

7. Ibid. III. 2.2. cf. Bṛhadā. IV. 4.5.

8. yaṃ yaṃ lokaṃ manasā saṃvibhāti viśuddha-sattvaḥ kāmayate yāṃśca kāmān; Tam tam lokaṃ jayate tāṃśca kāmān. . . . see also Chāndogya VIII. 1.5-6; VIII. 2. 1-10.

nor by intellectual power nor by much hearing. . . .nor can it be attained by one who is devoid of strength, thoughtfulness and right meditation."[1]

Similarly the Māṇḍūkya[2] formulation of four planes of consciousness seems to have some resemblance to Buddhist thought (e. g. Buddha's differentiation of kāmāvacara, rūpāvacara, arūpāvacara and lokuttara corresponding to the four pādas of Brahman in the Māṇḍūkya). The basis of the fourfold mode of meditation, analysed and amplified differently in Buddhism and the Yoga-Sūtra, can also be seen in this Māṇḍūkya mode of classification. Buddha's representation of the Taittirīya doctrine in the Brahmajāla sutta obviously follows the Māṇḍūkya line.[3] Even the highly developed doctrine of the Mādhyamika school that the highest truth lies beyond the fourfold modes of logic (catuṣkoti vinirmuktaḥ) is traceable in almost identical terms in the Māṇḍūkya.[4]

We find not only similar ideas in the Upaniṣads and Buddhism, but some of the expressions and analogies also are quite similar. We may just look at a few of them:—

Similar Expressions

	Upaniṣad	Buddhism
1.	Kaṭha V. 15 ; Muṇḍaka II. 2. 10 and Śvetā. VI. 14:—Na tatra sūryo bhāti na candra-tārakaṃ	Ud. I. 9—Na tattha sukkā jotanti ādicco nappakāsati; Na tattha candimā bhāti tamo tattha na vijjati.
2.	Bṛhadā. II. 4. 5. ; IV. 5. 6. ; Chāndogya VI. 1. 3. ; VI. 4. 5. darśanena śravaṇena, matyā, vijñānena.	M. I. 3. diṭṭhaṃ, sutaṃ, mutaṃ, viññātaṃ.
3.	Kauṣ. III. 1 . . . na mātṛ-vadhena, na pitṛ-vadhena nāsya pāpaṃ . . .	Dh. 294 & 295. Mātaraṃ pitaraṃ hantvā. . . . anigho yāti brāhmaṇo.

---

1. Muṇḍaka III. 2. 3-4.
2. It is, however, doubtful whether the Māṇḍūkya is pre or post-Buddhistic.
3. cf. Barua—A History of Pre-Buddhistic Indian Philosophy. p. 183.
4. Nāntaḥ prajñaṃ no bahiṣprajñaṃ nobhayataḥ prajñaṃ. . . .na prajñaṃ nāprajñam.—Māṇḍūkya. 7.

	Upaniṣad	Buddhism
4.	Kaṭha. II. 1. Anyac-chreyo anyad utaiva pr-eyaḥ....	Dh. 75. Aññā hi labhūpanisā aññā nibbāna-gāminī.... cf. M. I. 161ff. Dve'mā bhikkhave pariyesanā: ar-iyā ca..anariyā ca.
5.	Kaṭha VI. 17 . Aṅguṣṭha-mātraḥ puruṣo'ntarātmā sadā janānāṃ hṛdaye sanniviṣṭaḥ, taṃ svācchariīrāt pravṛhet mu-ñjād iveṣīkāṃ dhairyeṇa. cf. Taitt. 6. Sa ya eṣo'-ntarhṛdaya ākāśaḥ, tasmin-nayaṃ puruṣo manomayaḥ.	D. I. 77. Idañ ca pana me viññāṇaṃ ettha sitaṃ ettha paṭibaddhaṃ ti....rūpiṃ manomayaṇ sabbaṅgapac-caṅgiṃ ahīnindriyaṃ.. seyyathāpi puriso muñjamhā īsīkaṃ pavāhey-ya cf. M. II. 17-18.
6.	Chāndogya IV. 14. 2. spiritual attainment is guessed by shining face:— Brahmavid iva saumya, te mukhaṃ bhāti	S. II. 275: Vippasannāni kho te.... indriyāni, pari-suddho mukhavaṇṇo pariyodāto santena... ajja vihārena vihāsī ti.
7.	Chāndogya I. 8. 8. ; I, 10. 11 & I. 11. 5 & 9. Speak-ing of the head falling off if things are carried on in discourse without proper knowledge (mūrdhā te vipatiṣyatī ti) cf. Bṛhadā. III. 7. 1.	M. I. 231. Yo koci tathā-gatena yāvatatiyaṃ saha-dhammikaṃ pañhaṃ puṭṭho na vyākaroti etthevassa sattadhā mud-dhā phalatī ti.

We may again compare the following analogies occurring in the Upaniṣads and the Pali Nikāyas:—

Just as in Bṛhadā. IV. 5. 9. the peculiar relation between the body and soul is explained through the analogy of the conch and its sound, so also in D. II. 337-8 (Pāyāsirājañña Sutta) the same analogy of the conch and its undiscovera-able sound (saṅkha dhama) is put forward to explain the fact that under certain conditions alone can the body live and move. The body is likewise said to be lying 'like a log of wood' when all the vital forces leave it (śuskaṃ dārubhūtam śiṣye, Kaus. II 14 ; yathā kaṭṭhaṃ acetanaṃ, M. 1.296). Every verse of the Uraga-sutta (Sn. 1-3) contains the analogy of the snake casting off its old slough (uraga jiṇṇamiva tacaṃ purāṇaṃ) which is the same as that of Bṛhadā. IV. 4. 7. Similarly the analogy of the chariot and charioteer along with the senses as the horses found in Kaṭha. III. 3-9 is reflected in the Rathopama Sutta (S. IV. 176). Then the analogy of the reed being taken out from the sheath (pravṛhen muñjād iveṣīkām), as found in Kaṭha VI. 17, is used in the same context and in the same language in D. I. 77 and M. II. 17-18. Similarly the relation between the body and soul explained through the analogy of house and house-dweller (Śvetā. III. 18) frequently occurs in the Nikāyas, e. g. in the Hāliddikāni Sutta (S. III. 9.) the physical body is called 'Oka' and Viññāṇa is called 'Okasārī' and again in the Kiṃsukopama Sutta (S. IV 194-5) the physical body is called 'nagara' and Viññāṇa is called 'nagarassāmī'. Then again the analogy of producing fire with two pieces of wood is common both to the Upaniṣads (e. g. Śvetā. I. 14) as well as Buddhism (e. g. M. I. 240-5). The analogy of the lotus-leaf remaining detached from water found in Chāndogya IV. 14. 3. (yathā puṣkara-palāsa āpo na śliṣyante) is frequently used in the Nikāyas (e. g. Vāri pokkhara patte, va—Dh. 401 ; Seyyathā pi.... uppalam...udake jātaṃ..anupalittaṃ udakena S. III. 140). The analogy of the blind led by the blind as found in Muṇḍaka I. 2. 8. and Kaṭha II. 5 also occurs frequently in Buddhist texts (e g. M. II. 170, 200). These are not all but only some of the more striking analogies which have been used almost in the same contexts and very much in similar languages.

We, therefore, cannot but arrive at the conclusion that Buddhism was deeply influenced by the non-ritualistie trends of the Upaniṣads. This explains why Buddhism took an idealistic and absolutistic trend so early as the beginning of the first century. The ideas towards which some of the Upaniṣads had only vaguely felt their way were led to the logical culmination in Buddhism, and were given a definite and systematic shape. It would, however, be incorrect and misleading to say that Buddhism was influenced by the

Upaniṣads as a whole, in view of there being some orthodox tendencies also in them which Buddhism discards.

(F) *The Influence of Buddha's Contemporaneous Thoughts*:—

Buddhism was also influenced by its diverse contemporary currents of thought. We have seen how by the time of Buddha a host of theories were being preached with the utmost subtlety of reasoning and sophistry, with the result that there appeared a bewildering atmosphere of conflict. The reference to 62 erroneous theories made by the Brahmajāla-Sutta, and 363 theories by the Jain texts is indicative of it. The Nikāyas contain references, on the one hand, to logicians and dialecticians engaged in displaying their argumentative skill and, on the other, to sceptics and agnostics like Sañjaya Belaṭṭhiputta evading all answers to philosophical questions. Materialists like Ajitakesakambala, considering perception as the only valid means of knowledge, were questioning all moral values and the efficacy of human effort. The Nigaṇṭhas, on the other hand, were advocating extreme physical tortures. Buddha could not but be influenced by these current thoughts, but his genius lies in avoiding all these extremes and following a middle path in which the partial truths of the various rival schools were synthesised without jeopardising his own position.

Thus the emergence of the early Buddhist thought is the result of a criticism, acceptance and synthesis of different streams of thought. The greatness of Buddha lies in adopting a balanced attitude to and taking what is of value from the diverse views of his time, and in using his discerning intellect to give a practical and rationally consistent shape to the wisdom of the past.

In the light of what has been said, the views of Rhys Davids and Radhakrishnan on the one hand that "Gotama was born and brought up and lived and died a Hindu"[1] "Buddhism grew and flourished within the fold of orthodox belief"[2], "Buddhism in its origin at least, is an offshoot of

1. Rhya Davids—Buddhism p. 83.
2. Ibid. p. 85.

Hinduism"[1] and those of G. C. Pande on the other that "Buddhism and Jainism spring from pre-Vidic non-Aryan stream."[2]—both seem to be unwarranted generalisations in opposite directions Buddhism may more appropriately be regarded as originating from the confluence of the Vedic and non-Vedic culture which was embodied in the non-ritualistic trend of the Upaniṣads. In fact, it was only natural for the greatest protagonist of the middle path to have taken a middle position here also as elsewhere. It is, again, difficult to regard it as a 'lay-movement'[3] as Rhys Davids thinks. It is evidently, as alredy shown, a world-renouncing movement completely classless and casteless. Again it cannot be regarded as a movement of revolt against Hinduism originating from a reformative zeal (like that of the Ārya-Smāja of Dayānanda Sarasvatī or Brahm-Samāja of Kesava Sen). Its real originating motive was one of discovery and not of revolt or reform, and in effect it was a departure from the orthodoxy of the tradition, though not from the tradition as a whole.

1. Radhakrishnan—Indian Philosophy, Vol. I.p. 361.
2. Studies in the Origins of Buddhism, p. 327. Dr. Pande, however, regards Buddhism as deeply influenced by the Vedic stream.
3. Buddhist India p. 159.

Section B.

THE SOURCES OF THE BHAGAVADGĪTĀ

The Compromising Character of the Bhagavadgītā :—

While tracing the development of Indian thought in the preceding section, we noted that the ritualistic religion of the Vedas and Brāhmaṇas received a jolt when some of the Upniṣadic seers heralded a new and independent line of approach. Under the impact of this new knowledge the Upaniṣadic speculation took, broadly speaking, three alternative lines : (i) the ritualistic line of orthodox tradition (karma mārga) ; (ii) the radically anti-ritualistic intellectual and intuitionist line of knowledge (jñāna mārga); and (iii) a compromising line of the two (jñāna-karma-samuccaya-mārga). The second line, viz., the anti-ritualistic path of knowledge (jñāna mārga) had two forms: one the absolutistic, as embodied in the earlier Upaniṣads like the Bṛhadāraṇyaka and Chāndogya etc., which later on developed into what is known as 'Vedānta' ; and the other dualistic, traces of which are found in the later Upaniṣads like the Kaṭha and Śvetāśvatara etc., which later on came to be systematised under the name 'Sāṅkhya'. Notwithstanding the different accounts of the origin and development of the world-process, both of them alike emphasise the cultivation of knowledge and avoidance of ritualism. As regards the the question of acquiring knowledge (jñāna), we have already seen in the preceding section that the method of yoga was prescribed by some of the Upaniṣads.[1] Some of them spoke of the method of devotion and divine grace as well[2], which we delibrately omitted in the course of our discussion about the origin of Buddhism, for it had no positive hearing on that. Buddhism, as we have already seen, had much in common with that aspect of the Upaniṣads which emphasised knowledge, and utilised yoga as a means to it. Utilising these

---

1. Kaṭha II. 12; III. 13; VI. 9-11; VI. 18; Muṇḍaka II. 2.7ff; III. 1.8; Svetā I.3 and II.8-14.

2. Kaṭhā II. 20; II. 23; Muṇḍaka III. 2.3; Svetāśvatara III. 20; IV. 21; V. 14; VI. 18; VI. 21 and VI. 23.

two and taking due caution from the current extreme views of its time, it developed this branch of thought (jñāna mārga) into a practical philosophy. The B. G., on the other hand, representing a conciliatory scheme of things (jñāna-karma samuccaya-mārga) tried to absorb and assimilate all these different forms and methods of knowledge (jñāna), namely, Vedānta, Sāṅkhya. Yoga and Bhakti by making some alterations and adjustments in them and further adding to them a new concept of karma, viz., disinterested action (niṣkāma-karma). It seeks to combine the knowledge of the Sāṅkhya dualism and the Upaniṣadic absolutism along with the method of yoga and bhakti with the Brahmanical ritualism by giving the latter a new meaning, and avdocating thereby a new doctrine of 'niṣkāma karma'. It, thus, intends to counteract the growing influence of radical renunciation and atheism advocated by various sects and so strongly championed by Buddhism and Jainism by putting forward a philosophy of theistic activism rooted in traditionol orthodoxy and yet adjusted to new ideas.

We shall now see how these diverse elements are assimilated and appropriated in the B. G., and how far they are modified and altered in the process. It is not sufficient for our purpose to know in a general way that the B. G. has been influenced by the ideas of the Upaniṣads, Sāṅkhya and Yoga etc., which has already been pointed out by some scholars. We must make a further examination of the different elements found in the B. G. and see how far and in which senses these various thought-currents have been utilised by the B. G.

Elements of Ritualism:—

For an objective surveyor, it is not difficult to see that the B. G., though it undermines the value of rituals and sacrifices, it does not reject them *in toto*. It rather accepts and absorbs them into its scheme by modifying their concepts. Only those types of sacrifices are condemned and rejected which are performed without any inner piety. Such sacrifices which consist of mere external formalities are only nominal (nāmayajña), improperly performed, out of pride and prestige[1], and they will only lead the sacrificer to fall in-

1. B.G. XVI. 17.

to a foul hell.[1] But sacrifices, if duly performed, can lead to heaven where the sacrificer will enjoy heavenly pleasures.[2] But ultimately he will again have to come down to the world of mortals after the exhaustion of his merit, thus still remaining under the cycle of birth and death.[3] Sacrifices, therefore, cannot lead to the highest goal of immortality, and as they entail a desire for pleasure and prosperity, their pursuit rather distracts the mind from the meditative repose leading to the highest attainment.[4] It is remarkable, however, that notwithstanding this usual disparaging treatment of sacrifices, the B. G. considers them as essentially purifying (pāvanāni)[5], and gives them a new meaning in order to fit them in with the path of knowledge. The word 'sacrifice' (yajña) is used to connote perfect detachment based on knowledge (jñānayajña) which is the best of all sacrifices.[6] Thus, ultimately yajña is interpreted in the sense of the disinterested or selfless discharge of all duties (niṣkām-karma), and both knowledge and action are synthysised. In this sense it is said that actions other than yajñas alone can cause bondage[7], and yajñas performed in the selfless manner will lead to the highest goal.[8] Thus the sacrifice is taken in three different senses, rejected in the first sense, undermined in the second and accepted in the third sense ; in the first it leads to hell, in the second to heaven and in the third to final salvation.

It is clear that the B.G. in its attempt to bring the ritualistic religion in conformity with knowledge makes these alterations and adjustments in the meaning of yajña, and develops its important theory of detached or disinterested action (niṣkāma-karma). It cannot, however, be said that the idea was altogether new. The disparaging note to ordinary ritualism is traceable in some of the Upaniṣads. The general tone and even some of the words used in this

1. B.G. XVI. 16.
2. B.G. IX. 20; III. 10-12.
3. B.G. IX. 21.
4. B.G. II. 42-46.
5. B.G. XVIII. 5; III. 13.
6. B.G. IV. 33; IX. 15; XVIII. 70.
7. B.G. III. 9.
8. B.G. IV. 33ff; XVIII. 6.

connection by the Muṇḍaka is similar to that cf the B. G.[1] The special meaning attached to yajña (jñāna-yajña) is also an extension of the symbolic interpretation of the sacrifice commenced in the Upaniṣads. The teaching of disinterested action also is traceable in some of the Upaniṣads. The Īśa, for examle, states that man should desire to live a hundered years doing all his duties, and in that way and no other will action not contaminate him.[2] The Chāndogya.[3] Bṛhadā.[4], and Kauṣītaki[5] also speak of an elevated state of mind when actions do not contaminate the doer. But it is undoubtedly in the B. G. that the conception gains prominence and becomes one of its central themes.

Elements of the Upaniṣads:—

The influence of the Ups. on the B. G. is only too patent. The entire description of the eternity and immortality of Ātman, the absoluteness and transcendence of Brahman, its negative and paradoxical characterisation, the references to lordly powers and the supreme nature of God (Paramātman), the symbolic meditation of 'Om' (Śabda-Brahman), the description of the two pathways of pitṛyāna and devayāna, the ultimate unity behind the multiplicity of the world, an abiding and imperishable element behind the impermanent and perishing features of it, the nature and the state of nirvāṇa and the ideal conduct of sthita-prajña—in short, most of the metaphysical elements of the B. G. are drawn from the Ups. Not only are the ideas taken but very many verses as well, literally or with some variations, are the same as those of the Ups. Besides, there are numerous other short passages, words and expressions which clearly seem to be borrowed from the Ups. Some images also of the B. G.

---

1. Muṇḍaka, I. 2. 7—10 and B.G. II. 46; III. 11—12.
Nānyad śreyo vedayante (Muṇḍ. I.2.10)—nānyad astīti vādinaḥ (B. G. II. 42). Vedayante pramūḍhaḥ (Muṇḍ. I.2.10)—pravadanti avipaścitaḥ (B.G. II. 42). Vayaṃ kṛtārthā ity abhimanyanti bālāḥ (Muṇḍ. I.2.9)—puṣpitāṃ vācaṃ pravadanti avipaścitaḥ (B.G. II. 42).

2. Iśa. I. and 2 (tyaktena bhuñjīthāḥ; na karma lipyate nare).

3. Chāndo. IV. 14.3 (evaṃvidi pāpaṃ karma na śliṣyate).

4. Bṛhadā IV. 3. 22-30; IV. 4. 23. (na lipyate karmanā pāpakeṇa)

5. Kaus. III. 1. (sa yo māṃ veda na ha vai tasya kenacana karmaṇā loko mīyate).

are similar to those of the Ups. We may point out here the important verses, passages, expressions and images which will indicate the magnitude of this influence.

The passages occurring *verbatim* or with some variations:-

	B.G.	Ups.
1.	II. 19, ya enaṃvetti hantāram	—with little variation in the first line the verse is literally the same as Kaṭha. II. 19.
2.	II. 20, na jāyate mriyate vā kadācin . . .	—with little variation in the first line the verse is literally the same as Kaṭha. II. 18.
3.	II. 55. prajahāti yadā kāmān sarvān pārtha manogatān...	—corresponds to Kaṭha. VI. 14 and Bṛhadā. IV. 4. 7 : yadā sarve pramucyante kāmā ye'sya hṛdi śritāḥ.
4.	III. 42 and VIII. 20. indriyāṇi parāṇy āhuḥ...	—the verse is taken with slight variation from Kaṭha III. 10 and 11;VI. 7 and 8: indriyebhyaḥ parā hy arthā. . . .
5.	IV. 14, iti māṃ yo abhijānāti karmabhir na sa badhyate	—similar to kauṣītaki. III. 1, sa yo māṃ veda na ha vai tasya kenacana karmaṇā loko mīyate
6.	V. 10, lipyate na sa pāpena padmapattram iva'mbhasā	—closely corresponds to Chāndogya IV. 14. 3, yathā puṣkarapalāśa āpo na śliṣyante evaṃ evaṃvidi pāpaṃ karma na ślisyata iti.
7.	V. 13, nava dvāre pure dehī. . . with its epithet 'vaśī'	—exactly the same as in Śvetā. III. 18
8.	VI. 29, sarvabhūtastham ātmānam sarvabhūtāni cā'tmani	—exactly the same as in Kaivalya 10 ; Īśa 6, sarvāṇi bhūtānyātmani. .sarvabhūteṣu cā'tmānaṃ. . .

	B.G.	Ups.
9.	VII.4, bhūmir āpo'nalo—vāyuḥ..	with some modification similar to Muṇḍaka II. 1.3; Praśna VI. 4, etasmāj jāyate..khaṃ vāyur jyotir āpaḥ....
10.	VIII. 9, āditya varṇaṃ tamasaḥ parastāt	exactly the same as in Śvetā. III. 8.
11.	VIII. 9, aṇor aṇīyāṃsam	exactly the same as in Śveta. III. 20.
12.	VIII. 11, yad akṣaraṃ vedavido vadanti..	with some variation in the first line the verse is the same as Kaṭha. II. 15.
13.	XI. 28, yathā nadīnāṃ—bahavo'mbuvegāḥ samudram evā'bhimukhā dravanti	quite similar to Muṇḍaka. III. 2. 8, yatha nadyapaḥ syandamānāḥ samudre astaṃ gacchanti..cf. Praśna. VI. 5.
14.	XIII. 13, sarvataḥ pāṇi—pādṃ..	the entire verse is exactly the same as Śveta. III. 16.
15.	XIII. 14, sarvendriya—guṇābhāsaṃ sarvendriyavivarjitam	the whole line is axactly the same as Śvetā. III. 17.
16.	XIII. 15, dūrasthaṃ ca'n—tike ca tat	almost the same as Īśa 5, ṭaddūre tadvantike, and Muṇḍaka III.7., dūrāt sudūre tadihāntike ca.
17.	XIII. 17, jyotiṣāmapi taj—jyotiḥ	the same occurs in Bṛhadā. IV. 4. 16, jyotiṣāṃ jyotiḥ
18.	XIII. 32, sarvatrā'vasthito—dehe tathātmā no'palipyate	very much similar to Kaṭha. V. 11, ekas tathā sarva-bhūtāntarātmā na lipyate lokaduḥkhena bāhyaḥ
19.	XV. 1, ūrdhva mūlam—'adhaḥ śākhamaśvatthaṃ prāhur avyayam	almost same as Kaṭha. VI. 1. ūrdhvamūlo'vāk-śākha eṣo'-śvatthas sanātanaḥ

	B. G.	Ups.
20.	XV. 6, na tad bhāsayate sūryo..	—quite similiar to Kaṭha. V. 15 ; Muṇḍaka II. 2. 10 & Śvetā VI. 14, na tatra sūryo bhāti..
21.	XV. 15, Vedaiś ca sarvair ahameva vedyo vedāntakṛt..	—with the substitution of the word 'vedairanekaiḥ, in place of 'Vedaiś ca sarvaiḥ,' the entire line is exactly the same as in Kaivalya 22.
22.	XVIII. 17, hatvā'pi sa imāṃllokān na hanti na nibadhyate	—resembles Kauṣītaki III. 1, na bhrūṇa-hatyayā, na mātṛvadhena, na pitṛ-vadhena nāsya pāpaṃ..

Besides, there are a number of other passages conveying the same ideas and having somewhat similar expressions. We may just compare the following:—

	B. G.	Ups.
1.	II. 29, āścaryavat paśyati..	—clearly reminds of Kaṭha. II. 7 śravaṇāyāpi..āścaryo vaktā..
2.	II. 42-44 undermines	the value of rituals almost in the same way as Muṇḍaka I. 2. 7—10.
3.	II. 70, samudram āpaḥ praviśanti yadvat	—clearly resembles Muṇḍaka III. 2. 8, yathā nadyaḥ syandamānāḥ samudre astaṃ gacchanti. cf. PraśnaVI. 5.
4.	II. 71, Vihāya Kāmān yaḥ sarvān pumāṃ ścarati..	—echoes the idea of Kaṭha. VI. 4 & Bṛhadā. IV. 4.7., yadā sarve pramucyante kāmā ye'sya hṛdi śritāḥ
5.	VI. 11-13, describing the place posture and procedure of yoga like ..'śucau deśe pratiṣthāpya ....'samaṃ kāyaśirogrīvaṃ'	—has obvious similarity to Śvetā. II. 8-10. 'Same śucau....' 'trirunnataṃ sthāpya samaṃ śarīraṃ....'

	B.G.	Ups.
6.	VI. 31, sarva bhūtasth-itaṃ yo māṃ bhajaty ekatvam āsthitaḥ..	—is similar to Īśa. 7, yasmin sarvāṇi bhūtāni..ekatvam anupaśyataḥ.
7.	VII. 2; jñānaṃ..vakṣyāmy aśeṣataḥ, yaj jñātvā ne'ha bhūyo'nyaj jñātavyaṃ avaśiṣyate	—reminds at once of the all-revealing knowledge of Chāndo. VI. 1. 3. and Bṛhadā. IV. 5. 6., II. 4. 5., yena aśrutaṃ śrutaṃ bhavati..avijñātaṃ vijñātam iti.
8.	VIII.4 and 7, bhūmirāpo'nalo vāyuḥ.. mattaḥ parataraṃ nā'-nyat.. mayi sarvam idaṃ protaṃ....	contain similar ideas as Muṇḍaka. II. 2. 5. yasmin dyauḥ pṛthivī cāntarikṣam otaṃ
9.	VIII. 13. and XVII.24, aum ity ekākṣaraṃ brahma vyāharan....; tasmād aum iti udāhṛtya	prescribes the same meditation and remembrance of śabda-Brahma as found in Muṇḍaka. II. 4. 5, Māndūkya. 12 and Śvetā. I. 14. cf. Kaṭha. II. 15-17 and Praśna V. 1-5.
10.	VIII. 24-27 and IX. 25., have the similar description of devayāna (śukla gati) and pitṛyāna (kṛṣṇa-gati)	—as found in Chāndo. IV.15; V. 10;Bṛhadā. VI.2. 15ff; Praśna I. 9ff; Kauṣītaki I. 2ff and Muṇḍaka. I. 2. 9ff.
11.	IX. 20 and 21, te taṃ bhuktvā svargalokaṃ viśālaṃ kṣīṇe puṇye martyalokaṃ viśanti	—is stated similarly in Muṇḍaka. I. 2. 10, nākasya pṛṣṭhe te sukṛte'nubhūtvemaṃ lokaṃ hīnataraṃ vā viśanti

	B.G.	Ups.
12.	XI. 10ff, 'śaśi sūrya netram' etc. describing cosmic form of Kṛṣṇa	—carries similar ideas as in Muṇḍaka II. 1. 4, agnir mūrdhā cakṣuṣī candra sūryau..
13.	XV. 16-18. The tripartite distinctions of kṣara, akṣara and Paramātma	—is traceable in Śvetā. I. 10, kṣaraṃ pradhānam amṛtākṣaraṃ haraḥ kṣarātmānāv īśate deva ekaḥ.

Many of the images also of the B. G. are quite similar to those of the Ups. The analogy of the river merging into the ocean in B. G. II. 70 and XI. 28 is similar to that of Muṇḍaka. III. 2.8. Detachment is compared both in B. G. V. 10 and Chāndogya IV. 14.3 to the noncontamination of the lotus-leaf from water. The analogy of the Aśvattha tree of B. G. XV. I is found in Kaṭha. VI. I, as also in Maitrī. VI. 4. The world is generally conceived as a sea, and the different means to salvation are imagined as boats which take men across it. B. G. IV. 36, for example, speaks of going across through the boat of knowledge (jñāna plavenaiva ..saṃtariṣyasi) and Muṇḍaka. I. 2. 7 calls the boats of eighteen-fold sacrifices as insecure (plavā hy ete adṛḍhā yajñarūpāś aṣṭādaśoktam avaraṃ yeṣu karma). Again the body is imagined as a house with nine doors having the soul as the indwelling being (navadvāre pure dehī) both in B.G. V. 13 and XIV. 11 as well as in Śvetā. III. 18. The analogy of horses, chariot and charioteer found in Kaṭhā III. 3-9 with regard to the relation of senses, mind and intellect etc., is suggested, though not clearly stated by the B. G. in its various expressions like II. 60, 67, 68; III. 7, 41 and VI. 24-26. It has been suggested that "the famous figure of Ātman as the chariot-driver in the parable referred to is responsible for the Gītā episode itself of the Mahābhārata".[1] All these go to prove that the B. G. derives much of its material from the Ups.

1. I.H.Q., Vol. 6, p. 503.

It should not, however, be thought that the entire B. G. is nothing but a jumble or collection of all the diversified elements of the Ups. Firstly, it takes material from other sources as well; secondly, its aim being the reconciliation of the paths of knowledge and action (jnāna-karma-samuccaya) it takes only those materials from the Ups. which are suited to its purpose; and thirdly, some of the ideas traceable here and there in the Ups. as stray hints or occurring in them infrequently are for the first time brought into focus and propounded prominently by it. This may be illustrated by referring to its distinctive doctrines of devotion (bhakti) and disinterested action (niṣkāma karma). Except for the Śvetāśvatara which Deussen[1] considers the leading example of the theistic teachings of the Ups., and which has been styled by Barth[2] as a kind of Śaivite Bhagavadgītā, no other Ups. has that pronounced tone of devotion as is found in the B.G. Similarly the doctrine of disinterested action, though hinted at here and there in the Ups., as already indicated, was nowhere given that place and prominence which is given to it in the B.G. It is with a view to fitting in the knowledge of the Ups. with the special doctrines of disinterested action and devotion that the B.G. shapes and sharpens the relevant ideas of the Ups. Besides, it also utilises the ideas of the Sāṅkhya and Yoga much more than any of the Ups., and tries to mould them in such a way that they might be brought in conformity with its largely adopted Upaniṣadic ideas. Thus, it is a deliberate appropriation, adjustment and synthesis of some of the Upaniṣadic ideas relevant to its syncretic doctrine. Therefore, the oft-quoted verse[3] indicating the B. G. as being exclusively derived from the Ups., representing all the Ups. as cows, and the Gītā as the milk derived out of them, is to be taken as a very general statement, and should be accepted only with reservations.

Elements of Saṅkhya:—

Let us now look at the elements of Sāṅkhya which the

1. I.H.Q., Vol. 6, p. 507.
2. Religions of India (English Translation), p. 207.
3. Sarvopaṇiṣado gāvo dogdhā gopālanandanaḥ
Pārtho vatsaḥ suddīr bhoktā dugdham gītāmṛtaṃ mahat.

B. G. makes use of. It is not difficult to see how the fundamental tenets of the Sāṅkhya system are combined with those of the Vedānta and interwoven in the metaphysical scheme of the B. G. The nature of prakṛti and puruṣa, their relation causing the world-process, the nature and function of the three guṇas, the twentyfour principles together with the puruṣa as the twentyfifth and the discriminative knowledge of prakṛti and puruṣa leading to emancipation—all are clearly accepted and assimilated in the B. G.. We find specific mention of prakṛti and puruṣa as two beginningless entities (B. G. XIII. 19)[1] the contact of which is said to be the source of all things and beings (B. G. VII. 6; XIII. 26)[2]. Puruṣa, however, is not an active participant and is regarded as inactive (akarttā—B. G. XIII, 29; III. 27), indifferent, pure witness (udāsīna, sākṣī—B. G. XIV. 23; IX. 18), beyond qualities (guṇātīta, nirguṇa—B. G. XIV. 25; XII. 31) and unique (Kevala..B.G. XVIII. 16). One can easily see that these epithets are precisely the same as those used for purusa in the Sāṅkhya philosophy.[3] It is only when the puruṣa is deluded by ahaṅkāra, an evolute of prakṛti that he falsely takes himself for the doer (B. G. III. 27). Prakṛti alone is the active principle (B.G.III. 27; XIII, 29),[4] the three guṇas of which constitute the whole universe (B. G. VII. 13; XIII. 19).[5] The function of the world is explained in terms of these very guṇas (B. G. III. 27, 28, 29; XIV. 23).[6] Again the knowledge (jñāna) leading to salvation consists in the discrimination of puruṣa from prakṛti (B. G. XIII. 2, 18, 23 and 34)[7] which are also called Kṣetrajña and Kṣetra respectively.

---

1. Prakṛtim puruṣaṃ caiva viddhy anādī ubhāv api.
2. etadyonīni bhūtāni sarvānī'ty upadhāraya;
yāvat saṃjāyate Kiñcit sattvam sthāvara jaṅgamam
Kṣetra-kṣetrajña-saṃyogāt tad viddhi bharatarṣabha.
3. Sāṅkhya-Kārikā 19:—tasmācca viparyāsāt siddhaṃ sākṣitvamasya puruṣasya; Kaivalaym mādhyasthyaṃ drasṭṛtvaṃ akartṛbhāvaśca.
4. prkṛtyaiva ca karmāṇi kriyamāṇani sarvaśaḥ.
5. tribhir guṇamayair bhāvair ebhiḥ sarvamidaṃ jagat.
6. guṇā guṇesu varttante.
7. Kṣetra kṣetrajñayor evam antaraṃ jñāna cakṣuṣā. . .ye vidur yānti te param.

With slight variation in the scheme of classification the twentyfour principles of Sāṅkhya together with puruṣa as the twentyfifth are accepted by the B. G. According to Sāṅkhya the classification of these 25 principles is broadly subsumed under four heads, viz. (a) the original primal matter which is never an evolute (mūla prakṛtir avikṛtiḥ), (b) the seven principles like mahat etc. which are evolvent in relation to the sixteen principles, namely, the eleven senses and the five tanmātṛas, and evolutes in relation to the primal matter or prakṛti (prakṛtir vikṛtayaḥ), (c) the sixteen evolutes which are never evolvents but only evolutes (vikārāḥ), and (d) the puruṣa who is beyond both these evolvents and evolutes (na prakṛtir na vikṛtiḥ).[1] Thus, out of these four grades, prakṛti and puruṣa are placed in two separate grades. Then there iv a third group of seven, 'prakṛtir vikṛtayaḥ', i. e. mahat, ahaṅkāra and five subtle elements. The fourth group consists of the sixteen evolutes, viz. the eleven indriyas and five gross elements.

The B. G. makes slight modifications in this broad scheme of the Sāṅkhyan classification in view of its persistent affiliation with the Vedāntic metaphysics. Admitting, as it does, the absolute supremacy of the non-dual Brahman, it does not regard puruṣa and prakṛti as two ultimate and independent entities, but considers them as only two forms, higher and lower, of the same supreme Reality (VII. 4-6). Therefore, puruṣa and prakṛti are not entirely separeted in its broad scheme of classification. Again, instead of assigning a separate class for the sixteen evolutes, it tries to merge them into the class of seven principles called by Sāṅkhya 'prakṛtir vikṛtayah'. Out of these sixteen, five gross elements are supposed to be implied by five tanmātras, and so need not require any separate mention. Regarding the remaining eleven indriyas, it takes the chief of them, namely, mind as a representative (implying all of them), and adds it to the group of seven, thus making the total number eight. This is how it comes to formulate the eightfold (aṣṭadhā) division of prakṛti and simplifies the mode of broad classification.

Now according to it, the supreme Reality, like that of

1. mūla prakṛtir avikṛtiḥ mahadādyāḥ prakṛtir vikṛtayaḥ sapta. ṣoḍaśakastu vikāro na prakṛtir na vikṛtiḥ, puruṣaḥ, Sāṅkhya-Karikā 3.

the Vedānta, is only one having two forms, lower (aparā) and higher (parā), called prakṛti and puruṣa respectively, and the former is spoken of as being of eight kinds (aṣṭadhā, B. G. VII. 4 and 5). The latter being essentially identical with the Supreme (B. G. XIII. 2)[1] no division or distinction can be spoken of it. After this adjustment, the B. G. fully accepts the Sāṅkhyan enumeration of 24 principles excluding the puruṣa (B. G. XIII. 5). It can thus be clearly seen that the B. G. in order to bring the Sāṅkhyan principles in harmony with those of the Vedānta, introduces this little modification in the scheme of broad classification, and then finds it easy to accept the Sāṅkhyan enumeration of tattvas.

We may at a glance clearly see the nature of these two schemes of classification in the following tables :—

Sāṅkhya Classification

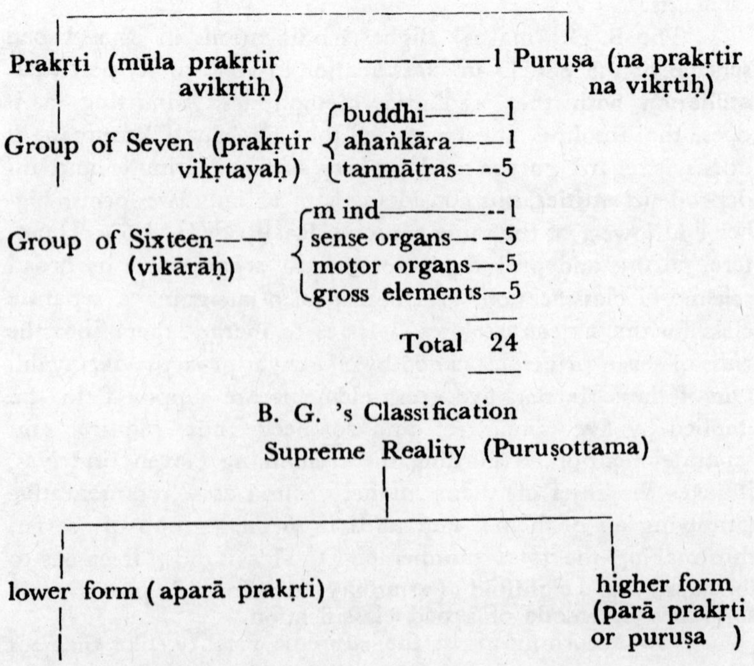

1. Kṣetrajñaṃ cā'pi māṃ viddi sarvakṣetreṣu bhārata.

lower form (aparā prakṛti) ———1

eightfold division (aṣṭadhā prakṛti)
- 1. earth : its gross and subtle forms ———2
- 2. water : do do———2
- 3. fire : do do———2
- 4. air : do do———2
- 5. ether : do do———2
- 6. indriyas: 5 sense-organs, 5 motor-organs, and 1 mind—11
- 7. egotism——— ——— 1
- 8. intellect——— ——— 1

Total 24

Thus the Sāṅkhyan categories along with the important tenets of Sāṅkhya are absorbed by the B. G. and fitted into the metaphysical scheme of the Vedānta which it largely follows. The term 'Sāṅkhya' itself occurs in the B. G. as often as seven times (II. 39; III. 3; V. 4; V. 5; XIII. 24; XVIII. 13 and XVIII. 19) but it must not be forgotten that the B. C. makes use of the Sāṅkhyan material in its own way. We cannot find here an unmitigated form of the later atheistic Sāṅkhya philosophy. In fact the term 'Sāṅkhya' is hardly used in the B. G. in the sense of that atheistic system. It is rather constantly used in the sense of a doctrine based on knowledge (jñāna) which is placed as an alternative to yoga i. e. a doctrine based on action (karma). Even in chapter XVIII in which alone the term 'Sāṅkhya' occurs without its usual alternative doctrine, yoga, it does not seem to indicate the well known Sāṅkhya system of subsequent times, for the five causes spoken of by B.G. XVIII.13 in the name of the Sāṅkhya doctrine do not appear in the later Sāṅkhya system known to us.

It has already been pointed out that the B.G. does not admit the ultimacy of prakṛti and puruṣa, and adds above them a supreme principle known as Paramātmā, Uttama-Puruṣa or Puruṣottama (B.G. XV.16-18). Thus neither the prakṛti nor the puruṣa remains strictly and exclusively Sāṅkhyan. The prakṛti which is also known as avyakta (B.G. VIII. 18, 20) is at once identified with the Vedāntic māyā (B.G. VII. 14.) and Kṣetra (B.G. XIII. 5-6, 26), and at times spoken of as Svabhāva (B.G. V. 14). Puruṣa also, like the Vedāntic Ātman, is said to be essentially identical with the supreme (B.G. XIII. 2, XIII. 22 and 31). Besides, the terms 'prakṛti' and 'puruṣa' are not always used in their strict philosophical sense. They are at times found to assume some meanings of common usage. The term prakṛti, for example, is used in B.G. III. 33, VII. 20, IX. 12 and 13 in the sense of 'natural tendency' and in B.G. XI. 51 in the sense of 'normal state'. Similarly, Ātman is used indiscriminately in the senses other than soul as well. In B.G. V. 21; VI. 10, 36, 47 and XIII. 24, it is used in the sense of the limited empirical self or individuality. Ātmā in B.G. IV. 21 and VI. 10 is interpreted by Rāmānuja in the sense of mind[1] and Śaṅkara takes it in the sense of body.[2] At any rate, it does not and cannot mean the philosophical concept of Ātmā or Puruṣa. Similar loose uses of terms like buddhi, ahaṅkāra and manas also can be shown. Besides denoting the Sāṅkhyan meaning, viz. the internal organs, buddhi and manas occur in the sense of heart, understanding and view (e.g. B.G. II. 39; III. 2 and I. 30; XI. 45 and XVII. 16); and ahaṅkāra is taken, at times, in the sense of general pride (e.g. B.G. XVI. 18 XVIII. 59).

From this, two things are indicated: firstly, the B.G. while accepting the fundamental tenets of both the Ups. and Sāṅkhya makes some necessary modifications in their ideas, terms and concepts; and secondly, it does not always use the different philosophic terms in their technical senses. The former indicates its synthetic and compromising character and the latter, its non-logical and poetic treatment of the subject.

Elements of Yoga :—

We may now examine the elements of yoga as found in the B.G. Like the term 'yoga' the term 'Sāṅkhya' also is not always used in the B.G. in its strict technical sense, as it is found in the subsequent Yoga-system of Patañjali, where it is

---

1. With regard to the word 'yatacitt*ātmā*' occurring in these two verses Rāmānuja gives the words 'yatacitta*manāḥ*' (R.B.G. IV. 21) and 'yatacitta*manaskaḥ*' (R.B.G.VI. 10) as its synonyms.

2. Commenting on the word 'yatacitt*ātmā*' in B.G. IV. 21 Śaṅkara says: "Cittam antaḥkaraṇam ātmā *bāhyaḥ kārya-kāraṇa-saṅghātaḥ*." (S.B.G. IV. 21) Again commenting on the same word in B.G. VI. 10, he says: "Cittam antaḥkaraṇam atmā dehaḥ." (S.B.G. VI. 10).

defined as 'the restraint of the mental operations' (citta-vṛtti-nirodhaḥ). It is loosely used in the B.G. in so many senses and at places the meanings so imperceptibly pass into one another that it becomes difficult to ascertain as to which meaning rightly conveys the intended sense of the author. In fact, some commentators have been led to diverse interpretations of the B.G. on account of the fluidity of this and other such important terms. In the VIth chapter, for example, most of the discussion about yoga is in the sense of the practice of self-restraint, but both in the opening and closing few verses of the chapter it is taken in the sense of karma-yoga.[1] But this transition from one sense to another is so swift and silent that the author seems to have passed almost unnoticed from one neaning to another. No wonder, therefore, that even commentators like Śaṅkara and Rāmānuja are eluded in the interpretation of the important verse of the chapter, viz. VI. 46 where Arjuna is asked to become a yogī (tasmād yogī bhavārjuna), and yoga is preferred to jñāna. Evidently, here 'yoga' means 'karma-yoga' or 'niṣkāma-karma' which the B. G. uniformly holds in preference to mere jñāna, and unambiguously asks Arjuna to follow it.[2] But both

1. The chapter opens up with an unmistakable definition of yogī as "one who does the prescribed work regardless of its fruit" (anāśritaḥ karma-phalaṃ kāryaṃ karma karoti yaḥ—B.G. VI.1). This sense of the word 'yoga' is carried on upto B.G. VI. 9 where the equanimity of intellect (samabuddhiḥ) is emphasised and yogī is said to conduct himself among his friends and foes with equanimity (B.G. VI.9). It is precisely in this sense that 'yoga' was earlier defined as 'equanimity' and 'skilful action' (Samatvaṃ yoga ucyate—B.G.II. 48; yogaḥ Karmasu Kauśalam—B.G. II. 50). It is again in this sense of the word that Arjuna is asked to be a yogī towards the close of the chapter (Tasmād yogī bhavā' rjuna, B.G. VI. 46). Evidently, Kṛṣṇa cannot ask Arjuna to retire from the battle and go to the forest for practising Pātañjala yoga. But right from VI. 10 to VI. 41 the B.G. uses the word 'yoga' in the sense of Pātañjala yoga and describes the place, posture and procedure of it, referring to 'practice' and 'detachment' (abhyāsa and vairāgya—B.G. VI. 35) as the means of acquiring self-restraint—precisely the same as prescribed in the Yoga-Sūtra of Patañjali (abhyāsa vairāgyābhyāṃ tan nirodhaḥ—Yoga-Sūtra I. 12). The latter i.e. Pātañjala yoga seems to be described as a means to the former i.e. karmayoga.

2. Preference to karmayoga over jñāna is clearly shown in B.G. III. 7 and 8 (karmayogam. . .viśiṣyate; niyataṃ kuru karma tvaṃ) as well as in B.G.V.2. (tayos tu karmasaṃnyāsāt karmayogo viśiṣyate). In the second chapter itself kṛṣṇa asks Arjuna to work as a yogī (yogasthaḥ kuru karmāṇi—B. G. II. 48) as he does in the present verse (tasmād yogī bhavā'rjuna—B.G. VI. 46). cf. B.G. III. 9; IV. 42 (muktasaṅgaḥ samācara; yogam ātiṣṭho' ttiṣṭha bharata).

Śaṅkara and Rāmānuja, holding up their own respective positions of jñāna and bhakti, attach a differnt meaning to jñāna and remain ambiguously silent about yoga, indicating thereby its continued sense of Pātañjala-yoga.[1] We must, therefore, understand the different senses in which the term 'yoga' is used in the B.G.

On careful examination of the various passages relating to yoga, we find as many as four differeut senses in which the term has been used in the B.G. :—

(1) The first and most important use of the term, in keeping with the highest teaching of the B.G., is in the sense of the disinterested or selfless discharge of one's duty. It is in this sense that the term occurs for the first time in the B.G. (II. 39) where, as at many other places, it is placed as an alternative to Sāṅkhya or jñāna. As this yoga enjoins the relentless discharge of one's actions, it is, at times, joined with the word 'karma', and is thus more fully known as karma-yoga (III, 3,7; V. 2 and XIII. 24) as against Sāṅkhya-yoga or jñāna-yoga (XIII. 24; III. 3) which stands for renunciation of actions. Still another name for this karma-yoga is buddhi-yoga (II. 49), for in it, it is the state of buddhi which matters and not the mere outward action. It is in this sense that the term is throughout used in the second chapter and defined as the "equanimity of mind" (samatvaṁ yoga ucyate, II. 48) or "skilful action" (yogaḥ karmasu kauśalam II. 50) when actions are so "skilfully performed that they do not contaminate the doer. This sense of yoga is very frequently used in the B.G. e.g. II. 39,48-50, 53; III. 3. 7; IV. 38, 41, 42; V. 1, 2, 4-7, 11; VI. 1-4, 46; IX. 28; XIII. 24 etc.

It may be noted here that when the term 'yoga' is preceded by some other term, it leaves its independent meaning of 'niṣkāma-karma' and signifies a general sense, viz.

1. Śaṅkara commenting on B.G. VI. 46 where the supremacy of yoga (karmayoga) over jñāna is clearly stated (. . . .yogā jñānibhyo'pi mato'dhikaḥ), tries to give a different twist to the word, 'jñāna' and takes it in the sense of mere scriptural scholarship (jñānam atra-śāstra-pāṇḍityam S.B.G. VI. 46) and leaves the word 'yoga' unexplained. Rāmānuja also does not enlighten about the meaning of the word 'yoga', and very much like Śaṅkara takes the word 'jñāna' in the sense of knowledge other than the true knowledge of the Self (ātmā-jñāna-vyatiriktaiḥ jñānaiḥ R.B.G. VI. 46).

'by means of' as is clear from such uses as Sāṅkhya-yoga (XIII. 24), jñāna-yoga (III. 3), karma-yoga (III. 3, V. 2; XIII. 24), buddhi-yoga (II. 49; X. 10; XVIII. 57), abhyāsa-yoga (VIII. 8), saṃnyāsayoga (IX. 28) and bhakti-yoga (XIV. 26).

(2) In order to fit in with the devotional aspect of the B.G., yoga is again used in the sense of 'complete self-surrender' to God which, of course, in effect demands a similar disinterested discharge of action in the name of God. Thus in the devotional context the terms 'yoga' and 'yukta' indicate total surrender to God, as in the following verses: VII. 1; IX. 14; X. 10; X. 22 etc.

(3) Then, in relation to God, yoga has also a developed conception of action, viz. the wondrous powers. In this sense, it is also known as yoga-māyā, e.g. VII. 25; IX. 5; X. 7, 17, 18; XI. 4, 8, 9, 47 and XVIII. 75 and 78.

(4) Then there are passages where yoga has been used in its technical sense of controlling the mental operations and practising concentration, as found in Pātañjala-yoga. We may cite the following instances: IV. 27-30; V. 27-28; VI. 10 ff; VIII. 10, 12-14; and XVIII. 33.

It is thus clear that although the B G. borrows ideas from Yoga, it does not keep it confined merely to its technical sense of the practice of concentration and mental restraint, but extends its meaning in order to fit in with its special doctrines of disinterested action, perfect devotion and resignation to God.

It has already been pointed out in the previous chapter, in the course of comparing the B. G.'s ideas of yoga with those of the Yoga-Sūtra, that the former's explanation of yoga (in the fourth sense i.e. in the sense of self-control) is rather scrappy, and seems to be an earlier stage of the fully developed and systematised yoga of the Pātañjala-Yoga-Sūtra. Though it prescribes like the latter 'practice' (abhyāsa) and 'non-attachment' (vairāgya) as means to control the fickle and fugitive mind,[1] it does not discuss in detail the nature, modification and classification of them as found in the Yoga-Sūtra. Similarly when it comes to deal with the practical guidance regard

1. B.G. VI. 35 compare Yoga-Sūtra I- 12.

ing place and posture of the practice of yoga[1], it gives merely some direction without caring overmuch to be thorough and systematic. But the same, as shown earlier, has been very elaborately discussed in the sādhana-pāda of the Yoga-Sūtra, and the eightfold yoga (aṣṭāṅga-yoga) has been systematically formulated.

Thus, although the ideas of Sāṅkhya and Yoga are taken by the B.G. from the current thought, they are modified and adjusted in order to be brought under its largely adopted Upaniṣadic or Vedāntic[2] thought. It is the ideas of the Ups. which throughout dominate the teachings of the B.G. We have seen how the terms Sāṅkhya and Yoga, though they occur so many times in the B.G. are more frequently used in a sense other than what is signified by the later systems under those names. It is difficult, therefore, to accept the view of Garbe who thinks that "the teachings of the Sāṅkhya-Yoga constitute almost entirely the foundation of the philosophical observations of the Bhagavadgītā. In comparison with them the Vedānta takes a second place."[3] We have seen that the real position is just the reverse. The B.G. is mostly found to be dominated by the Vedāntic ideas, and the author always seems to be anxious to appropriate and subordinate the atheistic and dualistic ideas of Sāṅkhya along with the method of Yoga under a theistic and non-dualistic philosophy of Vedānta.

Elements of Buddhism :—

The question of the Buddhist influence on the B.G. is not so easy to decide, for we do not get any direct and clear reference to Buddha or Buddhism in the B.G. Most of the scholars have, therefore, either left this question out of account or have given a negative answer to it. Indian

1. B.G. VI. 10ff.

2. The term 'Vedānta' is used in the B.G. only once in XV. 15. It is, however, wrong to think on that ground that the B.G. is a work of post-Vedāntic period. The term is used, in the B.G., as also in some other Ups. like Muṇḍaka (III. 2.6) and Śvetā (VI. 22) in the sense of the speculative thought of the Ups. This clearly shows that the term was in usage long before the emergence of the lately known Vedānta school.

3. Quoted by Radhakrishnan—Indian Philosophy Vol. I. p. 527; cf. Indian Antiquary Vol.47, Suppl. p. 6.

scholars like K.T. Telang, R.G. Bhandarkar, B.G. Tilak, R.D. Ranade, S. Radhakrishnan etc, are not inclined to see any Buddhist influence on the B.G. The eminent German scholar, Garbe, who is known for his critical attitude to the Gītā, and who assigns it a date as late as 200 A.D., and speaks of the influence of so many thought-currents on it, has also nothing better to say. He remarks that "Buddhist influence .. might be regarded as very much doubtful, resting at most on very far-fetched reasons."[1] Telang speaks of two possible alternatives and accepts the first one according to which the B.G. being an earlier thought, cannot be conceived to have been influenced by Buddhism. To use his own words : "Either the Gitā and Buddhism were alike the outward manifestation of one and the same spiritual upheaval which shook to its centre the current religion, the Gitā being the earlier and less thorough-going form of it; or Buddhism having already begun to tell on Brahmanism, the Gitā was an attempt to bolster it up, so to say, at its least weak points, the weaker ones being altogether abandoned. I do not accept the latter alternative.."[2] He further says : "The Ups. with the Gītā and the precepts of Buddha appear to me to be the successive embodiments of the spiritual thought of the age, as it became more and more dissatisfied with the system of mere ceremonial, then dominant."[3] According to R.G. Bhandarkar "the B.G. is the result of development of the religious and philosophic speculation that prevailed before the rise of Buddhism."[4] Regarding the occurrence of the term 'Brahma-nirvāṇa' also he says that "though the Gītā speaks of the Brahma-nirvāṇa, it might not be supposed that it borrows this doctrine of final peace and serenity from Buddhism."[5] B.G. Tilak also makes an unambiguous statement that "the elements of the B.G. are not borrowed from the Buddhist religion."[6] R. D. Ranade referring to the alleged influence of the ethical virtues of Buddhism, viz., mettā and karuṇā

1. Indian Antiquary Vol. 47, Suppl. p. 28.
2. S.B.E. Vol. VIII. p. 25.
3. S.B.E. Vol. VIII. p. 27.
4. Collected Works of Bhandarkar, Vol. IV. p. 39.
5. Ibid. p. 38.
6. Gitā Rahasya (Hindi Edition) p. 585.

on the B.G., says : "The very fact that these virtues are so elaborately treated in the Buddhist scriptures is itself an indication of their later development."[1] Radhakrishnan, even though he admits that "some of the views of the Gītā are like those of Buddhism" and "the word nirvāṇa occurs in the Gītā", he clearly says that "this does not show any borrowing from Buddhism, since it is not peculiar to it."[2] Senart is of the opinion that Buddhism itself has been influenced by the devotion of Viṣṇu-Kṛṣṇa. Comparing the two religions, he says that "the affinities are undeniable" and "Buddhism is undoubtedly the borrower."[3] According to him "if there had not existed a religion made up of the doctrines of yoga, the legends of Viṣṇu and devotion to Viṣṇu-Kṛṣṇa worshipped under the name of Bhagavat, Buddhism would not have come into existence."[4]

Now we have already shown while discussing the chronology of the B. G. that it is of later origin than Early Buddhism and if so, the influence of the former on the origin of the latter is altogether out of question. We have further, while dealing with the sources of early Buddhism in the previous section, made it quite clear that the arguments of Senart regarding the alleged influence of the Viṣṇuite-Kṛṣṇaite cult on Buddhism are more ingenious than convincing, and are based on superficial similarities devoid of a proper historical perspective.

It is not insignificant in thi s regard to note that the B. G. is nowhere referred to in the early Pali Nikāyas[5] which allude to so much preceding and contemporary thought. The theism with which the older portions of the Nikāyas seem to be acquainted is at best the idea of Mahābrahmā as creator

1. The Bhagavadgītā, p· 116.

2. Indian Philosophy, Vol. I. pp. 526-7.

3. I.H.Q. Vol. 6.p. 672.

4. Ibid· p. 673.

5. Reference to Vāsudeva and Baladeva by the Buddhist work, Niddesa, which is evidently commentatorial in nature, does not necessarily presuppose the composition of the B.G. cf. Collected Works of Bhandarkar, Vol. IV, pp. 5-6.

and controller of the world.[1] They nowhere refer to such a doctrine or belief according to which Kṛṣṇa is regarded as the Supreme Deity, having Brahma and Śiva along with others rooted in Him. (B. G. XI. 15). Thus our view about the later origin of the B. G. is supported by this negative evidence of the Pali Nikāyas. This negative evidence finds a positive support when, on closer examination, we find a somewhat clear allusion to Buddhism by the B. G. In B. G. XVI. 8, 14 and 23 we find descriptions not only of materialists who regard this world as a place of sensual enjoyment but also of the followers of such a sytem of thought according to which the world is unsubstantial or unreal, without God and caused by desires. Such people call themselves lord, fully accomplished, mighty and happy, and follow their own way setting aside the scriptures. This seems to be a reference to the Buddhists.[2] But Śaṅkara simply passes it by with the remark that it is the view of the materialists (lokāyatikadṛṣṭiḥ iyam—S. B. G. XVI. 8). Rāmānuja attributes it to atheists in general who transgress the commandments of God (bhagavad ājñā' tivṛtti śīlāḥ—R. B. G. XVI. 4) Later interpreters also think it convenient to fall in the line.[3] It is true that some of these ideas are common to both materialists and Buddhists, but the former do not consider this world to be unreal, rather, they think it to be the only reality; nor do they regard this world as caused by desires.[4] So it is quite plausible to read into these verses an allusion to Buddhism.

This is generally admitted that Buddhism and the B.G. have certain ideas in common. Some of them, of course, can be explained in the light of the Ups. being their common source, which we have already shown. But there are some

1. D.I. 18: tatra bhikkhave. . .tassa evaṃ hoti—ahamasmi brahmā, mahābrahmā abhibhū anabhibhūto aññadatthudaso vasavattī issaro kattā nimmātā seṭṭho sañjitā vasī pitā bhūtabhabyānaṃ. See also M. I. 326-7.

2. cf. The views of Buddha as reproduced by Raṭṭhapāla : 'Upanīyati loko addhuvo. . . anabhissaro. .. .assako. . .ūno loko atitto tanhādāso ti'—M. II. 68.

3. cf. Telang—S.B.E. Vol. VIII. Introduction; Radhakrishnan also quotes Saṅkara—The Bhagavadgītā, p. 337.

4. The word 'kāmahaitukam' occurring in B.G. XVI. 8 which we have taken to mean as 'caused by desire' may, however, have an alternative meaning, viz. 'for the sake of sensuous enjoyment' in which case it would be treated as a reference to Materialists and not to Buddhists.

other ideas, words and expressions which are not found in the Ups. or, at least, are not so articulate there, and yet they are so strikingly peculiar to Buddhism and the B. G. that it is very difficult to consider them as mere coincidences. There are again some pointed statements made in the B. G. which clearly seem to be intended to counter those of the Nikāyas. Now, if there is any cogency in the evidence set forth above as well as in that of the previous chapter where the later origin of the B. G. was established, then these remarkable similarities and reactions would quite reasonably suggest the impact of Buddhism on the B. G.

We may first point out here some of the important words, ideas and passages of the B. G. which indicate its familiarity with Buddhism. The term 'nirvāṇa', even though its verbal form (nis+vā) is found in the Vedic period,[1] seems to have been used for the first time in its strict technical sense in Buddhism. In the whole of the pre-Buddhistic Ups., it is nowhere found. So to ignore its occurrence in the B. G. (as has been done by most of the scholars) in which it is used as many as five times[2] does not seem justified. Again, virtues like nirvaira (XI. 55) adveśa, karuṇā and maitrī (XII. 13) also are striking peculiarities of the B.G. and Buddhism, and these words do not occur in the Ups. Similarly 'rāga and dveṣa' occur in compound in the B.G. (II. 64; III. 34 and XVIII. 51) just as in the Pali texts. The way in which they are used B.G. II. 64 and Dhammapada 369[3], as well as in B. G. XVIII. 51 and Dhammapada 377[4] has a close resemblance. The epithets used for a muni in the B. G. like aniketa (XII. 19), nirmama (II. 71; III. 30; XII. 13 and XVIII. 53), nirāśi (III. 30; IV. 21), nirāśraya (IV. 20) nirāhāra (II. 59), naiṣkarmya (III. 4; XVIII. 49), sama-duḥkha-sukha (II. 15, 38; XII. 13, 18; XIV. 24), tulya-nindā-stuti (XII. 19; XIV. 24), tulya-mānāpamāna (XIV. 25) etc. are exactly the same as their corresponding Pali

1. Pali-English Dictionary by Rhys Davids and Stede (P.T.S.), under the words 'nibbāna' and 'nibbāpeti'.
2. B.G. II. 72; V. 24: V. 25; V. 36 and VI. 15.
3. B.G. :—rāga-dveṣa viyuktais tu. . . prasādam adhigacchati
Dh. :—chettvā rāgañ ca dosañ ca tato nibbāṇam ehisi.
4. B.G. :—rāga-dveṣau vyudasya ca
Dh. :—rāgañ ca dosañ ca vippamuñcetha.

words of the Nikāyas.[1] None of these words is traceable in the pre-Buddhistic Ups. Then the vices like krodha, mada, dambha, atimānitā and asūyā enumerated in the B. G. (XVI. 3, 4, 10 and 18) are strikingly similar to those found in the Āmagandha Sutta (kodho, mado, thambho..usuyyā.. mānātimāno—Sn. 44), and people having such vices are alike called 'narādhama' (B. G. XVI. 19 and Sn. 44. Again just as Buddha regards ñāṇa-yañña (D. I 147 and Kūṭadanta Sutta) to be the best of all sacrifices, so also the B G. (IV. 33) speaks of the jñāna-yajña as the best. Similarly the teachings of 'samacariyā' in Buddhism (D. I. 3: M. I. 125-9, 423-4) is well reflected in the teachings of 'samatva' in B. G. II. 38 and XIV. 24 and 25. Again the middle path of Buddhism is adopted in the B. G. while prescribing the practice of yoga (VI. 11, 16 and 17). The gradual psychological stages in the process of concentration as described in Buddhism (D. I. 73; M. I. 37), vix. pāmujjam, pīti, passaddhi and sukha are somewhat similarly found in B. G. II, 64-66. Then the life has been characterised as suffering in the typical Buddhistic style (B. G. XIII,8: janma-mṛtyu-jarā-vyādhi-duḥkha-doṣānudarśanam). Besides, there are a number of passages betraying similarity or close affinity between the B. G. and the Nikāyas. We may take here some of the important ones for illustration:—

B.G.	Nikāyas
1. II. 46, yāvān artha udapāne sarvataḥ samplutodake	Ud. 79, kiṃ kayirā udapānena āpā ce sabbadā siyuṃ.
2. II. 16 and 28, avyaktādīni bhūtāni...avyaktanidhanāny eva tatra kā paridevanā. ubhayor api dṛsto'ntaḥ...	Sn. 113, yassa maggaṃ na jānāsi āgatassa gatassa vā, ubho ante asampassaṃ niratthaṃ paridevasi
3. III. 17 and VI. 22, tasya kāryaṃ na vidyate. yaṃ labdhvā cā param lābhaṃ manyate nādhikaṃ tataḥ	M.I. 249; II. 280, kataṃ karaṇīyaṃ nāparaṃ itthattāyā'ti.

1. For corresponding Pali words of the Nikāyas—see Pali—English Dictionary (P.T.S.).

	B.G.	Nikāyas
4.	VI. 5, uddhared ātmanā' tmānam.	Dh. 379, attanā codaya'ttānaṃ
5.	VI. 5 and 6. ātmaiva hy ātmano bandhur ātmaiva ripur ātmanaḥ. bandhur ātmā'tmanas tasya ...vartetā'tmai'va śatruvat	Dh. 42 and 43, diso disaṃ yaṃ taṃ Kayirā verī vā pana verinaṃ.. na taṃ mātā pitā kayirā...
6.	VI. 32. ātmaupamyena sarvatra..	Dh. 129-130; Sn. 137: attānaṃ upamaṃ katvā na haneyya na ghātaye.
7.	II. 58 yadā saṃharate cāyam kurmo' ṅgānī' va sarvaśaḥ	S.I.7. kummo va aṅgāni sake kapāle
8.	VI· 34. cañcalam hi manaḥ Kṛṣṇa...	Dh. 33ff. phandanaṃ capalaṃ cittaṃ......
9.	VI. 40 na hi kalyāṇakṛt kaścid durgatiṃ tāta gacchati, and IX. 31. na me bhaktaḥ praṇaśyati	S.I. 27, ye keci Buddhaṃ saraṇam gatāse, na te gamissanti apāyabhūmiṃ
10.	II. 11 aśocyān anvaśocas tvaṃ...gatāsūnagatāsūṃśca nā'nuśocanti paṇḍitāḥ	S.I. 5. atītaṃ nānusocanti nappajappanti nāgataṃ, anāgatappajappāya atītassānusocanā etena bālā sussanti......
11.	II. 56. duḥkeṣvanudvignamanāḥ sukheṣu vigataspṛhaḥ	S.IV. 71. phassena phuṭṭho na sukhena majje dukkhena phuṭṭho pi na sampavedhe.
12.	III. 11 and 12 devān bhāvayatā'nena...śreyaḥ paramavāpsyatha. iṣṭān bhogān hi vo devā dāsyante yajña bhāvitāḥ	D. II. 88-89. yā tattha devatā āssuṃ tāsaṃ dakkhiṇamādise; tā pūjitā pūjayanti mānitā mānayanti naṁ; devatānukampito poso sadā bhadrāni passatī ti.
13.	III. 4. na karmaṇām anārambhān naiṣkarmyaṃ puruṣo' śnute...	Dh. 271-272. na sīlabbatamattena vivitta sayanena vā, phusāmi nekkhamma sukhaṃ......
14.	III. 24 utsīdeyur ime lokā..	D. II. 37 nassati vata bho loko vinassati vata bho loko...

	B.G.	Nikāyas
15.	VI. 10ff. ātmānaṃ rahasi sthitaḥ ekākī...sthiramāsanam...samaṃ kāya śirogrīvaṃ dhārayan.........	M.I. 421. araññа gato vā rukkhamūla gato vā, suññāgāra gato vā nisīdati pallaṅkaṃ ābhujitvā ujuṃ kāyaṃ paṇidhāya...
16.	VII. 3. manuṣyāṇām sahasreṣu kaścid yatati siddhaye	S.V. 24, appakā te manussesu, ye janā pāragāmino.
17.	VII. 25. nā'haṃ prakāśaḥ sarvasya yogamāyā samāvṛtaḥ	D.II, 36 rāgarattā na dakkhinti tamokhandhena āvuṭā ti.
18.	XI. 8. na tu māṃ śakyase draṣṭum anenaiva svacakṣuṣā, divyaṃ dadāmi te cakṣuḥ	D, II. 329. na kho rājañña evaṃ paro loko daṭṭhabbo yathā tvaṃ maññasi maṃsacakkhunā...te dibbena cakkhunā...passanti...
19.	XII. 15. yasmān no'dvijate loko lokān no'dvijate ca yaḥ	Sn. 37 arosaneyyo so na roseti kañci...
20.	XVI. 4. and 18. dambho darpo' timānaśca krodhaḥ pāruṣyam eva ca	Sn. 44, Kodho mado thambho..
21.	XVI. 19 and 16. tān ahaṃ dviṣataḥ...narādhamān, prasaktāḥ kāmabhogeṣu patanti narake'śucau	Sn. 43 narādhamā ye'dha Karonti Kibbisaṃ......... patanti satta nirayaṃ avaṃsirā

These similarities of expressions and ideas are sufficient indication to the fact that the B. G. has assimilated all those Buddhistic elements which could be conveniently fitted into its scheme. But in other matters, like atheism and renunciation etc., it sharply reacts against the Buddhist approach. We may, for example, compare the dialogue of Asurendra Vepacitti and Surendra Śakra (which is almost the same as that of Mātali and Śakra)[1] with that of Arjuna and Kṛṣṇa. Here one can at once see that the arguments of Asurendra Vepacitti (or of Mātali) are utilised by Kṛṣṇa to win over Arjuna who uses the arguments similar to those of Śakra.

1. Saṃyutta I. pp. 221-4.

A battle is said to have been fought between gods and demons in which the latter are defeated and their chief Vepacitti is caught and brought by gods before their king, Śakra. But Vepacitti, even though a captive, is abusing Śakra off and on in his very presence. At this Mātali tells Śakra that it would be simply weakness and fear on his part if he tolerates such abuses of Vepacitti, but Śakra replies that it would be unbecoming of an enlightened being like him to care for such fools.[1] Mātali tells him that not to fight and control evil is to give encouragement to it, but Śakra emphatically says that to remain awakened and silent at the anger of others is alone the best way to control it.[2] Mātali further argues that by so doing he will not only be betraying his fear and weakness but will also earn ill fame to which Śakra replies that fame or ill fame, praise or slander are immaterial to the really enlightened one. To resist force with force is only brutal, and is really an indication of weakness. For the enlightened ones, it is tolerance and forgiveness which matter most.[3] To fall victim to anger is a sin. The real victory lies in victory over anger. One who does not give way to anger does good both to himself as well as to others.[4]

Now one can find a clear echo of the same ideas when Arjuna places his point before Kṛṣṇa saying that he at least, who is sensible enough to realise the inherent sin and evil of the brutal act of fighting, should not behave like his

---

1. Mātali :— bhayā nu maghavā Sakka dubbalyā no titikkhasi, suṇanto pharusaṃ vācaṃ sammukhā Vepacittino ti.
   Sakka :— nāhaṃ bhayā na dubbalyā khamāmi Vepacittino, kathaṃ hi mādiso viññū bālena paṭisaṃyuje'ti.—S.I. 221.
2. Mātali :— bhiyyo bālā pakujjheyyuṃ no cassa paṭisedhako, tasmā bhusena daṇḍena dhīro bālaṃ nisedhaye'ti.
   Sakka :— etad eva ahaṃ maññe bālassa paṭisedhanaṃ, paraṃ saṅkupitaṃ ñatvā yo sato upasammatī ti.—Ibid. I. 221
3. Sakka :— abalaṃ taṃ balaṃ āhu yassa bālabalaṃ balaṃ, balassa dhammaguttassa paṭivattā na vijjati. sada tthaparamā atthā khantyā bhiyyo na vijjati.—Ibid. I. 222.
4. Sakka :— tasseva tena pāpiyo yo kuddhaṃ paṭikujjhati, kuddhaṃ apaṭikujjhanto saṅgāmaṃ jeti dujjayam. ubhinnaṃatthaṃ carati attano ca parassa ca.—Ibid. S.I. 222.

opponents who are stupid and deluded by greed.[1] But Kṛṣṇa using the arguments of Mātali asks Arjuna to stick to his 'svadharma' and not to betray futile weakness of heart and fear.[2] It is remarkable that the very same words namely 'bhaya' and 'daurbalya' are used by Kṛṣṇa in relation to Arjuna (B. G. II. 3 & 35), which were used by Mātali in relation to Śakra (*bhayā* nu maghavā Sakka *dubbalyā* no titikkhasi, S. I. 221). Kṛṣṇa further reminds Arjuna of the evil consequences of ill fame and slander[3] as Mātali had done. But in the light of the Buddhist approach Mātali was silenced when it was pointed out to him by Śakra that the man by meeting anger with anger only incurs sin (tasseva tena pāpiyo yo kuddhaṃ paṭikujjhati, S. I. 222). The B. G., on the other hand, takes just the opposite stand when Arjuna is reminded by Kṛṣṇa of his 'svadharma' which when violated brings about sin, besides spoiling the wordly fame.[4] The deciding factor, it may be noted, both in Buddhism as well as in the B. G., is the moral consideration of 'sin' (tasseva tena pāpiyo—S. I. 222; pāpam avāpsyasi—B. G. II. 33), but the measuring rod of sin, as indicated above, is different in the two systems.

It can now be clearly seen that Arjuna takes the position of Śakra which is nothing but the representation of the Buddhist stand. Kṛṣṇa counters this stand and wins over Arjuna by fully utilising the arguments of Mātali. What is held inferior in Buddhism is, thus, given an upper hand in the B. G.

Similarly the statements of Buddhism and the B. G. regarding the future of the warriors killed in the battlefield are in sharp opposition to each other. According to Buddhism such soldiers cannot but go to hell or be born in an animal species, whereas the B. G. promises heaven for

---

1. yadyapy ete na paśyanti lobhopahata cetasaḥ,
.... kathaṃ na jñeyam asmābhiḥ pāpād asmān nivartitum.—B.G.I. 38-39.
2. klaibyaṃ mā sma gamaḥ Pārtha, nai'tat tvayy upapadyate, kṣudraṃ hṛdaya-daurbalyaṃ tyaktvo'ttiṣṭha Paraṃtapa—B.G. II. 3.
3. akīrtiṃ cāpi bhūtāni kathayiṣyanti te'vyayām,—B.G.II. 34.
bhayād raṇād uparataṃ maṃsyante tvāṃ mahārathāḥ—B.G. II. 35.
4. atha cet tvam imaṃ dharmyaṃ saṅgrāmaṃ na kariṣyasi, tataḥ svadharmaṃ kīrtiṃ ca hitvā pāpam avāpsyasi—B.G. II. 33.

them.[1]

Thus, it appears that the B. G., though absorbs some of the tems, concepts and ideas of early Buddhism which it finds convenient to make room for in keeping with its doctrine of jñāna-karma-samuccayavāda, it, nevertheless, tries to counteract the Buddhist tenets of atheism, anattā and renunciation by putting forward opposite theories along the lines of orthodox tradition. So the influence of early Buddhism on the B. G. seems to be not only of assimilation but also of reaction, and in fact, it is the latter aspect which is more ponounced. In other words, we find in the B. G. more a reaction against than an adoption of the fundamental tenets of Buddhism.

The Uniqueness of the B.G. and its Primary Source:—

The true nature of the B. G. can hardly be conceived without understanding its dominating tenets of devotion and niṣkāma-karma. The element of devotion along with that of niṣkāma-karma is so characteristically unique to the B. G. that unless its real origin is traced, one cannot claim to have discovered the primary source of B. G. So it is desirable to discuss this point at some greater length.

Obviously, devotion is foreign to atheistic systems like Buddhism and Sāṅkhya. In the system of Yoga also, God is rather loosely fitted in; at least, He does not occupy a prominent place there. In fact, it is more plausible to think here with Garbe that the Yoga system itself "has taken over the idea of God from the Bhāgavat religion"[2] and this will explain why it is so loosely knit in the scheme of Yoga. Regarding the Ups., we find, of course, in some of the later ones like the Kaṭha[3] and Iśa[4] some theistic leanings, but even in them the references are hardly prominent enough to be treated as the source of the B. G's preponderant tenet of devotion. In the Śvetāśvatara, no doubt, we find a dominant note of theism and divine grace[5], and bhakti

1. S. IV. 309-311 :—dvinnaṃ gatīnaṃ aññataraṃ gatiṃ vadāmi: nirayaṃ vā tiracchānayoniṃ vā ti. Compare B.G. II. 37: hato vā prāpsyasi svargam.

2. Indian Antiquary Vol. 47. Suppl. 22.

3. Kaṭha. II. 20; II. 23.

4. Īśa 1, 13, 15-18.

5. Śveta. III. 20; IV. 21; V. 14 and VI. 18.

or devotion also is clearly prescribed[1], but it must not be forgotten that its highest Deity is Rudra, Maheśvara or Śiva[2] and not Vāsudeva, Puruṣottama or Kṛṣṇa, as found in the B. G. In other words, the former is Śaivaite, while the latter is Vaiṣṇavite. This indicates that we must look for the main source of the B. G. in something other than the Sāṅkya, Yoga, Ups. and Buddhism to account for its emphasis on devotion.

It is, no doubt, possible, as we have ourselves said, to find some theistic and devotional references in the Ups., just as some elements of 'niṣkāma-Karma' also are traceable in them, but they can hardly be met with in any of the Ups. to the extent they are found in the B. G. As a matter of fact, the Ups. are the compilation of the diverse speculations of many generations of seers and saints presenting different creeds, and hence they are found to contain germs of different and diverse thoughts. But in order to account for subsequent development of only some of the selected ideas of them, one has to look for some source over and above them which could have provided the basis for a new synthesis.

We have already seen that although the B. G. takes various elements from the Ups., Sāṅkhya, Yoga as well as Buddhism, it invariably brings about some modifications and adjustments in them. This also shows that the B.G., inspite of utilising materials from them, does not directly develop from any one of them. Its fountain-spring seems to be something else which supplies its essential tenets, and leads it to combine in a specific way the knowledge both of the Ups. and Sāṅkhya along with the methods of yoga, and couch them with the dominant doctrines of disinterested action and devotion.

It may be remembered here that even before the B. G. a compromising trend was visible in some of the later Ups. like the Kaṭha, Śvetā. Muṇḍaka and Īśa, from which, indeed, a considerable material has been availed of by the B. G., as is evident from the parallel passages collected already from them. But it must be very clearly borne in mind that none

1. *Ibid.* VI.23.
2. Ibid. III. 2, 4,5; IV, 10,14, 16, 21, 22; V. 14 and VI.7

of them combines the entire elements all at the same time, as is done by the B. G. The Kaṭha, though alluding to some Sāṅkhya ideas along with its absolutistic ideas, makes but a bare reference to bhakti. The Śvetā., though theistic and devotional and combines ideas of Sāṅkhya and Vedānta, it neglects the tenet of niṣkāma-karma, besides being Śaivaite in character. The Muṇḍaka also does not refer to this special doctrine of disinterested action. The Īśa, although it provides for the doctrine of jñāna-karma-samuccaya, and has also a theistic leaning, it does not contain other elements of Sāṅkhya and Yoga. Again, the manner of their compromise and extent to which these elements are combined are hardly similar to those of the B.G. Thus none of the Ups., either separately or collectively, can be said to be the prototype of the B.G. from which it may be supposed to have derived its special line of thought. This does not mean that the utilisation of the Upaniṣadic material is questioned here. Indeed, it is so patent and unquestionably clear that none can doubt it. But the question is whether the B. G. has directly come out of the Ups., or represents primarily a different religion in which the ideas of the Ups. etc. are combined. In other words, the question is: What can be regarded as the primary source of the B. G.'s essential and unique philosophy of niṣkāma-karma and bhakti?

A clue to its answer is got from the internal evidence of the B. G. itself which, while tracing the tradition of its doctrine (B.G. IV. 1-2), mentions exactly the same tradition as does the Nārāyaṇīyopākhyāna of the M. B. (M. B. Śānti. 348. 51-52)[1] in the course of tracing the tradition of the Bhāgavata dharma. Almost all the traditional commentators as well as the modern translators of the B. G. pass over these important verses (i. e. B. G. IV. 1 and 2) after giving their mere translation[2]. They seem to have either no intention of discussing this point or they ignore it deliberately, lest the B. G. would be treated as a

1. tretāyugādau ca tato Vivasvān Manave dadau,
Manuś ca lokabhṛtyartham sutāya Ikṣvākave dadau,
Ikṣvākuṇā ca kathito vyāpya lokān avasthitaḥ,
gamiṣyati kṣayānti ca punar Nārāyaṇam nṛpa.—M.B. Śānti 348. 51-52. Compare this tradition with that of the B.G. (IV. 1 and 2.).

2. B.G. Tilak, however, has pointed out this fact in his Gītā Rahasya, pp. 669-770.

sectarian work of a particular cult, viz., the Bhāgavata religion, and would lose its universal character. But to an objective and impartial mind these verses are highly informative, and contain a clear proof of the fact that the B. G.represents the tenets of the Bhāgavata religion. This alone explains why the B. G. deriving so much material from the Ups. does not mention their names in tracing its tradition. Even Janaka of the Bṛhadāraṇyaka who is cited in the B. G. (III. 20) as an example of the syncretic cult of jñāna-karma, is not included when the tradition of the B. G.'s religion is traced. The sage Ghora Āṅgirasa also, who according to the Chāndogya (III. 17. 6) is supposed to have been the teacher of Kṛṣṇa, the son of Devaki, is not mentioned in that list. It is difficult to ascertain whether Kṛṣṇa of the Chāndogya and that of the B. G. are the same person, but in any case, it is by no means an unimportant fact that while enumerating the names of the teachers handing down the tradition of the Gītā-doctrine, the B. G. makes no mention of the teachers or followers alluded to by the Ups., but in their place the names of those teachers and disciples are mentioned which are found in the tradition of the Bhāgavata religion. This is a sufficient indication of the fact that B. G. belongs to the Bhāgavata school of thought, for no two religions are associated with the same tradition of teachers. The same is further confirmed by the clear statement of Vaiśaṃpāyana who, while speaking of the source of the Bhāgavata dharma direct from Nārāyaṇa, says to Janamejaya: "It is this great religion, O king, that has already been taught briefly to you in the Harigītā"[1] (which is, evidently, another name for the B. G.). Still another statement pointing out the occasion of this teaching is made in the same Nārāyaṇīyopākhyāna which says:—"The Gītā was taught by Bhagavata Himself on the occasion when Arjuna had become despondent in face of the drawn-out armies of the Kauravas and Pāṇḍavas".[2] The name of the work, viz.

1. evameṣa mahān dharmaḥ sa te pūrvaṃ nṛpottama,
kathito Harigītāsu samāsavidhi kalpitaḥ—M.B. Śānti 346. 10

2. samupoḍheṣv anīkeṣu kurupāṇḍavayor mṛdhe
Arjune vimanaske ca Gītā Bhagavatā svayam.—M.B. Śānti 348.8.

the 'Bhagavat'-Gītā also signifies that it represents the doctrine of Bhagavat or Nārāyaṇa as embodied in the Bhāgvata or Nārāyaṇīya-dharma. Of course, the B.G. is said to contain, besides this Bhāgavata-doctrine, the tenet of renunciation as well.[1]

Now, the B.G. being primarily a work of the Bhāgavata religion, its true spirit and approach cannot be adequately grasped without comprehending the true nature of the original Bhāgavata cult. We may, therefore, disscuss this point briefly in the light of the available material.

The chief available sources of the Bhāgavata dharma which is variously known as Nārāyaṇīya, Sātvata, Ekāntika and Pāñcarātra dharma are the Bhagavadgītā, the Nārāyaṇīya section of the M. B. (i.e. M.B. Sānti 334-351), the Śāṇḍilya Sūtra, the Bhāgavata Purāṇa, the Nārada Pāñcarātra and the Nārada Sūtra. We may leave out later works like those of Ālvārs and Rāmānuja which may not be useful for our purpose of determining the original nature of the Bhāgavata dharma. Now, the Nārada Pāñcarātra is definitely of later origin than the B.G., the M.B. and the Bhāgavata Purāṇa, for it mentions their names along with others as the chief works on the subject (Nārada Pāñcarātra II.7.28-32; III.14.73; IV.3.154). The Nārada-Sūtra which refers to Vyāsa and Śuka (Nār. Sūtra-83) and the Śāṇḍilya-Sūtra which quotes freely from the B.G. (Śāṇḍ. Sūtra 9, 15,83)—are also to be placed after the B. G., the M. B. and the Bhāgavata Purāṇa. The Bhāgavata Purāṇa also is clearly said to have been composed after the B. G. and the M. B. In the very beginning (Bhāg. Skandha I. 4-5) it is stated that the purpose of its composition is to bring into full prominence the element of devotion which according to the author had not been given its rightful place in the M. B. including the B.G., where it was somewhat subordinated to niṣkāma-karma.[1] Thus, ultimately we have to fall back on the B. G. and the Nārāyaṇīya section of the M.B., which seem to be the

---

1. yatīnāṃ cā'pi yo dharmaḥ sa te pūrvaṃ nṛpottama
kathito Harigītasu samāsa-vidhi-kalpitaḥ.—M.B., Śānti 348.53

2. Bhāgavata Purāṇa 1.5.12 and34 (naiṣkarmyam apy acyutabhāva-varjitaṃ na śobhate jñānamalaṃ nirañjanam).

earliest available accounts of the Bhāgavata religion. The fact that the Nārada Pāñcarātra (IV. 3. 156-159; IV. 8. 81) and the Bhāgavata Purāṇa (I. 3. 24) mention Buddha as an incarnation of Viṣṇu, whereas he is not included in the incarnation-account of the Nārāyaṇīya section of the M. B. (Śānti 339. 100) also tends to suggest the greater antiquity of the Nārāyaṇīya account. So in order to determine the original character of the Bhāgavata religion, we have no other choice but to take recourse to the Nārāyaṇīya account of it and that of the B. G. along with the relevant references made to them by some later ancient works.

Now, the very fact that the whole teaching of the B. G. and the Nārāyaṇīya section of the M. B. is woven in the background of the Pāṇḍavas fighting against the Kauravas for their just cause, makes the intention of the author sufficiently clear. One can hardly doubt that the whole purpose seems to highlight and enhance the worth of the performance of rightful actions and not the renunciation thereof. According to the Nārāyaṇīya section of the M. B., the religion was taught to the warrior tribe known as Sātvatas. Vāsudeva himself is said to belong to this tribe (M.B. Ādiparva 218. 12) and is known as a Sātvatarṣabha (Bhāg. Purāṇa IX. 58. 42 and IX. 27. 5). Other warriors like Kṛtavarman (Ādiparva 221. 31) and Sātyaki (Droṇa-parva 97. 36), besides the well known Bhīṣma and Arjuna—are all said to come of the same tribe and follow the same Sātvata or Bhāgavata dharma. The religion itself is supposed to have been named as 'Sātvata' after the name of the tribe. Again, in the course of describing the tradition of this religion, both the B. G. and the Nārāyaṇīyopākhyāna mention names of people who are all well known Kṣatriya-kings, and who are known to have led an active worldly life. Thus, from the very nature and character of the narrative (both of the B. G. as well as of the Nārāyaṇīya section of the M.B.), as also from the life of the people who preached and practised this religion, its activism is amply indicated. An unambiguous and explicit affirmation of the same is found in the Nārāyaṇīya section of the M. B. (Śānti 347. 81) which clearly declares that "activism is the characteristic mark of the Nārāyaṇīya-dharma".[1]

It is, however, very important to remember that this doctrine of action (pravṛtti) is securely based on dharma, and we are repeatedly reminded that all our pursuits should be in accordance with this dharma. This has been very pointedly referred to by the M.B. towards its close when it exhorts people to attain all happiness and wealth through dharma alone.[2] The Gītā also begins with the mention of 'Dharma Kṣetra' which is the name given by it to the Kurukṣetra, the well known battle-field of the M. B. This makes it clear that in order to defend righteousness or dharma, wars also can be justifiably waged according to this religion. Arjuna is said to be deluded regarding dharma (B. G. II. 7 dnarmasaṃmūḍhacetāḥ), and Kṛṣṇa also is instructing him about his dharma (II. 31, 33 svadharmam api cā'vekṣya). While exhorting Arjuna to fight, Kṛṣṇa repeatedly calls it as 'dharma-yuddha' or fight for righteousness (B.G. II. 31 and 33).[3] Thus, this religion teaches the relentless discharge of duties with utter disregard to consequences and with perfect resignation or surrender to the highest deity known as Hari, Nārāyaṇa, Vāsudeva or Bhagavat. Here the philosophy of action is saturated with a deep theistic sentiment. It is on account of this high devotional element that the religion is known by the name of Nārāyaṇīya or Bhāgavata dharma. As it is a devotion to a monotheistic conception of God, it is also called an Ekāntika dharma. Thus, the teaching of selfless or disinterested action is given a pronounced theistic tinge which, we think, is the unique feature of the original Bhāgavata dharma. We find no basis for making any other conjecture with regard to the original nature of the Bhāgavata dharma. Later on, of course, devotion is emphasised more and more, and the Bhāgavata dharma came to be regarded as an exclusive cult of bhakti or devotion. This is fully

1. pravṛtti-lakṣaṇaścaiva dharmo nārāyaṇātmakaḥ; cf. Radhakrishnan, Indian Philosophy, Vol. I. p. 491, footnote 4. See also M.B. Śānti. 217. 2. (pravṛttilakṣaṇaṃ dharmaṃ ṛṣir nārāyaṇo'bravit.)

2. ūrdhvabāhur viraumy eṣaḥ na ca kaścic chṛṇoti mām;
dharmād arthaś ca kāmaś ca sa dharmaḥ kiṃ na sevyate?

3. dharmyād dhi yuddhāc chreyo'nyat kṣatriyasya na vidyate;
atha cet tvam imaṃ dharmyam saṅgrāmaṃ na kariṣyasi......

confirmed from the statement of the Bhāgavata Purāṇa, already alluded to, according to which, since the element of bhakti was not given the highest place in the B. G. and the M. B. (on account of the combination and prominence of niṣkāma-karma), the composition of a fresh independent work, namely, the Bhāgavata Purāṇa had to be undertaken. Thus, it is clear that the original Bhāgavata dharma embodied a philosophy of action based on devotion. In other words, it was a combination of niṣkāma-karma and bhakti. But conservative in its approach as it was, it had not shaken off the doctrine of renunciation, as is explicitly stated in the Nārāyaṇīya section of the M. B.[1] Thus, it is clear that both the path of action (pravṛtti) as well as of renunciation (nivṛtti) are synthesised in the B. G., the former being the special feature of it.

Śaṅkara also alludes to some commentaries of the B. G. earlier than his (which unfortunately are no more available) according to which the original Bhāgavata dharma, as embodied in the B. G., was regarded as a synthesis of pravṛtti and nivṛtti.[2] In fact it is so clear that it was impossible even for Śaṅkara to deny it[3], but in order to suit his own special theory of knowledge and renunciation, he twists and turns the sense, and tries to show that pravṛtti is meant for the people of lower order only, and is a means to the lower goal, whereas the highest goal can be realised by following the path of nivṛtti alone[4]. But this position cannot be accepted. The real position is that the B. G. incorporates the tenet of knowledge and renunciation in its special doctrine of niṣkāma-Karma and bhakti, and thus the

1. yatīnāṃ cā'pi yo dharmaḥ sa te pūrvaṃ nṛpottama;
kathito harigītāsu samāsa-vidhi-kalpitaḥ.—M.B. Santi 348. 53.

2. kecit tu...jñāna-karmaṇoḥ-samuccayo gītāśāstre nirūpitaḥ, S.B.G. Introduction to the IIIrd. Chapter. Tatra kecid āhuḥ...karma-sahitād jñānāt kaivalya-prāptiḥ iti sarvāsu gītāsu niścitaḥ artha-iti.,S.B.G. II.10.

3. dvividho hi vedokto dharmaḥ, pravṛttilakṣaṇo nivṛttilakṣaṇaḥ ca ...vaidikaṃ hi dharmadvayam Arjunāya...upadideśa.—S.B.G., Introduction to the Ist Chapter.

4. pravṛtti lakṣaṇo dharmo...devādi sthāna prāptihetuḥ...sattva śuddhaye bhavati phalābhisandhi-varjitaḥ—S.B.G., Introduction to the Ist Chapter. Tasmāt Kevalād eva jñānad mokṣa iti....bhinna pusuṣānuṣṭheyatvena...jñāna-karmaṇoḥ samuccayānupapattiḥ.—S.B.G. Introduction to the IIIrd. Chapter.

tripartite path of jñāna, karma and bhakti is presented by it. In fact, from the time of its very inception the Bhāgavata dharma seems to have made use of the knowledge of the Ups., Sāṅkhya and Yoga, perhaps in order to have a wide popular appeal for its special doctrine of selfless action and self-surrender to God (niṣkāma-karma and bhakti). The very name Pāñcarātra is said to signify this synthetic character of the religion. While accounting for the name Pāñcarātra, it has been said in the same Nārāyaṇīya section of the M. B. that it is so called because it synthesises the four Vedas and the Sāṅkhya and Yoga as the fifth.[1] All these scriptures with the Vedas and Āraṇyakas (inclusive of the Ups.) are said to be supplementary parts of one another.[2]

Thus from all these statements of the Nārāyaṇīya section of the M. B. as well as from an objective analysis of the different elements of the B. G. and other supporting evidences from the later works referring to them, it becomes clear that the original form of the Bhāgavata dharma was synthetic in nature, having disinterested action and devotion as its special feature, and an assimilation and adoption of knowledge as a mark of its compromising and conservative character. It is this form of the religion which the B. G. represents.

The same is confirmed from the story described in the Ṇārāyanīya section. Exigencies of space precludes the possibility of giving the whole story here, but a brief reference to its main events may prove useful.

The story begins with Nārada going to Badrikāśrama to see Nara and Nārāyaṇa. There he is astonished to find the latter engaged in some religious rites, and enquires of him as to whom he worships. He is told that he worships his original substance of which Nara and Nārāyaṇa, Kṛṣṇa and Hari are the forms. Nārada eager to seeth at Original Substance goes to Śvetadvīpa and praises the Great Being for His purity and grandeur and the latter manifests Himself to him saying that none else who is not so exclusively devoted to Him (Ekāntin) can get his vision. He then explains to Nārada the religion of

1. M.B. Śānti. 339. 107,
2. Ibid. 348. 82.

Vāsudeva. At the creation of each Brahmā this dharma is said to be revealed by Nārāyaṇa and at the end of Brahmā it is lost.

The story of the glorious king, Vasu Uparicara is then related in this connection. This king used to worship God according to Sātvatavidhi. He performs an extensive horse-sacrifice in which no animal is killed. The oblations devised in accordance with the Āraṇyakas are directly received by God of gods Himself who reveals Himself only to Vasu without showing Himself to anybody else. His priest, Bṛhaspati gets angry thereupon, but he is told by Ekata, Dvita and Trita, sons of Prajāpati, who were present at the sacrifice, that the Great God is not to be revealed before those who are not favoured by His grace. Then they relate their own experiences as to how they practised austerities for four thousand years, and on failing to perceive Him even after that, a further set of austerities for another hundred years,' when a voice resounded, "Go you away as you came. That Great Being is not to be seen by one who is not devoted to Him" and they had to return without a vision of Him.

One more incident is narrated about Vasu Uparicara. He is represented as a mediator in a religious controversy between the gods and ṛṣis in which the gods held that at a sacrifice at least a goat must be killed, while the ṛṣis maintained that no animal should be sacrificed, but only vegetable grain should be offered. Vasu is said to have sided with the gods as a result of which he is described as lying in a hole in the earth. He, however, by virtue of his devotion to Nārāyaṇa, is ultimateby saved when the Garuḍa of Nārāyaṇa lifts him up and takes him to Brahmaloka.

Giving an account of the Bhāgavata dharma in the present Kalpa of the seventh Brahmā, the tradition of Vivasvata, Manu and Ikṣvāku is related, and it is said that that great eternal dharma difficult to be known and followed is professed by the Sātvatas.

Now from this story also, if one tries to pick up its chief elements leaving out the mythical and legendary accretions, one can clearly see that all the essentials of the Bhāgavata dharma as represented by this story are much the same as those contained in the B.G. We find here that (1) the religion is practised by the the great king, Vasu Uparicara, and in the present Kalpa, the names of Vivasvan, Manu and Ikṣvāku are enumerated. Evidently, they were all men of action who had not taken to renunciation. Exactly the same is true of the B.G. Of course, the doctrine of niṣkāma-karma is not as much emphasised here as it is in the B.G. In fact, not long after the composition of the B.G. there was a tendency to emphasise bhakti more and more. This is reflected here also and is made quite evident in the subsequent literature of the religion. (2) God is repeatedly said to be revealed only to those who are solely devoted to Him. The very same thing is stated by Kṛṣṇa to Arjuna in B.G. XI. 54. (3) Neither the sacrificial mode of worship, which Bṛhaspati adopted nor the practice of austerities, as the ṛṣis like Ekata, Dvita and Trita followed could lead to the highest revelation, which could be had only through wholehearted devotion, which Nārada and Vasu Uparicara had developed. The B.G. also represents the same view (XI. 48 and 53). (4) Vasu had to suffer the curse of lying in a hole of the earth for siding with the view of animal-sacrifice. On the other hand, when he devotedly performs the horse-sacrifice in which no animal is killed, he gets the vision of the highest God. Similarly, it is remarkable that the B.G., while enumerating various kinds of sacrifices, omits animal-sacrifice altogether (IV. 24-33), and speaks of the sacrifice of the thoroughly devoted man who reaches the Supreme (B.G. IV. 24 brahmārpaṇam brahma havir...brahmaiva tena gantavyaṃ...). (5) The oblations are devised in the sacrifice in accordance with the teachings of the Āraṇyakas which include the Ups. The B.G. also is equally conservative and accepts the ways of the scriptures (XVI. 24 śāstravidhānoktaṃ karma...).

From this it is clear that this religion inculcates a combined pursuit of karma and bhakti. It rejects animal sacrifice and undermines the value of outward formalities as well as austere asceticism. It, however, does not disregard the scriptures like the Āraṇyakas and their knowledge. Incidently, it may be noted here that Buddha most probably came to be treated as an incarnation of Viṣṇun in the later

Bhāgavata works[1] chiefly because he had also made an emphatic protest against animal sacrifice and austerities, and had led a life of active service to humanity.

In spite of very marked affinities between the B.G. and the Nārāyaṇiya account, we must note that there are some points of divergences as well, which are indicative of the fact that a considerable time had passed between the composition of the two works. The fact that the B.G. is frequently referred to in the Nārāyaṇīya section is a proof of the greater antiquity of the former. Now the first thing which we have noted in the course of the Nārāyaṇīya account of the Bhāgavata dharma is its greater emphasis on bhakti. The second point which one may point out is the absence of a reference to the Sātvata or Bhāgavata dharma by name in the B.G. Thirdly, the four vyūhas mentioned in the Nārāyaṇīya section are not mentioned in the B G. Of course, the Nārāyaṇīya also speaks of these Vyūhas as being optional. It is admitted in it that different views about the nature and number of these Vyūhas or forms of Divinity were entertained by people (M.B. Śānti 348.57). All this, however, only confirms our view that the B.G. is the earliest systematisation of the doctrines of the Bhāgavata school when its various names had not crystalised. In the subsequent period the religion underwent some changes and modifications, as is usual with regard to almost any religion. We can, therefore, reasonably expect to see the original Bhāgāvata dharma in its highest available purity in the B.G. just as we expect to find the purest available form of Buddhism in the Nikāyas.

Conclusion :—

Thus we can conclude that the B.G. is the first available work of the Bhāgavata religion which, in keeping with its avowed aim, seeks to compromise knowledge (both of the Ups. and the Sāṅkhya along with the method of Yoga and bhakti) with action. Being reconciliatory in character, it, inspite of its primary emphasis on non-renunciation or action,

---

1, Bhāgavata Purāṇa I.3.24; Nārada Pāñcarātra IV. 3. 156-159; IV. 8. 81.

does not discard renunciation, and in so doing comes to advocate the doctrine of niṣkāma-karma. It is this niṣkāma-karma or the theory of disinterested action which can be regarded as the crux of the B.G.'s teachings, and which the B.G. tries to fortify both with a philosophic theory of knowledge (jñāna) as well as a popular doctrine of devotion (bhakti). Adopting the poetic style of the Ups. (from which, indeed, it draws much of its material), it tries to blend these diverse elements and reconcile their differences, though on purely logical examination one may encounter some difficulties.

Section C

The Converging and Diverging Linces of the B.G. and Buddhism :—

Now, in the light of this account of the historical back ground of both the B.G. and early Buddhism, we can clearly see how and why they bear some striking similarities in spite of their divergent approaches to some other problems. They are found to share a certain common cultural heritage, though they take different stands, and voice different points of view with regard to man's attitude to life and its problems.

As a matter of fact, both Buddhism and the B.G. seem to have emerged from that new thought-milieu which was heralded by the Kṣatriyas in the Upaniṣadic period, and in which a departure from the hitherto dominating ritualism of the Brāhmaṇas and a fresh approach to the philosophical problems were initiated. We have already seen in the preceding section that some Kṣatriyas of the Ups. claimed new knowledge hitherto unknown to the Brāhmaṇas[1] and both Buddhism and the B.G. represent to some extent the continuation and development of that thought. In the B.G. evidently a Kṣatriya (Kṛṣṇa) is teaching another Kṣatriya (Arjuna) his svadharma or the Kṣatriya-vidyā saying that there is no higher good than the righteous fight for a Kṣatriya.[2] In tracing the ancient tradition of its teaching the same tradition of the Kṣatriya sages (rājarṣayaḥ) is mentioned.[3] Again in the chapter IX of the B.G. the teaching is called 'rāja-vidyā' and 'rāja-guhya.[4] The pāth of deva-yāna and pitṛ-yāna referred to in the Bṛhadā., and Chāndogya as special Kṣatriya-vidyā (Bṛhadā. VI. 2.8-16; Chāndogya V.3.7—V.10.4) is also described here[5], and Sanat Kumara or Skanda of Chāndogya VII. 26. 2, who taught the Brahmin sage Nārada, is also mentioned as the greatest of the war-champions (senānīnām...

1. Bṛhadā VI. 2.8; Chāndo. V.3.7.
2. B.G. II. 31.
3. B.G. IV. 1-2.
4. B.G. IX.2.
5. B.G. VIII. 24-26.

Skando).[1] The same is confirmed from the identical tradition mentioned in the Nārāyaṇīyopākhyāna which is but another description of the same religion, as well as from a remarkable statement made in the M.B. in which Madhusūdana is called the saviour of the rājarṣis who following their duty never turn back from the fight.[2]

Similarly Buddhism also is propounded by a person of the Kṣatriya clan, and the repudiation of the Brahmanical system of thought is quite patent from his teachings. It is also remarkable that the superiority of the Kṣatriyas in mundane matters is uniformly affirmed in Buddhism, and Sanat Kumara is frequently quoted in support of it.[3] As against the traditional enumeration of castes, placing Brāhmaṇas as the first, the Buddhist Canons invariably mention Kṣatriya as first,[4] just as we find in the Bṛhadā. I.4.11. In fact no single individual has caused as much set back to Brahmanical religion as has been done by Buddha alone.

We have also seen that both of them owe something to the common cultural heritage of the Upanisads. This would account for various similarities in their epistemological, ontological and ethical ideas even without any direct borrowing. At the same time the B.G. seems to have conveniently utilised some ideas, terms and concepts of Buddhism, as has already been pointed out.

In spite of these common elements there are other important factors which make their approach quite different from each other. The B.G., firstly, on account of its uniform compromising nature is incapable of making a radical and full-throated departure from traditional thought; secondly, due to its synthetic character contains heterogeneous elements; and thirdly, it has some special doctrines of its own which Buddhism is either not interested in or has no room for. We shall consider all these points in detail in our comparative

1. B.G. X. 24.

2. rājarṣīṇām udārāṇām āhaveṣva nivartinām;
sarvadharmapradhānānāṃ tvaṃ gatir madusūdana.—M.B. VI. 3044-5 (Calcutta Edition).

3. Khattiyo seṭṭho jane tasmiṃ ye gotta-paṭisāriṇo-D. I. 99; III. 97-98; M.I. 358; S.I. 153; II. 284.

4. e.g. D. I.91; III. 96-97; M. II. 87-89; II. 149-153; II. 182-184.

treatment of the subject in the seqel. But in order to indicate the nature of these three types of differences, we may briefly refer to one or two illustrations here. Although, while furthering the non-Brahmanical trends of the Ups., the B.G. makes its teachings accessible to all castes, and promises salvation to all without distinction,[1] it nevertheless maintains the traditional hierarchy of castes placing Brāhmaṇas as the first[2], and speaks of the four-fold caste as originating from the Supreme.[3] But Buddhism discards altogether the idea of any divine origin of caste, and places all the four castes on an equal footing (cattāro vaṇṇā samasamā—M. II. 85). With regard to sacrifice also, though the inadequacy of ordinary rituals and austerities is commonly accepted, the B.G. tends to retain sacrifices and austerities by calling them purifying[4], whereas Buddhism has hardly any place for them. Again, the B.G. continues to regard scriptures as authoritative, whereas Buddhism inculcates no such credulity. Then again the B.G. seeks to combine the metaphysical theories of Sāṅkhya and Vedānta, and justifies its ethical teachings in relation to the immutability of Ātman, and accounts for the world-process in the light of the Sāṅkhya metaphysics. All these are of no interest to Buddhism. Then there are some new tenets of the B.G., namely, duty for duty's sake or activism and devotion to God, to which Buddhism gives no place. On the other hand, it is atheistic and favours renunciation. It is precisely in respect of this atheism and renunciation that the B.G. seems to run counter to Buddhism. In fact, this appears to be an important reason why the B.G. was composed.

It is undeniable that during the time of the rise of Buddhism as well as before and after it, there was a widespread tendency to give up worldly life and take to the life of homelessness, and it was greatly valued by such influential systems as Jainism and Buddhism. Renunciation was considered the first step to a higher life. Again, many of the systems that flouri-

1. B.G. IX. 32.
2. B.G. XVIII. 41-44.
3. B.G. IV. 13.
4. B.G. XVIII. 5.

shed during this time were atheistic and indulged in mere moral discourse unassociated with any theistic faith. The B.G. seeks to counteract these tendencies by advocating a philosophy of active worldly life coupled with a firm faith in God. It utilises its conservatism to collect the scattered theistic ideas of the Ups. and combining them with the sectarian elements of faith, puts forward an easier way of redemption.

In the light of these facts and circumstances, we can now have a clearer idea of the respective approaches of these two systems of thought to many of the problems of life tackled by them.

Chapter III

THE EPISTEMOLOGY OF THE B. G. AND EARLY BUDDHISM

General Introduction

(A) *Epistemology as an Indispensable Basis of Philosophy* :—

Both the B.G. and early Buddhism are primarily concerned with the practical problems of human life. Their direct aim, therefore, is to offer solutions for the proper guidance of human conduct, and suggest ways and means for attaining the state of supreme perfection. But in order to do so, the knowledge of truth and reality is indispensable, which in its turn necessitates explicit or implicit consideration of the problems of knowledge. Any genuine philosophy of life, thus, has to take into account the problems of knowledge directly or indirectly. Epistemology, indeed, in some form or other, serves as the basis of ethics and metaphysics. So Buddhism and the B.G. also are found to deal with the problems of epistemology in a direct or indirect manner, with more or less emphasis. The B.G., however, being a much smaller work of only 700 verses, explaining within this short compass the complex questions of metaphysics and ethics (Brahma-vidyā and Yoga-śāstra)[1], the epistemological elements in it are few and far between. But if closely examined with their implications, they can, nevertheless, give a fair idea of its epistemological position. Scholars, however, whether Eastern or Western have not hitherto thought it worthwhile to make a detailed and systematic study of this topic, despite their long discussions about the teachings of the B.G. But it would be useful for our purpose to give a separate account of this problem, howsoever scanty the material available from the text may be, for, as stated above, epistemology has often a close relation with metaphysics and ethics, and it constitutes their basis to a great extent. As regards early Buddhism, the bulk of the Pali

1. See the colophon at the end of each chapter of the B.G.

Canon being relatively larger, we are likely to get here more material which, besides clarifying its own position, may be helpful in enabling us to see the epistemological ideas of the B.G as well in a clearer light. We, thus, propose to discuss here the epistemological position of the B.G. and early Buddhism in a comparative way in the light of the material available from their respective texts.

(B) : *Knowledge Commonly Emphasised by the B.G. and Early Buddhism*:—

We have seen (supra p. 81) that the emphasis on knowledge had gradually gained ground in the Upaniṣadic period which was led to its culmination in the Buddhist thought. The B.G. also utilises this Upaniṣadic knowledge, though it seeks to combine it with its dominant teaching of disinterested action (karm-yoga), thus putting forward a syncretic philosophy of knowledge and action (jñāna-karma-samuccaya-vāda). Anyway, the element of knowledge remains a common possession of both the B.G. and early Buddhism.

This emphasis on knowledge is well indicated from the respective texts of the B.G. and Buddhism. In the B.G. from the very beginning, Arjuna is represented as being keen on having the *knowledge* and insight into things before he decides the proper course of his action. He says to Kṛṣṇa "Although these people (the Kauravas) do not *see* (na paśyanti) having their mind overpowered by greed...why should we not have the *knowledge* to turn away from this sin?"[1] Like the Upaniṣadic seeker of knowledge who discards all wealth and pleasure (preya) for the sake of what is better (śreye)[2], Arjuna also is ready to give up all worldly and heavenly pleasures, gain and victory and even his life[3] for the sake of the latter. His mind is all the time intent on the knowledge of 'śreya'

1. B.G. I. 38 and 39.

2. cf. Kaṭha II. 1 & 2 (Anyac chreyo anyad utaiva preyaḥ...śreyo hi dhīro' bhipreyaso vṛṇīte, preyo mando yoga-kṣemād vṛṇīte); II. 15 (yad icchanto brahmacaryaṃ caranti); Bṛhadā. IV. 4.22 (etam eva viditvā munir bhavati...pravrajanti...vidvāṃsaḥ prajāṃ na kāmayante): IV. 5.3. (amṛtatvasya tu nāśāsti vitteneti).

3. na kāṅkṣe vijayaṃ Kṛṣṇa na ca rājyaṃ sukhāni ca...kiṃ bhogair jīvitena vā (B.G.I.32);...rājyaṃ surāṇām api cā'dhipatyam (B.G. II.8).

and since he is himself unable to see[1], he asks Kṛṣṇa about it.[2] Kṛṣṇa also is found to impart the same knowledge to him which the wise (paṇḍitāḥ) are said to follow.[3] He explains to him the metaphysical knowledge of the immutable and eternal soul (B.G.II, 11-25) knowing which one is not liable to grieve.[4] Kṛṣṇa in clear and unambliguous terms is found to emphasise over and over again the highest value of knowledge, and its necessity for final release.[5] Thus there is no doubt that the B.G. recognises the great importance of knowledge and seeks to base its dominant teaching of disinterested action (niṣkāma-karma) on the foundation of the philosophic knowledge of the Self.

The Buddhist texts also are full of references which very clearly bear out the fact that Buddhism upholds the path of knowledge, (jñānamārga). Buddha is said to have renounced all worldly pleasures for the sake of knowledge or enlightenment (Abhiññāya, sambodhāya M.I. 431). Whatever he learns from Aḷāra Kālāma and Uddaka Rāmaputta, he claims to have directly known and seen (aham pi kho āvuso ettāvatā imaṁ dhammaṃ sayam abhiññā sacchikatvā upasampajja viharāmī'ti—M.I. 166). On the final realisation of the supreme goal also, he likewise claims in unmistakable terms that he has attained knowledge and insight (ñāṇam ca pana me dassanaṃ udapādi M.I. 167). The same is described in detail in the Mahāsaccaka Sutta where Buddha speaks of the gradual awakening of the threefold higher knowledge in the three successive watches of the night[6]. It is only after having directly known and seen the highest truth which is difficult to see and understand (duddaso duranubodho, M.I. 167)

1. na ca śreyo 'nupaśyāmi (B.G.I. 31); na cai' tad vidmaḥ Kataran no garīyo (B.G.II.6).

2. yac chreyaḥ syān niścitaṃ brūhi tan me (B.G.II.7); tad ekaṃ vada niścitya yena śreyo'ham āpnuyām (B.G. III.2); V.1.

3. B.G. II. 11.

4. tasmād evaṃ viditvai 'naṃ nā' nuśocitum arhati (B.G. II. 25); yaj jñātvā na punar moham evaṃ yāsyasi pāṇḍava (B.G. IV. 35).

5. na hi jñānena sadṛśaṃ pavitram iha vidyate (B.G. IV. 38); sarvaṃ jñānaplavenai 'va vṛjinaṃ saṃtariṣyasi (B.G. IV. 36). jñānaṃ labdhvā parāṃ śāntim acireṇādhigacchati (B.G. IV. 39).

6. rattiyā paṭhame yāme paṭhamā vijjā...majjhime yāme dutiyā vijjā...pacchime yāme tatiyā vijjā adhigatā, avijjā vihatā vijjā uppannā, tamo vihato āloko uppanno......M.I. 248-9.

and is intelligible only to the wise (paṇḍitavedanīyo, loc. cit.), that Buddha preaches it to the people.[1]

Buddha seems to be fully conversant with the two well known paths followed by his predecessors and contemporaries, viz. the path of ritualism (karma-mārga) and that of knowledge (jñāna-mārga). This distinction is referred to in the Pali Canon.[2] So when Buddha calls himself a perfectly enlightened one (sammā-sambuddha, M.I. 171) and knower of all (sabba vidū, loc. cit.), he is not unaware of the technical meanings of these words. Not only does he himself claim to be enlightened and a knower but he is acclaimed as such by others as well. Acela Pāṭika Putta, for example, while comparing himself to Buddha, describes himself as well as the latter as the followers of the path of knowledge (samaṇo Gotamo ñāṇa-vādo ahaṃ pi ñāṇa-vādo-D. III.12). The word 'knower' (ñāṇī) is but another name of the Tathāgata (ñāṇī ti..Tathāgatassa etaṃ adhivacanaṃ, A. IV. 340). He is described as one who "knowing, knows and seeing, sees having become sight and knowledge" (jānṃ jānāti passaṃ passati cakkhubhūto ñāṇabhūto, M.I. 111). Thus the fact that Buddha was a jñāna-vādin or a follower of the path of knowledge is beyond question, and it is needless to cite further textual evidence in support of this fact.

The Nature of Knowledge :—

(A) : *The Emphasis on Paranormal Knowledge* :—

Knowledge undoubtedly was highly valued in some of the Ups. in as much as it was acknowledged that it alone could secure immortality or final release from the bondage of the world.[3] It is, however, important to remember that its nature was not conceived alike in all the Ups. We have

---

1. atthi bhikkhave aññeva dhammā gambhīra duddasā duranubodhā santā paṇītā atakkāvacarā nipuṇā paṇḍitavedanīyā, ye Tathāgato sayam abhiññā sacchikatva pavedeti, D. I. 12.

2. yañña-pathe appamattā—Sn. 200; ñāṇa pathāya sikkhe—Sn. 169.

3. Kena II.4 (Vidyayā vindate amṛtam): Iśa. 11. (Vidyayāmṛtam aśnute); Bṛhadā. II. 4.5. (ātmano vā are darśanena śravaṇena matyā vijñānena idaṃ sarvaṃ viditam); Chāndogya VI. 1. 3. (yenāśrutaṃ śrutaṃ bhavati amataṃ matam, avijñātaṃ vijñātam iti).

already pointed out in the previous chapter that the knowledge emphasised in the early Ups. was mostly intellectual or rational, whereas in the later Ups. it is intuitonal or mystical knowledge which was emphasised most. Yājñavalkya in the Bṛhadāraṇyaka after having instructed Janaka exclaims, "You have reached the state of fearlessness".[1] In the Chāndogya Śvetaketu requests his father to repeat the instruction till he comprehends them.[2] After listening to the instructions one was asked to reflect and comprehend intellectually. Yājñavalkya says to Maitreyī : "Ātman should be looked into, listend to, reflected on and contemplated upon. Verily by the seeing of, by the thinking of, by the understanding of the Self, all is known."[3] But when we come to the later Ups., we find that all this instruction, intellectual refeetion and hearing is said to be of no avail[4] and knowledge is supposed to be revealed in a strange mystic manner[5], sometimes described theologically in terms of the grace of God (dhātuḥ prasādāt).[6] The aspirant of knowledge is almost taken by surprise, and not comprehending the true significance of this experience, regards it as a somewhat unaccountable mysterious experience or a special favour of God. It is only in a few passages of the later Ups. that references to a somewhat systematic and accountable type of samādhi-consciousness are met with.[7] Thus, we must first differentiate between the intellectual knowledge of the early Ups. and the intuitional (paranormal) knowledge of the later ones, and again in the latter we should distinguish between the unaccountable mystical knowledge often taken as the divine revelation and the other which is described as a somewhat natural development of the higher consciousness. Now it will be seen that it is not the intellec-

1. abhayaṃ vai Janaka prāpto'si, Bṛhadā. IV. 2.4.
2. bhūya eva mā bhagavān vijñāpayatu iti, Chāndogya VI. 5.4; VI.6.5; VI. 8. 7ff.
3. Bṛhadā. II. 4.5.
4. nāyam ātmā pravacanena labhyo na medhayā, na bahunā śrutena, Kaṭha. II. 23.
5. yam evaiṣa vṛṇute tena labhyas tasyaiṣa ātmā vivṛṇute tanūṃ svām, Kaṭha. II. 23; Muṇḍaka III. 2.3.
6. Śvetā. III. 20.
7. Śvetā. II. 8-15; Kaṭha. III. 13; VI. 7-11; VI. 18(labdhvā.... yoga vidhiṃ ca kṛtsnam).

tual but the intuitional or paranormal knowledge which is greatly valued in the B.G. and Buddhism[1], and which they consider as the means to salvation. But the difference between the B.G. and Buddhism lies in the fact that the former is largely fascinated by the mystical intuition associated with divine grace, whereas the latter adopts and develops the systematic and naturalistic type of paranormal knowledge. We shall substantiate this point in the following pages through their respective textual references.

Another important element which the B.G. and Buddhism share in common with the Ups. is the acceptance of moral discipline as a prerequiste of attaining higher knowledge. The moral preparedness in the form of faith, control of the senses and mind and cleansing oneself of impurities was considered necessary by the Ups. in order to attain the true knowledge.[2] Indra and Virocana are asked to practise several years of 'brahmacarya' before being considered fit to be imparted higher knowledge.[3] The word 'brahmacarya' here assumes a broad meaning signifying the moral conduct conducive to the attainment of the highest truth. It is in this sense that the B.G. refers to the practising of brahmacarya (yad icchanto brahmacaryaṃ caranti—B.G. VIII. 11), and the Pali Nikāyas speak of bhikkhus undergoing brahmacarya under Buddha (tassa ñāṇāya dassanāya pattiyā sacchikiriyāya bhagavati brahmacariyaṃ vussatī ti, A. IV. 384; cf. M.I. 147). The highest knowledge and insight which is the means to salvation is supposed to follow the rapt contemplative gaze of the mind when it is cleansed of its impurities.[4] To attain it various methods of self-control, discipline and yoga are prescribed.[5] We shall see that both the B.G. and Buddhism

---

1. The word 'intuitional' on account of some mystical meaning attached to it, does not suit the Buddhist context as it does the context of the B.G. We, therefore, consider it more correct to use the word 'paranormal' in the Buddhist context since it is free from mystical associations.

2. Muṇḍaka III. 1. 5; Praśna I. 15.

3. Chāndogya VIII. 7-11; cf. Kaṭha. II. 15 (yad icchanto brahmacaryaṃ caranti).

4. Muṇḍaka. III. 1.8; Kaṭha VI. 9.

5. Kaṭha speaks of adhyātma-yoga (II. 12), defines yoga as 'sthirām indriya-dhāraṇām' (VI. 11) and refers to 'yoga-vidi' (VI. 18). Śvetā. prescribes 'dhyāna-yoga' (I.3.).

accept this moral discipline in some degree as an essential precondition of the higher knowledge.

Let us first substantiate from the B.G. what we have said with regard to its approach to the nature of knowledge. Arjuna is represented as deluded as regards the determination of his rightful duty (dharmasammūḍha-cetāḥ, B.G. II. 7). In the light of his mundane knowledge he is sentimentally attached to his kith and kin, friends and relatives[1] but at the same time he talks in terms of higher knowledge exhibiting absolute detachment from all worldly objects, wealth and victory.[2] In such a situation Kṛṣṇa smilingly (prahasanniva) points out the utter confusion of Arjuna who, though speaking words of higher knowledge, was yet grieving for things which the truly wise never grieve for.[3] This is the occasion when Kṛṣṇa starts his philosophic teaching so that Arjuna may view things in the light of the higher knowledge. Evidently, the knowledge imparted to Arjuna is not ordinary, sensory or intellectual knowledge but the supramundane intuitive knowledge of the metaphysical self. Ordinary people led by normal mundane experience make distinctions of subject and object, killer and killed, and tend to miss the undying imperishable element underlying all phenomena. Kṛṣṇa points out that those who are moved by these passing vicissitudes of life, do not really perceive the truth about the undying spirit who neither kills nor is killed.[4] The entire subsequent discussion about vīnāśī and avināśī (perishable and imperishable, B.G. II. 17 ff), vyakta and avyakta (manifested and unmanifested, B.G. II. 25 ff), kṣara and akṣara (destructible and indestructible, B.G. VIII, 3 ff) and kṣetra and kṣetrajña (field and the knower of the field, B.G. XIII. 1 ff) pertains to metaphysical knowledge, said to be realised by the wise contemplative seers of the Reality (jñāninaḥ tattvadarśinaḥ, B.G. IV. 34) and the persevering yogins (yatantaḥ yoginaḥ, B.G. XV. 11). It is claimed to be a higher knowledge which "the deluded ones (vimūḍhāḥ) do not see, and (only) those

1. B.G. I. 25-30.
2. B.G. I. 32; II. 5 & 8.
3. B.G. II. 10-11.
4. B.G. II. 19 (ubhau tau na vijānīto nā'yam hanti na hanyate).

who have the eye of wisdom (jñānacakṣuṣaḥ) see."[1] Words like 'mūḍha', 'vimūḍha' or 'saṃmūḍha' are used for those whose knowledge is confined to the mundane level and who are ignorant of the higher wisdom.[2] But the knowledge which the B.G. talks about is that which having been known, nothing else is left to be known.[3]

This metaphysical knowledge seems to be of a mystical nature where the mystic is taken by surprise. The B.G. itself says : "one looks upon it amazingly."[4] The fact that it is often characterised as the most secret knowledge (guhyatamaṃ jñānam. B.G. IX 1) or more secret than all secrets (guhyād guhyataram. B.G. XVIII. 63) also suggests the same idea. Then again the Upaniṣadic notion of divine grace also is frequently associated with it.[5] All this leads to the conclusion that the knowledge taught by the B.G. is not intellectual but intuitional in character and is more or less of the type of a mysterious mystical experience. We use the word 'more or less' because the B.G. is not quite uniform and consistent in explaining the nature of this knowledge. At places a somewhat naturalistic account of knowlege also is found indicating different stages of concentration (samādhi)[6] and yogic practices[7] preceded by the control of the senses and mind along with other moral disciplines.[8] Thus what is conceived at one place as the mystic revelation occasioned by divine grace[9] is mixed up with the naturalistic account of the development of mental and spiritual faculties. We shall discuss this point at greater length when we deal with the process of knowledge in the sequel.

---

1. B.G. XV. 10. (vimuḍhā nā'nupaśyanti, paśyanti jñānacakṣuṣah.)
2. cf. B.G. II. 7. (dharma-saṃmūḍha); VII. 25 (mūḍho'yaṃ nā') bhijānāti); XI. 11 (avajānanti māṁ mūḍha).
3. B.G. VII. 2 (yaj jñātvā ne'ha bhūyo'nyaj jñātavyam avaśiṣyate).
4. B.G. II. 29 (āścaryavat paśyti kaścid enam. . . . .)
5. B.G. X. 11 (tesām evā'nukampārtham aham ajñānajam tamaḥ nāśayāmi); XI. 8 (divyaṃ dadāmi te cakṣuḥ); XVIII. 56 (mat prasādād avāpnoti śāśvataṃ padam avyayam); XVIII. 58, 62 & 66.
6. B.G. II. 55-72,
7. B.G. VI. 10-29.
8. B.G. II. 57, 58, 61, 64, 68; III 37-43; V. 26-28; XVIII. 51-55.
9. B.G. X. 10, 11; XI. 8; XVIII. 56, 58, 62, 66.

As regards the Buddhist conception of knowledge, it hardly needs evidence to show that it attaches the highest value to paranormal knowledge. It is well known that Buddha after testing and trying different methods ultimately attained the highest knowledge through meditation.[1] He claimed himself to be a perfectly enlightened one (sammā-sambuddha) only when he had a direct knowledge and insight into things as they are. He is reported to have said : "So long as, monks, I did not thoroughly understand things as they really are...I did not declare myself to be truly enlightened, unsurpassed in the world with its devas, its Māras, its Brahmas, among the host of recluses and brahmins and of devas and men. But when, monks, I thoroughly understood them as they really are...then I declared myself to be truly enlightened, unsurpassed in the world with its devas, its Māras..."[2] It is only after having himself known and realised this highest wisdom that he teaches it to others (sayaṃ abhiññā sacchikatvā pavedeti, D-I. 12). Obviously this knowledge cannot be confused with mere sensory or intellectual knowledge, and Buddha himself describes it as "profound, difficult to see and comprehend, serene, excellent, superrational, subtle and comprehensible (only) by the wise (gambhīrā, duddasā, duranubodhā santā paṇītā atakkāvacarā nipuṇā paṇḍita-vedanīyā, D.I. 12). In fact we are inclined to think that close to the period of the later Ups., the very term, 'jñānavāda' had come to signify the doctrine of higher supra-mundane knowledge and it is in this sense that the words like 'jñānin' or 'jñānavādin' are used in the later Ups., Buddhism, the B.G. and other contemporaneous thoughts. Puraṇa Kassapa and Nigaṇṭha Nātaputta who claim direct supra-mundane knowledge and profess omniscience are called jñāna-vādins.[4] It is again in this sense that Pāṭika Putta calls himself as well as Buddha jñāna-vādins and proposes to have a competitive display of their respective super-human powers.[1] It is again by virtue of this very higher knowledge

1. M.I. 167; M.I. 247-9.
2. S. III. 28.
3. A. IV. 429.
4. Samaṇo pi Gotamo ñāṇa-vādo aham pi ñāṇa-vādo, ñāṇa-vādo kho pana ñāṇa-vādena arahati uttari-manussa-dhammā iddhi-paṭihāriyaṃ dassetuṃ. —D. III. 12.

that the arhat disciples of Buddha, besides the Master himself are supposed to have direct knowledge and insight into things including the fourfold Noble Truth (ariya saccāni avecca passati, Sn. 40; Cattāri ariya saccāni sammappaññāya passati, Dh. 190) and the nibbāna (nibbānam passeyyam, M.I. 511).

Thus, the B.G. and Buddhism seem to be in perfect accord in attaching the highest value to paranormal knowledge. They again accept in common (as we shall see later) that moral discipline is a necessary pre-condition for attaining such knowledge. But they differ as regards the way in which this knowledge arises, as also regarding orientation towards it and evaluation of it. We shall see in the sequel how Buddhism in contradistinction to the partly naturalistic and partly theological approach of the B.G., offers a thoroughly naturalistic and systematic account of the emergence of this higher knowledge.

(B) *Due Recognition to Normal Knowledge* :—

The fact that paranormal knowledge is accorded the highest place in the B.G. and Buddhism should not be taken to mean that normal sensory knowledge is ignored by them. In fact, its value is fully recognised by both of them. They only point out that its range and value are limited. It cannot go beyond the range of our senses and cannot reveal the higher truths of life. For ordinary purposes, however, both of them agree that normal sensory knowledge suffices.

In the B.G. Kṛṣṇa and Arjuna are represented as conversing together, seeing and hearing themselves as well as the entire events of the battle-field which are no hallucinations but facts. Though the word 'māyā' or 'yoga-māyā' occurs in the B.G. (VII. 14, 15 and 26), it is used only as a synonym of Prakṛti representing the three guṇas or as a creative power of God. That is why it is called divine (daivī, B.G. VII. 14) and endowed with guṇas (guṇamayī, loc. cit.). Rāmānuja very explicitly points out that the word māyā is not indicative of illusion but is a real power of God.[1] Even Śaṅkara

1. ato māyā śabdo na mithyārtha-vācī....eṣā guṇamayī pāramārthikī bhagavan-māyā eva, R.B.G. VIII. 14.

while commenting on the word 'yoga-māyā' admits that it is used here in the sense of an admixture of guṇas.[1] Professor Das Gupta rightly notes this point when he says : "The Gītā ..does not assert anywhere that Brahman is the only reality, and all else that appears is false and unreal".[2] Indeed, for all practical purposes of mundane life the validity of normal sense-perception is duly recognised in the B.G. It is only with regard to knowing things beyond the range of the senses that it evokes the service of intuitional knowledge. Sañjaya, in order to have the direct personal knowledge of the events of war from the royal palace, had to be endowed with paranormal perception.[3] Arjuna had to be provided with the 'divine eye' (divya cakṣu) in order to have the direct vision of the cosmic form of Kṛṣṇa imperceptible to ordinary eyes.[4] Similarly in order to perceive the higher metaphysical truth leading to salvation one is said to acquire the eye of wisdom (jñāna cakṣu).[5] Thus higher knowledge is emphasised in the B.G. only with a view to enhancing the power of our normal faculties and enabling us to realise the highest truth, and there by the supreme goal of life.

In Buddhism the validity of normal sensory preception is more explicitly admitted. It is through one's normal sense-perception that the sufferings of birth, old-age, disease and death are experienced and one is led to look for the higher truth. In fact, it is a truism that commonsense constitutes the basis of philosophy, and the normal mundane knowledge paves the way for paranormal supra-mundane wisdom. Naturally, the latter includes the former. In day-to-day practical life, people have to be directed through their normal sense-experience. Thus paranormal knowledge is taught by Buddha for the sake of realising the higher truths of life and directing ourselves to the right path culminating in Nibbāna.

---

1. yogo guṇānāṃ yuktiḥ ghaṭanaṃ, sā eva māyā-yogamāyā, S.B.G. VII. 25.

2. A History of Indian Philosophy, Vol. II. p. 478.

3. B.G. XVIII. 7.

4. B.G. XI. 8.

5. B.G. XV. 10 (paśyanti jñānacakṣuṣaḥ) XIII. 34. (....evam....ye vidur yānti te param).

(C) *Qualitative Difference Between Normal and Paranormal Knowledge* :—

It is clear that higher knowledge is emphasised in the B. G. and Buddhism on account of its greater power and value. But this greater capacity and utility is so vital that it amounts to a qualitative difference rather than a difference in degree. The knowledge gained through higher faculties is found to be qualitatively different from the knowledge gained through ordinary sensory means. What is desirable and pleasant for a man with normal sensory knowledge, may be quite undesirable and painful to the man with paranormal vision; what is happiness for the former may be suffering for the latter; what one takes to be stable, the other may take to be thoroughly unstable; and what is considered substantial by one may be regarded as wholly insubstantial by the other. Thus higher knowledge may result in a fundamental difference in the whole outlook of man. The entire perspective is changed and the total personality is transformed. We may understand this even in the light of our normal experience. Blood, for example, looks like a red liquid to our naked eyes, but the same when viewed under a microscope assumes a different nature. It looks like a swarm of innumerable small corpuscles. Many such instances may be multiplied. This gives an idea as to how a higher faculty of knowing may produce a knowledge quite different in kind. It is in the light of this enhanced or higher knowledge of blood that its maladies are properly diagnosed, a cure is effected and the limitations of ordinary perception are realised. Likewise, it is in the light of the higher paranormal knowledge that the malady of life is clearly seen, its cure is found and the limitations and shortcomings of ordinary mundane knowledge are realised. Then the latter may be so shaped, controlled, changed, modified and adjusted as not to prove any impediment in the way of attaining the highest goal of life. This indicates the supremacy of the paranormal knowledge over the normal, and suggests a clue to understand why both the B. G. and Buddhism call those people ignorant(mūḍhāḥ or bālāḥ)[1] who,

---

1. Dh. 60-74 (bāla-vaggo); Dh. 28,136; B. G. VII. 25, IX. 11, XV. 10.

disregarding the higher knowledge altogether, view things differently.

Instances are many both in the B. G. as well as in Buddhism to indicate that according to them, quite an opposite conception of things arises on account of an utter disregard for higher knowledge. It is pointed out by the B. G. that a man devoid of true knowledge, considers the apparent pleasures of the world begotten of sense-object-contact (saṃsparśajāḥ) to be delightful which in reality are sources of suffering and which the truly wise abhors. Kṛṣṇa clearly points out : "Whatever pleasures are born of contact are only sources of suffering. They have a beginning and an end, O son of Kunti (Arjuna), no wise man delights in them".[1] It is in the light of this very teaching that Arjuna is asked to learn to rise above apparent pleasure and pain born of contacts.[2] The same has been conveyed in so many ways and through so many analogies in Buddhism too. The man deriving pleasure out of sense-object contact has been compared to a leper who is scratching his wound and heating it over a fire and deriving momentary pleasure thereby, which ultimately worsens his wound and augments his trouble all the more.[3] The same is suggested by the analogy of a dog, lustily gnawing at a fleshless piece of bone, and gaining ultimately nothing but pain and suffering.[4] The fool, not realising the inherent painfulness of apparently pleasant objects, enjoys them like honey (madhu'vā maññati bālo.... Dh. 69). This indicates that the wise and the fool have quite opposite views with regard to the same things. Buddha clearly states : "What others call happiness, the wise call misery, and what others call misery, the wise know it to be happiness".[5] The Dhamma- pada conveys the same idea when it refers to the ignorant man conceiving good (bhadraṃ) as evil (pāpam), and evil as good.[6] The B. G. also seems

1. B.G. V. 22.
2. B.G. II. 14.
3. M.I. 507.
4. M.I. 364.
5. S. IV. 127; Sn. 149.
6. Dh. 119, 120 & 69.

to suggest a similar idea when it says : "What is night for all beings is the time of waking for the disciplined man, and what is the time of waking for all beings is night for the sage with insight."[1] It should not, however, be forgotten that Buddhism in contradistinction to the B. G. does not indulge in any metaphysical speculation about the nature of reality which is basic to the B. G.

(D) *Reasons for the Superiority of Paranormal Knowledge* :—

Now, in view of the great emphasis laid on this paranormal or extra-sensory knowledge both in the B. G. and Buddhism, if one were to ask why it should be given preference over ordinary sensory knowledge, specially when the nature of objects as presented by ordinary sense-perception is different from what it known through paranormal or extra-sensory perception, the simple answer, as we have suggested, would be to appeal to the greater capacity and utility of the latter. But if one further raises the query as to why it should be taken as more reliable and useful for higher purposes, we cannot but point to the acclaimed greater clarity and directness of paranormal knowledge. It is important in this connection to note that both in the B. G. and Buddhism, paranormal knowledge is conceived as extra-ordinary direct perception analogous to visual perception. Knowing in this sense is used as a synonym of *seeing*.

There is little doubt about the fact that perception is the most direct and authentic of all the sources of knowledge. It is invariably mentioned as first among the various sources of knowledge. It is so open and obvious that even the Materialists, who denounce all other sources of knowledge, accept it.[2] Now among the different kinds of sensory perception, the visual perception appears to be the most direct and authentic. In fact the term 'pratyakṣa' (perception) itself literally means (prati =pertaining to+akṣa

1. B.G. II. 69.

2. There was, however, one School of Materialists who denied perception as well. cf. K.N. Jayatilleke—Early Buddhist Theory of Knowledge, pp. 72, 79—92.

=eye) 'knowledge pertaining to eye' i.e. visual perception. But there has been an extension in the meaning of the word so as to signify knowledge pertaining to the senses in general.[1] It is remarkable that even in the Ups. the verdict of visual knowledge is regarded as more authentic and reliable than any other. In the Bṛhadāraṇyaka, for example, it is said : "Verily, truth is sight. Therefore, if now the two persons come disputing, one saying, 'I saw'. and the other, 'I heard', we should trust the one who says, 'I saw' "[2] The same attitude seems to be adopted by the B. G. and Buddhism. Arjuna, after having heard from Kṛṣṇa about the divine glories of the latter, wants to *see* them directly. He says : "The origin and decease of beings, as also your inexhaustible glory have been heard (śrutau) by me in detail from you, O Kṛṣṇa. As you have declared yourself to be, even so it is, O Supreme Lord. But I desire to *see* your divine form (draṣṭum icchāmi te rūpam), O Supreme Person."[3] In Buddhism too, this idea of having greater conviction through the evidence of visual perception is well brought out in the following statement of Buddha : "Who would believe that this earth and the majestic mountain, Sineru would be consumed by fire except on the evidence of sight ?"[4] It is thus clear that perception is considered to be the most reliable among the different sources of knowledge, and among different kinds of perceptual knowledge, it is the visual perception which carries the highest reliability.

Now it is worthy of note that the highest knowledge through which the ultimate goal is to be realised, is conceived both in the B. G. and Buddhism as extra-ordinary visual perception attainable through the eye of wisdom. One is to know and *see* the truth directly. It may be useful here to draw attention to the Buddhist account of six kinds of supernormal capacities attainable after the fourth stage of medita-

1. cf. Vātsyāyana's explanation of the word 'Pratyakṣa' who states : "Pratyakṣa means the operation of the sense-organs, each in relation to its object" (akṣasyā'kṣasya prati-viṣayaṃ vṛttiḥ pratyakṣam, Nyāya Bhāṣya, I. 1.3.).

2. Bṛhadā. V. 14.4.

3. B.G. XI. 2 & 3.

4. A. IV. 103.

tion (jhāna).[1] Of these the first, viz., the super-normal power to act according to one's will (iddhi-vidhā) is not strictly cognitive in the sense of 'knowing that'[2] and so it has come to be dissociated from the rest which are together known as the five kinds of higher knowledge (pañcābhiññā). Out of these five, all except the first, viz., the extraordinary auditory knowledge (dibbasota dhātu) are conceived in terms of extraordinary visual perception. They are the following :

1. cetopariyañāṇa, i. e. telepathic knowledge
2. pubbenivāsānussatiñāṇa, i. e. retrocognitive knowledge.
8. dibbacakkhu, i. e. clairvoyance (also known as cutūpapātañāṇa i. e. knowledge of the decease and survival of beings).
4. āsavakkhaya ñāṇa, i. e. knowledge of the destruction of defiling impulses.

In order to account for the direct vision of these extraordinary perceptions, Budddhism conceives of extraordinary 'eyes', viz., thc divine eye (dibbacakkhu) and the eye of wisdom (paññācakkhu). The Niddesa commenting on the verb 'addakkhi' which means 'he saw' says that it could mean "he saw with his telepathic knowledge....retrocognitive knowledge....his human eye or divine eye (paracitta ñāṇena vā addakkhi, pubbenivāsānussatiñāṇena vā.... maṃsacakkhunā vā....dibbena cakkhunā...., Nd. I. 323). The similes which Buddha has given in order to explain the nature of these four kinds of knowledge also suggest that they are intended to be taken as a kind of extraordinary visual perception. The nature of telepathic knowledge or that of knowing others' minds is companed to *seeing* one's face in a mirror or a pan of water and noticing whether there is a mole or not.[3] The nature of retrocognitive knowledge also is explained in terms of the remembrance of direct experience

1. D.I. 77-84.
2. On the distinction of 'knowing how' and'knowing that' see G. Ryle, The Concept of Mind, Chapter II, pp. 25-60. cf. K.N. Jayatilleke, Early Buddhist Theory of Knowledge, p. 438.
3. D. I. 80.

of a man who goes from village to village and subsequently remembers all about his journey.[1] It is like 'seeing' the past. The nature of clairvoyance through which one sees (passati) the decease and survival etc. of beings is explained through the simile of a man with eye-sight (cakkhumā puriso) who stationing himself on the terrace of a palace situated on the cross-roads sees people sitting or loitering about, coming or going from one direction to another.[2] Lastly, the nature of the knowledge of the destruction of defilements which is said to be had through the eye of wisdom (paññāya passati, Dh. 277-9, 190) is compared to the *seeing* of shells, conches, swimming fish etc., in a clear transparent and tranquil pool of water on the hill-top by a man of vision (cakkhumā puriso) standing at its bank.[3] In the B. G. also one is said to see the higher truth through the divine eye or the eye of wisdom, though these different kinds of higher knowledge are not clearly and systematically enumerated in it. Arjuna had to be endowed with the divine eye (divya-cakṣu) in order to see the divine cosmic form (divyāni rūpaṇi, XI. 5: rūpam aiśvaram, XI. 3) of Kṛṣṇa.[4] Again, there are numerous verses which speak of the direct vision of the highest truth (metaphysically conceived as Ātman or Brahman) through the eye of wisdom (jñāna-cakṣuṣā) which alone can lead to salvation. Kṛṣṇa, after imparting knowledge of 'Kṣetra' and 'Kṣetrajña' to Arjuna, says : "Those who perceive thus by the eye of wisdom (jñāna-cakṣuṣā), the distinction between the field (kṣetra) and the knower of the field (kṣetrajña), and the deliverance of beings from nature (prakṛti), they reach the Supreme".[5] Only those having the eye of wisdom (jñāna-cakṣuṣaḥ) are said to *see* (*paśyanti*) the truth which is hidden from the sight of ordinary people.[6] One who is possessed of yoga is said to *see* the truth (*īkṣate* yoga yuktātmā, B. G. VI. 29). "The persevering yogins *see*

1. D. I. 81-82.
2. D. I. 83.
3. D. I. 84.
4. B.G. XI. 8.
5. B.G. XIII. 34.
6. B.G. XV. 10.

him. . . ." (yatanto yoginaścainaṃ *paśyanti*. . . ., B. G. XV. 11). "When he *sees* (anupaśyati) the manifold states of beings as centred in the One, and from that alone the entire expansion, then he attains Brahman."[1] Thus it is evident that both in the B. G. and Buddhism the higher knowledge is conceived as extraordinary direct perception. Such direct vision or insight attained through the divine eye or the eye of wisdom, as a result of cleansing the mind of impurities and attaining concentration, is claimed to be more penetrating than the ordinary vision of the normal eyes, and hence more reliable and convincing than the latter.

One can now see the significance of the use of knowing as a synonym of seeing in Buddhism and the B. G. Buddha frequently uses the word 'seeing' along with 'knowing' (tam ahaṃ jānāmi passāmi, MI. 329). 'The Knowing and seeing One' (jānata passatā, M.II.111) is, indeed, a characteristic description of Buddha. The central truths of Buddhism are *seen*. One is said to comprehend and *see* the Noble Truths (ariyasac cāni avecca *passati*, Sn. 40; cattāri ariyasaccāni sammappaññāya *passati*, Dh. 190; cf Dh. 277-9). The final truth is directly realised and *seen* (paramasaccaṃ sacchikaroti, paññāya ca ativijjha *passati*, M. II. 112, 173). Nibbāna also is said to be seen (nibbānaṃ *passeyyan* ti, M. I. 511) in a sense analogous to the seeing of a man who, though born blind, has been treated and cured by the physician (loc. cit). Buddha emphatically claims that he teaches about the destruction of defilements after knowing and *seeing*, and not without knowing and seeing (jānato'ham bhikkhave *passato* āsavānaṃ khayaṃ vadāmi no ajānato no appassato, S. II. 29). He is represented as one who 'has the knowledge and *insight* into all things' (sabbesu dhammesu ca ñāṇa-*dassī*, Sn. 84), and the religious life is led under the Exalted One for the knowledge and *insight*, attainment, realisation and comprehension of what is not known not *seen* not attained, not realised and not comprehended.[2] In the B. G. also, as stated already, higher knowledge is conceived as 'seeing'. The final truth both about 'sat' and 'asat (real and unreal) is said to have been

1. B.G. XIII. 30.
2. A. IV. 384.

seen (*dṛṣṭaḥ*) by the seers of Reality (tattva darśibhiḥ).[1] The reality as it is in itself (tattva) is to be known and *seen* (jñātuṃ *draṣṭum* ca tattvena, B. G. XI. 54).

Now this knowledge which is thus obtained through direct vision is considered both by the B. G. and Buddhism as objective, not dependent on or determined by the subjective mode of perception. That is why it is called 'tattvajñāna' by the B. G. and 'yathābhūta-ñāṇa' by Buddhism.

It is true that both the B. G. and Buddhism speak of it as direct *personal* knowledge. Buddha claims to know and see things *personally* (tam *ahaṃ* jānāmi passāmi, M.I. 329; tathāgato *sayaṃ* abhiññā sacchikatvā pavedeti, D. I. 12), and likewise Kṛṣṇa also declares that he has direct *personal* knowledge of things (tāny *ahaṁ* veda sarvāṇi, B.G. IV.5.). But this does not in any way warrant the conclusion that it is subjective, differing from person to person. It is nowhere suggested that it is an exclusive or a private possession of Buddha or Kṛṣṇa, inaccessible to others. On the other hand, it is quite clearly shown both in the B.G. and Buddhism that it is equally open to all and objective in character.

Both the B.G. and Buddhism prescribe certain moral disciplines and practices of concentration by following which one is said to attain this capacity of knowing and seeing directly and personally. Whosoever fulfils the condition can realise the goal. It is thus open to all and not limited to a selected few. In the B.G. Kṛṣṇa after having explained the worthlessness of ordinary vicissitudes of life, says : "Whosoever is not troubled by these, O Arjuna, whosoever remains the same amidst pain and pleasure, and is wise, is entitled for immortality."[2] Similarly, it is said : "He who is without affection on all sides, who is neither pleased nor displeased as he obtains good or evil, he obtains the unwavering wisdom.[3] When the B.G. speaks of this knowledge as attainable by the persevering yogins (B.G.XV. 11), it also makes it clear as to how yoga is attained[4] or how one can be a yogin.[5] Thus

1. B.G. II 16.
2. B.G. II. 15.
3. B.G. II. 57.
4. B.G. II. 53; VI 10ff.
5. B.G VI. 1, 32; V. 11.

the knowledge which is said to be directly and personally realised by Kṛṣṇa is not an exclusive or private possession of his own, but is open equally to all who practise the method of yoga, and follow the prescribed code of discipline. In fact, we find references to the seers and yogins, besides Kṛṣṇa, who are said to have actually seen and realised the final truth.[1] It is thus clear that the direct *personal* knowing and seeing is emphasised in order to indicate its authenticity and not its subjectivity.

The same is conveyed in Buddhism with greater clarity and certitude. The dhamma is decribed as "bearing fruit in the present life, before long, an invitation to come and see, leading to the goal and comprehensible personally by the wise."[2] Buddha quite unambiguously points out that what he has personally known and seen is the objective truth which is equally open to all who try for it. He says "Let an intelligent person come to me, sincere, honest and straightforward; I shall instruct him and teach the doctrine so that on my instruction he would conduct himself in such a way that before long he would himself know and himself see."[3] Buddha claims only to have seen and discovered the truth and the way to it which others have seen and traversed in the past (purāṇaṃ maggaṃ purāṇañjaaṃ pubbakehi manussehi anuyātam, S. II. 106), which is objectively there, and is open to all[4], and is not a private or subjective experienie of his. The Pali Canon itself refers to so many other arhat bhikkhus having perfected themselves, besides the Master, in all the sixfold higher forms of knowledge (chaḷabhiññā), spoken of by the latter.[5]

Again both the B. G. and Buddhism clearly characterise the highest truth as 'objective'. According to them it presents the reality as it is in itself (tattvena, B. G. IX. 24; XI. 54 or yathābhūta, S. II. 30; A. V. 37). Those who

1. B.G. II. 16; III. 20; IV. 1 & 2; VI. 29; XIII. 24 & XV. 11.
2. M.I. 37.
3. M. II. 44.
4. Etena maggena atariṃsu pubbe,
Tarissanti ye taranti ca oghan ti. —S.V. 168.
5. S. II. 217, 222; see also the definite reference to the attainment of the sixfold knowledge by sixty monks in S.I. 191 (saṭṭhi bhikkhū chaḷabhiññā).

attain this highest knowledge are called in the B. G. the seers of reality in its objectivity (tattva-darsī, B. G. II. 16). The word 'tattva-jñāna', which is used in the B. G. for the highest knowledge, literally means knowledge of 'thatness' (tat = that or object + tva = ness) i. e. knowledge of 'the thing or object as it is' The B. G. uniformly uses it in this very sense. For example, it is said : "He who thus knows it as it is (tattvataḥ) does not fall into rebirth after leaving off the body".[1] "Thereafter, having known me as I am (tattvato) he forthwith enters into me"[2] Again Kṛṣṇa says : "By unswerving devotion to me, O Arjuna, I can be thus known and seen as I am (tattvena) and (then) entered into, O Arjuna."[3] This hardly leaves any doubt about the fact that the highest knowledge leading to salvation is considered in the B. G. as an objective truth, revealing reality as it is in itself (tattvataḥ). It is also added that without attaining this objective knowledge there is no possibility of final release. Kṛṣna says : "They do not know me truly (tattvena) and therefore they fall away".[4] In fact, the B. G. regards that knowledge as 'tāmasa' (of inert nature) which presents things in a non-objective way (atattvārthavad)[5].

The same is true of Buddhism as well. We find frequent references to knowledge and insight of the object as it is (yathābhūta ñāṇa-dassana, S. II. 30; V. 432; A. IV. 336). The word 'yathābhūta' (yathā = as + bhūta = it was) means 'as it was' i. e corresponding to the fact (or the object as it was). Thus the word 'yathābhūta-ñāṇa' used by Buddhism is really a synonym of the word 'tattva-jñāna' used by the B. G. The Pali Canon itself makes its sense clear when it says that the yathābhūta-ñāṇa consists in knowing "what exists as existing and what does not exist as not existing" (santaṃ vā atthī'ti ñassati asantaṃ vā natthī'ti ñassati, A. V. 36). It is further added that "knowing things as they are and wherever they are is the

1. B.G. IV. 9.
2. B.G. XVIII 55.
3. B.G. XI. 54.
4. B.G. IX. 24,
5. B.G. XVIII. 22.

highest knowledge" (etad ānuttariyaṃ....ñāṇānaṃ yad idaṃ tattha tattha yathābhūto-ñāṇaṃ, A. V. 37). Thus the highest knowledge is stated to be objective and not dependent on the subject. With regard to the truth preached by him, Buddha himself makes this explicit statement : "Whether the Tathāgata preaches the dhamma to his disciples or does not preach it, the dhamma remains the same".[1]

Now, what is the ground on which the claim of clarity and objectivity is made by the B .G. and Buddhism? This claim is made because this knowledge is said to arise in a state when the mind is purged of all impurities and defilements, and is made free from all biases and prejudices which distort the vision and impede clear and objective knowledge. Unlike ordinary sensory knowledge, this higher knowledge is said to be attained only when one has gone a long way in the practice of concentration (samādhi). This in its turn is made possible by following some moral disciplines and practices of self-control (śīla) and thereby cleansing oneself of impurities and overcoming one's normal emotional and sentimental weaknesses, biases and prejudices. In other words, it is through the successive practice of moral discipline and concentration (śīla and samādhi) that the true knowledge(prajñā) is attained, and the supreme goal(vimukti) is finally realised. It is well stated in the Pali Canon according to which one first cultivates virtue (śīla sampadaṃ ārādheti, M. I. 200-2), then achieves concentration (samādhi sampadaṃ ārādheti, loc. cit.), and subsequently knowledge and insight (ñāṇa-dassanaṃ ārādheti, loc. cit.) and through this knowledge, perfect emancipation is attained (sammā-ñāṇassa sammāvimutti pahoti, M. III. 76). Thus moral preparedness is essential for attaining true wisdom, or as a well-known Pali saying puts it "Wisdom shines forth with conduct" (apadāne sobhati paññā, A. I. 102). The same idea is conveyed by the statement: "Wisdom is cleansed by virtue and virtue is cleansed by widom; where there is virtue there is wisdom and where there is wisdom there is virtue; virtue and wisdom

3. M.I. 331.

are held in the highest regard in the world".[1]

Similar ideas are expressed in the B. G. as well. The need for self-control and moral discipline is emphasised for securing the state of concentration whereby knowledge and consequent salvation are said to be attained. It is said that the mind cannot be steadily fixed in concentration (samādhau na vidhīyate) so long as it is running after worldly pleasures and powers, and is distracted thereby.[2] It is only when the mind stands unshaken and stable in concentration (samādhau) that the equanimity (yoga) is achieved.[3] Various moral virtues and disciplines are enumerated, conducive to concentration (dhyāna-yoga)[4] whereby one attains the state fit to realise the Supreme (Brahmabhūyāya kalpate, B.G. XVIII. 53). It is at this stage that the highest knowledge leading to salvation (or what the B.G. in view of its theological approach would like to call, 'merger with the Supreme') arises (tato māṃ tattvato jñātvā viśate tad anantaram, B.G. XIII.55). Again the idea that virtue, wisdom and salvation are interlinked, is also well expressed in the following verse: "The man of faith endeavouring with the control of senses (saṃyatendriyaḥ) attains wisdom (labhate jñānam), and having attained wisdom, he in no time achieves salvation or supreme Peace (parāṃ śāntim)".[5]

This indicates that in order to attain true knowledge, the mind, by means of proper discipline, has to be first made free from all impurities and obstructions which are obstacles to clear and objective vision. Many such obstructing factors are referred to in the B.G., though they are not systematically enumerated. In the very first chapter the Kauravas are said not to see things on account of greed (lobha).[6] Similarly the

---

1. Sīlaparidhotā....paññā paññāparidhotaṃ sīlaṃ, yattha sīlaṃ tattha paññā yattha paññā tattha sīlam...Sīla paññānañ ca pana lokasmiṃ aggamakkhāyati, D.I. 124.

2. bhogaiśvarya prasaktānāṃ tayā'pahṛtacetsām. . . .buddhiḥ samādhau na vidhīyate, B.G. II. 44.

3. śruti vipratipannā te yadā sthāsyati niścalā,
samādhau acalā buddhis tadā yogam avāpsyasi, B.G. II. 53

4. B G. V. 25-29; XVIII. 51-53.

5. B.G. IV. 39.

6. . . . .ete na paśyanti lobhopahatacetasaḥ, B.G. I. 38.

need for giving up delusion (moha)[1] and desire (kāma)[2] is emphasised in order to attain concentration and see things rightly. Then again we find mention of attachment, fear and anger (rāga, bhaya and krodha) which are to be eliminated in order that the intellect should be firmly fixed in concentration.[3] In some other verses emphasis is laid on giving up attachment and hatred (rāga and dveṣa)[4]. Thus taking them all together we find seven emotional impediments generally spoken of by the B.G., viz. desire, anger, greed, attachment, hatred, delusion and fear (kāma, krodha, lobha, rāga, dveṣa. moha and bhaya). Of these the first four which are said to be interlinked[5], may in a general way be indicated by the word 'desire' (kāma) or attachment (rāga). In that case we find that according to the B.G. there are four major impediments to knowledge, viz. attachment, hatred, delusion and fear (rāga, dveṣa, moha and bhaya) which are almost the same as those mentioned in the Pali texts. Buddha is said to have spoken of the very same four ways of falling into injustice or untruth (agati gamanāni, A.II. 18), viz. out of attachment (chanda), hatred (dosa), delusion (moha) and fear (bhaya). Now, the first impediment spoken of by the B.G., viz. 'rāga' is not different from 'chand' as used in Buddhism. These words along with others are used in the Pali texts indicating almost the same sense.[6] Thus, the B.G. and Buddhism seem to be in agreement in pointing out the impediments of concentration and consequent higher knowledge. It is essential according to both to rise above all these subjective emotions which alone can lead to perfect equanimity, and give rise to objective truth free from the distortion and prejudice, likes

1. B.G. II. 52; VII. 13.
2. B.G. II. 55; III. 37.
3. B.G. II. 56; VI. 10.
4. B.G. II. 64; XVIII. 51.
5. B.G. II. 62; III. 37 & 38 make it clear that anger is caused by desire, and again the keen desire for a thing causes attachment and greed.
6. Cf. rūpe avigata rāgassa . . .chandassa. . . .pemassa. . .pipāsassa. . . parilāhassa. . . . .taṇhassa tassa rūpassa vipariṇāmaññathābhāvā uppajjanti. . . .S. III. 107. Similarly it is said : 'rūpe bhikkhave yo chando, yo rāgo, yā nandi, yā tanhā ye upāyupādānā, cetaso-adhiṭṭhānā abhinivesā'nusaya, te pajahatha', S. III. 161-2.

and dislikes. As the B.G. says: "He who is free from affection (emotion) on all sides and is neither elated nor depressed as he obtains good or evil, his wisdom, indeed, is firmly set in."[1] Such an ideal man (sthita-prajña) is said to be even-minded in pain and pleasure (samaduḥkhasukhaḥ, B.G. II. 15, 56; XII. 13, 18; XIV. 24), the same in honour and dishonour (sama or tulyamānāpamānayoḥ B. G. XII. 18; XIV. 25) alike in blame and praise (tulya nindā stutiḥ, B.G. XII. 19; XIV. 24) and equal to friends and foes (tulyo mitrāripakṣayoḥ, B.G. XIV. 25, XII. 18). The same is true of Buddhism. The ideal man (arhat) is not misled by anyone of the four misguiding ways.[2] Buddha himself claims to be neither pleased at the praise of others nor displeased at their abuse, and instructs his disciples to adopt the same attitude.[3] On one occasion when the bhikkhus are discussing among themselves after having heard the mendicant, Suppiya and his disciple, Brahmadatta speaking respectively ill and well of Buddha, Dhamma and Saṅgha, Buddha approaches and gives them the following admonition: "If others were to speak ill of me, the Dhamma and the Order, do not bear any hatred or ill-will towards them or be displeased at heart ..it will be a danger to you.., for if you were to be enraged and upset, will you be able to know whether these statements of others were fair or unfair?"[4] On the other hand, "if others were to speak in praise of me, the Dhamma or the Order, you should not be happy, delighted and puffed up at heart..it will only be a danger to you..you should understand fact as fact and realise that 'this is true and this is false'.."[5] Even Sāriputta when he says in the praise of the Master: "I have such faith in the Exalted One that I do not think that there ever has been or will there ever be or is now a recluse or brahmin who has greater understanding and

1. B.G. II. 57.
2. D. III. 133.
3. tatra ce...pare Tathāgataṃ akkosanti...tatra....Tathāgatassa na hoti āghāto...tatra ce...pare Tathāgataṃ sakkaronti...na hoti ānando... Tasmātiha...tumhe ce pi pare akkoseyyuṃ...tatra tumhe hi na āghāto... karaṇiyo...pare sakkareyyuṃ...tatra tumhe hi na ānando...karaṇīyaṃ, M.I. 140
4. D.I.3.
5. D.I. 3.

knowledge than the Exalted One,"[1] he is quietly rebuked by Buddha with the remark: "Have you examined the minds of the perfectly enlightened Exalted Ones of the past...the future.. or my own mind in the present?"[2] To this Sāriputta had to say: "Not so Lord," and thereupon Buddha remarks: "Why then have you uttered a statement so grand and bold, made categorical claim and uttered a lion's roar?"[3] All this clearly shows to what extent it is considered necessary according to Buddha to rise above one's subjective likes and dislikes, biases and prejudices in order to know and see objective truth. This emphasis on getting rid of subjective prejudices and habits of mind which make people fall into error is reminiscent of Bacon's idols[4] which, according to him, hinder the objective approach of the individual. Of course, the purging of the mind prescribed by the B.G. and specially by Buddhism is too penetrative and thorough-going to be expected in Bacon's note of caution which was meant for attaining objectivity only in our intellectual knowledge.

It is only after surmounting all these misleading and impeding elements that one attains the tranquility and serenity of mind required for clarity and objectivity of vision.[5] In the B.G. we do not find a clear and analytic account of the different states of concentration, but according to Buddhism which elaborately analyses the different states of concentration, it is in the fourth stage of concentration (jhāna) that one is said to turn and direct his mind for the attainment of the true objective knowledge and insight (ñāṇa-dassanāya cittam abhinīharati abhininnāmeti, D.I.76). We shall take up this point when we next discuss the process of knowledge. For the present it suffices to show that the claim of clarity and objectivity made in the B.G. and Buddhism about the paranormal knowledge is based on rational considerations.

---

1. D. III. 99.
2. D. III. 99-100.
3. D. III. 100.
4. Bertrand Russell-A History of Western Philosophy, p. 566.
5. B.G. II. 64, 68, 70 & 71 (prasādam adhigacchati, tasya prajñā pratiṣṭhitā, śāntim adhigacchati.)

(E) *The Differences Between the B.G. and Buddhist Approach to Paranormal Knowledge* :—

Despite the aforesaid similarities between the B.G. and Buddhism, it may be noted that the former in emphasising the impact of desire on knowledge does not seem to be as penetrative and thorough-going as the latter. It has been pointed out in Buddhism that some of our subjective desires and habits of mind, if not completely purged off, may influence us even in the meditative state of mind, and may lead to wrong interpretation and evaluation of the knowledge gained through paranormal vision. Thus, unlike the B.G., Buddhism envisages the possibility of error even in the meditative knowledge. Buddha points out that the different metaphysical theories about the Self or Ātman are really based on wrong interpretations of the meditative experiences of the seers,[1] which perhaps are traceable to the influence of desire for immortality (bhava-diṭṭhi). In one of the causal statements made by Buddha it is pointd out that "on account of desire there is clinging (taṇhā paccayā upādānaṃ, M.I. 261). This clinging is said to be of four kinds, viz. clinging to (i) sense-pleasures (kāmupādānaṃ), (ii) to rituals (sīlabbatupādānaṃ), (iii) to metaphysical beliefs (diṭṭhupādānaṃ) and (iv) to soul or substance-theories (attavādupādānaṃ). Now, the last two are specially important for our purpose, since the doctrines of the B.G. embody metaphysical beliefs including a belief in the soul. The desires are analysed as three-fold, viz. the desire (i) for sense-gratification (kāma-taṇhā, M.I.48, 299, III. 250), (ii) for personal immortality (bhava-taṇhā, loc. cit.), and (iii) for annihilation[2] (vibhava-taṇhā, loc. cit.). The correlation of these specific desires (taṇhā) with the specific forms of clinging (upādāna) is not shown in the Pali texts, but it appears that the desire for sense-gratification

1. D.I. 13-16. The retrocongnitive knowledge of some previous states of life is shown to have led the man in meditation to conceive erroneously of an abiding and eternal substance called 'Ātman'.

2. The word 'vibhava-taṇhā' is also interpreted as 'desire for power'. Since the word 'vibhava' has both meanings (cf. P.T.S. Dictionary), both interpretations are possible. But 'annihilation' is the usual interpretation given in the commentaries (cf. Dialogues III. 208). At D.I. 22, we find 'vibhava' used as a synonym of uccheda (annihilation) and vināsa (destruction) : "Sato sattassa ucchedaṃ vināsaṃ vibha vaṃ..."

(kāma-taṇhā) would have been thought to produce clinging to sense-pleasures (kāmupādāna), and the desire for personal immortality and annihilation would have been considered to give rise respectively to the belief in the eternalistic and annihilationist theories of metaphysics. There was no need for showing specific correlatation of these desires with silabbatupādāna, diṭṭhupādāna and attavādupādana separately, perhaps because these three, on ultimate analysis, are found to be associated with the diṭṭhi or belief in some sort of metaphysical theories, either eternalist or annihilationist. The different rules of rituals and moral virtues (silabbata) are associated with one or the other of the metaphysical theories, and the substance-theory of the soul (attavāda) also is after all one of the metaphysical theories (diṭṭhi), otherwise known as 'sakkāya-diṭṭhi'. The latter, however, seems to have been separately mentioned on account of the wide-spread and deep-rooted belief in it.[1] Thus, according to the Buddhist analysis, it appears that the strong desire for personal immortality (bhava-taṇhā) would have led people to believe in a theory of personal immortality (bhava-diṭṭhi, A.I.83), while the strong desire for annihilation would have led them to believe in an annihilationist or materialistic theory (vibhavadiṭṭhi, M.I. 65). If this analysis is accepted, then the entire eternalistic theory of soul, advocated by the B.G., would appear to be rooted in a strong desire for personal immortality.

It is interesting to see that L.S. Stebbing also gives a similar analysis of the origin of the soul-theory. She observes: "There seems to be a deep-rooted tendency in the human mind to seek what is essential, in the sense of something, that persists through change..Hence the search for an *underlying* identity, a persistent stuff, a substance that is conserved... Hence, the popularity of substance theories in science."[2]

Besides this impact of desire, our linguistic habit of

---

1. According to the Buddhist view, the belief in 'I' or the sakkāya-diṭṭhi is so deep-rooted and vital that all the 62 erroneous theories enumerated in the Brahmajāla Sutta are said to be ultimately traceable to it. It is explicitly stated : Yāni cimāni dvāsaṭṭhi diṭṭhigatāni Brahmajāle bhaṇitāni...saākkyadiṭṭhiyā sati honti, sakkāyadiṭṭhiyā asati na honti ti, S. IV. 287.

2. A Modern Introduction to Logic, pp. 404-5.

calling ourselves 'I' must also have further facilitated the confusion between this grammatical subject and a metaphysical substance. We shall discuss this topic in detail in our subsequent chapter on metaphysics. Here we only wish to point out that in spite of the marked similarity between the B.G. and Buddhism in conceiving the higher knowledge as objective as well as in assigning reasons for this objectivity, they, nevertheless, differ as regards the thoroughness of the mental and moral preparedness, and, consequently, in relation to the nature and content of this knowledge.

Let us now exanine how they differ with regard to the nature and content of the higher knowledge. The higher knowledge claimed by the B.G., as already stated, is predominantly mystical as against the thoroughly naturalistic conception of Buddhism. Then again, what is revealed by this knowledge is also differently conceived. The B.G. (unlike Buddhism) identifies it with the ultimate Reality which, more often than not, is given a theological interpretation. The entire approach of the B.G. is metaphysical, whereas that of Buddhism is empirical and practical. The latter claims to have observed the essentially changing and transitory nature of things, their painful and unsubstantial character, and with the knowledge of the fourfold truth, it claims to realise the state of Nibbāna. But the B.G. claims to have discovered a permanent and blissful substance behind the transitory and painful elements of the world, on the basis of which it constructs its entire metaphysical and theological theories about Ātman, Brahanm and God.

Putting forward the theory of the permanent substance behind the changing phenomena of the universe, Kṛṣṇa asks Arjuna to realise, on the one hand, the worthlessness of the passing vicissitudes of life, which "come and go, are transitory, ...and are sources of suffering" (āgamāpāyino'nityāḥ, B.G.II. 14 and duḥkhayonayaḥ, B.G. V. 22) and to visualise, on the other hand, the importance of the true Reality, which is "indestructible permanent..unborn and unchanging" (avināśinaṃ nityaṃ..ajam avyayam, B.G. II. 21). The final truth of both the unreal (asat) and real (sat) is said to have been seen by the seers of the Reality (ubhayor api dṛṣṭo'ntas tv anayos tattvadarśibhiḥ, B.G. II. 16.). Now the eternal substance said to have been seen (supposedly through intuitive vision) is no other than the supreme Reality which is spoken of at times as personal[1] and at times as impersonal[2]. It is from this Reality that all beings proceed (yataḥ pravṛttir bhūtānām, B.G. XVIII. 46. cf. VII.6), are sustained (jīvanaṃ sarvabhūteṣu, B.G. VII.9) and to which ultimately all return (pralayas tathā, B.G. VII. 6). It is the all-inclusive Reality which excludes nothing[3], and so the true realisation of its nature means a complete merger with it,[4] known as salvation.

Buddhism, on the other hand, does not indulge in any such metaphysical or theological speculations. It simply claims to have gained insight into the dynamic and impermanent nature of the entire conditioned objects of the universe (sabbe saṅkhārā aniccā, Dh. 277), their painful character (sabbe saṅkhārā dukkhā, Dh. 278) and the unsubstantiality of all elements (sabbe dhammā anattā, DH. 279). It claims to have realised the four Noble Truths[5] and visualised the state of final deliverance or Nibbāna.[6] It emphatically repudiates the view that there is anything permanent and abiding discoverable in the universe.[7] There is no attempt here to construct a speculative theory of metaphysics. The highest truth, viz., Nibbān abeing essentially supra-mundane is considered inexplicable in terms of logic (atakkāvacara, D.I. 12), and is said to be an object of direct realisation and verifi-

1. B.G. VII. 6, 7; X. 8, 41 and 42.

2. B.G. VII. 24 and 25.

3. Mattaḥ parataraṃ nā'nyat kiñcid asti Dhanañjaya, B. G. VII. 7.

4. . . . .jñātuṃ draṣṭuṃ ca tattvena *praveṣṭuṃ* ca paraṃtapa, B. G. XI. 54; tato māṃ tattvato jñātvā *viśate* tadanantaram, B.G. XVIII. 55.

5. cattāri ariyasaccāni sammappaññāya passati Dh. 190; ariya saccāmi avecca passati, Sn. 40.

6. nibbāṇaṃ passeyyan ti, M. I. 511.

7. Attani ca bhikkhave attaniye ca saccato thetato anuplabbhamāne yaṃ pi idaṃ diṭṭhiṭṭhānaṃ—so loko, so attā, so pecca bhavissāmi nicco, dhuvo, sassato, aviparināmadhammo. . . .kevalo paripūro bāladhammo'ti M. I. 138.

cation by the wise.[1] In any case, there is no attempt to interpret this highest experience as the centre of the origination, sustenance and merger of all things and beings.

It is true that the B.G., in common with Buddhism, considers true knowledge as indispensable means to salvation[2], yet it is important to note that the sense in which knowledge is regarded as means to salvation in the B.G. is not quite the same as it is in Buddhism. The B.G., following its dominant metaphysical theory, believes that this knowledge consists in the realisation of the essential identity between the individual and the universal Soul.[3] As soon as one realises that the entire multiplicity is essentially centred in the One, salvation is secured.[4] The Soul is described in the B.G. as a transcendent principle which is always above change and mutation (avyayaḥ and avikāryaḥ, B.G. II. 17, 21, 25), and hence in reality it is never sullied by worldly impurities. Once this true nature of the Self is realised, one finds oneself released. There is nothing to acquire afresh, but only to recognise and realise what already stands accomplished and fulfilled. That is why the B.G. says: "To the knower of the Self, salvation exists all around"[5] or "the knower of Brahman is established in Brahman".[6] On theological plane the same is spoken of as merger of the individual self with the supreme Self or Paramātmaṃ.[7] This is how knowledge is supposed to bring about salvation according to the B.G.

But in Buddhism, the highest knowledge not being conceived metaphysically or theologically, the picture is quite

1. Sandiṭṭhiko akāliko ehipassiko opanayiko paccattaṃ veditabbo viññūhī ti, M. I. 37.

2. B.G. V. 29 (jñātva māṃ śāntim ṛcchati); IV. 32 (evaṃ jñātvā-vimokṣyase); XIII. 12 (yaj jñātvā'mṛtam aśnute) cf. M. III. 76 (sammā-ñāṇassa sammāvimutti pahoti).

3. sarvabhūtastham ātmānaṃ sarvabhūtani cā'tmani, B.G. VI. 29. VI. 30 and 31; kṣetrajñaṃ cā'pi māṃ viddhi, B.G. XIII. 2.

4. yadā bhūtapṛthagbhāvam ekastham anupaśyati
...Brahma saṃpadyate tadā, B.G. XIII. 30.

5. abhito Brahma nirvāṇaṃ vartate viditātmanām, B.G. V. 26.

6. Brahmavid Brahmaṇi sthitaḥ, B.G. V. 20.

7. bhaktyā tv ananyayā śakya aham evaṃvidho'rjuna
jñātuṃ draṣṭuṃ ca tattvena *praveṣṭum*, ca paraṃtapa, B G. XI. 54
bhaktyā mām abhijānāti. ..*viśate* tadanantaram, B.G. XVIII. 55.

different. Salvation consists in the destruction of all defilements (āsavakkhaya) which results from perfect insight into the cause of defilements and suffering and the way leading to their cessation. With the realisation of the fourfold Noble Truth, one clearly knows and sees the suffering, the cause of suffering, the cessation of suffering and the way leading to the cessation of suffering (Dh. 190-1), and with this knowledge and insight his "mind is freed from the defilements of sense-pleasures..defilements of becoming..defilements of ignorance. Being freed, the knowledge that 'freedom is achieved' dawns upon him. He knows, 'rebirth is exhausted, fulfilled is the holy-life, done what was to be done and nothing more is beyond this".[1] Thus, the entire approach of Buddhism is thoroughly practical, comepletely dissociated from metaphysical theorisation. What the B. G. claims to know and see in its intuitive vision (dhyānenā'tmani paśyanti kecid ātmānam ātmanā, B.G. XIII. 24; VI. 20, 29; XV. 11) is emphatically denied by Buddhism. It is declared in unequivocal terms: "Whatever is seen, heard, reflected, known, attained, searched for and contemplated upon by mind—that also is not mine, not the 'I' and not my self."[2] Again, unlike the B.G., the realisation of salvation by means of this knowledge is not conceived by Buddhism as a mere passive recognition of the eternally fulfilled and perfected state of the Self. On the other hand, it is considered as an active attainment, and realisation of what was hitherto unattained and unrealised. Buddha exhorts monks to strive "for the attainment of what is not attained, for knowledge of what is not known and the realisation of what is not realised".[3]

Thus we find that, in spite of knowledge being regarded as objective and as a means to salvation in both, its nature, content as well as its operational mechanism are conceived differently by the B.G. and Buddhism; the one conceives knowledge chiefly in an intuitive or mystical way, while the

1. M. I. 249.
2. M. I. 136.
3. S. II. 29; cf. A. IV. 385 (aññātam adiṭṭhaṃ appattaṃ asacchikataṃ, anabhisametaṃ, tassa ñāṇāya dassanāya pattiyā sacchikiriyāya, abhisamayāya Bhagavati brahmacariyaṃ vussatī ti)

other gives a naturalistic account of it; the one claims to have seen the true Ātman through it, while the other emphatically denies this; the one gives a metaphysical orientation to it, while the other confines itself to the observational data and direct practical considerations; the one claims to have recognised and realised what was already there, while the other declares to have attained and realised what was hitherto unattained and unrealised.

The process of knowledge :—

In Buddhism we find a thoroughly analytic, causal and naturalistic account of the process of knowledge, but in the B.G. no systematic analysis is met with, and causal and naturalistic explanations are often mixed up with mysterious, divine or supernatural elements. Besides, the details of the process are generally skipped over. It would, therefore, be more convenient to present first the Buddhist account of the process of knowledge and then to see in its light the position taken by the B.G.

(A) *The Buddhist Account of the Process of Knowledge*:—

The first striking peculiarity of the Buddhist account is its thoroughly naturalistic explanation of knowledge and its process. Not only with regard to normal sensory experience, but also in relation to the paranormal extra-sensory knowledge, the same naturalistic explanation is offered. As the Pali Canon puts it: "It is *in the nature of things* (dhammatā) that a person in the state of (meditative) concentration knows and sees the thing as it is. A person who knows and sees the thing as it is, does not need to make an effort of will to feel disinterested and renounce. It is *in the nature of things* that a person who knows and sees the thing as it is, feels disinterested and renounces. One who has felt disinterested and has renounced does not need to make an effort of will to realise the knowledge and insight of emancipation (vimutti-ñāṇadassanaṃ). It is *in the nature of things* that one who has felt disinterested and renounced, realises the knowledge and insight of emancipation".[1] Thus the explanation is always

1. A. V. 3, 313.

natural and not supernatural.

The second important characteristic feature of Buddhism is its uniformly causal explanation of things. Nowhere is an attempt made to explain things in a mysterious, mystical or unaccountable way. All things and events of the universe are supposed to be necessarily conditioned by other phenomena. This, indeed, is the central tenet of Buddhism which is explained in the words of Buddha himself as follows:—"This occurring, that occurs; this arising, that arises; this not occurring, that does not occur; this ceasing to be, that ceases to be".[1] The pivotal importance of this principle can well be realised from the fact that its knowledge is identified with the knowledge of the Dhamma itself. Buddha is said to have observed: "Whosoever sees the causal genesis of things (paṭiccasamuppādaṃ) sees the Dhamma and whosoever sees the Dhamma, sees the causal genesis of things."[2] It is, therefore, quite natural for Buddha to explain everything including the attainment of the highest knowledge and insight in well defined causal terms. He says : "A moral man..endowed with virtue is *causally* matured (upanisasampanno) for right concentration, having right concentration the man endowed with right concentration is *causally* matured for the true knowledge and insight, having true knowlege and insight the man endowed with true knowledge and insight is *causally* matured for renunciation and dispassion, having renunciation and dispassion, the man endowed with them is *causally* matured for the knowledge and insight of emancipation".[3] In fact, everything that Buddha teaches whether the knowledge of worldly suffering, or of the successive stages of moral discipline leading to concentration, or of the various stages of concentration, or of the higest state of the destruction of defilements (āsavakkhaya), he claims to teach in a 'causal way' (sa-upanisaṃ no anupanisaṃ, S.II.30).

---

1. Imasmiṃ sati idaṃ hoti, imass'uppādā idaṃ uppajjati; imasmiṃ asati idaṃ na hoti; imassa nirodhā idaṃ nirujjhati, M. III. 63.

2. Vuttaṃ kho pan'etaṃ Bhagavatā : Yo paṭiccasamuppādaṃ passati so dhammaṃ passati, yo dhammaṃ passati so paticcasamuppādaṃ passati, M. I. 190-1.

3. A. III. 20, 200.

The causes and conditions for the emergence and non-emergence of knowledge are dealt with in a detailed manner. It is said in this connection :—"When one dwells with one's mind obsessed with and given to passion and one does not truly know and see the elimination of the passion that has arisen, it is a cause of one's failure to know and see..(likewise) ill-will, sloth and torpor, excitement and perplexity, and doubt (are causes of one's failure to know and see.)"[1] On the other hand, the seven factors of enlightenment (satta-bojjhaṅga) are described as the cause and condition for the emergence of knowledge and insight.[2]

The five factors mentioned above as the factors responsible for the lack of knowledge and insight are the same as what is frequently described in the Nikāyas as 'the five impediments' (pañcanīvaraṇa, D.I.73; III. 234; M.I. 60, 144, 276; III. 4, 295). These five impediments constituting the cognitive, conative and affective factors[3], not only prevent the mind from being concentrated, and thus effect the emergence of extra-sensory or meditative (jhānic) perception, but also prove obstacles in the way of normal consciousness. A Brahmin named Saṅgārava asks Buddha: "What is the cause and reason, why at times even hymns which have been recited for a long time are not clearly recollected, not to speak of hymns not so recited; while at other times, even hymns not recited for a long time are easily recollected, not to speak of hymns recited for a long time?"[4] It is replied that this happens when the mind is affected by one or more of the five impediments which tend to cause forgetfulness.[5] Now

1. Yasmiṃ...samaye kāmarāgapariyuṭṭhitena cetasā viharati kāmarāgaparetena uppannassa ca kāmarāgassa nissaraṇaṃ yathābhūtaṃ na jānāti, na passati, ayam pi...hetu ayam paccayo aññāṇāya adassanāya... byāpāda...thīnamiddha...uddhaccakukkucca...vicikicchā..., S.V. 127.

2. S.V. 127-8.

3. Unlike the four 'agatigamanāni' (discussed earlier) which are emotional obstructions in the way of right knowledge, the five impediments enumerated here are the general causes of the lack of proper knowledge, taking into consideration the emotional factors as well as mental and physical lassitude (thīnamiddha).

4. A. III. 230.

5. A. III. 230-6.

the applicability of the same causal factors to both normal as well as paranormal knowledge shows that Buddha offers a natural and not a supernatural explanation for the emergence or nonemergence of both sensory as well as meditative experience. The same is indicated from the way in which these five impediments are often characterised in the Nikāyas. They are described as 'the defilements of the *mind* and factors which weaken *wisdom* (*cetaso* upakkilese *paññāya* dubbalīkaraṇe M.I. 181, 270, 276, 521; II. 28). Evidently, the word 'paññā' (wisdom) refers to the higher faculty of cognition in contradistinction to the normal mental faculty of cognition.[1]

When the mind is emancipated from these five defilements, it becomes lustrous (pabhassaraṃ, A. III. 17). This is explained with the simile of gold-ore. Gold-ore is said to have the defilements (jatarūpassa upakkilesā, A. III. 16) of iron, copper, tin, lead and silver, but when it is purified, it shines with its natural lustre.[2] Similarly the elimination of these five impediments is said to clear the way for the development of the pure meditative states (jhānas) of the mind. This process is gradual and is described as follows:- "When these five impediments are eliminated, he looks within himself and gladness (pāmujjaṃ) arises in him, and with gladness, joy (pīti), with his mind overjoyed his body becomes at ease (passambhati), and with his body at ease he experiences happiness (sukhaṃ), being happy his mind becomes concentrated (samādhiyati)".[3] Thus the state of concentration is preceded by the gradual stages of gladness, joy, bodily ease and happiness (pāmujjaṃ, pīti, passaddhi and sukhaṃ). Then follows the description of the first up to the fourth jhānas It is at this stage, on the attainment of the fourth jhāna "when the mind is concentrated, pure, cleansed, free from blemishes, purged of adventitious defilements, supple, pliant, steady and unperturbed" (evaṃ samāhite citte parisuddhe pariyodāte anaṅgaṇe vigatupakkilese mudubhūte

1. P.TS. Dictionary; cf. Mrs. Rhys Davids—Buddhism pp. 94, 103 and 201.

2. See also S. V. 92 and 93.

3. D. I. 73.

kammaniye ṭhite āneñjappatte, D I. 76) that he is said to "turn and direct his mind to knowing and seeing" (ñāṇadassanāya cittaṃ abhinīharati abhininnāmeti, loc. cit.). It is said that in this state the mind has a direct introspection of one's consciousness associated with the body.[1] Then he proceeds to the attainment of the following sixfold higher knowledge (Chaḷabhiññā) :—

1. iddhividhā i.e. psychokinesis e.g. assuming multiple forms, moving at one's will, etc.
2. dibbasotadhātu i.e. clairaudience.
3. cetopariyañāṇa i.e. telepathic knowledge.
4. pubbenivāsānussatiñāṇa i.e. retrocognitive knowledge.
5. dibbacakkhu or cutūpapātañāṇa i.e. clairvoyance or the knowledge of the decease and survival of beings.
6. āsavakkhayañāṇa i.e. knowledge of the destruction of defiling impulses.

Thus, it is clear that according to Buddhism, the attainment of wisdom (paññā) and consequent salvation (vimutti) by means of concentration (samādhi) is conceived as naturalistic, causally accountable and capable of clear and systematic analysis. There is nothing mystical, mysterious or supernatural about it. Buddha points out how by using one's own efforts and powers one is gradually led to the highest goal, viz., the enlightenment and emancipation. Addressing the monks he exhorts as follows :—"O monks, there are these five powers..the power of faith (saddhābalaṃ), the power of energy (viriyabalaṃ), the power of mindfulness (satibalaṃ), the power of concentration (samādhibalam), and the power of insight (paññābalaṃ)..., a monk who cultivates and makes much of these five powers is one who flows to Nibbāna, slides to Nibbāna and tends to Nibbāna."[2] Obviously these five are man's own natural faculties which he is asked to use for the realisation of the highest goal. That is why they are also known as 'the five faculties' (pañcindriyāni). Buddha just

---

1. Ayam kho me kāyo rūpi...idañ ca pana me viññāṇaṃ ettha sitaṃ ettha paṭibaddhaṃ ti. D.I. 76.

2. S. V. 249.

after the attainment of perfect enlightenment (paṭhamābhisambuddho) reflects about the process of his own attainment as follows: "There are five faculties which cultivated and made use of plunge one into the Deathless, have their end and culmination in the Deathless. What five? The faculty of faith...energy...mindfulness...concentration...and insight."[1] Thus the highest knowledge with the consequent emancipation is said to be realised gradually in a natural way by awakening and harnessing one's own faculties.

(B) *The Approach of the B.G. as Compared with that of Buddhism*:—

In the light of the Buddhist account of the process of knowledge we may now examine the B. G.'s point of view.

The B. G. account does not follow any one strict line. At places, we find some naturalistic and causal explanations analysing things stage by stage. But elsewhere this method seems to be abandoned, and a supernatural or divine colouring given to the whole account. Besides, the details of the process are often skipped over, and the discussion pertaining to a topic is not carried on systematically. We shall first see whatever naturalistic, causal and analytic accounts of the process of knowledge are to be had in the B.G., and then judging them in the light of the Buddhist account, try to point out how, unlike the latter, it has been mixed up with the elements of theological and mystical explanations.

A naturalistic accuont seems to be offered when the B.G. emphasises the role of man's own desire (kāma) in the emergence and non-emergence of knowledge. It is pointed out in a general way that man is deluded when his knowledge is covered up by ignorance (ajñānena).[2] Now, the main factor responsible for this ignorance is said to be the desire (kāma) which blurs the vision and leads one to commit evil deeds. Kṛṣṇa points out : "Wisdom is enveloped O Arjuna, by this insatiable fire of *desire* which is the constant

1. S. V. 232.
2. Ajñānenā'vṛtaṃ jñānaṃ tena muhyanti jantavaḥ. B.G. V. 15.

foe of the wise."[1] It is this which leads man astray and impels him to commit sin.[2] Therefore an aspirant who practises yogic concentration with a view to attaining higher knowledge is asked to "abandon without residue all desires born of selfish thought."[3] One has to free oneself of all desires (kāmān...sarvān) in order to attain true knowledge and real peace.[4]

After having stated that desire is the root cause of the lack of knowledge and the consequent evil, the B. G. propounds its main thesis of desireless action (niṣkāma-karma), through which right knowledge and consequent salvation are said to be attained. It is pointed out : "Nothing is here purifying like knowledge, and that (knowledge), in course of time, is naturally attained by one who has perfected himself in the yoga (of desirelessness)."[5] Thus the man free from desire attains knowledge and consequent salvation, and is not bound by his actions (na karmāṇi nibadhnanti, B. G. IV. 41).

This shows that the B. G. here tries to explain the emergence or non-emergence of knowledge in a natural way in terms of one's mind being free from or overpowered by selfish desires. It is indicated that the *natural factor* responsible for ignorance and bondage is one's own lustful action (karma) which when neutralised or destroyed by desirelessness, the right vision or knowledge with the consequent salvation is attained. It is worth noting that like Buddhism, the B. G. also takes into consideration the vital force of karma (gahanā karmaṇo gatiḥ, B. G. IV. 17). In fact, it is its primary purpose to suggest ways and means for the attainment of that knowledge whereby one may cut away the bond of karma (buddhyā yukto yayā pārtha *karmabandhaṃ* prahāsyasi, B.G. II. 39). The B.G., despite its dominant theological emphasis, seems to be anxious to say that the Divinity

1. B.G. III. 39.
2. B.G. III. 36-37.
3. Saṅkalpaprabhavān kāmāṃs tyktvā sarvān aśeṣataḥ, B.G. VI. 24
4. Vihāya kāmān yaḥ sarvān. . .sa śāntim adhigacchati. B.G. II. 71; cf. B.G. III. 36-43 (...jahi śatruṃ mahābāho kāmarūpaṃ durasadam).
5. B.G. IV. 38.

does not come in the way of the natural law of karma.[1] God is only the custodian of karmas who disinterestedly (udāsīnavat, B G. IX. 9) operates them without any bias or favour.[2] It is an important point to note, for it is chiefly through this method that the B. G. seeks to suggest a compromise between its purely naturalistic and dominantly theological utterances.

Although it is not quite relevant for our purpose to discuss here in detail the compatibility or non-compatibility of the naturalistic utterances with the supernaturalistic ones, it may be useful to keep in mind the general line of compromise suggested by the B. G. As pointed out above, the B. G. believes in the potency of karma. It explicitly points out that the righteous and non-righteous actions have their respective good and evil consequences. "The fruit of good action, they say, is good and pure in nature, while the fruit of passion is pain, and the fruit of dullness is ignorance."[3] This natural account of the karmic law is sought to be reconciled with the pronounced theological stanzas[4] by conceiving God as a disinterested regulator of karmic processes. Kṛṣṇa says: "I am impartial to all beings. None is hateful or dear to me" (B. G. IX. 29). In highly coloured passages where God is regarded as "the final goal, supporter, lord, witness, abode, shelter, friend, origin and dissolution, ground, resting place and imperishable seed",[5] Kṛṣṇa tries to clarify the position by saying: "These actions do not bind me, O Arjuna, for I hold myself as if indifferent and unattached to these actions";[6] "the all pervading Spirit (Vibhu) does not take on the sin or merit of anyone. Creatures are bewildered because their knowledge

1. B.G. IV. 14; V. 14, 15 (Na kartṛtvaṃ na karmāṇi lokasya sṛjati prabhuḥ. . . ., Nā'datte kasyacit pāpaṃ na cai'va sukṛtaṃ vibhuḥ)

2. B.G. IX. 7-9 (Na ca māṃ tāni karmāṇi nibadhnanti dhanañjaya, udāsīnavad āsīnam asaktaṃ teṣu karmasu); VIII. 18 and 19.

3. B.G. XIV. 16.

4. B.G. XII. 7; XVIII. 56-58.

5. B.G. IX. 18ff.

6. B.G. IX. 9.

is enveloped in ignorance."[1] When Kṛṣṇa makes the statement, "my devotee is dear to me" (madbhaktaḥ sa me priyaḥ, XII. 14 ff) in flagrant contradiction to his previous statement, "none is hateful or dear to me" (na me dveṣyo'sti na priyaḥ, IX. 29), he tries to reconcile it by pointing out that the devotee deserves this love by virtue of his own righteous deeds (XII. 14-20). So this love or favour is shown to coincide with simple justice. Even when the B. G. refers to "a man of most vile conduct worshipping God" (IX. 30), it is said that "he soon converts himself into a righteous man' (kṣipraṃ bhavati dharmātmā, IX. 31) by virtue of his rightly settled (samyag vyavasitaḥ, IX. 30) mind.[2] All these statements indicate that the B. G. is all the time anxious to suggest a way of reconciling the apparent contradictions between its naturalistic and supernaturalistic propositions. It is, however, yet to be seen how far it succeeds in doing so.

The cause-effect relation also is a general presupposition of the B.G., and the action undertaken without considering its effect or result (anubandhaṃ) among other things is said to be of inert nature (tāmasam).[3] The factors leading to the failure of knowledge are causally analysed[4] and the gradual processes leading to concentration (samādhi)[5] and knowledge (prajñā)[6] are also explained

1. B.G. V. 15.

2. Śaṅkara points out that one soon becomes a righteous man "by abandoning external evil conduct through his internal power of right resolve" (utsṛjya ca bāhyāṃ durācāratām antaḥ-samyagvyavasāyasāmarthyāt, Introduction to S.B.G. IX. 31).

3. B.G. XVIII. 25. The teaching of disinterested or desireless action (niṣkāma-karma) requires only the renunciation of selfish desires or lustful attachment to the fruit. It does not enjoin blind action, having no idea of the result whatsoever. M.K. Gandhi tries to clarify the position as follows :"...renunciation of fruit in no way means indifference to the result. In regard to every action one must know the result that is expected to follow, the means thereto and the capacity for it. He, who being thus equipped, is without desire for the result and is yet wholly engrossed in the due fulfilment of the task before him, is said to have renounced the fruits of his action...Renunciation means absence of hankering after fruit..." —Gita the Mother pp. 9-10.

4. B.G. II. 62-64.

5. B.G. II. 64-66.

6. B.G. II. 61, 68.

through the cause-effect relation, though these discussions are not as detailed and distinct as they are found in the Pali Nikāyas.

Let us now look to the causes and conditions spoken of by the B. G. for the emergence and non-emergence of knowledge and the processes involved in them. As stated, already, we cannot find here a systematic enumeration of the various factors leading to the emergence or non-emergence of knowledge at one place. We have already noted that desire (kāma) is one of the basic obstacles in the way of knowledge, which envelops the latter (āvṛtaṃ jñānam etena, B. G. III. 39), and distracts the vision (kāmaiḥ..hṛtajñānāḥ, B. G. VII. 20). The passionate desires are said to create delusion (moha) and perplexity or bewilderment (citta-vibhrama)[1], and therefore they also are mentioned as impediments of knowledge. Arjuna, for example, fails to have the proper knowledge of his duty (na cai' tad vidmaḥ.., B. G. II. 6) because of his deluded mind (saṃmūḍhacetāḥ, B. G. II. 7). Similarly in order to attain meditative vision mind has to be made free from perplexity (anudvignamanāḥ, B. G. II. 56). Again on account of passionate selfish desire (kāmabhoga) one develops attachment (rāga) for some and aversion or hatred (dveṣa) against others. Therefore, one is asked to be perfectly free from them.[2] Remaining free from hatred or ill-will in relation to all beings (adveṣṭā sarvabhūtānām, B. G. XII. 13), is counted as the first virtue among the various virtues enumerated by the B. G., and wise men are said to be men of equanimity (paṇḍitāḥ samadarśinaḥ, B. G. V. 18). Only he who sees all alike is said to see things aright (samaṃ sarveṣu bhūteṣu..yaḥ paśyati sa paśyati, B.G. XIII. 27). All these are, evidently, emotional impediments of knowledge. But besides them, the B.G. speaks of physical and mental lassitude as well, which when not surmounted, prove impediments in the way of the emergence of proper knowledge. Thus, in the course of prescribing conditions for concentration (yoga) aimed at higher knowledge,

---

1. Aneka *citta vibhrāntā moha*jāla, samāvṛtāḥ, prasaktāḥ *kāmabhogesu*. . ., B.G. XVI. 16; *Kāmāt* krodho'bhijāyate, krodhāt bhavati *saṃmohaḥ*, saṃmohāt *smṛti-vibhramaḥ*..., B.G. II. 62 and 63.

2. B.G. II. 64 (Rāgadveṣa viyuktais tu.....)

it is pointed out that it can be attained by one "whose attempts at actions are regulated" (yuktaceṣṭasya karmasu, B.G. VI. 17). The same is confirmed when sloth or inactivity and negligence (apravṛtti and pramāda) are listed along with non-illumination and delusion (aprakāśa and moha) as the products of the preponderant state of dullness (tamasi vivṛddhe, B.G. XIV, 13), and knowledge is said to be produced by its opposite, namely, sattva (sattvāt saṃjāyate jñānam, B.G. XIV, 17). Dullness (tamas) only gives rise to negligence, delusion and ignorance or lack of knowledge (pramāda, moha and ajñāna, loc. cit). Besides this negligence sloth or inactivity, the B.G. further asks us to give up doubt which, if not duly removed, may lead to ruin (saṃśayātmā vinaśyati, B.G. IV. 40). Therefore doubt must be dissipated by developing proper knowledge (jñānasaṃchinna-saṃśayam, B.G. IV. 41).

Now if we put together all these factors mentioned by the B.G. as impediments of knowledge, we can see that they include under one name or another, all the five impediments of knowledge enumerated by Buddhism. As the words used by these systems of thought had not till then assumed strict technical rigidity, it would be too much to demand from them the use of exactly the same word to convey a particular idea. Thus, granting some liberty for the use of synonyms, we can see that their approach to the problem of the emergence and non-emergence of knowledge is close to each other. We may give below the words used by the B.G. as corresponding to the five impediments spoken of by Buddhism :—

	Buddhism	B.G.
1.	kāmarāga	kāma or kāmabhoga (passionate desire)
2.	byāpāda	dveṣa (ill-will or hatred)
3.	thīnamiddha	aceṣṭā, apravṛtti or pramāda (sloth, inactivity or negligence).
4.	uddhaccakukkucca	udvignamanaḥ, cittavibhrama or moha (perplexity, bewilderment or delusion)
5.	vicikicchā	saṃśaya (doubt)

It is evident, however, that the account of the B.G., in contradistinction to that of Buddhism, is scattered and unsystematic.

After bringing the senses under control and cleansing the mind of impediments and impurities, one is gradually led to the stage of concentration which entitles him to attain the state of sthita-prajña (settled wisdom). In the B.G., however, unlike Buddhism, the successive stages leading to concentration (samādhi), viz. pāmujjaṃ. pītī, passaddhi and sukhaṃ are not clearly and systematically enumerated. The reference seems to be made in a general way as follows: "A man of disciplined mind who moves among objects, with the senses under his control and free from attachment and aversion, comes to attain *gladness* (prasādam). With gladness arisen all his troubles (caused by the contact with outer nature[1]) come to an end, for the mind being *overjoyed* (prasannacetaso) his intellect soon attains stability. He who is uncontrolled has no intelligence nor has he (serenity of) thought. Having no such thought, he can have no *peace* (śāntiḥ) and for the unpeaceful, how can there be *happiness* (sukha)?"[2] But when all these conditions are fulfilled, one is said to enter the state of concentration in which he attains unwavering meditative wisdom (tasya prajñā pratiṣṭhitā, B.G. II. 68). Now, although the above quoted verses do not clearly and systematically enumerate the successive stages leading to concentration, they yet seem to follow a line similar to that of Buddhism. We may compare the stages mentioned above by the B.G. with those of Buddhism as follows:—

Buddhism	*B.G.*
pāmujjaṃ	prasādam (gladness)
pīti	prasannatā (joy)
passaddhi	śānti (peace)
sukha	sukha (happiness)

It is, of course, not possible to be very definite whether

1. Rāmānuja takes it in this very sense. To quote his words: "*prakṛti-saṃsarga-prayukta* sarvaduḥkhānāṃ hāniḥ, "R.B.G. II. 65.
2. B.G. II. 64-66.

all these corresponding words of the B.G., as presented here, have accurately the same import as those of Buddhism. Again it is doubtful whether the words 'prasāda' and 'prasannatā' used by the B.G. are intended to be taken as synonyms, as Śaṅkara[1] understands them, or as two successive stages as suggested above. In case the idea suggested above is not accepted and Śaṅkara's interpretation is favoured, then the second stage, viz., 'joy' will have to be considered as having been skipped over by the B.G. But in any case, it cannot be denied that both the B.G. and Buddhism mention similar stages leading to concentration, and that the difference is mainly one of clarity and systematisation.

Buddhism, however, as usual follows its analytic method even in describing the various stages of concentration (samādhi), and, according to it, one directs one's mind for the attainment of higher knowledge only after the fourth stage of concentration. But in the B.G. no such analysis of the stages of samādhi is found, though all the six kinds of higher knowledge spoken of by Buddhism are accepted by it, as we shall see in the sequel.

In the Buddhist account of knowledge we have noted that the highest knowledge and consequent salvation is attainable by the use of man's own powers or faculties viz. saddhā, viriya, sati, samādhi and paññā.Now, we can see that all these five are mentioned by the B.G. as well, though as usual, they are stated unsystematically. It is, however, possible to see how they are supposed to be connected according to the B.G. There is no doubt about the fact that the highest truth is said to be attainable through the faculty of wisdom (jñāna or prajñā). It is stated: "Those who are deluded, do not see; those who have the eye of *wisdom* (jñāna-cakṣuṣaḥ) see,"[2] and "those who know through the eye of *wisdom* (jñāna cakṣuṣā)...reach the highest".[3] This highest vision is said to be realised through *concentration*

1. Śaṅkara clearly says : "Prasādaḥ prasannatā..." —S.B.G. II. 64. Rāmānuja, however, takes the word 'prasāda' in the sense of inner purity (nirmalāntaḥkaraṇo, R.B.G. II. 64).

2. Vimūḍhā na'nupśyanti, paśyanti jñāna-cakṣuṣaḥ, B.G. XV. 10.

3. ...jñānacakṣuṣā...ye vidur yānti te param, B.G. XIII. 34.

(dhyānenā'tmani paśyanti, B.G. XIII. 24). Only "he who has harmonised himself by yoga can see" (īkṣate yoga yuktātmā, B.G. VI. 29). It is for this reason that the man who has reached the state of *concentration* (samādhistha) is said to have established himself in *wisdom* (sthita-prajña).[1] His intellect is said to be firmly established or stabilised (tasya prajñā pratiṣṭhitā, B.G. II. 68, or buddhiḥ paryavatiṣṭhate, B.G. II. 65). But if this intellect (buddhi) is misguided, it leads to spiritual ruination (buddhināśāt praṇa yati, B G. II. 63). This misguidance is said to be caused by *perversity of remembrance* (smṛtibhraṃśāt buddhināśo, loc. cit.). In other words, the right setting of the intellect in meditative peace is supposed to be conditioned by proper remembrance or *mindfulness* (Smṛti). But at the same time this also is made clear by the B.G. that without proper effort and energy it is not possible to attain yoga or concentration. Yoga or concentration can be attained only by him "who makes proper *effort*" (yukta ceṣṭasya, B.G. VI.17). Only the *striving* yogins can attain the meditative vision (yatanto yoginaś cai'naṃ paśyanti, B.G. XV. 11) Again, it is necessary to follow the spiritual pursuit with *faith* (śraddhā) and not with doubt, for the doubtful one is said to meet with ruin (saṃśayātmā vinaśyati, B.G. IV. 40), whereas the person with faith with proper effort and sense-control is said to attain knowledge (śraddhāvāṃl labhate jñānam, B.G. IV. 39).

Thus we see that according to the B. G. one is supposed to reach the highest goal gradually by making use of śraddhā (faith), ceṣṭā (effort), smṛti (remembrance or mindfulness), samādhi (concentration) and jñāna or prajñā (wisdom) which are almost the same as the five powers or faculties (pañcabalāni or pañcindriyāni) of Buddhism. We shall, however, see in the sequel that the concept of faith (śraddhā) in the B. G. and Buddhism is not quite the same.

From what has been shown above, it is clear that B. G. also, somewhat like Buddhism, suggests a naturalistic and causal account of the process of knowledge. The various

1. B.G. II. 54.

impediments of knowledge, the stages leading to concentration as well as the utilisation of various faculties to realise the true wisdom and consequent salvation are also described approximately in similar ways. But the two accounts have certain differentiating features as well which must not be overlooked. Buddhism, as we have found, is quite straightforward, thorough, systematic and clear in its accounts, whereas the B. G. is mostly vacillating, scrappy, unsystematic and at places ambiguous. In order to get a complete picture of the B.G. position with regard to any problem, we have seen, one has to collect the scattered references from the entire body of the text and then to examine them by arranging relevant matters in their proper order. But in Buddhism, position is mostly clear, distinct and well analysed. Then again, the B. G. can be most sharply distinguished from Buddhism on account of the amalgamation of metaphysical and theological elements in its explanations. The true knowledge revealed to the seer in the state of meditation is metaphysically conceived as the revelation of the Supreme Ātman or Brahman[1], and is theologically considered as the result of God's grace[2]. God is said to destroy the ignorance of his devotees, and arouse knowledge in them by his grace.[3] Arjuna is clearly told: "By unswerving devotion, O Arjuna, I can be thus truly known, seen and entered into, O Arjuna."[4] These and other such highly devotional verses apparently seem to overthrow all its causal and naturalistic accounts of knowledge and salvation, though the B. G., as indicated above, tries to suggest a line of compromise between them. As a matter of fact, the B. G. seldom cares to follow an uniform explanation, and the demand for rational or logical consistency is often ignored or drowned amidst its dominantly poetic and mystical utterances. But Buddhism on account of its thoroughly naturalistic and rational approach, does not at any stage bring in theological considerations, and thus keeps itself free of all such difficulties.

1. B.G. VI. 29, XIII. 24, XV. 11.
2. B.G. X. 10, 11; XI. 47, 54; XVIII. 55, 56, 58, 62 and 73.
3. B.G. X. 10 and 11.
4. B.G. XI. 54.

The Sources of Knowledge :—

The B. G. is found to rely on three independent sources of knowledge, viz., perception (normal and para-normal), inference (based on both kinds of perception) and authority or testimony. But in early Buddhism only the first two are accepted as the valid sources of knowledge. The third one is criticised and rejected.

According to S. Radhakrishnan, however, "Early Buddhism. . . . seems to have accepted analogy and authority also."[1] It is later that "Maitreya discarded analogy and Dignāga discarded authority."[2] Radhakrishnan bases his view on the account given in Sarvasiddhāntasārasṅgraha[3] which, obviously, cannot carry much weight if its views are at variance with those expressed in the Pali Nikāyas. Now, the Nikāyas are clearly against considering analogy and authority as separate independent sources of knowledge. Analogy is supposed to be just an aid to understanding. It is used with a view to elucidating the meaning of a statement, to facilitate the understanding of the ideas expressed, and not as a separate and independent way of knowing. It is clearly stated: "A simile...is employed in order to make clear the sense" (upamā...katā atthassa viññāpanāya, M. I. 155; III. 275; It. 114) or that "some intelligent people understand the meaning of what is said by means of a simile" (upamāya pi idhekacce viññū purisā bhāsitassa attham ājānanti, D. II. 324, 330). Then, the criticism of the different forms of authority is so patent in the Nikāyas (A. I. 189; II. 191-3) that it can hardly be considered as an independent means of knowledge acceptable to early Buddhism. It is, however, true that authority has not been rejected on the ground of being definitely false (as is done by the materialists), but on the ground of being doubtful, i. e. being either true or false (and so undependable as a primary and independent source of knowledge). It is admitted that if one has 'personal knowledge' (attanā vā jāneyyātha A. II. 191), he may take into account the views of the wise

---

1. Indian Philososphy, Vol, I, 462 footnote 3.
2. Ibid p. 462 footnote 3; J.A.S. of Bengal, 1905, p. 179.
3. Sarvasiddhāntasārasaṅgraha III. 4.4. 18-22.

and see whether it has been deprecated or appreciated by them (viññūgarahitā vā viññūpasatthā vā, loc. cit.) But this can only mean that early Buddhism grants a secondary or confirmatory value to testimony of others based on their experiences. But it cannot be taken to mean that authority is recognised by early Buddhism as an independent valid source of knowledge. As a matter of fact, within certain limits reason or *a priori* argument (takka) also has been utilised by Buddhism, as also by the B. G., but this does not mean that any one of them regards it as a separate independent source of knowledge. Buddha, on the other hand, calls his Dhamma as 'beyond pure reasoning' (atakkāvacaro, D. I. 12; M. I. 167) being based on his direct personal experience (ye Tathāgato sayaṃ abhiññā sacchikatvā pavedeti, D. I. 12). His non-acceptance of authority and reason as independent valid means of knowledge (pramāṇa) is well evidenced from his address to the Kālāmas (A. I. 189) and to Bhaddiya Licchavi (A. II. 191-3) where he criticises six ways of knowing based on authority and four ways of knowing based on reason. It is also clearly borne out from the threefold classification[1] made by Buddha of his predecessors and contemporaries in respect of the ways of knowing, viz., (i) the Traditionalists (Anussavikā), (ii) the Rationalists and Metaphysicians (Takkī and Vimaṃsī) and (iii) the Experientialists, from among whom he associates himself with the last ones.[2] This class is said to consist of those seers who professed the doctrines on direct personal experience. The B. G. also despite its reliance on authority, may with some justification be classed along with the Buddhists in the last group, since, like Buddhism, it also lays claim to direct personal knowledge of the higher truths.[3] The first category to which the Tevijja (followers of the three Vedas) belong, does not suit it,

1. See for a detailed discussion of the threefold classification, Early Buddhist Theory of Knowledge by K. N. Jayatilleke, pp. 170 ff.

2. M. II. 211.

3. tāny ahaṃ veda sarvāṇi, B. G. IV. 5; Dhyānenā'tmani paśyanti, B.G. XIII. 24; Yatanto yoginaś cai'nam paśyanti. . ., B.G. XV. 11.

since it clearly looks down upon the Vedas.[1] The second class of the Rationalists also does not fit it, since 'reason' according to it is considered inadequate to realise the higher truths.[2]

Thus we see that early Buddhism recognises only two sources of valid knowledge, viz., perception and inference, and the B. G. believes in three, viz., perception, inference and authority or testimony. We shall now make a comparative assessment of these ways of knowing as they appear in Buddhism and the B. G.

(*A*): *Perception*:—

We have already noted that both the B. G. and Buddhism, notwithstanding their emphasis on paranormal perception for the higher holy life, recognise the validity of normal perception for practical life. The value of the latter is so evident that it has been simply taken for granted. It is regarded as the very basis and presupposition of all knowledge. But the range and value of it being limited, a greater emphasis is laid on paranormal perception.

The Pali Canon refers to the sixfold higher knowledge which Buddha[3] and some of his disciples[4] are found to have attained. It is mentioned that "out of five hundred monks, sixty have attained the sixfold higher knowledge"[5]. This sixfold knowledge enumerated already (supra. p. 187) is said to be attained gradually after the fourth jhāna.

In the B. G., unlike Buddhism, there is no attempt to enumerate the different kinds of higher knowledge (paranormal perception) systematically, but in the course of its dialogue, the B. G. directly or indirectly refers to all the six kinds of it described by Buddhism. We shall first see how they occur in Buddhism and the B. G. and then point out the differences in their treatment.

The first kind of this higher knowledge consists according

1. B.G. II. 42-46; IX. 20, XI. 53 (nā'ham Vedair na tapasā...).

2. The true Reality is said to be beyond reason (acintya, B.G. II. 25; VIII. 9.)

3. M. I. 69.

4. S. II. 217, 222.

5. Pañcannaṃ bhikkhusatānaṃ....saṭṭhi bhikkhū chaḷabhiññā, S.I. 191.

to Buddhaghosa in the manifestations of various 'powers of will' (adhiṭṭhānā iddhi, Vm. 405), e. g. to assume multiple forms, to appear or disappear at will, to move freely without obstruction in or on earth, water and sky, and so forth. Their nature and significance have been discussed in detail by Lindquist.[1] We find references to Buddha and some of his disciples displaying some such powers[2] when there is any need for them, though normally such demonstrations are discouraged.[3] In the B. G. also we get a glimpse of these powers when Kṛṣṇa on the request of Arjuna assumes cosmic-form which is "a hundred-fold, a thousand-fold, various in kind, divine, of various colours and shapes. . . with numberless arms, bellies, faces and eyes" etc.[4]

The second higher knowledge, viz., the clairaudience is conceived as a paranormal capacity to hear sounds of both human and non-human beings, whether far or near. As the Nikāyas put it : "With one's clairaudience, clear and paranormal, one hears both sounds—human and divine—far and near".[5] It is thus an extension of the normal auditory capacity, both in degree (extent) as well as in quality (depth or intensity). It is by means of this faculty that Buddha is said to have heard the conversation between the Brahmin, Bhāradvāja and the wandering ascetic Māgandiya while sitting far away beneath a tree in the forest.[6] Even his disciple Mahāmoggallāna claims to have had direct discourse with Buddha while the former was staying at Rājagaha and the latter at Sāvatthi by utilising their respective powers of clairvoyance and clairaudience.[7] Then again, we find Buddha

1. Siddhi und Abhiññā, pp. 12-65.

2. D. II. 89, M.I. 253-4, 326, 330.

3. Buddha disapproving the idea of displaying such powers says to Kevaḍḍha:—"Na kho ahaṃ Kevaḍḍha bhikkhūnaṃ evaṃ dhammaṃ desemi : 'Etha tumhe bhikkhave gihīnaṃ odātavasanānaṃ uttari-manussa-dhammā iddhi-pāṭihāriyaṃ karothā' ti," D.I. 211.

4. B G XI. 5 ff.

5. dibbāya sotadhātuyā visuddhāya attikkantamānusikāya ubho sadde suṇāti, dibbe ca mānuse ca, ye dūre santike ca. D.I. 79; M. II. 19.

6. M.I. 502.

7. S. II. 276.

explaining to Oṭṭhaddha as to why Sunakkhatta after following three years of training in the Order could attain the ability of only seeing beautiful figures and not of hearing their voices, though the latter also was equally possible to attain.[1]

This kind of clairaudience seems to be the presupposition of the B.G. as well. As a matter of fact, the whole of the B.G. is presented in the form of a narration of war-events to Dhṛtarāṣṭra by Sañjaya who is endowed with the capacity of seeing and hearing directly whatever is taking place in the distant battle-field. Not only does he hear the dialogue between human beings like Duryodhana and Droṇācārya (B.G. II. 2-11) and ordinary sounds like those of conches, kettle-drums, tabors and trumpets (B.G. II. 12-19) but he also listens to the divine discourse of Kṛṣṇa himself when the latter speaks to Arjuna in his cosmic form (B.G. XI. 5ff, 32ff). Sañjaya himself tells about this power of clairaudience bestowed upon him by Vyāsa as follows : "Thus have I *heard* (aśrauṣam) this wonderful and horripilating dialogue between Vāsudeva (Kṛṣṇa) and the high-souled Arjuna. By the grace of Vyāsa I have *heard* (śrutavān) this supreme secret of Yoga being told directly (sākṣāt) by Kṛṣṇa, the Lord of Yoga, himself.".[2]

The next higher knowledge enumerated in the Pali Canon is telepathic knowledge (cetopariya-ñāṇa). Two types of description of this knowledge are presented by the Nikāyas which seem to suggest that two kinds of telepathic knowledge are known to early Buddhism : the one revealing the general state of another's mind, and the other disclosing the specific thoughts and ideas of it. According to the first description, it is said that "he comprehends with his mind the mind of other beings (cetasā ceto paricca pajānāti), a passionate mind he knows to be passionate, a dispassionate mind he knows to be dispassionate, (like-wise) he knows a mind full of hatred and free from hatred, ignorant and devoid of ignorance, attentive and inattentive, exalted and unexalted, inferior and superior, concentrated and distracted, emancipated and unemancipated."[3]

1. D.I. 152 ff.
2. B G. XVIII. 74-75.
3. D.I. 80-81.

By means of this knowledge Anuruddha, the well known disciple of Buddha tells the latter about the spiritual attainments of his fellow-monks, Nandiya and Kimbila. On being interrogated by them as to how he could know about their attainments without being told by them, Anuruddha says : "I know by my mind the minds of the venerable ones, to the effect that the venerable ones are acquirers of this and that meditative attainment" (M.I. 210). Utilising this very power of knowing the other's mind, these three fellow-monks live together adjusting their minds in such a way as to have veritably one mind, despite having different bodies (Nānā hi kho no...kāyā, ekañ ca pana maññe cittam, M.I. 207). According to another description it is said that "one can read the mind, the states of mind, the thoughts and the trains of thought of other beings and individuals" (parasattānaṃ parapuggalānam cittaṃ pi ādisati cetasikam pi...vitakkitam pi...vicāritaṃ pi..., D.I. 213). We get numerous such examples where Buddha is said to have known the specific thoughts of others' minds. He comes to know, for example, the specific thought in the mind (ceto parivitakkaṃ) of the Brahmin student, Kāpaṭhika who, being anxious to put questions to Buddha, was desiring that the latter should look to his side. Buddha turns his eyes towards Kāpaṭhika by knowing the specific thought of his mind (Bhagavā Kāpaṭhikassa māṇavassa cetasā ceto parivitakkam aññāya yena Kāpaṭhiko māṇavo tena cakkhūni upasaṃhāsi, M. II. 169). Similarly Buddha knows the specific thought of the mind of the Brahmin Soṇadaṇḍa who was thinking within himself that Buddha should question him in his own field of the Vedic learning (sake ācariyake tevijjake pañhaṃ puccheyya, D.I. 119), and accordingly asks him what he wanted. When Sunakkatta, at the sight of the behaviour of the naked ascetic, Korakkhattiya takes him for a perfect saint (arahaṃ samaṇo), Buddha at once knows this specific thought of his mind, and rebukes him for his wrong notion.[1]

The Pali Canon describes four ways of knowing another's mind (both in the normal and paranormal senses): (i) by

1. D. III. 6-7.

observing external signs (nimittena, A.I. 170), (ii) by getting information from human or nonhuman beings (manussānaṃ vā amanussānaṃ vā..saddaṃ sutvā, A.I. 171), (iii) by listening to the vibration of the thoughts of another, as the other thinks and reflects (vitakkayato vicārayato vitakkavipphārasaddaṃ sutvā, loc. cit.) and (iv) by observing directly how the mental dispositions are placed in the mind of another (yathā..manosaṅkhāre paṇihitā imassa cittassa anantarā amun nāma vitakkaṃ, loc. cit.). It may be noted here that up to the third way of knowing another's mind, knowledge is indirect, for one has to depend either on external signs or on hearing sounds (whether of other beings or of thought-vibrations). But the last one is direct. Here one is supposed to *see* the mental dispositions directly. It is this last type of telepathic knowledge which seems to be described in the Nikāyas as the next higher knowledge after clairaudience. This explains why it is compared to *seeing* one's face in a mirror or a pan of water and noticing directly whether there is a mole or not.[1] It has been already pointed out that the authenticity of seeing is supposed to be greater than that of hearing (Supra pp. 164-5).

It is needless to look for such an analytic picture of telepathic knowledge in the B.G. where epistemological ideas are purely incidental to the main theme. But if one accepts the general background of the B.G. that it is a narration based on the extra-sensory perception of Sañjaya, then it may be possible to say that telepathic knowledge in a general sense is presupposed by it, since we find Sañjaya describing the mental states of people along with other heard and seen events of the battlefield. Thus Sañjaya is supposed to have known the mind of Duryodhana or Arjuna on different occasions when they are elated, depressed or horrified. For example, he notices the elation of Duryodhana when Bhīṣma blows his conch vigorously with a lion's roar,[2] and the terrified state of the Kauravas' mind when various conches are tumultuously sounded from the other side.[3] Again he describes Arjuna in a

1. D. I. 80.
2. B.G. I. 12.
3. B.G. I. 14-19.

sorrowful state (viṣīdan) and as moved by tender sentiments (kṛpayā parayā' viṣṭo) at the sight of his kinsmen.[1] He further speaks of Arjuna as having his mind overwhelmed with grief (śokasaṃvignamānasaḥ)[2]. He is again described to be in great fear (bhītabhītaḥ) at the sight of the terrible form (ugrarūpa) of Kṛṣṇa.[3] All these descriptions of the different states of the mind appear, of course, to presuppose telepathic knowledge on the part of Sañjaya, the describer. Beyond this, we find nothing in the B.G. to enlighten us further on the nature of telepathic knowledge.

The remaining three kinds of higher knowledge (tisso vijjā) are of special value to Buddhism, for it is through them that one is supposed to have a direct realisation of the central truths of Buddhism, viz., (a) the doctrine of Saṃsāra or the great cycle of previous births and rebirths (b) the doctrine of Karma regulating appropriate decease and survival of beings and (c) the four Noble Truths leading to the final deliverance from all defilements and suffering.

Through retrocognitive knowledge one is supposed to recall one's innumerable previous lives with full details. It is said that, "he recalls his manifold past experiences, one birth, two..three..hundred..thousand...lac..for many periods of world-evolution and dissolution as follows: 'I was in such a place with such a personal and family name, such a status, having such and such food, such and such experiences and such a term of life. Dying there I was born in such and such a place; there too I had such a name..Dying there I was born here'—thus he recounts his manifold previous experiences in all their aspects and details."[4] In the B.G. also the claim of knowing manifold past lives is made. Kṛṣṇa points out to Arjuna: "Many lives of mine as well as of yours have been spent, O Arjuna. You do not know them but I know them all, O Arjuna."[5]

Through clairvoyance (dibbacakkhu) one is said to have

1. B.G. I. 28.
2. B.G. I. 47.
3. B G. XI. 31 and 35.
4. D.I. 81.
5. B.G. IV. 5.

direct vision of the decease and survival of beings along with the insight into the workings of Karma. It is stated: "With his clear and paranormal clairvoyant vision he sees beings dying and being reborn, the low and the high, the fair and the ugly, the good and the evil, each according to his karma..."[1] When King Pāyāsi doubts the existence of other worlds and the survival of beings after death merely on the ground that they are not seen through his normal vision, the monk Kassapa points out to him: "The other world O King, is not to be seen like this through these normal eyes of the flesh, as you think. Those recluses and Brahmins who...purify the divine eyes, they through the divine eye see this world as well as the other; as also the spontaneously born beings."[2] Those who are devoid of this paranormal vision cannot see certain divine beings even when they are close by. Further, through this paranormal eye one is supposed to see things which are too distant to be perceived through normal eyes. Buddha, just after his enlightenment claims to see through this clairvoyant vision the group of five monks dwelling near Benares at Isipatana in the deer park.[3] Anuruddha who is considered the chief among those disciples who had attained clairvoyance (A.I. 23) is believed to have the power of seeing a thousand worlds (sahassaṃ lokānaṃ voloketi, M.I. 213). Thus the clairvoyant vision is conceived as an enhanced visual capacity both in quality as well as in extent so that one may perceive through it the supra-mundane things invisible to normal vision as well as things which are too distant in space. Now in the B.G. also we find reference to clairvoyance in both these senses. When Arjuna expresses his desire to see the divine forms of Kṛsṇa, he is told by the latter (just as King pāyāsi was told by the monk Kassapa) that it was not possible to see the divine forms (divyāni rūpāṇi, B.G. XI. 5) by means of the ordinary eye. Kṛṣṇa says: "You cannot see me through this (normal) eye of yours. I bestow on you the divine eye; thereby, behold my

1. D.I. 82.
2. D. II. 329.
3. M. I. 170.

divine wonder."[1] Then he is shown the supreme divine form (paramaṃ rūpam aiśvaram, B.G. XI. 9) in which he sees among other things, "all the gods and the varied hosts of beings, Brahmā and Śiva (Īśa) seated on the lotus-throne, as also all the sages and heavenly nāgas."[2] Besides this perception of divine beings, we have already referred to the clairvoyant vision of distant things of the battle-ground by Sañjaya. Thus, the clairvoyant vision in its dual aspect is accepted by the B.G. as well. The Jaina conception of 'avadhi-jñāna' also resembles this clairvoyant vision, though according to it avadhi-jñāna is possible irrespective of the time factor as well.[3]

The last is the highest state of knowledge when one is supposed to be endowed with the eye of wisdom (paññā-cakkhu) and to apprehend with it the four Noble Truths. It is called 'āsavakkhaya-ñāna' in Buddhism, because one is said to know by means of it the destruction of all defiling impulses. He knows the nature of defilements, their cause, their cessation and the path leading to their cessation. Having known and seen thus, he becomes free from all defilements and there arises in him the knowledge of emancipation (vimuttasmiṃ 'vimuttam' iti ñāṇaṃ hoti, D.I.84). This clear vision of the four Noble Truths and consequent salvation is said to be had through the eye of wisdom.[4] Of the three kinds of eyes (tīṇi cakkhūni) spoken of in Buddhism[5], viz., the normal eye of the flesh (maṃsa cakkhu), the divine eye (dibba cakkhu) and the eye of wisdom (paññā cakkhu), the last is evidently the best and clearest of all. In the B.G. also we find reference to these three kinds of eyes of which the last one is valued most, since through it alone the highest goal is said to be realised. Of course, the difference is there in view of the metaphysical and theological approach of the B.G. We have just referred

1. B. G, XI. 8.
2. B. G. XI. 15. See also XI. 5-30.
3. Tatia—Studies in Jaina Philosophy. p. 61.
4. Cattāri ariya saccāni samma*ppaññāya* passati., Dh. 190.
Sabbe saṅkhārā aniccā...Sabbe saṅkhārā dukkhā...sabbe dhammā anattā'ti yadā *paññāya* passati; Atha nibbindati dukkhe esa maggo visuddhiyā. Dh. 277-9.
5. D. III. 219.

above to the distinction made by the B.G. between the normal human eye and the divine eye. It is through the latter that Arjuna was enabled to see divine form of Kṛṣṇa, and Sañjaya was in a position to have a direct vision of the events of the distant battle-field. Then we find reference to the eye of wisdom (jñāna-cakṣu) through which one is said to attain the highest discriminative knowledge and realise the supreme goal. It is said: "Those who know thus by their eye of wisdom (jñāna-cakṣuṣā) the distinction between the field (kṣetra) and the knower of the field (kṣetrajña), and the deliverance of beings from Nature (Prakṛti), they attain to the Supreme."[1] Through this effulgent light of wisdom (jñāna-dīpena bhāsvatā) the darkness born of ignorance (ajñānajaṃ tamaḥ) is said to be desroyed.[2] The truth cannot be seen by ignorant people, only they who have the eye of wisdom (jñāna-cakṣuṣaḥ) can see.[3] It is to be seen by the persevering yogins.[4]

In spite of this general resemblance between the B.G. and Buddhism regarding normal and paranormal means of perception, we cannot ignore the differences that they exhibit in the treatment of this knowledge. We have already pointed out that the Buddhist account is systematic, analytic and thoroughly intelligible in terms of the natural development of the normal human faculties. The B.G. account, on the other hand, is mixed up with mystical and theological notions.

We may here elucidate how the B.G. unlike Buddhism associates theological notions with almost all the different kinds of paranormal knowlede. The display of psychokinetic powers is evidently made by Kṛṣṇa, represented as God himself (B.G. IX. 16ff). The same is the case with the retrocognitive knowledge (B.G. IV.5). The divine eye (divya cakṣu) as well as the eye of wisdom (jñāna cakṣu) also are said to be obtainable through divine grace. It is Kṛṣṇa who favours Arjuna with the divine eye (divyaṃ dadāmi te

1. B·G XIII. 34.
2. B.G X. 11.
3. B·G, XV. 10.
4. B.G. XV. 11.

cakṣuḥ, B.G. XI. 8) and shows his supreme form through his grace (Mayā prasannena tavā'rjune'daṃ rūpaṃ paraṃ darśitam ātmayogāt, B.G. XI. 47). Similarly he bestows 'the light of wisdom' and removes 'the darkness of ignorance' out of compassion for his devotees.[1] Besides this grace of Divinity, the B.G. refers to the grace of enlightened seers as well. Sañjaya is said to have acquired the powers of clairaudience, clairvoyance and telepathic knowledge by the grace of Vyāsa (Vyāsaprasādāt, B.G. XVIII. 75). The B.G., however, tries to reconcile it with the naturalistic explanation by indicating that the divine favour goes to those devotees who deserve it by virtue of their righteous conduct (B.G. XII. 14-20). Arjuna himself is presented in the form of a great devotee,[2] free from ill-will[3] and born with divine endowments.[4] It may also be noted that the paranormal capacities bestowed on Arjuna and Sañjaya are only temporary and not a permanent possession of theirs.

Then again, Buddhism tries to offer empirical explanations both for normal as well as paranormal perceptions, and avoids metaphysical explanations, whereas in the B.G it is the latter which play a dominant part. All knowledge, whether normal or paranormal, partial or full, obscure or clear—is sought to be explained with the help of the metaphysical Self whose existence is always presupposed. In this respect the B.G. seems to adopt the Sāṅkhya method traceable to the Kaṭhopaniṣad. Though the B.G. skips over some of the details of the Kaṭha, yet it is found to follow the same hierarchy of the senses, mind, intellect and the Self which are said to be controlled in descending order, with a view to attaining proper knowledge and keeping oneself to the right path.[5] The B.G. first sounds a warning by emphasising the forceful nature of

---

1. Teṣām evā'nukampārtham aham ajñānajaṃ tamaḥ,
   Nāśayāmi ātmabhāvastho jñāna-dīpena bhāsvatā., B.G. X. 11
   Teṣāṃ . . .bhajatāṃ prītipūrvakam,
   Dadāmi buddhiyogaṃ tam. . ., B.G. X. 10.
2. B.G. IV. 5 (Bhakto'si me. . .).
3. B.G. IX. 1. (Idaṃ tu te guhyatamaṃ pravakṣyāmy *anasūyave*).
4. B.G. XVI. 5 (. . .saṃpadaṃ daivīm abhijāto'si Pāṇḍava).
5. Compare Kaṭha. III. 10 and 11 with B.G. III. 42 and 43, and again Kaṭha. III. 13 with B. G. VI. 24-26.

the senses which tend to carry away the mind.[1] Then "the mind, if it runs after the roving senses, carries away the intellect even as wind carries away a boat on the waters"[2] and with the intellect gone wrong, one is doomed to destruction.[3] It is said that the inherent luminosity or consciousness of the self is covered by the cloud of passionate desire or anger.[4] "The senses, the mind the intellect are said to be its seat. Through them it (passionate desire) deludes the embodied soul by covering up the wisdom."[5] In this way the B.G. tries to show that the ignorance or delusion is caused when the different faculties of man, namely, the senses, the mind and the intellect operate in an order just opposite to what they should. The B.G., therefore, prescribes the right way to regulate them. It points out that the senses, howsoever forceful, may be controlled by the mind, and the mind by the intellect, which, when purified, would get clear reflection (wisdom) from the conscious principle, the Self.[6] Accordingly, Arjuna is told: "The senses are said to be high (subtle or powerful), higher than the senses is the mind, higher than the mind is the intellect and that which is higher than the intellect is he (the Self). Thus realising him as higher than the intellect, control yourself by the Self. ."[7] The right way of regulating the different faculties of man is to begin with the control of the lowest faculties, the senses, through the next higher faculty, namely, the mind, and the mind has to be regulated through the intellect, and the intellect is to be directed to the Self. Then alone can one attain the proper wisdom or knowledge. As the B.G. says:

---

1. Indriyāṇi pramāthīni haranti prasabhaṃ manaḥ., B.G. II. 60.
2. B.G. II. 67.
3. B.G. II. 63 (. . buddhināśāt praṇaśyati).
4. B.G. III. 37-39.
5. B.G. III. 40.
6. Dasgupta's view that the B.G. "does not seem anywhere to refer to it (the Self) as a self-conscious principle" (A History of Indian Philosophy, Vol. II. p. 471) can hardly stand in view of B.G. X. 4,5 (Buddir jñānam asaṃmoham. . .bhavanti bhāvā bhūtānāṃ matta eva pṛthagvidhāḥ) and B.G. XV. 15 (Sarvasya ca'haṃ hṛdi saṃniviṣṭo mattaḥ smṛtir jñānam apohanaṃ ca).
7. B.G. III. 42-43.

"Therefore O Bharatarṣabha (Arjuna) *first regulate your senses* (Tasmāt tvam indriyāṇy ādau niyamya Bharatarṣabha) and slay this sinful (desire), the destroyer of wisdom and discrimination."[1] "Having abandoned all desires completely born of selfish will and *having well regulated the host of the senses from all sides through the mind* (Manasai've'ndriyagrāmaṃ viniyamya samantataḥ), one should gradually attain tranquility by *directing the mind through the steadfast intellect* (..buddhyā ..ātmasaṃsthaṃ manaḥ kṛtva)". [2] Then ultimately he should *bring it under the control of the Self alone* (ātmany eva vaśaṃ nayet).[3] It is only when people direct themselves in the above manner that their ignorance is said to be destroyed by wisdom, which lights up in them like the sun (tesāṃ ādityavaj jñānaṃ prakāśayati tat param)[4] and "their sins being washed away by wisdom, they reach a state from which there is no return (Gacchanty apunarāvṛttiṃ jñānanirdhūtakalmaṣāḥ).[5] This metaphysical account of the B.G. along with the hierarchical gradation of the different faculties reminds one of similar ideas expressed in the Kaṭha, through the analogy of the chariot. The body is imagined as the chariot and the Soul is the rider. The senses, the mind and the intellect are compared respectively to the horses, rein and the charioteer. They are to be properly controlled in order to reach the right goal.[6] It is in this metaphysical background of the eternally conscious soul that the B.G. seeks to account for all normal and paranormal perceptions, their obscurity as well as clarity.

Such metaphysical explanations are out of question in Buddhism. Buddha brushes aside the very hypothesis of the Self as an unobservable entity within, and seeks to explain all normal and paranormal perception in the light of empirical facts. Dr. Sarathchandra has rightly noted this empirical

1. B.G. III. 41
2. B.G. VI. 24-25.
3. B.G. VI 26.
4. B.G. V. 16.
5. B.G. V. 17.
6. Ātmānaṃ rathinam viddhi, śarīraṃ ratham eva tu,
Buddhiṃ tu sārathiṃ viddhi manaḥ pragraham eva ca.
Indriyāṇi hayān āhuḥ. . . . . . . , Kaṭha. III. 3-13.

approach of the Buddha when he says: "What is most interesting in the analysis of mind contained in this literature is its empiricist approach,"[1] though the reason for the adoption of this attitude has not been rightly evaluated by him. According to him "Buddhism having cast the current conceptions about the soul, had to advance an alternative hypothesis.."[2] This view of Dr. Sarathchandra is somewhat misleading in as much as it gives the impression that the empirical approach of Buddha was a result of his repudiation of the soul. The fact, however, is just the other way round. The rejection of the soul itself was the result of his empirical attitude and not *vice versa*.[3] We have already shown how even in explaining the emergence of paranormal perception, Buddha follows a strictly natural account, not to speak of his explanation of normal perception, which evidently is thoroughly factual. In order to explain the emergence of normal visual perception, for example, he mentions three conditions: (i) an unimpaired internal sense organ of sight (ajjhattikaṃ..cakkhu aparibhinnaṃ hoti, M.I. 190), (ii) external visible forms entering into the field of vision (bāhirā ca rūpā āpāthaṃ āgacchanti, loc. cit.) and (iii) an appropriate act of attention on the part of the mind (tajjo ca samannāharo hoti, loc. cit.) When these conditions are fulfilled "there arises consiousness pertaining to that" (tajjassa viññāṇabhāgassa pātubhāvo hoti, loc. cit.). None of these conditions should be lacking. It is said that if only the first condition is fulfilled and not the second and third; or if the first and second are fulfilled and not the third, the knowledge will not arise.[4] This example should make it clear how the Buddhist account of knowledge, in contradistinction to that of the B.G., is thoroughly empirical and non-metaphysical. According to the B.G., however, it is on account of the Self at the centre that the empirical factors bring about knowledge.

---

1. Buddhist Psychology of Perception—Introductory note, p. viii.
2. *Ibid.* p. 3.
3. K.N. Jayatilleke—Early Buddhist Theory of Knowledge, pp. 432ff.
4. M. I. 190.

(*B*) *Inference*:—

The second source of valid knowledge accepted by the B. G. and early Buddhism is anumāna (inference). The term 'anumāna' which is usually translated by the word 'inference' must, however, be taken in a comprehensive sense signifying a combined deductive-inductive process. In Aristotelian logic where the distinction between formal and material truth is emphasised, we find corresponding to them two kinds of inference, viz., deductive and inductive. The former which aims at formal truth is classified into immediate and mediate, syllogistic and non-syllogistic, pure and mixed etc. But in the context of Indian philosophy where philosophising means seeking for objective or material truth leading to emancipation from snffering, mere formal truth is empty. According to it truth must be material or corresponding to the reality which, of course, is assumed to be consistent or formally valid. It is this basic motive force of Indian philosophy which distinguishes the Indian concept of anumāna (inference) as a means of valid knowledge or truth from the Western conception of it. Anumāna, as a means of valid knowledge, must therefore be based on the knowledge of objective truth and should consistently aim at achieving further objective truth. In other words, anumāna is a combined deductive-inductive process in which (i) on the basis of some knowledge already arrived at, one (ii) passes from this known to something unknown and, thus, obtains some new knowledge. If the first condition is lacking, the second cannot be fulfilled. If there is no basis in some ascertained truth, mere consistency of reasoning cannot be considered as evidence of valid knowledge.

The method of showing mere formal consistency is known as 'takka' (Sk., tarka) which has only a limited value and application. Having no basis in ascertained truth, it cannot be expected to lead unmistakably to objectively valid knowledge. It is for this reason that 'takka' (pure reasoning or *a priori* argument) is not considered as a means of valid knowledge either in Buddhism or in the B. G.

It may incidently be noted that in the Nyāya system also tarka (hypothetical argument) is distinguished from pramā (valid knowledge).[1] Its value, however, as an indirect proof or as a means of suggesting hypotheses is not denied. S. Radhakrishnan, in this connection, has rightly pointed out that "tarka is not by itself a source of valid knowledge, though it is valuable as suggesting hypotheses."[2] This limited value of it is accepted both by the B. G. and Buddhism. Both of them, as we shall see in the sequel, (infra, pp. 236-241) use it as a method of indirect proof by means of which the absurdity of the opposite view is exposed, and thereby (indirectly) one's own position is established.

That anumāna is a combined deductive-inductive process having its basis in some other knowledge is indicated by the very etymology of the word (anu = after + mān i. e. $\sqrt{\text{mā}}$ = measure). Thus it signifies that knowledge which follows (comes after) some 'other knowledge'. Now the question is: What is that 'other knowledge'? Usually it is supposed that this 'other knowledge' is perceptual which precedes inferential knowledge.[3] It is in this sense that anumāna is understood in early Buddhism. According to it perception (both normal and paranormal) provides the basis for inference. But the B. G. which regards scriptural authority also as a means of valid knowledge, bases inference both on perceptual as well as scriptural knowledge.

In the Pali Canon according to Mrs. Rhys Davids "anumāna apparently does not occur at all."[4] It is surprising how she has failed to notice it when one Sutta itself of the Majjhima Nikāya is named as 'Anumāna Sutta' (M. I. 95ff) where one is asked to infer (anuminitabbaṃ) in the following way: "An evil person who is swayed by evil thoughts is disagreeable to and disliked by me; now if I were to be evil and swayed by evil thoughts, I too would be disagree-

---

1. Nyāya-Sūtra I. 2.1. It must, however, be taken note of that in Buddhism 'takka' is not taken exclusively in the Naiyāyika sense of the term (hypothetical argument directed mainly at demolishing the opponent's theory), but it has a positive connotation as well, and hence it should be taken in the sense of a general *a prioi* argument or reflection. cf. K. N. Jayatilleke—Early Buddhist Theory of Knowlede, p. 206.

2. Indian Philosophy, Vol. II. p. 114.

3. Nyāya-Sūtra I. 1. 5. cf. S. C. Chatterjee-Nyāya Theory of Knowledge pp. 254-5.

4. Encyclopaedia of Religion and Ethics, Vol. 8. p. 133, fn. 4.

able to and disliked by others".[1] Obviously this interefence is based on direct perception that 'an evil person...is disliked by me'. One who is conversant with the five-membered syllogism of Indian logic can easily see that this constitutes the example (udāharaṇa) of the general proposition 'All evil persons are disliked'. Thus relying on the 'Uniformity of Nature' this inferential knowledge of 'myself being disliked' has been arrived at. In brief we may express it as follows:—

All evil persons are disliked.
I am an evil person.
Therefore, I am disliked.

We know that an inference is based on an universal proposition. In early Buddhism this universal proposition is sought to be established on the basis of the causal connections which are to be discovered by observing the phenomena of nature. Thus perception supplies the data for establishing causal connections. We have already noted that the theory of causation is one of the central tenets of early Buddhism, so much so that it was indentified with the Dhamma itself.[2] Some western scholars, however, find it difficult to accept this truth. R. E. Hume, for example, observes that "neither Buddha nor the Buddhist writings had any interest in the problems of...scientific causation."[3] E. J. Thomas thinks that 'in Buddhism causation was never applied as an "universal philosophical principle."[4] Keith feels that "the chain of causation is essentially an explanation of misery; it tells us nothing regarding physical causes."[5] According to Kern, in the "chain of causation", "the difference between *post hoc* and the *propter hoc* is utterly ignored."[6] These views

---

1. Tatra...evaṃ anuminitabbaṃ : yo khvāyaṃ puggalo pāpiccho pāpikānaṃ icchānaṃ vasaṃgato ayaṃ me puggalo appiyo amanāpo; ahaṃ c'eva kho pan'assaṃ pāpiccho pāpikānaṃ icchānaṃ vasaṃgato, ahaṃ p'assaṃ paresaṃ appiyo amanāpo ti., M.I. 97.

2. Yo paṭiccasamuppādaṃ passati so dhammaṃ passati,
yo dhammaṇ passati so paṭiccasamuppādaṃ passati, M.I. 190-1.

3. 'Miracles in the Canonical Scriptures of Buddhism' in J.A.O.S, Vol. 44, p. 162.

4. Life of Buddha, p. 199.

5. Buddhist Philosophy, p. 112.

6. Manual of Indian Buddhism, p. 47.

do scant justice to the texts which we have already referred to. K. N. Jayatilleke, adducing various textual evidences bearing on this subject, has clearly shown the untenability of these and other such views.[1] We may, therefore, only point to the scientific formulation of the causal theory found in the Pali texts. It is said: "This being present, this occurs; this arising, this arises; this being absent, this does not occur; this disappearing, this disappears."[2] Obviously this takes into consideration both agreement in presence as well as agreement in absence. If the cause is present, effect is present; if the cause is absent, the effect is absent. This unambiguously embodies the scientific view of causation signifying a regular sequence between cause and effect where one cannot occur without the other. This is what Stebbing calls the scientific view of a 'one-one relation' as distinct from the commonsense view.[3] This is a never-failing relation which is objectively valid and is not merely a subjective imposition on the phenomena. To emphasise these points, four characteristics of a cause are enumerated in the Pali Canon, viz: "objectivity, necessity, invariablity and conditionality."[4]

In this connection it is interesting to note the reference to 'anvaye ñāṇaṃ' (S. II. 58; D. III. 226: Vbh. 329) in the Pali texts, which most probably indicates how by having an insight into the essential nature of things (dhamme ñāṇaṃ) or into their causal conditionality one arrives at the universal proposition which is true for the past and future as well, besides the present. In the Saṃyutta Nikāya

---

1. Early Buddhist Theory of Knowledge, pp. 445-457.

2. Imasmiṃ sati idaṃ hoti; imass'uppādā idaṃ uppajjati; imasmiṃ asati idaṃ na hoti; imassa nirodhā idaṃ nirujjhati. —M. I. 262-264; III. 63.

3. To quote the very words of Stebbing: "The practical agent, however, is content with a relation that is determinate only in the direction *from* cause to effect : *wherever X occurs, E occurs.* But the scientific investigator wants to find a relation that is equally determinate in either direction, that is, he seeks a one-one relation : *wherever X occurs, E occurs, and E does not occur unless X has occurred.*" A Modern Introduction to Logic, p. 264.

4. tathatā avitathatā anaññathatā idappaccayatā ayaṃ vuccati... paṭiccasamuppādo, S. II. 26.

(II. 57-58), after describing various causally related phenomena and having shown how their origin and cessation are causally related, it is said that this knowledge into the essential causal conditionality of things is to be considered as the knowledge of the dhamma (dhamme ñāṇaṃ, S. II. 58), and it is further pointed out that after knowing this one understands that the same holds good for the past and future as well. This latter knowledge is called 'anvaye ñāṇaṃ'. This indicates that by having an insight into the nature of present phenomena, along with a belief in the postulate of the Uniformity of Nature, one knows that the same holds good in relation to the past and future as well. Thus, the how and why of arriving at the universal proposition (true for all times) seems to be explained here.

After having mentioned various causally related phenomena, the text gives the following illustration: "With the arising of birth, there is the arising of decay and death, and with the cessation of birth, there is the cessation of decay and death...When, monks, the noble disciple knows in this (causal) way the decay and death...the origin of decay and death... the cessation of decay and death... the path leading to the cessation of decay and death, *this is his knowledge into the dhamma* (idam assa dhamme ñāṇam). By seeing, knowing, realising before long and impenetrating into this dhamma, he draws the conclusion (nayaṃ neti) in relation to the past and future as follows: 'All those recluses and Brahmins who thoroughly understood the nature of decay and death, its cause, its cessation and the path leading to its cessation, did so in the same way as I do at present; all those recluses and Brahmins who in future will thoroughly understand the nature of decay and death... will do so in the same way as I do at present'—*this is his generalised knowledge or induction* (idam ass anvaye ñāṇaṃ)."[1] This description shows how analytic and scientific was the approach of early Buddhism regarding causation and induction. Here the universal proposition is established by means of knowing the essential nature (causal conditionality)

1. S. II. 57-58.

of things in the present and then extending its applicability to the past and future with reliance on the Uniformity of Nature. This method of establishing universal propositions (true for all times) by means of discovering the essential nature or causal conditionality of present things (dhamme ñāṇaṃ) and thereby knowing its validity for all times (anvaye ñāṇam), is somewhat similar to the Naiyāyika's method of establishing universal proposition through Sāmānyalakṣaṇa-Pratyakṣa[1], though there is an important difference in as much as the Naiyāyikas conceive of Sāmānya as a distinct category inhering in individuals, which is not the case with the *dhammatā* of Buddhism.

After having seen that early Buddhism depends on causal relation in order to draw inference on the basis of observed facts, we may now see how it bases its inference both on normal as well as paranormal perceptions. Let us first take some examples of inference based on normal perception.

We come across a number of inferences in the Pali texts drawn on the basis of normal perception. The well-known statements like, 'all conditioned things are impermanent[2]' 'all conditioned things are sorrowful[3],' 'on account of birth there is decay and death[4],' etc. are, to begin with, purely empirical generalisations based on normal perception. Even before going forth from home to homelessness, one is supposed to arrive at these empirical generalisations on the basis of what one normally perceives in the world. With this, the noble-search (ariya pariyesanā, M. I. 161) is said to begin. As Buddha says : "Someone, monks, being himself subject to birth..old age..disease..and death, having known the consequences of what is subject to birth..old age..disease.. and death starts the search of nibbāna, the unborn and the unsurpassed state of peace and security."[5] It is these truths which are first placed before people to make them see the truth of the Buddhist doctrine in the light of their own em-

1. See for a detailed discussion on 'Sāmānyalakṣaṇa-Pratyakṣa'—The Nyāya Theory of Knowledge—by S.C. Chatterjee pp. 228-38 and 272.
2. Sabbe saṅkhārā aniccā, Dh. 277.
3. Sabbe saṅkhārā dukkhā, Dh. 278.
4. Jātipaccayā. . .jarāmaraṇam, S. II. 25.
5. M. I. 162-3.

pirical knowledge.[1] Quoting the example, 'all conditioned things are impermanent' Wijesekera pertinently points out : "This is not given as a result of metaphysical inquiry or of any mystical intuition but as a straight-forward judgment to be arrived at by investigation and analysis. It is founded on unbiased thought and has a purely empirical basis."[2] It is, no doubt, true that subsequently this truth is comprehended and verified by means of the highest wisdom (paññā) (sabbe saṅkhārā aniccā..dukhā..yadā *paññāya passati*; atha nibbindati dukkhe.., Dh. 277-9), but at the beginning, this generalisation is based on what is known and seen in ordinary life. This may be illustrated from a reference in the Majjhima Nikāya where the universal proposition : 'all grief is rooted in attachment' is demonstrated on the basis of the observed facts. Buddha, on being asked whether he holds the view that "grief, lamentation, mental agony, sorrow and anxiety arise and originate from attachment" (M. II. 108), affirms it, and further adds that "it should be understood in this way" (tad aminā p'etam..pariyāyena veditabbaṃ, loc. cit.). He then enumerates many observed instances from among the people of Sāvatthi indicating how they were led to grief because of their attachment to their loved ones.[3]

Similarly the denunciation of caste-distinction among human beings is based on a careful observation of nature. It is said that the grasses, trees. worms, moths, ants, four-footed creatures, serpents, fishes, birds etc., possess "characteristics denoting species" (liṅgaṃ jātimayaṃ, Sn. 117-8) and so among them we find different species (aññamaññā jātiyo, loc. cit.). But among human beings such characteristics denoting species are not there (evaṃ natthi manussesu liṅgaṃ jātimayaṃ puthu, Sn. 118) in respect of their hair, head, ears, eyes, face, nose etc. So it is concluded that there is no caste or species among human beings (manussesv' etaṃ na vijjati, Sn. 119). This is a clear case of anumāna (inference) based on normal perception.

1. M.I. 230-233, 261-264; S. II. 25.
2. The Three Signata, pp. 1-2.
3. M. II. 108-9.

Instances of inference based on paranormal perception also are not lacking. The theory of karma itself is a noteworthy example of it. The correlation between the actions of men and their future states of life is said to be perceived through clairvoyant vision. It is stated that "he sees some beings endowed with bodily, verbal or mental misconduct who reproach the holy men, hold false views and act in accordance with false views being born in a state of decline, in an unhappy condition, in a state of downfall and a lower state at death on the dissolution of the body"[1]; and likewise he sees other beings endowed with good bodily, verbal or mental conduct etc. being "born in a happy state, in a heavenly world at death on the dissolution of the body."[2] On the basis of this observed correlation between bad conduct and the unhappy future state, on the one hand, and between good conduct and happy future state, on the other, he arrives at the induction "as the man sows, so he reaps... beings are the inheritors of their karmas" (yaṃ karoti tena upapajjati..kammadāyādā sattā, M.I. 390). This is the meaning of the statement that "he knows beings fairing according to their karmas" (yathā kammūpage satte pajānāti, M. I. 82).

Instances can be multiplied to indicate that inductions were established and inferences drawn on the basis of such direct paranormol perceptions. We find Buddha asking monks to cultivate the Fourfold Mindfulness (cattāro satipaṭṭhānā) or practise the Eightfold Path (aṭṭhaṅgiko maggo) etc. on the basis of the universal proposition arrived at by means of his own paranormal knowledge. He makes such general statements: "By whomsoever, monks, the four kinds of mindfulness are neglected, by them is neglected the Noble Path leading to the perfect destruction of suffering. By whomsoever, monks, the four kinds of mindfulness are undertaken, by them is undertaken the Noble Path leading to the perfect destruction of suffer-

1. D.I. 82.
2. D.I. 82.

ing."[1] Similarly it is stated in a general way that "whenever a monk cultivates the Noble Eightfold Path, makes much of the Noble Eightfold Path, it leads him to Nibbāna, inclines towards Nibbāna and takes him on to Nibbāna."[2] All such statements are said to be based on the direct paranormal perception of Buddha himself (Tathāgato sayaṃ abhiññā sacchikatvā pavedeti, D.I. 12).

It is, however, important to note that Buddha points out the possibility of error in drawing infernces if they are not based on thorough and comprehensive observations. This error is possible in relation to inferences based on both normal and paranormal perceptions. For example, he points out that the inference drawn by certain recluses and Brahmins that 'all those who kill living creatures experience pain and sorrow in the present life itself' (yo koci pāṇam atimāpeti sabbo so diṭṭheva dhamme dukkhaṃ domanassam paṭisaṃvediyati, S. IV. 343) is erroneous, for some people are found to be honoured in this very life, if they kill the king's enemies (loc. cit.). Even with regard to inference based on clairvoyant vision, erroneous inferences can be drawn. Buddha points out (M.III. 209-212) how four different generalisations are made by four different recluses or Brahmins on the basis of their respective clairvoyant vision. It is said that a certain recluse or Brahmin sees in his clairvoyant vision a sinful man being born after death in an unhappy state, and at once arrives at the following four inferences: (i) there are evil acts (ii) there are evil consequences for evil acts(iii)all those who perform evil acts are born after death in an unhappy state and (iv) only those who know this are correct, others are wrong.[3] Another

---

1. yesaṃ kesañci bhikkhave cattāro satipaṭṭhānā viraddha, viraddho tesam ariyo aṭṭhaṅgiko maggo sammādukkhakkhayagāmī. Yesaṃ kesañci....āraddhā, āraddho tesam ariyo aṭṭhaṅgiko maggo ..., S.V. 179-180.

2. Evaṃ... bhikkhu ariyam aṭṭhaṅgikaṃ maggam bhāvento.... bahulī karonto nibbānaninno hoti, nibbānapoṇo nibbānapabbhāroti, S.V. 38.

3. Atthi...pāpakāni kammāni; atthi duccaritassa vipāko ;...yo... pāṇātipātī adinnādāyī...sabbo so kāyassa bhedā paraṃ maraṇā apāyaṃ duggatiṃ vinipātaṃ nirayaṃ uppajjati; ye evaṃ jānanti te sammā jānanti, ye aññathā jānanti micchā tesaṃ ñāṇaṃ ti, M. III. 210.

recluse or Brahmin sees in his clairvoyant vision a sinful man being born after death in a happy state and reaches another four conclusions as follows: (i) there are no evil acts (ii) there are no evil consequences for evil acts (iii) all those who perform evil acts are born after death in a happy state and (iv) only those who know this are correct, others are wrong (M.III. 211). Similarly the third recluse or Brahmin having the clairvoyant vision of a virtuous man being born after death in a happy state runs to four dogmatic conclusions (loc. cit.), and so does the fourth, after having found the virtuous man being born after death in an unhappy state (M.III. 212). Buddha does not deny what they claim to have perceived in their clairvoyant vision. They, according to Buddha, have rightly seen the sinful or virtuous man being born after death in one or the other state. But some of the inferences drawn on the basis of their respective visions are not correct. They make dogmatic inferences claiming exclusive validity on the basis of their solitary experience. Buddha points out that on a comprehensive and long-range clairvoyant vision, it can be seen that the sinful man's immediate birth in a happy state or the virtuous man's immediate birth in an unhappy state are traceable to their respective good or bad deeds performed sometime or another in their past lives or they are due to a change of their heart at the moment of death (pubbe vā'ssa taṃ kataṃ hoti..pacchā vā... maraṇakale vā'ssa hoti..,M. III. 214-5). Thus the apparent exceptions do not upset the general law of karma according to which righteous and unrighteous deeds are followed by happy and unhappy consequences in the future, as the case may be. This shows how careful Buddha was in drawing inferences from normal and paranormal perceptions, and how much he emphasised the need for comprehensive observation and verification in discovering true knowledge.

It is interesting to note that Buddha, with a view to avoiding erroneous inferences, is found to test and verify the data of paranormal perception in a way analogous to the testing of a hypothesis. For example, in the Mahāsīhanāda Sutta we find him testing the validity of karma-theory in the light of what he sees through his telepathic knowledge and clairvoyant vision (M.I. 74).[1]

This emphasis on careful observation and verification is particularly important in view of the fact that direct personal knowledge is claimed by many of Buddha's contemporaries, predecessors or successors without caring much for correct inference and verification. It is mainly on this ground that Jaina ascetics are criticised and ridiculed by Buddha when he finds them preaching certain things which they had never tested or verified.[2]

In the light of this Buddhist account of inference, let us now examine the position of the B.G. in this respect.

We have already said that according to the B.G. both perceptual as well as scriptural knowledge are utilised as the basis of inference. We have also shown that the causal relation is presupposed by the B.G. and, at places, events are enumerated one after another in a causal sequence,[3] though unlike Buddhism, we do not find here a scientific formulation of the causal theory. Anyway, both of them believe in causation and make use of it in establishing the universal proposition on the basis of perception.

Let us take an illustration. Just as in Buddhism, contact with objects is said to be the cause of pleasant or painful experience (phassa paccayā vedanā, M.III. 63; S. II. 25), so also in the B.G. it is stated : "Contacts with objects, O Arjuna, give rise to...pleasure and pain."[4] Now, Buddhisn, on the basis of normal experiences finds these objects to be impermanent, implying thereby the impermanence of the experiences arising out of their contact. Then it points out tnat whatever is impermanent is sorrowful[5] and on this basis the painful character of worldly objects is asserted (sabbe saṅkhārā dukkhā, Dh. 278). The B.G. also is found to follow the same line of argument. After having stated that "Contacts

1. K. N. Jayatilleke—Early Buddhist Theory of Knowledge, pp. 460-1.

2. M. I. 92-93.

3. B. G. II. 62-66.

4. Mātrāsp. śās tu Kaunteya. . .sukhaduḥkhadāḥ B.G. II. 14.

5. Yaṃ panāniccaṃ dukkhaṃ vā taṃ sukhaṃ vā ti ? Dukkham. . . . —M.I. 138, 233.

with objects give rise to...pleasure and pain" it at once adds that "they come and go and are impermanent" (āgamāpāyino'nityāḥ, B.G. II.14), and so it declares in the same Buddistic way that "whatever pleasures are born of contact (with objects) are only sources of sorrow, (for) they have a begining and an end (i.e. they are impermanent)."[1] This shows how closely the B.G. here follows the Buddhist reasoning.

In the light of this close correspondence, it appears that the B.G. also, like Buddhism, relies on the causal theory in establishing universal propositions on the basis of observational data. It is, of course, not possible to find in the B.G. an analytic treatment of the causal theory, but the general assumption of causation is present. We may now see how the B.G. draws inferences on the basis of perception (normal as well as paranormal) and authority.

Let us first take an example of inference based on the data of normal perception. We have just noted that the induction, namely, 'whatever pleasures are born of contact are only sources of sorrow' was arrived at as an empirical generalisation. Then again, some of the arguments used by Arjuna are also found to be based on normal perception. To take one illustration, Arjuna declares that he would not fight (na yotsya iti, B.G. II.9) on the ground that he has no desire for victory, kingdom or pleasures (na kāṅkṣe vijayaṃ Kṛṣṇa na ca rājyaṃ sukhāni ca, B.G.I.32). This implies the following inference :

> Those who fight, desire victory, kingdom or pleasures,
>
> I do not desire them,
>
> Therefore, I do not fight.

This generalisation is based on normal perception and not on mystic experience.

We also come across inferences based on paranormal perception. Arguments used by Kṛṣṇa to dispel the distress and despondency of Arjuna are mostly metaphysical and are

3. Ye hi saṃsparśajā bhogā duḥkhayonaya evate,
ādyantavantaḥ Kaunteya. . ., B.G. V. 22.

supposed to be based on paranormal mystic perceptions of seers. Let us take a few examples:

Kṛṣṇa says: "He (the Self) is said to be unmanifest, unthinkable and unchanging. Therefore, knowing him as such, you should not grieve".[1] This statement may be fully expressed as follows:—

> All those who know him (the Self) to be unmanifest, unthinkable and unchanging, do not grieve,
> You know him to be such.
> Therefore, you are not to grieve.

Here the basis of the inference is not normal perception but the paranormal perception of the seers. They are said to perceive this Self in yogic meditation. This is clear from the repeated statements of the B.G.: "By meditation some perceive the Self in the self by the self"[2]; "the striving yogins perceive him (the Self) as established in the self"[3]; "he whose self is harmonised by yoga sees the Self abiding in all beings and all beings in the Self"[4]; "when, he (thus) sees the diversified beings as centred in the One...he attains Brahman"[5] and "having attained Brahman he becomes happy and he neither grieves nor desires."[6] Thus, it is evident from the text that the basis of the above inference is the paranormal perception of the yogins.

Let us take another instance, Kṛṣṇa says: "He who knows this (Self) to be indestructible, eternal, unborn and undecaying, how can he, O Arjuna, slay anyone or cause anyone to slay?"[7] This statement when stated in syllogistic

---

1. Avyakto'yam acintyo'yam avikāryo'yam ucyate;
tasmād evaṃ viditvai'nam nā'nuśocitum arhasi, B.G. II. 25.
2. B. G. XIII. 24.
3. B.G. XV. 11.
4. B.G. VI. 9.
5. B.G. XIII. 30.
6. B.G. XVIII. 54.
7. Vedā'vināśinaṃ nityaṃ ya enam ajam avyayam;
kathaṃ sa puruṣaḥ Pārtha kaṃ ghātayati hanti kam ? B. G. II. 21.

form will read as follows :—

All who know the Self to be indestructible eternal etc. cannot slay anyone or cause anyone to slay,
You know the Self as such,
Therefore, you cannot slay anyone or cause anyone to slay.

These metaphysical arguments of Kṛṣṇa represent inferences which are supposed to be based on paranormal perception.

Let us now take an instance of inference based on scriptural knowledge. There is no doubt about the fact that Kṛṣṇa, besides using metaphysical arguments, appeals to scriptural testimony as well (Tasmāc chāstraṃ pramāṇaṃ te, B.G. XVI. 24). Thus with tacit reference to scriptural authority[1], he reminds Arjuna of his prescribed-duty (svadharma) as a Kṣatriya. He says: "In consideration of your own prescribed-duty also, you should not falter, since nothing for a Kṣatriya is a higher good than the righteous fight."[2] Now, it may be expressed in the following form :—

Nothing for a Kṣatriya is a higher good than the righteous fight,
You are a Kṣatriya
Therefore, nothing for you is a higher good than the righteous fight.

Or, to put the same in a positive form:—

All Kṣatriyas have the righteous fight as their highest good.
You are a Kṣatriya
Therefore, you have the righteous fight as your highest good.

---

5. The scriptural authority in the B.G., however, does uot strictly include the Vedic authority which is undermined by the B.G. (II. 42-46; IX. 20 and 21). It perhaps refers to post-Vedic scriptures including the Dharmaśāstras(which deal with the duties of different classes). Besides, the B.G. relies on some other forms of authority as well, like tradition, convention, etc.

1. Svadharmam api cā'vekṣya na vikampitum arhasi ;
dharmyād dhi yuddhāc chreo'nyat Kṣatriyasya na vidyate,
B.G. II. 31.

The basis of this inference cannot be said to be perception, whether normal or paranormal. It is evidently impossible to see through sense-perception what happens beyond this life. Nor does the B.G. claim to have seen through clairvoyant vision that the soldiers killed in the battle-field go to heaven. So the only basis for this claim seems to be the traditional belief which is preserved in the MB. or the B.G. and is alluded to in the Pali Canon as well (S.IV. 308-311). To refer to a few statements of the MB. in this connection, it is said: "Verily the duty of a Kṣatriya consists in holding the sceptre (or protecting against evil by means of punishment) and not in shaven-headedness" (Daṇḍa eva hi rājendra Kṣatradharmo na muṇḍanam, Śānti-parva 23. 46). "As he protects against destruction, so, indeed, he is called a Kṣatriya" (Kṣatād yo vai trāyatī'tī sa tasmāt Kṣatriyaḥ smṛtaḥ, MB. XII.29. 138). The MB places a gallant warrior and a true yogin on the same footing. It says: "O, thou tiger among men, there are these two who pierce the constellation of the Sun (i.e., reach the sphere of Brahman): the one is the recluse who is steeped in yoga, and the other is the warrior who falls fighting in the battlefield."[1] It is on the basis of this traditional belief that the above inference seems to be drawn.

From these instances of inference found in the Pali Canon and the B. G., it would appear that inference (anumāna) which is taken in them as the means of valid knowledge is not exclusively deductive or inductive, but is a combined deductive-inductive process in which inductions are established on the ground of already known facts, and then conclusions are deduced from them. But the difference between Buddhism and the B. G. lies in the fact that according to the former, perception (normal and paronormal) alone can supply the data for induction; whereas according to the latter, besides perception (normal and paranormal,) authority also can be invoked for this purpose. Then again the data supplied by paranormal perception are also

---

1. Dvav imau puruṣavyāghra sūryamaṇḍala bhedinau;
parivrāṭ yogayuktaś ca raṇe cā'bhimukho hataḥ, MB., Udyoga-parva, 32. 65.

differently conceived. The B. G. claims insight into the eternal and imperishable Self, on which, indeed, many of its inferences are based. But according to Buddhism, such claims being repudiated, these inferences cannot but be considered misleading and futile. Buddhism envisages the possibility of error in deriving inferences, and, in keeping with its empirical approach, emphasises the need for comprehensive observation and verification of inference. The B. G. also, no doubt, admits the possibility of error in deriving inferences (in view of which Arjuna's position is shown to be incorrect), but on account of its metaphysical stand, the test that is applied by it for ascertaining the correctness or incorrectness of an inference is its conformity or non-conformity with metaphsical and scriptural truths, which are themselves controversial.

(*C*) *The Role of Reason*:—

We have stated that in spite of reason not being considered as an independent means of valid knowledge, a limited use of it is made both by Buddhism and the B. G. It would, therefore, be relevant to see how and to what extent it is used by them.

Before we discuss the role of reason in the B.G. and Buddhism, we must clarify the use of the term. Buddha himself has been characterised as a rationalist by different scholars in different senses.[1] We must, therefore, be clear and precise in which of the senses he can or cannot be considered a rationalist.

In modern philosophical language, rationalism is a school of philosophy opposed to empiricism. It is defined as "a theory of philosophy in which the criterion of truth is not sensory but intellectual and deductive—usually associated with an attempt to introduce mathematical methods into philosophy as in Descartes, Leibniz and Spinoza."[2]

---

1. V. Bhattacharya—The Basic Conception of Buddhism, pp. 9ff; Tatia—Studies in Jaina Philosophy, p. 7; Poussin—The Way to Nirvana, pp. 30ff : Keith—Buddhist Philosophy in India and Ceylon, p. 14; Jennings—The Vedantic Buddhism of the Buddha, p. xxiv; Radhakrishnan—Indian Philosophy, Vol. I., P. 359.

2. Runes—The Dictionary of Philosophy, s.v. 'Rationalism'.

In the light of this definition, Buddha is, evidently, not a rationalist. He is definitely opposed to a purely intellectual approach to truth. He has no self-evident axioms or premises from which conclusions are to be drawn in a deductive manner, as is the case with typical rationalists like Descartes, Spinoza and Leibniz. On the other hand, as we have noticed, he relies on direct experience and observation, and tries to verify things in the light of objective facts. He does not construct metaphysical theories on the basis of purely intellectual reflections or speculations, as is done by modern rationalists. In fact, he criticises such rational theorists and metaphysicians who are referred to in the Pali Canon under the names, 'takkī.' and 'vīmaṃsī'. The significance of these terms has already been examined by K.N. Jayatilleke who points out that "the term takki is quite clearly used of a 'rationalist' in the sense of a 'pure reasoner' (suddha-takkika) who constructed a metaphysical theory on the basis of reasoning. In this sense takkī and vīmaṃsī (investigator, or speculator) go together."[1]

In the Pali texts, we frequently find Buddha dissociating himself from this class of rationalists and criticising views which are said to be based on different forms of reasoning and reflection. In the Saṅgārava Sutta, as we have already seen, Buddha clearly dissociates himself from the class of traditionalists (anussavikā) and rationalists (takkī, vīmaṃsī), and claims to be an experientialist.[2] Again when Sunakkhatta tries to undermine the doctrine of Buddha by saying that "the recluse Gotama does not have a distinctive superhuman paranormal knowledge and insight, the recluse Gotama preaches a doctrine which is a product of reasoning, a result of speculation and based on mere self-reflection" (natthi samaṇassa Gotamassa uttarimmanussadhammā, alamariyañāṇadassana viseso; takkapariyāhataṃ samaṇo Gotamo dhammaṃ deseti vimaṃsānucaritaṃ sayaṃ paṭibhānaṃ, M. I. 68), Buddha disowns all this by pointing out that this is a slanderous statement made by him (Sunakkhatta)

1. Early Buddhist Theory of Knowledge, p. 264.
2. M. II. 211.

out of anger.[1] This amounts to disowning the appellation of being a rationalist. Besides, we find him criticising the four different kinds of knowledge based on various forms of reason or reflection, viz, (i) takkahetu (ii) naya-hetu (iii)ākāra-parivitakkena and(iv)diṭṭhi-nijjhānakkhanti.[2] In all these forms of reasoning their unreliability is pointed out on the ground that they may be well-reasoned or ill-reasoned, true or false. To use the words of the Canon itself, "Herein.. a certain teacher is a reasoner or speculator; he teaches a doctrine which is a product of reasoning, a result of speculation and based on self-reflection. But in case of a person who reasons and speculates, his reasoning may be good or bad, true or false."[3] This means that theories based on mere reason present a twofold difficulty: firstly, their consistency is subject to doubt; and secondly, even if they are consistent, their consistency is no guarantee of their factual truth. Thus with regard to rational theories there are four possibilities:—

1. sutakkitaṃ tathā i. e. well-reasoned true
2. sutakkitaṃ aññathā i. e. well-reasoned false
3. duttakkitaṃ tathā i. e. ill-reasoned true
4. duttakkitaṃ aññathā i. e. ill-reasoned false.

This means that on the ground of mere reasoning one can, at utmost, if he is very careful, claim consistency or formal validity for his theory. But thereby he can never be sure of having reached the objective truth, since even well-reasoned theories or consistent doctrines may be true or false. In short, pure reasoning cannot be relied on as a criterion of truth.

From what has been stated above, it is clear that the word 'takka' has been used in the Pali Canon in the sense of pure or *a priori* reason and takkī or vīmaṃsī is one who constructs theories on its basis. It is in this sense that

1. Kodhā ca panassa esā vācā bhāsitā, avaṇṇaṃ bhāsissāmī ti, M. I. 68.

2. A. I. 189; II. 191-3.

3. Idh'ekacco satthā takkī hoti vīmaṃsī, so takkapariyāhataṃ vimaṃsānucaritaṃ sayaṃ paṭibhānaṃ dhammaṃ deseti. Takkkissa kho pana. . .satthuno vīmaṃsissa sutakkitaṃ pi hoti duttakkitam pi hoti, tathā pi hoti aññathā pi hoti., M. I. 520.

Buddha criticises takka, and can, therefore, be regarded as a non-rationalist. Some scholars, however, have given inaccurate renderings of these words which are not supported by the usages of the Pali Canon. S. C. Vidyabhusana, for example, thinks that takkī in the Pali Canon refers to sophists. He says: "They were not logicians in the proper sense of the term but they appear to me to have been sophists who indulged in quibble and casuistry."[1] He uses the words 'sophist' and 'argumentationist' for takkī and 'casuist' for vīmaṃsī. (op. cit. p. 21). He is quoted by Keith who follows the same line. He says: "The old Pali texts ignore the names Nyāya or Vaiśeṣika: in the Brahmajāla Sutta we hear in lieu of them only of takkī, sophists and vīmaṃsī, casuists...."[2] Mrs. Rhys Davids brings in further confusion by using the words 'sophists' and 'sceptics' almost indiscriminately. We can see this indiscriminate usage in the following lines: "There appears to have been parallel with the Absolutist beliefs, a good deal of scepticism current when Buddhism arose...The most important of the *sceptic* schools was that of Ājīvakas." She then speaks of "another *sophistical* school headed by Ajita of the Hair-garment."[3] Oldenberg speaks of 'a species of Indian sophistic' and compares it with 'their Greek counterpart.' He observes: "Certain phenomena which developed themselves in the busy bustle of these ascetic and philosophizing circles, may be described as a species of Indian sophistic...The conditions under which this sophistic arose were quite similar to those which gave birth to their Greek counterpart."[4] He further goes on comparing this Indian sophistic with their Greek counterpart.

These descriptions do not square with the description of the takkī (rationalist) that we have given above on the basis of the Pali texts. Though it is not possible to examine at great length the various contexts in which takkī is used in the Pali Canon, a few important references would suffice

1. History of Indian Logic, p. 227.
2. Indian Logic and Atomism, p. 13.
3. Buddhism, pp. 85-86.
4. Buddha, Translatad by W. Hoey, p. 67.

to make it clear that the primary sense of the word, 'takkī' has been confused by these scholars. Nowhere do we find any evidence in the Canon to suggest that the takkīs of the texts are to be taken as sophists. The attempt of Oldenberg to compare these so-called Indian sophists with their Greek counterpart finds no basis in the texts. None can deny that the term 'sophist' implies a vain or fallacious reasoner who displays his argumentative skill merely with a view to getting victory over his adversary. Its meaning has its association with the peripatetic teachers of Greece in the 5th century B. C. who denied the objectivity of knowledge, and hence the possibility of any objective truth. The possibility of objective truth being denied, there remained, only one motive for their debates, and that was to defeat the rivals by means of rhetoric and fallacious reasoning. They, in fact, with this aim in view started schools and became paid teachers for training people in that art.[1] According to the Concise Oxford Dictionary, 'sophist' means "an ancient Greek paid teacher of philosophy and rhetoric, captious or fallacious reasoner, quibbler."

Now, the picture presented by the Pali texts of the Indian sceptics or the 'so-called' Indian sophists is quite different. Instead of entering into debate with the overt intention of using fallacious reasoning, most of the Indian sceptics are found to avoid it either on account of their intellectual cowardice or their scruples for truth. As the Pali Canon puts it, it was "due to fear or disgust at joining the issue" (anuyogabhayā anuyogaprijegucchā, D. I. 26). They felt that "the debate would lead to vexation" (vivāde sati vighāto, M. I. 499). Thus as against the Greek sophists who welcomed such debates and unscrupulously took delight in the intentional use of fallacious reasoning, we find these Indian sceptics shunning debate mainly on account of moral scruples like the fear of uttering falsehood (musāvādabhayā, D. I. 25). Probably they thought that if they are not openly committed to any particular thesis, they would remain immune to any attack by other theorists or, alternatively,

1. Russell—A History of Western Philosophy, p. 94ff.

they avoided dogmatic statements, because they themselves had not reached any definite conviction. In any case the approach of these Indian sceptics is one of moral scruple, abhorrence of debate and avoidance of fallacious reasoning, which is evidently the very opposite of what the Greek sceptics did. It is therefore, difficult to agree with Oldenberg who regards Indian sceptics as 'sophists' and compares them with 'their Greek counterpart'. The indiscriminate use of the words 'sceptic' and 'sophist' by Mrs. Rhys Davids also cannot be justified in the Indian context. Vidyabhusana and Keith also are found to be mistaken in using the words 'sophist' and 'casuist' for takkī and vīmaṃsī. Even if the approach of some other schools (whose position with regard to debate is not specifically stated in the Pali texts) is admitted to be sophistic, it must be noted that they are not characterised in the texts as 'takkī' but as 'titthiyas.' The word 'takkī' has quite a different connotation which has been lost sight of by these scholars who use the word 'sophist' as its synonym.

We have shown above on the basis of the contextual meaning that the word 'takkī' has been used in the Pali texts in the sense of pure reasoners who construct speculative metaphysical theories by means of *a priori* or pure reasoning. It is in this sense that Buddha dissociates himself from them and can be regarded as a non-rationalist.

There are, however, other senses in which Buddha may properly be called a rationalist. He is rationalist in the sense of being critical or non-dogmatic in his approach. Thus V. Bhattacharya says that Buddha "was an out and out rationalist," since "he would not like to give anything as dogmatic truth, but always based his views on the strong ground of reason."[1] N. Tatia also voices the same view.[2] Poussin considers him a rationalist on the ground that he is non-mystical and non-metaphysical in his outlook and explanation. He says: "If we were asked to characterize in a word the old Buddhist discipline of salvation and the old

1. The Basic Conception of Buddhism, pp. 9-10.
2. Studies in Jaina Philosophy, p. 7.

Buddhism as a whole, we should say that it is a form of rationalism. Every idea and every practice made use of by Śākyamuni to build up his theory and his rule of religious life have been freed from any tinge of mysticism."[1] Buddhism "succeeded in explaining the cosmos and human destiny without recourse to any metaphysical agent."[2] Again, he may be regarded as a rationalist in the sense of being opposed to supernaturalist explanations. As Radhakrishnan says:"...he is a rationalist, since he wished to study reality or experience without any reference to supernatural revelation."[3] Radhakrishnan, however, seems to go wrong when in his subsequent statement he observes that Buddha "wanted to establish a religion within the bounds of pure reason...He is a dialectician, arguing with his opponents to lead them to liberation."[4] We have already shown that Buddha does not construct his doctrines on the basis of pure reason. Lastly, one may call Buddha a rationalist in the sense of being an experientialist, opposing *a priori* reflection (takka). Here the meaning of rationalism is different. Radhakrishnan seems to have this sense of rationalism in mind when he says that "he (Buddha) relied on reason and experience... He presents to his followers the experience through which he himself has passed and exhorts them to verify for themselves his views and conclusions."[5] Thus his rationalism consists in his call for objective experience and verification.

After having seen the various senses in which Buddhism can and cannot be characterised as rationalism, we may now turn to the B.G. The position of the B.G. in relation to the philosophical use of the term rationalism seems to be quite similar to that of Buddhism. Although there is no reference to various schools of thought in the B.G., and we have no occasion to see a clear-cut stand taken by the B. G. in relation to the theories based on pure reason (takka), yet

1. The Way to Nirvāṇa, p. 30.
2. Ibid., p. 32.
3. Indian Philosophy, Vol. I. p. 359.
4. Ibid., p. 359.
5. Indian Philosophy, Vol. I. p. 359.

its attitude to pure reason or intellectual reflection is well indicated from its general approach to truth. We have seen that, according to the B. G., the truth is supposed to be mystically comprehended. In view of this general mystical approach, it is plausible to think that the B. G. cannot but be opposed to pure reason as the source of valid knowledge or truth, for mysticism and pure rationalism cannot go hand in hand. This is confirmed when we find the B. G. calling the reality or truth beyond thought or reason (acintyam, B. G. II. 25, VIII. 9; XII. 3) just as Buddha speaks of his dhamma as beyond reason (atakkāvacaro, M. I. 167, 487). The use of the word 'cintā' in the sense of 'tarka' (pure reason) is not uncommon. In Jaina epistemology also we find the word 'cintā' used as a synonym of 'tarka'.[1] Thus it appears that the B.G. also, like Buddhism, does not recognise tarka (pure reason) as an independent valid source of knowledge, though its limited value is not denied by any one of them and, as we shall see in the sequel, both of them make limited use of it.

But as against Buddhism, which may be called rationalistic in other senses of the term, the B. G. seems to be non-rationalistic in all senses except one. The very fact that the B. G. does not wholly dissociate itself from tradition, indicates its dogmatism and in this sense it may be regarded as non-rationalistic. Again owing to its mystical metaphysical and theological (supernatural) approaches it will have to be characterised as non-rationalistic in sharp contrast to Buddhism. Only with regard to the last sense, we find the B. G. making experientialist claims like Buddhism. But here also it parts company with the latter inasmuch as it does not permit any doubt, critical investigation or verification. In fact, the author of the B. G. would have us believe that it is the infallible God himself who speaks in the first person and so his utterances are beyond doubt or dispute. In Buddhism, however, Buddha neither believes in God nor

1. Tattvārthādhigama Sūtra. I. 13; see its commentary by J. L. Jaini who points out that mati-jñāna is inclusive of smṛti (remembrance), sañjñā or pratyabhijñā (recognition) *cintā or tarka* (reasoning) and abhinibodha or anumāna (inference).

does he claim himself to be one and so he talks as a man whose statements are open to verification.

From the above it is clear that reason (takka) in the modern philosophical sense of the term is not accepted by Buddhism and the B. G. as a means of valid knowledge. But despite its non-recognition as a full-fledged means of valid knowledge, its limited value is not ignored. It is perhaps in recognition of this very limited role of reason that religions based on reason (takka) are not counted by Buddha among those religions which are false (abrahmacariyavāsā, M. I. 514-518) but among those which are considered only unsatisfactory (anassāsikāni, M. I. 519-521). Still clearer evidence of the recognition of the limited role of reason is contained in the following statement of Buddha who addressing Ānanda says : "So far as anything can be ascertained by reason, O, Ānanda, you have ascertained" (yāvatakam kho, Ānanda, takkāya pattabbaṃ anuppattaṃ tayā, S.I. 56).

Now, what is this limited role of reason? The limited role consists firstly, in directing intelligent people (viññū purisā) to select their proper course in the light of it and secondly, in exposing the absurdity of the opposite view and thereby (indirectly) justifying one's own. Let us see how reason is used by Buddhism and the B. G. for both these purposes:—

In the Apaṇṇaka Sutta, we find Buddha asking the Brahmin house-holders to decide their own course of action on the ground of pure reason. Even if nothing definite is known about the reality, one can follow the proper path in reliance on reason. Buddha points out that there are two alternative theories: the one denying moral responsibility, survival and the other world etc., and the other affirming all this. Now, if a man chooses to live in accordance with the former alternative and if his view be really true (i. e. there is no other world etc.), then from the future point of view he has no cause for regret after death (kāyassa bheda sotthim attānaṃ karissati. M. I. 403) but from the present point of view, in this very life he is to be reproached by the elite as an immoral person and a disbeliever (diṭṭheva dhamme viññūnaṃ gārahyo, loc. cit.). But if his view be false (i. e. there is another world etc.), he loses in both ways (ubhayattha kaliggaho, loc. cit.): from the future point of view he will be doomed to be born in hell (kāyassa bhedā...nirayaṃ upapajjissati, loc. cit.) and from the present point of view he will be reproached by the elite in this very life. Thus, in adopting the first alternative, he suffers at least on one count (reproach by the elite) and runs the risk of suffering on both counts (reproach by the elite as well as falling into hell).

But, on the other hand, if he chooses to live in accordance with the latter alternative and if his view be really true (i. e. there is another world etc.), then from the future point of view, he will be born in heaven after death (Kāyassa bhedā.. . saggaṃ lokam upapajjissati, M. I. 404) and from the present point of view he will be praised by the elite in this very life (diṭṭheva dhamme viññūnaṃ pāsaṃso, loc. cit.)—thus he gains in both ways (ubhayattha kaṭaggaho, loc. cit.). And if his view be false (i. e. there is no other world etc.), then also from the present point of view he is at least praised by the elite in this very life and from the future point of view there is no question of gaining or losing. Thus in the case of adopting this second alternative he gains at least on one count (praise by the elite) and stands the hope of gaining on both counts (praise by the elite and birth in heaven).

Evidently, it is on purely rational grounds that Buddha asks people to decide their course of life, if they are not in a position to see the objective truth.

Now, if we turn to the B. G., we find that this limited role of reason is recognised by it as well. We find Kṛṣṇa trying to direct Arjuna in a particular way by means of a similar rational argument.

Arjuna is aggrieved to think that he, in the course of the battle, is going to slay his own kith and kin, friends and relatives.[1] Kṛṣṇa, in order to indicate that there is no reason for grief in the situation, points out that there are only two possibilities: either (i) the Soul is unborn and

1. B.G. I. 26-37; II. 4-9.

undying or (ii) it is always subject to birth and death. If the former alternative be true, it is wrong to think that anyone will be really killing anyone and so there is no reason for grief. And if the latter alternative be true, then birth and death are only inevitable and so it is futile to grieve for anyone. Thus, whatever be the case (truth), there is no reason to grieve. The verses read as follows: "One who knows that he (the Soul) is indestructible and eternal, unborn and undecaying, how can such a person slay anyone, O Arjuna, or cause anyone to slay?... Therefore, knowing him as such, you should not grieve. Even if you think that he (the Soul) is always subject to birth and death, then also, O Arjuna, you should not grieve, for death is certain for him who is born and certain is birth for him who has died. Therefore, you should not grieve for the inevitable."[1]

Thus we see that both Buddhism and the B. G. make use of reason in deciding the proper course of action. It is significant to note that the line of action is sought to be determined without prejudice to objective truth. This shows that according to them reason is considered helpful only in showing the proper direction but not in revealing objective truth. It can only be a pointer to the right path but not a discoverer of the ultimate truth. This explains why despite making limited use of it, none of them considers it as an independent means of valid knowledge.

The second purpose for which reason is utilised is to expose the absurdity of the opposite view by pointing out its inner inconsistency and thereby (indirectly) to show the validity of one's own position. Let us take some illustrations of it from Buddhism and the B. G.

It is argued in the Therīgāthā that "if water-baptism can free one of evil Karma (p), then the fishes, tortoises, frogs, etc.... will go straight to heaven (q)"[2] But q is absurd or false, which, therefore, implies the absurdity or falsity of the implicans, p. Thus by exposing the absurdity of the rival view that 'the external bath or purification can

1. B.G. II. 21, 25-27.
2. Therīgāthā, 240-1.

free one of evil karma' the validity of Buddha's own position, that evil karma can be washed out only through inner purification[1], is indirectly shown.

A similar argument in the *modus tollendo tollens* is used against the four theories, viz.: Materialism, Amoralism, Non-causal Fatalism and Determinism which are described as definitely false religions not to be pursued by the holy aspirant (abrahmacariyavāsā). It is argued that if these theories are true (p), then the austerities like "the nakedness, the shaving of the head, the exertion in squatting, the plucking out of the hair of the head and the beard, on the part of such teachers are superfluous (q)"[2]; for it would be all the same (in both the cases) whether they observe them or do not observe them.[3] But q is not the case, for those who observe these austerities, evidently would not have observed them in that case. So p is not the case.

Similar arguments are used against theism. To take one instance, it is argued: "If God designs the life of the entire world—its glory as well as misery, actions—good and evil (p), then man is only the doer of his bidding and God (alone) is contaminated." (q)[4] But q is absurd, for the freedom of man is an experienced fact and theists consider their God to be pure and uncontaminated. So p is false.

Thus merely by pointing out obvious absurdities or inner inconsistencies of rival views, their untenability is shown without bringing objective truth into consideration. At times, we find Buddha starting with an assumption of his opponent and by a series of questions leading the opponent to a position in which he contradicts himself. Then it is pointed out to him that his earlier statement does not tally with the later and *vice versa* (na kho te sandhīyati purimena

1. M. I. 39.

2. Atirekaṃ kho pana imassa bhoto satthuno naggiyaṃ muṇḍiyaṃ ukkuṭikappadhānaṃ kesamassulocanaṃ, M. I. 515-518.

3. akatena...kataṃ...ubho pi mayaṃ ettha samasamā sāmaññaṃ pattā, *Ibid.*, 515-518.

4. Issaro sabbalokassa sace kappeti jīvitaṃ;
iddhivyasanabhāvañ ca, kammaṃ kalyāṇapāpakaṃ;
niddesakāri puriso, issaro tena lippati, J.V. 238.

vā pacchimaṃ pacchimena vā purimaṃ, M. I. 376, 377, 378). It is through this method that Upāli, the well known adherent of Nigaṇṭha Nātaputta was made to realise the untenability of his teacher's position (loc. cit.)

In the B. G. the refutation of rival theories is not to be met with. Yet we can see a somewhat similar use of reason being made by Kṛṣṇa in the course of his attempt to show the untenability of Arjuna's position. In the very first remark of Kṛṣṇa about Arjuna's attitude an argument of the nature of *modus tollendo tollens* is implied. Kṛṣṇa tries to expose the absurdity of Arjuna's stand by pointing out the inconsistency of the latter who is grieving like an unwise person on the one hand, and uttering words of wisdom on the other. He says: "You grieve for those whom you should not grieve for, and yet speak like men of wisdom. Wise men do not grieve for the dead or for the living"[1] This remark implies the following argument—

If you are wise (p), you should not grieve (q)
But you grieve (q is not the case)
Therefore, you are not wise (p is not the case).

Similarly, we find the statement: "If one knows him (the Soul) to be indestructible and eternal, unborn and undecaying (p), how can such a person slay any one, O Arjuna, or cause any one to slay"[2] i. e. he cannot slay or cause to slay (q). Thus the absurdity of Arjuna's stand is shown by pointing out the inconsistency in his attitude in that while holding the view that the Soul is indestructible and eternal, he thinks that he can slay or cause to slay.

It may, however, be noted that through the above argument it is not the absurdity of the implicans (viz. the eternity of the Soul) which is sought to be exposed but only the absurdity of the man's stand who while holding this view does not carry it on consistently. Because, in the present case, the B. G. stands committed to p and so if there is any anomaly in q, it can only indicate the absurdity of the man's position who does not consistenly hold p. In Bud-

1. B G. II. 11.
2. B.G. II. 21

dhism, however, the opponent's view is consciously accepted as true with a view to exposing its absurdity in the light of the evident inconsistency.

It is evident that even in this limited sphere, reason has has to be used carefully, for, as Buddha has pointed out, rational argument may be well-reasoned or ill-reasoned (sutakkitam pi hoti duttakkitam pi hoti, M. I. 520). Thus, reason can offer right guidance and can rightly show the absurdity of the opposite view only when it is properly and consistently made use of.

(*D*) *The Attitude to Authority* :—

The B. G. and Buddhism differ with regard to authority as a means of valid knowledge. Buddha, in his resolute search for objective truth, casts aside the burden of the past, and refuses to accept authority as a safe and reliable means of valid knowledge. Whatever old ideas he retains of the tradition, he claims to retain on the basis of his own direct personal experience, and not on the ground of any authority. He clearly says : "I do not speak by hearing from other recluses and Brahmins, but I speak only that which I have myself known, myself seen and myself comprehended."[1] We have already seen that he claims to be an experientialist and dissociates himself from the traditionalists (anussavikā) and rationalists (takkī).[2] The B. G., on the other hand, is conservative and compromising and so does not break away completely from the tradition. Though it also lays claim to being an experientialist[3] and undermines the value and authority of the Vedas, yet it does not shake off authority altogether, and is found to accept it in its many forms.

The Pali Canon is analytic enough to delineate the different forms of authority. It presents a list

1. nāññassa samaṇassa vā brāhmaṇassa vā sutvā vadāmi, api ca yad eva mayā sāmaṃ ñātaṃ sāmam diṭṭhaṃ sāmaṃ viditaṃ tad evā'haṃ vadāmī ti, S.V. 390.

2. M. II. 211.

3. B.G. IV. 5. (Tāny ahaṃ veda sarvāni) ; XIII. 24 (Dhyānenā'tmani paśyanti) : XV. 1:. (Yatanto yoginaś cai'naṃ paśyanti).

of six kinds of authority which Buddha has criticised.[1] They are the following :—

(a) anussava i.e. the Vedic tradition

(b) paramparā i.e. tradition in general

(c) iti kirā i.e. report or hearsay

(d) piṭaka-sampadā i.e. scripture in general

(e) bhavyarūpatā i.e. eminence of the speaker

(f) samaṇo no garu i.e prestige of the speaker

If in the light of this list we try to look for the different forms of authority referred to in the B. G., we find that except 'a' (Vedic tradition) and 'c' (report or hearsay) all the rest are directly or indirectly accepted by the B.G. . Kṛṣṇa, while imparting the teaching of disinterested action (yoga) to Arjuna, speaks of its ancient tradition (paramparā, i.e. 'b') and refers to the teachers and followers of eminence (bhavyarūpatā, i.e. 'e') who commanded high prestige (samaṇo no garu, i.e. 'f'). To quote his statement : "I expounded this imperishable yoga to Vivasvān, Vivasvān told it to Manu and Manu spoke it to Ikṣvāku. Thus coming down through *tradition* (evam paramparā prāptam) this was known by the royal sages (rājarṣayah)."[2] Kṛṣṇa here tries to show the authoritativeness of this teaching on the ground that it has come down from the ancient *tradition*, and followed by men of *eminence* who enjoyed high *prestige*, as royal sages. Similarly he cites the example of the *eminent* King Janaka[3] who enjoyed the *prestige* of being a royal sage—thus again making use of eminence and prestige (bhavyarūpatā and samaṇo no garu).[4]

---

1. Kalāma Sutta, A. I. 189; Bhaddiya Sutta, A. II. 191-3.
2. B.G. IV. 1 and 2.
3. B.G. III. 20.
4. The separate mention of 'bhavyarūpatā' and 'samaṇo no garu' implies that the two are distinguished. Bhavyarūpatā means eminence of a person i.e. his intrinsic ability and merit. The commentary confirms the same (ayam bhikkhu bhabbarūpo, imassa katham gahetum yuttam, A.A. II. 305.) Samaṇo no garu (lit. the recluse is our respected teacher) means to accept a statement out of respect for the teacher, i.e. acceptance on the prestige value of the person speaking. As for example, we find the statement : 'satthā no garu, satthu gāravena ca mayṃ vadema' i.e. our teacher is respected, we speak out of respect for the teacher, M.I. 265.

Thus bhavyarūpatā seems to indicate the intrinsic worth of the speaker, while the latter signifies his reputation or prestige among people. At times both may go together and at times only one may be the case.

He further says : "Having known thus, the action was performed (karmayoga or the path of action was adopted) even by the previous seekers of emancipation. Therefore (tasmāt) you also should perform action itself, as the ancients did in former times."[1] Here we may note the significant use of the word, 'therefore' which clearly implies that the ancient tradition has been considered as a ground for adopting the same line of action. It is utilised as a weighty argument to let Arjuna see the truth and value of karmayoga. Besides., paramparā (tradition in general), bhavyarūpatā (eminence of the authority) and samaṇo no garu (prestige of the authority), the B. G. quite unambiguously refers to piṭaka-sampadā (authority of scriptures in general). It says : "He who discards the *scriptural law* (śāstravidhi) and acts according to the promptings of his desire does not attain either perfection or happiness or the supreme goal. Therefore let scripture be your authority (tasmāc chāstraṃ pramāṇaṃ te) for determining what should be done and what should not be done. Knowing the prescribed injunctions of the scripture, you should perform duty in this world."[2] Thus the authority of scripture is considered essential for having the knowledge of one's own rightful duties, without which the supreme goal or perfection cannot be attained. Subsequently, however, provision to attain heaven is made for the non-followers of scripture as well when it is said that men endowed with illuminative faith (sāttvikī śraddhā) can attain heaven by worshipping the gods even while discarding scriptural injunctions (śāstravidhim utsṛjya).[3]

Thus out of the six forms of authority criticised in early Buddhism, four are accepted in the B.G. Iti kirā (report or hearsay) is nowhere referred to, and the Vedic authority is undermined. But in spite of undermining the authority of the Vedas, the attitude of the B. G. towards it is quite different from that of early Buddhism. Since the authority of the Vedas is by far the most important (it is mentioned in the Nikāyas as the first among the six forms of authority)

1. Evaṃ jñātvā kṛtaṃ karma pūrvair api mumukṣubhiḥ; kuru karmai'va *tasmāt* tvam. . ., B.G. IV. 15.
2. B.G. XVI. 23 and 24.
3. B.G. XVII. 1-4 and IX. 23-25.

and the adherents of the Vedic tradition (anussavikā) are counted as the first among the threefold division of religious teachers on epistemological grounds, and also because the very same criticisms are applicable to all the other forms of authority, it is important to have a clear idea of the respective positions of the B.G. and Buddhism with regard to the authority of the Vedas

There is no doubt that the B.G. relegates the Vedas to an inferior position. The highest knowledge and the supreme goal cannot be attained by following the Vedic injunctions. They would rather prove an obstruction in the way of the the highest pursuit, since they abound in the elements of earthly and heavenly pleasure, which naturally tend to distract the mind from the path of real peace and tranquility. Arjuna is, therefore, asked to rise above the Vedic outlook. Kṛṣṇa says : "The Vedas have for their subject matter the threefold guṇas (i.e. they are concerned with the sphere of the objects, born of the threefold guṇas). But let yourself be free from this threefold nature, O Arjuna."[1] It is not possible to attain meditative repose and consequent knowledge and bliss unless the distracting thoughts of the Vedas are abandoned. It is said : "When your intellect which is bewildered (vipratipannā)[2] by the Vedas, shall stand unshaken and stable in concentration (samādhau) then shall you attain the equanimity (yoga)."[3] The B.G., therefore, repeatedly emphasises the inefficacy of the Vedas for the attainment of the highest goal. They are enumerated as the first among the various deficient means adopted generally by religious people. Kṛṣna says : "Neither by the Vedas, nor by sacrifices, nor by study, nor by charity, nor by ceremonial rites nor by severe austerities can I with this from be seen in this world of men..."[4] Thus the Vedas are considered not only inefficaious but also obstructive to the attainment of the

1. Traiguṇyaviṣayā Vedā nistraiguṇyo bhavā'rjuna, B.G. II. 45.

2. Śaṅkara means by 'vipratipanna' a state of bewilderment or misguidance (vikṣiptā), S.B.G. II. 53.

3. B.G. II. 53; The word 'yoga' is used to signify the state of 'equanimity' as already defined in B.G. II. 48 (smatvaṃ yoga ucyate)

4. B.G. XI. 48; cf. XI. 53.

highest knowledge. Nevertheless, their efficacy for securing heavenly pleasures is not denied nor is their divine origin questioned. They are said to be created by Prajāpati or Brahmā for the fulfilment of human desires. It is said : "In the beginning Prajāpati having created men along with sacrifice said : 'let you all flourish with this, let this be the giver of all your desired objects."[1] To say that Brahmā or Prajāpati is the creator of sacrifices amounts to saying that he is the creator of the Vedas, since the latter emobody them. The same is stated in a clearer way as follows :—"Sacrifices emerge out of injunctions, injunctions originate from Brahmā (the Vedas)"[2] Thus the limited value and validity of the Vedas are not denied by the B.G., though they are not accepted to be the source of the highest knowledge.

Since the Vedas are not based on true knowledge, the practice of the Vedic rites is said to produce limited merit leading to temporary sojourn in heaven. When the merit is exhausted one will have to come down to the cycle of birth and rebirth. As Kṛṣṇa says : "The followers of the three Vedas (traividyāḥ)...worshipping me with sacrifices pray for the heavenly state. They having acquired merit, reach the holy world of Indra and enjoy in heaven the divine pleasures of the gods. Having enjoyed the vast world of heaven, they, at the exhaustion of their merit, come down to the world of mortals. Thus, the desirers of enjoymement, having followed the doctrine of the three Vedas, come to the cycle of birth and death."[3] The *raison d'être* of their temporary stay in heaven and fall from there is said to be their lack of true knowledge. "Temporary is the fruit that is gained by these men of little understanding" (Antavat tu phalaṃ teṣāṃ tad bhavaty alpamedhasām, B.G, VII. 23). "They do not know me truly and hence they fall down" (na tu mām abhijānanti tattvenā'taś cyavanti te. B.G. IX. 24).

This attitude of the B.G. towards the Vedas at once reminds of the similar attitude of the Muṇḍakopaniṣad towards

---

1. B.G. III. 10.
2. Yajñaḥ karmasamudbhavaḥ; Karma Brahmodbhavaṃ viddhi. . ., B.G. III. 14-15. Śaṅkara commenting on the word 'Brahmodbhavaṃ' disjoins it as Brahma+udbhavaḥ, and takes the word 'Brahma' as a synonym of the Vedas.
3. B.G. IX. 20 and 21.

them, where the distinction between lower and higher knowledge is made[1], and the Vedas are said to embody the former[2]. We have already noted (supra p. 109, fn. 1) that not only the general tone of the B.G. but some of its words also are similar to those of the Muṇḍaka in this respect.[3]

Let us now see how the Vedas are looked upon in early Buddhism. First of all, Buddha discards the theory of the divine origin of the Vedas. The authors of the Vedas, according to him, are the ancient sages (pubbakā isayo mantānaṃ kattāro mantānaṃ pavattāro. D.I. 242. M. II 169, 170.) None of these sages and saints are said to lay claim to direct personal knowledge of the truth (natthi koci brāhmaṇānaṃ eka brāhmaṇo pi yo evam āha : 'aham etaṃ jānāmi, aham etaṃ passāmi', M. II. 170). So the Vedas lack an experiential basis. Nor can the Vedas be considered as a revelation from Brahmā, since none of the Brahmin sages claimed to have had a direct personal vision of Brahmā (natthi koci tevijjānaṃ brāhmaṇānaṃ eka brāhmaṇo pi yena Brahmā sakkhidiṭṭho, D.I. 238). The direct personal knowledge of Brahmā or of his abode being denied to the authors of the Vedas, the Vedic injunctions calculated to lead to the world of Brahmā or heaven cannot be relied on. Thus the claim for exclusive validity of the Vedas that "this alone is true, all else is false" (idam eva saccaṃ mogham aññaṃ, M. II. 170) turns out to be a mere baseless faith (amūlikā saddhā, loc. cit.). Buddha calls it a "blind tradition" (andhaveṇi paramparā, D.I. 239; M. II. 170) in which the blind are led by the blind.[4] The Vedic Brahmin who without knowing and seeing Brahmā prescribes the path for the communion with Brahmā (Brahmasahabyatāya, D.I. 241) is compared to a man who without having any idea whatsoever of the lady of his love, foolishly claims to

1. dve vidye veditavye. . .parā caivāparā ca., Mundaka. I. 1.4.

2. Muṇḍaka, I. 1. 5.

3. Compare further B. G. IX. 20 and 21 with Muṇḍaka I. 2. 10; see also Muṇḍaka I. 2. 7-9.

4. Seyyathā pi. . .andhaveṇi paramparāsaṃsattā purimo pi na passati, majjhimo pi na passati, pacchimo pi na passati, evaṃ eva kho... andhaveṇūpamaṃ maññe tevijjānaṃ brāhmaṇānaṃ bhāsitaṃ, D. I. 239, M. II. 170.

be in love with the imagined lady of the land.[1] The means prescribed in the Vedas for the realisation of such an unknown and unseen goal is compared to the construction of a staircase for a palace, the very location or size of which is not known.[2] The Vedic hymns and prayers invoking the favour of the deities are as futile as the calling of the other bank of the river to come to this side.[3] Thus the Vedic authority being devoid of the experiential basis cannot be considered dependable either for the realisation of the highest goal or for the attainment of heaven. It is just a belief which may be either true or false.

The attitude of Buddha towards the Vedic authority, as also towards some other forms of belief and reasoning is very clearly indicated in his analytic gradation of the stages of faith and knowledge. He says : "There are five things which have a twofold result in this life. What five ? (Belief based on) faith, likes, tradition, superficial reflection and approval of a theory reasoned about (saddhā, ruci, anussavo, ākāraparivitakko, diṭṭhinijjhānakkhanti)...; Even if one hears something on the profoundest tradition (svānussutaṃ yeva hoti), that may be empty, hollow and false, while what one does not hear on the profoundest tradition, may be factual, true and not otherwise. It is not proper for an intelligent person to come categorically to the conclusion in this matter that this alone is true and all else is false."[4] But if one has a non-dogmatic attitude to what he has learnt from tradition or authority and if he does not come to a categorical conclusion that "it alone is true, all is false" (idam eva saccaṃ mogham aññaṃ, M. II. 171), then he is said to safeguard the truth (ettāvatā saccam anurakkhati, loc. cit.). After this initial stage of saccānurakkhaṇā (safeguarding the truth), Buddha speaks of two subsequent stages of saccānubodha (knowing the truth) and saccānuppatti (realising the truth). The former is said to arise when one,

---

1. D.I. 241-2.
2. D.I. 243-4.
3. D.I. 244.
4. M. II. 170-1.

on critical inquiry and examination of the speaker, finds him free from greed, hatred and delusion (lobha, dosa and moha), and then having listened to him with trust, applies himself and gets the glimpse of the highest truth (param saccaṃ). The last stage is the stage of perfect realisation and verification of the truth resulting from the practice, cultivation and development of the same mental states (tesam eva... dhammānam āsevanā, bhāvanā, bahulīkammaṃ saccānuppatti hoti, M.II. 174). This shows that the knowledge through authority having no experiential basis, is itself subject to doubt and verification and cannot be considered as a source of valid knowledge.

The same is fully confirmed from the Sandaka Sutta where the religions based on authority or tradition (anussava) and reason (takka) along with two others (viz., Jainism and amarāvikkhepavāda) are characterised as unsatisfactory religions (anassāsikāni brahmacariyāni, M.I. 519-521). With regard to the religion based on tradition (anussava) it is said that "it may be well-remembered or ill-remembered; may be true or false" (sussutam pi hoti dussutam pi hoti; tathā pi hoti aññathā pi hoti, M.I. 520). It is exactly the same attitude which Buddha adopts with regard to knowledge based on pure reason, in relation to which he says that "it may be well-reasoned or ill-reasoned; may be true or false" (sutakkitam pi hoti duttakkitam pi hoti, tathā pi hoti aññathā pi hoti, loc. cit.). So, just as with regard to knowledge based on reason, so also with regard to knowledge based on authority there are four possibilities:—

1. sussutaṃ tathā i.e. well-remembered true
2. sussutaṃ aññathā i.e. well-remembered false
3. dussutaṃ tathā i.e. ill-remembered true
4. dussutaṃ aññathā i.e. ill-remembered false.

Thus there is a twofold difficulty with regard to the knowledge based on authority or tradition. Firstly, it is difficult to ascertain whether it is well-remembered or ill-remembered, and secondly, even if it is well-remembered, it is no guarantee of its truth; it may still be true or false and therefore doubtful and hence unreliable, since it is not based on direct personal verification. The same criticism holds good of all the six forms of authority mentioned in the Pali Canon.

Now one can clearly see how in spite of undermining the value of the Vedas, the attitude of the B. G. towards them is essentially different from that of early Buddhism. The B. G. considers the Vedas as having come down from Brahmā or Prajāpati for the worldly or heavenly welfare of man, and for that purpose their vailidity and efficacy are unquestionably accepted. It is only when people mistake them for the highest good that they are said to commit folly and are, therefore, characterised as ignorant or undiscerning (avipaścitaḥ, B. G. II. 42). In other words, the B. G. considers the Vedas to be definitely authoritative for lower knowledge, and definitely unauthoritative for higher knowledge. Buddhism, on the other hand, rejects the divine-origin theory of the Vedas and refuses to accept them as authoritative either for lower or higher purposes. The approach of the B. G. is one of definiteness and dogmatism, whereas that of Buddhism is one of doubt and criticism. The Buddhist approach, here also as elsewhere, remains empirical, whereas that of the B .G. is theological. But in view of its compromising attitude, the B. G. seems to have partly adjusted itself to the anti-Vedic move of the time, and accordingly undermined the value of the Vedas. In attacking the Vedas from the point of view of higher knowledge, it joins hands, as we have shown, with the later Ups., especially the Muṇḍaka, and on this score the tone of the B. G. along with the Muṇḍaka is very much similar to Buddhism despite radical differences in their approach.

Buddha's criticism of the Vedas must, however, be distinguished from that of the Materialists. Unlike the latter, Buddha does not make a downright condemnation of the Vedas and their authors.[1] According to Materialists "the authors of the three Vedas are knaves, buffoons and demons"[2], and the Vedas are full of falsity (anṛta), self-contradiction (vyāghāta) and repetition (punarukti). But, Buddha does not

---

1. cf. Oldenberg —Buddha, translated by Hoey, pp. 170ff.

2. Trayo vedasya kartāro bhaṇḍa dhūrta niśācarāḥ, Sarvadarśanasaṃgraha, p. 14.

question the honesty and piety of the Vedic seers, nor does he propose a wholesale rejection of their views. He recognises the value of their disciplined life and moral restraint (isayo pubbakā āsuṃ saññatattā tapassino, Sn. 51) and praises their virtue and rectitude (sīlaṃ ca ajjavaṃ..avaṇṇayuṃ, Sn. 51). Some of their views like belief in survival, moral values and moral retribution are found to be in conformity with the right philosophy of life (sammādiṭṭhi) as described by Buddha.[1] It is perhaps in due consideration of these things that the religion based on authority or tradition is not reckoned with those religions which are said to be false (abrahmacariyavāsā) but is counted among those which are considered only unsatisfactory (anassāsikāni brahmacariyāni, M. I. 520). Even with regard to sacrifices, Buddha is averse mainly to animal sacrifices and cumbrous and complicated rituals involving much of wasteful expenditure and energy. We find references to the arahants attending such sacrifices in which there is no slaughter.[2] The move to reinterpret the sacrifice which was started as early as the Chāndogyopaniṣad[2] is reflected in Buddhism as well, and we find Buddha explaining the nature of the best sacrifice.[3] The B. G., in view of its closer tie with traditional orthodoxy, is found to make a more concerted effort to provide a new meaning for the sacrifice.[4] Buddha, however, who was not labouring under the weight of tradition shows no excessive zeal for it and bases his criticism on epistemological grounds, being neither unnecessarily reactionary nor unduly credulous or dogmatic.

The attitude of the Materialists in this respect is diametrically opposed to that of the Mimāmsakas who are the greatest champions of the infallibility of the Vedic ritualism. According to the former the Vedas represent unmitigated falsity (anṛta), whereas according to the latter they are the

1. M. III. 72 (atthi dinnam, atthi yiṭṭham, atthi hutam, atthi sukatadukkatānaṃ kammānam phalaṃ vipāko...).
2. nirārambhaṃ yaññam upasaṅkamanti arahanto, S.I. 76; A.II. 43.
3. Atha yad yajña ity ācakṣate brahmacaryam eva tat, Chāndogya, VIII. 5. 1.
4. D.I. 134-147.
5. B.G. IV. 23-33.

embodiment of infallible and unquestionable truths. The Ups. the B. G. and Buddhism stand between these two extremes, but unlike Buddhism the tone of thc first two is subdued and not free from orthodoxy so that the Vedic authority is retained by them for certain purposes.

Thus we may conclude that the Buddhist attitude to authority is critical, whereas that of the B. G. is generally dogmatic. Out of the six kinds of authority criticised by Buddhism, the B. G. retains four of them, and the Vedic authority, though rejected as a means of higher knowledge, is, nevertheless, entertained for lower purposes.

An objection, however, may be raised and, in fact, has been raised against the aforesaid critical attitude of early Buddhism on the ground that faith (saddhā) plays as important a role in it as in any other religion. So it is necessary to examine the role of saddhā in early Buddhism in comparison with the B. G. and see whether it upsets the conclusion that we have arrived at.

(E) *The Role of Faith* (*Saddhā*):—

We have first to examine whether the concept of saddhā in early Buddism is compatible with the critical attitude adopted by Buddha in his address to the Kālāmas (A. I. 189) and Bhaddiya Licchavi (A. II. 191-3) and in his general teachings to people.

Scholars like Poussin, Keith and Mrs. Rhys Davids are inclined to read an element of faith and credulity in early Buddhism similar to what is found in other religions. According to Poussin, "Buddhism is a faith and creed" and in it faith is "the root of the correct view"[1], though inconsistently enough, "it considers critical inquiry as the one key to the comperhension of truth."[2] Thus Poussin tries to show that "Buddhism is contradiction itself"[3] He quotes the statement : "The Law saves the believer and destroys the

1. 'Faith and Reason in Buddhism' in Transactions of the Third International Congress for the History of Religions, Vol. II. p. 34.

2. *Ibid*, p. 33.

3. *Ibid*, p. 42.

unbeliever" (op. cit. p. 35) and on this basis thinks that "Buddha's word is to be believed without inquiry" (loc. cit.). Keith also holds a similar view. He thinks that "faith is an indispensable preliminary..the root of correct knowledge."[1] It is "the means by which a man may cross the depths of the river of existence to the safety of Nirvāna".[2] He also refers to the verse : "The teaching of the Buddha saves him who has faith but destroys the faithless" (loc. cit.). Unlike Poussin, Keith, however, maintains that "happily enough (there) is a bridge built between the final authority of the Buddha and the demand of the individual for respect to his intellectual independence", for "the Buddha's teaching.... appears as the occasion but not the cause of the knowledge" (loc. cit.). Mrs. Rhys Davids also follows the same line when she makes the following observation : "Years of study, in Buddhism has shown me that for it (Buddhism), faith is no less important than it is for all religions worthy of the name."[3]

Dr. Cyomroi-Ludowyk, on the other hand, says : "Wherever the word saddhā is met with in the early Pali texts a noteworthy difference between its importance and that of faith in Christianity will be observed."[4] According to her, Buddhā "does not prohibit criticism and judgment.. Absolute *a priori* faith is never demanded."[5] K. N. Jayatilleke is more inclined to agree with the theory of Dr. Gyomroi-Ludowyk than that of Poussin and Keith. He, however , points out that "it is necessary to distinguish at least two strata in the evaluation of saddhā within the Pali Canon. In what was probably the earlier stratum the acceptance of saddhā was strictly consonant with the spirit of the Kālāma Sutta, whereas in the next stratum it is not, although attempts are made to bring it in harmony with its outlook."[6]

---

1. Buddhist Philosophy in India and Ceylon, p. 34.
2. Buddhist Philosophy in India and Ceylon, pp. 34-35.
3. Wayfarer's Words, Vol. III, p. 1124.
4. The Valuation of Saddhā in the Early Buddhist Texts. U.C.R. Vol. 5, p. 37.
5. Ibid., p. 36.
6. Early Buddhist Theory of Knowledge, pp. 384-5.

In view of these conflicting evaluations, it is necessary to see what exactly the correct position is.

At first sight, it appears that the view expressed by Poussin, Keith and Mr. Rhys Davids is not untenable. We find so many references in the Canon itself which, if read with the presuppositions of the other religions, may tend to support this view. Saddhā is said to be the very first condition for entering into the Buddhist Order. Buddha while approving of some befitting behaviour of the monks or reproaching them for their unseemly behaviour, points to the saddhā whith which they came to lead the holy-life, renouncing their homes. He says : "It is, indeed, befitting of you noble ones, O monks, who have gone forth from home to homelessness *with saddhā*" (etaṃ kho tumhākam patirūpam kulaputtānaṃ saddhā agārasmā anāgariyam pabbajitānam. M.I. 161, 463.) Similarly he says: "It is not befitting of you noble one who has gone forth from home to homelessness" *with saddhā* (M.I. 123). Saddhā is said to be the best wealth of man in this world (saddhīdha vittam purisassa settham, S.I.42,214) and through saddhā one is said to cross the flood of the world (saddhāya tarati ogham, S.I.214). It is the first of the fivefold requisites leading to the cessation of suffering (pañc' imāni padhāniyaṅgāni..sammādukkhakkhayagāminiyā, M.II. 95.). Doubts (vicikicchā) in the teacher, the doctrine and the order are the first three of the five obstacles (pañca cetokhilā, M.I. 101), which must be replaced by corresponding sampasāda or saddhā. Vicikicchā (doubt) is again counted as the first of the five fetters (pāñc' orambhāgiyāni saṃyojanāni, M.I.432). It is clearly said: "Lack of faith is a sign of decline in the religion preached by the Tathāngata (assaddhiyam kho pana Tathāgatappavedite dhammavinaye parihānam etam, A.V.158) Buddha is supposed to have observed "Even those who have mere faith and affection in me, they are all bound for heaven (yesaṃ mayi saddhāmattaṃ pemamattaṃ sabbe te saggaparāyanā ti,M.I.142).

All such utterances leave little doubt in the great importance of saddhā in early Buddhism. It seems to be regarded as the first indispensable requisite without which no progress in the Dhamma can be made. But this does not imply a downright condemnation of the unbeliever as Poussin and Keith try to make out by saying that "the Law...destroys the unbeliever" (Poussin—op.cit.,p.35). or "the teaching of Buddha...destroys the faithless" (Keith—op.cit,p.35). K. N. Jayatilleke has shown that the above view of Poussin and Keith is based on a mistranslation of Pali passage.[1] The passage along with the context reads as follows :—....sabbadevamanussānaṃ imasmiṃ dhamme assaddhiyaṃ vināseti, saddhāsampadaṃ uppādeti. Ten' etaṃ vuccati :

'vināsayati assaddhaṃ saddhaṃ vaḍḍheti sāsane
evam me sutam icc' evaṃ vadaṃ Gotamasāvako.'

—D. A. I. 31.

In the light of the prose introduction it is not difficult to see that the meaning of the verse is different from what has been read into it by Poussin and Keith. The words 'assaddhiyaṃ' and 'saddhāsampadaṃ' in the prose introduction obviously mean 'disbelief' and 'the wealth of faith' (cf. P.T.S. Dictionary) and not 'the disbeliever' and 'the person having the wealth of faith' respectively. Accordingly the correct rendering would be as follows :—

"It destroys the lack of faith of all gods and men in this doctrine and it generates the wealth of faith. Therefore has it been said : "*It destroys lack of faith and promotes faith in the religion*—in this vein have I heard a disciple of Gotama speaking."

This shows that Buddhism does not sound a threat of destruction to the unbeliever as the aforesaid scholars have tried to make out. However, in the light of the passages quoted above, it is obvious that saddhā in Buddhism is regarded as an indispensable preliminary for a holy aspirant. But even this position may imply that Buddhism demands dogmatic faith which is incompatible with its avowed critical approach. The entire picture however, would appear different, if it is shown that faith (saddhā) which Buddhism conceives as the necessary preliminary or the basic factor of all moral and spiritual progress is different from what is

1. Early Buddhist Theory of Knowledge, p. 385.

usually understood by the term in other religions. We shall therefore, briefly examine the concept of saddhā in early Buddhism and show how it is in conformity with the critical attitude generally adopted by Buddha.

The sermons to Kālāma and Bhaddāli only emphasise the fact that no statement should be accepted on mere authority, for it may be either true or false. This only indicates that Buddha wanted people to verify the truth or falsity of any statement before its acceptance or rejection. In other words, he was averse to dogmatic acceptance or rejection and encouraged people to examine things critically before anything is accepted or rejected. Now, it would be seen that it is precisely the same attitude that he recommends with regard to saddhā as well. He does not ask people to place blind faith in anyone including himself without due scrutiny and examination. Saddhā being an initial stage in way to acceptance, it is said to be based on partial but personal examination of the veracity of the speaker. In other words, it is not a dogmatic or blind faith but a critical or rational belief based on evidence adequate for belief though inadequate for knowledge.

Buddha, while recommending saddhā as an essential requisite for moral and spiritual progress, warns against the danger of having faith (saddhā) in an inefficient or unenlightened teacher. In the Cūḷagopālaka Sutta, he compares the unenlightened teacher with a foolish cowherd who, while taking cattle to the other bank of the flooded river, drowns them in the midstream; whereas the enlightened teacher is compared with a competent cowherd who knowing the right place and the path for crossing, takes cattle safely to the other side. He then adds : "Whoever thinks the incompetent recluses or Brahmins..worth hearing and worth placing faith in (saddhātabbaṃ), that will be for their woe and suffering for long."[1] Contrariwise "whoever thinks the competent recluses or Brahmins ..worth hearing and worth believing, that will be for their welfare and happiness for long."[2] Similarly in the

1. M.I. 225.
2. M.I. 226.

Cūḷasīhanāda Sutta Buddha lays down the qualifications of the true recluse or Brahmin (M.I. 64-67) and says that trust or faith in the religion of such a teacher alone can be said to be well directed.

In the Vīmaṃsaka Sutta Buddha describes the practical ways in which a teacher has to be first tested before one goes to listen to his teachings and places trust or faith (saddhā) in him. It is said that "an inquiring monk, who does not know (or have the capacity to read) another's mind, should examine the Tathāgata to ascertain whether he is perfectly enlightened or not" (M. I. 317). The inquiry should proceed as follows :—

First, "the Tathāgata is to be examined in respect of two things, namely, of what can be known by seeing and by hearing (dvīsu dhammesu Tathāgato samannesitabbo cakkhu-sotaviññeyyesu dhammesu, M. I. 318). One should ascertain that he is not seen to have nor heard to have impure (saṅki-liṭṭhā) or partially corrupt (vītamissā) conduct but is found to have only pure (vodātā) conduct. Then he should examine further whether he has been so for a long time past or only recently (dīgharattaṃ samāpanno..udāhu ittarasamāpanno, loc. cit.). After he is satisfied from what he has seen and heard that the Tathāgata is endowed with pure conduct since long, he should further inquire if he is uniformly maintaining his pure conduct despite his reputation or fame, for blemishes are likely to arise when a monk gains fame and reputation (yato ca...bhikkhu ñattajjhāpanno hoti yasampatto ath' assa idh' ekacce ādīnavā saṃvijjanti, loc. cit.). Then he should further investigate whether he has taken to reclusehood out of fear and attachment or being free from them. After being satisfied with all these preliminary tests, one should approach such a teacher in order to listen to his doctrines (Evaṃ.. satthāraṃ arahati sāvako upasaṅkamituṃ dhammassavanāya, M. I. 319). This is just the initial stage of saddhā, which having arisen, one is said to approach the teacher (saddhājāto upasaṅkamati, M. I. 480). Then as he listens to the noble and excellent doctrine being explained in an analytic way, he gains more and more confidence in the doctrine, realising the truth of some of the teachings in the light of his higher knowledge. Then he reposes faith or trust in the teacher (yathā yathā..satthā dhammam deseti uttaruttarim panīta-panītam kaṇhasukkasappatibhāgaṃ tathā tathā so tasmiṃ dhamme abhiññāya idh' ekaccam dhammam dhammesu nitthaṃ gacchati, satthari pasīdati, M I. 319-320). About this well-grounded faith it is said : "That faith in the Tathāgata, O monk, which is thus fixed, rooted and established on these reasons, grounds and considerations, is known as 'rational faith' (ākāravatī saddhā) which is rooted in insight, firm and irremovable by a recluse or Brahmin, a god, Māra or Brahmā or anyone in the world."[1]

In the Caṅkī Sutta where the uncritical faith of Brahmins is characterised by Buddha as 'baseless faith' (amūlikā saddhā, M. II. 170), we find mention of three gradual stages in the course of which the development of knowledge from its initial stage to the final is described. The first stage is known as saccānurakkhaṇā (safeguarding of the truth). As has already been shown, it is a stage of provisional acceptance of a statement for the purpose of verificiation without any dogmatic assertion that 'it is the truth' (na tv' eva tāva ekaṃsena niṭṭhaṃ gacchati : 'idam eva saccam mogham aññam', M. II. 181). At this stage there is no saddhā or faith. But if one has faith at this very stage without examining the truth critically, (as was the case with the traditional Brahmins), such faith would be known as 'amūlikā saddhā' (baseless faith). According to Buddha, therefore, it is considered as a stage when, without acceptance or rejection, moral inquiries into the conduct and behaviour of the teacher (as described above) should be made, and it is only when one finds him pure on preliminary inquiries, that he may have faith in him (Yato naṃ samannesamāno visuddhaṃ.. samanupassati atha tam hi *saddhaṃ niveseti*, M. II. 173). The stages from this initial faith up to the first realisation of the truth or saccānubodha (which is mentioned as the second

---

1. Yassa kassaci bhikkhave imehi ākārehi imehi padehi imehi byañjanehi Tathāgate saddhā nivitthā hoti mūlajātā patitthitā, ayaṃ vuccati...ākāravatī saddhā dassanamūlikā daḷhā, asaṃhāriyā samaṇena vā brāhmanena vā devena vā mārena vā Brahmunā vā kenaci vā lokasmim., M. I. 320.

stage subsequent to the first, viz., saccānurakkhaṇā) are described as follows : "With faith arisen, he approaches and associates with (the teacher). thus associating he lends ear, lending ear he listens to the doctrine, listening to the doctrine he bears it in mind, he then examines the meaning of the doctrines borne in mind, examining the meaning he approves of it, with the approval of it, there arises liking (for it), with the liking arisen, he exerts himself, having exerted himself he reflects, having reflected he puts forth effort, putting forth effort he realises the highest truth personally and sees it having penetrated it with his wisdom."[1] This very first glimpse of the highest truth subsequently matures into the abiding attainment of the truth (saccānupatti) when the same mental states are fully developed.[2] This is the third or the last stage of the perfect realisation of the truth.

From this it is clear that the first or initial stage of saddhā when one reverentially approaches the teacher for instruction, and the second or rational stage of it (ākāravatī saddhā) when one is said to have the partial but personal knowledge of the truth—are the stages which come in between the stages of saccānurakkhaṇā (safeguarding of the truth) and saccānubodha (when one gets the first glimpse of the highest truth or 'paramasaccaṃ'). It would be noted that even the initial faith is said to follow a thorough moral scrutiny of the teacher, and cannot, therefore, be confused with dogmatic or blind faith which is explicitly condemned by Buddha as baseless faith (amūlikā saddhā, M. II. 170). It is this type of critical or partially verified belief which is considered in early Buddhism as a stepping stone to knowledge, and which an aspirant, to start with, is asked to cultivate. Doubt (vicikicchā) has to be replaced by this type of faith or conviction based on critical examination. But, if on the other hand, one simply goes on doubting dogmatically without caring to examine the teacher and ascertain the truth, he can evidently never gain confidence, and thus his doubt would prove an obstacle in the way of his moral and spiritual progress. It is

1. M. II. 173; cf. M. I. 480.

2. Tesaṃ yeva...dhammānaṃ āsevanā, bhāvanā. bahulikammaṃ saccānupatti hoti., M. II. 174.

due to this reason that after having described the process of gradual development from initial saddhā to the highest knowledge (as quoted above), Buddha at once adds that the initial faith being not cultivated, all the subsequent developments leading ultimately to the realisation of the highest truth are shut out for that man.[1] This explains why saddhā (trust or confidence based on critical examination) is considered in early Buddhism as the first essential requisite for moral and spiritual progress and doubt or vicikicchā (uncritical or dogmatic scepticism) is reckoned among the five hindrances of the mind (pañca cetokhilā, M. I. 101), the five impediments (pañca nivaranā, M. I. 269-270) and the five fetters (pañc' orambhāgiyāni saṃyojanāni, M. I. 432).

From what has been said above it is clear that even the initial faith commended in early Buddhism is intended to be critical. But the faith which is highly valued in early Buddhism is the subsequent one which is known as ākāravatī saddhā (rational faith) in which one has the partial but personal realisation of truth through his own higher knowledge. About it, it is said: "Saddhā becomes a friend of man when it is controlled by wisdom" (Saddhā dutiyā purisassa hoti paññā c'enam pasāsati, S. I. 38). It is this well-established faith which is characterised as 'good' (saddhā sādhu patiṭṭhitā, S. I. 36).

This rational faith is differently named, perhaps to signify its different aspects. We come accross the words 'cetaso-pasāda' or 'avecca-ppasāda' which appear to be the affective or emotional counterparts of 'ākāravatī saddhā' which is cognitive or intellectual in character. We have stated above that ākāravatī saddhā (rational faith) is a stage of partial but personal verification of truths which is prior to saccānubodha (knowledge of the highest truth). Now, in the course of the description of the process leading to saccānubodha, we find mention of a stage when, after examining the meaning of the doctrines borne in mind, there arises in the

1. Sā pi nāma...saddhā nāhosi, tam pi nāma...upasaṅkamanaṃ nāhosi...payirupāsanā nāhosi...sotāvadhānaṃ nāhosi...dhammasavanaṃ nāhosi...dhammadhāraṇā nāhosi...atthūpaparikkhā nahosi...moghapurisā apakkantā imamhā dhammavinayā, M.I. 480.

aspirant a liking or appreciation for the doctrine (dhāritānaṃ dhammānaṃ atthaṃ upaparikkhati, atthaṃ upaparikkhato dhammā nijjhānaṃ khamanti. . . . chando jāyati, M. II. 173). This appears to be the stage of what is known as 'cetaso-pasāda,' because the description given here is quite similar to that of 'cetaso-pasāda' which is as follows: "in-as much as he examines with his intellect the meaning of this doctrinal teaching, he obtains satisfaction and mental appreciation." (yato yato imassa dhammapariyāyassa paññāya atthaṃ upaparikkheyya, labheth'eva attamanataṃ, labhetha cetaso pasādaṃ M. I. 114). Thus the element of appreciation resulting from examination of the teaching is common to both these descriptions. In the case of ākāravatī saddhā also we find almost a similar description of mental joy emerging from the partial verification of the doctrine. It is said: "As the teacher instructs the doctrine. . . so he, having realised partially the truth of the doctrine with his higher knowledge, gains confidence in the doctrine and develops faith in the teacher (yathā yathā. . . satthā dhammaṃ deseti. . . tathā tathā so tasmim dhamme abhiññāya idhekaccam dhammam dhammesu nittham gacchati, satthari pasīdati, M. I. 319). Similarly 'aveccappasāda' seems to be another word for 'cetaso-pasāda', since 'avecca' means 'having understood' (e. g., yo ariyasaccāni avecca passati i. e. he having understood sees the noble truth, Sn. 40). This aveccappasāda (faith based on understanding) is said to arise after one's mind has become free from the defilements of the mind (Yato... cittassa upakkileso pahīno hoti, so Buddhe. . . dhamme... saṅghe aveccappāsādena samannāgato hoti, M. I. 37). Thus it appears that cetasopasāda or aveccappasāda (rational or intellectual joy) is the affective aspect of the same stage whose intellectual aspect is known as ākāravatī saddhā (rational faith).

After one has reached the stage of ākāravatī saddhā and has realised partially but personally and directly the the truth of the doctrine, he does not have any more to take things entirely on trust or confidence in the teacher. His initial saddhā has now enabled him to go on testing and verifying the entire truth of the doctrine freely on his own. It is perhaps for such a person that the word 'saddhā-vimutta' (M. I. 478) is used in the Canon. This view is strengthened by the indentical description of the man endowed with ākāravatī saddhā and the person who is said to be a saddhā-vimutta. In relation to both it is said in exactly indentical terms that their "faith in Tathāgata is fixed, rooted and established" (Tathāgate saddhā niviṭṭhā hoti mūlajātā patiṭṭhitā, M. I. 320 = M. I. 478).

In view of what has been said above, we find it difficult to agree with N. Dutt who considers aveccappasāda as a different path to salvation meant for the laity, and again with Professor Barua who takes the saddhā-vimutta in the sense of an Arhat. N. Dutt says that "in a few places in the Nikāyas, saddhā is recognised as the third path for the attainment of Nibbāna in spite of the fact that it does not go well with the rationalistic principles of which the Buddhists are the avowed champions. But this path which we may call the aveccappasāda path or process is particularly important for the laity. . ."[1] The main basis of his conjecture is the Vatthūpama Sutta. But the Sutta itself, as one can clearly see, is addressed to monks and not to the laity.[2] We have seen that this aveccappasāda is said to arise after the elimination of the various defilements of the mind (cittassa upakkilesā, M. I. 37). It is then that one can partially verify the truth of the doctrine. This only indicates its similarity to ākāravatī saddhā (rational faith), as we have shown above. Moreover, it is nowhere mentioned that it is by itself sufficient for salvation. So Dutt's conjecture in considering it a different path of salvation has no basis. Again Dutt contends that the jhānic processes of salvation are not mentioned here. But one may notice that despite the non-mention of the specific stages of jhānas, the stages leading to jhāna (meditation) are all clearly described here

1. Place of Faith in Buddhism, I. H. Q., Vol. 16. p. 640.
The two other paths, according to him are (i) the sīla-citta-paññā process and (ii) the sati-paṭṭhāna process—apparently quite an arbitray division.

2. M.I. 36 ff.

as elsewhere.[1] This amounts to an indirect reference to the jhānic state.

The indentification of saddhā-vimutta with the Arhat by Professor Barua[2] is also misleading. Dr. Gyomroi-Ludowyk[3] has already drawn attention to the fact that Buddha has considered the sadhā-vimutta as one who is in need of vigilant action (appamādena karaṇīyam'ti vadāmi, M. I. 478) which is not the case with an Arhat. We have already pointed out that saddhā vimutta (which is taken to mean 'emancipated by faith' in the P. T. S. Dictionary) and the man endowed with ākāravatī saddhā (rational faith) are described in identical terms in the Pali Canon. From this one can reasonably conclude that the two are meant to be taken as the same.

Although words like cetaso-pasāda, aveccappasāda, ākāravatī saddhā, saddhā vimutta, etc., signify the same stage of moral and spiritual progress, they nevertheless suggest, as hinted earlier, the different aspects of saddhā. On closer examination one can notice that saddhā has been conceived in early Buddhism in its affective, conative as well as cognitive aspects, though the post-Canonical literature from the Milindapañha onwards speaks mainly of the first two. For example, both the Milindapañha (34) and the Atthasālini (section 304) speak of saddhā as having the characteristics of appreciation (sampasādana-lakkhaṇa) and endeavour (sampakkhandana-lakkhaṇa)—representing the affective and conative aspects respectively. The word 'pasāda' signifies the affective aspect of saddhā. At times we come across the word 'pema' (filial affection) or even bhatti (devotion) to denote this aspect of saddhā (niviṭṭhasaddho niviṭṭhapemo... abhipasanno, A. V. 326; idha... ekacco puggalo ittarasaddho hoti, ittarabhatti ittarapemo, ittara-

1. The description of D. I. 73 viz. "pamuditassa pīti jāyati, pītimanassa kāyo passambhati, passaddhakāyo sukham vedeti, sukhino cittaṃ samādhiyati" is exactly the same as we find here i.e. in M.I. 37.

2. 'Faith in Buddhism' in Buddhistic Studies, edited by B.C. Law, pp. 345ff.

3. The Valuation of Saddhā in the Early Buddhist Texts, U.C.R. vol. 5. p. 40.

ppasāḍo, A. III. 165). Professor N. Dutt seems to be largely led by these Post-Canonical ideas when he considers saddhā to have "two distinct meanings (1) one is faith (pasāda) producing pīti (serene pleasure), and (2) the other is self-confidence producing viriya (energy)."[1] Obviously he is referring here to the affective and conative aspects of saddhā. But when he speaks of saddhā in the first sense as being an antidote to vicikicchā (doubt) and moha (delusion), he simply confuses the affective aspect with the cognitive aspect.

The cognitive aspect of saddhā has been clearly indicated by the Nettippakaraṇa which says: "Faith has the characteristic of trust and the proximate state of belief" (okappana lakkhaṇā saddhā adhimuttipaccupaṭṭhanā, 28). It is this cognitive aspect of saddhā that we have mainly discussed here in view of our epistemological context. Moreover, the Canon also lays special emphasis on this aspect of saddhā for the simple reason that Buddhism emphasises the path of knowledge. Saddhā is reckoned as a faculty conducive to the realisation of enlightenment. (saddhindriyaṃ bhikkhave bodhipakkhiyo dhammo, taṃ bodhāya saṃvattati, S. V. 227). It is this cognitive aspect of saddhā which is emphasised by Buddha when he points out to Bodhi Rajakumāra that a man may not be able to learn the art of elephant-riding and using the elephant-rider's hook if he lacks saddhā.[2] Thus saddhā in its cognitive aspect is regarded as the first stepping stone to knowledge.

There is no doubt that the valuation of knowledge is superior to that of saddhā in early Buddhism. This is clearly indicated from the dialogue between the householder Citta and Nigaṇṭha Nātaputta. The latter asks Citta whether he believes in the statement of Buddha that discursive or reflective thought ceases to be in a higher jhānic (meditative) state. Citta answers: "I do not accept this on *faith*" (na khvāhaṃ *saddhāya* gacchāmi, S. IV. 298) and poses the question to Nigaṇṭha Nātaputta as to "which of the two is better—

1. Place of Faith in Buddhism, I.H.Q. Vol. 16, p. 639.
2. M. II. 94.

knowledge or faith" (loc. cit.). To this the latter replies: "Certainly *knowledge is better than faith*" (loc. cit.). At this, the householder Citta who had the capacity to attain up to the fourth jhāna says: "Knowing and seeing thus why should I accept it on the ground of faith in any recluse or Brahmin?" (loc. cit.). Similarly we find Buddha telling Ānanda: "You say this out of faith, but it is a matter of knowledge for the Tathāgata (pasādā kho tvaṃ..vadesi ñāṇam eva h'ettha Tathāgatassa, D. II. 155; A. II. 180). Again we find Sāriputta saying to the Master: "I do not accept this on account of faith in the Lord..For whomsoever, Lord, is it unknown, unseen, uncomprehended, unrealised and untouched by wisdom, they in that respect may accept on the ground of faith in others..but in my case, Lord, it is known, seen, comprehended, realised and experienced by wisdom."[1]

Since saddhā is only a means to knowledge which culminates in knowledge, it should not be strange if the Arahant is described as being "free from faith" (assaddho, Dh. 97). As evident from the above statement of Sāriputta (admittedly an Arahant), an Arahant is one who is in a position to claim the highest knowledge without having to rely on faith (aññatra saddhāya..aññam vyākareyya, S. IV. 138). But at the same time, from a different point of view, one may speak of the fullest knowledge along with the fullest confidence (saddhā). Though it may sound paradoxical, but it is true. Just as the initial faith is converted into unshakable rational faith (ākāravatī saddhā) with the partial verification of the truth, so also it is quite consistent to think of the highest state of confidence (saddhā) with the perfect realisation and verification of the highest truth. Saddhā in that highest state would virtually merge into or culminate in knowledge so much so that it would be all the same whether one speaks of an Arahant as absolutely devoid of faith (in one sense) or absolutely endowed with it (in another sense). It is perhaps due to this reason or consideration that we find two kinds of description of an Arahant--completely devoid of as well as fully endowed with saddhā. The first type of

1. S. V. 221.

description we have just noted above, and the second type of it can be seen in the Saṃyutta Nikāya where the Arahant is said to be one in whom all the five faculties, viz., *saddhā*, viriya, Sati, samādhi and *paññā* are to be found in their fullest maturity (imesam..pañcannam indriyānaṃ samattā paripūrattā arahaṃ hoti, S. V. 202). Professor Barua is, thus, not unjustified when he says: "According to the Buddha Gotama, the higher is the place of cognition..the stronger are the expressions of faith. There are in other words degrees of faith corresponding to the degrees of knowledge."[1]

From what has been said above, it is clear that saddhā is an essential preliminary for the holy aspirant. It must not, however, be forgotten that it is only necessary but not sufficient for knowledge and salvation. By itself it can only lead to heaven (yesam mayi saddhāmattaṃ pemamattaṃ sabbe te saggaparāyanā, M.I. 142). But this is a state which is subject to decline (yam pi'ssa tam saddhāmattakam pemamattakam tamhā pi parihāyi, M. I. 444). It may also prove a hindrance to salvation if not carefully and critically directed. It may generate hatred for those who speak ill of the object or person loved. So it is said: "Affection breeds hatred (pemā doso jāyate, A. II. 213). It is said to produce five drawbacks (pañc' ime..ādīnavā puggalappasāde, A. III. 270).

Thus we conclude that saddhā is an essential or indispensable preliminary in early Buddhism, but it is never to be confused with uncritical blind faith. Buddha, indeed, is so much against blind acceptance of a doctrine that in the Apaṇṇaka Sutta (M. I. 400-411) he advises people that, in case they fail to have rational faith in any teacher or doctrine, they should choose their course of life by exercising their pure reason rather than by accepting anything blindly or uncritically. Thus saddhā, as conceived in early Buddhism, is in full consonance with the critical attitude adopted by Buddha towards authority.

When we turn to the B. G., we find that here also śraddhā is greatly emphasised. But in view of its recognition

---

1. 'Faith in Buddhism' in Buddhistic Studies, edited by B. C. Law, p. 345.

of authority as a source of vaild knowledge and its attachment to tradition, the treatment of śraddhā in it is evidently not as critical as it is in early Buddhism. Again, in the B. G., it is the affective aspect of śraddhā which is most emphasised, so much so that in its highest expression, viz., devotion, it is recognised as an independent path to the highest goal, though the cognitive and conative aspects of it are also not completely ignored.

Of the various paths leading to the attainment of truth and salvation, the path of devotion grounded on faith is said to be one. Those who fail to have direct access to the truth are advised to adopt the path of devotion and faith which is considered quite easy to practise. It is needless to repeat that the realisation of the truth consists, according to the B.G., in the knowledge of the Self. Thus it is said: "Some see the Self in the self by the self through meditation (dhyānena), others by means of knowledge (Sāṅkhyena yogena) and still others through the path of disinterested action (karma yogena). But those others who fail to know thus, worship (upāsate) *by hearing from others*, and they also, pursuing what they have heard, go beyond death."[1] Thus the men having no direct experience are recommended to take recourse to faith. It is said: "Learn that by humble reverence, by inquiry and by service. The men of wisdom who have seen the truth will instruct you in knowledge."[2] The B.G. then sounds a threat to the sceptics who, having neither direct knowledge nor faith in others, indulge in doubt. It says: "The man who is ignorant (devoid of direct knowledge) as well as faithless, such a doubting man is destroyed."[3] This statement at once reminds one of the verse in Buddhism, already referred to, viz. D. A. I. 31, which was mistranslated by Poussin and Keith as "the Law saves the believer and destroys the unbeliever,"[4] or

1. B.G. XIII. 24-25.
2. B.G. IV. 34.
3. Ajñaś cā'śraddadhānaś ca, saṃśayātmā vinaśyati, B.G. IV. 40.
4. 'Faith and Reason in Buddhism' in Transactions of the Third International Congress for the History of Religions, Vol. II. p. 35.

"the teaching of the Buddha saves him who has faith but destroys the faithless."[1] Curiously enough what Poussin and Keith observed with regard to Buddhism is found to be true in relation to the B. G.

From the above statements of the B.G. it appears that those who adopt the path of meditation (dhyāna), knowledge (jñāna or sāṅkya), and even disinterested action (karma-yoga) may not necessarily require śraddhā (faith), though it is always preferable even for them to have it. But the follower of the devotional path must always have it in its fullness (śraddhayā parayo' petāḥ, B. G. XII. 2.). In the course of his instruction about the path of devotion, Kṛṣṇa says: "Men who have no *faith* (asraddadhānāḥ) in this way (devotional way) return to the cycle of the mortal world, O Arjuna, without attaining to me."[2] But "those devotees who with *faith* (śraddadhānaḥ) hold me as their supreme aim and follow this immortal wisdom, they are exceedingly dear to me."[3] In this path of devotion, it is the degree of faith which determines the worth of devotion. "Man is verily of the nature of his faith. As is his faith so he becomes."[4]

Although faith does not seem to be essential or compulsory for the followers of other paths, the B. G., in view of its theological approach, considers it preferable if they also are given to faith and devotion. This attitude of the B.G. is clearly reflected in the following verses where the follower of disinterested action or karma-yoga, who is reckoned as the follower of the best path, is said to be preferred all the more if he is *faithfully* devoted to the Supreme. Thus Kṛṣṇa says to Arjuna: "The follower of disinterested action (yogin) is better than ascetics (tapasvibhyo), better also than men of knowledge (jñānibhyo) as well as men of rituals (karmibhyaḥ). Therefore, you do become a yogin, O Arjuna. And of all yogins (followers of disinterested action), him I hold to be the best

1. Buddhist Philosophy in India and Ceylon, p. 35.
2. B. G. XI. 3.
3. B. G. XII. 20.
4. B. G. XVII. 3.

who with his inner self given to me is devoted full of *faith* (śraddhāvān) to me."[1]

Again, it is important to remember that in contradistinction to early Buddhism where the cognitive aspect of saddhā is most emphasised, in the B. G. it is the affective aspect which is most prominently brought out. This, indeed, is only natural for it, since unlike Buddhism, it believes in the path of devotion. Then again, early Buddhism lays down a critical procedure to examine the teacher before reposing confidence (saddhā) in him. But the B. G. offers no such method of critical examination, and passes on by saying that "the men of wisdom who have seen the truth will instruct you in knowledge. Learn that by humble reverence, inquiry and service."[2] We must not, however, ignore that the B. G. also does not approve of all kinds of faith (śraddhā) and, as we shall see, it distinguishes among good, passionate and dull (sāttvikī, rājasī and tāmasī, B. G. XVII. 2) types of it. But its treatment on the whole, unlike Buddhism, is more conservative than critical.

In other respects their treatment of śraddhā (faith) seems to be similar. Just as in Buddhism we find three distinct aspects of saddhā, so also in the B.G., the three aspects of it, viz., cognative, conative and affective are to be met with. We may take here some examples of them. The cognitive aspect of śraddha is borne out from the statement that "the man of *faith* obtains knowledge" (Śraddhāvān labhate jñānam, B.G. IV. 39). Its conative aspect is suggested from the statement of Kṛṣṇa who exhorts Arjuna to discharge his duty with resignation and faith (śraddhāvanto). He says: "Resigning all your works to me, with your consciousness fixed in the Self, being free from desire and egotism, fight, delivered from your fever. Those men who full of *faith* (śraddhāvanto) and free from cavil *act* always according to this teaching of mine, they also are released from the bondage of karmas."[3] In fact, śraddhā is said to lead to knowledge only by prompting the faithful

1. B.G. VI. 46 and 47.
2. B.G. IV. 34.
3. B.G. III. 30 and 31.

man to act. It is for this reason that the B.G. says: "the man of *faith* (śraddhāvan) obtains knowledge *endeavouring for it* with controlled senses" (tatparaḥ saṃyatendriyaḥ, B.G. IV. 39). Śaṅkara commenting on the word 'tatparaḥ' makes it clear that it is indicative of endeavour on the part of the faithful man.[1] The affective aspect of faith leading to devotion is always very prominent and explicit. Kṛṣṇa says: "Those who fixing their mind on me worship me, ever earnest and possessed of *supreme faith* (śraddhayā parayo'petāḥ)—them do I hold as best devoted."[2] "The devotees fully given to me with *faith* (śraddadhānāḥ) are exceedingly dear to me."[3]

But despite this pronounced stress on śraddhā, the B.G. also, like Buddhism, does not consider it sufficient for the attainment of the truth and salvation. Firstly, it has to be properly placed in the right object or person, and secondly, the goal has to be resolutely and faithfully pursued. We have just referred to the three divisions of faith made by the B.G., namely, good, passionate and dull of which the B.G. approves of the first only. In order to develop this first type of faith, the B.G. demands purification of intellect, since it maintains that "the faith of every individual is in accordance with his intellect."[4] Only the first type of faith is directed towards the devotion of the gods. Those having the second type wor-

---

1. Śaṅkara says: "The faithful one obtains knowledge. But someone may remain sluggish despite his faith. That is why for the sake of the attainment of knowledge 'endeavour for that' is mentioned (śraddhāvān, śraddhāluḥ labhate jñānam. Sraddhālutve api bhavati kaścid mandaprasthānaḥ. Ataḥ āha 'tatparo.. jñānalabdhyupāye)., S.B.G. IV. 39.

2. B.G. XII. 2.

3. B.G. XII. 20.

4. Sattvānurūpā sarvasya śraddhā bhavati Bhārata, B. G. XVII. 3. Here the word 'sattva' means intellect. It is in this sense that we find it used in the Kaṭhopaniṣad from which, admittedly, the B. G. borrows many of its ideas, expressions and even some of its verses with slight modifications. The meaning of the word 'sattva' in Kaṭha. VI. 7 (Indriyebhyaḥ param mano, manasaḥ *sattvam* uttamam; *sattvād* adhi mahān ātmā...) becomes evident when we compare it with the word 'buddhi' occurring especially in Katha. III. 10. (Indriyebhyaḥ....paraṃ manaḥ; manasaś ca parā buddhir, buddher ātmā mahān paraḥ). Śaṅkara (S.B.G. XVII. 3) and Rāmānuja (R. B. G. XVII. 3.), however, use the word 'antaḥkaraṇa'(internal sense)for it, yet 'buddhi' cannot but be included in antaḥkaraṇa.

ship the demigods and the demons, and others having third type worship the spirits and ghosts.[1] Thus, in a general way, the B.G. recommends that faith which is begotten of purified intellect, and separates it from that faith which is based on passion and dullness.[2] The last type of śraddhā (faith) is virtually a state of faithlessness (śraddhāvirahitam).[3] It is in this sense that the apparently moral actions like sacrifice, charity, penance or other such actions are condemned, as they are performed in a faithless way. The B.G. says: "Whatever sacrifice, charity, or penance is performed or action done, without faith is known as 'futile' (asat), O Arjuna. That is of no avail either here or hereafter."[4] Thus in a general way the B.G. like Buddhism accepts the position that mere faith by itself is not sufficient. It must be regulated by purified intellect and must be intelligently placed in a proper object or person. Then again, in order to reach the highest goal, right effort or endeavour has to be faithfully developed. Merely reposing faith in something cannot secure the goal. This idea is clearly suggested in the verse quoted above where Kṛṣṇa points out: "Those men who *full of faith* and free from ill-will *constantly act* (nityam anutiṣṭhanti) according to this teaching of mine, they also are released from the bondage of karmas."[5] Similarly when he speaks of faith (śradhā) as leading to knowledge (jñāna), he does not forget to add that the faithful man must work for it with his senses well-controlled (tatparaḥ saṃyatendriyaḥ, B.G. IV. 39). Thus, according to the B.G. also, śradhā (faith), though greatly emphasised, is not by itself sufficient for the attainment of the goal.

Then again, in the B.G. also like in Buddhism, the superiority of knowledge (jñāna) over faith (śraddhā) is clearly recognised. The very fact that the latter is conceived as a means to the former and is recommended for those who find it difficult to follow directly the path of knowledge and meditation, makes this point clear. In Chapter VI when Kṛṣṇa is

---

1. B.G. XVII. 4.
2. B.G. XVII. 1-28.
3. Śraddhāvirahitaṃ yajñaṃ tāmasaṃ paricakṣate, B.G. XVII. 13.
4. B.G. XVII 28.
5. B.G. III. 31.

instructing Arjuna in the methods of yoga and the control of the mind (B.G. VI. 10-28), the latter thinks it difficult to pursue it[1] and frankly asks about the fate of those who fail to attain yoga, though possessed of faith (śraddhayo'peto).[2] Arjuna expresses his apprehension whether such a man deviating from the prescribed path perishes like a cloud broken by the wind (chinnābhram iva naśyati, B.G. VI. 38). Kṛṣṇa annuls his fear and adds : "Never does a virtuous man tread the path of woe, O dear one."[3] "Such a man who has fallen away from yoga, having attained to the heavenly states and dwelt there for very many years, is born in the house of the pure and prosperous or in the family of yogins themselves."[4] "Being fully cleansed of impurities, endeavouring assiduously and perfecting himself through many lives, the yogin, then, attains to the highest goal."[5] This shows that śraddhā by itself cannot lead a man beyond heaven. In order to reach tha highest goal "which is the consumate state of knowledge" (niṣṭhā jñānasya yā parā, B.G. XVIII. 50) one has to endeavour for so many lives, if he fails to put forth resolute and strenuous efforts in this life.

Similarly on another occasion when Kṛṣṇa is asking Arjuna to follow the prescribed path of the scripture,[6] the latter again wants to know about the fate of those who fail to follow the scriptural injunctions but perform sacrifice or worship *filled with faith* (śradhayā'nvitāḥ).[7] Here, in reply to Arjuna's question, Kṛṣṇa analyses faith (śraddhā) into three kinds, viz., good (sāttvikī), passionate (rājasī) and dull (tāmasī) and points out that men of good faith worship the gods (Yajante sāttvikā devān, B.G. XVII. 4), and by virtue of that they reach the gods i e. heaven (Yānti devavratā devān,

1. B.G. VI. 33 and 34.
2. Ayatiḥ śraddhayo'peto yogāc calitamānasaḥ
aprāpya yogasaṃsiddhiṃ kāṃ gatiṃ Kṛṣṇa gacchati., B.G. VI. 37.
3. na hi kalyāṇakṛt kescid durgatiṃ tāta gacchati, B.G. V 1. 40.
4. B.G. VI. 41 & 42.
5. B.G. VI. 45.
6. B.G. XVI. 24.
7. Ye śāstravidhim utsṛjya yajante śraddhayā' nvitāḥ
teṣāṃ niṣṭhā tu ka kṛṣṇa sattvam āho rajas tamaḥ, B.V. XVII. 1.

B.G. IX. 25). Likewise the men of passionate and dull faith worship demigods or demons and spirits or ghosts and are led accordingly to their respective abodes.[1] Thus here also it is confirmed that mere faith, even if it be of the best type, cannot take a man beyond heaven. The same is corroborated when tne B.G. says: "One who being endowed with faith (śraddhāvān) and free from ill-will listens to it, he also becomes free from sins and attains the holy worlds (śubhāṃl lokan) of the virtuous."[2]

The upshot of this is that those who find it difficult to follow any prescribed path strictly, they may adopt the easier path of faith whereby they may fare fairly well in any of the spiritual pursuits. But with mere faith they cannot go beyond heaven and it is clearly stated that heaven is a state of limited duration. The *raison d'être* of this limited gain is said to be the fact that the man of mere faith lacks true knowledge, and is motivated by desires. His desire is fulfilled on account of his faith, but the true goal is not achieved due to the lack of true knowledge. As the B.G. puts it: "Endowed with that faith he endeavours for the propitiation of that (deity) and as decreed by my own self, he obtains his desires from him. But the fruit of these men of little wisdom (alpamedhasām) is only temporary."[3] These faithful worshippers (bhaktā... śraddhayā'nvitāḥ) of the gods "fall down, since they do not truly know me (the Supreme)"[4]. Thus in considering knowledge as superior to faith and in thinking of the latter as leading only to heaven which is subject to decline, the B.G. and Buddhism are found to be in perfect accord. It is quite possible that the B.G., despite its greater stress on faith, might have found it difficult to go against the role of saddhā set up by early Buddhism, notwithstanding the fact that their conception of it is different in accordance with their respective critical and conservative approaches.

---

1. B.G. XVII. 4 and IX. 25.
2. B.G. XVII. 71.
3. B.G. VII. 22 and 23.
4. B.G. IX. 23 & 24.

The Limits of Knowledge :—

The question that we have to consider here is whether the range of human knowledge has any limit or is limitless (capable of knowing all). In other words, is it possible for human beings to be omniscient?

(A) *Buddha's Answer to the Question of Omniscience* :—

The question has been posed directly before Buddha and we find him answering both in a positive as well as negative way which seems to indicate that he is claiming omniscience in one sense and disowning it in another. The ascetic Vacchagotta pointedly inquires of him whether it is correct to describe him as an omniscient being. To this Buddha gives the following answer: "Those who say that the recluse Gotama is omniscient, and all-seeing and professes to have knowledge and insight without residue which is constantly and at all times present to him, whether be walks or stands, sleeps or keeps awake—are not reporting me correctly and misrepresent me falsely and untruly."[1] He further adds that one would report him properly by saying that "the recluse Gotama has a threefold knowledge" (Tevijjo samaṇo Gotamo ti, M. I. 482), namely (i) unlimited (as much as he likes) retrocognition, (ii) unlimited clairvoyance and (iii) knowledge of the destruction of the defiling impulses (loc. cit). This enumeration of the threefold knowledge can by no means be taken as exhaustive, since elsewhere in the Nikāyas (e.g. D.I. 78-84; S.I. 191) we find mention of other kinds of higher knowledge along with these, which monks are said to attain after the fourth jhāna. So the claim of only the last three kinds of knowledge is made here by Buddha presumably to indicate the highest value and importance of this threefold knowledge, and to signify that he, being in possession of it, is a perfectly enlightened one or an Arahant.

On another occastion when King Pasenadi inquires of him

---

1. Ye te...evam āhaṃsu : 'Samaṇo Gotamo sabbaññū sabbadassāvī, aparisesaṃ ñāṇadassanaṃ paṭijānāti, carato ca me tiṭṭhato ca suttassa ca jāgarassa ca satataṃ samitaṃ ñāṇadassanaṃ paccupaṭṭhitan' 'ti' na me te vuttavādino, abbhācikkhanti ca pana man te asatā abhutenā ti, M.I. 482.

whether it is true that he (Buddha) denies the possibility of omniscience, the latter answers as follows: "Those who say that the recluse Gotama denies the possibility of there being any recluse or Brahmin as omniscient and all-seeing are not reporting me properly and are accusing me falsely and untruly."[1] He then further clarifies his statement by pointing out that what he means to deny is the possibility of an omniscient person capable of knowing all at the same time. As he says: "It is not possible that a recluse or Brahmin would know and see all at the same time" (Natthi so samaṇo vā brāhmaṇo vā yo sakid eva sabbañ ñassati sabbaṃ dakkhiti, n'etaṃ ṭhānaṃ vijjatī ti. M. II. 127).

This makes the position clear as to why Buddha disowns omniscience and again at the same time accepts the validity of it. It appears that during Buddha's time the word 'omniscient' (sabbaññū or sabbadassāvī) was ambiguously used and, therefore, Buddha disclaimed omniscience in one sense and claimed it in another. It is important to note that Buddha disclaims it when it is attributed to him in the sense of knowing and seeing all at all times, whether walking or sleeping etc. But when King Pasenadi asks him about omniscience in a general way he does not deny it, and clarifies the position by pointing out that he denies only that concept of omniscience in which one claims to know and see all at once. It may be remembered that it is this latter type of omniscience which is said to be claimed by the Jain leader, Nigaṇṭha Nātaputta (M. II. 31), whose views are frequently criticised by Buddha.[2]

Thus it appears that omniscience in the dispositional sense, or in the sense of a capacity to know something if and when one desires to have this knowledge, is tacitly accepted by Buddha. One may raise doubts about it on the ground that Buddha in reply to the question of King Pasenadi has only granted its possibility in relation to other recluses and Brahmins and not its actuality with regard to his own self. But such doubt can hardly be sustained when it is made quite

1. M. II. 127.
2. M.I. 372-378, 519; II. 214-223.

clear in the Nikāyas that Buddha had attained the highest knowledge. None in the past, present or future is supposed to have knowledge superior to Buddha, and in the present none is said even to equal him, though in the past and future there were and there would be his equals. Sāriputta openly declares before Buddha: "I have such conviction in the Exalted One that I think that there never was nor would ever be nor is now a recluse or Brahmin who may excel the Exalted One in respect of knowledge"[1]. On being asked by the Master to account for this grand and bold statement (āsabhī vācā), Sāriputta explains it by comparing the highest state of knowledge with a king's fortress having only one door (eka dvāraṃ) so that anyone entering it must follow one and the same route.[2] Buddha then explicitly approves the statement of the latter by saying that "in speaking thus you will be reporting me properly and not misrepresenting me."[3] Sāriputta further says on the above-mentioned ground that the past and future Enlightened Ones were and would be equal to Buddha in knowledge, but in the present there can be none, on account of the fact that two perfectly Enlightened Ones cannot possibly be born at the same time in the same cosmos.[4] This statement also is likewise fully endorsed by Buddha.[5] In fact, we find Buddha himself making this unambiguous declaration: "Whatever has been seen heard, reflected, known, obtained, discovered and mentally contemplated by the world of the gods, Māra and Brahmā along with other beings including recluses, Brahmins, gods and men—is well known to the Tathāgata.[6]

This shows that Buddha's reluctance in claiming unqualified omniscience is mainly due to some prevalent misconceptions about the term. Besides this, there appears to be one more difficulty about it and that is about the know-

1. Evam pasanno ahaṃ bhante Bhagavati, na cāhu na ca bhavissati na c'etarahi vijjati añño samaṇo vā brāhmaṇo vā Bhagavatā bhiyyobhiññataro, yad idaṃ sambodhiyaṃ ti. D. II. 82; III. 99.

2. D. II. 83; III. 101.

3. D. III. 115.

4. Aṭṭhānam etaṃ anavakāso yaṃ ekissā lokadhātuyā dve arahanto sammāsambuddhā apubbaṃ acarimaṃ uppajjeyyuṃ netaṃ ṭhānaṃ vijjatī ti, D. III. 114.

5. D. III. 115.

6. D. III. 135.

ledge pertaining to the future. Buddha does not seem to claim unlimited precognitive knowledge of the future, possibly because of its partly undetermined nature. The courses of future events being partly dependent on those of the past and present, the futuie, evidently, cannot be considered as wholly determined, and hence to speak of omniscience in relation to future is to maintatin an impossible position. Thus in the Pāsādika Sutta Buddha himself states: "It is possible that other heretical teachers may say 'the recluse Gotama speaks of an enormous knowledge with regard to the past but not with regard to the future'."[1] Buddha explains it by pointing out that past is a matter of recall and so the Tathāgata recalls as much as he likes (ṣo yāvatakaṃ ākaṅkhati tāvatakaṃ anussarati, D. III. 134) but regarding the future his knowledge is based on his enlightenment (bodhiyaṃ ñāṇaṃ uppajjati, loc. cit.). So one can see by virtue of his present enlightenment, that there is no future rebirth for him (natthi'dāni punabbhavo ti, loc. cit.).

In the light of these difficulties one can clearly see why Buddha is reluctant to claim unqualified and unreserved omniscience. But he seems to have no objection in being called omniscient with these reservations. In fact, it is only in this sense that omniscience can reasonably be spoken of. The Milindapañha, (pp. 102ff), for example, ascribes omniscience to Buddha in this sense. In the Pali Canon also we find references to all-knowing Buddha which perhaps have to be understood in thıs light. In the Saṃyutta Nikāya, for example, Buddha is called "all-knowing" (sabbaviduṃ, S. I. 33), who having the eye (of wisdom) sees all(sabbaṃ passati cakkhumā, S. I. 134). Buddha himself claims before Baka Brahmā: "I am an Exalted One having infinite vision" (Anantadassī bhagavā'ham asmi, S.I. 143). The Suttanipāta describes Buddha as ' one who has the knowledge and insight into all things" (sabbesu dhammesu ca ñāṇa-dassī, Sn. 84). All this shows that omniscience is acceptable to Buddha provided the reservations suggested by him are made.

In the later stratum of the Canon, however, we come

---

1. D. III. 134.

across a real difference in this concept of omniscience. The Paṭisambhidāmagga and the Kathāvatthu, for example, ascribe unqualified and unreserved omniscience to Buddha. The former in its very first section known as 'Nāṇa-Kathā' takes the omniscience of Buddha for granted and proceeds to explain what constitutes the omniscience of the Tathāgata (Katamaṃ Tathāgatassa sabbaññutañāṇaṃ, 131). It points out that it consists in "knowing everything conditioned and unconditioned without residue (Sabbaṃ saṅkhatam asaṅkhatam anavasesaṃ jānāti ti, loc. cit.) including all knowledge about the past, present and future (atītaṃ..anāgataṃ..paccuppannaṃ sabbaṃ jānāti ti, loc. cit.), besides various other components of this omniscience. Then it proceeds to explain what is meant by 'all-seeing' (Kenaṭṭhena samantacakkhu, op. cit. p. 133) which curiously enough is taken in a still wider sense than the omniscience, for the latter (sabbaññutañāṇaṃ) is mentioned as one of the fourteen kinds of Buddha's knowledge (Cuddasa Buddhañāṇāni, loc. cit.). Similarly the Kathāvatthu includes the epithets, omniscient (sabbaññū) and all-seeing (sabbadassāvī) in the list of eight epithets ascribed to Buddha.[1]

This indicates that sometime before the final completion of the Pali Canon, unimlited knowledge or omniscience came to be ascribed to Buddha, but in the early record of the text it is ascribed only in a qualified sense. It is important to remember here that the attainment of this highest knowledge on the part of Buddha exemplifies the range of human knowledge, for he is said to attain it as a man by means of his normal human effort. It is clearly stated: "Whatever is attainable by a faithful steadfast and enterprising noble man through manly effort, manly vigour, manly endeavour and manly perseverance, that has heen attained by the Exalted One."[2] It is, however, accepted that this highest knowledge is difficult to attain. Buddha himself after attaining perfect enlightenment says: "With difficulty have I attained it" (Kicchena me adhigataṃ, M. I.

1. The list of the eight epithets is mentioned as follows:—Tathāgato, Jino, Satthā, Sammāsambuddho, *Sabbaññū Sabbadassāvī* Dhammassāmi, Dhammapaṭisaraṇo—Kathāvatthu, 228.

2. Yaṃ...saddhena kulaputtena pattabbam āraddhaviriyena thāmavatā purisathāmena purisaviriyene purisaparakkamena purisadhorayhena, anuppattaṃ taṃ Bhagavatā. D. III. 113.

168) There are only a few among men who really attain it and go to the other shore (Appakā te manussesu, ye janā pāragāmino, S. V. 24).

In the light of what has been said we cannot agree with Kern who in an unreserved manner ascribes omniscience to Buddha without distinguishing between the early and later strata of Buddhist thought, and goes to the extent of characterising it as a superhuman non-rationalistic system. To quote his own words: "Buddhism is professedly no rationalistic system, it being a superhuman (uttarimanussa) Law, founded upon the decrees of an omniscient and infallible Master."[1] Poussin[2] and Keith[3] also hold the same view and quote his above-mentioned line with approval. We have already explained the different senses in which Buddha's teaching can be regarded as rationalistic and shown that such views as those of Kern, Poussin and Keith are untenable.

We shall see later in our next chapter on metaphysics that the ten unanswered metaphysical questions (dasa abyākatāni) of the Pali texts, by no means imply the lack of knowledge on the part of Buddha, as Keith has wrongly taken them to mean.[4] It is not without reason that they were called 'unspeakable' and not 'unknowable'. The limits of speech, as also of pure reason (takka) do not necessarily imply limits of knowledge, and we shall see that in Buddhism this, indeed, is the case. Thus our conclusion about the qualified concept of omniscience in early Buddhism is not jeopardised by this consideration.

(*B*) *The B. G. Concept of Omniscience as Compared with that of Buddhism*:—

The B. G. here also as elsewhere, in keeping with its usual unanalytical approach, makes no critical examimtion of the concept of omniscience and, like the later stratum of the Buddhist texts, speaks of unqualified omniscience i.e., know-

1. Manual of Buddhism, p. 50.
2. Bouddhisme, p. 132, foot-note 3.
3. Buddhist Philosophy in India and Ceylon, p. 33.
4. Keith says : "It is quite legitimate to hold that the Buddha was a genuine agnostic...that he had no reasoned or other conviction on the matter." Buddhist Philosophy in India and Ceylon, p. 63.

ledge without any limitation. Besides, its entire approach is metaphysical and theological and this gives an entirely different orientation to the whole problem.

The highest knowledge is said to consist in the realisation of the Supreme Reality which is conceived at times impersonally as Brahman and at times personally as God. This Reality being conceived as all-inclusive and non-exclusive, the knowledge or realisation of it amounts to knowing all without residue. Thus, Kṛṣṇa while proceeding to impart the highest knowledge to Arjuna, speaks as follows: "Hear then, O Arjuna, how practising yoga with your mind centred in me, with me as your refuge, *you will know me entirely and indubitably* (asaṃśayaṃ samagraṃ māṃ yathā jñāsyasi tac chṛṇu). I shall expound to you this knowledge together with the reason *by knowing which nothing else will be left to be known here* (yaj jñātvā ne'ha bhūyo'nyaj jñātavyam avaśiṣyate)"[1] This is evidently a promise to bestow omniscience which is to be realised by knowing Kṛṣṇa (representing the Supreme Reality). There is no doubt that the B. G. conceives of this Reality, as all-embracing. As Kṛṣṇa puts it: "Nothing whatever is beyond me, O Arjuna. All this is woven in me as pearls in a thread"[2] "I hold this entire universe pervading it with a single fraction of myself."[3] An unqualified claim to know the past, present as well the future is made by Kṛṣṇa (vedā'haṃ samatītāni vartamānāni ca'rjuna, bhaviṣyāṇi ca bhūtāni...., B. G. VII. 26). Now, it is by knowing this all-comprehending and all-knowing Reality that all is said to be known without residue. Knowing is conceived in the B. G. as becoming one with the Reality. To know Reality is to become one with it. In other words, the B. G. conceives of the highest knowledge as the identification with the Supreme, known as Brahman or Paramātman. As it puts it: "The knower of Brahman is established in Brahman" (Brahmavid Brahmaṇi sthitaḥ, B.G.,V. 20) This point is repeatedly emphasised (e. g. Brahmaiva tena gantavyam, IV. 24; tasmād Brahmaṇi te sthitāḥ, V. 19; Brahma saṃpadyate tadā, XIII. 30.) The same state of merg-

1. B.G. VII. 1 & 2.
2. B.G. VII. 7.
3. B.G. X. 42.

ing is conveyed in theological terms as well (e. g. tato māṃ tattvato jñātvā *viśate* tadanantaram, XVIII. 55; cf. IV. 9; IX. 34; X. 55; XI. 54; XII. 8; XVIII. 65 & 68). It is difficult to agree with Garbe who disapproves of this merging and regards salvation as "a state of blissful freedom of the soul, existing on *individually*, in the presence of God."[1] He tries to read too much into the verse XV. 7 of the B. G. and observes: "The expression 'mamai'vā'ṃśo jīvaloke jīvabhūtaḥ sanātanaḥ (XV. 7) is so clear that one must be indeed a credulous follower of Śaṅkara to understand the word 'aṃśa' in this important passage, in a Vedāntic sense as equivalent to 'an imaginary, an apparent part".[2] He thinks that ' the individual soul..has *detached* itself as a part of the Divine Soul".[3] It is true that the B. G. does not subscribe to the māyā theory of Śaṅkara and does not regard things and beings of the universe as imaginary appearances,[4] yet there is no doubt that it regards the Soul as essentially one with the Supreme and not a *detached* part as Garbe thinks. The same Supreme Self or Principle is said to abide as one in all beings (sarvabhūtasthitam. ekatvam āsthitaḥ, B. G. VI, 31; Īśvaraḥ sarvabhūtānāṃ hṛddeśe'rjuna tiṣṭhati, XVIII. 61) and is explicitly said to be the same as the Self(Aham ātmā guḍākeśa sarvabhūtāśayasthitaḥ, B.G. X. 20; Kśetrajñaṃ cā'pi māṃ viddhi, XIII. 2.). The word 'aṃśa' (part), in relation to the Self has, therefore, to be understood in the sense of limited manifestation of the Supreme like the so-called part of the indivisible and all-pervasive ether (yathā sarvagataṃ saukṣmyād ākāśam no' palipyate, B.G. XIII. 32). This being so, man with the realisation of his unity and identity with the all-inclusive and all-knowing Supreme, naturally becomes

1. I.A., Vol. 47. Supplement, p. 27.

2. I.A. Vol. 47, Supplement p. 25.

3. Ibid., p. 25.

4. Cf. Prof. Dasgupta rightly observes : "The *Gītā*...does not assert anywhere that Brahman is the only reality and all else that appear is false and unreal. The word *māyā* is, no doubt, used in the *Gītā* in three passages; but its meaning is not what Saṅkara ascribes to it in his famous interpretation of Vedantic thought." A History of Indian Philosophy, Vol. II. p. 478.

all-knowing and attains entire knowledge without residue. As the B. G. explicitly states: "He who thus being free from delusion knows me as the Highest Person (Puruṣottamam) is all-knowing (sarvavid)".[1] Similarly, speaking of the all-comprehensive knowledge Kṛṣṇa says: "When you know it, you shall not fall again into such delusion, O Arjuna. By this you shall see all existences without residue (aśeṣeṇa) in the Self, then in me".[2]

It is thus clear that the B. G. concept of omniscience unlike that of early Buddhism is without reservation. Moreover, it gives a metaphysical and theological interpretation to it which is entirely different from the empirical and non-theological account of early Buddhism.

However, the B. G. agrees with Buddhism in accepting the fact that the attainment of this highest knowledge is very difficult and scarce. It says: "Among thousands of men scarcely one strives for perfection and of those striving aspirants scarcely one knows me truly (tattvataḥ)"[3] Even great recluses and the host of gods are said to be devoid of this highest knowledge. Speaking in theological terms, Kṛṣṇa says: "Neither the host of gods nor the great sages know me."[4] Arjuna also is found to speak in the same vein: "Neither the gods nor the demons, O Lord, know thy mainfestation"[5] Then again like Buddhism, the B. G. also regards the highest knowledge as incomprehensible to reason ('acintyam', as the B. G. calls it, II. 25; VIII. 9; XII. 3 and 'atakkāvacaro' as Buddha describes it, D. I. 17, 22, 39; M. I. 167), though one can attain it by proper perseverance[6] and meditation.[7]

1. B.G. XV. 19.
2. B.G. IV: 35.
3. B.G. VII. 3.
4. Na me viduḥ suragaṇāḥ...na maharṣayaḥ, B.G.X. 2.
5. na hi te Bhagavan vyaktiṃ vidur deva na dānavāḥ., B.G.X. 14.
6. yatanto yoginaś cai'naṃ paśyanti (B.G. XV. 11);
yuktaceṣṭasya karmasu. . .yogo bhavati duḥkhahā (B.G. VI. 17).
7. Dhyānenā' tmani paśyanti kecid ātmānam ātmanā, B.G. XIII. 24

Chapter IV

THE METAPHYSICS OF THE B.G. AND EARLY BUDDHISM

Buddha's Approach to Metaphysics, as Distinct from that of the B. G. :—

We observed in the beginning of the previous chapter that the outlook of the B. G. and early Buddhism is predominantly practical. They try to suggest practical ways and means to solve the pressing problems of life and to attain the state of absolute perfection. But it is interesting to notice the diversity of the approach despite the unity of their purpose. The approach of the B. G. is mainly metaphysical and it offers solutions mostly on the basis of traditional metaphysical presuppositions, whereas the approach of early Buddhism is thoroughly empirial in which the traditional metaphysical speculations are brushed aside. Naturally, therefore, in the B. G. we find explicit mention of different theories and concepts of metaphysics which, despite their unsystematic and synoptic treatment, clearly indicate the metaphysical position of the B. G. But in early Buddhism, where metaphysical problems are meticulously avoided (as evidenced from the ten unanswered metaphysical questions called 'abyākatāni,' M.I.426), a categorical answer to them is not to be found. Some reasons, however, are given as to why these questions are set aside and this enables one to understand the attitude and approach of Buddha towards them. Besides this indirect way of knowing his views on metaphysics, we find at places direct criticisms of very many metaphysical theories. On the basis of these direct and indirect sources we can ascertain Buddha's attitude to the major metaphysical problems and compare it with that of the B. G.

But Buddha's silence or his setting aside of metaphysical questions has been a subject of controversy among scholars and different views have been expressed about the meaning and significance of it. It is, therefore, necessary to examine first the nature and significance of his silence without which his attitude to metaphysical problems cannot be rightly understood or appreciated. After having examined this question, we can, with added informations from his explicit utterances and criticisms, determine his correct metaphysical position and compare it with that of the B. G. We, therefore, first propose to examine briefly the nature and significance of Buddha's silence.

The Nature and significance of Buddha's Silence:—

The chief metaphysical questions which Buddha is either silent about (Bhagavā tuṇhī ahosi, S. IV. 400)) or rejects (mā h'evaṃ, A. II. 161) or brushes aside (na kallo pañho, S. II. 61) are the questions pertaining to the duration and extent of the world, identity or non-identity of the soul and the body, and the existence or non-existence of the Tathāgata (liberated saint) after death. Thus altogether the following ten questions are enumerated in the Pali Canon (e. g., M. I. 426, 484-5) under the name abyākata pañhā (unanswered[1] questions):—

(1) sassato loko, the world is eternal
(2) asassato loko, the world is not eternal
(3) antavā loko, the world is finite
(4) anantavā loko, the world is infinite
(5) taṃ jīvam tam sarīram, the soul is indentical with the body
(6) aññaṃ jīvaṃ aññaṃ sarīram, the soul is different from the body
(7) hoti Tathāgato paraṃ maraṇā, the liberated one exists after death
(8) na hoti Tathāgato paraṃ maraṇā, the liberated one does not exist after death
(9) hoti ca na ca hoti Tathāgato param maraṇā, the liberated one does and does not exist after death
(10) n'eva hoti na na hoti Tathāgato paraṃ maraṇā, the liberated one neither exists nor does not exist after death.

1. It is more accurate both in word and spirit to translate the word 'abyākata' as 'unanswered' or 'unexplained', as has been done by Professor Jayatilleke (Early Buddhist Theory of Knoweldge, p. 471) and not as 'inexpressible' as Professor Murti has done (The Central Philosophy of Buddhism, p. 36).

Of these, evidently Nos. 1 and 2 concern the question of the duration of the world, Nos. 3 and 4, the extent of the world, Nos. 5 and 6, the identity or difference between the soul and the body and Nos. 7 to 10. the existence or non-existence of the liberated saint after death. In the Buddhist Sanskrit literature the number is extended to fourteen by giving four alternatives[1] each to the questions of the duration and extent of the world in place of only two assigned to them in the Pali Canon.

Now, there could be various reasons for not answering these questions. Opinions of scholars being widely divided on the issue, it is better to proceed with a clear analysis of the various considerations which may have led Buddha to refrain from making any categorical reply. Firstly, the questions may be answerable or may not be answerable by their very nature. In case they are answerable, it is possible that Buddha may not have known their answers (Scepticism, Naive Agnosticism), or he may have deliberately avoided them even while knowing the answers in view of their irrelevance for the purpose (Pragmatism). On the other hand, if they are unanswerable, their unanswerability may be either due to limited capacity of the human mind (Rational Agnosticism) or due to the inherent inappropriateness or meaninglessness of the questions themselves (Logical Positivism). We may express these possibilities in the form of a table as follows:—

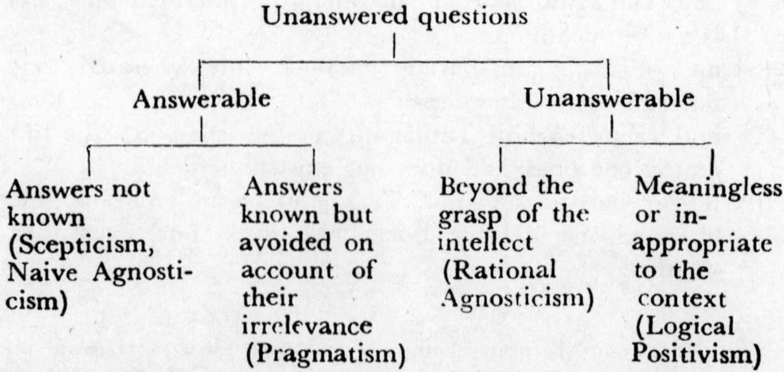

1. cf. Professor Murti—The Central Philosophy of Buddhism, p. 36, footnote 2.

Again one has to bear in mind the following considerations:—

(i) The reasons behind setting aside these questions may not be the same in all cases. Some questions may have been set aside for some reasons and others for other reasons.

(ii) Then again, the alternatives need not be mutually exclusive. An answer might be avoided on account of its irrelevance, besides at the same time being intellectually incomprehensible.

(iii) Again some of these questions might be ambiguous and liable to different interpretations, answerable in one sense and unanswerable in another so that any unreserved categorical answer could be misconstrued and be misleading.

According to A.B. Keith and A. J. Bahm the reason behind Buddha's silence was his lack of clear knowledge about the reality, besides his practical or pragmatic considerations. Jacob also seems to hold a similar view and reads into it an element of agnosticism analogous to that of Sañjaya. To quote their own words, Keith says: "It is quite legitimate to hold that the Buddha was a genuine agnostic...and that he had no reasoned or other conviction on the matter.[1] Keith is led "to the conclusion that agnosticism in these matters is not based on any reasoned conviction of the limits of knowledge; it rests on the twofold ground that the Buddha has not himself a clear conclusion on the truth on these issues, but is convinced that disputation on them will not lead to the frame of mind which is essential for the attainment of Nirvāṇa."[2] Thus Keith supports the first view, viz. the Naive Agnosticism, though recognising at the same time the validity of the Pragmatic approach. A.J. Bahm also favours a similar view. He, however, grants Buddha the credit of recognising the limits of human knowledge. He says: "Indeed, it is quite central to the nature of the philosophical enterprise...to grasp what is ultimate regarding the ability and inability of men to understand each other.

1. Buddhist Philosophy in Indian and Ceylon, p. 63.
2. *Ibid*, p. 45.

Gotama did not wholly understand reality, and it may be something to his credit, not that he did not try, but that he recognised, after trying, that expecting more understanding than we will get leads to unhappiness."[1] Jacobi arguing in favour of the Agnostic views of Buddha says "In support of my assumption that Buddha was influenced by contemparory Agnosticism, I may adduce a tradition..that the most distinguished pair of his disciples, Sāriputta and Moggalāna, had previously to their conversion, been adherents of Sañjaya, and had brought over to Buddha 250 disciples of their former teacher. This happened not long after Buddha's reaching Bodhi, i.e. at the very beginning of the new sect, when its founder must have been willing, in order to win pupils, to treat prevalent opinions with all due consideration."[2] It is needless to repeat that Sañjaya's Agnosticism was supposed to be based on utter ignorance and he was characterised as "the most foolish and stupid of all recluses and Brahmins" (ayañ ca imesaṃ samaṇabrāhmaṇānaṃ sabba-bālo sabba-mūḷho, D.I. 59). Jacobi's suggestion implies that Buddha in order to win pupils adopted a kind of agnosticism similar to that of Sañjaya.

This Naive Agnostic interpretation said to be based on ignorance can hardly find any support from the Pali texts, which, as we have already seen (supra pp. 273-276), ascribe omniscience to Buddha.

Keith (op. cit. p. 44, fn.3) points to three references in support of his view-Ud.II, S.V.437, D.I. 179. Of these the first and last contain no discussion of the 'avyākata' (unanswered) topics and the second one (S.V. 437) which mentions the parable of the Simsapa-leaves proves just the opposite of what Keith says. In this lattter context Buddha takes a handful of Siṃsapa-leaves and asks the monks whether the leaves in his hand or those in the forest were greater in number. The monks naturally reply that the leaves in the forest were obviously much greater in number, whereupon Buddha remarks: "Similarly, O monks, what I know and have not

1. Philosophy of the Buddha, p. 27.
2. Jaina Sūtras, S.B.E., Vol. 45, p. xxix.

taught is greater and what I have taught is very little." (S. V. 438).

Bahm's view that "Gotama did not wholly understand reality" seems to ignore the explicit passages of the Pali Canon describing Buddha as all-knowing (sabbaviduṃ, S.I.33; sabbam passati cakkhumā; S.I. 134; Anantadassī Bhagavāham asmi; S.I.143; sabbaṃ Tathāgatena abhisambuddhaṃ, D.III. 135; sabbesu dhammesu ca ñāṇadassī, Sn. 84) and having the highest wisdom.[1] Again Bahm does not seem to take note of the supra-rational or paranormal knowledge attained and taught by Buddha, and seems to regard rational or intellectual knowledge as constituting the limits of human understanding when he thinks of Buddha as holding the view that "expecting more understanding than we will get leads to unhappiness." It is true that Buddha recognises the limitations of normal conceptual knowledge but he does not consider such knowledge to constitute the limits of human understanding. On the other hand, he speaks of nonconceptual paranormal knowledge beyond reason (atakkāvacaro, M.I. 167), the expectation of which is not only desirable but indispensable for the attainment of the highest goal. It leads not to unhappiness but to supreme happiness or Nibbāna (Nibbānam paramaṃ sukhaṃ, Dh. 203 and 204.).

Jacobi (op. cit., p. xxix) refers in support of his view to the similarity between the questions put to Sañjaya by Ajātasattu in the Sāmaññaphala Sutta (D.I. 58-59) and the same put to the nun Khemā by Pasenadi in the Samyutta Nikāya (S.IV. 375). It is true that the questions are asked in identical terms but this does not mean that the answers given by Sañjaya and the nun Khemā are also identical. Sañjaya expresses his sheer ignorance while giving negative answers to all alternative questions about the existence or non-existence of the Tathāgata,[2] whereas the nun Khemā clearly points out the impropriety of the questions in the supra-

1. n'eva attano samasamaṃ samanupassāmi kuto bhiyyo, atha kho aham eva tattha bhiyyo yadidaṃ adhippaññati, D. III. 139.

2. hoti Tathāgato param maraṇā ti iti ce me assa...iti te naṃ vyākareyyaṃ...na hoti...hoti ca na hoti ca...nevahoti na na hoti Tathāgato param maraṇā ti iti ce me assa...iti te naṃ vyākareyyam. Evaṃ ti pi me no, tathā ti pi me no, aññathā ti pi me no, no ti pi me no, no no ti pi me no'ti., D.I. 59.

mundane context, and gives ample suggestions to indicate the profundity of the state realised by the Tathāgata. The five aspects of personality through which one is cognized or determined in terms of existence or non-existence are said to be abandoned by the Tathāgata, and thus he is said to go beyond the sphere of existence or non-existence and become profound, incomprehensible and unfathomable (gambhīro, appameyyo, duppariyogāho, S. IV. 376-9)[1] like the innumerable (particles of sand in the Ganges or the immeasurable water of the great ocean.[2] Thus we find that the views of Sañjaya are based on his ignorance and stupidity (mandattā momūhattā, D. I.27) whereas those of Buddha (as represented here by the nun Khemā) are based on his direct experience of the highest state. Therefore it is wrong to see any similarity in their view merely on the basis of the resemblance of the questions put to them. In fact, Buddha rejects the views of all the six titthiyas (sectarians) including those of Sañjaya and nowhere do we find him adopting a deliberately erroneous view "in order to win pupils" as Jacobi believes.

Besides, there is good evidence in the Pali Canon to show that Buddha's silence was not due to his ignorance. In the Cūḷa-Sakuludāyi Sutta we find Buddha claiming to know the answers to the questions pertaining to the beginnning and end (pubbantaṃ and aparantam) which he does not deliberately answer. He points out that those who have the capacity to see the past and the future without limit can surely answer these questions satisfactorily. To quote his own words: "He who recollects the various forms of previous lives, for example, one llfe, two lives..in all their modes, details and multiple forms, he may ask me a question pertaining to the beginning (pubbantaṃ) or I may ask him a question pertaining to the beginning, and he may satisfy me

---

1. yena rūpena Tathāgataṃ paññāpayamāno paññāpeyya taṃ rūpaṃ Tathāgatassa pahīnaṃ ucchinnamūlaṃ...rūpasaṅkhāyavimutto...Tathāgato gambhīro appameyyo duppariyogāho...vedanā...saññā...saṅkhāra...viññāṇasaṅkhāya vimutto...gambhīro, appameyyo, duppariyogāho, S. IV. 376-7.

2. atthi te koci gaṇako vā muddiko va saṅkhāyako vā yo pahoti Gaṅgāya vālukaṃ gaṇetum...mahāsamudde udakaṃ manituṃ, S. IV. 376.

by answering the question pertaining to the beginning or I may satisfy him by answering the question pertaining to the beginning. (Likewise) he who with his purified paranormal clairvoyant vision sees beings dying and being reborn, the low and the high, the fair and the ugly, the good and the evil, each according to his karma, he may ask me a question pertaining to the end (aparantaṃ) or I may ask him a question pertaining to the end and he may satisfy me by answering the question pertaining to the end or I may satisfy him by answering the question pertaining to the end. But leave aside, O Udāyi, the questions pertaining to the beginning and end. I shall teach you the Dhamma."[1] This statement of Buddha shows that he sets aside these questions not out of ignorance but due to some other consideration. It is important to note that Buddha offers to satisfy only those who have acquired the higher knowledge of retrocognition and clairvoyance. This most probably indicates that the answers pertaining to the beginning and end are supposed to be duly understood only by those who have acquired the higher faculty of knowing and gone beyond the level of mere conceptual knowledge. It is again in the light of this very higher knowledge about the beginning and end that in the Brahmajāla Sutta, Buddha is in a position to point out the errors of the 18 views pertaining to the beginning and 44 pertaining to the end. There he explains how, many of these views are based on only a limited knowledge of the past and future state of existence (taṃ pubbe nivāsaṃ anussarati tato paraṃ nānussarati, D.I. 18-20) and some are the product of mere conceptual reasoning and speculation (takka-pariyāhataṃ vimaṃsānucaritam..evam āha, D.I. 21, 27).

In the Cūḷa-Mālunkya Sutta we find Māluṅkyaputta telling Buddha in a straightforward manner that the latter should answer these unanswered (abyākatāni) metaphysical questions if he really knows their answers, and in case he does not know them, he should plainly confess his ignorance.[2]

1. M. II. 31-32.
2. Sace Bhagavā jānāti...me Bhagavā byākarotu. No ce Bhagavā jānāti...ajānato kho pana apassato etad eva ujukaṃ hoti yadidaṃ na jānāmi na passāmī ti, M.I. 427.

Here Buddha explains through the parable of the arrow as to why he refrains from answering these questions. He points out that the real need of the man pierced with a poisoned arrow is to get rid of it and be cured rather than to wait for a fruitless investigation about the nature of the arrow, the man shooting it and so on, and thus lose his life in the process.[1] At the end he clearly says: "It is not useful, not related to the basic disciplines of the holy-life, not conducive to detachment, dispassion, cessation, pacification, higher knowledge, enlightenment and Nibbāna. Therefore, has it not been answered by me."[2] This clearly shows that the pragmatic or practical consideration is an important factor in setting aside these questions. In view of this explanation as well as in the light of his other utterances claiming the highest knowledge, it is absurd to think that he is intellectually dishonest and is trying to conceal his ignorance by evading these questions. We cannot, therefore, accept the first interpretation, viz., Scepticism or Naive Agnosticism.

The second interpretation, viz., Pragmatism as conveyed through the parable of the arrow finds full support from the parable of Siṃsapa leaves (S.V. 437-8) as well that of the raft (M.I.134). It, indeed, appears to be a general consideration with Buddha whatever his other reasons for silence may be.

The position is further clarified in the Abhayarājakumāra Sutta (M. I.395) where, as K. N. Jayatilleke points out[3], Buddha himself describes what kind of propositions he does or does not assert. He claims to assert only the first two types of propositions out of the following :—

1. True useful pleasant
2. True useful unpleasant
3. True useless pleasant
4. True useless unpleasant
5. False useful pleasant
6. False useful unpleasant
7. False useless pleasant
8. False useless unpleasant

---

1. M.I. 429.
2. M.I. 431.
3. Op. cit., pp. 351-2.

Sheer pleasantness or unpleasantness is of no consideration to him. He does not assert untrue and useless propositions (7 and 8). It is, however, important to note that he does not speak all truths (as evident from the 3rd and 4th situations) but only the useful truths (1 and 2). We may note that Buddha omits the 5th and 6th possibilities where falsity is combined with usefulness. It may be that according to Buddha it is impossible for falsehood to be useful in the moral and spiritual sense of the term, since falsehood (musāvāda) is reckoned as one of the cardinal vices in the Buddhist moral teachings (sikkhāpadaṃ). This may have been the reason of ruling out the possibility of useful falsehood. We cannot, however, be certain about it, since the omission might have been only accidental and not intentional. Anyway, our point that Buddha does not assert useless truths (3 and 4) but only truths which are useful (1 and 2) is established in the light of this clarification from Buddha himself. It is precisely due to this reason that he is called kālavādī, bhūtavādī and atthavādī (the speaker in appropriate time, the speaker of the truth and the speaker of the useful).[1]

Thus the second solution finds full support from the Pali texts, and Keith is right in noticing at least this aspect of Buddha's teaching when he says that "disputation on them will not lead to the frame of mind which is essential for the attainment of Nirvāṇa."[2] Radhakrishnan also emphasises this pragmatic or practical approach of Buddha when he points out that "Buddha taught from motives of expediency."[3] This however, does not mean that it is an exclusive reason for Buddha's silence. To think so is to read too much into the parables of the arrow, Siṃsapa leaves and the raft and to ignore other legitimate possibilities like the inappropriateness

---

1. abhūtam ataccham anatthasaṃhitaṃ na taṃ Tathāgato byākaroti... bhūtam tacchaṃ anatthasamhitam tam pi Tathāgato na byākaroti...bhūtam tacchaṃ atthasaṃhitam tatra kālaññū Tathāgato hoti tassa pañhassa veyyākaraṇāya...Iti kho...Tathāgato kālavādi bhūtavādī atthavādī, D. III. 134-5.

2. Buddhist Philosophy in India and Ceylon, p. 45.

3. Indian Philosophy, Vol. I. p. 389.

or meaninglessness of the questions themselves, as also intellectual incomprehensibility of the answers. It is, indeed, misleading, since it assumes that all the ten questions are meaningful and answerable, and gives room for some scholars to read their own metaphysical views into the silence of Buddha.

Radhakrishnan himself is found to ascribe the positive metaphysical views of Ups. to Buddha which, he thinks, the latter did not explicitly state owing to his practical motive. He tries to show that the very same Upaniṣadic conception of the soul is presented in a practical form by Buddha. In his own words: "His (Buddha's) conceptions of life and the universe are derived from his severely practical outlook.. If.. we are divine, then there is nothing for us to aim at or strive for.. Man is not divine but has to become divine.. To tell him that there is a transcendental consciousness where scepticism and relativity are defeated from all eternity is not of much comfort."[1] It is from this "severely practical outlook" or "motives of expediency" that Buddha, though holding the Upaniṣadic view of the soul, does not explicitly state it. "The Upanisads arrive at the ground of all things by stripping the self of veil after veil of contingency. At the end of the process they find the universal self which is none of these finite entities, though the ground of them all. Buddha holds the same view, though he does not state it definitely."[2] Similarly Frauwallner thinks that ' these conceptions (those of the soul etc.) are ultimately connected with views which we are already familiar from the philosophy of the Upaniṣads... In both cases (Ups. and Buddhism) we come across the same ideas, only in Buddhism they are differently expressed and so to speak negatively formulated."[3] George Grimm also reads a somewhat similar idea of the soul into Buddha's doctrine of anattā. He says: "Everything is anattā, not the I, and does not belong to my innermost essence.. I am beyond all this, beyond the world. This was one of the

1. Radhakrishnan—Dhammapada, Introduction, p. 31.
2. Indian Philosophy, Vol. I, p. 388.
3. Quoted in Grimm's 'The Doctrine of the Buddha', Preface, pp. 3-4.

truths which the Buddha had to tell us."[1] From all this it is illustrated how some of the eminent scholars, owing to their exclusive reliance on the pragmative motive of Buddha, have been led into the temptation of supplying some positive metaphysical basis for the silence of the Master, disregarding altogether the possibilities of the questions being intellectually insoluble and logically meaningless. We find, however, a number of utterances of the Master himself which suggest rather clearly that some of these questions are insoluble by the intellect and some are by their very nature inappropriate or meaningless. In other words, they seem to favour the third and fourth solutions.

The third solution has been suggested by Beckh[2] and emphasised rather exclusively by Professor Murti who finds an articulation of Kantian antinomies in these unanswered questions. He says: "The similarity of the avyākṛta to the celebrated antinomies of Kant...cannot fail to strike us."[3] "That there are difficulties on either conception of reality on any conceptual pattern, no one realised perhaps more strongly than Buddha. He was thus led to discredit all attempts at *conceiving* reality, and in consequence to reject all speculative metaphysics. This is the sole meaning of his silence."[4]

We can agree only in part with Professor Murti. We also think that this rational agnostic interpretation is of particular significance with regard to the questions pertaining to the duration and extent of the world. But we find it difficult to agree with his view that "this is the sole meaning of his (Buddha's) silence." The pragmatic consideration of Buddha, we feel, can never be ignored in any case. It is due to this pragmatic consideration that whenever Buddha finds some other factor or factors causing genuine difficulties in the way of a categorical reply, he brushes aside the question. There are various factors, e. g , the limitation of intellectual capacity, the ambiguity

1. The Doctrine of the Buddha, p. 229.
2. Buddhismus, Vol. I., p. 120.
3. The Central Philosophy of Buddhism, p. 38.
4. The Central Philosophy of Buddhism, p. 35.

or misleading character of the problem and the inappropriateness or meaninglessness of the questioṇ as such, which may be singly or jointly responsible in different cases for creating genuine difficulties in the way of a categorical solution. Therefore, it would be wrong to think without further examination in the light of other relevant utterances of the Master that this or that interpretation alone has the sole validity in all cases.

The Pali texts seem to support the third interpretation, viz, Rational Agnosticism, in relation to the first four questions pertaining to the duration and extent of the world. It is clear from the Nikāya that both the thesis and antithesis were proved and disproved by the debaters during Buddha's time.[1] Buddha seems to have realised the antinomies of reason more clearly than any of the modern thinkers, for the clearest idea of the deep and interminable conflict of reason can be had only when one is in a position to look upon it from a higher perspective. So long as one is using reason itself implicitly or explicitly, one can understand its defects and limitations only vaguely. But when he has abandoned it and gone beyond the intellectual level, one may be expected to realise its shortcomings and limitations with greater clarity. It is probably due to this reason that, as we have already seen (supra, pp. 288-289) he claims to answer satisfactorily the questions pertaining to the beginning and end (pubbanta and aparanta) only before those who have acquired the higher knowledge of retrocognition and clairvoyance. The world perhaps has no beginning and end in time, and so to ask questions about the first beginning and the last termination of the world is to seek temporal solutions of that which transcends time. But since it is not possible for ordinary human beings to know things in a non-temporal and non-spatial manner, Buddha considers it expedient to set aside questions pertaining to

1. Idha, bhikkhave ekacco samaṇo vā brāhmaṇo vā takkī hoti vīmaṃsī. So takkapariyāhatam vīmaṃsānucaritaṃ sayaṃpaṭibhānaṃ evam āha: 'nevā' yaṃ loko antavā pana ananto. Ye te samaṇabrāhmaṇā evam āhaṃsu--antavā ayaṃ loko parivaṭumo ti, tesaṃ musā. Ye pi...evam āhaṃsu --ananto ayaṃ loko apariyanto ti, tesaṃ pi musā', D.I. 23-24.

the duration and extent of the universe. It is difficult to accept the position that the world has a beginning in time and Buddha is incapable of visualising it because of its remote ancestry. Such interpretation would flagrantly contradict the explicit claim made by Buddha to recollect the past as much as he desired (yāvad eva ākaṅkhāmi anekavihitaṃ pubbenivāsaṃ anussarāmi, M. I., 482. cf. D. III. 134.) We are, therefore, led to the conclusion that Buddha sets aside the questions pertaining to the duration and extent of the world on account of their intellectual incomprehensibility combined with the motive of expediency.

This rational agnostic interpretation is fully supported by the Pali Canon which explicitly says: "The beginning of the world is inconceivable (anamatagga = an + mat ($\sqrt{}$man) + agga), the first end (pubbākoti) is not comprehended."[1] The interpretation of the word 'anamatagga', of course, is not without its problems (P. T. S. Dictionary); the BHS. literature turns it into 'anavarāgra' i. e. "without beginning or end" (BHS. Dictionary), yet the difference in etymology does not seem to make any real change in the sense, for the sense is made clear in the subsequent qualifying words, viz., 'pubbākoti na paññāyati' (the first end is not comprehended, S. II. 178-181). Even if it is said that the world is rooted in ignorance, the problem is no nearer solution, for it is not possible to conceive temporally the beginning of ignorance. As it is clearly stated: "The first beginning of ignorance is not comprehended (such that we may say) 'before this there was no ignorance, after this it arose'."[2] Thus the references of the Pali texts suggest that the third solution (Rational Agnosticism) mainly accounts for setting aside the first four questions pertaining to the duration and extent of the world.

Of the remaining six unanswered questions, two refer to the identity or difference between the soul and the body, and the last four refer to the existence or non-existence of the liberated saint (Tathāgata) after death. Regarding the

1. Anamataggo'yaṃ...saṃsāro, pubbākoṭi na paññāyati, S. II. 178

2. purimā koṭi...na .paññāyati avijjāya, 'ito pubbe āvijjā nāhosi, atha pacchā sambhavī'ti', A.V. 113.

former, we feel that the chief responsible factor is the erroneous notion of the self or 'I', and regarding the latter the main reason appears to be the supramundane nature of the Tathāgata, besides the common consideration of moral expediency. These two sets of questions are closely related, because it is precisely under the delusion of the 'I-consciousness' that one asks personalistic questions in relation to the Tathāgata. When he gets rid of that error or delusion, he realises the meaninglessness or inappropriateness of the personalistic questions (like those of existence and non-existence) in the context of the Tathāgata. As Buddha clearly points out: "His ignorance being removed and knowledge arisen, he does not have the notion that 'I am' 'I am this'.. I shall be.. I shall not be..I shall be corporeal.. non-corporeal.. conscious.. non-conscious.. neither conscious nor non-conscious."[1] Buddha, therefore, takes all possible care to expose the untenability of the conceit of I or self (attā) to which people cling so tenaciously. We shall discuss this question separately under the next topic. Here we only wish to suggest that the questions pertaining to the identity or difference between the soul and the body were set aside owing to the fact that the soul itself was considered an erroneous concept.

There is no doubt that the notion of the self or soul is deeply rooted in man's natural desire. Diverse concepts of it, as the Pali texts tell us (D. I. 31-35; M. I. 300), were prevalent during Buddha's time. Generally it was believed that the real core of the human personality, the true 'I' or the self was eternal and blissful in nature. But Buddha, after a thorough analysis of the different constituents of the human personality, shows that nothing permanent and blissful is to be found in any or all of these various constituents which we may hold as our true 'I' or the 'self' saying, "this is mine, I am this or this is my self" (etaṃ mama, eso'ham asmi, eso me attā ti, S. II. 124-5). It is only on account of our clinging to or grasping of the five

1. Tassa avijjāvirāgā vijjuppādā asmī ti pi'ssa na hoti, ayam aham asmī ti pī'ssa na hoti, bhavissam ti...na bhavissaṃ ti...rūpī...arūpī...saññī...asaññī...nevasaññināsaññī bhavissaṃ ti pi'ssa na hotī ti...S. III. 47.

constituents that we develop this erroneous notion of I or the self.[1] But, since none of these constituents are found to be permanent and blissful, the notion of such a self cannot but be regarded as rooted in ignorance or a lack of proper knowledge.

Despite this analysis, man's clinging or attachment to his personality is so deep-rooted that he finds it difficult to shake off the notion of 'I' or the 'self' altogether and holds on to it in some form or the other. It is under this erroneous belief or assumption that an ordinary worldling raises the question whether the soul is identical with or different from the body. Obviously according to the Buddhist analysis, the question is inappropriate or meaningless, since it is not possible to speak of a relation (whether of identity or difference) between a fact (body) and a fiction (soul), between a thing and what is erroneously grasped about or superimposed upon it. But so long as this truth is not realised and understood by an average worldling in the light of the Buddhist theory of Paṭiccasamuppāda (dependent origination), the question will irresistably arise in him and any answer, whether positive or negative, is likely to confuse and mislead him further. The thoughtful Master, therefore, with due consideration to this misleading consequence, chooses to be silent about it.

This idea is fully borne out from the text as well as the commentary. When the wanderer Vacchagotta pointedly asks Buddha whether "the self is" (atthattā'ti, S. IV. 400) or "the self is not" (natthattā'ti, loc. cit.), Buddha remains silent (Bhagavā tuṇhī ahosi, loc. cit.) After his departure when Ānanda asks Buddha about the reason for his silence, he says that in case of his asserting the former, Vacchagotta would have taken him to mean that he accepted sassatavāda (eternalism) and in case of the latter, he would have confused it with ucchedavāda (annihilationism).[2] The first would have

1. upādāya...asmī ti hoti no anupādāya. Kiñca upādāya...? Rūpaṃ upādāya...vedanaṃ...saññaṃ...saṅkhāre...viññāṇam upādāya. S. III. 10?.

2. Ahaṃ c' Ānanda, Vacchagottassa paribbājakassa 'atthattā ti'puṭṭho samāno attheattā ti byākareyyaṃ...sassatavādā...saddhiṃ.abhavissa—natthattā ti byākaryyaṃ...ucchedavādā...saddhiṃ abhavissa, S. IV. 400.

gone against the basic teaching that "all things are soul-less" (sabbe dhammā anattā, S. IV. 401) and the second one would have caused further delusion to the already deluded Vacchagotta who would have thought, "I, indeed, had a self previously, which now is not" (ahu vā me nūna pubbe attā, so etarahi natthī'ti, loc. cit.). Thus any answer whether positive or negative would have been misconceived by him on account of his egoistic obsession which would have proved detrimental to his religious quest. Therefore, Buddha makes this declaration: "If, monks, the erroneous view that the soul is identical with the body is there, the holy life is not fulfilled; (likewise) if monks the erroneous view that the soul is different from the body is there, the holy life is not fulfilled."[1] The commentary on this passage explains the position as follows: "Whoever maintains the view that the soul is identical with the body, holds that with the destruction of the soul, the body is destroyed and with the destruction of the body, the soul is destroyed. The view of him who holds thus is known as Ucchedadiṭṭhi (annihilationism) on account of holding that the being is destroyed..In the second instance, whoever maintains the view that the soul is different from the body, holds that the body is destroyed here itself but the soul passes off at will like a bird out of the cage. The view of him who holds thus is known as Sassatadiṭṭhi (eternalism) on account of holding the view that the soul has passed from this world to another."[2]

Thus it seems clear that Buddha rejected the aforesaid questions about the identity or difference between the soul and the body chiefly on account of the erroneous and misleading concept of the soul. According to Buddhist wisdom, the questions are inappropriate or meaningless owing to the simple reason that a thing cannot be said to have a relation (either of identity or difference) with an illusory concept.

Coming to the last four unanswered questions about the existence or non-existence of the Tathāgata after death, we feel that they are rejected, on account of their inapplicability

1. S. II. 61-63.
2. S.A. II. 68-69 on S. II. 63.

or meaninglessness in relation to the Tathāgata. The question of existence or non-existence can legitimately arise only in relation to one who is endowed with the five aspects of personality. But the Tathāgata being devoid of all these aspects, the question of existence or non-existence ceases to be meaningful in relation to him. We find Buddha clearly explaining to Anurādha the impropriety of the question of existence or non-existence in relation to the Tathāgata who is in no way associated with any of the five constituents. He asks Anurādha whether the latter cognizes (samanupassati) the Tathāgata as the five aggregates, included within the five aggregates, possessing the five aggregates or including the five aggregates, and to each of these questions Anurādha answers in the negative.[1] Buddha, then points out to him that the Tathāgata being indeed undiscoverable in terms of any of the cognizable elements (ditṭheva dhamme saccato thetato Tathāgate anupalabbhayamāne, S. IV. 384) it is not proper to answer (Kallam..veyyākaraṇaṃ, loc. cit.) that the Tathāgata exists, does not exist, both or neither. Nor can it be said that any answer outside the four alternatives (aññatra imehi catūhi ṭhānehi, loc. cit.) is possible, since all the logical possibilities are exhausted by the four alternatives. This only shows that the question itself is inappropriate or meaningless in the context.

This interpretation is fully confirmed when Buddha with the simile of the fire explains the situation to Vaccha. Vaccha having found Buddha rejecting all the four logical alternatives of the question (viz, the Tathāgata is born, not born, both and neither) is apparently confounded because he thought that the four alternatives being mutually exclusive, one must necessarily be true. Buddha, however, explains to him by means of the simile of the fire how in that context the questions themselves were not fitting or were meaningless. He asks Vaccha: "If the fire in front of you were to go out, would you know, this fire in front of me has gone out?"[2] On

1. S. IV. 383.

2. Sace te...purato so aggi nibbāyeyya, jāneyyāsi tvaṃ—'ayaṃ me purato aggi nibbuto'ti ?, M. I. 487.

this Vaccha answers in the affirmative. Buddha then further questions him: "If some one were to ask you, 'this fire in front of you which has gone out, in which direction has it gone, eastern, western, northern or southern'—asked thus how would you reply?"[1] To this Vaccha answers: "(I would say), It does not fit the case. The fire which burnt on account of the fuel of grass and wood is reckoned as gone out (extinguished) when it has consumed it (the fuel) and is not fed with more fuel."[2] At this Buddha points out: "In the same way, O Vaccha, the corporeality (rūpaṃ) whereby one seeking to know the Tathāgata were to cognize him, that corporeality of the Tathāgata has been abandoned, cut off from the root, made unable to grow, rendered incapable of future becoming like an uprooted palm tree. So in relation to the Tathāgata who is free from the mark of corporeality (rūpa), it does not fit the case (na upeti) to say that he is born,.. not born,..born as well as not born,..and neither born nor not born."[3] [Similarly with regard to feeling (vedanā), perception (saññā), dispositions (saṅkhāra) and consciousness (viññāṇa)]. This illustration clarifies why all the four alternatives about the existence or non-existence of the Tathāgata were set aside. Just as it is inappropriate or meaningless to speak of the direction of the fire which being free from the fuel has gone out, so also it is inappropriate or meaningless to speak of the existence or non-existence of the Tathāgata who being free from all the cognizable marks has become indeterminable.

Thus we see that these last four questions were set aside because of their inapplicability or meaninglessness in the supramundane context. We must however distinguish between

1. Sace pana taṃ...evaṃ puccheyya—'yo te ayaṃ purato aggi nibbuto so aggi ito katamaṃ disaṃ gato, puratthimaṃ vā dakkhiṇaṃ vā pācchimaṃ va uttaraṃ vā'ti puṭṭho tvaṃ...kin ti byākareyyāsī ti ? loc. cit.

2. Na upeti...yaṃ hi so...aggi tiṇa-kaṭṭh upādānaṃ paṭicca ajali tassa ca pariyādānā aññassa ca anupāhārā anāhāro nibbuto t'eva saṅkhaṃ gacchatī ti., loc. cit.

3. Evam eva kho Vaccha yena rūpena Tathāgataṃ paññāpayamāno paññāpeyya taṃ rūpaṃ Tathāgatassa pahīnaṃ ucchinnamūlaṃ tālāvatthukataṃ anabhāvakataṃ āyatiṃ anuppādadhammaṃ. Rūpasaṅkhāvimutto... Tathāgato...upapajjatī ti na upeti, na upapajjatī ti...upapajjati ca na ca upapajjatī ti...neva upapajjati na na upapajjatī ti na upeti., M.I. 487-8.

the previous set of questions (pertaining to the identity or difference between the soul and the body) and the present one. In the case of the former, we vainly seek for a relation (either of identity or difference) between a fact (the body) and a fictitious thing (the soul). Thus the questions become misleading and meaningless, because the soul itself is a misconception having no actual *locus standi* whatsoever. In the case of the latter, on the other hand, we vainly try to ascribe the epithets of the five aggregates (viz., existence or non-existence) to that which is free from them. Thus the questions become inappropriate and meaningless because the mundane attributes do not apply to the transmundane reality (the Tathāgata).

Now we may briefly express our findings regarding the reason for Buddha's silence about the ten questions as follows:—

Questions No. 1 to 4:—irrelevant and intellectually incomprehensible.

Questions No. 5 to 6: –irrelevant and meaningless (due to misconception)

Questions No. 7 to 10:—irrelevant and meaningless (due to inappropriateness)

After having determined the nature and significance of Buddha's silence and seen thereby his general outlook to different metaphysical questions, we may now in the light of his other relevant utterances and occasional criticisms of diverse theories and concepts try to ascertain his position and compare it with the corresponding thought of the B. G. The ten metaphysical questions themselves pertain to three major metaphysical problems, viz., those of the world, the soul and salvation. We may add two more: one the question of rebirth which the metaphysicians tie up with the theory of the soul and the other, the problem of God which is central to the B. G. and irrelevant to Buddhism. We shall thus deal with the problems of the self (Soul), salvation, rebirth, world and God one by one.

The Problem of the Self:—

The Buddhist approach to the problem of the self,

though superficially simple, has proved to be one of the most intricate and intriguing topics of the Buddhist thought and scholars, more often than not, have misrepresented the Master in this respect. The problem is as controversial as it is important and, therefore, it is necessary to steer clear of the confusions about it before we compare the Buddhistic attitude to the self with the B. G. view of it.

(*A*) *Some Basic Confusions about the Notion of the Self*:—

We may briefly mention the views of some eminent scholars and show how on account of their metaphysical predilections and some basic confusions, they have misconstrued the oft-repeated utterances of the Master and thereby thrown overboard one of his most essential teachings, wherein, indeed, lies one of his unique contributions to Indian thought. Unable to free themselves from the long-prevalent traditional speculations about the self, these scholars appear to read into his utterances the very ideas of the tradition which Buddha intends to discard They display their ingenuity in constructing a positive soul theory, on the oft-emphasised anattā-doctrine (the dartrine of soullessness) of Buddha and try to establish that like the Ups. Buddha also preached the same identification of the self, reality and Nibbāna.

We have already mentioned the views of Frauwallner, Radhakrishnan and Grimm (supra, pp. 292-3) who are in favour of reading the Upanisadic conception of the soul into the Buddhist doctrine of anattā. Frauwallner has clearly said that both in the Ups. and Buddhism, "we come across the same ideas, only in Buddhism they are differently expressed and so to speak negatively formulated."[1] Radhakrishnan also explicitly supporting the same view, says: "Buddha clearly tells us what the self is not, though he does not give any clear account of what it is,"[2] and then comparing the views of Buddha with those of the Ups., he concludes: "Buddha holds the same view, though he does not state it definitely."[3]

1. Quoted in Grimm's 'The Doctrine of the Buddha', Preface, p. 4.
2. Indian Philosophy, Vol. I, p. 386.
3. *Ibid.*, p. 388.

Grimm declares in the Cartesian style:—"I am: that is the most certain axiom there is. It belongs to those axioms that are evident in themselves without any proof."[1] Then he proceeds to say, "This question as to our true essence may be approached from two sides: We may try to answer it directly or indirectly, namely, by determining what I am *not*, at all events. Which way is the better,.....this much is clear, that the indirect way is certainly the safer one...he (Buddha) prefers the safer indirect way."[2] Max Hoppe corroborating this, says: "Indeed, from the statement that everything perishable and sorrowful cannot be the self, one might sooner draw the deduction that the self is therefore imperishable and free from suffering, and that anyone arguing in this way presupposes the existence of such a soul."[3] Mrs. Rhys Davids sees a complete identity between the Upaniṣadic and the Buddhist view of the self and finds it inconsistent and illogical to think that in the same period of the sixth century B.C. the Buddhist and the Upaniṣadic tradition could have developed a different attitude to the same Indian word 'attā' or 'ātman'. She accuses the later tradition of Ceylon and modern interpretation in Europe for taking the word 'atta' in the sense of the reflexive pronoun 'yourself' and not in the sense of the metaphysical soul. Referring to the translation "Be ye a lamp unto yourselves, etc." (Dialogues of the Buddha, IIp. 108)[4] she says that "this is not the religious meaning such a sentence would have had in the sixth century B. C., however plausible a rendering it may be for Ceylon later, or for Europe now..It has always seemed to me illogical and inconsistent to render one and the same context in the Indian way, when found in the Upaniṣads; and in the European way, or at best in the secular, the nonreligious way of Ceylon, when it is found in the Pali."[5] She declares: "Never will the reader understand the original Buddhism if he imagines the first

1. The Doctrine of the Buddha, p. 112.

2. *Ibid.*, p. 114.

3. Preface to Grimm's 'The Doctrine of the Buddha', p. 5.

4. The text reads as follows : atta-dīpā viharatha, atta-saraṇā anañña-saraṇā, D. II. 100.

5. Buddhism : Its Birth and Dispersal, pp. 74-75.

Buddhists of the sixth century B. C. teaching religion in terms of either the late Pali tradition, or of Western ideals..The Indian, Brahman or Buddhist, never thought of the self as.. this hateful Me."[1] Not only does she find the Upaniṣadic self taken for granted in early Buddhism but she also sees here a distinction made between the great self and the little self. To quote her own words once again: "We find 'the self', not only taken for granted, but referred to in lofty terms as a more in the man than either the body, the mind-ways or the 'just himself.' We find 'self' called a great self co-existing with a little self."[2] Ananda K. Coomaraswamy and I. B. Horner also support this theory of the two selves, the great and the small, and collect various Pali texts which according to their interpretation imply the two-selves theory.[3] Radha-Krishnan also follows the same line and refers to the distinction of "the surface self" and "the true self" and thinks that Buddha only "disputes the reality of the surface self."[4] After having read the Upaniṣadic self into the Pali texts, it was only natural for these scholars to follow the same Upaniṣadic line of thinking in equating the self with Nirvāṇa. As Radhakrishnan puts it: "Nirvāṇa is.. a positive return of the self to itself";[5] or as Guenther says: "Nirvāṇa is the true nature of man" and "the Buddha meant the same by Nirvāṇa and Ātman".[6] It is curious to see that even the well-known commentator Buddhaghosa has been baffled at places with regard to this problem and is found to equate the liberated saint (the Tathāgata) with the soul (Tathāgato ti attā, Ud. A. 340). The last four questions pertaining to the existence or non-existence of the liberated saint (the Tathāgata) are taken to mean by him as the questions pertaining to the soul (hoti Tathāgato ti ādisu, satto Tathāgato ti adhippeto,

1. *Ibid.* p. 82.
2. Buddhism : Its Birth and Dispersal, p. 70.
3. The Living Thoughts of Gotama, the Buddha, pp. 147-163.
4. Indian Philosophy, Vol. I, p. 385.
5. *Ibid.*, p. 386.
6. Quoted by Professor H. Von Glasenapp in 'Vedanta and Buddhism', p. 8.

i. e. in the statements, 'hoti Tathāgato', etc., by Tathāgata is meant the soul, D. A. I. 118).[1]

It is evident from the above-mentioned views that Buddha's repeated teaching of the anattā-doctrine has been construed by these scholars veritably as an implicit attā-doctrine, indistinguishable from that of the Ups. We, however, have suggested in the course of our discussion about the unanswered (abyākata) questions that this is a misrepresentation of Buddha's real view. It is not only not in conformity with the fundamental Buddhist ideas, but it flagrantly contradicts the explicit utterances of the Master.

The crux of the problem seems to lie in some basic confusions about the notion of 'I' or 'self' (attā). We have in us a deep-seated conceit of 'I' which we uncritically and unquestionably accept.[2] We consider the existence of this 'I' as axiomatic and with this assumption proceed to inquire what its true nature is. In view of this extremely intimate attachment or clinging to this notion of I-ness or egotism, it is no wonder that even when meditative insight into the indescribable reality is had, one is led to give a personalistic or egoistic colour to it and think that the reality is only the true form of the 'I' or self, In other words, reality is identified with the self, and salvation is said to consist in the realisation of this identity. This is the line of thought adopted in the pre-Buddhistic tradition of the Ups. By the time of Buddha this tradition of ego-centric speculation about reality had become so firmly established that it had become almost impossible to conceive of reality distinct from the self. Thus, the word ātman or self had come to acquire a dual meaning, viz., (i) the 'I' or the self and (ii) the reality—ostensibly associated together.

(B) *Buddha's Analytical Approach to the Problem*:—

A radically new approach to the problem is heralded in Indian thought with the advent of Buddhism. What had hitherto uncritically passed for the self is now subjected to a

1. cf. Professor Jayatilleke—Early Buddhist Theory of Knowledge, p—244.

2. cf. Śaṅkara's statement: sarvo hy ātmāstitvaṃ pratyeti, na nā'ham asmī'ti, Sаṅkara's commentary on Brahma-Sutra, I. 1. 1.

critical analysis and examination. It is found after a thorough examination that the notion of the self is ultimately rooted in the subtlest and strongest desire of man for personal immortality (bhava-diṭṭhi), which leads him almost irresistibly to conceive of a permanent and blissful element in him. This erroneous conceit of a permanent and blissful 'I', indeed, is found to be the root of all confusion and suffering, and one is asked to break through this long-accepted notion of I-ness in order to see truth and reality in right perspective and attain the state of the absolute cessation of suffering, viz., Nibbāna.

Since man finds everything passing and leading to sufferring, there arises in him an ardent desire or craving for permanence (immortality) and bliss. This desire combined with his egoistic obsession leads him to imagine some permanent and blissful element in his personality which he fondly holds on or clings to. Thus on a penetrative analysis this conceit of 'I' or the self is found to be a mere clinging or attachment to an erroneous or imaginary element. So, Buddha calls this clinging or grasping 'attavādupādāna' (clinging to I-ness), and the erroneous speculative belief in some permanent element in personality which leads to this clinging is called 'sakkāyaditthi'.

Buddha in order to enable us to get rid of this erroneous belief (sakkāyadiṭṭhi) and vain clinging to I-ness (attavādupādāna) tries to show by analysing the entire personality of man that each one of its constituents is transiṭory and is source of suffering. There is nothing permanent and blissful in it. The notion of a permanent and blissful 'I' is only a product of imagination. Thus by exposing the absurdity of the sakkāyadiṭṭhi (the belief in some permanent element in personality) he trie to remove our undesirable clinging to it (attavādupādana) or, in other words, the erroneous conceit of the 'I' or the self. But it is precisely this very intention of the Master which appears to have been misunderstood by the above-mentioned scholars. Not forsaking the egoistic line of thinking, they continue to look for an attā (self) somehow and somewhere in man and thus disregard the clear declaration of the Master that "all elements are soulless" (sabbe dhammā anattā, Dh. 279).

It is only by ignoring some important passages, misconceving others and disregarding the contextual suggestions of some of them that they ascribe such a positive metaphysical concept of the soul to Buddha. It is not necessary to examine individually the view of all these scholars, for they mainly follow the same line of argument and refer mostly to the same Pali passages in support of their views. So if we carefully examine those passages and read them along with others in their proper contexts, it would not be difficult for us to see how and where these scholars are misled in interpreting the Master. In our attempt to understand the true significance of the anattā-doctrine, we shall try to point out what this doctrine seeks to deny and what it does not deny.

The Pali Canon is full of references where Buddha analysing the total personality of man into five ingredients, viz., rūpa (corporeality), vedanā (feeling), saññā (perception), saṅkhāra (dispositions) and viññāna (consciousness) explains that there is nothing permanent and blissful in them, and establishes the point that it is wrong to cling to anything and to have the conceit of 'I' in any or all of them. He is frequently found to proceed by asking whether corporeality (rūpa) is permanent or impermanent (taṃ kiṃ maññasi... rūpaṃ niccaṃ vā aniccaṃ vā ti, M.I. 232-233; S. III. 88, 118), and on the reply that it is impermanent, he further asks whether that which is impermanent is to be regarded as sorrowful or blissful (yaṃ pana aniccaṃ dukkhaṃ vā taṃ sukhaṃ vā ti, loc. cit.) To this the natural reply is that it is sorrowful. Then he asks : "Is it proper to look upon that which is impermanent, sorrowful and changeable as, 'this is mine, I am this, this is my self' ?" (yaṃ pana aniccaṃ dukkhaṃ vipariṇāmadhammaṃ, kallaṃ nu taṃ samanupassitum—'etaṃ mama, eso' ham asmi, eso me attā ti'?, loc. cit.), and then the obvious reply comes as, "certainly not, Lord" (loc. cit.). By applying the same formula with regard to the rest of the constituents he finally shows the absurdity of the conceit of the 'I' and 'mine' and remarks : "I (self) and mine (anything belonging to the self) not being truly and really discovered, is it not, monks, a perfectly foolish doctrine to hold the point of view, 'this is the world, this is the self; permanent, abiding, eternal, immutable shall I be after death. in eternal identity shall I persist ?"[1] This is, briefly speaking, the way in which Buddha tries to remove the erroneous notion of the 'I' or self.

But the scholars who do not shake off their egoistic line of thinking, seem to miss this basic point of the Master and try to discover a self or 'I' besides and beyond the five aggregates. It is argued that the statements declaring the five aggregates as soulless (anattā) seek to repudiate only the superficial views of the self but the true self is never intended to be denied. Thus, Mrs. Rhys Davids observes : "that the words, 'body is not the self, mind is not the self' cannot rationally be said to imply that there is no self (or soul, or real 'man'). As soon might I be held to be denying the existence of the captain, if I said on looking at two sailors, 'you are not the skipper'. Yet this is just the inference that Buddhism has come to draw from this monition. This belongs to the after-history."[2] We have already referred to the views of various other scholars (supra. pp. 292-3; 302-5) who also argue in the same vein. These scholars do scant justice to the above-quoted concluding utterance of Buddha (M.I. 138) in which he precludes the possibility of discovering anything permanent as I or mine. The very fact that they try to discover a self, while Buddha fails to do so, indicates that they misconceive the crucial point which the latter wants to drive in. Besides, we find a number of other utterances, still more explicit, where Buddha exposes the absurdity of the notion of 'I' or the self in all possible shape or form. These statements are so open and obvious that they are generally ignored by these scholars, and some of them are given a different twist.

First of all, it is made quite clear by Buddha that the conceit of the 'I' or the self is possible only in and through the five aggregates of the personality. He clearly says : "Any

1. Attani ca bhikkhave attaniye ca saccato thetato anupalabbhamāne yaṃ pi taṃ diṭṭiṭṭhānaṃ—'so loke so attā so pecca bhavissāmi nicco dhuvo sassato avipariṇāmadhammo sassatisamaṃ tatheva ṭhassāmī ti'—nanāyaṃ bhikkhave paripūro bāladhammo' ti?, M.I. 138.

2. Outlines of Buddhism, p. 46.

ascetic or Brahmin who variously conceives of the self, all of them conceive the five groups of grasping or anyone of them (as the self)."[1] The way in which the conceit of the 'I' or the self arises in its various forms is described as follows : "There is, O monks, an uninstructed worldling who has not seen the noble one, who has no knowledge of the noble doctrine, no training in the noble doctrine. He regards corporeality as the self, or the self as possessing corporeality, or the corporeality as being within the self or the self as within the corporeality. (Similarly with regard to the rest of the Khandhas). Seeing in this manner he forms the notion 'I am' ".[2] Just the opposite is said to be the case with regard to "the instructed noble disciple" (S III. 114, 165) who "does not regard corporeality as the self or the self as possessing corporeality, or corporeality as being within the self or the self within the corporeality (similarly with regard to the rest of the khandhas, loc. cit)" and accordingly "he does not grasp corporeality, does not cling to corporeality and does not hold (the view) that 'this is my self'. (Similarly with regard to the other four khandhas)."[3] Buddha then remarks : "Of such an instructed and noble disciple I say that he is no longer fettered by the bond of corporeality, internal or external, he is the seer of the other shore, the seer of the beyond and absolutely emancipated from suffering. (Similarly with regard to the other four aggregates)."[4] Discarding the validity of the conceit of the 'I' or the self in any possible shape or form, he says : "Any kind of cor-

1. Ye hi keci...samaṇā vā brāhmaṇā vā anekavihitam attānaṃ samanupassamānā samanupassanti, sabbe te pañcupādānakkhandhe samanupassanti etesaṃ vā aññataraṃ S. III. 46.

2. Idha bhikkhave assutavā puthujjano ariyānaṃ adassāvī ariyadhammassa akovido ariyadhamme avinīto...rūpaṃ attato samanupassati, rūpavantaṃ vā attānaṃ, attani vā rūpam, rūpasmiṃ vā attānaṃ; vedanaṃ... saññaṃ...saṅkhāre...viññānaṃ attato samanupassati...Iti ayaṃ ceva samanupassanā asmīti assa adhigataṃ hoti, S. III. 46.

3. So rūpaṃ na upeti na upādiyati nādhiṭṭhāti, 'attā me ti', vedanaṃ...saññaṃ...saṅkhāre...viññāṇaṃ na upeti...attā me ti, S. III. 115.

4. Ayaṃ vuccati...sutavā ariyasāvako na rūpabandhanabaddho na sāntarabāhirabandhanabaddho, tīradassī pāradassī parimutto so dukkhasmā ti vadāmi, S. III. 165.

poreality whatever, whether past, future or present, whether internal or external, whether gross or subtle, inferior or superior, whether far or near—all corporeality must with objective knowledge be regarded as 'this is not mine, this is not I, this is not my self. (Similarly with regard to the other aggregates)".[1] It is again said: "Whatever is seen, heard, reflected, known, attained, inquired and mentally contemplated—that also is to be viewed as 'this is not mine, this is not I, this is not my self.'"[2] Thus the attempts of the scholars to discover some kind of the self beyond or beside the five aggregates is shown to be baseless.

The same doctrine of utter soul-lessness is over and over again taught by means of various similes. It is said: "There is no corporeality whatever, O monks, no feeling, no perception, no dispositions, no consciousness whatever that is permanent, everlasting, eternal, changeless and identically abiding for ever. Then the Blessed One took a bit of cowdung in his hand and spoke to the monk: 'if, monk, even that much of permanent, everlasting, eternal, changeless selfhood (attabhāva), identically abiding for ever could be found, then living of a life of purity for the complete eradication of suffering would not be feasible,"[3] He makes similar statements by placing a particle of dust on the tip of his nail (nakhasikhāyaṃ paṃsuṃ āropetvā, S. III. 147). The five constituents of the personality, viz., corporeality, feeling, perception, dispositions and consciousness are respectively compared with a lump of foam (pheṇapiṇḍaṃ), a water-bubble (undaka-bubbulaṃ), a mirage (marīcikā), a trunk of a plantain tree (kadalikkhandhaṃ) and an illusion (māyaṃ), and it is expressly stated that there is no essence or substance in it (sāro ettha na vijjati).[4]

---

1. yam kiñci rūpaṃ atītānāgatapaccuppannam ajjhattaṃ vā bahiddhā vā olārikam vā sukhumaṃ vā hīnaṃ vā panītam vā, yam dūre santike vā sabbam rūpam netaṃ mama ne so'ham asmi na me so attāti evam etam yaṭhābhūtaṃ sammāppaññāya daṭṭhabbaṃ. . .yā kāci vedanā. . .saññā. . . saṅkharā. . .viññaṇaṃ. . ., S. III. 68.

2. yaṃ p'idaṃ diṭṭham sutam mutaṃ viññātaṃ pariyesitaṃ anuvicaritam manasā tam pi n'etam mama n'eso'ham asmi na meso attā ti samanupassati, M.I. 136.

3. S. III. 144.

4. S. III. 142-3

It is important to note that the characteristic of soullessness (anattā) is unsparingly applied even to consciousness (viññāṇa), which in the Ups. as well as in the B. G. is considered to be an eternal and immutable element. The question of the applicability of soullessness in relation to consciousness is very pointedly raised in the Saṃyutta Nikāya (IV. 166-168), and a definite positive answer is given with the illustration of the voidness of a plantain tree. As this point is of crucial importance we may give here an exact version of the text:—

"Just as with regard to this body, it has in diverse ways been stated, explained and shown by the Exalted One that 'this body is non-self' (anattā), is it possible in the same way to describe, teach, state, set forth, make plain, analyse and expound in relation to the consciousness also that 'this consciousness is not-self'?[1]"

"...it is surely possible in the same way to describe... that 'this consciousness also is non-self'".[2]

"Suppose... a man in need of the heart of the wood, in search of the heart of the wood, looking for the heart of the wood should roaming about enter a forest taking a sharp axe. There he sees a mighty plantain-trunk, straight up, new-grown and of towering height. He cuts it down at the root. Having cut it down at the root, he chops it off at the top. Having done so he thoroughly peels out the skin. But he would not find there even the pith, not to speak of the heart of the wood. Even so... a monk beholds no self or anything belonging to the self in the sixfold group of contact" (evam eva... bhikkhu chasu phassāyatanesu n'evattānam na attaniyaṃ samanupassati, S. IV. 168).

Exactly the same analogy of the essenceless plantain tree is given by Buddha when he, in his discussion with Saccaka, explains to the latter the utter voidness or self-

1. Yatheva nu kho. . .ayaṃ kāyo bhagavatā anekapariyāyena akkhāto vivato pakāsito, 'iti p'āyam kāyo anattā ti'sakkā evam evaṃ viññānam pidaṃ ācikkhitum desetum paññāpetum paṭṭhapetuṃ vivaritum vibhajitum uttānīkātum—'iti pidam viññāṇam anattā ti' ?, S. IV. 166.

2. . . .sakkā evam evaṃ viññāṇaṃ pidaṃ ācikkhitum. . .uttānīkātuṃ. —'iti pidam viññānaṁ anattā ti.', S. IV. 166.

lessness of all the five aggregates.[1] The same voidness is clearly indicated by the analogy of the empty village (suñño gāmo, S. IV. 174). Speaking allegorically of the empty village, Buddha remarks: "By empty village is meant the sixfold internal organs. The wise, instructed and intelligent one examines the eyes and finds them empty vain and void. (Similarly with regard to other five internal organs)"[2] Ānanda says to Buddha: "The empty world, the empty world they say lord. Why, Lord, is it known as the empty world?"[3] Buddha replies: "Because, Ānanda, the world is empty of the self and anything belonging to the self; so they call it as the empty world"[4]

These statements are in open contradiction to the view of Radhakrishnan who, in his attempt to indentify the Upaniṣadic and Buddhist approach to the self, remarks: "The Upaniṣads arrive at the ground of all things by stripping the self of veil after veil of contingency. At the end of the process they find the universal self which is none of these finite entities, though the ground of them all. Buddha holds the same view, though he does not state it definitely."[5] But here we find Buddha stating definitely in so many words and through so many analogies, especially through the analogy of the plantain tree, that after stripping oneself of layer after layer of contingency, nothing as essence or the self is left, and it is all empty, void or non-self.

It is made quite clear that this false conceit of the 'I' or the self arises only on account of our vain clinging to the fivefold aggregate of personality and, therefore, it must be completely shaken off in order to lead a really holy life and attain the state of the absolute cessation of suffering. Thus it is explicitly pointed out: "It is by clinging that the conceit of 'I' arises and not without clinging. By clinging to what..? It is by clinging to corporeality..feeling.. per-

1. M.I. 233.
2. S. IV. 174-5.
3. S. IV. 54.
4. loc. cit.
5. Indian Philosophy, Vol. I, p. 388.

ception..dispositions..consciousness that the conceit of 'I' arises, and not without clinging."[1] This conceit of 'I' is considered so detrimental to the religious quest that it is singled out as one which must be abandoned. With regard to the question as to "which one thing is to be got rid of" (katamo eko dhammo pahātabbo?, D. III. 273), it is said that "the conceit of 'I' is the one thing which is to be got rid of" (asmimāno-ayaṃ eko dhammo pahātabbo, loc. cit.). It is only by shaking off all conceit of 'I' in this conscious body as well as in all external objects that one becomes thoroughly free from all clinging and thereby attains unfettered salvation (anuppādā vimutti). The monk Kappa, therefore, asks Buddha: "Pray, Lord, how should one know, how should one see, so that in this body together with the consciousness, as well as in all objects external to it, the mind has gone away from all conceit of 'I' and 'mine', gone away from egotism, gone beyond all distinctions, is calmed and wholly released"?[2] To this Buddha replies: 'Whatever corporeality, Kappa, be it past, present or 'future.. you behold thus: 'this is not mine, this is not I, this is not my self'. So knowing things objectively as they are by perfect insight, one, having forsaken clinging, is free. (Similarly with regard to other four aggregates). Thus knowing, thus seeing, Kappa..., the mind has gone away from all conceit of 'I' and 'mine', gone away from egotism, gone away from all distinctions, is calmed and wholly released."[3] Since this conceit of 'I' is the result of attachment or lust for the five coggregates and consequent grasping of or clinging to them, aBuddha exhorts monks as follows: "Whatsoever desire, attachment, lust, craving.. there be monks, concerning corporeality, do ye abandon that. Thus will that corporeality be abandoned, cut down at the root, made like the stump of a palm tree, unable to grow in future. (Similarly with regard to other aggregates.)"[4] If in relation to corporeality

1. S. III. 105.
2. S. III. 170.
3. S. III. 170.
4. S. III. 161-2.

one is not free from attachment, desire, love, thirst, fever, and craving, there arise in him the sorrow, lamentation grief woe and despair (similarly in relation to other aggregates).... but one who is free from them, in him they do not arise."[1] It is thus made clear that the source of confusion lies in our vain grasping or clinging based on the erroneous notion of permanence or blissfulness in one or the other element of our personality. Buddha compares the grasping of the five aggregates of our personality with the holding of five kinds of grass by a man being washed away with the gushing current of the river. Each of the five grasses which the floating man fondly catches hold of with the hope that it would save him, proves feeble and is uprooted (palujjati) leading him to suffering all the more.[2] Buddha, therefore, declares: "I do not see. O monks, that form of clinging to 'I'-ness which having clung to, there would not arise sorrow lamentation suffering, agony and despair."[3]

This is the crux of the Buddhist approach to the problem of the self. The self being considered as the manifestation of the strongest and subtlest from of clinging, and clinging being regarded as the root cause of suffering, the greatest emphasis is naturally laid on the abandonment of the conceit of the self, It is a teaching of absolute detachment *par excellence*. One is asked not to have any clinging or the conceit of 'I' in anything including Nibbāna. Exhorting monks to give up clinging or conceit of the 'I' in all things in all possible ways, Buddha says: "One should not imagine oneself as being indentical with the totality of things (sabbaṃ), as being included in the totality of things, as being excluded from the totality of things as belonging to oneself. Thus not associating oneself, he does not cling to anything in the world; clinging no longer, he trembles not; trembling no longer, he realises in

1. S. III. 107.
2. S. III. 137-8.
3. aham pi kho taṃ bhikkhave attavādupādānaṃ na samanupassāmi yaṃ sa attavādupādānam upadiyato na uppajjeyyum soka-parideva-dukkha-domanass-upāyāsā, M. I. 137.

his own person the absolute emanciption (Nibbāna)."[1] In fact, this basic teaching of Buddhism is fully emphasised in the very first Sutta of the Majjhima Nikāya which, significantly enough, is named as the Mūlapariyāya Sutta (discourse on the root cause). There giving a long list of various categories or cencepts like the material elements, heavenly worlds, incorporeal spheres, everything seen, heard, reflected or known, the totality of things (sabbaṃ) and even the Nibbāna, Buddha points out that the ignorant worldling clings to them and has the conceit of 'I' in them in the abovementioned fourfold way; whereas the perfect saint having the right knowledge, does not have any clinging or the conecit of 'I' in anyway and, accordingly, he is absolutely emancipated.[2] It is significant to note here that even with regard to Nibbāna, it is clearly said that the conceit of 'I' in any of the four ways is not there. Thus Buddha says: "The Tathāgata, the Emancipated and rightly enlightened One having known Nibbāna as Nibbāna (as it is) does not imagine himself as identical with Nibbāna...included in Nibbāna...excluded from Nibbāna...Nibbāna as belonging to himself, (and thus) he does not cling to (or have lust or attachment for) Nibbāna. Why so? Because he knows that lust (rejoicing) is the root of suffering."[3] This Buddhist approach to Nibbāna as a state of perfect freedom and absolute detachment having no trace of 'I'-ness in it shows the untenability of the view of Radhakrishan who considers Nibbāna as "a positive return of the self to itself".[4] According to Buddha "it is impossible and cannot be that a man with right knowledge should look upon anything as the self..such a thing cannot happen. But it is certainly possible that an ignorant man should look upon something as the self."[5]

---

1. S. IV. 65-66.
2. M. I. 1-6.
3. Tathāgato pi. . .arahaṃ sammāsambuddho. ..nibbānaṃ nibbānato abhiññāya nibbānaṃ na maññati, nibbānasmiṃ na maññati, nibbānato na maññati, nibbānaṃ me ti na maññati, nibbānaṃ nā'bhinandati. Taṃ kissa hetu? Nandi dukkhassa mūlan ti—iti viditvā, M. I. 6.
4. Indian Philosophy, Vol. I, p. 386.
5. Aṭṭhānam etaṃ anavakāso yaṃ diṭṭhisampanno puggalo kiñci dhammaṃ attato upagaccheyya—n'etaṃ ṭhānaṃ vijjatī ti. . .Ṭhānañ ca kho etaṃ vijjati yaṃ puthujjano kiñci dhammaṃ attato upagaccheyya, M. III. 64.

Buddha, however, knows full well that it is extremely difficult to disentangle oneself completely from this notion of 'I'-ness or selfhood. The thirst or craving for the conceit of 'I' is so great that even when one is confornted with the contradictions and impossibility of self-identification with any of the five aggregates or groups of grasping, he still nurtures a craving for 'I'-ness, though he is unable to give any meaningful content to it. This is well indicated in the Khemaka Sutta where the monk Khemaka says: "I do not say anything as 'I' or 'mine' in corporeality or out of corporeality..in or out of feeling...in or out of perception...in or out of dispositions...in or out of consciousness, yet my conceit of 'I'-ness in the five groups of grasping is present, though I do not see, 'this is the I'."[1] An analogy is given to illustrate the nature of this highly persuasive ego-centric obsession. It is pointed out that a dirty and filthy cloth even after being thoroughly washed and made clean (parisuddaṃ pariyodātaṃ) by the washerman is still left with some smell. "Even so, though a noble disciple has put away the five lower fetters (including the sakkāyadiṭṭhi i. e. belief in something permanent in the five aggregates), yet there remains in him, from among the five groups of grasping, a subtle remnant of the conceit of the 'I' an attachment to the I, and a lurking tendency to think, 'I am' is still not removed from him".[2] It is said that the cloth is put with the sweet-scented coffer (gandhaparibhāvite karaṇḍake nikkhipanti, S. III. 131) for the sake of removing the smell which still clings to it. In the same way it is pointed out that "later on he (monk) lives contemplating the rise and fall of the five groups of grasping ...in this way as he lives in the contemplation of the five groups of grasping, that subtle remnant of the conceit of the 'I,' the

1. Na khvāhaṃ...rūpaṃ asmī ti vadāmi na pi aññatra rupā asmī ti vadāmi na vedanaṃ...na saññaṃ...na saṅkhāre...na viññāṇaṃ...na pi aññtra rūpaṃ...vedanaṃ...saññam...saṅkhāre...viññāṇaṃ...Api ca me...pañcasu upādānakkhandhesu asmī ti adhigataṃ, ayam aham asmī ti na ca samanupassāmi., S. III. 130.

2. Evam eva kho...kiñcāpi ariyasāvakassa pañcorambhāgiyāni saṃyojanāni pahīnāni bhavanti, atha khvassa hoti yo ca pañcasu upādānakkhandhesu anusahagato asmī ti māno, asmī ti chando, asmī ti anusayo asamūhato, S. III. 131.

attachment to the 'I' and the lurking tendency to think, 'I am' which was not removed from him is absolutely removed."[1]

This discourse is important particularly in relation to some of the passages of the Ups. and the B. G. which seem to entertain a lurking conceit of the 'I'. They speak of the self in negative terms, divesting it of all cognisable contents[2] and yet persist in calling it the 'I' or the self (ātman). They seem to satisfy their last lingering attachment to permanence and immortality by imagining a soul to which they themselves fail to give any meaningful content. We have already seen (supra, pp. 177-8) how, according to the Buddhist analysis, the B. G. concept of the soul or the self is to be regarded as being rooted in the strong desire for personal immortality (bhavadiṭṭhi). Since no idea of the self, howsoever subtly conceived, can escape falling within the five groups of grasping, any attempt to speak of its validity is foredoomed to failure. If the words like I, ego, self or soul etc. should have a meaning at all, any form of it, howsoever abstract and rarefied, must necessarily be associated with the personalistic or egoistic content. But, from what could that content be derived if not from the only available data of experience, analysed by Buddha into five aggregates? Nyanaponika Thera has rightly observed: "To speak of a self devoid of such differentiating attributes, having therefore nothing to characterize it and to give meaningful contents to the word, will be entirely senseless and in contradiction to the accepted usage of these terms, 'self', 'ego', etc."[3] This explains why Buddha refuses to call the highest truth, the undifferentiated (nippapañca) Nibbāna as the 'I' or the self, and why the Pali Canon is permeated with the relentless exhortation to abandon the vain conceit of the 'I'.

(C) *The Conventional Use of the word, 'Attā'*:—

The denial of the validity of the self or 'I' does not prevent a right-meaning person from using these words as

---

1. So aparena samayena pañcasu upādānakkhandhesu udayabbayānupassi viharati...tassa imesu pañcasu upādānakkhandhesu udayabbayānupassino viharato yo pissa hoti pañcasu upādānakkhandhesu anusahagato asmī ti māno, asmī ti chando, asmī ti anusayo asamūhato so pi samugghātaṃ gacchatī ti., S. III. 131.

2. cf. Bṛhadā. II. 3.6; VI. 4. 22; Tait. II. 7; Kaṭha. III. 15 and B.G. II. 20, 21, 23-25.

3. Anattā and Nibbāna, p. 20.

the current modes of speech without being misled by them. In using them, he only conforms to convention, but has no misapprehension about the sense of the words. Buddha himself states in this connection that "they are merely popular expressions, popular terms of speech, designations in common practice and usages prevalent in the world, which the Tathāgata makes use of without being misled."[1] It is further said: "The monk who has become Arahant (liberated), who has done whatever was to be done, who has purged himself of defilements and is carrying the last body...whose conceits have fallen off, who has no knots, whose all egoistic bonds are dissipated and who has gone beyond all conceits and deemings—such a wise one might use the expression: 'I say, this is mine'. But knowing well the popular expression of the world, he in so doing only conforms to current usage."[2] Buddha in unambiguous terms clarifies the position as follows: "Beings are only names (designations) for expression, and they consist (only) in this expression. They, not rightly understanding this expression, come under the yoke of death. But he who rightly understands this expression does not have the conceit of the speaker (subject) of the expression."[3] The statement of the nun Vajirā also which is quoted by Nāgasena (Milindapañha, II. 1) represents the same view of the Master. It says: "Just as the assemblage of parts constitutes the word 'chariot' so also when the aggregates appear together, the phrase 'being' is used."[4]

But despite all these clarifications the scholars who ascribe a positive theory of the self to Buddha try to read a Upaniṣa-

1. Imā kho...loka-samaññā loka-niruttiyo loka-vohārā loka-paññattiyo yāhi Tathāgato voharati aparāmasan'ti, D. I. 202.

2. Yo hoti bhikkhu arahaṃ katāvī khīṇāsavo antimadehadhārī...
pahīnamānassa na santi ganthā vidhūpitā mānaganthassa sabbe
Sa vītivatto yamataṃ sumedho ahaṃ vadāmīti pi so vadeyya,
mamaṃ vadāmīti pi so vadeyya,
loke samaññaṃ kusalo viditvā vohāramattena so vohareyyāti., S.I. 14-15.

3. Akkheyyasaññino sattā akkheyyasmiṃ patiṭṭhitā,
akkheyyam apariññāya yogam āyanti maccuno
akkheyyañ ca pariññāya akkhātāraṃ na maññati, S.I. 11.

4. yathā hi aṅgasambhārā, hoti saddo ratho iti,
evaṃ khandhesu santesu, hoti satto ti sammuti, S.I. 135.

dic meaning into the Buddhist use of the word 'attā'. Whenever Buddha, in the course of either emphasising his teaching of self-reliance or deprecating the habit of leaning on others, makes use of this word, these scholars run after it and quote it enthusiastically in support of a soul-theory in Buddhism. They, thus, try to make out that Buddha's criticism of the self is directed only against what they call the 'little' or 'small' self and not against the true or great self. Ananda K. Coomaraswamy and I. B. Horner have collected a number of such passages from the Pali texts under the heads: "(a) The two selves; (b) The Great Self; (c) The Small Self".[1] This collection contains almost all the passages that are frequently used by scholars to ascribe a theory of the self to Buddhism. But the clarification made by the Master hardly leaves room for a metaphysical exploitation of a purely linguistic difficulty.

We need not examine each and every such passage to expose the untenability of the interpretation of these scholars, since the very same meaning of the word 'attā' is applicable in all the cases. We may take just a few examples and show how the contextual meaning goes against any metaphysical twist of the term.

Frequent reference is made by these scholars to the following exhortation of Buddha: "atta-dīpā viharatha, atta-saraṇā, anaññasaraṇā" (D. II. 100; S. III. 42, V. 163), which they generally translate as "go along having the self as lamp, the self as refuge and none other refuge."[2] Paying little attention to the context, they at once take it for granted that the word 'atta' must necessarily refer to the metaphysical soul or self. But if one cares to look into the context, it would not be difficult to see that the word 'atta' is used here as a convenient current expression indicating self-reliance. The context is as follows: Some time before the Parinibbāna, Buddha was seriously ill. After his recovery, Ānanda, referring to that illness says to the Master: "On account of the illness

1. The Living Thoughts of Gotama, the Buddha, pp. 147-163.

2. Cf. Ananda K. Coomaraswamy and I. B. Horner—The Living Thoughts of Gotama the Buddha, p. 151; Radhakrishnan—Dhammapada (Introduction) p. 45: Mrs. Rhys Davids —Buddhism, its Birth and Dispersal, p. 73.

of the Exalted One, my body became languid, I could not see the directions, nor could I remember the Dhamma."[1] At this Buddha says: "What does, Ānanda, the Order of monks expect of me. The Dhamma has been taught by me, Ānanda, without making any distinction between exoteric and esoteric. The Tathāgata does not have the closed fist of a teacher with regard to the Dhamma. Surely, Ānanda, if there were one who were to harbour the thought that it is he who should lead the Order or that the Order is dependent on him, he, indeed, would give out guidance in anything concerning the Order. But the Tathāgata thinks not so..I am now, Ānanda, old, full of years, I have lived my span and am at the close of my days. I am turning eighty years of age. And just as a worn-out cart, Ānanda, can be kept going only with the help of thongs, so methinks, the body of the Tathāgata can be kept going only by bandaging it up....Therefore, Ānanda, 'live as a lamp unto yourself, refuge unto yourself and no other refuge, the Dhamma as a lamp, the Dhamma as a refuge and no other refuge" (Tasmāt ih, Ānanda atta-dīpā viharatha, atta-saraṇā, anañña-saraṇā, dhamma-dīpā, dhamma-saraṇā, anañña-saraṇā).[2]

It is clear from the above context that Buddha, in view of his impending death (Parinibbāna), was advising Ānanda not to lean on him (Buddha) or, for that matter, on anyone else for light and help but to depend on his own self and the noble teaching (Dhamma). The light and help have to be had through one's own effort and the practice of the Dhamma. Self-reflection and self-help alone can bestow knowledge and peace on oneself and there is no other refuge (anañña-saraṇā, loc. cit.) The same idea is expressed with greater clarity by Buddha in his last words: "It may be, Ānanda, that (after my passing away) you might think: 'gone is the doctrine of our Master, we have no Master any more'. But you should not think so, Ānanda, for the Doctrine (Dhamma) and the Discipline (vinaya) which I have taught to you will be your

1. D. II. 99.
2. D. II. 100.

Master after my death."[1]

It is in the same vein that a number of passages occur in the Dhammapada. One is said to consider oneself as the lord of oneself and no other lord,[2] oneself to be a light (or an island) for oneself,[3] and oneself to rouse up or restrain oneself.[4] We do not find any passage anywhere in the Pali Canon which may prove the acceptance of a metaphysical self in early Buddhism. On the other hand, if the metaphysical interpretation of the word 'atta' (which in essence is supposed to be identical with Nibbāna) were to be thought correct, then one would wonder how one can make sense of such passages as, "evil done by (one-) self brings (one-) self to grief" (Attanā'va kataṃ pāpaṃ attanā saṅkilissati, Dh. 165) or "evil done by (one-) self, produced by (one-) self, born of (one-) self oppresses the evil-minded even as the thunderbolt does to the diamond-stone" (Attanā'va kataṃ pāpaṃ attajaṃ attasambhavaṃ, abhimanthati dummedhaṃ vajiram'va smamayaṃ maṇiṃ, Dh. 161). It is absurd to think that evil is done by the pure metaphysical self or Nibbāna and man is put to grief by the self or Nibbāna.

The fact that the grammatical subject ('I' or self) is confused with a metaphysical one, only shows that our deep-rooted desire or craving for some sort of abiding 'I' or the self gets facilitated by our *linguistic* modes of expression. Professor Wittgenstein is right when he says: "Now the idea that the real 'I' lives in my body is connected with the peculiar grammar of the word 'I' and the misunderstandings this grammar is liable to give rise to."[5] On account of this linguistic habit one tends to look for a real distinction between the subject and something belonging to the subject, between a metaphysical substance and its attributes when, in fact, the distinction is only verbal. Thus the question, "what is

1. Siyā kho pana, Ānanda, tumhākaṃ evam assa: 'atītasatthukaṃ pāvacanaṃ, natthi no satthā ti'. Na kho panetaṃ, Ānanda, evaṃ daṭṭhabbaṃ. Yo vo, Ānanda, mayā dhammo ca vinayo ca desito paññatto, so vo mamaccayena satthā., D. II. 154.

2. Attā hi attano nātho ko hi natho paro siyā, Dh. 160. cf. Dh. 380.

3. So karohi dīpam attano..., Dh. 236 & 238.

4. Attanā codayā'ttānaṃ paṭivāse attam attanā, Dh. 379 cf. Dh. 159, 161 and 165.

5. The Blue and Brown Books, p. 66.

decay and death and of whom is this decay and death?" (katamaṃ nu kho...jarāmaraṇaṃ, kassa ca panidaṃ jarāmaraṇaṃ?, S.II.60) is declared by Buddha as a misleading question (no kallo pañho, S. II. 61), and it is pointed out that "if one were to say, decay and death is one thing and this decay and death belongs to another, both these mean the same, only the expression is different" (ubhayam etam ekatthaṃ vyañjanam eva nānā, loc. cit.). Similarly the question: "who feeds on the food of consciousness" (ko nu kho..viññāṇāhāraṃ āhāreti, S. II. 13) is set aside by Buddha as not a legitimate question (no kallo pañho, loc. cit.). In the like manner, we find that when Buddha declares, "any kind of corporeality, feeling, perception, dispositions and consciousness, whether past, future or present, gross or subtle, internal or external, inferior or superior, far or near—should, with objective knowledge, be regarded as 'this is not mine, this is not 'I' and this is not my self,' "[1] a monk wonders, "to what self will the actions done by non-self touch (affect)?" (anattakatāni kammāni kam attānaṃ phusissantī ti?, M. III. 19; S. III. 103). It is then pointed out by Buddha that only a foolish and untrained person who is under the sway of ignorance and craving would transgress the discipline of the Master in such a way.[2]

Thus the Buddhist doctrine of anattā (soullessness) makes it clear that notion of the 'I' or the self (permanent ego) is faulty and so the question of its being annihilated or existing for all eternity is meaningless. The theories of annihilationism (uccheda-diṭṭhi) and eternalism (sassata-diṭṭhi) are considered as two extreme views based on fundamentally erroneous approaches to truth.[3] The denial of the self, however, should not be taken to mean the denial of the non-personalistic reality. viz. Nibbāna. It is precisely with a view to realising this non-personalistic or uncharacterisable state that Buddha emphasises the need for breaking through all personalistic or egoistic notions. We have stated (supra, p. 305) that due to the age-old egocentric line of speculation,

1. M. III. 19; S. III. 103.
2. moghapuriso, avidvā avijjāgato taṇhādhipateyyena cetasā satthusāsanaṃ atidhāvitabbaṃ maññeyya, M. III. 19, S. III. 103.
3. S. II. 17, 76; III. 135.

the word 'ātman' (self or soul) had come to be ostensibly associated with the supreme reality. Naturally, therefore, Buddha's theory of anattā (soullessness) was likely to be misunderstood as a nihilistic doctrine. In fact, accusations to this effect were made during Buddha's own time. But Buddha clearly dissociates himself from any such view.[1] It is precisely with a view to avoiding this dangerous misconception that, as we have already seen (supra pp. 297-298), Buddha refrains from either affirming or denying the reality of the self before an undiscerning man like the wanderer Vacchagotta. He, however, affirms in unmistakable terms the reality of Nibbāna for which, indeed, the entire holy life is led (Ud. 80), though he perfers to use negative expressions in relation to it with a view to avoiding any mundane misconception about it. We shall discuss this question separately under the next topic.

(D) *The B.G.'s Attempt to Highlight the Traditional View*:—

Contrary to the Buddhist approach, we can at once notice the orthodoxy of the B. G. in upholding the traditional Upaniṣadic concept of the metaphysical self. Despite Buddha's persistent attempt to dispense with the notion of the self and dissociate reality from all egoistic approaches to it, the B.G. harps back to the same old theme and considers the self as the inmost essence of man, essentially identical with the supreme reality. Buddha, as we have already seen, himself knew how difficult it is to free one's mind completely from the conceit of the 'I' and, therefore, he laid the fullest possible emphasis on his teaching of the non-self doctrine. But the egocentric desire proved too deep to be completely eradicated from the mind of posterity, and apart from the B.G. which, in adherence to orthodoxy, disregards this teaching, the philosophical speculation in India with the solitary exception of Materialism (which did not believe in anything beyond the present life) clung to the idea of the self. Even some later schools of Buddhism itself found it difficult to uphold and preserve the word and spirit of the Master.[2] Whitehead's observation that

1. M. I. 140.
2. Cf. Professor Wijesekera—The Three Signata, p. 13; Nyanaponika Thera—Anattā and Nibbāna, pp. 4-5.

"Philosophy never reverts to its old position after the shock of a great philosopher,"[1] could not be true with regard to this problem of the self.

Buddha, as we noted, showed through a thorough analysis of all cognisable elements, whether internal or external, gross or subtle that there is nothing permanent and blissful in whatever we can conceivably call as the 'I' or the self and, therefore, the realisation of Nibbāna, the timeless and non-spatial, undifferentiated and non-personalistic reality can only be had by giving up all that we erroneously consider as the 'I' or the self. This notion of the self, he has made it clear, is possible only in and through the five aggregates (pañcakkhandha), and not without them. Now the B.G. agrees with Buddhism in holding that all the ingredients of human personality upto the empirical consciousness (cetanā)[2] are non-self. The entire organism (saṅghāta, S.B.G. XIII. 6) including the psychical elements like desire, hatred, pleasure, pain, steadfastness and even the manifest consciousness are said to be the modifications of the changeable kṣetra or Prakṛti.[3] But still somehow it holds on to the belief that there is an extremely subtle self, subtler than the senses, the mind and the intellect, which is the true essence of the self in man[4] by knowing which one attains immortality or the supreme goal (yaj jñātvā' mṛtam aśnute, B.G. XIII. 12; tato yāti parāṃ gatim, B.G. XIII. 28). It is here that Buddhism and the B.G. are found to be in diametrical opposition to each other. Buddha after his penetrative analysis, makes a definite assertion that nothing permanent and blissful is to be found in the whole of our personality and, therefore, it is absolutely foolish to speak of any permanent and eternal 'I' or self (attani ca...attaniye ca saccato thetato anupalabbhamāne...

1. Process and Reality, p. 14.

2. The transcendental consciousness belongs to the self. The empirical consciousness seems to be regarded by the B.G., following the Sāṅkhya theory, as the reflection of the self in the intellect. As Śaṅkara, commenting on the word 'cetanā' of B.G. XIII. 6, observes: "abhivyaktā antaḥkaraṇavṛttiḥ tapte iva lohapiṇḍe agniḥ ātmacaitanyābhāsarasaviddhā cetanā", S.B.G. XIII. 6.

3. B. G. XIII. 6.

4. B.G. III. 42 and 43.

so attā, so peccā bhavissāmi nicco dhuvo...kevalo paripūro bāladhammo ti, M.I. 138). The B.G., on the other hand, declares that the self as the eternal and immutable reality is definitely there, though it is not cognised due to its extreme subtlety (sūkṣmatvāt tad avijñeyam, B.G. XIII. 15) and lack of qualities (nirguṇatvāt, B.G. XIII, 31). The persevering yogins are said to perceive it within themselves through meditation (yatanto yoginaś cai'naṃ paśyanty ātmany avasthitam B.G. XV. II; dhyānenā'tmani paśyanti, B.G. XIII. 24; īkṣate yogayuktātmā, B.G. VI, 29), and those who fail to perceive it are branded as 'deluded' and 'ignorant' (*vimūḍhā* nā'nupaśyanti, B.G. XV. 10; nai'nam paśyanty *acetasaḥ*, B.G. XV. 11).

It is not possible for us to verify the validity or invalidity of the respective claims of the B.G. and Buddhism, but in view of the Buddhist account of the meditative stages of perception being more thorough and systematic (supra. pp. 183-188) and the notion of the 'I' or the self being well analysed and clearly defined, it appears less likely that Buddha has been led astray in his meditative perception. It appears more likely that the B.G., as also the Ups., not being completely free from an egoistic bias have confused their vague meditative awareness of the undifferentiated reality with some personalistic or egoistic element, and thereby claimed to have seen the true nature of the self. We have already shown (supra. pp. 188-197) that the B.G. account of the meditative processes is not as systematic and clear-cut as that of Buddhism, nor is the meaning of the self well-defined and precisely formulated by it. It is perhaps owing to this unanalytic and vague meditative experience of the B.G. and the Ups. that we find their concept of the self as mystical, having hardly any cognisable content. Thus the B.G., despite its agreement with Buddhism in considering every cognisable content of personality as impermanent and non-self, does not abandon the conceit of the 'I', and goes on speaking mystically of some incognisable and unmanifest (aprameya, II. 18; avyakta, II. 25) self as the inmost essence of man. This type of lingering of the conceit of the 'I' or the self, as we have seen (supra, pp. 316-317), has been compared in Buddhism with the lingering smell of the cloth even after the dirt and filth of it are washed away by the washerman.

In the course of tracing the source of the B.G., we have pointed out (supra, pp. 109-114) that its conception of the self is largely Upaniṣadic, and very many verses also are bodily taken from the Ups. Now, the highest point in the development of the Upaniṣadic concept of the self is reached when the self is spoken of negatively (neti neti),[1] paradoxically[2] and analogically.[3] The soul or self is said to be that in which all contradictions are reconciled[4] and which passes beyond all opposites.[5] It is said to transcend all thought and speech and silence alone is considered as its adequate expression.[6] This indescribable and ineffable self (ātman) is identified with the supreme reality, Brahman.[7] This description hardly conveys any idea of the self or 'I' which is necessarily associated with some element of differentiation, separatedness or particularity. It is, indeed, by giving up all such egoistic notions that one can have the realisation of the universal undifferentiated reality, metaphysically known as Brahman which, as we shall see in the sequel, has some striking points of resemblance with the Buddhist concept of Nibbāna But the Upaniṣadic seers, pioneers as they were in the field, could not disentangle themselves from the weight of the traditional egocentric speculation and the deep-seated egoistic desire, and thus appear to have been led into the error of conceiving the impersonalistic and undifferentiated reality in a somewhat personalistic and differentiated manner. It is here that Buddha tries to steer clear of the confusion and marks out clearly the elements which really lie at the base of the conceit of the 'I' or the self. Thus, he is in a position

---

1. Bṛhadā. II. 3. 6; IV. 4. 22; Tait. II. 7; Kaṭha. III. 15.
2. Kena. II. 1-3; Kaṭha II. 21; Iśa 4; Śvetā. III. 19.
3. Bṛhadā. IV. 3. 7.
4. Bṛhadā. IV. 3. 22 ff; IV. 4. 5; Tait. II. 6; Kaṭha. II. 20; Īsa. 5.
5. Bṛhadā. III. 8.8; Kena. I. 3; Kaṭha. II. 14; Īsa. 10 and 13; Śvetā. IV. 18; Māṇḍūkya. 7.
6. Kena I. 3; Tait. II. 9; Kaṭha II. 8; Muṇḍaka III. 1. 7; Māṇḍūkya. 7 (acintyam avyapadeśyam...prapañcopaśamaṃ śāntam).
7. Kaṭha II. 16; IV. 5-9.

to see clearly that the realm of reality goes beyond whatever is considered as the 'I' or the self. But the Ups. owing to their failure to demarcate the realm of the self could not arrest the egoistic shadow looming large in their conception of reality, and were thus led to confuse and misconceive the self as the reality. Thus, it seems that the Ups. in their highest stage of development were tending to deny whatever one can meaningfully call a self, but they were not clear enough to see the implications of their own thought.

From what has been said above, it appears that the similarity between the Ups and Buddhism does not consist in the identical affirmation of the self, but in a somewhat similar view of the reality. As regards the self, the Ups. despite their pull in the direction of the non-self theory, propound ultimately a philosophy of the self (ātma-vidyā), whereas Buddhism preached a philosophy of non-self (anattā).

Now, the B.G. conception of the soul being essentially Upaniṣadic, what is true of the Ups. is true largely of the B.G. as well. There is hardly any doubt that the entire approach of the B.G. concerning the self is mystical like that of the Ups. The self or soul is identified with the reality, described mostly in negative (B.G. II. 12-30) and paradoxical (B.G. XI. 37; XIII. 12-16) terms and unambiguously called the universal divine principle indwelling all beings (sarvabhūtāśayasthitaḥ, B.G. X. 20; hṛdi sarvasya dhiṣṭhitam, B.G. XIII. 17; sarvagataḥ, B.G. II. 24; XIII. 32; samaṃ sarveṣu bhūteṣu tiṣṭhantaṃ parameśvaram, B.G. XIII. 27; sarvasya cāhaṃ hṛdi saṃniviṣṭaḥ, B.G. XV. 15; cf. XIII. 2, 22 and XVIII. 61). This universal and unified principle can hardly be conceived as something individualistic or personalistic. The same is stated also in clear words: "Though it appears divided among beings, it is (really) undivided" (avibhaktaṃ ca bhūteṣu vibhaktam iva ca sthitam B.G. XIII. 16). "When one sees that the manifold state of beings is centred in the One and from that alone is the entire spreading out, then he attains Brahman."[1] Comparing the self with the all-pervading ether, the B.G. says : "As the all-pervading ether is not

1. B.G. XIII. 30.

tainted on account of its subtlety, so also the self that is present in every body is not touched (tainted)."[1] In this description, the word 'I' or 'self' is bereft of all meaning which can conceivably be attached to it. One is reminded of the criticism of Vasubandhu who, in order to show the meaninglessness of the Vatsīputrīyas' belief in some kind of individual (pudgala) separate and distinct from the skandhas, argues that rain and sun have no effect on mere vacuous space; they are of use only to the skin. If the individual is like the skin, a determiner of the value of experiences, then it must be accepted as external; if it is like vacuous space, then no purpose is fulfilled by accepting it.[2] The same may be said in relation to the B.G. concept of the self which like the vacuous space loses all meaning as a self or 'I'.

(E) *Points of Fundamental Difference Between the B.G. and Buddhism:—*

The lack of a clear connotation of the concept of the self along with the consequent confusion between the self and the reality brings about a fundamental difference of approach between the B.G. and Buddhism. One cannot minimise the importance of this difference by saying that it consists simply in extending the meaning of the word 'self' to the reality, and that it is merely a verbal difference. Had it been so simple, Buddha would not have harped untiringly on the doctrine of the non-self. We have seen that the real motive behind preaching this doctrine of the non-self was to instil the lesson of perfect detachment or non-clinging, the conceit of the 'I' being the manifestation of the subtlest and strongest form of clinging.[3] So long as this clinging to 'I'-ness in any shape or form persists, there can be no real emancipation or salvation. We have pointed out how significantly in the very first sutta of the Majjhima

1. B G. XIII. 32.
2. Vātsīputriyāṇāṃ tīrthikā-dṛṣṭiḥ prasajyate niṣprayojanatvaṃ ca varṣāta-pābhyāṃ kiṃ vyomnaś carmaṇy asti tayoḥ phalam carmopamaś cet sa nityaḥ khatulyaś ced asatphalaḥ., MS. of Yaśomitra's commentary, p. 338.
cf. Dasgupta, Indian Philosophy, Vol. II. p.59.
3. upādāya. . .asmīti hoti. no anupādāya, S. III. 105.

Nikāya, viz., "the discourse on the root cause" (Mūlapariyāya Sutta) where Buddha teaches the root-causes of all dhammas (sabba-dhamma-mūlapariyāyaṃ...desessāmi, M.I. 1), he emphasises the need for absolute abandonment of the conceit of the 'I' in all. things (sabbaṃ) including the Nibbāna, and concludes by saying that the Tathāgata, the liberated saint and the truly enlightened one does not have the conceit of the 'I' or the self in the Nibbāna in any of the four possible ways.[1] He clearly says :"Not to see 'I am this' that is all round freedom—above and below."[2] It is said : "Happy, indeed, are those perfect ones who have no craving, whose conceit of 'I am' is eradicated and the net of delusion rent asunder."[3] "Curbing of the conceit of 'I am' is, indeed, the bliss supreme."[4] As against this Buddhist concept of salvation where no trace of selfhood is left, the B.G., like the Ups., conceives of salvation as a state of self-realisation[5] which seems to indicate its lurking subtle clinging or attachment to some personalistic element.

It is, no doubt, true that the B.G. also speaks of the eradication of the conceit of 'I'-ness which it calls 'egotism' (ahaṅkāra)[6], but one wonders what is meaningfully left in the word 'self' when this egotism in all possible senses of of the term is completely removed from it. If the word 'I' or 'self' should have a meaning at all, any form of it, howsoever diluted, must contain some element of individuality, differentiation or ego-conception. But when all ego-conception or egotism is completely abandoned, the self is reduced to naught. Does then not the B.G. by still retaining some sort of 'self' give an indication of the fact that despite the pull of its thought being in the direction of the non-self theory, it is too steeped in orthodoxy to see the tendency of its own

1. Md. I. 6.
2. Uddhaṃ adho sabbadhi vippamutto ayam aham asmī ti anānupassī, Ud. 74.
3. Sukhino vata arahanto, taṇhā tesaṃ na vijjati;
asmimāno samucchinno, mohajālaṃ padālitaṃ, S. III. 83.
4. asmimānassa yo vinayo, etaṃ ve paramaṃ sukhan'ti, Ud. 10; Vin. I. 3.
5. cf. ātmavān (B. G. II. 45); ātmavantam (B.G. IV. 41); tṛptātmā (B.G. VI 8); yuktātmā (B.G. V. 21; VI. 29).
6. B.G. II. 71; III; 27; XII. 13; XVIII. 17.

thought ? It seems that the B.G. in view of the contradictions involved in the conceit of 'I'-ness tries to abandon it in the form of ahaṅkāra (egotism), but is not aware of the fact that the same is making its re-entry under the guise of an elevated self (ātman), and thus only obscures the confusion.

It is mainly through this concept of the so-called disconceited (nirahaṅkāraḥ, B.G. II. 71; XII. 13) self that the B.G. provides a metaphysical basis for its doctrine of disinterested action. Thus according to it "the self considers itself to be the doer when it is deluded by egotism" (ahaṅkāravimūḍhātmā kartā' haṃ iti manyate, B.G. III. 27). But 'he who is free from egotism and whose intellect is not sullied, even when he slays these worlds, he neither slays nor is he bound".[1] In the light of this concept of the self, "he who thinks that this (self) slays and he who thinks that this is slain, both of them do not realise (the truth) that this can neither slay nor can be slain."[2] It is on this ground that Arjuna is asked to kill his enemies in a disconceited or disinterested way. In Buddhism also one is asked to give up egotism (ahaṅkāra) or the conceit of 'I'-ness, but according to it, it is impossible that a man free from egotism would indulge in killing or commit evil deeds.[3] Here the abandonment of egotism is thorough and perfect, and it is said to secure absolute calmness or tranquility leading to the final release. In reply to the question of Rahula as to "how the mind is freed from all conceit of 'I' and mine, freed from all egotism, freed from all distinctions and is calmed and perfectly released" (kathaṃ...ahaṅkāra-mamaṅkāra-mānāpagataṃ mānasaṃ hoti vidhā samatikkantaṃ santaṃ vimuttan ti, S.II.253), Buddha says : "Whatever corporeality....feeling... perception...formations...consciousness, Rahula, be it past, present or future, internal or external, gross or subtle, inferior or superior, far or near—all you should behold 'this is not mine, this is not I, this is not my self'. Thus knowing,

1. B.G. XVIII. 17.
2. B.G. II. 19.
3. yo so...arahaṃ khīṇāsavo...vimutto, abhabbo so nava ṭhānāni ajjhācarituṃ..., sañcicca pāṇaṃ jīvitā voropetuṃ..., D. III. 133.

Rahula, thus seeing objectively through perfect insight, being free from clinging one is released. Thus...the mind in relation to this body together with its consciousness as well as in relation to all objects external to it is freed from all distinctions, is calmed and perfectly released."[1] This difference is again indicative of the fact that the B. G. is not completely free from the conceit of the 'I', though paradoxically enough, it over and over again professes the same. But for some lurking element of selfhood or 'I'-ness, it would not have been possible for the B. G. to speak of the compatibility between disconceitedness and violence.[2]

In this connection, we may remember how Buddha himself envisages the possibility of professing some doctrine, not realising its full truth and implications. The mendicant Aggivessana Dīghanakha, for example, says to Buddha: "All is not pleasing to me"[3] (sabbaṃ me na khamatī ti, M. I. 497). Buddha at once asks him, "This view of yours, Aggivessana 'all is not pleasing to me'—is not this view of yours pleasing to you?" (loc. cit.). At this Dīghanakha answers: "Well Gotama, if this view were pleasing to me, then also it would be all the same, it would be all the same" (M. I. 497-8). Thereupon, Buddha makes the following remark: "Well Aggivessana, there are very many people in the world who speak thus: 'it would be all the same, it would be all the same' but they do not get rid of that view and cling to another view. There are only a few rare people in the world who speak thus: 'it would be all the same, it would be all the same' and really get rid of that view and do not cling to another view" (M. I. 498). This indicates how people despite speaking of perfect detachment or utter disinterest-

1. S. II. 253.

2. It is interesting to see that even Gandhi, one of the most faithful followers of the B.G., feels the anomaly in this teaching of the B.G. He frankly says : "Let it be granted that according to the letter of the Gītā, it is possible to say that warfare is consistent with renunciation of fruit. But after 40 years' unremitting endeavour full to enforce the teaching of the Gītā in my own life, I have in all humility felt that perfect renuciation is impossible without perfect observance of Ahimsa in every shape or form.", Gītā the Mother, p. 12.

3. This literal translation should not be mistaken for an 'O' proposition, for it really means, 'none of the theories is pleasing to me'.

edness are still found to be under the influence of some subtle attachment and clinging.

Similarly we come across some mendicants of other sects who claim to teach the same doctrine as that of Buddha and wonder what special feature there is in Buddha's teaching. They say: "The recluse Gotama teaches the true understanding of sense-pleasures (kāmānaṃ pariññaṃ paññāpeti); so do we teach the true understanding of sense-pleasures. The recluse Gotama teaches the true understanding of feelings (vedanānaṃ); so do we....what then is the uniqueness, what difference is there between the recluse Gotama and us regarding the teaching of doctrines or codes of discipline?"[1] Buddha later on explains to the monks the distinctive characteristics of his doctrines and disciplines and shows how they differ from those of the other mendicants, notwithstanding the claim of the latter to preach indentical doctrines and disciplines.[2]

On another occasion when Buddha pronounces the utterance, "Health is the highest gain, Nibbāna is the highest bliss" (ārogya paramā lābhā, Nibbānaṃ paramaṃ sukhaṃ, M.I. 508), the mendicant Māgaṇḍiya enthusiastically acclaims it, saying that he also has heard the earlier mendicants, teachers and instructors speaking the same (mayā pi kho etaṃ...sutaṃ pubbakānaṃ paribbājakānaṃ ācariyapācariyānaṃ bhāsamānānaṃ, M.I. 509). But on being asked what he understands by it (loc. cit), he has nothing better to speak of than physical health and happiness. Buddha thereupon remarks: "This solemn utterance was pronounced by the previous Arahants and perfectly enlightened ones but it has now come down to worldlings[3]".

All these discourses show the possibility of understanding the same teaching in a different light. It should not, therefore, be surprising if the B.G., in spite of imparting a teaching of the abandonment of egotism (ahaṅkāra) in a way

1. M. I. 84.
2. M. I. 85-90.
3. Pubbakehesā...arahantehi sammāsambuddhehi gāthā bhāsitā... sā etarahi anupubbena puthujjanagatā. M. I. 510.

similar to that of Buddhism, does not abandon it as thoroughly as the latter does.

The B.G. theory of the self, in fact, appears to be identical with one of the six erroneous views of the self enumerated by Buddha in the Sabbāsava Sutta. This view is described in the Sutta as follows: "Thus owing to wrong mindedness one or other of the six wrong views emerges in him.. 'I perceive the self by the self' (attanā va attānaṃ sañjānāmī ti), this wrong view emerges in him as a true and correct one."[1] Now, the B.G. view of the self seems to fit in with the above description. It is said: By meditation *some perceive the self by the self* within the self" (dyānenā'tmani *paśyanti kecid ātmānam ātmanā,* B.G. XIII.24). The B.G. speaks of a state "where one is satisfied within the self by *perceiving the self by the self*" (yatra cai'*vā tmanā' tmānaṁ paśyann* ātmani tuṣyati, B.G. VI. 20).

It is true that some statements of the B.G. describing the self in negatative terms (B.G.II. 12-30) and calling it indefinable or ineffable (B.G. II. 29; XII.3 XII.3 XIII. 15) have something in common with the Buddhist description of Nibbāna, but it must not be forgotten that Buddhism unlike the B.G.does not confuse the self with Nibbāna and uniformly considers the self as an erroneous concept. The B.G., on the other hand, holding fast to its theory of the self, seems to have given a personalistic colour to its doctrine of the Absolute.

Moreover, the B.G. weaves out a speculative metaphysical theory on the basis of its acceptance of a mystical self. The self which is said to be unborn, eternal, everlasting and ancient (B.G.II.20) and considered essentially identical with the supreme reality (B.G.X.20, XIII, 17, 22, 27, 31 and XVIII. 61) is said to be responsible for the emergence of the entire universe, and the ignorance and knowledge of its true nature are said to be the cause respectively of bondage and liberation.[3] Being conceived as the all-pervasive subtle principle

---

1. M. I. 8.
2. Yāvat saṃjāyate kiṃcit sattvaṃ sthāvarajaṅgamaṁ kṣetrakṣetrajñasaṃyogāt tad viddhi bharatarṣabha, B.G., XIII. 26.
3. B.G. XIII. 28-30, 34.

like the ether (B.G. XIII. 32), it is said to be both inside as well as outside of all beings (bahir antaś ca bhūtānām, B.G. XIII. 15). "It neither acts nor is tainted, though stationed in the body".[1] In short, the etnire account of the self on which the metaphysical speculation is bascd is simply baffling. The B.G. itself acknowledges its strange nature (āścaryavat, II.29). Radhakrishnan quite appropriately remarks: "About the nature of the supreme self, the Gītā account is rather puzzling."[2]

In Buddhism, we do not find any room for speculative metaphysics. The wanderer Vacchagotta pointedly asks Buddha whether the latter entertains any speculative view (atthi pana bhoto Gotamassa kiñci diṭṭhigatan'ti, M.I. 486). Buddha answers explicitly: "A speculative view as such has been abandoned by Tathāgata" (diṭṭhigatan' ti..apanītam etaṃ Tathāgatassa, loc. cit.) Thus, in contradistinction to the B.G., early Buddhism keeps itself completely free of metaphysical speculation.

Then again, true to his empirical approach, Buddha does not try to conceptualise what is non-conceptual. He would leave the transcendental or supramundane for direct and personal experience and verification. S. Radhakrishan, despite his attempt to ascribe a positive theory of the self to Buddha, recognises this attitude of the latter when he says: "Buddha exhorts us to be philosophical enough to recognise the limits af philosophy"[3] As Wittgenstein would put it: "Where of one cannot speak, thereof one must be silent."[4] The B.G. and the Ups. also, no doubt, indicate their awareness of the limits of thought and speech, yet they are found to indulge in mystical and metaphysical descriptions. The B.G. speaks of the self as incomprehensible, unknowable, unthinkable and indefinable (aprameya, II.18; avijñeya, XIII. 15, acintya II. 25, VIII.9 and anirdeśya, XII.3) and yet, for the most part, it abounds in mystical the orisations about the nature of the self. Likewise the Ups. also, notwithstanding their declaration that the supreme reality is indescribable

1. B.G. XIII. 34.
2. Indian Philosophy, Vol. I. p. 535.
3. Indian Philosophy, Vol. I, p. 387.
4. Tractatus Logico-Philosophicus, p. 189.

and ineffable,[1] fail to refrain from indulging in mystical utterances. The credit, indeed, goes to early Buddhism for having kept itself aloof from all speculative metaphysics and mystical descriptions and confined itself to the experiential or the empirical.

It would be seen in the sequel how this difference with regard to the problem of the self influences the respective conceptions of salvation and survival in the B.G. and early Buddhism.

The Problem of Salvation :—

(A) *Nibbāna, the Ultimate Goal of Holy Life* :—

Undoubtedly, the ultimate purpose of the holy life both according to Buddhism and the B.G. is the attainment of salvation (Nirvāṇa). "Nibbāna is the kernel of the holy life, brother Visākha, Nibbāna is its purpose and its goal,"[2] says the nun Dhammadinnā with the approval of Buddha.[3] Buddha himself clearly states: "The purpose of this holy life does not consist in acquiring alms, honour and fame, nor in attaining virtue, concentration or the knowledge and insight. That unshakable deliverance of the heart—that, indeed, monk, is the object of the holy life, that is its essence, that is its goal."[4] It is described as "the state of unsurpassed peace and safety" (anuttara-yogakkhema, S.II. 195, 226). No state of comfort is higher than and superior to this comfort (imamhā phāsuvihārā uttaritaro vā paṇītataro vā phāsuvihāro natthī ti, M.I. 209). "Nibbāna is the supreme—declare the Buddhas" (nibbānaṃ paramaṃ vadanti Buddhā, Dh. 184). Therefore, at the attainment of Nibbāna, one realises: "Exhausted is rebirth, lived the holy life, done whatever was to be done and

1. Bṛhadā. II. 4, 14; Muṇḍaka. III. 2. 3; Kaṭha. II. 8 and 9.

2. Nibbānogadhaṃ hi, āvuso Visākha, brahmacariyaṃ, nibbānaparāyanaṃ nibbānapariyosānaṃ, M. I. 304; cf. S.V. 218.

3. Mamaṃ ce pi tvaṃ, Visākha, etam atthaṃ puccheyyāsi, ahaṃ pi tam evam eva byākareyyaṃ yathā taṃ Dhammadinnāya bhikkhuṇiyā byākataṃ, M.I. 304-5.

4. nayidaṃ brahmacariyaṃ lābhasakkārasilokānisaṃsaṃ, na sīlasampadānisaṃsaṃ, na samādhisampadānisaṃsaṃ, na ñāṇadassanānisaṃsaṃ. Yā ca kho bhikkhave akuppā cetovimutti, etad atthamidaṃ, bhikkhave brahmacariyaṃ etaṃ sāraṃ etaṃ pariyosānam, M.I. 197.

nothing further remains after this."[1] "The liberated saint has nothing (to accomplish). The liberated saint has done whatever is to be done."[2]

Similar utterances in relation to salvation are found in the B.G. as well. It is spoken of as the supreme goal (parāṃ or paramāṃ gatim, B.G. VI. 45; VIII. 13; XIII. 28). It is "that state which the sages freed from passions enter and desiring which they lead the holy life."[3] "Having attained that one realises that there is no gain higher than this."[4] "For him neither is there any interest in the actions done nor in the actions undone."[5] "For him there exists no work that needs to be done."[6] He is enlightened and has done whatever was to be done.[7] Thus in quite similar terms Nirvāṇa is spoken of as the highest goal both by Buddhism and the B.G.

But do they mean the same when they speak of it as the supreme goal? Let us first see how it is understood in Buddhism and then compare it with the B.G. view of it.

(B) *The Etymological Significance of Nibbāna* :—

Etymologically different derivations of the term, 'Nibbāna' are possible, and passages in support of each one of the derivative meanings are present in the Pali texts. The earliest use of it in the sense of 'blowing off' (nir + vā) is found in the Ṛg-Veda X. 16[13] (nirvāti)[8] which is supported by the Sutta Nipāta. The passage of the Sutta Nipāta reads as follows: "Just as the flame of a lamp struck by a gust of wind disappears and cannot be traced, so also does a perfect saint freed from name and form disappear without leaving any

---

1. M.I. 23; S. II. 51; IV. 66.

2. Natthi kiccaṃ brāhmaṇassa, katakicco hi brāhmaṇo, S. I. 47.

3. viśanti yad yatayo vītarāgāḥ, yad icchanto bramacaryam caranti B.G. VIII, 11.

4. Yaṃ labdhvā cā'paraṃ lābhaṃ manya'e nā' dhikaṃ tataḥ B.G. VI. 22.

5. Nai'va tasya kṛtenā'rtho nā'kṛtene'ha kaścana, B.G. III. 16.

6. tasya kāryaṃ na vidyate, B.G. III. 17.

7. etad buddhvā buddhimān syāt kṛtakṛtyaś ca bhārata, B.G. XV. 20.

8. P.T.S. Pali English Dictionary —vide, 'nibbāpeti'.

trace."[1] But the more commonly used metaphor is that of the extinguishing of the fire by the exhaustion of the fuel and being not fed with fresh fuel. Thus, Buddha himself explains the incomprehensible and unfathomable state of Nibbāna as follows: "The fire which blazed on account of the fuel of grass and wood comes to be reckoned as 'gone out' (nibbuto), since it had consumed the fuel and was not fed with more fuel, so also the Tathāgata...being freed from the marks of corporeality...feeling..perception..dispositions.. and consciousness becomes deep, incomprehensible and unfathomable".[2] Evidently in this metaphor the word 'Nirvāṇa' is sought to be explained through the root 'vṛ' and not through √vā. It is this metaphor which largely governs the early Buddhist concept of Nibbāna. Still another derivation is ni + vāna. 'Ni' is a negative particle and 'vāna' means desire, lust or craving (lit. forest).[3] Thus it means freedom from desire or craving. As the Dhammapada puts it: "By cutting down the forest and bushes (of craving), be emancipated, O monks."[4]

One can, however, notice that despite these various derivations of the word 'Nibbāna' the meaning conveyed by each one of them is very much the same, i.e. the going out of a lamp or fire, the fire of craving. The world is said to be in flames (ādīpito loko, S.I. 31; niccaṃ pajjalite, Dh. 146) and it is the fuel of craving which keeps it ablaze.[5] So the Nibbāna consists in extinguishing the fire of craving or desire. Thus it is said: "It is the eradication of craving which is known as Nibbāna" (taṇhāya vippahānena nibbānam iti vuccatī ti, S.I. 39). "By destroying craving with root, one being free from hunger attains the perfect Nibbāna" (samūlaṃ taṇhamabbhuyha nicchāto parinibbuto ti, S. III. 26). "It is due to desire that man is bound and it is by surmount-

1. Accī yathā vātavegena khitto atthaṃ paleti na upeti saṅkhaṃ; evaṃ munī nāmakāyā vimutto atthaṃ paleti na upeti saṅkhaṃ, Sn. 195.
2. M. II. 487-8.
3. P.T.S. Pali English Dictionary, vide. the word 'vana'.
4. chettvā vanañca vanathañca nibbānā hotha bhikkhavo, Dh. 283.
5. S. II. 85-87.

ing (the self-same) desire that he is liberated" (icchāya bajjhatī loko icchāvinayāya muccati, S.I. 40). "By the destruction of desire or craving all bonds are cut off" (icchāya, or taṇhāya vippahānena sabbaṃ chindati bandhanaṃ ti, S.I. 40). "He who destroys craving overcomes all suffering" (taṇhakkhayo sabbadukkhaṃ jinātī, Dh. 354). It is this extinction of suffering which is taught by Buddha in the third Noble Truth as follows: "What, monks, is the Noble Truth of the extinction of suffering? It is the complete fading away and extinction of this craving, its forsaking and abandonment, freedom and emancipation from it."[1]

It should not be forgotten that it is this desire or craving which manifests itself in three forms, viz., lust or attachment, hatred and delusion. It is well-known that according to Buddhism, feeling is the cause of craving (vedanā paccayā taṇhā, S.II. 25, 116). Now this feeling is said to be of three kinds—pleasant, unpleasant and neither pleasant nor unpleasant (sukhā, dukkhā and adukkhamasukhā, M.I. 302) which respectively tend to produce attachment, hatred and delusion. It is said: "To the pleasant feeling, the inclination to attachment adheres, to the unpleasant one, the inclination to hatred, and to the feeling neither pleasant nor unpleasant, the inclination to delusion."[2] This explains why at times Nibbāna is described in terms of the destruction of this tripartite division of craving. "Nibbāna, Nibbāna, they say, friend Sāriputta; what now means Nibbāna friend?[3] "That which is the destruction of attachment, friend, the destruction of hatred, the destruction of delusion, that is called Nibbana."[4]

There is still another way to describe the same. It is a matter of common place that the root cause of all our craving and consequent suffering is ignorance, and so, it is said that "whatever evil things are there, they are all rooted in ignorance (ye keci akusalā dhammā sabbe te avijjāmūlakā, S.

1. Katamaṃ ca, bhikkhave, dukkha-nirodhaṃ ariyasaccaṃ ? Yo tassāyeva taṇhāya asesa virāga nirodho cāgo paṭinissaggo mutti anālayo, D. II. 310.

2. M.I. 303.

3. S. IV. 251, 261.

4. Yo kho, avūso rāgakkhayo dosakkhayo mohakkhayo—idaṃ vuccati nibbānaṃ ti. loc. cit.

II. 263). This ignorance (avijjā) consists in the lack of proper knowledge about the five aggregates and the consequent clinging to them which gives rise to the conceit of 'I'-ness. "Ignorance, ignorance, they say, Lord; what, Lord, is ignorance and how does one fall into ignorance"?[1] "There is, monk, an uninstructed worldling who does not properly know corporeality, the origin of corporeality, the cessation of corporeality and the path leading to the cessation of corporeality. (Similarly with regard to feeling, perception, dispositions and consciousness). This, monk, is called ignorance and this is how one falls into ignorance."[2] This lack of proper knowledge gives rise to the conceit of 'I'-ness which constitues bondage and, therefore, liberation is said to consist in getting rid of this conceit of 'I'-ness."There is, monks, an uninstructed worldling...who regards corporeality as the self, or the self as possessing corporeality, or corporeality as being within the self or the self within corporeality (Similarly with regard to other aggregates)." This, monks, is known as being bound with corporeality, bound with internal and external fetters, non-perceiving the shore, non-perceiving the beyond. He is born with bondage, dies with bondage and with bondage does he go from this world to another (Similarly with regard to other aggregates)."[3] Therefore, "whatever corporeality, be it past, future or present....you should behold thus, 'this is not mine, this is not I, this is not my self. So seeing things as they are, through proper insight, one being free from clinging, is thoroughly released (Similarly with regard to other aggregates)."[4] We have already seen that the conceit of 'I'-ness is the subtlest form of clinging (attavādupādāna) caused by our desire or craving for personal immortality (bhavataṇhā) and, therefore, it is quite understandable why Nibbāna is indiscriminately described as the destruction of craving or of the conceit of 'I'-ness.

The Buddhist analysis of suffering and its cessation

1. S. III. 162.
2. S. III. 162-3.
3. S. III. 164-5.
4. S. III. 170.

(Nibbāna) being thoroughly causal, based on the doctrine of Paṭiccasamuppāda (dependent origination), the destruction of one link in the series naturally leads to the destruction of the subsequent links. As Buddha himself points out: 'Through the total fading away and extinction of craving (taṇhā), clinging (upādāna) is extinguished; through the extinction of clinging, the process of becoming (bhava) is extinguished; through the extinction of the process of becoming, rebirth (jāti) is extinguished and through the extinction of rebirth, decay, death, sorrow, lamentation, suffering, grief and despair are extinguished. Thus comes about the extinction of this whole mass of suffering."[1] This accounts for the various descriptions of Nibbāna, stated in the Pali texts, each with different purpose in view. As a matter of fact, the Budddhist concept of Nibbāna is so deep, unfathomable and many-sided that it is difficult to bring out its full import through any one single description. We cannot agree with T. W. Rhys Davids and W. Stede who think that "Nibbāna is purely and solely an ethical state."[2]

(C) *Negative and Positive Descriptions of Nibbāna and its Ineffability*:—

It may be noticed that all the above-mentioned descriptions, in keeping with the etymological meanings of the term, speak of Nibbāna only in negative terms, and try to avoid a positive description of the really indescribable and ineffable state. George Grimm, despite his mistaken attempt to see a state of true self-realisation in the Buddhist concept of Nibbāna[3], has rightly emphasised this negative approach of Buddhism. He says: "Liberty is a negative conception, not a positive one. It indicates only that we are set free from something, more exactly, from some hindrance or limitation, but not what we then are, when in this manner we are freed.".[4] This negative approach of early Buddhism is particularly im-

1. S. II. 72.
2. Pali English Dictionary (P.T.S.), vide 'Nibbāna'.
3. According to him the liberated saint, "after having freed himself from every kind of sensation. . .had remained what he is from all eternity", The Doctrine of the Buddha. p. 251.
4. The Doctrine of the Buddha, p. 235.

portant in view of the predominantly positive approach of the B. G., which we shall see in the sequel.

The negative approach of Buddhism, however, should not be taken to mean that Nibbāna is a state of nothingness or utter annihilation. It is only by misconstruing the analogy of the extinction of fire that some scholars have given such an interpretation to it. The views of these scholars have already been thoroughly criticised by Poussin[1] and Heiler[2] and so it is not necessary to deal with them here at length. Perhaps no modern scholar now adheres to the nihilistic interpretation. The fact that we do not come across any school of Buddhism preaching the ideal of utter annihilation shows that the nihilistic interpretation is averse to all Buddhist trends of thought. It is precisely with a view to avoiding such misconceptions that the Pali Canon makes use of some positive expressions also along with the negative ones. We may notice, for example, the following epithets (in italics) used for Nibbāna in the Saṃyutta Nikāya:—"This is the Nibbāna, the uncompounded, *the ultimate*, free from defilements, *the truth*, *the further shore*, *the subtle*, very difficult to see, the unfading, *the stable*, the undecaying, the ineffable, the undifferentiated, *the peaceful*, the deathless, *the excellent*, *the good*, *the security*, destruction of craving, *the wonderful*, *the marvellous*, free from ill, the state free from ill, the harmless, the passionless, *the purity*, the release, the non-attachment, *the island*, *the cave*, *the protection*, *the refuge* and *the goal* which the well-accomplished One has taught."[3]

Yet the positive epithets of Nibhāna also, no less than the negative ones, have been misunderstood. Many scholars who energetically denounce the annihilationist view of Nibbāna go to the other extreme, and try to give an eternalistic interpretation to it. Poussin himself, in the course of criticising the annihilationist view, has been led to this error. According

1. Etudes Sur L'Histoire de Religions.
2. Die Buddhistische Versenkung, pp. 36-42.
3. Asaṅkhatam anatam anāsavaṃ saccaṃ ca pāraṃ nipuṇaṃ sududdasaṃ, ajajjarantaṃ dhuvam apalokitaṃ anidassanaṃ nippapañca santaṃ, amataṃ paṇītañca sivañca khemaṃ taṇhākkhayo acchariyañca abbhutaṃ, anītikaṃ anītikadhammaṃ nibbānam etaṃ sugatena desitaṃ,

abyāpajjo virāgo ca suddhi mutti anālayo,
dīpaṃ lenañca tāṇañca saraṇañca parāyanan'ti S. IV. 373.

to him, "Nirvāṇa meant a simple faith in soul's immortality, its blissful survival in a paradise, a faith emerging from practices of obscure magic."[1] George Grimm also observes that "after having freed himself from every kind of sensation, he (the liberated saint) has not become nothing..but he had remained what he is from all eternity."[2] Similarly Professor Keith says that "the extinction of fire was not that which occurs to us of utter annihilation but rather the flame returns to the Primitive pure invisible state of fire, in which it existed prior to its manifestation in the form of visible fire."[3] Radha krishnan also pronounces the same view. He says: "Nirvāṇa is not a lapse into a void but only a negation of the flux and a positive return of the self to itself."[4]

All this clearly shows that these scholars while countering the annihilationist view of Nibbāna are carried away by their own arguments to the opposite extreme of eternalism. It is, indeed, very difficult to steer clear of these two opposite views of annihilationism and eternalism and keep close to the Middle Path shown by Buddha. Buddha is well aware of this difficulty, and so he repeatedly warns against the danger of falling into these basic misconceptions which occur again and again in many and varied ways. He says: "This world Kaccāna, usually leans upon a duality: upon (the belief in) existence or non-existence...Avoiding these two extremes, the Tathāgata shows the doctrine in the middle."[5] It is, therefore, wrong to read too much into either of the two sets of epithets and expressions which seem to be more suggestive than descriptive. In the words of Nyānaponika Thera, "they are evocative and not truly descriptive."[6] By means of their mutual qualification, they only serve the purpose of suggesting the indescribable and ineffable nature of Nibbāna.

---

1. Quoted by Stcherbatsky—The Conception of Buddhist Nirvāṇa, pp. 1-2.
2. The Doctrine of the Buddhā, p. 251.
3. Buddhist Philosophy. pp. 55-56.
4. Indian Philosophy' Vol. I. p. 386.
5. S. II. 17; cf. S. II. 76; III. 135; IV. 400.
6. Anattā and Nibbāna, p. 26.

The fact that Nirvāṇa is truly ineffable and uncharacterisable (anidassanaṃ, nippapañca, S. IV. 373) is made quite clear in the very first utterance of Buddha after the attainment of his unshakable salvation (akuppā vimutti, M. I. 167). He speaks of his attainment as "profound, difficult to see, difficult to comprehend, tranquil, subtle, beyond reason, excellent and realisable by the wise."[1] It is wonderful and marvellous (acchariyaṃ abbhutaṃ, S. IV. 373) in the true sense of the term and cannot be communicated through any of our conceptual modes of description. Thus our positive or negative descriptions, strictly speaking, are only conventional, though they serve a useful purpose if understood in the right perspective. It is precisely with a view to indicating the profound and ineffable nature of Nibbāna that the negative descriptions are preferred. They by denying everything mundane and conceptual to Nibbāna, suggest its supramundane and non-conceptual nature in the best possible way, though the positive expressions also are useful in so far as they assert the reality of Nibbāna and allay the fears of the nihilistic conception.

In the light of this approach of Buddhism, we can now understand why, even while making categorical assertions about the reality of Nibbāna, the Pali texts frequently make use of negative expressions. Thus the Itivuttaka says: "There is, O monk,the unborn, the unbecome, the uncreated, the unformed."[2] Similarly it is stated in the Udāna: "There is an unborn, unbecome, uncreated, unformed. If there were not this unborn... an escape from the born, the become, the created, the formed could not be known."[3] It is further said: "Truly, there is a realm where there is neither the earth nor water, neither fire nor air, neither ether nor consciousness..neither this world, not any other world, neither sun nor moon. This I call neither arising nor passing away, neither continuing, nor being born nor dying. There is neither foothold nor development nor any basis. This is

1. adhigato kho myāyaṃ dhammo gambhīro duddaso duranubodho santo paṇīto atakkāvacaro nipuṇo paṇḍitavedanīyo, M.I. 167.

2. Atthi, bhikkhave, ajātam abhūtam akatam asaṅkhataṃ, It. 37.

3. Ud. 80.

the end of suffering."[1] "There the stars shine not nor does the light of the sun. Neither is there the illuminatian of the moon nor is there any darkness."[2] "The form, location, age and measure cannot be given of Nibbāna—the state that is truly real."[3] All these utterances only point to the fact that Nirvāṇa is regarded in Buddhism as a snpramundane state strictly incomprehensible in any conceptual manner. It can only be directly and personally realised by the wise (paccattaṃ veditabbo viññūhī ti, M. I. 37). We have already shown, while discussing the last four of the unanswered (abyākata) questions (supra. pp. 298-301), that it is this incomprehensibility of Nibbāna which is sought to be conveyed through the inapplicability of the fourfold negation.

Again, the positive descriptions also should not be regarded as positively determining or characterising the state of Nibbāna in any mundane sense. The well-known utterance of Buddha, "Nibbāna is the supreme happiness" (Nibbānaṃ paramaṃ sukhaṃ, M. I. 508), for example, was erroneously conceived by the mendicant. Māgaṇḍiya in the sense of mundane happiness. Buddha thereupon exposes his folly and remarks: "The utterance was pronounced by previous Arahants, the perfectly enlightened ones, which has now come down to the worldling."[4] In fact the significance of the positive utterance also can be better understood in terms of negation. Thus Buddha himself explains the meaning of the happiness of Nibbāna as follows: "Dispositions are impermanent, by nature originating and decaying. They arise and perish. Their stilling (cessation) is the Happiness."[5] It is made further clear from the statement of Sariputta. The monk Udāyi, after having heard, "Blisss is Nibbāna, bliss is Nibbāna", asks in astonishment: "How can there be bliss where there is no feeling?" (A. IV. 415). Sariputta answers: "This

1. Ud. 80.
2. na tattha sukkā jotanti ādicco nappakāsati,
na tattha candimā bhāti tamo tattha na vijjati, Ud. 9.
3. Atthi-dhammass'eva nibbānassa na sakkā rūpaṃ vā saṇṭhānaṃ vā vayaṃ vā pamāṇam vā ..upadassayitum, Milindapañha, 316-7.
4. M.I. 510.
5. D. II. 199.

precisely, O friend, is bliss that there is no feeling" (etad eva khvettha, āvuso, sukhaṃ yadettha natthi vedayitaṃ, loc. cit,)

It is, thus, clear that the positive descriptions also cannot be understood in the sense of ascribing some mundane attributes to Nibbāna. They can only be taken to suggest a definite supramundane state of reality to which all mundane epithets are inapplicable. Nibbāna in itself is, thus, a strictly inexpressible or incommunicable supramundane state of reality which one can only realise directly and personally.

The negative and positive modes of description, thus, serve useful purposes and are in a way indispensable. Briefly speaking, we may say that in view of our language and thought being basically unsuited for the proper expression and comprehension of the true nature of Nibbāna, the negative statements are most appropriate, since they consist in eliminating whatever is inapplicable to and incommensurate with Nibbāna. The negative descriptions like 'the destruction of attachment, hatred and delusion' etc. serve a practical purpose by indicating what needs to be done in order to realise Nibbāna (which, indeed, matters most for the holy aspirant). Similarly the positive descriptions also are intended to serve a purpose. They preclude the possibility of a nihilistic interpretation of Nibbāna. They allay the fears of those who have not as yet adequately grasped the subtle truths of the Buddhist doctrines of anattā and paṭiccasamuppāda, and are at a loss to find repose in the negative descriptions of Nibbāna. They emphatically convey the truth that Nibbāna is a definite goal capable of attainment, and is truly desirable.

In the light of this Buddhist account of Nibbāna, when we turn to the B. G. view of it, we come across some striking similarities between them, though unlike the former, the latter brings in metaphysical and theological elements, and lays more emphasis on positive rather than on negative description. The word Nirvāṇa or Brahma-Nirvaṇa occurs in the B. G. (II. 72; V. 24-26 and VI. 15) as a synonym of such words as Brāhmīsthiti (II. 72; V. 19, 20), Brahmabhūta (V. 24; VI. 27; XIII. 54), matparāyaṇaḥ (IX. 34), madbhāvam āgataḥ (IV. 10), ātmavān (II. 45; IV. 41), tṛptātmā (VI. 8) yuktātmā (V. 21; VI. 29) and guṇātīta (XIV. 25) etc. which seems to indicate that the B. G. is trying to appropriate the Buddhist concept of Nirvāṇa in such a way as to make it conform to its dominantly metaphysical and theological view of the self and God. While using the similes of the fire and lamp, the B. G. in contradistinction to Buddhism makes a positive rather than a negative approach.

Speaking of wisdom (jñāna) which is nothing but the realisation of the supreme metaphysical reality, Ātman or Brahman (B. G. VII. 1-3, 29, 30), manifesting itself as witness (sākṣī, B. G. IX. 18) or the knower of the Field (kṣetrajñam, B. G. XIII. 2), the B. G. says: "Just as the blazing fire reduces the, fuel to ashes, so also the fire of wisdom (jñānāgniḥ) turns the entire (lustful) karmas to ashes."[1] Evidently, the simile is almost the same as that of Buddhism, and just as in Buddhism it is the fuel of desire, craving or lust which keeps the fire ablaze,[2] so also it is the fuel of lust or desire behind the action which is meant to be burnt out here. Śaṅkara commenting on this verse has made it clear that it is not the action as such, but its root motive-force or the seed which is burnt to ashes by means of the true knowledge.[3] It is made clear in the B. G. itself that the root cause of all deluded actions is the desire or lust which burns as an insatiable fire.[4] On ultimate analysis, it is on account of the uprising of desire and hatred that men are deluded and come to the cycle of birth and death in the world.[5] We have already noticed that according to Buddhism also, "the world is bound by desire"[6] or "one is led to the world by craving."[7] Thus the B. G. and Buddhism seem to be in perfect accord up to this

1. Yathai' dhāṃsi samiddho' gnir bhasmasāt kurute 'rjuna,
jñānāgniḥ sarva karmāṇī bhasmasāt kurute tathā, B.G. IV. 37.
2. S. II. 85.
3. Na hi sākṣād eva jñānāgniḥ karmāṇi indhanavad bhasmīkartuṃ śaknoti, tasmāt samyagdarśanaṃ sarvakarmaṇāṃ nirbījatve kāraṇam iti abhiprāyaḥ, S.B.G. IV.37.
4. Āvṛtaṃ jñānam etena jñānino nityavairiṇā,
kāmarūpeṇa kaunteya duṣpureṇā'nalena ca.. B.G. III. 39.
5. Icchādveṣasamutthena...sarvabhūtāni saṃmohaṃ sarge yānti paraṃtapa, B.G.VII. 27.
6. Icchāya bajjhati loko, S.I. 40.
7. Taṇhāya nīyati loko, S.I. 39.

point, but after this the B. G. parts company with the latter. Buddhism, in keeping with its doctrine of non-self (anattā), suggests through this simile that the fuel of craving or desire being exhausted, the huge mass of fire is extinguished (mahā aggikkhandho..anāhāro nibbāyeyya, S. II. 85) leaving no determinable trace behind. Thus, it conveys the indeterminable nature of Nibbāna through its predominantly negative approach. But the B. G., conspicuously enough, gives no hint to the extinction of the fire. It, on the other hand, seems to suggest that the self-luminous, ever-brilliant fire of knowlege after consuming the fuel of lust or desire shines forth with the purest lustre. Salvation thus consists in the true realisation of the Supreme who is described as "the light of all lights" (jyotiṣām api taj jyotiḥ, B. G. XIII. 17) This is how the B. G., despite its acceptance of the word 'Nirvāṇa' (ni + vā) and also the simile of the fire and fuel, stresses its own positive metaphysical theory.

The same is evident in the use it makes of the simile of the lamp and wind. Buddhism, as we saw, following the derivation of the word Nirvāṇa (ni + va) compares the liberated saint freed from name and form with the lamp blown out by the wind (accī yathā vātavegena khitto, Sn. 195). But the B.G. takes it (ni + vā) in the sense of non-flickering or the steadiness of the lamp not disturbed by the wind. It says: "As a lamp in a windless place does not flicker, the same simile is said to apply to the yogin of subdued thought who practises union with the self."[1] Here the predominantly positive conception of Nirvāṇa based on a belief in a metaphysical self is clearly brought out.

This, however, does not mean that the negative descriptions of Nirvāṇa and suggestions of its being an ineffable and indeterminable state are not to be met with at all in the B. G. In fact, the B. G. also, in a somewhat Buddhistic manner, gives negative descriptions of Nirvāṇa and indicates its supramundane and incomprehensible nature. But, as it believes like the Ups. in a

1. Yathā dīpo nivātastho ne'ṅgate so'pamā smṛtā,
yogino yatacittasya yuñjato yogam ātmanaḥ, B.G. V

positive metaphysical and theological principle indwelling in man[1], Nirvāṇa according to it is ultimately nothing but a state of self-realisation.[2] On closer examination, it would appear that the B. G., true to its synthetic and compromising character, is trying to absorb and assimilate both the Buddhistic as well as the Upaniṣadic concept of salvation, giving prominence to the latter.

Let us first see how, like Buddhism, it makes use of the negative descriptions. We have noted that like Buddhism it also lays great emphasis on the abandonment of lust or desire (B. G. III. 39, VII. 27). It is, in fact, on this basis that it formulates its central doctrine of desireless or disinterested action (niṣkāma karma). Naturally, therefore, like Buddhism which speaks of Nibbāna as the destruction of desire or craving (taṇhāya vippahānena nibbānam iti vuccatī ti, S. I. 39; icchāya vippahānena sabbaṃ chindati bandhanan'ti, S. I. 40), the B. G. also declares that the attainment of Nirvāna can be had by abandoning all desires. It says: "He who abandons all desires and acts free from longing without any sense of mineness or egotism, he attains to Peace."[3] It may also be noticed here that in a Buddhistic way the abandoning of the conceit of 'I'-ness and 'mine'-ness (nirmamo nirahaṅkāraḥ, loc. cit.) also is spoken of by the B. G. as a necessary condition for the attainment of this supreme state, though, as shown above (supra, pp. 329-333) it does not seem to realise its full implications owing to its adherence to the Upaniṣadic concept of the self Thus despite its repeated exhortation for giving up desire and egotism (B. G. III. 27; XVIII. 17), it persists in clinging to the self, so much so that salvation itself is regarded by it as a state of self-absorption. It is explicitly stated: "When a man casts aside all the desires of his mind and

1. B.G.X. 20; XIII. 2, 17, 22, 27, 32; XV. 15 and XVIII. 61.

2. The liberated saint, therefore, is described as 'ātmavān' (B.G. II. 45; IV. 41); 'tṛptātmā' (B.G. VI.8) and 'yuktātmā' (B.G.V. 21, VI.29).

3. Vihāya kāmān yaḥ sarvān pumāṃś carati niḥspṛhaḥ,
nirmamo nirahaṅkāraḥ sa śāntim adhigacchati, B.G. II.71.

feels himself satisfied in the self itself (ātmany evā'tmanā tuṣṭaḥ), then he is called a man of settled wisdom (sthitaprajñaḥ)".[1]

Similarly like Buddhism, the B. G. speaks of the destruction of attachment, hatred and delusion (rāga, dveṣa and moha), but again all this is intended to seek refuge in the self wherein, indeed, lies the true salvation. It says: "Being free from the attachment and hatred (rāga dveṣa viyuktaiḥ) the man of accomplished self (vidheyātmā) and self-control attains to serenity, even while letting his senses move among the objects."[2] It is further said: "When your intellect shall cross the mire of delusion (mohakalilam), then shall you reach the state of detachment which is beyond what has been heard and what is yet to be heard."[3] It is interesting to see that some of the expressions also of the B. G. and Buddhism in this connection have remarkable similarity. We may compare the following:—

B. G. II. 64, Rāgadveṣaviyuktais tu..prasādam adhigacchati—Dh. 369 chettvā rāgañca dosañca tato nibbāṇam ehisi.

B. G. XVIII. 51, rāgadveṣau vyudasya ca—Dh 377 rāgañca dosañca vippamuñcetha.

Again like Buddhism, the B. G. speaks in a general way of ignorance which envelops the wisdom and leads people to delusion (ajñānenā'vṛtaṃ jñānaṃ tena muhyanti jantavaḥ, B. G. V. 15), and consequent suffering. In a typical Buddhist style, true knowledge is said to consist in "seeing the evils of birth, death, old age, disease and suffering" (janmamṛtyujarāvyādhiduḥkhadoṣānudarśanam, B.G. XIII. 8). Ignorance being the root of suffering, salvation here also is said to consist in the destruction of ignorance by means of true knowledge. Kṛṣṇa tells Arjuna: "Therefore, cut off the doubt of your heart born of ignorance with the sword of knowledge,"[4] and it is stated

1. B.G. II. 55.
2. B.G. II. 64.
3. B.G. II. 52.
4. B.G. VI. 42.

further that "by attaining that knowledge immortality (or salvation) is achieved."[1]

Then again, like Buddhism, the B. G. also uses a number of negative epithets such as unborn, undying, unbecoming, incomprehensible, unmanifest, etc.,[2] though in keeping with its metaphysical approach, they are used in relation to the self in the realisation of which lies true salvation.[3]

The inexpressibility of Nirvāṇa also is suggested by the B. G. in a metaphysical or theological context. Nirvāṇa is said to consist in the indentification or unification with the metaphysical reality called Ātman or Brahman (B. G. V. 19, 20, 24; XI. 54; XVIII. 55), theologically spoken as Paramātman, Īśvara or Puruṣottama (B. G. XV. 17, 18). This reality being regarded as incomprehensible (aprameya, II. 18), unthinkable (acintya, II. 25, VIII. 9, XII. 3), undefinable (anirdeśya, XII. 3) and marvellous (āścaryavat or āścaryamaya, II. 29, XI. 6, 11), one is supposed to attain the same state by its realisation. This reality is spoken in paradoxical terms (B. G. XI. 37; XIII. 12-16) where all conceptual contradictions and oppositions are resolved.

The positive description of this highest state is quite evident all through the text and salvation is frequently described as "abiding and absolute bliss" (sukhaṃ akṣayam V. 21; sukham ātyāntikam. VI. 21; sukham aikāntikam, XIV. 27.), supreme peace (parāṃ śāntim, IV. 39; XVIII. 62), the highest goal (parāṃ gatim, VI. 45; VIII. 13; XIII. 2.), the eternal abode (śāśvataṃ padam or sthānam, XVIII. 56, 62) supreme perfection (paramāṃ siddhim, XVIII. 49) and so on. The positive realisation of the Ātman or Brahman is, indeed, the dominant note of the B. G. view of salvation.

1. yaj jñātvā'mṛtam aśnute, B.G. XIII. 12.

2. B.G. II. 17-25 (na jāyate mriyate vā kadācin nā'yaṃ bhūtvā bhavitā vā na bhūyaḥ, ajo. . .avināśi, avyaya, aprameya, acintya, avyakta etc.)

3. B.G. II, 55; VI. 20; XIII. 12; XIV. 2; XVIII. 55.

(*D*) *Some Basic Differences Between the Buddhist and the B. G. Approach to Nibbāna*:—

The above discussion makes it clear that there is a general agreement between the B. G. and Buddhism with regard to their negative and positive descriptions of Nirvāṇa as well as in respect of their references to the inexpressibility or incomprehensibility of this highest state. But despite this general agreement and the common use of some words and epithets, there are some basic differences between their respective concepts of Nirvāṇa. In the B. G. all the negative descriptions as well as the indications of ineffability hinge on one positive metaphysical entity, known as Ātman or Brahman. It is essentially the very same principle which is psychologically conceived as Ātman, metaphysically known as Brahman and theologically spoken as Paramātman or Puruṣottama. It is this dominantly positive metaphysical and theological approach which sharply distinguishes the B. G. concept of Nirvāṇa from that of Buddhism. We have seen that the concept of the self is repudiated by Buddhism and all metaphysical speculations are set aside. In keeping with its strict empirical approach, Buddhism refrains from all metaphysical speculations or mystical descriptions of the truly indescribable, which according to it is a matter of direct personal experience and verification (ehipassiko, paccataṃ veditabbo, M. I. 37). As a result, the Buddhist approach to Nibbāna is predominantly negative whereas that of the B. G. is largely positive. This is mainly on account of the fact that the B. G. tries to blend the Buddhistic ideas with its dominantly Upaniṣadic view of the self which, as we have shown (supra pp. 328-333), appears to be a manifestation of a subtle but srong attachment or clinging to personality.

Thus owing to the difference in their basic approaches the treatment of Nirvāṇa finds a different orientation in the B. G. and Buddhism. Psychologically Nirvāṇa of the B. G. consists in the realisation of the self,[1] metaphysically in the

1. ātmany evā'tmanā tuṣṭaḥ sthitaprajñaḥ tado'cyate, B.G. II. 55: yatra cai'vā'tmanā'tmānaṃ paśyann ātmani tuṣyati, B.G. VI. 20; cf. XIII. 24, 25.

indentification with Brahman[1] and theologically in the unification with God.[2] In Buddhism, however, since the concepts of the self and God are rejected and metaphysical speculation is set aside, the entire outlook is quite different. Nibbāna primarily consists in the eradication of the conceit of the self, sundering all attachment or clinging, and the consequent emancipation from all suffering.

Then again, according to the B. G., since the self is considered as essentially perfect and accomplished, eternally free and immortal, ever-uncontaminated and unchangeable, salvation is supposed to consist in the mere realisation or recognition of this ever-present truth. It is not a new acquisition or a fresh attainment but what the Vedāntins would say, 'the attainment of what is already attained' (prāptasya prāptiḥ). So the B. G. declares: "Salvation is present all around to the knower of the self" (abhito Brahmanirvāṇaṃ vartate viditātmanām, B. G. V. 26). "The knower of Brahman is established in Brahman" (Brahmavid Brahmaṇi sthitaḥ, B. G. V. 20). But according to Buddhism, salvation is not just a recognition of the eternally fulfilled or perfected state of the self, but is a real attainment of what is hitherto unattained. So Buddha exhorts monks to endeavour to attain what is unattained, and to realise what is unrealised (tasmāt iha, bhikkhave, viriyam ārabhatha appattassa pattiyā...asacchikatassa sacchikiriyāya, S. II. 29).

In this connection it is useful to pay attention to a somewhat uncommon description of Nibbāna found in the Pali Canon where it is spoken of as infinite consciousness (viññāṇaṃ...anantaṃ, D.I. 223, M.I. 329). At first sight it appears to be quite similar to the Upaniṣadic or the B.G. view of Nirvāṇa as self-realisation, a state of pure infinite consciousness.[3] It is, therefore, worth examining if by this des-

1. B.G. IV. 24 (Brahmai'va tena gantavyam); V. 19, 20 (Brahmaṇi te sthitāḥ); XIII. 30 (Brahma saṃpadyate tadā).

2. B.G. IV. 9; XI. 55 (mām eti); XII. 8 (niv. siṣyasi mayy eva) VII. 23; VIII. 7; XI. 34; XVIII. 65, 68.

3. We have already shown (supra. pp. 115-8) that the B.G. conception of the self is quite akin to the Sāṅkya conception of Puruṣa as pure consciousness, with the Upanisadic view of the Absolute superadded.

cription, Buddha indicates a departure from his usual conception of Nibbāna. We may quote here the entire stanza which Buddha is supposed to have uttered referring to the highest state of Nibbāna. It reads as follows:—

Viññāṇaṃ anidassanaṃ anantaṃ sabbatopabhaṃ
ettha āpo ca paṭhavī tejo vāyo na gādhati.
ettha dīghañ ca rassañ ca aṇuṃ thūlaṃ subhāsubhaṃ
ettha nāmañ ca rūpañ ca asesaṃ uparujjhati
viññāṇassa nirodhena etth'etaṃ uparujjhatī ti.

—D.I.223

"It is consciousness (viññāṇa) which is signless, infinite and radiant on all sides[1] where water, earth, fire and air have no footing, where long and short, fine and coarse, good and bad along with name and form cease to be, without residue. On account of the cessation of consciousness (viññāṇa), all this ceases to be."

Obviously the word 'viññāṇa' of the first and the last lines is not used in the same sense, since the first viññāṇa spoken of as 'signless, infinite and radiant on all sides' is said to be a state where the second viññāṇa ceases to be. There can be hardly any doubt that the second viññāṇa refers to the fifth constituent of our personality, for elsewhere also in unmistakable terms all the five constituents are said to cease in the state of Nibbāna (M.I. 487-8; S. III. 107-8, 111-2, 118-9, 122-4). But the difficulty remains about the first viññāṇa which is equated with Nibbāna.

Buddhaghosa offers the solution that its meaning should be understood on the basis of the root ñā (to know), i.e. that which is to be known, viz., Nibbāna. In other words, viññāṇa is only another name for Nibbāna (tathā viññātab-

---

Like the Sāṅkhya the B.G. calls the self as draṣṭā or sākṣi (XIV. 19; IX. 18), udāsīna or madhyastha (XIV. 23; VI. 9) and Kevala (XVIII. 6). It is also called as kṣetrajña (XIII. 2) and vettā (XI. 38) and regarded as the source of all knowledge (XV. 15). We cannot, therefore, agree with S.N. Dasgupta to whom "it does not seem that the Gītā describes the self as pure consciousness". (A History of Indian Philosophy Vol. II, p. 471).

1. J.d 'Alwis' suggestion of 'pabham' for 'paham' has been preferred here. For a note on this, see S.B.B. Vol. II. p. 282, footnote 2.

ban'ti viññāṇaṃ, nibbānassa taṃ nāmaṃ).[1] Regarding the second viññāṇa, he also accepts that it is one of the five constituents.[2]

Whatever be the reason of calling Nibbāṇa as viññāṇa (consciousness), this, at least, is evident that it is not to be confused with any element constituting our personality, and this at once shows that the Buddhist view of viññāṇa (consciousness) as a synonym of Nibbāna is not the same as the B.G. view of realising the inmost consciousness of one's own self. According to Buddhism, it is made quite clear that all the constituents of our personality along with the viññāṇa disappear completely in this state of Nibbāna. Thus the last consciousness (viññāṇa) of an arahant ceases like the flame of a lamp and passes into a state of signlessness or indistinguishability. Just as fire is discerned or distinguished only so long as it finds fuel as its support, and is extinguished or becomes incomprehensible after the exhaustion of the fuel, so also the viññāṇa is to be found only in the presence of the other four constituents as its support, on the exhaustion of which it loses all distinction and becomes incomprehensible. This is what we call in Buddhism the state of Nibbāna in which viññāṇa being without support (appatiṭṭhita viññāṇa), becomes incomprehensible or untraceable Buddha refers to the wicked Māra who was searching in vain for the viññāṇa of the arahant monks Godhika and Vakkali just after their death (Māro pāpimā viññāṇaṃ..samanvesati, S.I. 122; III. 124). Māra fails in his attempt because they had attained Parinibbāna leaving no support for viññāṇa (appatiṭṭhitena.. viññāṇena..parinibbuto ti, loc. cit). Obviouly, this incomprehensible and characterless 'viññāṇa', if one still likes to call it as such, is not the same as one with which we are familiar as an element of our personality. Thus this signless (anidassanaṃ) or supportless (appatiṭṭhitaṃ) viññāṇa only refers to the supramundane, incomprehensible, uncharacterisa-

1. Sumaṅgalavilāsinī II. 393; The Papañcasūdani (II. 413) also commenting on the two words, 'viññāṇam anidassanaṃ'says the same: "Padadvayena pi nibbānam eva vuttaṃ".

2. Tathā viññāṇan ti carimaka-viññāṇaṃ pi abhisaṅkhāra-viññāṇan ti, Visuddhimagga, 689.

ble and indistinguishable state of pure viññāṇa which is comparable to the pure fire without fuel, and hence is used as a synonym of Nirvāṇa. The sense of 'appatiṭṭhita-viññāṇa' (supportless consciousness) is made clear in the Saṃyutta Nikāya in which it is said to arise when all attachment to the five constituents is completely removed.[1] This supportless viññāṇa is devoid of growth, unconstituted and absolutely free (tad appatiṭṭhitaṃ viññāṇaṃ avirūḷhaṃ anabhisaṅkhārañ ca vimuttaṃ, S.III. 53-54).

It is, thus, clear that this so called consciousness (viññāṇa) as a synonym of Nibbāna is not to be confused with our inmost consciousness, as the B.G. and the Ups. would have it. It is a state beyond the meditative state known as 'the sphere of infinite consciousness' (viññāṇañcāyatanaṃ M.I. 352, 399, 436; II. 13) and cannot be equated even with the state called 'the sphere of neither consciousness nor nonconsciousness (nevasaññānāsaññāyatanaṃ, M. I. 399; II. 13). So it is not entirely without justification that Buddhaghosa calls it merely another name for Nibbāna.

A passage occurring in the Nibbāna Sutta of the Udāna which is substantially similar to the stanza of the Dīgha Nikāya (I. 223) under reference, and which makes use of the word 'appatiṭṭhaṃ', fully supports the view that we have stated above. Here Buddha declares: "There is that sphere, O monk, where there is neither earth nor water nor fire nor air; neither is there the sphere of infinite space, of infinite consciousness, of nothingness or of neither consciousness nor non-consiousness. There is neither this world nor the other world, nor the sun and the moon. That I say, monks, neither coming nor going, neither continuity nor decay nor origin. It is supportless (appatiṭṭhaṁ), free from the cycle (of birth and rebirth) and without basis. This is the end of suffering."[2] The close resemblance of this passage with that of the Dīgha Nikāya (I.223) suggests that it is the same 'supportless' state, which is referred to in the latter as 'infinite consciouseness'. Evidently, it is so called only in a special

1. S. II. 65-67; III. 53-58.
2. Ud. 80.

supramundane sense. It is precisely in order to convey this supramundane sense that in the aforesoid stanza the significant addition of the word 'anidassanaṃ' (signless) is made to the word 'viññāṇa'.

It is, no doubt, true that the B.G. also speaks of the incomprehensible and supramundane nature of the supreme state but it confuses it entirely with the inmost self, and that makes all the difference. Buddha, on the other hand, is thoroughly opposed to confusing it with any form of the self. This is well brought out in the dialogue between Poṭṭhapāda and Buddha. Poṭṭhapāda after having heard from Buddha about the highest state of conscious meditation (sampajāna samāpatti, D.I.180-185) inquires of him whether this consciousness is the same as the self of man or is something different (saññā nu kho, bhante, purisassa attā udāhu aññā saññā añño attā' ti? D. I. 185). Buddha, thereupon asks Poṭṭhapāda as to what the latter means by the self (kiṃ pana tvaṃ, poṭṭhapāda, attānaṃ paccesī'ti? loc.cit.), and poṭṭhapāda puts forward one after another various concepts of the self such as the corporeal (oḷārikaṃ) mental (manomayaṃ) and the formless conscious self (arūpī attā saññāmayo). But in each case Buddha rejects the possibility of it being identical with the meditative consciovsness (evaṃ santam pi kho te, Poṭṭhapāda, aññā va saññā bhavissati añño attā, D.I. 186-7) and ultimately remarks: "It is hard, indeed, Poṭṭhapāda, for you, holding a different view, having a different attitude, a different inclination, striving after a different perfection, trained in a different system of doctrine to comprehend whether the consciousness is the same as the self of man or the consciousness is one thing and the self another."[1] This clearly shows that Buddha, in contradistinction to the B.G., does not identify the highest meditative consciousness with any form of the self. It is especially remarkable that the last concept of the self put forward by Poṭṭhapāda as the formless conscious self (arūpī attā saññāmayo, D. I. 187) is quite similar to the B.G. view of the self which is spoken of as unmanifest (avyakta, II. 25), subtle like the ether (yathā sarvagataṃ saukṣmyād ākāśam, XIII. 32; sūkṣma-

1. D.I. 187.

tvāt tad avijñeyam, XIII. 15) and the conscious principle appearing in the form of the witness (sākṣī, XI. 18), the pure spectator or knower (draṣṭā,vettā, kṣetrajña, XIV. 19; XI. 38, XIII.2).

Indeed, the keynote of Buddha's teaching is the complete eradication of the conceit of the 'I' or the self, whereby alone the total destruction of attachment, hatred and delusion (rāga, dosa and moha) and consequent suffering can be effected and the highest goal, viz., Nibbāna realised. We have made it clear that it is this basic difference regarding the self which largely governs the respective concepts of salvation in the B.G. and Buddhism, and is responsible for many of their differences.

(E) *The Realisation of Nibbāna in One's Life-time* :—

Notwithstanding this difference in approach and orientation to salvation, both Buddhism and the B.G. maintatin that it is a state realisable in one's life-time. Thus Buddha speaks of Nibbāna as "realisable in this life, immediate and inviting to come and see" (sandiṭṭhiko, akāliko, ehipassiko, D. II. 93, 217, 228; M.I. 265). On the attainment of Arahatship, the saint experiences the complete extinction of impurities and so the state is called kilesa-parinibbāna (Dh. A. I. 286; IV. 194). As the body of the liberated saint (Arahant) constituted of five aggregates (pañcakkhandha) still remains, this life-time liberation is also known as 'sa-upādi-sesa-nibbāna' (Dh. A.II. 163) in contradistinction to 'anupādi-sesa-nibbāna' (Dh. A. II. 163; D. III. 135; M. I. 148; Vin. II. 239) or 'khanda-parinibbana'. These, in fact, are not two different 'kinds of Nibbāna but the very same Nibbāna receiving two names according as it is experienced before and after death.

In the B.G. also these two phases of Nirvāṇa are clearly accepted. Referring to the state of supreme Peace (śāntim, B.G. II. 70, 71) attained by the perfected saint in his very life-time, the B.G. says: "This is the supreme state (Brāhmī sthitiḥ), O Partha (Arjuna), having attained which one is no more liable to be deluded. Having remained in this state, one even at the time of death attains supreme deliverance (Brahmanirvāṇam)"[1]. Śaṅkara commenting on this verse points out that one attains the second phase of Nirvāṇa at the expiry of his life-span (ante vayasi), and the first phase of Nirvāṇa is experienced by him so long as he lives (yāvaj jīvaṃ..Brahmaṇi eva avatiṣṭhate).[2] Radhakrishnan also in his note on this verse observevs: "Even while alive, the sage rests in Brahman, and is released from the unrest of the world."[3] There is no doubt about the fact that words like sthitaprajñaḥ, Brahmasthitaḥ, Brahmabhūtaḥ, ātmavantaḥ, tṛptātmā, yuktātmā, muktātmā, guṇātītaḥ etc. (cf. supra, 345-6) are synonymously used by the B.G. for the liberated saint in keeping with its metaphysical and theological views. In various ways it is pointed out that such a saint has attained liberation in his very life-time. Thus it is said: "Even here (in this world) they whose mind is established in equanimity have overcome the cycle of becoming..and, therefore, they are established in Brahman."[4] Nirvāṇa, consisting as it does in the self-realisation or the knowledge of the Supreme (Brahma), is said to be attained as soon as this knowledge arises. Thus like the famous utterance of the Muṇḍaka (Brahma veda Brahmaiva bhavati, III. 2.9), the B.G. also declares: "The knower of Brahman is established in Brahman" (Brahmavid Brahmaṇi sthitaḥ, V. 20). "To the Knower of the self, Nirvāṇa is present all around" (abhito Brahmanirvāṇaṃ vartate viditātmanām. V. 26). "He is ever free who has cast away desire, fear and anger" (vigatecchābhayakrodho yaḥ sadā mukta eva saḥ, V. 28). He has attained blessedness before giving up his body (prāk śarīravimokṣaṇāt..sa sukhī naraḥ, V. 23). Thus both Buddhism and the B.G. consider Nirvāṇa as a reality attainable here and now in this very life.

(F) *The life and Behaviour of the Liberated Saint* :—

Not only do they agree in considering Nirvāṇa as a

1. B.G. II. 72.
2. S.B.G. II. 72.
3. The Bhagavadgītā, p. 130.
4. B G. V. 19. See also B.G.V. 21, 24, 25; XIII. 30.

state realisable in one's life-time, but they also give a somewhat similar description of the life and behaviour of the liberated saint, though the description of B.G. has a metaphysical and theological colour and it lays special emphasis on its doctrine of disinterested action (niṣkāma karma). We may briefly point out here the striking similarities of their descriptions.

According to both Buddhism and the B.G., the liberated saint has altogether a changed perspective to life. Though, he is in the world, he is as it were completely cut off from it. The diverse vicissitudes of life no longer affect him and he remains absolutely calm and tranquil, utterly unperturbed and detached like a lotus leaf in water (vāri pokkharapatteva, Dh. 401; Sn. 117; cf. padmapattram ivā'mbhasā, B.G.V. 10). As he has accomplished whatever there is to accomplish, he has nothing else to desire for or aspire after.[1] The perfect equanimity which is to be realised by the liberated saint is well expressed in the following utterance of Buddha. "Coming in contact with the pleasant one should not rejoice nor should he feel aggrieved when touched by the unpleasant. Being indifferent to the pleasure and pain of these contacts, one should neither like nor abhor anything."[2] Overcoming both attachment and hatred, O monks, pass ye beyond the bounds of birth and death."[3] A similar description is found in the B.G. of the saint of steadfast wisdom (sthita prajña). It is said: "He whose mind is untroubled in sorrows and who is disinterested amidst pleasures, he, being free from attachment, fear and anger, is called a sage of settled wisdom. He who is without attachment on all sides, who neither welcomes nor abhors as he obtains good or evil, his wisdom is firmly

---

1. natthi kiccaṃ brāhmaṇassa katakicco hi brāhmaṇo, S.I. 47; kataṃ karaṇīyaṃ nāparaṃ itthattāyāti, M.I. 23; S I.V. 64-67; cf. nai'va tasya kṛtenā'rtho nā'kṛtene'ha kaścana, B.G. III. 18; tasya kāryaṃ na vidyate, B.G. III. 17.

2. Phassena phuṭṭho na sukhena majje dukkhena phuṭṭho pi na sampavedhe;
phassa dvayam sukhadukkhe upekho anānuruddho aviruddha kenaci, S. IV. 71.

3. te rāgadose abhibhuyya bhikkhavo bhavattha jātimaraṇassa pāragā'ti, S. IV. 71.

settled."[1] "One should neither be elated by getting the pleasant nor be depressed by obtaining the unpleasant."[2] Such a man of perfect self-control being free from attachment and hatred (rāgadveṣaviyuktaḥ) is said to reach the state of serenity.[3]

It is, no dout, true that the liberated saint also feels sensations like all other people, but the difference is that he is not affected by them. The entire outlook of the perfect saint is so disciplined that he acquires the power to neutralise the effect of the various sensory experiences. Thus, even when he is amidst them and apparently not free from them,he stands really as a free man towards them. He is no longer under the control of the senses; the senses are under his control. He does not, however, control the senses by stopping their operation forcefully. If the stopping of the operation of the senses were the mark of sense-control, then, as Buddha points out, "the blind and deaf ought to be treated as men of sense-control" (andho... badhiro bhāvitindriyo bhavissati. M. III. 298). He explains to Ānanda the way in which a true saint controls his senses. He says: "How, Ānanda, may a noble one dominate his senses? There, Ānanda, the monk has seen a form with his eye,...has heard a sound with the ear,..has smelt an odour with the nose,..has tasted a flavour with the tongue,..has touched something tangible with the body,..has thought an idea with the mind, and thus he is moved pleasantly, unpleasantly and partly pleasantly and unpleasantly. And he wishes: 'the repugnant I will perceive unrepugnant' and there he perceives unrepugnant. He wishes: 'the repugnant I will perceive repugnant' and there he perceives repugnant. He wishes: 'the partly repugnant and partly unrepugnant I will perceive unrepugnant' and there he perceives unrepugnant. He wishes: 'the repugnant and the unrepugnant both I will banish from me and I will remain detached, thoughtful and clearly consious' and there he becomes detached thoughtful and

1. B.G. II. 56-57.
2. Na prahṛṣyet priyaṃ prāpya no'dvijet prāpya cā'priyam, B.G.V. 20. cf. B.G. II. 38; XII. 15, 17; XVIII. 10.
3. B.G. II. 64.

clearly conscious. Thus, Ānanda, does a saint dominate his senses."[1]

In the B.G. also, in a somewhat similar way, the idea of stifling the senses is deprecated, and it is pointed out how by being free from attachment and hatred the perfect saint endowed with true knowledge remains even-minded and detached, even while letting his senses function in a natural way. It is said : "Even the man of wisdom, acts in accordance with his own nature. Beings follow their nature. What can repression accomplish ? Every sense is linked with attachment and hatred in relation to its object. One should not come under their sway, for they are his waylayers."[2] Thus, the B.G. also teaches sense-control and detachment, not by stopping the operation of the sense-organs, but by giving up all attachment and hatred in relation to the sense-experience. Like Buddhism, it also refers to the detached and disinterested attitude of the accomplished saint towards the operation of the senses, though unlike Buddhism, it brings in its metaphysical concept of the non-agency and unchangeability of the self for the purpose. Thus it says : "The man of unified vision, the knower of the truth (tattvavit) thinks while seeing, hearing, touching, smelling, tasting...that only the senses are operating with the sense-objects and 'I do nothing at all.' "[3] Thus, except for its metaphysical orientation, it also gives a similar description of the detached outlook and behaviour of the liberated saint.

As a result of this utterly detached or disinterested outlook, the liberated saints are endowed with the capacity of extreme endurance. As Buddha himself says : "The monk is an endurer of cold, heat, hunger, thirst, wind, rain and biting of mosquitoes, wasps, crawling creatures and snakes. He tolerates ill-spoken abusive words and patiently endures the arising of the painful feeling of the body, violent, harsh, piercing, disagreeable, tedious and causing death-like pain."'[4]

---

1. M. III. 301-2.
2. B.G. III. 33 & 34.
3. B.G.V. 8 & 9.
4. M. III. 137.

In the B.G. also, the reference to this idea is found. Kṛṣṇa says : "Contacts with objects, O Arjuna, give rise to cold and heat, pleasure and pain. They come and go and are transitory. Endure them, O Arjuna. The man who is not troubled by these, who remains alike in pain and pleasure, such a man of endurance is fit for the immortal state."[1] To be free from the affliction of the pairs of opposites is considered an important feature of the liberated saint (nirdvandvo, B.G. II. 45; dvandvātīto, B.G. IV. 22; dvandvair vimuktāḥ, B.G. XV. 5).

In view of his equanimity, detachment and perfect endurance, the accomplished saint treats all impartially showing no ill-will or disfavour to anyone. As Buddha referring to his own self says : "Those who cause me pain and those who cause me pleasure, towards all of them I behave in the same way; affection or aversion I know not. In joy and sorrow I remain unmoved; in honour and dishonour, everywhere I am the same. This is the perfection of my equanimity."[2] In the B.G. also we find a number of verses teaching this equanimity to all. Kṛṣṇa says : "He who is equal-minded among companions, friends and foes, among those who are neutral and impartial, among the jealous and well-wishers, among saints and sinners, he is excellent."[3] "He is equal to friend and foe, the same in honour and dishonour and alike in cold and heat, pleasure and pain and absolutely free from attachment."[4] The attitude of equality and utter disinterestedness is frequently emphasised in the B.G. (XIV. 24-25; XII. 13, 15-17, 19; IV. 22; V. 25, 26) and equal treatment to the entire sentient creation is said to be the mark of the truly wise. It says : "Men of wisdom see with equal eye, a learned and humble Brahmin, a cow, an elephant and even a dog and one who cooks dogs (an outcast)."[5]

Thus the utter detachment, perfect equanimity, extreme

---

1. B.G. II. 14 & 15.
2. Cariyāpitaka, 102.
3. B.G. VI. 9.
4. B.G. XII. 12.
5. B.G.V. 18.

endurance and absolute impartiality are considered to be the chief characteristic marks of the liberated saint both in Buddhism and the B.G.

The B.G., however, does not seem to be quite strict and consistent in upholding this view, since it vouchsafes the possibility of fighting with equanimity. Its central teaching, viz., the doctrine of disinterested action or 'karmayoga' is said to consist in equanimity (samatvaṃ yoga ucyate, B.G. II. 48) and the B.G. thinks that it is possible to fight enemies with equanimity. Thus, Arjuna is told : "Treating alike pleasure and pain, gain and loss, victory and defeat, get ready for the battle. Thus you shall not incur sin."[1] But in Buddhism, as we shall see in the next chapter on Ethics, this teaching of perfect equanimity and endurance is not compatible with warfare. This difference seems to indicate that in the B.G. the teaching of detachment is not as thorough and perfect as it is in Buddhism. The same conclusion we have arrived at in the course of our discussion about their respective attitudes to the self (supra, pp. 328-333). The B.G. shows a pronounced preference for the life of a householder as against the Buddhist preference for the life of a mendicant, and this also must have influenced their views in this respect. In any case, the general statement of Radhakrishnan that "in the descriptions of the ideal man the Gītā and Buddhism agree,"[2] must be qualified by the considerations that the B.G., unlike Buddhism, sanctions disinterested fighting in the event of aggression by the enemy, and further justifies its position on unverified and unverifiable metaphysical presuppositions.

The Problem of Rebirth:—

With regard to the problem of rebirth, the B.G. and Buddhism are found to have much in common, yet their positions are well-differentiated on account of the basic belief of the B.G. in a metaphysical self and its theological faith in a gracious God.

1. B.G. II. 38.
2. Indian Philosophy, Vol. I, p. 527.

(A) *The Karmic Forces Responsible for the Recurrence of Rebirth* :—

In general, both the B.G. and Buddhism agree that beings are born again and again in different spheres of life driven by their karmic forces. As long as these karmic forces operate the chain of rebirth continues. The physical death, therefore, does dot imply a gap or break in the perpetual flux of life. Like many other events of the present life, death also is a normal event in the continuous stream of life flowing down since a time the beginning of which is not known (anamataggo'yaṃ...saṃsāro, pubbā koti na paññāyati ...sattānaṃ...sandhāvataṃ saṃsarataṃ, S. II. 178-180). Speaking of death and rebirth as normal features of life, the B.G. says : "Just as the self passes in this body through childhood, youth and old age, so also is the passing on to another body."[1] The successive process of birth and death is incessantly and inevitably flowing on in this world.[2]

Usually one looks upon death as the annihilation of the world for oneself and, therefore, one desires to prolong the duration of one's stay in the world as much as possible. One does not realise that life is assured to everyone so long as one only wills for it. The real problem as George Grimm aptly puts it "is not how to remain in the world as long as possible, but how to escape from it as soon as practicable."[3] This position is accepted in common by both Buddhism and the B.G.

(B) *Ignorance and Desire Feeding the Karmic Forces*:—

Karmic forces leading to the cycle of birth and rebirth are generated by ignorance and the consequent craving or desire for worldly objects. This is what Buddha points out when he speaks of beings being reborn for an inconceivable length of time owing to the veil of ignorance and the fetter of craving.[4] We have already noted (supra. pp. 346-7;

---

1. B.G. II. 13.
2. B.G. II. 27.
3. The Doctrine of the Buddha, p. 255.
4. pubbā koti na paññāyati *avijjānīvaraṇānam* sattānaṃ *taṇhāsaṃyojanānaṃ* sandhāvataṃ saṃsaratam, S. II. 178-180.

349-350) that the B.G. also like Buddhism regards ignorance and desire as the cause of deluded actions which are responsible for the continued chain of existence.[1] Thus, according to both of them, it is ignorance resulting into craving or desire which leads to clinging and the consequent chain of becoming. Both of them, therefore, lay great emphasis on the attainment of true knowledge and the destruction of craving or desire. Buddha claims final release from the chain of rebirth (khiṇā jāti...M.I. 249; ayam antimā jāti, natthi dāni punabbhavo'ti, M.I. 167) only when ignorance is destroyed and knowledge has arisen (avijjā vihatā, vijjā uppannā, M.I. 249; ñāṇañ ca pana me dassanaṃ udapādi, M.I. 167). He clearly points out that "one is entangled in the world on account of desire and it is by overcoming desire that one is liberated."[2] "By destruction of craving all bondage is cut off."[3] In the B.G. also, in many and varied ways, the same attainment of knowledge and destruction of desire are emphasised for the same reason. Kṛṣṇa says : "You shall cross over all sins by the boat of knowledge alone...the fire of knowledge turns all karmas to ashes...having attained knowledge, one at once reaches the supreme Peace."[4] It is also said : "He who abandons all desires and acts free from longing, without any conceit of 'I' or 'mine', attains Peace."[5] From all this it is evident that Buddhism and the B.G. broadly agree with regard to the general cause of rebirth.

(C) A Comparative Account of the Mechanism of the Process of Rebirth:—

Notwithstanding this similarity, it is important to note one difference even with regard to this general agreement concerning the cause of rebirth. According to Buddhism karma is the sole controlling factor in rebirth and there is

1. ajñānenā'vṛtaṃ jñānaṃ tena muhyanti jantavaḥ, B.G.V. 15; āvṛtaṃ jñānam etena. . .kāmarūpeṇa. . .,B.G. III. 39; icchādveṣasamutthena. . .saṃmoham sarge yānti paraṃtapa, B.G. VII 27.

2. icchāya bajjhatī loko, icchāvinayāyā muccati, S.I. 40.

3. tanhāya vippahānena sabbaṃ chindati bandhanaṃ, S.I. 40.

4. B.G. IV. 36, 37 and 39.

5. B.G. II, 71; cf. II. 55.

no supernatural interference whatsoever. It declares without any reservation: "By karma revolves the world, by karma revolves mankind. Like the nail holding the rolling chariot-wheel, beings are held by karma."[1] Beings, O monks, are responsible for their deeds, are heirs to deeds, having deeds for matrix, deeds for kin, deeds for refuge. Whatsoever deed they do, be it good or evil, they become its heir."[2] It is, therefore, proclaimed in the Dhammapada: "Neither in the sky nor in mid-ocean, nor by entering the mountain-cave can be found a place in the universe where having stationed, one may escape one's evil deeds."[3] The B.G. also, no doubt, believes in the karma-theory, imparts teaching about right, wrong and neutral deeds (karmaṇah, vikarmaṇaḥ and akarmaṇaḥ, B. G. IV. 17) and speaks of the intricate working of the karma (gahanā karmaṇo gatiḥ, loc. cit.). It, nevertheless, introduces God, the supreme lord, creator, controller and supporter[4] who promises to free his devotees from all sins[5], secure all attainment and safety to them[6] and take even the man of most vile conduct to the highest goal.[7] One wonders how the strict law of karma can be made compatible with the belief in a gracious God. The B. G., however, as already pointed out (supra. pp. 190-191) seems anxious to suggest a way out of this difficulty. It intends to emphasise that the true devotion to God is itself a righteous action, for the mind of an exclusively devoted (ananyabhāk, B. G. IX. 30) person is rightly concentrated (samyag vyavasito, loc. cit.), and thus by his intense

---

1. Kammunā vattati loko, kammunā vattati pajā
kamma nibandhanā sattā rathassāṇīva yāyato., Sn. 120.

2. Kammassakā, bhikkhave, sattā, kammadāyādā,
kammayonī, kammabandhū, kammapaṭisaraṇā; yaṃ kammam
karonti, kalyāṇaṃ vā pāpakaṃ vā, tassa dāyādā bhavanti, A.V. 288.

3. Dh. 127.

4. Pitā'ham asya jagato. . .,B.G. IX. 17; Gatir bhartā prabhuḥ sākṣī. . .B·G. IX. 18.

5. ahaṃ tvā sarvapāpebhyo mokṣayiṣyāmi mā śucaḥ., B.G. XVIII. 66.

6. teṣāṃ nityābhiyuktānāṃ yogakṣemaṃ vahāmy aham, B.G. IX. 22

7. Api cet sudurācāro. . .;ye'pi syuḥ pāpayonayaḥ. . .te'pi yānti parāṃ gatim, B.G. IX. 30-32.

devotion, he is supposed to convert himself soon into a virtuous man and realise the supreme peace by virtue of his own noble deed.[1] It is further pointed out that God is only an impartial regulator of the karmic-process. The law of karma is only the manifestation of the nature of God which operates without favour or disfavour. Kṛṣṇa says: "The Lord does not create agency or actions of the people nor does he bring about connection between action and the fruit. It is only nature which operates. The all-pervading God, (therefore), does not take on the sin or the merit of anyone."[2] He further says: "Actions do not defile me, nor do I have yearning for their fruit."[3] "I am seated as if indifferent and unattached in those actions."[4] "I am equal to all beings. None is hateful nor dear to me."[5] All this may or may not be a satisfactory solution of the problem created by the introduction of a gracious or merciful God, but at any rate there is no denying the fact that the B. G. makes a conscious effort to resolve this difficulty which Buddhism safely avoids by rejecting the concept of any such supreme controller or governor. In strict fidelity to the empirical appproach, Buddhism seeks to explain everything in terms of natural laws and principles without calling for any supernatural interference.

By far the most distinctive feature of the Buddhist concept of rebirth lies in its denial of the self which sharply distinguishes it from all traditional concepts of rebirth found in any other Indian system of thought. With the denial of the traditional self, the idea that a self transmigrates from life to life automatically falls to the ground. We may briefly notice here how Buddha explains the event of rebirth

---

1. Kṣipraṃ bhavati dharmātmā śaśvacchāntiṃ nigacchati., B.G. IX. 31.
2. Na kartṛtvaṃ na karmāṇi lokasya sṛjati prabhuḥ
na karmaphalasaṃyogaṃ svabhāvas tu pravartate.
Nā'datte kasyacit pāpaṃ na cai'va sukṛtaṃ vibhuḥ, B.G.V.14-15.
3. Na māṃ karmāṇi limpanti, na me karmaphale spṛhā., B.G. IV. 14.
4. udāsīnavad āsīnam asaktaṃ taṣu karmasu., B.G. IX. 9.
5. Samo'haṃ sarvabhūteṣu na me dveṣyo'sti na priyaḥ., B.G. IX. 29.

in contradistinction to the traditional view represented by the B. G.

Buddha claims to base his theory of rebirth on his direct paranormal knowledge. In the course of his resolute pursuit for perfect enlightenment, he at last attained the threefold higher knowledge (tevijjā) during the three watches of one particular night.[1] The first of these three forms of higher knowledge known as 'pubbenivāsānussatiñāṇa' (retrocognitive knowledge) is said to have afforded him a clear recollection of his innumerable past lives. He then knew through his direct knowledge that rebirth is a fact. But he could not as yet realise the exact mechanism of the process of rebirth. It is only when he attained the second of the three higher knowledge known as 'dibbacakkhu' (clairvoyance) or cutūpapātañāṇa (knowledge of the decease and survival of beings) that he saw "through his clear paranormal clairvoyant vision, beings dying and being reborn, low and high, the fair and the ugly, the good and the evil, each according to his karma"[2] and, thus, realised the mechanism of the process of rebirth. He could have a clear and direct vision as to how through the instrumentality of karmic forces fed by ignorance and craving beings are born again and again after death. Thereafter he had the final realisation of the truth as to how these defilements could be destroyed (āsavakkhayañāṇa) and the process of rebirth could be stopped once for all.

The B. G. also evokes the support of direct supernormal experience for its theory of rebirth, but this theory is remarkably different from that of Buddhism. Asserting the fact of rebirth, Kṛṣṇa says: "Many are the lives that are past of mine and thine, O Arjuna. All of them I know, though thou knowest not, O Arjuna."[3] Upto this point the B. G. and Buddhism are in agreement. But the process of transmigration of the self is also claimed by the B. G. to be directly perceived through the eye of wisdom

1. M.I. 248-9.
2. M.I. 248.
3. B.G. IV. 5.

(jñānacakṣuṣā) and it is here that the B. G. differs from Buddhism. The B. G. says: "The deluded ones do not see its passing out, staying in or experiencing, in contact with the modes (guṇas); but those who have the eye of wisdom see it."[1] Thus the migration of the embodied self or its passing from one body to another is claimed by the B. G. to be a fact directly witnessed by the seers. Elaborating the same idea through a simile, the B. G. says: "Just as a person casts off worn out garments and puts on others that are new, even so does the embodied self cast off worn-out bodies and take on others that are new."[2]

This poetic expression of the migrating self is nothing but a reaffirmation of the old traditional idea that we come across in the Ups. and the Saṅkhya school of thought. In the Bṛhadāraṇyaka, for example, it is said:"Just as a leech after having come to the end of a blade of grass, and having made an approach to another, contracts itself, so also does the self, after having thrown away this body and having approached another, withdraw itself (from the previous body)."[3] In the Sāṅkhya also this idea of transmigration is clearly accepted.[4] The true self being regarded as all-pervasive (sarvagataḥ, B. G. II. 45; XIII. 32), unmoving (sthāṇur, acalo, B. G. II. 24), unchanging (avyayaḥ, B. G. II. 17, 21) unborn and undying (na jāyate mriyate va, B. G. II. 20; ajaḥ, avināśi, B. G. II. 17-21), the transmigration is ascribed to the empirical self which owing to its association with the modes of Prakṛti appears in the form of an embodied self (jivabhūtaḥ, B. G. XV. 7). Thus, according to the traditional philosophy of the Ups., the Saṅkhya and the B. G., when a man of non-discriminative knowledge dies, only the gross component parts of his personality are dissolved. Of the twenty-three total evolutes of Prakṛti, as enumerated in Sāṅkhya, and accepted in the B. G. (XIII. 5), only the five

1. B.G. XV. 10.
2. B.G. II. 22.
3. Bṛhadā. IV. 4. 3.
4. Sāṅkhyakārikā 40 and 41.

gross elements are said to be dissolved after death. The remaining eighteen elements (intellect, egotism, eleven indriyas and five subtle elements) technically known as the subtle body (sūkṣma or liṅga śarīra) persist even after death and pass away from the dying body to a new body. This is how transmigration is generally understood in the traditional thought. But, when the perfect discriminative knowledge is attained and the true nature of Puruṣa as distinct from Prakṛti is realised, then there takes place the total dissolution of all the elements of Prakṛti which is known as mokṣa or kaivalya (emancipation), the absolute deliverance from the process of rebirth.[1]

It is not difficult to see that the same idea of transmigration is accepted in the Ups. as well as the B. G. with slight adjustments and modifications. The Bṛhadāraṇyaka, while referring to the migrating self, speaks of its association with the five subtle elements, the senses, the mind and the intellect and also refers to its being accompanied by the vital breaths as well as the meritorious and demeritorious actions.[2] The Sāṅkhya, however, does not make separate mention of the vital breaths and the meritorious and demeritorious actions, since according to it the vital breaths (prāṇāḥ) are said to be operated by the three internal instruments (antaḥkaraṇāḥ), viz., the intellect, ahaṅkāra and mind, and all actions whether meritorious or demeritorious are said to be performed through the intellect assisted by the senses.[3] Thus they are supposed to be included within the eighteen elements constituting the subtle body. The same Sāṅkhya idea of the subtle-body, as described in Sāṅkhyakārikā, 40 (mahadādi sūkṣmaparyantam...), occurs in similar terms in the Maitrī (mahadādyaṃ viśeṣāntam.., VI. 10), supposedly a later Upaniṣad. The transmigration is accounted for by the Bṛhadāraṇyaka in terms of the desire of man. It says: "The object to which the mind is attached,

1. B.G. XIII. 34. cf. Sāṅkhyakārikā, 64.
2. Bṛhadā. IV. 4.5.
3. Sāṅkhyakārikā, 35-37.

the subtle self goes together with the deed, being attached to it alone...This is so for the man who desires. But the man who does not desire, who is without desire, who is free from desire, whose desire is satisfied, whose desire is fulfilled in the self, his breaths do not depart. Being Brahman he goes to Brahman."[1]

The same idea is asserted in a condensed form in the B. G. where Kṛṣṇa says: "It is my own eternal fragment[2] which appearing in the world of beings as embodied self[3] draws the senses together with the mind as the sixth, which lay there in Prakṛti. When the self departs from a body and assumes another, it goes taking away these (senses) just as the wind carries away smells from their abodes."[4] Thus the old idea of the Ups. and the Sāṅkhya, that the embodied self in association with the subtle elements migrates from the dying body to a new body is upheld by the B. G. The only difference that can be noticed is that in place of eighteen elements comprising the subtle body (sūkṣma or liṅga śarīra), the B. G. refers only to six. But this does not make much difference so far as the general theory is concerned. Morever, it appears quite plausible to accept the suggestion of B. G. Tilak[5] according to which the six elements of the B. G. really imply all the eighteen elements that are traditionally believed to constitute the subtle body. A synoptic description is not an uncommon feature of the B. G.. We have already shown (supra, pp. 117-119) how the Sāṅkhya enumeration of the twentyfour elements

1. Bṛhadā. IV. 4.6.

2. The word 'aṃśa' (fragment or fraction) in relation to the indivisible and partless supreme is to be understood in the sense of a limited manifestation of the one all-pervasive Reality. It is like the apparent limitation of the all-pervasive space in a jar or a house. The B.G. itself suggests this idea in XIII. 32. Śaṅkara supports this interpretation in full. He says: "yathā vā ghaṭādyupādhiparicchinno ghaṭādyākāśa ākāśāṃśaḥ ...evam". S.B.G. XV. 7.

3. jīvabhūto—bhoktā kartā iti prasiddhaḥ, S.B.G. XV 7.
jivabhūtaḥ tu atisaṅkucitajñānaiśvaryaḥ, R.B.G. XV,7.

4. Mamai 'vā'ṃso jīvaloke jīvabhūtaḥ sanātanaḥ
manaḥṣaṣṭhānī' ndriyāni prakṛtisthāni karṣati
śarīraṃ yad avāpnoti yac cā'py utkrāmatī'śvaraḥ
gṛhitvai'tāni saṃyāti vāyur gandhān iva'śayāt., B.G. XV. 7 and 8.

5. Gitārahasya, p. 805.

excluding the Puruṣa is subsumed by the B. G. in the eightfold (aṣṭadhā) Prakṛti. It is, therefore, quite likely that in the present case also, all the eighteen elements might have been intended to be subsumed under the six elements. In view of several ideas being freely utilised by the B. G. from the Ups. and the Sāṅkhya, this difference cannot, at any rate, be taken to indicate a difference in theory.

Now, for the traditional thinkers working upon the theory of a static or changeless self, nothing perhaps could have been a better explanation of the event of rebirth than the theory of transmigration. But this static conception of a permanent and changeless self in man being rejected outright by Buddha, the process of rebirth finds a different explanation in Buddhism in the light of its dynamic conception of the world-process.

The individual, according to Buddha is a psycho-physical organism described as 'name and form' (nāma-rūpa). The former i.e., nāma is a complex composed of feeling and mental states, and the latter i.e., rūpa is the manifestation of different material forces and qualities. This entire psycho-physical organism is in perpetual flux like an ever-revolving wheel. Just as the running wheel rests on the ground only for a moment even so do we live for just one thought-moment. We are always in the present and this present is ever slipping into the irrevocable past. This dynamic Buddhist outlook contradicts the attitude of the B.G., according to which the persons who fail to perceive the migration of the indwelling (ātmany avasthitam, B.G. XV. 11) and changeless (avyayam, B.G. II. 21) self are to be branded as deluded (vimūḍhāḥ)[1] and ignorant (acetaṣaḥ).[2]

The entire mechanism of the process of rebirth envisaged by Buddha can be understood empirically. When a man dies, his physical organism is dissolved but the flux of the psychical stream goes on to form a new conglomeration, since the ignorance and craving which feed the karmic forces have not been destroyed. Impelled by the karmic

1. vimūdhā nā'nupaśyanti, B.G. XV. 10.
2. nai'naṃ paśyanty acetasaḥ., B.G. XV. 11.

forces, the last moment of the series of psychical states finds a new matrix suited to it. Evidently, it is not some identical entity (the soul) which passes from one to another place but the ever-changing forces which disappear in one state and appear in another. This renewed state is the result of the preceding state and so it inherits the character of its predecessor. Thus there is nothing identical or lasting in the being which is reborn, yet there is continuity of character. The whole process is to be understood in the light of the Buddhist theory of Paṭiccasamuppāda. When the monk, Sāti, not understanding this ever-revolving process puts forward his erroneous view that it is this very consciousness that runs on, fares on as non-different (tadevidaṃ viññāṇaṃ sandhāvati saṃsarati anaññan'ti., M. I. 256), he is at once admonished by Buddha. The latter then explains the theory of Paṭiccasamuppāda (dependent origination) at a great length and shows how the ever-changing process goes on producing different states one after another. The consciousness (viññāṇa) which is said to form the psycho-physical organism (nāma-rūpa) is itself the result of the preceding state known as 'conative dispositions' (saṅkhāra) which in its turn is rooted in ignorance (avijjā). It is in the light of this ever-revolving process that Buddha's statements like, "due to the growth of consciousness (viññāṇa) the coming rebirth-formation takes place"[1], "the food of consciousness is the cause of the coming rebirth-formation"[2], "it is the psychic state which runs on"[3] etc., have to be understood.

It is in this sense that the last thought-moment of the dying creature in the form of what is known as 'gandhabba' is said to vitalize the combination of the sperm and ovum of the parents and give rise to a renewed existence. Thus, accounting for the event of rebirth, Buddha says: "Where, monks, three are found in combination, there a seed of life is planted. Thus, if a father and mother come together, but it is not the mother's period, and the being to be born

1. viññāṇe virūḷhe āyatiṃ punabbhavābhinibbatti hoti, S.II. 65.
2. viññāṇāhāro āyatiṃ punabbhavābhinibbattiyā paccayo, S.II.13.
3. cittam assa vidhāvati, S.I.37.

(gandhabba) is not present, then no seed of life is planted. Or, if father and mother come together, and it is the mother's period, but the being to be born is not present, then again no seed of life is planted. But when, monks, a father and mother come together, and it is the mother's period, and the being to be born is also present, then by the combined agency of these three, a seed of life is planted."[1]

The use of the word 'gandhabba' by Buddha has tempted some scholars to read into it the affirmation of the traditional concept of the subtle body (sūkṣma śarīra). Referring to the view of Sarvāstivādins, Keith observes "that the intermediate being must be treated as quasi-material, with a transporting (ātivāhika) body, analogous to the subtle body of the Sāṅkhya".[2] Mrs. Rhys Davids goes still further in indentifying the gandhabba with the subtle body and says: "In this tradition (i. e. of gandhabba) I see the advent of the soul, self or man, encased in the invisible 'subtle body' of Indian belief, into the mother in the fifth month of foetal life."[3] Such interpretation, it goes without saying, amounts to falling back on the old traditional ideas of the self and its transmigration. Professor Wijesekera, after discussing the problem at a great length, has ably shown that the term gandhabba is used by Buddha only "to denote a particular state of saṃsāric consciousness"[4] (viññāṇa). "This saṃsāric viññāṇa is no other than the 'stream of consciousness' (viññāṇasota) extending into both wolrds[5], called also

---

1. M.I. 265-6; cf. M.II. 157.

2. Buddhist Philosophy, p. 207.

3. The Birth of Indian Psychology and its Development in Buddhism p. 250; cf. Indian Religion and Survival—Mrs. Rhys Davids, p. 63. It may be noted that the gandhabba of the Majjhima Nikaya is said to enter the womb at the very moment of coitus and does not wait till the fifth month of foetal life, which goes against the identification of gandhabba and the self.

4. Vedic Gandharva and Pali Gandhabba, U.C.R., Vol. III. No. I. p. 95.

5. Atikkamma ca purisassa chavimaṃ salohitaṃ aṭṭhim paccavekkhati purisassa ca viññāṇasotaṃ pajānāti ubhayato abbocchinnaṃ idhaloke patiṭṭhitañ ca paraloke patiṭṭhitañ ca, D. III. 105.

'bhava-sota'[1] or 'stream of becoming', implying constant change."[2] It is this stream of consciousness which, in the Majjhima Nikāya (II. 262 ff), is technically called 'saṃvattanika viññāṇa' or 'the consciousness that evolves (into the next world)' and for which the term 'paṭisandhi viññāṇa' is substituted in the scholastic period (P. T. S. Dictionary).

Thus the difference of the Buddhist view of rebirth from that of the B. G. consists in the fact that the former (a) abandons the traditional concept of a permanent self and dissolves static entities into dynamic processes; and (b) gives an empirical account of the processes of rebirth in place of a mysterious metaphysical explanation offered by the B. G. But in other respects, as already pointed out, they are quite in agreement. They (a) assert the validity of rebirth on the basis of paranormal experience and (b) hold in common that karma is responsible for the event of rebirth which in turn is due to ignorance and desire.

(D) *The Psychic Body (Manomayaṃ Kāyaṃ) of Buddhism and the Migrating Subtle Body (Sūkṣma Śarīra) of the B.G.* :—

In this connection we wish to put forward a suggestion which appears as a further point of approximate agreement between Buddhism and the B.G. We are inclined to think that the claim of the B. G. of having a yogic perception of indwelling self is acceptable to Buddhism as well, though the former gives a different orientation and evaluation of it. According to the Sāmaññaphala Sutta, after the fourth stage of meditation, a monk is said to have a clear observation of his consciousness, as different from his body, but enveloped and bound by it (so evaṃ pajānāti: ayaṃ kho me kāyo rūpī cātumahābhūtiko idañca pana me viññāṇaṃ ettha sitam ettha paṭibaddhanti, D.I. 76-77). He is then said to develop a psychic body, having form and endowed with all senses and faculties (so imamhā kāyā aññaṃ kāyaṃ abhinimmināti, rūpiṃ manomayaṃ sabbaṅgapaccaṅgiṃ ahīnindriyaṃ, D.I. 77).

1. S. IV. 291.

2. Vedic Gandharva and Pali Gandhabba, U.C.R. Vol. III, No. I, p. 93.

This psychic body (manomayaṃ kāyaṃ, loc. cit) is distinguished from the gross physical body as clearly as the reed from the muñja grass (seyyathāpi muñjamhā isīkaṃ pavāheyya.. ayaṃ muñjo, ayaṃ isīkā, añño muñjo aññā isīkā..evaṃ eva, loc. cit.). It is only after the development of this psychic body that one is said to attain the psychokinetic powers, e. g. moving unobstructed anywhere and everywhere, reaching the sun and the moon and the world of Brahmā etc.[1]

Now this Buddhist concept of the inner consciousness associated with the body seems to correspond roughly to the embodied inner self (jīvātmā or antarātmā) of the Ups. and the B.G., and its concept of the psychic body (manomayam kāyaṃ) endowed with all senses appears to be somewhat similar to the migrating subtle body (sūkṣma śarīra or liṅga śarīra) of the latter. The Ups. and the B.G., perhaps, mistook the observation of consciousness on the part of the yogin as the vision of the self and further, due to the lack of a dynamic conception of the world-process, considered the psychic body as an entity migrating from body to body. It is interesting to note that in the Kaṭhopaniṣad, from which, indeed, very many ideas and even some of the verses are taken *verbatim* by the B.G., a clear reference to this inner self is made with the same simile of the reed and the muñja grass, which is found in the Pali Canon. The verse reads as follows : "The puruṣa of the size of a thumb, the inner self abides always in the hearts of men. Him one should draw out with firmness from the body, like the reed from the muñja grass. Him one should know as the pure, the immortal."[2] The same is described as the migrating self by the MB. which refers to the taking out of the Self of Satyavān by Yama, the king of death. It Says : "Yama drew out forcibly the Puruṣa (Self) of the size of a thumb."[3] The B.G. also refers perhaps to a

1. D.I. 77-78.
2. Aṅguṣṭhamātraḥ puruṣo'ntarātmā sadā janānāṃ hṛdaye sanniviṣṭaḥ;
taṃ svāc charīrāt pravṛhen muñjād iveṣīkāṃ dhairyeṇa;
taṃ vidyāc chukram amṛtaṃ taṃ vidyāc chukram amṛtam iti, Katha. VI. 17.
3. Aṅguṣṭhamātraṃ puruṣaṃ niścakarṣa yamo balāt, M.B., Vana Parva, 296. 16.

similar indwelling inner self which is said to be perceived by the presevering yogins[1] and the migration of which is claimed to be seen through the eye of wisdom.[2]

The Problem of the World :—

We have seen (supra, pp. 294-5) that of the ten unanswered (abyākata) metaphysical questions, the first four, which pertained to the duration and extent of the world, were set aside primarily on account of their intellectual incomprehensibility. But in spite of avoiding vain speculations about the ultimate origin and the limit of the universe, the Pali texts do not lose sight of the vastness of space and the immensity of time. We find Buddha occasionally indicating the utter insignificance of the span of human life and of the position of human beings in the vast universe by pointing out the immensity of cosmic time and space. In the B.G. also, though the cosmological discussions are not directly taken up, we find some significant references to the duration of the universe. Regarding the extent of the universe, however, the B.G. provides very little information and we have largely to depend on a few words of doubtful connotation. Its answer to the question of the universe is purely metaphysical. It is, however, interesting to note that some of the views of Buddhism and the B.G. compare favourably with modern astronomical findings.

(A) *The Extent of the Universe* :—

According to Buddhist cosmology, the human world of of ours forms a very insignificant part of the vastness of cosmic space containing innumerable worlds within it. It is said : "As far as these suns and moons revolve, shedding their light in space, so far extends the thousandfold universe. In it there are a thousand suns (sahassaṃ suriyānaṃ), a thousand moons, thousands of inhabited regions with diverse

1. Yatanto yoginaś cai'naṃ paśyanty ātmany avasthitam, B.G. XV. 11.

2. Utkrāmantaṃ sthitaṃ vā'pi...paśyanti jñānacakṣuṣaḥ, B.G. XV. 10.

social orders...thousands of heavenly worlds of varying grades. This is the thousandfold minor world-system (Cūḷanikā lokadhātu). A thousand times the size of the thousandfold minor world system is the twice-a-thousand middling world-system (Majjhimikā lokadhātu). A thousand times the size of the middling world-system is the thrice-a-thousand major world-system (Mahā lokadhātu)".[1] This description appears stupendous, but those conversant with modern astronomical research will observe how it bears a resemblance to the modern conception of the universe. We may here take the liberty of quoting a few observations of A.C.B. Lovell, Professor of Radio Astronomy in the University of Manchester and Director of the Jodrell Bank Experimental Station. He says : "We live on one of the smaller planets of a typical star. Our solar system is minute by cosmic standards...Not only are we cosmically small, we are in a rather undignified position amongst the stars of the Milky Way. Our telescopes of the twentieth century have shown that the Milky Way contains about ten thousand million stars...This Milky Way is itself only a local galactic system..Wherever we look in space we see these nebulae and within the region of the cosmos which we study with our modern telescopes they are almost countless — certainly thousands of millions and probably billions — all stellar systems made up of thousands of millions of stars...The galaxies exist in great groups of clusters. In the same way that the earth and planets are bound to the sun and move as a unit through space, so on an inconceivably vaster scale we think that the galaxies are contained in clusters as connected physical system."[2] Though present astronomical findings have not as yet been claimed as final, the representation of the universe containing galaxies and clusters of galaxies and the entire universe as consisting of innumerable clusters is comparable to what is described in the Buddhist texts as the minor world-system (Cūḷanikā lokadhātū or sahassī-lokadhātu) the middling world-system (Majjhimikā lokadhātu) and

1. A.I. 227-8.
2. The Individual and the Universe, pp.4-6.

the major world-system or the great cosmos (Mahā lokadhātu).

The above statement of Buddha is said to be based on his clear paranormal observation and not on any imaginary speculation. Even Anuruddha, one of his disciples claims: "By virtue of cultivating and developing fourfold mindfulness, I know the thousandfold world (catunnaṃ satipaṭṭhānānaṃ bhāvitattā bahulīkatattā sahassaṃ lokaṃ abhijānāmī'ti, S,V. 299).

Various kinds of celestial abodes, strewn within the vast cosmos, differing from one another in glory and grandeur are spoken of.[1] It appears from the Brahmanimantanika Sutta (M.I. 326ff) that the great Brahmā (Mahā Brahmā) is the lord of the thousandfold world-system (sahassi lokadhātu) which is but another name for the minor world-system (Cūḷanikā lokadhātu). This is indicated from the identical description of the two.[2] Brahmās also are many and of different grades. We find mention of Brahmās as lords of one thousand, two thousand, three thousand, four thousand, five thousand, ten thousand and hundred thousand world-systems.[3] But even the highest Brahmā is within the range of time and is subject to rebirth. It is only on account of his limited knowledge that he considers himself to be the eternal and supreme lord.[4] It is pointed out that there are other worlds which are beyond the ken of Brahmā and of which he is utterly ignorant.[5]

Besides men, gods and Brahmās, there are numerous other varieties of beings. At times, some attempts are made to classify the vast range of beings from different standpoints. According to one such classification, there is a class of beings who are different and distinguishable from each other in mind

1. M.I. 289; III. 100-103.
2. The descriptions of the Brahmanimantanika Sutta (M.I. 328) and that of A. I. 227 both read as follows:—
"Yāvatā candimasuriyā pariharanti disā bhānti virocanā,
tāva sahassadhā loko."
3. M. III. 101-102.
4. D.I. 17-18; M. I. 326-9
5. Atthi kho Brahme aññe tayo kāyā tattha tvaṃ na jānāsi.
na passasi tyāhaṃ jānāmi passāmi .., M.I. 329

and body. The other class consists of those groups of beings who are different in body but one in mind. Still others are alike in body but different in mind, while there are some who are alike both in mind and body.[1] Then according to another classification, beings are grouped as the no-footed, the two-footed, the four-footed, the many-footed, those having or lacking material form, having or lacking consciousness and those without consciousness or unconsciousness.[2]

This vast span of the cosmos with its innumerable worlds and inconceivably wide varieties of beings is said to provide different grades of happiness and unhappiness, but one cannot attain the supreme blessedness or Nibbāna so long as one is bound within the spatio temporal universe. We have seen that Nibbāna is described as that "where the stars shine not nor does the sun shine. Neither is there the illumination of the moon nor is there any darkness."[3] It is a state of supramundane or signless consciousness, infinite and resplendent, where there is no penetration of earth, water, air or fire."[4] So in order to attain this highest state it is considered necessary to go beyond the spatio-temporal universe,but obviously not by means of physically traversing through it, which is simply an absurdity as well as impossibility. Buddha points out that even if a man endowed with supreme pace and speed (paramena javena ca samannāgatā paramena padavītihārena, A. IV.429) were to go across the universe with the speed of a shaft or storm, in spite of his continuous travel for a full span of a hundred years, he would not find the end of the universe but would die on the way. (vassasatāyuko vassasatajīvī vassasataṃ gantvā appatvā va lokassa antaṃ antarā kālaṃ kareyya, loc. cit.) Then he adds: Not by such journeying do I say that the end of the universe is to be known, seen or reached, and yet I do not maintain that without reaching the end of

1. A. IV. 39-40.
2. A. III. 35.
3. na tattha sukkā jotanti, ādicco na ppakāsati;
na tattha candimā bhāti tamo tattha na vijjati, Udāna. 9.
4. viññāṇaṃ anidassanaṃ anantaṃ sabbatopabhaṃ
ettha āpo ca pathavī tejo vāyo na gādhati., D.I. 223.

the universe there would be an end of suffering."[1]

The B.G., in spite of presenting the cosmic form (viśvarūpa, B.G.XI. 16) of Kṛṣṇa does not throw much light on the nature of this cosmos. It provides only a poetic and figurative depiction of the Cosmic Person rather than a realistic description of the cosmos. There is, however, no doubt about the fact that it conceives of the universe as boundless and infinite. In his cosmic state Kṛṣṇa is described as "infinite in form on all sides....without beginning, middle or end" (sarvato'nantarūpam, nā'ntaṃ na madhyaṃ na punas tavā'dim, B.G.XI. 16; anādimadhyāntam, B.G. XI.19). The entire universe with its vast space in all directions is said to be pervaded by this infinite form.[2] It is said to contain manifold divisions (pravibhaktaṃ anekadhā, B.G. XI. 13)—hundredfold, thousandfold (śataśo' tha sahasraśaḥ, B.G.XI.5) with the various gods, and with varied hosts of beings, Brahmā, Śiva, all the sages and heavenly nāgas.[3] Besides the hosts of gods (surasaṅghāḥ, B.G. XI. 21) and great saints and seers (maharṣi-siddhasaṅghāḥ, loc. cit.), we find various other celestial beings like the Rudras, the Ādityas, the Vasus the Sādhyas, the Viśvedevas, the Aśvins, the Maruts, the Manes and the hosts of Gandharvas, Yakṣas, Asuras and Siddhas.[4] They all seem to be located in various worlds, for it is said that the worshippers of the various gods (devavratāḥ), the manes (pitṛvratāḥ) and the spirits (bhūtejyāḥ) go to their respective abodes as a result of their worship.[5] Besides, we find separate mention of the earthly abode of man (mānuṣe loke, B.G. IV. 12; nṛloke, B.G. XI. 48) and the heavenly abode of Surendra (Surendra loke. B.G.IX.

1. Nā'haṃ...evarūpaya sandhāvanikāya lokassa antaṃ ñāteyyaṃ daṭṭhayyaṃ pattayyaṃ ti vadāmi, na cā'haṃ ...appatvā va lokassa antaṃ dukkhassa antakiriyaṃ vadāmi., A. IV. 430.
2. vyāptaṃ tvayai'kena diśaś ca sarvāḥ., B.G. XI. 20; tvayā tataṃ viśvam anantarūpa, B.G. XI. 38; sarvaṃ samāpnoṣi tato'si sarvaḥ., B.G. XI. 40; sarvam āvṛtya tiṣṭhati., B.G. XIII. 13.
3. B.G. XI. 15.
4. B.G. XI. 21 and 22.
5. B.G. IX. 25.

20) as well as of Brahmā (Brahma loka, VIII. 16), which indicates that these divisions most probably are meant to be taken as the different worlds of these beings. Reference to the three worlds (loka trayam, B.G. XI.20; XV. 17; I.35) is also made and this may correspond to the three world-systems of the Buddhist texts. The B.G., however, is not quite clear on this point. The classical commentaries also throw little light on the exact import of the word 'lokatrayam'. Śaṅkara, while commenting on the verse XI. 20, leaves this word unexplained and passes on by saying 'lokānāṃ trayaṃ, lokatrayam' (lokatraya—is the triad of worlds). Rāmānuja gives a queer explanation. He says that he means by 'lokatraya' the unfavourable, favourable and indifferent forms of beings from amongst Brahmā, etc., the gods, the demons, the Manes, the Siddhas, the Gandharvas, the Yakṣas and the Rākṣasas.[1] However, while commenting on the first line of the verse, he refers to the plurality of worlds situated in the space both above and below us[2] and speaks of "that space in which all worlds are located" (yasmin avakāśe sarve lokāḥ tiṣṭhanti, R.B.G.XI. 20). Some information is given by Śaṅkara when in the verse XV. 17 he comments on this word. Here he points out that the word 'lokatraya' means the three worlds known as Bhuḥ, Bhuvaḥ and Svaḥ.[3] But this interpretation does not seem to be convincing because these three are only the first three of the fourteen lokas referred to in the Vedantic literature.[4] Rāmānuja, giving the etymology of the word 'loka' says that whatever is observed is the 'loka' (lokyata iti lokaḥ, R.B.G. XV. 17) and takes the word 'lokatraya' to signify the three worlds comprising the unconscious (inanimate matter), conscious associated with the unconscious (animated matter) and

---

1. Brahmādi devā'sura-pitṛgaṇa-Siddha-gandharva-yakṣa-rākṣaseṣu pratikūlā'nukūla-madhyastharūpaṃ lokatrayam., R.B.G. XI. 20.

2. dyu-śabdaḥ pṛthivī-śabdas' ca ubhau uparitanānām adhastanānāṃ ca lokānāṃ pradarśanārthau., R.B.G. XI. 20.

3. lokatrayaṃ bhūrbhuvaḥsvarākhyam, S.B.G. XV. 17.

4. etebhyaḥ pañcīkṛtebhyo bhūtebhyo bhūr bhuvaḥ svar mahar janas tapaḥ satyam ity etan nāmakānām uparyupari vidyamānānām; atala vitala sutala rasātala talātala mahātala pātāl nāmakānām adho'dho vidyamānānāṃ lokānām...co'tpattir bhavati, Vedānta Sāra, p. 68; cf. Dasgupta-Indian Philosophy, Vol. II. p. 76.

the disembodied pure consciousness (liberated soul).[1] It is thus difficullt to determine what exactly is meant by this word. But in view of the fact that the B.G. itself on other occasions speaks of more than three worlds and refers to the divisions of cosmic form as manifold, hundredfold and thousandfold, it appears more plausible to hold that this word signifies three systems or groups of world rather than just three worlds.

Now, whatever be the range and pattern of the cosmos according to the B.G., it agrees with Buddhism at least in holding the view that the ultimate goal of man consists in going beyond the spatio-temporal universe. It speaks of that supra-cosmic goal "which is illumined neither by the sun nor by the moon nor by the fire and reaching which they do not return (to the world)."[2] On this point both the B.G. (XV.6) and Buddhism (Ud.9) are in agreement with the Upaniṣadic statement found in Muṇḍaka II.2. 10, Kaṭha V. 15 and Śvetā VI. 14. This vast universe along with Brahmā Śiva and the hosts of gods and saints (B.G. XI. 15, 21, 22), is considered by the B.G. as the manifestation of only a fraction of the Supreme,[3] and it is maintained, as in Buddhism, that the grades of existence upto the Brahma-loka are subject to the cycle of birth and death. Kṛṣṇa clearly points out: "Upto the realm of Brahmā, all worlds are subject to rebirth, only by reaching me, O Arjuna, is there no return to birth again."[4]

(B) *The Origin and Duration of the Universe* :—

As regards the origin and duration of the universe, it is pointed out by Buddha that the span of human life is insignificantly small in comparison with cosmic time. Through various analogies like those of the dew-drop, the water-bubble, the line drawn on water etc. the utterly insignificant and

---

1. lokatryam :—acetanaṃ, tat saṃsṛṣṭaḥ cetaro, muktaḥ ca iti, R. B.G. XV. 17.
2. Na tad bhāsayate sūryo na śaśāṅko na pāvakaḥ yadgatvā na nivartante..., B.G. XV. 6.
3. viṣṭabhyā'ham idaṃ kṛtsnam ekāṃśena sthito jagat, B.G.X. 42.
4. B.G. VIII. 16.

trifling nature of the span of human life is indicated.[1] The duration of the present universe which is incalculably long, is conceived in Buddhism as only a link in the inconceivably long chain of previous evolutions (vivaṭṭa) and dissolutions (saṃvaṭṭa). The time taken in the process of one evolution of the universe is immensely long and is known as a kappa (aeon). This kappa is so immeasurably long that Buddha does not speak of its length in terms of a hundred. thousand or even of hundreds of thousands of years. He says: "Long, indeed, O monk, is an aeon. It is not easy to count in terms of so many years,....so many hundred years,.....so many thousand years....and so many hundreds of thousand years."[2] He conveys its immense length by means of various similes. He says: "Suppose, monk, there were a great mountain, one yojana in length, one yojana in breadth and one yojana in height without chasms or clefts—a solid mass. And a man at the end of every hundred years were to rub it once each time with a Kāsi-cloth. Well, the mountain in this way would be sooner rubbed out and destroyed than an aeon. So long, monk, is an aeon."[3] Similarly he gives the analogy of a city of iron-walls (āyasa ṃnagaraṃ), one yojana in length, and the same in breadth and height, filled up to the top with mustard-seed from which one is to take out one seed at the end of every hundred years. The entire pile may thus be exhausted but not the aeon.[4]

It is further stated that innumerable such aeons have elapsed and it is difficult to reckon them. Again some analogies are given to convey the idea of innumerable aeons already past. Buddha says: "Suppose, monks, there were four disciples of a life-span of a hundred years, living here for a hundred years. They were to recollect everyday a hundred thousand aeons. Thus recollecting aeons, the four disciples of a hundred years' life-span, living for a hundred years may die without

---

1. ussāvabindūpamaṃ...udakabubbuḷūpamaṃ...daṇḍarājūpamaṃ jīvitaṃ manussānaṃ parittaṃ lahukaṃ., A. IV. 136-8.
2. S. II. 181.
3. S. II. 181.
4. S. II. 182.

finishing the counting. Thus, monks, many aeons have passed and gone by. It is not easy to count them up—as so many aeons, so many hundred aeons, so many thousand aeons and so many hundred thousand aeons "[1] Similarly he gives the analogy of counting the sand-particles of the river Ganges[2], and at last concludes by saying: "Unthinkable is a beginning of this universe, the first end is not comprehended."[3]

This conception of the immensity of time is again not based on any theoretical speculation but on retrocognitive knowledge. Buddha says that he recalls the manifold past existences as much as he likes (yāvad eva ākaṅkhāmi anekavihitaṃ pubbenivāsaṃ anussarāmi, M. I. 482). Some of his disciples also claim to have personally verified this experience.[4]

We are further informed that the life-span of beings in different abodes of existence is not the same, nor is the life of different worlds of equal duration. We are told that one hundred years of men are equivalent to one day and night of the Tāvatiṃsa-gods and according to the measurement of their own year they live for a thousand years.[5] Similarly in another heavenly world, one day and night is said to be equal to fifty earth-years, and in yet another a day and night is equivalent to no less than sixteen hundred earth-years.[6] Nay, even more, we are told that there are beings in the world of Radiance (ābhāsvara loka) who live fors even aeons, though after that they also have to be reborn. Referring to a religious teacher, Sunetta, Buddha points out: "Sunetta, the religious teacher, cultivated thoughts of amity for seven years and (as a result) for seven world-cycles or aeons, he did not return to this world. He arose in the sphere of Radiance....Then in Brahma's sphere..as Mahā Brahmā.. yet, monks, although Sunetta lived so long, he was not freed

1. S. II. 183.
2. S. II. 184.
3. anamataggo'yaṃ...saṃsāro, pubbākoti na paññāyati...,S.II. 184.
4. S. II. 213, 216; V. 303.
5. yaṃ kho pana...mānussakaṃ vassasataṃ, devānaṃ tāvatiṃsānam eso eko rattindivo...tena saṃvaccharena dibbaṃ vassasahassaṃ devānaṃ tāvatiṃsānaṃ āyuppamāṇaṃ., D. II. 327.
6. A. IV. 252-4.

from birth, old age and death...."[1] This indicates that according to the Buddhist concept of the universe, some world-systems can last longer than the others. This is also supported by the Brahmajāla Sutta in which Brahmā along with others is said to remain for long in the world of Radiance even after the dissolution of this world-system. Then, in the course of time after the exhaustion of his merit or the span of life, he is said to be reborn in this world-system at the time of its next evolution.[2]

It is to be noted in this connection that Buddha by explaining the origin of Brahmā himself, discards the traditional theory, occurring in the Ups.[3] and the B. G.[4] that in the beginning there was one who desired to be many and through his desire the manifold beings were brought into existence. Though, Buddha also refers to the emergence of the empty Brahma-vimāna (suññaṃ Brahma-vimānaṃ pātubhavati, D. I. 17) and Brahmā appearing there as the first-born (paṭhamaṃ upapanno, D. I. 18) being, he nevertheless, offers a natural explanation of the entire process of evolution and dissolution, and does not speak of a creation of the universe.

Turning to the B. G., we find that it is in general agreement with Buddhism as regards the duration of the universe. Like Buddhism it also speaks of the universe as being without beginning or end (nā'nto na cā'diḥ, XV. 3) when it refers to it in terms of the simile of the cosmic tree (aśvattha-tree) alluded to in the Kaṭha (VI. 1). Again like Buddhism it does not consider the universe as a static unit, but only as a member in a successive series. It says: "At the commencement of the day (of Brahmā) all manifested things come forth fromt he Unmanifested and at the commencement of the night, they merge in that same, known as the 'Unmanifested'. Thus the self-same multitude of existences evolves and dissolves over and over again."[5] Then again, here also, as in Buddhism, the knowledge of the innumerable past existences

1. A. IV. 104-5.
2. D.I. 17-18.
3. Ait. I. 1; Tait. II. 6.
4. B.G. III. 10.
5. B.G. VIII. 18 and 19; see also IX. 7 and 8.

is claimed to be based on direct personal experience. Kṛṣṇa says to Arjuna: "Many are the lives past of mine and thine. I know them all, O Arjuna, though thou knowest not."[1] The difference in the life-span of earthly and heavenly beings, as well as in the duration of different worlds also is accepted by the B. G. It refers to people living in some heavenly abode for a very long period (śāśvatīḥ samāḥ)[2] when they are born there as a result of their meritorious karmas.[3] The one day of Brahmā is said to be of one thousand yugas and the same is the duration of his night. With the dawn of his day, as indicated above, our world issues forth from the Unmanifested (Prakṛti) and at the approach of the night it merges into it.[4] This is what is known as an aeon (kalpa) for our world.[5] This verse which speaks of the duration of the day and night of Brahmā (B. G. VIII. 17), is exactly the same as that which occurs in the MB. (Śānti 231. 31) and this provides a clue to the measurement of time acceptable to the B. G. The fuller description of what the B. G. says here is to be seen in the MB. (Śānti 231) and it will be useful to refer briefly to a few relevant passages of the latter which can help us to ascertain the length of an aeon (kalpa) as alluded to in the B. G.

Leaving aside the details of the divisions of time, we may note the following: "A year of human beings (360 days and nights) is equal to a day and night of the gods....The learned say that 12000 years of the gods constitute what is called a 'yuga'. A thousand such yugas compose a single day of Brahmā. The same is the duration of Brahmā's night. With the commencement of Brahmā's day our world begins

1. B.G. IV. 5.

2. The word, 'śāśvatīḥ samāḥ' is not to be taken here literally in the sense of 'eternity', since the text (B.G. VI. 41) makes it quite clear that after the expiry of that period (śāśvatīḥ) the man concerned has to be reborn.

3. Prāpya puṇyakṛtām lokān uṣitvā śāśvatiḥ samāḥ., B.G. VI. 41

4. Sahasra yugaparyantam ahar yad Brahmaṇo viduḥ
rātriṃ yugasahasrāntāṃ te'horātravido janāḥ
Avyaktād vyaktayaḥ sarvāḥ prabhavanty aharāgame
rātryāgame pralīyante tatrai'vā' vyaktasaṃjñake., B.G. VIII. 17 and 18.

5. B.G. IX. 7.

to unfold itself into life. During the period of its dissolution the creator sleeps having recourse to yoga-meditation..Thus, those who know that the day of Brahmā is of the duration of a thousand years (of gods) and that the night also extends for a thousand years, they are the knowers of day and night,"[1] (this last verse is exactly the same as that of B.G. VIII. 17).

Now the single day of Brahmā which is said to consist of the thousand yugas of gods is equivalent to one aeon (kalpa, B. G. IX. 7) of the human world, after which the dissolution begins. The dissolution of our world, however, does not mean the dissolution of the entire cosmos, since our one aeon is only a day for Brahmā. The same is said to be the length of his night, and 360 similar days and nights of Brahmā will constitute a year for him and in terms of this measurement of his year, his life-span is said to be a hundred years.[2] It is at the expiry of this long life-span of Brahmā that the final great dissolution of the entire universe is supposed to take place.

If we calculate the life-span of our own world (an aeon or a day of Brahmā) in terms of human years it comes to 4, 320 million years as shown below:—

1 day and night of gods = 1 year of human beings

1 year or 360 days and nights of gods = 360 years of human beings

1 yuga or 12000 years of gods = 12000 × 360 = 4,320,000 years of human beings

1000 yugas of gods or 1 day of Brahmā or 1 aeon of human beings = 4320,000 × 1000 = 4320,000,000 years of human beings.

The question of the duration of the universe has not, as yet, been accurately and unanimously settled by astronomers and their opinions are widely divided. According to Professor E. J. Opik "the universe exploded 4,500 million years ago from a superdense state: this was the beginning

---

1. MB., Sānti-Parva, 231. 17-31.
2. Viṣṇu-Purāṇa, I.3.

of our present universe."[1] He further states that "our sun with its planetary system came into being soon after the start of the present expansion, and can now look back upon more than one half of its lifetime; from what we know about stellar structure and evolution, it will not last for more than a further 3,000 to 4,000 million years. Life may disappear from the surface of our planet long before that."[2] Professor Lovell, however, thinks "that the explosion or disintegration of the primeval atom must have occurred between twenty thousand million and sixty thousand million years ago."[3] Working on this theory he suggests that "about nine thousand million years ago...the galaxies began to form and the present period of expansion began."[4] In fact, there are several astronomical theories in the field and so the various calculations, at this stage, cannot but be regarded as matters of tentative guess-work. In view of such a wide range of difference in the calculations of the modern astronomers themselves, it is not altogether insignificant that the B. G. calculation of 4,320 million years as the life of our world is more than the half of Professor Opik's calculation. In early Buddhism, however, the mathematical calculation in this respect is not encouraged and Buddha conveys the immensity of time through various analogies.

As regards the origin of the universe, the approach of Buddhism and the B. G. is quite different. Buddhism, as we have seen, speaks of the world as of inconceivable beginning, and explains the innumerable series of its evolutions and dissolutions in terms of purely natural processes without evoking the aid of any supernatural being.[5] But, the B. G., in spite of regarding the processes of evolution and dissolution as without beginning and end, holds the view that God or the Supreme Lord is the guiding principle behind the entire process of evolutions and dissolutions. Thus, it offers a theological account of it. Kṛṣṇa says: "Under my guidance, the

---

1. The Oscillating Universe, p. 120.
2. *Ibid.* p. 123.
3. The Individual and the Universe, p. 90.
4. The Individual and the Universe, p. 90.
5. D.I. 17-18; III. 84ff.

Prakṛti (Nature) gives birth to all animate and inanimate objects. By this means, O Arjuna, the world revolves."[1] "All beings, O Arjuna, return to my own Prakṛti (Nature) at the end of the aeon (kalpakṣaye) and at the beginning of the aeon, I send them forth. (Thus) taking hold of Prakṛti which is my own, I send forth again and again (punaḥ-punaḥ) all this multitude of beings."[2]

Both Buddhism and the B. G., however, agree about the inconceivable beginning of the successive process of evolution of the world. Then again, they both agree that the dissolution of our world does not necessarily mean the dissolution of the entire cosmos. According to the B.G., our world is supposed to pass through various evolutions and dissolutions before the world of Brahma is dissolved. In Buddhism also, we have seen that long after the dissolution of our world, beings are found in the world of Radiance.[3] The religious teacher, Sunetta is said to have lived there for seven aeons of this world.[4] Again the B.G. conception of 'Mahad Brahma' or primal Matter as the womb of the universe in which the seed is placed by the Supreme (B. G. XIV. 3) has some resemblance to the Buddhist conception of the mansion of Brahmā (Brahmavimāna) in which Brahmā appears as the first-born (paṭhamaṃ upapanno) being,[5] although in the former unlike the latter, the ideas are expressed in theological terms.

The Problem of God:—

Much can be said and, indeed, has been said both for as well as against the belief in the existence of God. However, our main purpose here is to show how the B. G. and Buddhism are fundamentally opposed to each other in this respect. It may, however, be fruitful for our purpose to understand in brief what exactly is meant by the word 'God' in the B. G. and in Buddhism when they respectively accept and reject it.

1. B.G. IX. 10.
2. B.G. IX. 7 and 8.
3. D.I. 17; III. 84.
4. A. IV. 104-5.
5. D.I. 17-18.

It would, then, be possible for us to see clearly whether there is any sense in which their views can be reconciled.

(A) *The Development of the Concept of Divinity in Pre-Buddhistic Indian Thought*:—

The idea of God seems to have been primarily conceived to account for the origin and existence of the world, as also for its order and arrangement. In the famous Puruṣa-Sūkta of the Ṛg-Veda (Rv. X. 90) the world is said to have come out from a quarter of the Divine Person (pādo'sya viśvabhūtāni, loc. cit.). In subsequent literature, the creator and controller of beings is quite often called Prajāpati. The Brāhmaṇas, usually indentify him with Brahmā (Prajāpatyo Brahmā, Tait. Brāh. III. 3. 8. 3; Gopatha Uttarabhāga III. 18), though in the Chāndogyopaniṣad (VIII. 15), he is distinguished from the latter. Along with Brahmā, the personal Creator-God, the conception of Brahman, the impersonal Divine Principle is referred to in the Brāhmaṇas.[1] But it is difficult to maintain that the two concepts were clearly distinguished.[2] It is only at a later period when the importance of ritualism was undermined and the value of knowledge was emphasised in the Ups. that Brahmā, the deliverer of the Vedas and the personal Creator-God of the world is relegated to an inferior position. But as rightly pointed out by Professor Jayatilleke, "even when in the Middle and Late Upaniṣads the personal conception of Brahmā (masc.) came to be sharply distinguished from Brahman (neut.), the importance of this personal conception of Brahmā as the first deliverer of the Vedas and the creator of the world was so great that the earlier idea was still retained."[3] Thus, in spite of the fact that the supreme position now goes to the impersonal Absolute or Brahman, and Brahmā is regarded as having been created and imparted the knowledge of the Vedas by the

1. A. B. Keith—Ṛg-Veda Brahmanas: Translated H.O.S. Vol. XXV, p. 27

2. K. N. Jayatilleke—Early Buddhist Theory of Knowledge, p. 179.

3. *Ibid*, p. 179

former[1], Brahmā does even then remain as the first born among the gods and the creator and the preserver of the universe,[2] though it is true that the unborn or self-caused Brahman also is, at times, spoken of as the cause or ground of the origin and existence of the universe[3] (perhaps because Brahmā is merely instrumental in executing the work ordained to him by the Prime Principle). Brahman, however, for the most part is referred to in the Ups. as an indefinable, ineffable, impersonal Principle, devoid of all assignable marks[4], in relation to which only negative modes of speech (neti-neti) could be used.[5] The reality of the phenomenal world in the absolute sense being denied,[6] worldly epithets like creator and controller in relation to Brahman lose their literal significance. But all the same, the Ups. persist in calling this impersonal absolute Reality (Brahman) as the supreme Self, indwelling and animating all things and beings (antarātma).[7] This, in brief, is the process of the gradual development of the concept of Divinity in pre-Buddhistic Indian thought.

(B) *The Acceptance or Rejection of God by the B.G. and Buddhism in Various Senses* :—

Now we have to see in which of its various senses the idea of God or Divinity is rejected or accepted by Buddhism and the B.G. From the Buddnist criticisms, it would appear that Buddhism is averse to the idea of God in a theological, teleological or metaphysical sense. God, whether he is conceived as a personal creator and controller, a moral governor and dispenser of justice, or as an indwelling principle in man

1. yo Brahmāṇaṃ vidadhāti pūrvaṃ: yo vai Vedāṃś ca prahiṇoti tasmai; Śvetā. VI. 18.
2. Brahmā devānām prathamaḥ sambabhūva viśvasya kartā bhuvanasya goptā, Muṇḍaka, I. 1. 1
3. Sa viśva-kṛd viśva-vid ātmayoniḥ... Saṃsāra-mokṣa-sthiti-bandhanahetuḥ, Śvetā., VI. 16; tasmin lokāḥ śritāḥ sarve, Kaṭha, VI. 1.
4. Bṛhadā. II. 4. 14; IV. 5. 15; Tait. II. 9; Muṇḍaka, I. 1. 6; III. 1 8; Kaṭha. III. 15; VI. 12.
5. Bṛhadā. II. 3.6; III. 9; 26; IV. 2. 4; IV. 4. 22; IV. 5. 15.
6. Katha. IV. 10, 11. (neha nānāsti kiñcana).
7. Kaṭha. II. 12; V. 9, 10, 11 (sarvabhūtāntarātma); VI. 17 (antarātmā).

known as the self, is unacceptable to Buddhism. There is, however, one sense, namely the sense of an ineffable and indefinable supreme Reality, in which the idea of God appears to be compatible with Buddhist thought. We may see the Buddhist position in a clearer light if we first understand the B.G. approach to the problem of God.

The B.G., having the Ups. and the Bhāgavatadharma as the chief source-material in this respect (supra. pp. 109-114, 134-145), tries to combine the Absolutism of the former with the theism of the latter. Thus the word 'Brahman' is taken by it as a synonym of Īśvara, Paramātmā or Puruṣottama[1] and a compromise is sought between the impersonal and the personal conception of Divinity. Following the Bhāgavata or Aikāntika tenet of devotion to a monotheistic God, the B.G. highlights the personal conception of God and gives a very prominent place to the single-minded devotion to God. Kṛṣṇa speaking in the form of the incarnate God, says : "He who worships me with unwavering devotion, transcends all guṇas and is fit to become Brahman."[2] The single-minded devotion is said to surpass all forms of worship (ekabhaktir viśiṣyate B.G. VII. 17). Even a man of most vile conduct (sudurācāro, B.G. IX. 30) is said to convert himself into a virtuous man and attain abiding peace[3], if he is given to single-minded devotion (bhajate mām ananyabhāk, B.G. IX. 30). It is through unswerving devotion (ananyayā bhaktyā, B.G. VIII. 22; XI. 54) that he in the form of the Supreme Person (Puruṣaḥ paraḥ, B.G. VIII. 22), can be truly known seen and entered into (jñātuṃ draṣṭuṃ ca tattvena praveṣṭuṃ ca paraṃtapa, B.G. XI. 54). Kṛṣṇa, therefore, repeatedly exhorts Arjuna : "Fix thy mind on me, be devoted to me, be resigned unto me, bow down to me. Having thus directed thyself to me as thy goal, thou shalt come to me."[4] "Let thy mind be absorbed in me, let thy

1. B.G. XV. 17 and 18.
2. B.G. XIV. 26.
3. kṣipraṃ bhavati dharmātmā śāśvacchāntiṃ nigacchati, B.G. IX. 31.
4. B.G. IX. 34; XVIII. 65.

intellect dwell in me."[1] "Abandoning all vacillating tendencies, come to me alone for refuge. Be not grieved, I shall release thee from all sins."[2] All this hardly leaves any doubt about the fact that the B.G. emphasises faith and devotion of a monotheistic type.

Impressed by these utterances some scholars have come to the conclusion that in the B.G. the devotion to the personal God is held higher than the meditation on the impersonal Absolute, and that knowledge (jñāna) is only subordinate to devotion (bhakti). Garbe, for example, remarks that "the characteristic feature of the B. G." is that "devotion to God is the climax of all knowledge."[3] In the same vein K.N. Mitra remarks that in the B.G. "intellect is more or less an auxiliary of the emotion."[4] Similarly Professor Ranade observes : "The general upshot of the teaching of the B.G. in this respect seems to be that the Saguṇa Upāsanā might be regarded as even higher than the Avyakta Upāsanā."[5]

But we must look to the other side as well before pronouncing judgment on the point. There can be hardly any doubt about the fact that the entire description of Brahman, as found in the B.G., is Upaniṣadic. Like the Ups., Brahman is considered as the absolute Reality which transcends all oppositions and in which all contradictions are reconciled. Thus, it is spoken of as both existent and nonexistent as well as beyond them.[6] Again, it is said to be neither existent nor non-existent.[7] At one time it is said to be incomprehensible, unthinkable, undefinable and unknowable (aprameya, II. 18; acintya, II. 25; VIII, 9; anirdeśya, XII. 3; avijñeya, XIII. 15) and at another time it is spoken of as knowable (jñeya, XIII. 12) "by knowing which immortality is attained" (yaj jñātvā'mṛtam aśnute, loc. cit.). It is said to be the knower as well as that which is to be known (vettā'si

1. B.G. XII. 8.
2. B.G. XVIII. 66.
3. Indian Antiquary, Vol. 47, Supplement, p. 21.
4. The Evolution of Vaiṣṇavism, B.C. Law, Vol. I, p. 678
5. The Bhagavadgītā as a Philosophy of God-Realisation, pp. 230-1
6. sat asat tatparaṃ yat, B.G. XI. 37.
7. na sat tan nā'sad ucyate, B.G. XIII. 12.

vedyaṃ ca, XI. 38) ; the knowledge, the object of knowledge, as also the goal of knowledge (jñānaṃ jñeyaṃ jñānagamyam, XIII.17). It is described as having hands, feet, eyes, head, mouth and ears everywhere in the world[1] and yet in the very next verse, it is added: "Though it appears to have the qualities of all senses, it is devoid of all senses, it is unattached and yet supporting all, free from all guṇas (modes of Prakṛti) and yet the enjoyer of the guṇas."[2] "It is inside as well as outside of all beings, it is unmoving as well as moving...it is far away and yet quite near, it is undivided and yet seems to be divided in beings."[3] We have already shown (supra. pp. 109-114) that almost all these verses, as also some other expressions and epithets of the B.G. are traceable to the Ups. Professor Dasgupta is not unjustified when he observes that "the whole concept of Brahman, as herein (i.e. in the B.G.) stated, is directly borrowed from the Upaniṣads."[4]

In considering the supreme Reality as the all-pervading Self (sarvagataḥ, II. 24; XIII. 32; aham ātmā sarvabhūtāśayasthitaḥ, X. 20, hṛdi sarvasya dhiṣṭhitam, XIII. 17, cf. XIII. 2, 22, 27, 32, XV. 15, XVIII. 61) also, the B.G. follows the lead of the Ups. Again like the Ups., it refers to Brahmā or Prajāpati as the personal creator and preserver of the world, as also the deliverer of the sacrificial injunctions of the Vedas.[5] It also adds that Brahmā has come out of the Imperishable or the supreme Reality (Brahman).[6] Thus, the supreme Reality is explicity said to be superior even to the first-creator, Brahmā (garīyase Brahmaṇo'py ādikartre, XI. 37) In the cosmic form of Kṛṣṇa also, Brahmā along with Śiva and hosts of other beings, sages and heavenly nāgas, has been shown to be contained in the supreme God.[7] The attainment of Brahma-loka is no freedom from the bond of rebirth.[8] But at the same time, it cannot be ignored that the supreme God also is spoken of as the ground, cause,

1. B.G. XIII. 13.
2. B.G. XIII. 14.
3. B.G. XIII. 15 and 16.
4. A History of Indian Philosophy, Vol. II, p. 475.
5. B.G. III. 10.
6. Brahmā'kṣarasamudbhavam, B.G. III. 15.
7. B.G. XI. 15.
8. Ābrahmabhuvanāl lokāḥ punarāvartino'rjuna, B.G. VIII. 16.

father and creator of the universe[1], and further the personal God is rather indiscriminately called the impersonal Brahman.[1] Thus the theistic element of the Bhāgavata-dharma is fused with the absolutistic idea of the Ups.

How should one reconcile this dual approach of the B.G.? In view of its indiscriminate use of terms, it appears at first sight, difficult to decide whether the personal God (Īśvar) or impersonal Absolute (Brahman) is given a higher place in it. But, on closer examination, it is found that the B.G. itself suggests a solution. In Chapter VII, which opens with the promise of disclosing the spiritual wisdom together with intellectual knowledge without any residue (jñānaṃ te' haṃ savijñānam idaṃ vakṣyāmy aśeṣataḥ, VII.2), it is declared by Kṛṣṇa "Not knowing my immutable and supreme higher nature, ignorant men consider me, the Unmanifest as having manifestation. Veiled by cosmic ignorance (yogamāyā), I am not revealed to all (in my higher unmanifest form). This deluded world knows me not, the Unborn and the Unchanging."[3] "This whole world deluded by these three modes (guṇas of Prakṛti) does not truly know me who am above them, the Imperishable."[4] These utterances show that when Kṛṣṇa, the personal God calls himself Immutable, Unborn and Supreme, he says so with reference to his higher unmanifest or unpersonified nature. It is in this sense that he calls himself "the abode of Brahman, the Immortal, the Imperishable, the eternal Law and the absolute Bliss,"[5] and urges that unflinching devotion to him would make one fit for becoming Brahman (māṃ ca yo'vyabhicāreṇa bhaktiyogena sevate, sa..Brahmabhūyāya kalpate, XIV. 26).

1. B.G. VII. 6, 7; IX. 17, 18; XI. 43; XIV. 3,4.

2. B.G. X. 12, XIV. 27; Professor Dasgupta has rightly noticed that "in IV. 24 and 25...the word 'Brahman' is in all probability used in the sense of God. In V. 6, 10, 19 also the word 'Brahman' is used in in the sense of God or Īśvara; and in most of the other cases the word is used in the sense of God." A History of Indian Philosophy, Vol. II, p. 474.

3. B.G. VII. 24 and 25 (Avyaktaṃ vyaktim āpannaṃ manyante mām abuddhayaḥ...)

4. B.G. VII. 13.

5. Brahmaṇo hi pratiṣṭhā'ham amṛtasyā 'vyayasya ca,
śāśvatasya ca dharmasya sukhasyai'kāntikasya ca., B.G. XIV. 27.

This explains the sense in which Kṛṣṇa or Puruṣottama, speaking as God in person, and Brahman, the impersonal Principle are to be treated as synonyms. It may also be interesting to note here that in the above verse (i.e. B.G. XIV. 27), the word eternal Law (Dharma) is used by the B.G. as one of the synonyms of Brahman. This reminds us of the similar use of terms, 'Brahma' and 'Dhamma' in Buddhism (Dhammakāyo, Brahmakāyo, Dhammabhūto,'D.III. 84), which we shall discuss in the sequel.

A regards the question as to how the Unmanifest Supreme can manifest itself and be the ground, the cause, the father and the creator of the universe (B.G. IX. 17, 18), Kṛṣna makes the following statements: "Though (in my higher form) I am unborn, essentially imperishable and the lord of all beings, yet taking hold of my own nature, I manifest myself through māyā."[1] "Taking hold of my own nature, I send forth (visṛjāmi) again and again this entire multitude of beings which under the control of nature (Prakṛti) helplessly come out."[2] Beings are helpless on account of their own vehicle of actions and the supreme Lord is indifferent and detached in sending them forth under the force of their own actions. It is for this reason that the word 'visṛjāmi' (to refashion) is used here instead of the word 'sṛjāmi' (to create afresh) used in B.G. IV.7 where God is said to manifest himself anew without any pre-existent germinating force of the karmas. The fact that the supreme Reality in its higher form remains ever detached and indifferent to the acts of creation and dissolution is clearly asserted by Kṛṣṇa in the very next verse: "These acts (of creation and dissolution) do not bind me, O Arjuna, for I am seated as if indifferent and unattached in these actions."[3] Thus it is suggested that attributes like creator, controller, sustainer, etc. are ascribed to God only in a phenomenal sense. Those who truly understand the imperishable nature of the Supreme are not deluded by this cosmic ignorance (yogamāya) and, being free from the qonds of phenomenal actions, transcend the realm of sāṃsāric

1. B.G. IV· 6.
2. B.G. IX. 8.
3. B.G. IX.9.

existence. As the B.G. puts it: "Actions do not defile me, nor do I have yearning for their fruits. He, who thus truly knows me, is not bound by actions."[1] "This divine māyā of mine, consisting of the guṇas (modes of Prakṛti) is hard to overcome. But those who take refuge in me alone, cross beyond it."[2]

Thus the B.G. seems to make out that the manifestation of the Supreme in the personal form and its being described as the creator of the universe have only a phenomenal validity. Revelation of the cosmic form by Kṛṣṇa also is likewise said to be a display of his divine yoga (yagam aiśvaram, ātmayogam, B.G. XI. 8, 47) which is nothing other than the aforesaid divine māyā (daivī māyā, B G.VII. 14, or yogamāyā, B.G. VII. 25). This is fully corroborated from the account of the Nārāyaṇīyadharma where also in a somewhat similar manner Kṛṣṇa displays his cosmic form to Nārada and after having done so, speaks of it as follows:

> "The form in which you see me is only the *māyā* created by me. You should not consider me thus endowed with the qualities of all beings."[3]

The word 'māyā' in the B.G. should not, however, be taken to imply a meaning which Śaṅkara attaches to the term. It only intends to indicate that the manifestation of the Absolute into God, as also the phenomenal facts of the cosmic manifestation are not as real as the Absolute or Brahman, and that these phenomenal manifestations of the Supreme are inscrutable mysteries to the average man. The Śaṅkarite sense of self-deception or illusory superimposition is not suggested either in the B.G. or in early Buddhism (where also the word 'māyā' occurs to indicate the transient character of worldly elements, e.g. etādisāyaṃ santāno *māyā*'-yam bālalāpinī, S.III. 143; *māyū*pamañ ca viññāṇaṃ, S. III. 142). The statement of Radhakrishnan, therefore, that "the Gītā asserts the truth of an advaita or non-dualism in philo-

---

1. B.G. IV. 14.
2. B.G. VII. 14.
3. Māyā hy eṣā mayā sṛṣṭā yan māṃ paśyasi Nārada, sarvabhūtaguṇair yuktaṃ nai'vaṃ tvaṃ jñātum arhasi, M.B. Śānti Parva, 339. 45-46.

sophy"[1] can be accepted only with qualifications. We consider the view of S.N. Dasgupta to be quite correct in this respect when he observes: "The word māyā is, no doubt, used in the Gītā..., but its meaning is not what Śaṅkara ascribes to it in his famous interpretation of Vedāntic thought ...Śaṅkara's paraphrasing of it as deception (chadmanā) is quite inappropriate."[2] This being so the idea of God as a divine being is not a wilful deception, though in the grade of reality its place is subordinate to that of the supreme impersonal Brahman. But at the same time the B.G. makes an important statement in favour of the personal God., viz., that the devotion to the personal God, as a means to salvation is easier than the meditative method of knowing the impersonal Absolute. For the average man devotion to the personified God is easier to practise (susukhaṃ kartum, B.G. IX. 2), whereas those who follow the meditative method of attaining to the unmanifested Supreme have to face greater difficulty (kleśo 'dhikataras teṣām, B.G. XII.5). The B.G. thus seems to suggest that it is easier to realise the highest unmanifested nature of the Supreme through the devotion of the manifested form of it. It is perhaps on account of this approach that through unswerving devotion (avyabhicāreṇa bhaktiyogena, B.G. XIV. 26) to God, one is said only to be fit for becoming Brahman (Brahmabhūyāya kalpte, loc. cit). After one has known the true nature of God (as Unmanifest) through devotion, one is said to reach the highest goal in no time (acireṇa).[3] Thus the B.G. seems to assert only the greater utility but not the greater reality of the personal God. This seems to be the way in which the B.G. reconciles its devotional fervour with its open declaration that "nothing is here equal in purity to knowledge (na hi jñānena sadṛśaṃ pavitram iha vidyate, IV.38).

In the light of this approach of the B.G., we find it difficult to accept the view of Garbe that in the B.G.

---

1. Indian Philophy, Vol.I., p. 537.
2. A. History of Indian Philosoph, Vol. II, p. 478.
3. Śradhāvāṃl labhate jñānaṃ...jñānaṃ labdhvā parāṃ śāntim acireṇā dhigacchati, B.G. IV. 39; Bhaktyā māṃ abhijānāti... tato māṃ tattvato jñātvā viśate tadanantaram, B.G. XVIII. 55.

"devotion to God is the climax of all knowledge"[1] or that of K.N. Mitra that in it, "intellect is more or less an auxiliary to emotion."[2] As regards the remark of Professor Ranade that "the Saguṇa Upāsanā might be regarded as even higher than the Avyakta Upāsanā,"[3] we would like to suggest the replacement of the word 'higher' by the word 'easier'. We find the statement of Radhakrishnan quite reasonable in this respect when he concludes: "It is therefore wrong to argue that according to the Gītā the impersonal self is lower in reality than the personal Īśvara, though it is true that the Gītā considers the conception of a personal God to be more useful for religious purposes."[4]

One may not be rationally satisfied with the B.G.'s way of reconciling the theistic concept of God with the absolutistic idea of Brahman, since the gulf between the two is sought to be bridged over by means of what is called 'yogamāyā' which is more a mystical than a rational concept. It only takes for granted what is found to be rationally inexplicable and, therefore, its solution may not appeal to one who is not mystically inclined. But the mystics who fervently believe that all contraditcions and incompatibilities are resolved on the realisation of God, may find the utterances of the B.G. emotionally appealing. It is perhaps on account of such an approach that Professor Ranade enthusiastically observes: "The Bhagavadgītā is one of the greatest works on mysticism the world has ever seen and when God-realisation has been fully stressed, everything else will follow in its wake."[5]

(C) *A Polemic Between Buddhism and the B.G. in Relation to God* :—

Now, whatever be the strength or weakness of the B.G. conception of God, its constant attempt to vindicate its

1. Garbe's introduction to the Bhagavadgītā, Indian Antiquary, Vol. 47 Supplement, p. 21.
2. The Evolution of Vaiṣṇavism, B.C. Law, Vol. I, p. 678.
3. The Bhagavadgītā, as a Philosophy of God-Realisation, pp. 230-1.
4. Indian Philosoy, Vol. I., p. 544
5. The Bhagavadgītā, as a Philosophy of God-Realisation, p. 138.

theistic position against all possible objections, seems to indicate that it is aware of the criticisms usually levelled against God by Buddhists and others. Whether it meets them or not, it is in any case interesting to see how in reliance on its mystical explanations, it tries to escape the criticisms of the Buddhists. These criticisms would also reveal the Buddhist approach to the problem of God vis-a-vis that of the B.G.

In the very first Sutta of the first book of the Sutta Piṭaka (i.e. the Brahmajāla Sutta of the Dīgha Nikāya) Buddha exposes the unsoundness of the theory of world-creation by Brahmā. He points out how at the beginning of the world-process (vivaṭṭamāne loke) a being, on account of the exhaustion of his life-span or merit falls from the world of Radiance and is born in the empty mansion of Brahmā (atha kho aññataro satto āyukkhayā vā puññakkhaya vā ābhassarakāyā cavitvā suññaṃ Brahma-vimānaṃ upapajjati, D.I. 17). After having lived there alone for a very long period, while he wishes for other beings to come and join him, other beings also due to the exhaustion of their life-span or merit are reborn there. This, according to Buddha, gives rise to delusion on the part of the first-born being who thinks: "I am Brahmā, the great Brahmā, the supreme One, the mighty, the all-seeing, the ruler, the lord of all, the maker, the creator, the chief of all assigning to each his place, the controller, the father of all that are and are to be"[1]. The beings who are born later, they also under the same delusion take him to be such.[2] This explanation of Buddha exposes the absurdity of the widely prevalent traditional belief about Brahmā as the first creator, a belief that finds a place both in the Ups.[3] and the B.G.[4]

It is, however, true that the B.G. does not regard Brahmā as the Supreme Lord and to that extent the above criticism may not be regarded as a criticism of the B.G.'s concept of God who is said to be superior to the creator-God, Brahmā (garīyase Brahmaṇo'py ādikartre, B.G. XI. 37). But

1. D.I. 18.

2. D.I. 18.

3. Bṛhadā. I. 4. 1-7; Tait. II. 6 (so'kāmayata, bahu syām prajāyeyeti, sa...idaṃ sarvam asṛjata); Muṇḍaka I. 1.1 (Brahmā devānāṃ prathamaḥ sambabhūva, viśvasya kartā).

4. Sahayajñāḥ prajāḥ sṛṣṭvā puro'vāca prajāpatiḥ, B.G. III. 10

it does affect the B.G.'s theory of world-creation by Brahmā. Moreover, the supreme God also is spoken of, at times, by the B.G. as the father or creator of the universe, of course, in a phenomenal, or say, in a mystical sense. But in any sense, if God is considered as responsible for the origin of the world, the above criticism of Buddhism holds good, since according to it all beings including the first-born being, are said to have come into existence on account of their own past deeds (āyukkhayā vā puññakkhayā vā, D.I. 17). It is perhaps to avoid this very difficulty that the B.G. takes recourse to its mysticism and speaks of the supreme God as being detached and indifferent to the acts of creation and dissolution (udāsīn-avad āsīno asaktaṃ teṣu karmasu, B.G. IX.9). "The supreme Lord does not create agency in people, nor the works, nor the connection between works and fruits. It is Nature that operates."[1]

But on other occasions, the B.G. in colourful passages declares: "I am the source of all, from me do all proceed."[2] "The diversified states of beings. such as understanding, knowledge,..pleasure and pain, existence and non-existence, fear and fearlessness,..fame and ill-fame, are derived from me alone."[3] If the B.G. were not to deviate from this declaration by taking recourse to mystical utterances, the following objections of Buddhism charging the supreme Being with the moral responsibility for all ills, will fall heavy on the B.G.'s God. Buddha says: "There are recluses and Brahmins who maintain and believe that whatever a man experiences, be it pleasant, unpleasant or neutral—all that is caused by God's act of creation..If that is so, then people commit murder, theft and unchaste deeds due to God's act of creation, they indulge in lying, slanderous, harsh and idle talk due to God's act of creation, they are covetous, full of hate and hold wrong views due to God's act of creation."[4] Similar arguments are found in the Jātaka too. It is said: "If God designs the

1. B.G. V 14, see also B.G. IV. 14, V. 15.
2. Ahaṃ sarvasya prabhavo mattaḥ sarvaṃ pravartate, B.G. X. 8.
3. B.G. X. 4 and 5.
4. A. I. 173-4.

life of the entire world—the glory and the misery, the good and the evil acts, man is only the doer of (God's) biddings and God (alone) is tainted thereby (Issaro tena lippati)."[1] Showing the utter incompatibility of the belief in the creator-God with the prevailing evils of the world, it is said: "If, indeed, Brahmā is the lord of the whole world and creator of the multiple beings, then why has he not made the entire world happy without ordaining any misfortune in the world?... Why has he made the world full of injustice, deceit, falsehood and conceit...The lord of beings, then, is evil, since he has ordained unrighteousness when there could have been righteousness."[2]

Such arguments, commonly known in the modern times as 'the arguments from evil' are quite often used by the critics of the divine-origin-theory of the world and, indeed, there hardly seems to be any satisfactory rational reply to these objections.[3] The B.G., however, tries to free itself from them in the light of its mystical conception of God. God being only the impartial operator of the universal law of karma which is nothing but the manifestation of his own nature (Prakṛti or svabhāva),[4] it is held by the B.G. that God is not tainted by actions (na māṃ karmāṇi limpanti, B.G. IV. 14), for he has no yearning for the fruits of actions. Thus, Kṛṣṇa declares: these actions do not bind me, O Arjuna (na ca māṃ tāni karmāṇi nibadhnanti dhanañjaya), for I am seated as if indifferent and unattached in those actions."[5] As regards the objection of God being responsible for all the good and evil of the world, the B.G. says: "The all-pervading spirit does neither take on the sin nor the merit of anybody. Knowledge is enveloped by ignorance, thereby creatures are

1. J.V. 238.
2. J. VI. 208.
3. cf. Antony Flew, 'Divine Omnipotence and Human Freedom' in New Essays in Philosophical Theology, pp. 144-169.
4. Sarvabhūtāni kaunteya *prakṛtiṃ* yānti māmikām. B.G. IX. 7; *Prakṛteḥ* kriyamāṇāni guṇaiḥ karmāṇi sarvaśaḥ, III. 27; na kartṛtvaṃ na karmāṇi lokasya sṛjati prabhuḥ...*svabhāvas* tu pravartate, V. 14.
5. B.G. IX. 9.

deluded."[1]

It is again pointed out by Buddhism that the reliance on the supernatural creator is detrimental to moral incentive and self-effort. "Those who fall back on God's act of creation as the essential factor, lack the impulse and effort regarding what should be done and what should not be done."[2] Such people relying on God's mercy and help, abandon efforts and offer vain prayers for the fulfilment of their desires. These prayers, Buddha points out, are as futile as calling on the other shore of the river to come to the opposite side.[3]

The B. G. tries to escape this difficulty by giving an activistic orientation to its theistic ideas. Work itself is considered the best worship of God. It is said that "man attains perfection by worshipping him (God) through his own action" (svakarmaṇā tam abhyarcya siddhiṃ vindati mānavaḥ, B. G. XVIII. 46). God himself in the B. G. is conceived as ceaselessly active, placing his ideal before men.[4] With this introduction of activism into the tenet of devotion, the B. G., as against Buddhism, preaches absolute dedication or surrender to God. Kṛṣṇa says: "With perfect resignation to me, one while doing all actions attains by my grace the eternal undecaying abode."[5] Arjuna is, therefore, asked to perform his duty to the best of his ability by dedicating all his works to God (sarvakarmāṇi mayi saṃnyasya, B. G, XVIII. 57). In respect of prayer, devotion and worship, the B. G., in strict adherence to its theistic belief takes an attitude which is diametrically opposed to that of Buddhism. As against Buddhism which ridicules the idea of prayer or worship, the B. G. strongly recommends it[6] and asserts

1. B.G. V. 15.
2. A.I. 174.
3. D.I. 244.
4. B.G. III. 22-24.
5. Sarvakarmāṇy api sadā kurvāṇo madvyapāśrayaḥ matprasādād avāpnoti śāśvataṃ padam avyayam, B.G. XVIII. 56.
6. Manmanā bhava madbhakto madyājī māṃ namaskuru, mām evai'ṣyasi satyaṃ...B.G. XVIII. 65, cf. IX. 27, 34; XII. 8; XVIII. 57.

that the life of an atheist is realy doomed. Using bitter words, it observes: "The evil-doers, stupid and mean-men, possessed of demoniac nature, do not seek refuge in me on account of their minds being carried away by ignorance."[1] "They say that the world is without God" (jagad āhur anīśvaram[2], B. G. XVI. 8) and "act recklessly" (vartate kāmakārataḥ, B. G. XVI. 23) and as a result "these fools are born in demoniac species life after life and, not attaining to me (God), go down to the lowest state."[3]

(D) *A Meeting Point Between Buddhism and the B.G.*

It may be pointed out here that these respective attacks of Buddhism and the B. G. do not fall on each other with full force, because there seems to be a meeting ground where Buddhism ceases to be atheistic and the B. G. ceases to be theistic. Buddhists are evidently not atheists in the sense in which the Materialists (cārvākas) are. They do not denounce the codes of morality, nor do they live a reckless life, for which the B.G. bitterly attacks the atheists. In the B. G. also, we have seen, that God in his higher form ceases to be personal and becomes wholly ineffable and incomprehensible. It then comes closer to the Buddhist concept of Nibbāna. Buddha does not seem to be averse to the idea of a supreme impersonal Reality known as Brahman, provided it is viewed without any metaphysical or theological strings which relate it to the conditioned world of phenomena. Any attempt to bring the Absolute into relation with the relative makes the Absolute itself relative. That is the reason why Buddha rejects the notion of a creator or controller-God, as also the idea of an indwelling Divinity of Whatsoever from—personal or impersonal, individual or universal (jīvātmā or sarvabhūtāntarātmā). The views of God as creator or father, comrade or lover belong to the theology of the finite which con-

1. Na māṃ duṣkṛtino mūḍhāḥ prapadyante narādhamāḥ, māyayā'pahṛtajñānā āsuraṃ bhāvam āśritāḥ., B.G., VII. 15.

2. cf. loko anabhissaro'ti (the world is without a God), the view said to have been taught by Buddha., M.II 68.

3. Āsurīm yonim āpannā mūḍhā janmani janmani, mām aprāpyai'va kaunteya tato yānti adhamāṃ gatim B.G. XVI. 20

fuses the reality of God with the finite modes of human thought. God or the supreme reality is there not by virtue of any relationship to or comparison with other things, but in its own right as a reality of a quite different nature. So Buddha sets himself against all relative conceptions of ultimate Reality, against all modes of conditioning the Unconditioned, against all means of conceptualising the Unconceptual. He is against such prayers and worships which take the character of private communications and selfish bargainings and present God on the model of worldly beings, meting out earthly favours to men. These relative associations being left out, only the true reality divested of all contingencies shines forth and this is nothing other than the highest truth called Nibbāna. This is a point where the distinction between 'theism' and 'atheism' tends to get obliterated and the B. G. and Buddhism share in common the idea of the highest truth. This truth or reality, in the strictest sense of the term, is incommunicable and uncharacterisable and the only possible way to suggest it is the negation of whatever we can normally speak and conceive of.

In this sense Buddha is not only not opposed to the word 'Brahman' but he also makes use of it as a synonym of Nibbāna, the supreme reality and the Dhamma, the highest truth. One who has attained Nibbāna (nibbuto) is clearly said to have become Brahman (Brahmabhūto).[1] Buddha himself is described as one who has attained Brahman (Brahmapatta, M. I. 386). The Tathāgata is said to have the Dhamma as his body, Brahma as his body, he is one with the Dhamma, one with the Brahma (Dhammakāya, Brahmakāya; Dhammabhūta, Brahmabhūta).[2] There is hardly any doubt that these words are used for the highest state of Nibbāna, since along with them some other words indicative of the supreme state of enlightenment such as 'cakkhubhūto, ñāṇabhūto' (M. III. 195, 224) also are indiscriminately used.

1. diṭṭheva dhamme nicchāto nibbuto...Brahmabhūtena attanā viharati, M.I. 344.

2. Tathāgatassa he taṃ. . .adhivacanaṃ, dhammakāyo iti pi, Brahmakāyo iti pi, dhammabhūto iti pi, Brahmabhūto iti pi, D. III. 84; cf. M. III. 195, 224.

The eightfold path leading to Nibbāna is indifferently called Dhammayāna or Brahmayāna.[1] Buddha is described as turning the wheel of the Dhamma or the Brahman.[2] To dwell in Dhamma is to dwell with Brahman.[3]

The concept of the Dhamma, the absolute Law or Truth as identical with Nibbāna, the supreme Reality, seems to have gradually evolved from the Vedic idea of 'ṛta'. In the Bṛhadāraṇyaka, Dharma is said to be the highest and is indentified with the Truth. "There is nothing higher than the Dharma, that which is the Dharma is the Truth (Dharmād paraṃ nāsti...yo vai sa dharmaḥ satyaṃ vai tat, Bṛhadā., I. 4. 14). Notwithstanding metaphysical and mystical descriptions of Brahman or the Reality, we find passages in the Ups. where Brahman is spoken of in terms of only the Truth, the Knowledge or the Reality (satyaṃ jñānaṃ anantaṃ Brahma, Tait. II. 1. 1; tad vai tat...satyam Brahmeti, Bṛhadā., V. 4), Truth is said to be the abode of Brahman (satyam āyatanam, Kena. IV. 8) and the highest Truth is said to be incapable of being seen, spoken of, and grasped; it is considered as being witnout any distinctive marks and is regarded as the pacification of the world, the pure silence.[4] It is this line of approach which seems to have been developed and carried out systematically in Buddhism, giving no room for metaphysical or mystical speculation. On the other hand, in the B. G., it is the metaphysical and mystical elements which dominate for the most part. Even when the B. G. speaks of the eternal Law (Dharma) and absolute Bliss as synonyms of Brahman, it ties them up with its theological ideas, and considers Dharma as grounded in God.[5] In Buddhism, un-

---

1. imass'eva kho...ariyassa aṭṭhaṅgikassa maggassa adhivacanaṃ, Brahmayānaṃ iti pi, dhammayānaṃ iti pi, S.V.5

2. Tathāgato...Brahmacakkaṃ pavatteti. S. II. 27; Bhagavatā... Dhammacakkaṃ pavattitaṃ, S. V. 423

3. Brahmunā saddhiṃ saṃvasati....dhammena saddhiṃ, saṃvasati, A.I. 207-8.

4. adṛṣṭam avyavahāryam agrāhyam alakṣaṇam acintyam avyapadeśyam...prapañcopaśamam śāntam, Māṇḍūkya, 7.

5. Brahmaṇo hi pratiṣṭhā'ham amṛtasyā'vyayasya ca,
śāśvatasya ca *dharmasya* sukhasyai'kāntikasya ca., B.G. XIV. 27.

like the B.G., the supreme Law (Dhamma) is independent of God or gods. To make it dependent on any being, be it supernatural or divine, would possibly amount to make it subjective or relative in some sense.

Chapter V

THE ETHICS OF THE B.G. AND EARLY BUDDHISM

Ethics as the Basic Foundation of the Holy Life:—

Early Buddhism and the B.G are noted in the history of Indian thought for their severely practical outlook and ethical doctrines. With a view to enabling man to secure the supreme end of life, both of them draw attention to the unsatisfactory nature of mundane existence and exhort people to seek deliverance from it. Considering Nirvāṇa as the highest goal of life, they suggest practical ways and means of attaining it. Thus, it is for the sake of attaining the highest that ethical codes of conduct and behaviour are emphasised by Buddhism and the B.G. Ethics is considered by them as an indispensable means for the consummation of the holy life. It is the very foundation, on which the superstructure of holy life culminating in Nirvāṇa is built.

The Basis Of Ethics:—

Nirvāṇa being the ultimate goal of ethics, the ethical ideas of both the B.G. and Buddhism are shaped in accordance with their respective concepts of it. We have seen (supra, pp-351-352) that the Buddhist approach to Nibbāna is thoroughly empirical having no element of metaphysics or theology associated with it. Buddha, therefore, prefers to call it the state of the extinction of suffering and refrains from any speculative description of it. But the B.G. looks upon it from a metaphysical and theological standpoint and speaks of it as a state of the fulfilment of the self, dwelling in Brahman, union with or merging in God (tṛptātmā or yuktātmā, Brahmīsthiti, maddhāvam āgataḥ) etc. (supra, pp. 345-346). This difference in attitude is, naturally, reflected in their approach to the problems of ethics. Thus, notwithstanding some of their common ideas, they view the problems of ethics in different perspectives.

Analysing every aspect of the inner or other experience, Buddha shows that it is all impermanent (aniccaṃ), sorrowful (dukkhaṃ) and soulless (anattā). We have seen that every cognisable element, whether internal or external, gross or subtle (ajjhattaṃ vā bahiddhā vā, oḷārikaṃ vā sukhumaṃ vā, S.III.68) is said to have these three characteristics. They are applicable, without exception, to "everything that is seen, heard, reflected, known, attained, inquired into and mentally contemplated."[1] This, indeed, constitutes the basic teaching of Buddhism which controls the entire Buddhist view of life, without comprehending which it is not possible to comprehend either the idea of Buddhist Nibbāna or the principles of its ethics. Buddha, therefore, repeatedly harps on this theme and is frequently found to start his exhortation with this formula of impermanence, suffering and soullessness (or unsubstantiality).[2]

With the realisation of this fundamental fact of experience one is said to be possessed of the right view (sammā diṭṭhi) which marks the beginning of the holy life, and is described as the first step of the eightfold path to Nibbāna. As Buddha says: "When, monks, the monk sees the impermanent corporeality, feeling, perception, volitions and consciousness as impermanent (subject to suffering and without a self) in that case he is possessed of the right view" (sā'ssa hoti sammādiṭṭhi, S.III.51). "When, monks, one sees the impermanent eye (and the rest) as impermanent, in that case he is possessed of the right view. Seeing rightly, one is detached. With the destruction of lust, passion is destroyed and with the destruction of passion, lust is destroyed. With the destruction of lust and passion, the mind is said to be perfectly freed.[3]" Thus, it is the right view (sammā diṭṭhi) or the proper realisation of the transient character of worldly existence which constitutes the basis of Buddhist ethics.

Without recourse to any metaphysical or theological presupposition, Buddha, on the basis of purely empirical

1. M.I. 136.
2. M.I. 232-3; S. III. 88-89, 111-112, 118-119; S. IV. 382-4.
3. S. IV. 142.

analysis shows how the suffering of mundane life follows from the transient nature of worldly objects and how through proper self-control and discipline in the light of right understanding, the final release from suffering can be attained. In the course of his causal analysis, he points out that all our feelings are due to the sense-object-contact (phassa paccayā vedanā, M.I.261-2; S.II.25). But, since both the objects and the sense-organs are transitory or impermanent (anicca), our feelings produced by their contact are also transitory or ever- lapsing.[1] One cannot feel secure with any object of sense and this insecurity is an unmistakable mark of suffering. Thus, the fact of suffering follows from the impermanent nature of worldly things. It is the abandonment of this painful existence or suffering which constitutes the goal of the holy life (i.e. Nibbāna) and for the attainment of which ways and means (i.e. ethical codes) are enunciated by Buddha. But Buddha in order to emphasise fully the need for utter detachment goes further to deduce the doctrine of anattā (soullessness) from these facts of impermanence and suffering. He asks:"Is it proper to look upon that which is impermanent, sorrowful and changeable as 'this is mine, I am this, or this is my self'?" and gets the reply, "certainly not, sir".[2]

It has already been shown in the previous chapter that absolute detachment and consequent release from suffering is not possible so long as one does not abandon this subtle clinging to the 'I' or selfhood (attavādupādāna), because lust, attachment or clinging is the very root of suffering.[3] Buddha, therefore, clearly says: "I do not see that form of clinging to I-ness which having clung to, there would not arise sorrow, lamentation, suffering......"[4] But with the realisation of the great truth of anattā, "one finds estrangement in corporeality (and the rest). With estrangement arisen, passion fades away.

1. S. III. 225-8; IV. 67-69.

2. M. I. 232-3; S. III. 88, 118; S. IV. 25.

3. Chandajaṃ dukkhaṃ, S.I. 22; or, chando hi mūlam dukkhassā'ti, S. IV. 330 and pañcupādānakkhandhā chandamūlakā'ti, S. III. 10.

4. M.I. 137.

With the fading away of passion, he is liberated. When liberated, there arises in him the knowledge that he is liberated. He knows, "exhausted is rebirth, fulfilled is the holy life, done what was to be done with nothing more beyond'."[1] Thus, beginning with the right view or proper understanding of the threefold characteristics of worldly objects, one is gradually led to shake off all attachment, and by getting rid of this root cause of suffering, is ultimately released. But if one is ignorant of this fundamental fact of experience, one drifts towards the evil course of life, since ignorance is the root of all evil things (ye keci akusalā dhammā sabbe te avijjāmūlakā, S. II. 263).

From the above approach of Buddhism, it is clear that the belief in anything as permanent, blissful and the self is to be reckoned a wrong view (micchā diṭṭhi) as against the right view (sammā diṭṭhi) which is said to coustitute the basis of Buddhist ethics. The right view, thus does not consist in the knowledge of any metaphysical or theological priniciple, but in the correct appraisal of the fundamental facts of our experience. Defining it in a more practical form Buddha says: "That, monks, which is the understanding of suffering, the understanding of the origin of suffering, the understanding of the extinction of suffering and the understanding of the path leading to the extinction of suffering is called the 'right view'."[2] Since all bodily, verbal and mental actions, whether good or bad, rest on the respective right or wrong view (sammā diṭṭhi or micchā diṭṭhi) of the man, we are told in a yet more practical way that the right view consists in the true understanding of righteous and unrighteous action and their root causes Thus, the Sammādiṭṭhi Sutta reads as follows: "Right view, right view, they say, friend. How is the noble disciple possessed of the right view?"[3] "When, friends, the noble disciple understands unrighteous action and the root of unrighteous action, righteous action and the root of rightous action, then he is posses-

1. M. I. 139; S. III. 68.
2. D. II. 312: cf. M.I.48
3. M.I. 46.

sed of the right view."[1] With regard to the question as to what constitute the righteous and unrighteous actions and their respective roots, it is pointed out that greed (lobha), hatred (dosa) and delusion (moha) are the roots of all unrighteous actions and their opposites are the roots of righteous actions. The bodily, verbal and mental actions, righteous and unrighteous, arising from their respective roots are enumerated as follows[2]:—

(A) Unrighteous bodily actions:—	(A) Righteous bodily actions:—
1. Destruction of life	1. To abstain from the destruction of life
2. Stealing	2. To abstain from stealing
3. Sexual misconduct	3. To abstain from sexual misconduct
(B) Unrighteous verbal actions:—	(B) Righteous verbal actions:—
4. Speaking falsehood	4. To abstain from speaking falsehood.
5. Slandering	5. To abstain from slandering
6. Speaking harsh words	6. To abstain from speaking harsh words
7. Talking frivolously	7. To abstain from talking frivolously
(C) Unrighteous mental actions:—	(C) Righteous mental actions: —
8. Covetousness	8. Absence of covetousness
9. Ill-will	9. Absence of ill-will
10. Wrong view	10. Correct view

This account makes it evident that the ethical code of Buddhism is based on an empirical analysis of the nature of things and not on extraneous sanctions from any other autho-

1. Yato kho āvuso ariyasāvako akusalaṃ ..akusalamūlaṃ. . .kusalaṃ kusalamūlañ ca pajānāti. ettāvatā pi kho. . .sammā diṭṭhi hoti, M.I. 46-47.

2. M.I. 47, 286-8, 489-490.

rity such as God, the Church, the self, conscience, convention tradition or the state. The natural law of karma operating universally and independently is thought sufficient to explain the fact of moral retribution in the universe. Thus, the ethics of Buddhism is essentially autonomous in character and cannot be reduced to any form of Intuitionalism.[1] Professor S. Tachibana also, though he does not enter into the theoretical discussion of the ethical problems,[2] takes note of this autonomous character of Buddhist ethics and remarks: "The Buddhist morality.....is in its foundation autonomous."[3]

It was a current belief of the tradition that there could not possibly be ethics without a metaphysics. We find Māluṅkyaputta declining to lead the holy life under Buddha, if the latter does not tell him whether the world is eternal or non-eternal, finite or infinite; whether the body is the same as or different from the soul, whether the liberated saint exists after death or does not exist, etc. Buddha points out the folly of Māluṅkyaputta by means of the simile of the man pierced by the poisoned arrow and, thus, shows the irrelevance of metaphysical speculations and the urgency of direct and straightforward action.[4] He says: "Whether there be the theory that the world is eternal,.....non-eternal,.... finite,....infinite, (in any case) there certainly exists birth, decay, death, sorrow, lamentation, pain, grief and despair, the destruction of which, I teach, in the present life itself."[5] Thus, Buddha proposes an ethics which is valid on its own right, irrespective of any theory of metaphysics. He is definitely opposed to any *a priori* theorisation. He clearly tells Udāyī that questions pertaining to the beginning (pubbanta) and the end (aparanta), besides being irrelevant to the urgent

1. For a description of the different forms of Intuitionalism according to what they regard as the predominant source of moral and religious truth, see Encyclopaedia of Religion and Ethics, Vol. 7, vide 'Intuitionalism', pp. 397-398.

2. cf. Tachibana's 'The Ethics of Buddhism', Preface, by Prof. Wijesekera, pp. viii-ix.

3. The Ethics of Buddhism, p. 64.

4. M.I. 427-430.

5. M.I. 430.

need of ethical life, are not to be solved by the mere exercise of the intellect or reason. They are soluble only through the attainment of the higher knowledge (vijjā or abhiññā) which cannot be developed without proper adherence to an ethical discipline.[1] Thus, it is clear that the *raison d'être* of Buddhist ethics is nothing but the fundamental fact of mundane experience. It does not base itself on any metaphysical speculation or *a priori* theorisation.

But when we look at the B. G., we find that its ethics is chiefly derived from its metaphysical and theological views, though some obvious empirical facts pointed out in Buddhism are also incorporated in it. In an almost Buddhistic manner, it speaks of the impermanence of worldly objects and considers all feelings resulting from the sense-object-contact as sources of suffering. Accordingly, it also, like Buddhism, imparts the teaching of detachment from all pain and pleasure of mundane life. But, unlike Buddhism, it does not deduce the doctrine of anattā (soullessness) from the facts of impermanence and suffering. On the contrary, it continues to assert the metaphysical doctrine of the self, which, more than anything else, provides the basis for its ethical code. We may briefly elucidate this point in the light of the explicit utterances of the B. G.

Kṛṣṇa asking Arjuna to adopt an attitude of detachment to pleasure and pain, says: "Contacts (sparśāḥ) with objects, O Arjuna, give rise to cold and heat, pleasure and pain. They come and go and are impermanent (anityāḥ). Endure them, O Arjuna."[2] "Whatever pleasures are born of contacts (saṃsparśajāḥ) are only sources of suffering (duḥkhayonayaḥ). They have a beginning and an end, O Arjuna. No wise man delights in them."[3] Thus, it appears that the B. G., like Buddhism, arrives at the fact of worldly suffering from the impermanence of worldly objects and imparts the teaching of detachment from them. But the B G does not go all the way with Buddhism and parts company with it in respect of

1. M. II. 31-32.
2. B.G. II. 14.
3. B.G. V. 22.

the last characteristic of soullessness. It is here on this crucial point that it gives up the empirical approach and harks back to the traditional metaphysical notion of the self.

This concept of the self is of pivotal importance in the B. G. and, indeed, its entire metaphysical and theological speculations rest on it. Metaphysically the self is considered as identical with the supreme reality or Brahman (B. G. XIII. 2, 17, 22: XV. 15) and theologically it is spoken of as the manifestation of God (B.G.X. 20; XIII. 27; XV. 7; XVIII. 61). Accordingly, the supreme end of man is said to consist in realising the essential identity of the Ātman with Brahman (B. G. IV. 35; V. 20, 24; XIII. 20) or in seeking union with Iśvara or God (B. G. IV. 9; VII. 23; VIII. 7 8; IX. 34; XI. 55; XII. 8, XVIII. 65, 68). It is to this metaphysical or theological end that all ethical efforts and disciplines are to be directed. The entire ethical code, therefore, is to be evolved in the light of this metaphysical or theological goal. In other words, theology and metaphysics are made the fundamental basis of ethics in the B. G. in contradistinction to its purely empirical basis in early Buddhism. Though it is true that the B. G. also, like Buddhism, refers to the right view of life and speaks of true knowledge as the basis of pursuing a proper course of action and avoiding delusion,[1] yet the true view of life, according to it, consists in realising the true nature of the permanent (nityaḥ, B. G. II, 20, 21) and blissful self (prasannātmā, B.G. XVIII. 54), which according to Buddhist analysis is nothing but delusion. But the B. G., on the other hand, asserts that the "persevering yogins perceive it (the Ātman) as established in the self, though the ignorant ones (acetasaḥ) do not see it."[2] According to it "they who have the eye of wisdom see it, the deluded ones (vimuḍhāḥ) do not see."[3] Thus, on the basis of the knowledge of this permanent and indestructible soul Arjuna is exhorted to discharge his duty of fighting (B. G. II. 11-25).

---

1. B.G. IV. [illegible].
2. Yatanto yoginaś cai'naṃ paśyanty ātmany avasthitam, B.G. XV. 11.
3. vimūḍhā nā'nupaśyanti paśyanti jñānacakṣuṣaḥ, B.G. XV. 10.

It may be easily noticed how even when the B. G. and Buddhism preach some identical ethical precepts, they try to establish them on the basis of their respective metaphysical and empirical considerations. In the course of prescribing the virtue of non-injury, Buddha speaks of treating all creatures like oneself, promoting happiness to all and refraining from doing any harm to them. The *raison d'être* of treating all creatures like oneself, according to Buddhism, is just the empirical fact that all living beings like ourselves have a natural liking for life and happiness, and they dislike death and pain. On the basis of this empirically observed common trait of their nature, Buddha lays down the ethical principle of non-injury or non-violence, and directs one to treat all beings like oneself. He says: "All tremble at punishment, all fear death,....to all life is dear. Comparing others with oneself, (attānaṃ upamaṃ katvā), one should neither kill nor cause to kill."[1] Thus, the principle that one should not do unto others what one does not wish others to do unto oneself, is not derived by Buddha from any metaphysical or theological assumption but is considered a simple inference derived from one's own experience. As Buddha clearly points out in the Anumāna Sutta: "Here one should oneself infer as follows: 'an evil person who is swayed by evil thoughts is disagreeable to and disliked by me; now if I were to be evil and swayed by evil thoughts, I too would be disagreeable and disliked by others.' "[2]

The same teaching of treating all like oneself in promoting happiness and refraining from inflicting injury to others is taught by the B.G. as well. But it does so on the basis of its metaphysical and theological concepts of the all-pervading Self and God. The perfect yogin of the B. G. is said to look upon the happiness and suffering of others like his own. The *raison d'être* of it is that the same Self (speaking metaphysically) or God (speaking theologically) is found by the yogin to pervade all the multiple creatures of the world. As the B. G. puts it: "He who has absorbed himself in meditation (yoga), sees the Self abiding in all beings and all beings in

1. Dh. 129 & 130.
2. M. I. 97.

the Self; he sees with equality everywhere (sarvatra samadarśanaḥ)."[1] In the next verse the same idea is repeated in theological terms: "He sees me (God) everywhere and sees all in me."[2] Thus, after showing the fundamental unity and equality of all beings on metaphysical and theological grounds, the aforesaid ethical principle is derived as follows: "He, O Arjuna, who perceives equally everywhere in respect of pleasure and pain, comparing others to oneself (ātmaupamyena) is to be considered as a perfect yogin."[3]

The same is true of the condemnation of asceticism or self-mortification by Buddhism and the B. G. Buddhism, as usual, exposes the absurdity of self-mortification by appealing to empirical facts. Referring to the Nigaṇṭhas who indulged in severe self-mortification under the belief that thereby they would expiate their past sins, prevent new ones, and thus extricate themselves from all suffering and attain perfect bliss (salvation), Buddha points out that in the process of their present self-imposed torture the Nigaṇṭhas, evidently, experience tremendous suffering. How then, can this suffering be said to have been caused by the past deeds and how can they thereby be led to the cessation of suffering and attainment of bliss?[4] He, then observes: "If, monks, (they hold that) beings experience pleasure and pain on account of previous actions, indeed then, O Monks, the Nigaṇṭhas were the performers of heinous actions in the past, for which they are now experiencing such painful, severe and bitter sensations."[5] He, by questioning them further, shows how the self-torture of the Nigaṇṭhas has no real basis in experience whatsoever. He asks them the following questions: 'Do you know whether or not you existed in the past.....whether you did or did not do any evil deed in the past....what kind of evil deed you did in the past....what amount of suffering has been spent

1. B.G. VI. 29.
2. B.G. VI. 30.
3. Ātmaupamyena sarvatra samaṃ paśyati yo'rjuna,
sukhaṃ vā yadi vā duḥkhaṃ sa yogī paramo mataḥ. B.G. VI. 32.
4. M. II. 219.
5. M. II. 222.

what amount remains to be spent and what amount of suffering was altogether necessary (for expiation).....whether the expiation of evil deeds and attainment of meritorious deeds are to take place in the present life."[1] The Jain ascetics are found to have no knowledge of any of these questions and thus their whole practice is shown to be devoid of any empirical basis. Buddha, on the basis of his own personal experience, found this practice of self-mortification as non-efficacious.[2] Again he points out that the ascetic, on account of the lack of right knowledge, is likely to be proud, puffed up, greedy, desirous of praise and fame, jealous, covetous and given to anger.[3] Even when he is free from these evils, he has not got at the true core or essence of righteousness but is only on the surface of it like finding the superficial bark of a tree (na kho....ettāvatā tapojigucchā aggappattā ca hoti sārappattā ca, api ca kho papaṭikappattā hotī ti, D. III. 48), for there has been no inner purification on the basis of right knowledge. Thus, asceticism or self-mortification is rejected by Buddha in the light of empirical facts.

The B. G. here also, as in the previous case, takes the metaphysical and theological stand. It condemns self-mortification or austerity on the ground that it is painful to the indwelling Divinity and is against the injunctions of the scriptures (supposedly of divine origin, B.G. III. 10, 15). It says: "Those men, who possessed of pride and egotism and impelled by the force of lust and passion perform austere penances, not sanctioned by the scriptures, do know these fools to be of demoniac nature, (since) they torture the group of elements in the body and also me (God) abiding in the body."[4]

Thus the ethics of the B.G. is grounded in the supreme Divinity which in various forms provides the basis for its moral doctrines. As the all-pervading inmost self it is the inner light (antarjyotiḥ B.G.V.24), showing the right course

1. M. II. 214-5.
2. M. I. 242-6.
3. D. III. 42-45.
4. B.G. XVII. 5 & 6

of action; as the supreme ground, upholder and the lord(gatir bhartā prabhuḥ, B.G.IX.18) it is the director (B.G.XVIII.61) and law-giver of the universe. As Kṛṣṇa says: "I am the origin of all, from me do all proceed."[1] "Non-violence, equal-mindedness, contentment, penance, charity, fame and ill-fame are different states of beings proceeding from me."[2] It is through the proper exercise of this same universal and indwelling divine principle that one is supposed to have the right congnition of the inviolable law of morality.[3] It is again this Divinity which reveals itself in the form of scriptures. So Arjuna is advised: "Let, therefore, the scripture be your authority for determining what should be done and what should not be done."[4] Thus the B.G. takes recourse to different forms of Intuitionalism[5] in order to establish the validity of its ethics. Besides, it invokes the help of tradition and convention[6] for the same purpose. Thus, as against Buddhism which erects the edifice of its ethics on the basis of the fundamental facts of experience, the B.G. seeks extraneous sanctions from such sources as the metaphysical self, a theological God, scriptural authority, tradition and convention.

This difference concerning the basis of ethics is important not only in its theoretical aspect but also in its practical bearing on moral life. Though, it is true, that some of the ethical precepts can be shown to follow alike from the empirical as well as metaphysical considerations, as in the cases mentioned above, it must be noted that the metaphysical presuppositions and *a priori* speculations, if made the fundamental grounds of ethics and carried out to their furthest limits, may lead ethics to a position where its very purpose is defeated. This is well evidenced from some of the teach-

1. Ahaṃ sarvasya prabhavo mattaḥ sarvaṃ pravartate, B.G. X.8.

2. B.G. X. 5.

3. B.G. XV. 15.

4. Tasmāc chāstraṃ pramāṇaṃ te kāryākāryavyavasthitau, B.G. XVI. 24.

5. For a description of the different forms of Intuitionalism according to what they regard as the predominant source of moral and religious truth see Encyclopaedia of Religion and Ethics, Vol. 7, vide 'Intuitionalism', pp. 397-398.

6. B.G. III. 20; IV. 1, 2 & 15.

ings of the B.G., as also of the Kauṣītakī Upaniṣad, where virtue is swamped by the over-emphasised knowledge of the Ātman. In the Kauṣītakī it is stated: "Whosoever knows me as thus (i.e. as the prajñātmā [1], by no deed whatsoever of his is the world injured, not by stealing, not by killing an embryo, not by the killing of his mother, not by the killing of his father."[2] The B.G.also adopts exactly the same line of thought when it exhorts Arjuna to slay his enemies in view of the metaphysical knowledge of the indestructible and immutable self. It says:"He who knows that it (the self) is indestructible and eternal, unborn and unchanging, how can such a person slay anyone, O Arjuna, or cause any one to slay...Weapons do not cut it, fire does not burn it, waters do not make it wet nor does the wind make it dry."[3] The indwelling Divinity, or the self being absolutely eternal, unattached and immutable, its knowledge makes a man free from the bonds of action. As Kṛṣṇa says:"He who knows me thus, is not bound by actions."[4] "Even if he slays these worlds, he neither slays nor is he bound."[5] It is, thus easy to see how morality is reduced to nought on account of its dependance on an absolutist metaphysics. The inherent defect of ethics based on metaphysics can best be seen in these implications Even Professor Ranade and Belvalker, the two noted champions of the Upaniṣadic thought, have realised this inherent weakness of the absolutist pantheism of the Ups. They observe: "Here, indeed, is touched what may be called the danger line of Upnishadic ethics. To say that the Ātman dies not is legitimate. To say that weapons cannot cut him nor fire burn him is also a legitimate varying of the phrase. But to argue that, therefore, the murderer is no murderer, and there is nobody really responsible for his action is to carry this 'Śāśvata' or 'Akriyā' doctrine to a point which, if seriously preached, would be subversive of all established social institutions and religious

1. prajñātmā taṃ māṃ āyur amṛtam ity upāsva, Kaus. III.2.

2. sa yo māṃ veda na ha vai tasya kena cana karmaṇā loko mīyate, na steyena, na bhrūṇa-hatyayā, na mātṛ-vadhena, na pitṛ-vadhena.... Kaus. III.1.

3. B.G. II. 21, 23.

4. iti māṃ yo'bhijānāti karmabhir na sa badhyate, B.G. IV. 14.

5. hatvā'pi sa imāṃl lokān na hanti na nibadhyate B.G. XVIII. 17.

sacraments."[1]

In fact, the transcendental truth of supramundane unity where the multiplicity of the world melts away, has to be realised in one's own direct experience by means of gradual development of the natural faculties through proper ethical conduct. Ethics is, thus, only the means to the transcendental or 'metaphysical' plane (if we may at all use the word 'metaphysical' in this special sense). It is only on that higher plane that ethics loses its significance, for it can have meaning only in the midst of multiplicity or society of individuals. But if one, instead of going from ethics to metaphysics reverses the process and proceeds from some *a priori* metaphysical assumptions to ethics, one will inevitably be caught in contradictions. Buddhism, therefore, cautions people against muddling metaphysics with ethics which is a matter of direct personal experience and not of any *a priori* speculation and assumption. It is the apex to be reached slowly and gradually through the holy life based on ethics, which having been attained, the mundane life is transcended and the ethical life is lived out. But in any case, if one has to deal with the world of multiplicity, whether he be a perfected saint or an average man, one has to follow ethical codes based on the empirical facts of mundane life. The B.G. by confounding ethics with metaphysics ignores the boundary between the two, and is thereby involved in ethical absurdities. The very fact that the same metaphysical presupposition of the eternal, immutable and all-pervading self is invoked to justify two mutually opposed lines of action, viz., the saving of life as well as the slaying of beings, shows the inner contradictions of the speculative basis of ethics.

3. *The Summum Bonum of Life and the Major Ingredients of the Holy Pursuit*:—

As indicated above, ethics is the initial requirement of the holy life which prepares the ground for the development of higher faculties by means of which true knowledge is attained and Nirvāṇa realised. It is, evidently, not an end in itself but only a means leading to the state of inner purification and concentration whereby the supreme end or the *summum*

1. History of Indian Philosophy, II, p. 399.

bonum of life (Nirvāṇa) is attained. The beginning, therefore, must be made with the correct view of life and all efforts must be directed towards the attainment of this goal. This right view (sammādiṭṭhi) of life, as already explained, does not consist, according to Buddhism, in accepting any *a priori* metaphysical or theological hypothesis but in a critical understanding of the fundamental facts of experience. The need for proceeding with the correct view of life is, no doubt, accepted in the B.G. as well, but it is said to consist in understanding the metaphysical and theological ideas rather than in comprehending the true nature of the empirical life.[1] So it ultimately falls back on the traditional concepts of the Soul and God. It is this basic presupposition and bias for tradition which primarily differentiates the ethical approach of the B.G. from that of Buddhism. Notwithstanding this difference, however, there are some significant similarities in their ethical doctrines and disciplines. Ethics, according to both of them, is regarded as the initial stage of the holy life and the *summum bonum* of life is said to consist in the attainment of Nirvāṇa.[2]

A devout holy pursuit in Buddhism has to be undertaken with trust or confidence. Since the deeper significance of the unsatisfactoriness of mundane life and the efficacy of the path leading to the absolute deliverance from it has to be understood by the beginner in reliance on the experience of the perfect ones, saddhā or confidence is recomended in Buddhism as an essential preliminary for the holy life. But this saddhā, as we have already shown (supra, pp. 251-265) is not the same as blind or baseless faith (amūlikā saddhā, M.II. 170) but is a confidence based on critical examination. We have seen how in early Buddhism a critical procedure for the examination of a teacher is laid down through which the teacher must

1. cf. yaj jñātvā na punar moham evaṃ yāsyasi pāṇḍava, yena bhūtany aśeṣeṇa drakṣyasy ātmany atho mayi., B.G. IV. 35.

2. Nibbānogadhaṃ hi. . .brahmacariyam, nibbānaparāyanaṃ nibbānapariyosānam, M.I. 304; S.V. 216; nibbānāya. . . anuttarassa yogakkhemassa adhigamāya, S. II. 195, 196. see also Dh. 184, 204. cf. sukham ātyantikaṃ yat tat, B.G. VI. 21; yaṃ labdhvā cā'paraṃ lābhaṃ manyate nā'dhikaṃ tataḥ, VI. 22; yad icchanto brahmacaryaṃ caranti, B.G. VIII. 11.

first be tested before one is to approach him with faith (saddhājāto upasaṅkamati, M.I.480). Subsequently after having listened to him and having personally verified some of his teachings, one is said to start his religious career under him with a rational faith in the Noble Doctrine (dhamme aveccappasādena samannāgato hoti, M.I 37). It is this verified knowledge of the basic principles and consequent confidence in the Doctrine (Dhamma) which marks the beginning of the holy life in early Buddhism, and is known as the right view of life (ettāvatā...ariyasāvako sammādiṭṭhi, hoti,...dhamme aveccappasādena samannāgato, M.I.47).

In the B. G. also this initial faith is recommended and people are advised to follow the instructions of the enlightened seers with faith and reverence. It is said: "The men of wisdom (jñāninaḥ) who have seen the truth will instruct you in knowledge. Learn that by humble reverence, by inquiry and by service."[1] "The faithful one (śraddhāvān) attains knowledge with his senses subdued and being devoted to that (knowledge)."[2] But unlike Buddhism, it does not lay down a critical procedure to examine the teacher acclaimed as the knower and seer of the truth (jñānī, tattvadarśī, B. G. IV. 34). On the other hand, it is asserted that the seer of the truth is one who sees the imperishable and abiding self in all perishable creatures (B. G. XIII. 27; cf. II. 16). Thus the faith recommended in the B.G. cannot be regarded as rational and critical as that of early Buddhism.

With rational faith firmly rooted and established (mūlajātā patiṭṭhitā...ākāravatī saddhā, M. I. 320), a holy aspirant in Buddhism is said to follow the Eightfold Path leading to salvation. It is a path which avoids the two extremes of self-indulgence and self-mortification and is, therefore, also known as the Middle Path (majjhimā paṭipadā). As Buddha himself points out in the Dhammacakka-

1. Tad viddhi praṇipātena paripraśnena sevayā,
upadekṣyanti te jñānaṃ jñāninas tattvadarśinaḥ., B.G. IV. 34.

2. Śraddhāvāṃl labhate jñānaṃ tatparaḥ saṃyatendriyaḥ, B G. IV. 39.

ppavattana Sutta: "The two extremes, monks, are not to be followed. What are the two? To give oneself up to indulgence in sensual pleasure (kāmesu kāmasukhallikānuyoga), which is base, common, vulgar, unholy and unprofitable; or to give oneself up to self-mortification (attakilamathānuyoga), which is painful, unholy and unprofitable. Avoiding both these extremes, the Tathāgata has shown the Middle Path, which is to make for insight and knowledge, to lead to peace, discernment, enlightenment or Nibbāna. What, monks, is that Middle Path? It is the very same Noble Eightfold Path (ayam eva ariyo aṭṭhaṅgiko maggo)."[1] This path consisting of eight steps is broadly subsumed under three heads, usually known as the three sampadās or khandhas, viz. sīla (practical morality), samādhi (concentration) and paññā (wisdom). Within these three stages of holy life, the whole of the Eightfold Path is included, as the learned nun, Dhammadinnā explains to Visākha.[2]

We do not propose here to discuss at any length the Eightfold Path of Buddha which is well-known to students of Buddhism. We only wish to point out here that with regard to the three major ingredients of the holy life, viz., sīla, samādhi and paññā as well as in relation to its chief feature of avoiding the extremes and following the Middle Path, the B. G. is found to be in general agreement with Buddhism. According to Buddhism, the highest knowledge (paññā) leading to final deliverance (vimutti) is to be attained through meditation (samādhi), which in its turn requires prior purification of mind by means of moral virtue and discipline (sīla). Thus, in early Buddhism, sīla, samādhi, paññā and vimutti are causally conditioned, and represent the progressive stages of the holy path. One is first said to cultivate moral virtue (sīlasampadaṃ ārādheti, M. I. 200), then enter into concentration (samādhi sampadaṃ ārādheti, M. I. 201), through which he acquires knowledge and insight (ñāṇadassanaṃ ārādheti, M. I. 202), and having attained perfect knowledge, he is finally released (sammāñāṇassa sammāvimutti pa hoti, M. III. 76). Thus, the virtuous

1. S. V. 421.
2. M.I. 301.

life is a preparation for attaining true wisdom. As it is said: "Wisdom is adorned by conduct" (apadāne sobhati paññā, A. I. 102). The intimate and invariable relation between virtue and knowledge is well indicated in the famous saying of Buddha; "Wisdom is cleansed by virtue and virtue is cleansed by wisdom; where there is virtue there is wisdom and where there is wisdom there is virtue; the virtuous one has wisdom and the wise one has virtue; virtue and knowledge are reckoned in the world as the best."[1]

In the B. G. also the need for virtue, self-control and discipline is emphasised in order to reach the state of concentration (samādhi), whereby knowledge and salvation are said to be attained. It is pointed out that the intellect cannot be established in meditation (buddhiḥ samādhau na vidhīyate, B. G. II. 44) so long as the mind is engrossed in worldly enjoyment and power, and is distracted by them (bhogaiśvaryaprasaktānāṃ, tayā'pahṛtacetasām, loc. cit.). So the B. G. starts with the control of the senses (tasmāt tvam indriyāṇy ādau niyamya bharatarṣabha, B.G. III. 41) and asks the holy aspirant to restrain the mind and the intellect in the proper manner.[2] It is only when the intellect stands unshaken and stable in meditation that the equanimity needed for the placid vision of truth is attained.[3] Various moral virtues like abandoning egotism, violence, pride, lust, anger, accumulation and possession are mentioned along with the cultivation of the tranquillity of mind (B. G. XVIII. 53) as disciplines conductive to concentration (dhyānayoga), which having been duly practised, one is said to be fit to realise the supreme state (Brahmabhūyāya kalpate.)[4]. After this the aspirant is said to attain true wisdom whereby he is led to final release which is characterised by the B. G. as a merging with the Supreme (tato māṃ tattvato jñātvā viśate tadanantaram, B. G. XVIII. 55). Thus, despite the account of

1. Sīlaparidhotā...paññā, paññāparidhotaṃsīlaṃ; yattha silaṃ tattha paññā, yattha paññā tattha sīlaṃ. Sīlavato paññā, paññavato sīlaṃ. Sīlapaññāṇaṃ ca pana lokasmiṃ aggamakkhāyati, D.I. 124.

2. B.G. III. 40-43; VI. 24-26.

3. B.G. II. 53.

4. B.G. XVIII. 51-53; V. 25-29.

the B. G. being not quite clear, systematic and methodical, as has already been pointed out (supra, pp. 183-197), there can be no doubt that it agrees, at least, in general with the Buddhist account of the successive stages of progress in the holy life. The fact that the holy life is to begin with faith and pass through the successive stages of virtue, wisdom and salvation is well brought out in the following verse of the B. G. : "The man possesed of faith (śraddhāvān) endeavouring with the control of the senses (saṃyatendriyaḥ) gains wisdom (jñānam) and having gained wisdom he, in no time, attains salvation or the supreme Peace (parāṃ śāntim)."[1]

The avoidance of the two extremes, viz. self-indulgence and self-mortification is also quite clearly accepted by the B. G. We have just noted that according to it concentration (samādhi) is impossible so long as the intellect is engrossed in worldly enjoyments and powers and distracted thereby.[2] The B. G., therefore, emphasises that the intellect has to be withdrawn from distracting desires in order to be firmly and unshakably established in samādhi (B. G. II. 53). But, for that purpose, it does not advocate the practice of forceful repression or the stifling of the senses.[3] It, on the other hand, considers those people as ignorant (acetasaḥ) and of a demoniac will (āsuraniścayān) who indulge in violent austerities and self-mortification.[4] Kṛṣṇa clearly says: "Yoga is attained neither by him who is given to excess in eating nor by him who does not eat at all. Again, O Arjuna, it is not to be attained by him who sleeps too much or keeps awake too much. The yoga leading to the destruction of suffering is attained by him who is moderate in food and recreation, whose effort in discipline is regulated and who is moderate in sleep and keeping awake."[5] All this shows that the disciplines prescribed in Buddhism and the B. G. for the

---

1. B.G. IV. 39.
2. Bhogaiśvaryaprasaktānāṃ tayā'pahṛtacetasām,
   vyavasāyātmikā buddhiḥ samādhau na vidhīyate., B.G. II. 44.
3. prakṛtiṃ yānti bhūtani nigrahaḥ kiṃ kariṣyati., B. G. III. 33.
4. B.G. XVII. 5and 6
5. B.G. VI. 16 & 17.

realisation of their respective ideals of holy life follow a similar pattern, though there are differences in emphasis and details, as we shall see in the sequel.

Buddhist and the B. G. Ideals of Holy Life as Compared with the Ethical Ideals of the West:—

It is clear from the foregoing discussion that ethics is considered by Buddhism and the B. G. only as an essential preliminary for practising the higher holy life. Both of them, therefore, envisage a stage when the life of practical morality is transcended. Buddha in his discourse with Pañcakaṅga, the carpenter refers to this stage where all good acts of practical morality are stopped without residue (kusalā sīlā aparisesā nirujjhanti, M. II. 27). It should not, however, be thought that Buddha thereby sanctions an immoral life to the holy aspirant after a particular stage, as had been wrongly understood by Ariṭṭha.[1] What Buddha really means to convey by this is that the purpose of practical morality is fulfilled for such an elevated aspirant who has gone over to the next higher stage. At that stage he is no more moved by the distracting thoughts prompting immoral actions. He has become what is known as 'asekha'[2] (requiring no more moral training), since he is no more liable to fall (abhabhā..pamajjituṃ, M. I. 47). The relative purpose of the different stages of the holy life is well conveyed through the parable of the relays of chariots (rathavinītaṃ), each having a purpose only in so far as it leads to the next stage.[3] The ideal stage thus does not consist merely in mastering morality but in going beyond it. It is in this vein that Buddha says: "Not by mere virtues and ceremonies (na sīlabbatamattena), nor by much learning, nor even by gain of concentration, nor by lonely lodging, do I enjoy the bliss of dispassion (nekkhammasukhaṃ) resorted to by the non-worldling."[4] Virtuous deeds and obser-

1. M.I. 130ff.
2. Catunnam.. satipaṭṭhānānaṃ samattaṃ bhāvitattā asekho hoti., S.V. 175.
3. M.I. 149-150.
4. Dh. 271, 272.

vances (sīlabbata) are necessary but not sufficient for the attainment of the ideal state of holy life.[1] To feel conceited merely by fulfilling virtuous deeds and observances is only an undue clinging to them (sīlabbatupādāna, D. II. 58) and is, therefore, disapproved by Buddha. Professor Wijesekera rightly notices this feature of Buddhist ethics when he remarks: "Early Buddhism administers a warning to the aspirant to master morality but not allow morality to get the better of him,"[2] Obviously, then the early Buddhist ideal of the holy life cannot be equated with the ethical Perfectionism of some of the Western moralists.

In this respect the view of the B.G. also is quite similar to that of early Buddhism, notwithstanding some differences concerning the details of practical morality. In it also practical morality consisting of the control of the mind and the senses is needed only for the sake of attaining equanimity and concentration. When a man has put away all the desires of his mind and has become a man of established wisdom (sthitaprajña)[3], he is said to have transcended the realm of morality. As the B.G. explicitly states: "Being endowed with such an intellect, he casts away even here both moral and immoral action."[4] Speaking in metaphysical terms, the B. G. further adds: "The man who delights in the self, who is contented with the self, satisfied within the self, for him there is no act that needs to be done,"[5] (i. e. no moral action is any more needed for him). "He has no purpose whatsoever to be achieved in the world either by action or by inaction. He has no interest to be served in all these living beings."[6] This shows that the B. G. also, like Buddhism, does not limit itself to the goal of ethical Perfectionism.

---

1. Na diṭṭhiyā na sutiyā na ñāṇena *silabbatenā'* pi na suddhim āha,
adiṭṭhiyā assutiyā aññāṇā *asilatā abbatā* no pi tena,
ete ca nissajja anuggahāya santo anissāya bhavaṃ na jappe.,
Sn. 157-8.

2. 'Buddhist Ethics' in 'Knowledge and Conduct' (The Wheel Publication, No. 50), p. 18.

3. Prajahāti yadā kāmān sarvān pārtha manogatān,
atmany eā'tmanā tuṣṭaḥ sthitaprajñaḥ tado'cyate., B.G. II. 55.

4. Buddhiyukto jahātī'ha ubhe sukṛtaduṣkṛte, B.G. II. 50.

5. B.G. III. 17.

6. B.G. III. 18

It must, however, be noted that according to the B. G. this state of the transcendence of morality can be reached not only through the practice of a single pattern of moral discipline, as Buddhism would have it, but also through other means like devotion and disinterested action. Thus, besides the aforesaid method of self-control and moral discipline leading to concentration (B. G. II. 53 ff; VI. 9ff), the B. G. refers to the devotional means as follows: "Dedicate all that to me, O Arjuna, whatever you do, whatever you eat, whatever oblation you offer, whatever charity you give, whatever penance you observe. Thus shall you be free from the bonds of action bearing good and bad fruits (śubhāśubhaphalair evaṃ mokṣyase karmabandhanaiḥ)."[1] The same state of moral transcendence known as 'naiṣkarmyasiddhi' is said to be attained also through the performance of disinterested actions (karma-yoga). Kṛṣṇa after asking Arjuna to discharge his bounden duties (B. G. XVIII. 48), asserts in the next verse: "The man having a detached intellect everywhere, who is self-restrained and whose desires are removed, he attains the supreme state of the transcendence of actions by means of desireless action (saṃnyāsena)."[2] After reaching this stage of transcendence through disinterested action,one is to proceed further in order to realise the subsequent stage leading to the highest goal which is characterised as "the supreme consummation of wisdom" (niṣṭhā jñānasya yā parā, B. G. XVIII. 50). Another distinguishing feature of the B. G., which we may note in this connection, is that the man at this stage, according to it, can perform even some morally defective (sadoṣam api) actions,[3] in certain circumstances, which are never sanctioned by Buddhism. We shall discuss this point further in the sequel. Again the B. G., as usual, views this state metaphysically as a state of rejoicing in the self (B. G. II. 55; III. 17) and theologically

1. B.G. IX. 27 and 28.

2. B.G. XIII. 49; The meaning of the word 'saṃnyāsa' occurring in the present verse has been explained in the beginning of the XVIIIth canto where it is defined as "the abandonment of actions prompted by desire" (kāmyānām karmaṇām nyāsam, XVIII. 2).

3. Sahajaṃ karma kaunteya sadoṣam api na tyajet, B.G. XVIII. 48; cf. Kṛṣṇa's exhortation to Arjuna in B.G. II. 38.

as dwelling and delighting in God (B. G. V. 19-21; X. 9), which is not the case with Buddhism.

We have already seen that the ultimate goal of the holy life, viz., Nirvāṇa is considered both by Buddhism and the B. G. as inconceivable in terms of mundane experience. Both of them, therefore, make use of negative descriptions to indicate its supramundane nature. But in order to indicate that it is the most desirable end and the culmination of the holy quest, they also speak of it as the supreme bliss (Nibbānaṃ paramaṃ sukhaṃ, M. I. 508; Dh. 203 and 204. cf. sukham ātyantikam, B. G. VI. 21, 28; sukham uttamam, B.G. VI. 27; sukham akṣayam, B. G. V. 21). This expression perhaps has led Dr. Pratt to classify Buddhism as a form of Hedonism.[1] But a little reflection will show that neither Buddhism nor the B. G. can fall under any of the hedonistic theories, as understood by most of the Western hedonists. Without entering into any discussion of the different forms of hedonism, it can at once be pointed out that the Buddhist or the B. G. ideal of the highest bliss is not the mundane happiness with which the Western hedonists chiefly concern themselves. According to Buddhism when the aspirant, in the gradual process of the holy pursuit, reaches the first stage of concentration, he is said to experience inner happiness which is distinct from any sensuous happiness of the world.[2] This latter form of happiness depending as it does on the senses is deprecated as "low, vulgar and ignoble" and is required to be abandoned by the holy aspirant.[3] Even the inner happiness along with its opposite is to be abandoned and the aspirant has to develop a state of perfect indifference to pleasant and painful hedonic tone at the stage of the fourth jhāna.[4] Thus, the Buddhist concept of supreme happiness as the goal of holy life trans-

1. Dr. Pratt remarks : "His (Buddha's) system may be classed as a form of altruistic hedonism in which the higher spiritual pleasures are rated much more important than those of the body."—Pilgrimage of Buddhism and a Buddhist Pilgrimage, p. 20.

2. D. I. 73; M. III. 233.

3. M. III. 230, 233.

4. Sukhassa ca pahānā dukkhassa ca pahānā...adukkhamasukhaṃ upekkhāsatiparisuddhiṃ catutthaṃ jhānaṃ upasampajja viharati, D.I. 75.

cends not only the sensuous happiness which is erotic in character (kāma) but also the inner jhānic happiness which is non-erotic (nekkhamma) in nature. It is a supramundane happiness which results from the cessation of all inner and outer feelings (saññāvedayitanirodha). It is, indeed, incomprehensible in terms of any mundane experience of happiness. In fact, it is the happiness resulting from the extinction of renewed mundane existence. The monk Udāyi astonished by Sāriputta's exclamation, "Bliss is Nibbāna, bliss is Nibbāna," asks: "How can there be bliss, where there is no feeling?" Sāriputta replies: "This precisely, O friend, is bliss that here there is no feeling."[1] This explains why this bliss is characterised by Buddha as "the stilling of all volitions"[2] or "the Peace."[3] Even though in the highest form of hedonism as conceived by Mill, the qualitative difference among happiness is acknowledged and the superiority of mental over bodily pleasure is granted,[4] it never goes beyond the mundane concept of happiness. Radhakrishnan is right when he distinguishes the Buddhist ideal of happiness from that of the hedonists and remarks: "Modern hedonists contend that happiness is found in the increase of life in its length and breadth. The Buddhists claim that it lies in the dissolution of the conditions of.....renewed existence."[5]

What has been said above in relation to Buddhism holds good on the whole with regard to the B. G. as well. The bliss which is spoken of by the B. G. as 'supreme and absolute' (sukham ātyantikam, VI. 21, 28; sukham aikāntikam, XIV. 27), 'excellent and undecaying' (sukham uttamam, VI. 27; sukham akṣayam, V. 21) can hardly be confused with any kind of worldly happiness, since the world as a whole is declared by the B. G. as impermanent and sorrowful (anityam

1. A. IV. 414-5.

2. Aniccā vata saṅkhāra...tesam vūpasamo sukho'ti, II. 199.

3. natthi santiparaṃ sukhaṃ, Dh. 202.

4. Granting the superiority of refined human pleasure over the gross brutal one, Mill observes: "It is better to be a human being dissatisfied than a pig satisfied; better to be a Socrates dissatisfied than a fool satisfied." —*Utilitarianism*, p. 9.

5. Indian Philosophy, Vol I, pp. 429-430.

asukhaṃ lokam, IX. 33). Referring to the ignoble sensuous pleasures of the world the B. G. clearly says: "Whatever pleasures are born of contacts are only sources of suffering, they have a beginning and an end, O Arjuna, no wise man delights in them."[1] In order to reach the highest state one has to transcend the pairs of opposites (pleasure and pain etc.) and be completely free from the threefold mode of prakṛti producing pleasure, pain and indifference.[2] The word 'nirdvandvaḥ' (B. G. II. 45), as Śaṅkara explains it, is to indicate the stage of complete freedom from pleasure and pain produced by objects of opposite nature;[3] or as Ramānuja puts it: "it is a stage of being completely free from all mundane nature" (nirgatasakala sāṃsārikasvabhāvaḥ, R. B. G. II. 45). Only when one reaches the stage of equanimity and indifference to pain and pleasure, is one said to be fit for realising the state of immortality (samaduḥkhasukhaṃ dhīraṃ so'mṛtatvāya kalpate, B. G. II. 15). We have noticed (supra, 194-195) that both Buddhism and the B. G. speak of quite similar stages leading to concentration. Now it is added in the B. G. with regard to the ever-contented yogin of self-restraint and unshakable determination (saṃtuṣṭaḥ satataṃ yogī yatātmā dṛḍhaniścayaḥ, B. G. XII. 14) that he is free from joy, anger, fear and agitation (harṣāmarṣabhayodvegair mukto, B. G. XII. 15), completely unconcerned, pure, competent, indifferent and untroubled (anapekṣaḥ śucir dakṣa udāsīno gatavyathaḥ, B. G. XII. 16), neither pleased nor displeased (yo na hṛṣyati na dveṣṭi, B. G. XII 17) and is alike in cold, heat, pleasure and pain, and is absolutely detached (śītoṣṇasukhaduḥkheṣu samaḥ saṅgavivarjitaḥ, B. G. XII. 18). This indicates that the yogin has not only gone beyond the sensuous pleasures but has also reached a stage of complete transcendence of inner and outer feelings, called by the B. G., 'the stage of supreme perfection of disinterestedness' (naiṣkarmyasiddhiṃ paramām, B. G. XVIII. 49).

1. B.G. V. 22.
2. nirdvandvo nityasattvastho niryogakṣema ātmavān B.G., II. 45.
3. sukhaduḥhahetū sapratipakṣau padārthau, dvandvaśabdavvandvo, S.B.G. II. 45.

The ultimate goal, however, is not reached even then, and a still higher stage of development has to be gone through before he reaches the supreme end, described by the B. G. as the culmination of wisdom (niṣṭhā jñānasya yā parā).[1] It is quite apposite, therefore, that the B. G. also, like Buddhism, should call this state, "the Peace, the supreme Nirvāṇa" (śāntiṃ nirvāṇaparamām, VI. 15, cf. IV. 39, IX. 31; XVIII. 62).

This leaves little doubt about the fact that the word 'happiness' (sukha) is used by Buddhism and the B. G. only in an exceptional sense. This is well indicated by the B. G. when it speaks of this happiness as beyond the ken of the senses and realisable only by the understanding (sukham ātyantikaṃ yat tad buddhigrāhyam atīndriyam, VI. 21). According to Buddhism also, it cannot be experienced outwardly and has to be realised inwardly by the wise (paccattaṃ veditabbo viññūhi, M. I, 37). But in view of the B. G.'s frequent characterisation of this happiness as the realisation of the inmost self (B. G. II. 55, III. 17, VI. 20), we are inclined to think that the B. G. perhaps has only a vague and sporadic realisation of the highest state, which Buddhism seems to be in full and firm possession of. In any case, however, there can be no doubt that the supramundane happiness of either the B. G. or of Buddhism is beyond the range of any form of hedonistic ideal.

Though Eudaemonism is distinguished from Hedonism, inasmuch as it is defined as a theory according to which "the ethical end, the ultimate object to be achieved by action and conduct, the standard and final criterion of what ought to be, is welfare,"[2] yet it cannot be denied that the term 'welfare' has been generally understood and employed in the sense of some sort of happiness. It is, of course, true that following Aristotle, the noted exponent of Eudaemonism (who observes that "well-being is founded and rooted in well-doing"[3]), a greater emphasis is laid in it on moral excellence, but as

1. B.G. XVIII. 50-55.
2. Encyclopaedia of Religion and Ethics, Vol. V, p. 571.
3. cf. Ibid, p. 571.

Professor Wundt has rightly pointed out, "if we adhere to the generally accepted principle that the end of all moral action is the welfare of our fellow-men, then the striving for perfection ultimately reduces itself to the principle of the maximum of happiness."[1] We have, however, seen that in Buddhism and the B. G. the end of holy life far transcends even the finest form of worldly happiness and, therefore, it does not seem proper to reduce their ideals to Eudaemonism. Eudaemonism is said to come quite close to Perfectionism insofar as it lays great stress on the moral development of man and points out that 'well-being is founded and rooted in well-doing'. But we have already noted that the Buddhist and the B. G. ideal transcends even Perfectionism which is granted, at least, a 'formal superiority' over Eudaemonism in this respect.[2]

We are, thus, led to the conclusion that the highest ideal of holy life, both according to Buddhism and the B. G., cannot strictly be indentified with any of the Western ideals of ethics. This, however, does not mean that happiness, welfare or perfection of oneself or others is ignored by Buddhism and the B.G. In fact, each of them is found both in Buddhism and the B. G. in its truest form, only it is so sublimated and refined that it transcends its usual mundane concept. Again, unlike the above mentioned ethical ideals which emphasise one or the other of these elements, almost in an exclusive manner, Buddhism and the B. G. seem to hold an all-round view taking into consideration not only the outward consequence and mundane attainments but also the inner motives and the supramundane goal. In the subsequent discussion of the Buddhist and the B. G criteria of morality, we shall further notice how they take a comprehensive view of life and look at the moral problems from the standpoint of oneself as well as of others seeking the good and welfare, the happiness and perfection in the highest sense of these terms.

---

1. Ethical Systems, translated by Margaret Floy Washburn, p. 187.

2. Referring to Perfectionism, J.M. Schulhof observes that "practically it coincides with Eudaemonism, though with the formal superiority that it lays more stress on the duty of moral self-development..." Encyclopaedia of Religion and Ethics, Vol. V. vide, 'Eudaemonism', p. 572.

The Criterion of Morality:—

Redemption from the pervasive ill and suffering of mundane existence constitutes the goal of life both in Buddhism and the B.G. and, accordingly, their most fundamental criterion of morality is derived from this supreme consideration. All forms of conduct, which promote the release of man from the mundane suffering and tend to secure the bliss of immortality are good, and their opposites are bad. In holding this fundamental criterion, Buddhism and the B. G. do not go against the basic psychology of man's nature. It is, indeed, in recognition of the self-same psychological urges and tendencies of human mind that Buddhism and the B. G. denounce the undue repression and mortification of the senses and enjoin the ethics of the Middle Path, elevating and sublimating the mind gradually to a stage where finally the normal levels of experience are transcended. Specially in Buddhism, the systematic processes of discipline and meditation are found to be based on a sound psychological basis. The same seems to be accepted in general by the B. G. as well, though it does not discuss the problem methodically. Its teaching of the triple paths of holy life, namely, the paths of knowledge, action and devotion (jñāna, karma and bhakti) seems to be based on the tripartite division of the mind into intellect, will and emotion. We do not propose here to go into a digression by discussing in detail the psychological basis of the Buddhist and the B. G. ethics. But we only wish to point out briefly that Martineau is mistaken when he thinks that "psychological ethics are altogether peculiar to Christendom."[1] It is true that the ultimate ideal of holy life in Buddhism and the B. G. is to reach a stage where the ordinary psychological feelings undergo transformation and mundane modes of conduct are modified, yet it may be noticed that their ethical teachings are founded on the psychological analysis of the nature of man.

Both Buddhism and the B. G. proceed with the realisation of the fundamental fact of psychology that the spring of all moral conduct is the inner will. Buddha is said to

1. Types of Ethical Theory, Vol. I, p. 14.

have made the statement that the willed or volitional (sañcetanika) act alone is ethically significant.[1] It is pointed out that the action of an infant who is devoid of this capacity, can have no moral significance.[2] The intensity of the act is said to depend on the extent to which it is performed deliberately (sañcicca).[3] Thus, there is clear recognition of the fact that only those actions which are voluntary, that is to say, willed by the agent are liable to be called either morally good or bad. In view of the inner will or volition being the prime spring of moral action, what one outwardly does (karoti) or says (bhāsati) has a secondary or indirect ethical significance, whereas what one thinks or wills is of primary or direct ethical value. This Buddhist approach, assigning greater ethical significance to the mental or volitional act (mano-kamma) than to the verbal and bodily act (vacī-kamma and kāya-kamma) is well borne out in Buddha's discussion with the Jain Dīghatapassī and Upāli who held the opposite view.[4] The Dhammapada also opens with the same assertion. It says : "All mental states are preceded by will, led by will and made by will. If one *speaks* or *acts* with an evil will, suffering follows him like the wheel following the foot of the drawer,..if one *speaks* or *acts* with a good will, happiness follows him like the ever-following shadow.[5]" Thus, it is made clear that the root (mūla) of all meritorious and demeritorious actions (kusala and akusala kamma) is the inner purity or impurity of the mind. It naturally follows from it that according to Buddhism we cannot call an act morally good or bad merely on the basis of its external consequences without taking into consideration the inner motive from which it springs.

The inner roots of all meritorious and demeritorious actions are pychologically analysed in early Buddhism and it

1. Cetanā'haṃ bhikkhave kammaṃ vadāmi, cetayitvā kammaṃ karoti—kāyena vācāyā manasā, A. III 415; sañcetanikaṃ...kammaṃ katvā kāyena vācāya manasā...sukhaṃ...dukkhaṃ...adukkhamasukhaṃ so vedayatī ti, M. III. 207; cf. M.I. 377.

2. M. II. 24-25.

3. D. III. 133; M.I. 523; II. 103.

4. M.I. 373, 376-8.

5. Dh. 1 and 2.

is pointed out that all demeritorious actions, whether manifested outwardly (i. e. verbal or bodily actions) or harboured within, without outer manifestation (i. e. mental actions),[1] are rooted in three unwholesome or undesirable states of mind, viz., lust or attachment (lobha or rāga), hatred (dosa) and delusion (moha) which are, therefore, known as 'akusala-mūla' (roots of demeritorious actions). The opposites of them are the roots of the corresponding meritorious actions which are, therefore, called 'kusala-mūla' (roots of meritorious actions).[2] As bondage or release is the result of our own wrong or right actions, as the case may be, the roots of these actions are naturally considered the roots of bondage and release. Thus, as we have seen in the course of the discussion of Nibbāna, bondage is said to be caused by attachment, hatred and delusion and deliverance is defined as the destruction of the self-same evil states of the mind.[3] Now, deciding the moral worth of an action in terms of its being conducive to or subversive of the highest end, viz. Nibbāna, it is maintained in early Buddhism that such actions which lead to the conquest of attachment, hatred and delusion are good and those which lead to their promotion are evil, and, accordingly, a great emphasis is laid on their eradication.[4] One has, therefore, to see introspectively whether one's actions are prompted by attachment, hatred or delusion, and thereby determine whether one's actions are good or evil.

It is in this context that the need of self-reflection has been emphasised by Buddha, and the mind has been compared with a mirror wherein one should introspectively see whether one's action is aimed at the good of oneself and others. In his admonition to Rāhula, Buddha says:

> "What do you think, Rāhula, for what purpose is a mirror"?

1. For the list of all these actions, see supra, p. 413.
2. M. I. 47; 489-490.
3. rāgakkhayo dosakkhayo mohakkhayo—idaṃ vuccati nibbānan'ti S. IV. 251, 261.
4. Dh. 369, 377; S. IV. 251.

"For the purpose of reflecting (paccavekkhaṇattho), Lord."

"Similarly, Rāhula, having reflected thoroughly should bodily action be done,...verbal action be done,..mental action be done..If Rāhula, when reflecting you realise: 'This bodily action of mine, that I am desirous of doing would lead to my own obstruction or harm (byābādhāya) or to the obstruction or harm of others or to that of both'—demeritorious is this bodily action, entailing suffering and productive of pain. Such an action with the body, Rāhula, you must on no account perform. If, on the other hand, Rāhula, when reflecting you realise: 'This bodily action that I am desirous of doing would be conducive neither to the obstruction or harm of myself, nor to that of others nor to that of both'—meritorious is this bodily action, entailing joy and productive of happiness'. Such bodily action, Rāhula, you should perform. (Similarly with regard to verbal and mental actions)."[1] Thus, along with the inner motive the outer consequencc has to be kept in view wherein, indeed, the former finds expression. Of course, the inner side being the primary and direct spring of action, it is considered ethically more important than the outer manifestation of it, which is relatively secondary or indirect. But even this outer side or the overt action can in no case be altogether ignored, as is done by the B. G. in certain contexts.

It is significant to note that the word, 'byābādha' used by Buddha in the above criterion of morality means both harm to the individual as well as obstruction to his spiritual progress. This may indicate the comprehensive attitude of Buddha which takes into cognisance not only ordinary harm done to oneself and others but also obstruction in the way of spiritual progress, which, indeed, is the greatest harm to one-self and others. It is needless to mention that any harm done to others obstructs the path of spiritual progress and, thus, both being linked together, they have to be jointly taken into consideration in determining the moral worth of an action. This shows how Buddha

1. M.I. 415-6.

keeps an eye on the highest end even while laying down the criterion of practical morality.

It is in keeping with this comprehensive approach that Buddha exhorts monks to work for the happiness and welfare of many (bahujana hitāya bahujana sukhāya, Vin. I. 21). It is evident that the word 'sukha' (happiness) which is used as a synonym of 'hita' (welfare) is not merely mundane pleasure or gain but true happiness and welfare which Buddhism always stands for. Naturally, its meaning is deeper and higher than what is meant by it in Utilitarianism and Eudaemonism. Like the distinction of preya (pleasure) and śreya (good) in the Kaṭhopaniṣad. Buddhism also clearly distinguishes between piya (pleasure) and sukha (happiness or good). The Kaṭha says: "Different is the good and different, indeed, is the pleasant..the wise man reflecting on them chooses the good in preference to the pleasant."[1] In the like manner Buddhism also declares: "Different is the path leading to worldly gain and different, indeed, is the way which leads to Nibbāna. Understanding thus, the monk, the disciple of Buddha should not delight in worldly gain but should cultivate the good of discernment."[2] Thus, it is clear that the happiness or welfare of many which in Buddhism is declared as the guiding principle of morality is not taken in the sense of ordinary sensuous pleasure or mundane happiness but in the sense of the highest good and the sublimest happiness.

In view of this comprehensive approach to the ethical problem one may think that the Buddhist criterion of morality is too complicated to provide a clear test of ethical conduct. But Buddha, thoroughly practical as he is, lays down a very simple guiding principle to determine what is morally good and bad. Fully realising the psychological nature of man in seeking for happiness and avoiding pain or obstruction, he lays down a simple test of morality which holds good for all stages of spiritual life. This consists in

1. Kaṭha. II. 1 and 2.

2. Dh. 75; see also Chapters XV and XVI of the Dhammapada dealing with 'sukha' and 'piya' respectively.

behaving with others just as one wants others to behave with oneself. He says: "All tremble at punishment, all fear death,..life is dear to all. Comparing others to oneself, one should neither kill nor cause to kill."[1]

Though we apparently find different criteria of morality stated here, it is not difficult to see that they all keep the same supreme end of life in view, and so all of them are in mutual harmony, and serve the same purpose of enabling man to determine whether an action is conducive to spiritual elevation, moral goodness and true happiness.

In the B. G. also, the most fundamental criterion of morality is derived from the supreme consideration of the highest end, viz., Nirvāna, though in view of its teaching of the tripartite path to salvation, it differs in certain respects from Buddhism, which we shall consider in the sequel. The supremacy of inner will over outer action is here also emphasised quite clearly. Kṛṣṇa says : "Far inferior indeed, O Arjuna, is mere action to the discipline of intellect."[2] In fact, it constitutes one of the most fundamental teachings of the B. G. on which its cardinal doctrine of desireless or disinterested action (niṣkāma karma) rests. Again, like in Buddhism, in the B. G. also attachment, hatred and delusion (rāga, dveṣa and moha) are regarded as the basic roots of all actions, by abandoning which one's actions are said to become free from all defilements, and one is said to realise the supreme serenity. It is stated: "A man of self-restraint who moves among the objects with the senses under his control and free from attachment and hatred (rāgadveṣaviyuktaiḥ), he attains the serenity."[3] It is also added by kṛṣṇa "When thy intellect shall cross the mire of delusion (mohakalilam), then shalt thou go beyond what has been heard and what is yet to be heard."[4] There is, however, one important difference between the approach of Buddhism and the B.G. The B.G. seems to lay an almost exclusive emphasis on the control of the inner will or desire so much so

1. Dh. 129-130.
2. Dūreṇa hy avaraṃ karma buddhiyogād dhanañjaya. B.G. II. 49.
3. B.G. II. 64.
4. B.G. II. 52.

that all actions are said to become ethically insignificant if one gets perfect control over one's desire.[1] It is under this plea that the B.G. sanctions even somewhat morally defective (sadoṣam api, XVIII, 48) actions and justifies them in the name of 'the duty for the duty's sake'.

Notwithstanding this difference, the B.G. also has a comprehensive approach to morality which takes into consideration, the true happiness and welfare of man along with normal happiness and well-being. Like the Kaṭhopaniṣad and Buddhism, it also keeps clear of worldly gain and pleasure in contradistinction to the true happiness and the good (śreya). Arjuna is found to rise above all considerations of worldly and heavenly gains (B.G.I.32, 35; II.18) and ask repeatedly about the real good or śreya (yac chreyaḥ syān niścitaṃ brūhi tan me. B.G.II.7.; yena śreyo' ham āpnuyām, III.2; see also I.31, II. 35, V.1). Kṛṣṇa also in reply imparts him the teaching whereby he would attain the true good (śreyaḥ param avāpsyatha, III.11) being free from what is merely pleasant or unpleasant (priyaṃ..cā' priyam, V.20). Though the B.G., in keeping with its central teaching of disinterested action (niṣkāma karma), lays undue emphasis on the inner will or desire, it does not seem to ignore altogether the consideration of outer consequences in normal cases, since it is said: "The action which is undertaken through ignorance, without regard to consequences or to loss and injury and also without regard to human capacity, that is said to be of inert nature (tāmasam)."[2] Again, just as in Buddhism monks are advised to go about for the happiness and welfare of people so also in the B.G. people are instructed to be absorbed in rendering good to all beings (sarvabhūtahite ratāḥ. V.25, XII.4) and remain free from enmity or ill-will to all(nirvairaḥ sarvabhūtesu,XI.55; adveṣṭā sarvabhūtānām, XII.13), though this teaching does not go well with its doctrine of 'svadharma'

1. yasya sarve samārambhāḥ kāmasaṃkalpa varjitāḥ...
karmaṇy abhipravṛtto'pi nai'va kiñcit karoti saḥ, B. G. IV. 20; see also B.G. IV. 21-23; VI. 1.

2. Anubandhaṃ kṣayaṃ hiṃsām anavekṣya ca pauruṣam,
mohād ārabhyate karma yat tat tāmasam ucyate, B. G. XVIII. 25.

taught to Arjuna (B.G.II.31-38; XVIII. 43, 47-49). The B.G. holds that men having abandoned all attachment, hatred and delusion, and being thoroughly pure and free from defilements and doubts, realise within themselves the essential unity of all beings, and with this realisation dedicate themselves to the service of all creatures. As the B.G. puts it: "The sages whose defilements are destroyed and doubts dissipated, they, engaged in the welfare of all beings, attain to Brahmanirvāṇa."[1] It may be noted here that the B.G., in order to justify its teaching of universal service brings in the metaphysical idea of the all-pervasive universal self[2], whereas in Buddhism the same idea of the essential unity of beings is established purely on the basis of observed psychological similarities of all creatures.[3]

Lastly, the simplest test of morality, viz., to look upon others as oneself, is also taught by the B.G. It says: "He who sees everywhere alike comparing others to oneself (ātma-upamyena) in relation to pleasure and pain, he is to be considered as a perfect yogin."[4] This criterion here also has an universal application and it can be used as a golden principle at all stages of spritual progress to determine what one should and should not do to others.

In the light of what has been said, it is clear that the criterion of morality, as envisaged by Buddhism and the B.G., is a comprehensive one and it is wrong to equate it with the hedonistic criterion of morality in any of its froms. Kassapa Thera seems to have ignored the inner aspect of the Buddhist criterion of morality when he observes: "Buddhism judges by results; therefore its moral standpoint may be said to be utilitarian."[5] It is not difficult to see that the utilitarian criterion of morality, as conceived by its noted exponent, Mill, is different from that of Buddhism and the B.G. According to Mill, "he who

---

1. B G. V. 25; cf. XII. 4.
2. Sarvabhūtastham ātmānaṃ sarvabhūtani cā'tmani īkṣate yogayuktātmā sarvatra samadarśanaḥ, B. G. VI. 29; see also B.G. VI. 30-31.
3. Dh. 129-130.
4. B.G. VI. 32.
5. Advice to Rahula, The Wheel Publication, No. 33, p. 9.

saves a fellow creature from drowning does what is morally right, whether his motive be duty or the hope of being paid for his trouble."[1] But both Buddhism and the B.G., in contradistinction to this attitude of Mill, duly consider the inner motive of the agent as well, which, in fact, is more important according to them than the mere outer manifestation of it. The moral worth of the action of the poor Ghaṭikāra, the potmaker, who gives simple alms and straw for roofing the hut of the Venerable Kassapa is rated much higher by Buddha than that of king Kikī of Kāsi who gives much wealth.[2] The reason is that the former does it with much greater inner piety. Similarly, king Pāyāsi who orders the distribution of alms to recluses, Brahmins and beggars etc. is said to be born after death in an inferior celestial region, for he was not doing it quite reverentially, not with his own hands, not mindfully, but negligently (asakkaccaṃ, asahatthā, acittīkataṃ, apaviddhaṁ, D.II. 356); whereas Uttara Māṇava who was deputed by the king for the same and who was only instrumental in carrying out the king's order is said to be born in a higher celestial region, for he was distributing alms with reverence, with his own hands, mindfully and not negligently (D. II. 357). We have already noticed that Buddha in contradistinction to the Nigaṇṭha Nātaputta lays greater emphasis on mental than on bodily action (M.I. 373, 376-8) and calls the will the forerunner of all psychological states (Dh. 1 & 2).

According to the B.G. also the worth of charity is said to depend on the inner motive and feeling of the agent rather than on the mere outward deed. It is said : "The charity done with a feeling that it is one's duty to give, given to one from whom no return is expected, given in proper place, time and to a worthy person, that charity is called good (sāttvikam). But the charity done with the motive of a return, with the expectation of future gain or is given with uneasiness, is called mediocre (rājasam). And the charity which is given with disrespect and contempt, at an improper place and time, to an unworthy person, that is called mean (tāmasam)."[3]

1. Utilitarianism, p. 17.
2. M. II. 49-54.
3. B.G XVII. 20-22.

This shows that the B.G. and Buddhist criterion of morality cannot be equated with the Utilitarian criterion.

Besides, according to Utilitarianism, the final criterion of morality is 'the greatest good of the greatest number'. But neither Buddhism nor the B. G. can approve of this mere numerical principle determining the moral worth of actions. According to them action promoting happiness to one noble man is better than one promoting happiness to a thousand knaves. Buddha who was hesitant after his enlightenment whether he should preach the Noble Doctrine or not, was led to decide in favour of preaching, out of the consideration for those few noble beings who would be lost if they did not hear the Doctrine.[1] He did not abandon his noble mission because a multitude of people were displeased and unhappy with what he was doing. "At that time well-known young people from the noble families of Magadha under the guidance of the Exalted One led the life of purity. Thereby the people were perturbed, became ill-disposed and grumbled : 'the recluse Gotama has come to make us childless..to make women widowed,..to cause families to die out."[2] But Buddha carried on his mission. His concept of happiness and good was not to be regulated according to the utilitarian code of 'the greatest number'. In the B.G. also this code is not accepted. Had this numerical consideration weighed before Kṛṣṇa, he would have made every effort to secure the victory and happiness of the Kauravas whose numerical strength was greater than that of the Paṇḍavas. Notwithstanding some differences between the Buddhist and the B.G. view of morality, it is obvious, that Arjuna's argument of not destroying the multitudes of criminals (ātatāyinaḥ) including his friends, relatives and elders.[3] could not find any serious consideration with Kṛṣṇa who offers a different criterion of morality.

In hedonistic ethics there is no clear way to determine wherein consists the real happiness of men. In fact, so

1. M.I. 168-9.
2. Vin. I. 43.
3. B.G. I. 36-45.

long as mundane happiness is the only consideration and men are to adjudge the worth of moral action in the light of worldly gain and loss, it is difficult to find a dependable criterion of right and wrong actions.

In the above discussion, we have noted that the B.G. is in agreement with the criteria of morality adopted by Buddhism. But in its attempt to effect a synthesis of the different paths of salvation, the B.G. provides room for some exceptions, adjustments and reservations which make its position considerably different from that of early Buddhism. A man in the course of discharging his normal worldly duties may perform certain action which none of the above criteria of morality would approve of and yet the B.G. would consider it perfectly moral in pursuance of its doctrine of 'duty for duty's sake' (B.G. II. 33, 38; IV. 21). Similarly, the sins of a devotee of God may be condoned, if he performs his actions in dedication to God (B.G.V. I0; IX. 27, 28, 30, 31; XVIII. 56-58). Thus, some important changes are brought about by the B.G. in the course of its advocacy of a diversity of paths, as against the one and only path taught by Buddhism. It may, therefore, be useful to see how the B.G. seeks a reconciliation of the various paths and how far in so doing it comes to differ from early Buddhism.

Unity Versus Diversity of the Path

(A) *Buddha's Advocacy for only one Holy path* :—

Buddhism, in unmistakable language, declares that the supreme truth that we aim at, the supreme goal that we aspire after, is only one and the path leading to it is also one. Referring to numerous conflicting theories put forward by different theorists, it is asked in the Suttanipāta : "Why do they put forward diverse theories,..are truths many and various..? (kasmā nu saccāni vadanti nānā..saccāni su tāni bahūni nānā?, Sn. 173), and the explicit answer is given : "Truths, indeed, are not many and various." (na h'eva saccāni bahūni nānā, Sn. loc. cit). It is made clear: "Truth is one without a second" (ekaṃ hi saccaṃ na dutiyam atthi, Sn. 172). This truth or reality is nothing other than Nibbāna or the final release, the absolute cessation of suffering (etaṃ hi..paramaṃ ariyasaccaṃ yad idaṃ amosadhammaṃ Nibbānaṃ, M. III. 245).

Now, there is only one path which, according to Buddha, leads to this goal, that is the Eightfold Path comprising of sīla (virtue), samādhi (concentration) and paññā (wisdom). Referring to this Eightfold Path, Buddha explicitly declares : "This is the only path, there is none other for the purity of vision..Treading upon this path you shall make an end of suffering."[1] Repeatedly we find Buddha emphasising : "This is the only way, monks, for the purification of beings, for the overcoming of sorrow and lamentation, for the cessation of suffering and grief, for the attainment of true knowledge, for the realisation of Nibbāna."[2] It is said : "The all-compassionate One knows the path, the only one, for ending rebirth. By this path have men previously crossed the Flood, shall cross, and do cross now."[3] Nibbāna is compared with a city (nagaraṃ) surrounded by strong foundations, strong walls and towers, having a single gate (eka dvāraṃ), having no other hole or entrance to allow even a cat to slip through, so that any creature of sizable stature must enter the city through the very same gate.[4] Thus, like the Śvetāśvatara Upaniṣad which declares : "There is no other path for going there" (nānyaḥ panthā vidyate'yanāya, Śvetā., III. 8), Buddhism also upholds the validity of one and only one path and no other.

(B) *Absolute Detachment as the Crux of the Buddhist Path* :—

The crux of this path is, undoubtedly, absolute detachment. In the very first sutta of the Majjhima Nikāya,

---

1. Eso'va maggo natth'añño dassanassa visuddhiyā
...etaṃ hi tumhe paṭipannā dukkhass'antaṃ karissatha, Dh. 274-275.

2. Ekāyano ayaṃ, bhikkhave, maggo sattānaṃ visuddhiyā, sokapariddavānaṃ samatikkamāya, dukkhadomanassānaṃ atthagamāya, ñāyassa adhigamāya, nibbānassa sacchikiriyāya, M. I. 56; S.V. 141, 167.

3. Ekāyanaṃ jātikhayantadassi maggaṃ pajānāti hitānukampī, etena maggena tariṃsu pubbe tarissanti ye ca taranti oghan ti, S. V. 168.

4. S.V. 160-161.

namely, the Mūlapariyāya Sutta, Buddha points out that the perfect saint freed from all defilements (arahaṃ khīṇāsavo) having truly realised the nature of all things in all respects (sabbaṃ sabbato abhiññāya, M.I. 5), finds no delight in the whole universe and is, in no way, attached to any of its objects (sabbaṃ na maññati, sabbasmiṃ na maññati, sabbato na maññati, sabbaṃ me ti na maññati, loc. cit). It is, indeed, with a view to bringing home the very same fundamental teaching of detachment that Buddha untiringly emphasises the utter transitoriness, sorrowfulness and insubstantiality of worldly objects. One feels attached to and is engrossed in worldly things only so long as one does not keenly realise their aforesaid nature. Buddha, therefore, analysing this triple character of objects, is frequently found to add : "Having seen thus, O monks, the instructed noble disciple finds estrangement in corporeality, in feeling, in perception, in volitions and in consciousness. Being estranged, he is detached. Being detached, he is freed. Being freed, the knowledge arises in him that he is free. 'Exhausted is rebirth, fulfilled is the holy life, done what was to be done, nothing other is beyond this'—thus he knows"[1] S. Radhakrishnan[2] and E. J. Thomas[3] are right when they speak of renunciation or detachment as essential for realising the Buddhist ideal of life.

It is with a view to effecting this perfect detachment from the enjoyment of worldly objects that Buddha exposes their true character and points out how very despicable and repulsive they really are, though apparently they look pleasant and delightful. Through various similes he tries to show that worldly enjoyments with which we feel so delighted, are at bottom nothing but sources of suffering. The man engrossed in worldly enjoyment is compared to a dog who is lustily

---

1. S. III. 68, 90; cf. S. IV. 65-66.

2. Radhakrishnan referring to "the quintessence" of the Buddhist ideal observes : "Insistence on renunciation is necessary for all healthy life."—Indian Philosophy, Vol. I., p. 435.

3. E. J. Thomas speaking of the Buddhist and Jain way of life refers to their "making renunciation of worldly life essential for final release."—The History of Buddhist Thought, p. 12.

gnawing a fleshless bone which far from appeasing his hunger, only adds to his pain and discomfort.[1] He is again compared to a man going with a blazing bundle of grass against the wind (ādittaṃ tiṇukkaṃ ādāya paṭivātaṃ gaccheyya) which is sure to burn his hand, arm or other parts of his body, if he does not quickly throw it away.[2] The man seeking delight in the sensuous pleasures of the world is likened to a leper who finds pleasure in scratching his wound with his nails and warming it at the fire, which ultimately augments his trouble all the more.[3] A very deplorable picture of worldly life is painted by Raṭṭhapāla realising which he successfully resists all worldly temptations.[4] Even in accepting things for the bare maintenance of physical existence, a simple offering of food, for example, a monk is not to take delight in it. He is to eat it with utter detachment considering it as an unavoidable need for maintaining life. Explaining how material food is to be looked upon (Kathaṃ ca, bhikkhave, kabalīkāro āhāro daṭṭhabbo, S. II. 98), Buddha relates the story of a couple, going with their only son through a forest with scanty provisions, which having run short, they were compelled to take the flesh of their only son (puttamaṃsaṃ), lest all the three would have perished. "Even so should material food be looked upon" (evam eva..kabalīkāro āhāro daṭṭhabbo, S. II, 99). This indicates the kind of detachment that was required for reaching the goal of the holy life.

The entire Eightfold Path comprising of sīla (virtue), samādhi (concentration) and paññā (wisdom) aims at realising this state of perfect detachment leading to final deliverance from mundane existence. Buddha realising full well the nature of the deep-rooted attachment which has been affecting our whole being and misguiding our entire conduct (bodily, verbal and mental) since time immemorial, lays down a systematic code of discipline which aims at leading gradually to both inner and outer purification and eradicating fully and

1. M. I. 364.
2. M. I. 365.
3. M. I. 506.
4. M. II. 64-65, 72-74.

finally all traces of attachment which manifests itself in three forms, namely, passion, hatred and delusion.[1] The mind, as pointed out earlier, is considered primarily responsible for all evil actions, because it is this which harbours lust or passion (lobha or rāga), hatred (doṣa) and delusion (moha), admittedly the root of all wrong actions (akusala mūla).[2] But Buddha knows that it is as difficult to control and purify the mind as it is important and essential. He clearly says : "The mind is fickle, flitting, difficult to guard, difficult to check, difficult to control, swift and slipping at will...very hard to perceive, extremely subtle and wandering wherever it desires, moving far, going alone, incorporeal and lying in the cave."[3] But adds : "It is good to control the mind, the controlled mind is conducive to happiness...the wise man should guard the mind, the guarded mind is conducive to happiness,...those who restrain the mind are freed from the bond of Māra"[4] So the Eightfold Path begins with the control or correction of the mental outlook (sammādiṭṭhi, ujugatadiṭṭhi, M. I. 46ff) and making a firm resolve (sammā saṅkappa) to purify it. But Buddha, at the same time, is conscious of the psychological fact of the interrelation between mind and body and their reciprocal actions and reactions. He knows that so long as one is engrossed in outer sense-indulgence, it is difficult for him to have inner control and purity of mind. Therefore, along with the control of mind, he prescribes perfect control of the outer actions of body and speech which are embodied in the three subsequent steps known as right speech (sammāvācā), right action (sammākammanta) and right livelihood (sammā-ājīva), and are generally classed under the broad term 'sīla' (virtue), as the learned nun, Dhammadinnā explains to Visākha.[5] But the control of mind being far more difficult and at the same time extremely vital on account of its being the primary source of

1. M. I. 303; cf. supra, p. 415.
2. M. I. 47; II. 26.
3. Dh. 33, 35, 36, 37.
4. Dh. 35-37.
5. M. I. 301.

all evil, Buddha further prescribes constant effort and mindfulness (sammāvāyāmo, sammāsatī) and lastly, various stages of concentration (sammāsamādhi), after passing through which one attains the highest state of Saññāvedayitanirodha when all mundane consciousness ceases and the aspirant reaches the supreme goal. It is stated in the Pali Canon that in the course of concentration when the aspirant reaches the fourth stage of jhāna, he rises above both happiness and its opposite, and attains a state of pure indifference (upekkhāsatipārisuddhiṃ catutthaṃ jhānaṃ upasampajja viharati, D. I. 75). But the highest goal of absolute detachment is not reached even then, and he is said to ascend still higher and higher and transcend even this indifference centred on unity (yā'yaṃ upekkhā ekattā ekattasitā taṃ pajahatha, taṃ samatikkamatha, M. III. 220), which, indeed, is the climax of detachment when the mind is thoroughly purged and there remains not even the slightest trace of any mundane attachment. The whole being of such a perfected saint, both inwardly and outwardly, is purified and controlled. All traces of passion, hatred and delusion are destroyed and as a result of absolute detachment from all mundane conditions, the highest enlightenment dawns upon him, and he realises the supramundane goal once for all. This is known as perfect deliverance free from all clingings (anupādā vimutti)[1], unshakable salvation, the true Nibbāna (akuppā vimutti, amosadhammaṃ nibbānaṃ).[2]

(C) *Buddha's Exhortation for the Utmost Strictness:—*

There is no doubt that the detachment aspired after in early Buddhism is comprehensive and perfect. No stage which falls short of the highest state of perfect detachment and complete eradication of defilements is to be delighted in. Buddha says : "Do not rest content, O monks without reaching the destruction of defilements" (bhikkhū vissāsa mā pādi appatto āsavakkhayaṃ. Dh. 272). He fervently exhorts : "It may occur to you, O monks, 'accomplishing this much

1. S. III. 61.
2. M. III. 245.

is enough, doing this much is enough, fulfilled (thereby) is our recluse life, nothing beyond is left to be done by us'—by that much you may find contentment. I declare to you, O monks, I instruct to you, O monks, while following the recluse life, do not stop with anything short of the goal of the recluse life, leaving anything beyond to be done."[1] A monk is to fear even a little bit of vice (aṇumattesu vajjesu bhayadassāvī, D. I. 63; III. 78), because even that much of defect may prove detrimental and dangerous. Buddha gives the simile of a man pierced by a poisoned arrow, who, only because the arrow has been taken out, moves about carelessly, not protecting his still unhealed wound and, as a result, comes to grief once again.[2] Buddha, therefore, emphatically urges us to maintain utmost care and vigilance till the goal is finally attained, lest the consequences may be grave. He does not permit any slackness or complacency in the course of following the holy path, for, according to him, "a slack recluse scatters dust (defilements) all the more" (sithilo hi paribhājo bhiyyo ākirate rajaṃ, Dh. 313). Elucidating the need for the utmost care, he gives the simile of a man who has to go with a bowl of oil, full to the brim, amidst the jolting and pushing crowd of people gathered to see the dance of the renowned public dancer, when a man with a drawn sword is following him ready to chop off his head in case even a little oil is spilt over (yattheva naṃ thokaṃ pi chaḍḍessati tattheva te siro patessatī'ti, S.V. 170). Thus, he exhorts people to pursue the path resolutely so long as all the fetters, great or small (aṇuṃ thūlaṃ, Dh. 31) are not rent asunder and the ultimate goal is not reached. Having explained to Udāyi, the successive stages of spiritual advancement up to the highest stage of 'Saññāvedayitanirodha', Buddha says : "Do you see Udāyi any fetter, great or small, the getting rid of which I do not speak of ?" (passasi no tvaṃ Udāyi taṃ saṃyojanaṃ aṇuṃ vā thūlaṃ vā yassāhaṃ no pahānaṃ vadāmī'ti?, M. I. 456) and Udāyi answers : "Not so, Lord" (no hetaṃ, bhante, loc. cit.). Thus, Buddha preaches absolute detachment and

---

1. M. 271 ff.
2. M. III. 256-7.

sanctions no relaxation or rest at any stage lower than the final deliverance.

It is pointed out that the higher the aspirant ascends in the spiritual path, the lesser does he delight in the preceding stage, and when he reaches the final supramundane goal, his detachment to mundane existence is at a climax, from which there is no fall, no more attachment for anything (abhabbo parihāṇāya, Dh. 32; abhabbā te pamajjituṃ M.I. 477). Various similes in this connection are given by Buddha. As a sere leaf loosened from its stalk cannot become green again, as a rock broken into two cannot become whole again, as a man having thrown away the remains of his food after finishing his meal cannot desire it once again, so also is the case with the aspirant who, casting aside the inferior stages, ascends gradually to higher and higher stages, ultimately reaching the highest goal, Nibbāna and becoming like a palm tree having its top completely cut off and made unable to grow any more.[1]

It is at the attainment of this goal that the aspirant is said to have reached the stage of absolute security, requiring no more care and vigilance. As Buddha says : "I, O monks, do not speak of all monks that they should act with vigilance. Those monks, O monks, who are perfect ones, free from defilements, to such monks, O monks, I do not say that they should act with vigilance. What is the reason for it? They have done (what was to be done) with vigilance. They are incapable of being negligent."[2] This statement, however, should not be taken to imply that Buddha recommends a licentious way of life for an accomplished saint giving him the latitude to commit morally wrong actions. The monk Ariṭṭha is chastised by Buddha for having misunderstood Buddha's teachings in that way. Ariṭṭha says: "I so understand the dhamma taught by the Blessed One that even by indulging in those things called 'obstacles' by the Blessed One, there is no obstacle."[3] Buddha reprimanding him says: "To whom

1. M. II. 254-256.
2. M. I. 477.
3. M. I. 130.

do you, foolish man, know that the dhamma was taught thus by me? Have I not spoken in many ways of obstructive things as obstructive, the indulgence in which would ever cause obstruction?...You foolish man, by your own erroneous grasp accuse me and cause harm to yourself and incur much demerit. It will be, foolish man, for your woe and suffering for long."[1] In fact, the true purport of the aforesaid teaching of Buddha lies only in indicating the fact that the perfect saint is so much above attachment, that it is no more possible for him to come under the sway of any temptation or to feel attached to anything. He is simply incapable of doing any wrong deed either through his body, speech or mind.

When king Pasenadi asks Ānanda whether Buddha can perform such bodily, verbal or mental actions which are deprecated by recluses, Brahmins and the wise, Ānanda gives a definite negative answer.[2] Addressing Cunda, Buddha says: "It may happen, Cunda, that teachers of other sects and wanderers may say thus: 'The Sākyan recluses are moving about unestablished in the Dhamma. To these teachers of other sects and wanderers, so speaking, you should reply thus: ...one who is arahant, free from defilements...is incapable of lapsing in respect of these nine things (abhabbo so imāni nava ṭhānāni ajjhācaritum ti), viz. deliberately depriving a living creature of life, taking what is not given (theft), sexual impurity, deliberately telling lies, indulging in worldly pleasures as he used to do as a householder, being misled by prejudice, hatred, ignorance and fear'."[3]

It is these infallible arahants whom Buddha calls upon to preach the Noble Doctrine, lovely in the beginning, lovely in the middle and lovely in the end for the welfare and happiness of many.[4] According to early Buddhism, it is only these perfect saints who are capable of moving about in the world with absolute detachment like water on a lotus leaf (vāri pokkharapatte'va, Dh. 401). Referring to his own detached

1. M. I. 132.
2. M. II 113-4.
3. D. III. 133.
4. Vin. I. 21.

way of moving about in the world and preaching the Dhamma to people, Buddha says: "Just as, monks, a dark blue lotus, or a white lotus, born in the water, developed in the water, rises above the water and stands untouched by the water (ṭhāti anupalittaṃ udakena), even so, monks, the Tathāgata having been born in the world, developed in the world, transcending the world, moves about uncontaminated by the world (viharati anupalitto lokenā'ti)."[1] Because of the absolute fading away of all lure and attachment, the perfect saint is ever free. Though apparently he is in contact with the mass of people, he is, as it were, all alone. As Buddha, addressing the monk, Migajāla, points out : "With the fading away of lure, there is no attachment, where there is no attachment, there is no contact. Being absolutely free from the fetter of lure, Migajāla, a monk is called a 'lonely-dweller' (eka vihārī)...Thus dwelling, Migajāla, a monk, even though he dwells amidst the village crowded with monks and nuns, lay-brethren and lay-sisters, kings and councillors, teachers of the other sects and their followers, he is called a lonely-dweller."[2] Such a saint, absolutely detached and free, moves about in the world accumulating no potentialities, whether meritorious, demeritorious or impassible. As Buddha says: "When, monks, the ignorance of the monk is destroyed and knowledge has arisen, he, on account of the destruction of ignorance and the emergence of knowledge, does not incur either meritorious potentialities or demeritorious potentialities or impassible potentialities. Not incurring, not accumulating, he does not feel attached to anything. Being not attached, he trembles not, not trembling, he realises Parinibbāna within himself."[3] Thus, Buddha envisages the possibility of detached action, but he makes it clear that it is possible only in the case of a thoroughly liberated or perfected saint. Again, it is to be noted that according to early Buddhism, the perfected one, in the course of discharging his disinterested service to humanity, can on no account perform an action which is morally wrong.

1. S. III. 140.
2. S. IV. 37.
3. S. II. 82.

The holy path outlined above is the only path according to early Buddhism which can lead one to the highest goal. It is the same path which all individuals, irrespective of class, creed, occupation or profession, have to follow as far as it is possible for them. Whether one is a householder or a recluse, the spiritual advancement depends strictly on the extent to which one has been able to practise the discipline of the path. Since, however, the ideal state of perfection demands absolute detachment, it can be wholly realised only by a recluse who has altogether renounced the world. As a householder one can, at best, expect to realise the state nearest to Nibbāna, known as Anāgāmitā.[1] Since the final deliverance attainable through absolute detachment is grounded in true knowledge, it is quite apposite to characterise the holy path of early Buddhism as a path of detachment or renunciation (nivṛtti mārga or saṃnyāsa mārga) or the path of knowledge (jñāna mārga). In fact, the true knowledge has been considered so essential for absolute detachment or renunciation[2], that the path of renunciation (nivṛtti or saṃnyāsa mārga) is usually taken as a synonym for the path of knowledge (jñāna mārga), and it is precisely in this sense that the two words (viz. saṃnyāsa and jñāna) are used indiscriminately by the B.G. too.[3]

(D) *The B.G. Technique of Compromise and Reconciliation*: —

In the light of the above account of the one straight path of renunciation or knowledge (saṃnyāsa or jñāna) preached by early Buddhism, we can now see how the B.G. in keeping with its synthetic character tries to evolve a compromise between the tenets of renunciation (nivṛtti or saṃnyāsa) and worldly action (pravṛtti) and advocates a triple path consist-

---

1. Anāgāmi is one who does not return to this world any more and is to attain Nibbāna by being born once as a celestial being. (opapātiko tattha parinibbāyī anāvattidhammo tasmā lokā'ti, M. I. 490).

2. cf. etam eva viditvā munir bhavati. etam eva pravrājino lokam icchantaḥ pravrajanti...prajāṃ na kāmayante...atha bhikṣācaryaṃ caranti, Bṛhadā. IV. 4. 2.; see also Bṛhadā. II. 4. 1 ff; Chāndogya. VIII. 7-11.

3. jñānayoga (B.G. III. 3) and saṃnyāsa (B.G.V. 2) are evidently used as synonyms.

ing of disinterested action (karmayoga), devotion (bhaktiyoga) and knowledge (jñānayoga). Evidently, in so doing, it makes certain adjustments, additions and alterations which differentiate its position from that of early Buddhism.

It is, no doubt, true that the B.G. also, like Buddhism, speaks of Nirvāṇa as the only goal of the holy life (B.G. II 72, V. 24, 25, 26; VI. 15), regards the world as transient and a vale of misery (anityam asukhaṃ lokam, B.G. IX. 33) and considers detachment as essential for the holy life (na hy asaṃnyastasaṅkalpo yogī bhavati kaścana, B.G. VI. 2; cf. IV. 20, VI. 1, 4). It, nevertheless, gives a different orientation to all these concepts so as to fit them into its diverse approach and bring about a compromise among different strands of thought. We have already seen (supra, pp. 345-346) how in keeping with its pronounced metaphysical and theological attitude the B.G. describes the same state of Nirvāṇa as Brāhmīsthiti, Brahmabhūta (B.G. II. 72, V. 19, 20, 24; VI. 27, XVIII. 54), tṛptātmā, yuktātmā or ātmavanta (B.G. IV. 41; V. 21; VI. 8, 29; VII. 18) and madbhāvamāgataḥ (B.G. VI.10), besides speaking of it, in common with Buddhism, as a state of absolute bliss (sukham ātyantikam, B.G. VI. 21) and freedom from all suffering (duḥkhasaṃyoga viyogaṃ, B.G. VI. 23). This seems to indicate that the B.G. is trying to seek reconciliation with Buddhist thought as far as it is possible within the limits of its metaphysical and theological setting. The same tendency is largely exhibited with regard to most of its other teachings as well.

Let us take the case of detachment. We have noticed above that detachment is the crux of the Buddhist life and all desire or attachment in the form of lust, hatred or delusion (rāga, doṣa or moha) has to be completely shaken off in order to realise the goal. With this aim in view the transient, sorrowful and insubstantial or soulless (aniccaṃ dukkhaṃ and anattā) nature of the world is repeatedly emphasised in Buddhism. Now the B.G., as pointed out earlier (supra, pp. 415-416), agrees with Buddhism in holding the view that all worldly objects are transitory and sorrowful but it discards the Buddhist doctrine of soullessness (anattā), since this goes against its avowed theory of the soul (ātmā). Thus, in spite of emphasising the transitoriness and sorrowfulness of the world, the B.G. asserts the permanence and blissfulness of the self. Again, agreeing with Buddhism that detachment or renunciation is essential for the holy life, and freedom from all passion, hatred and delusion is necessary for the realisation of the highest goal, the B.G. gives its own definition of renunciation so that it may be possible for it to reconcile it with the active life of the world, which the B.G. so emphatically recommends. We may now see how with this purpose of reconciliation in view, the B.G. adopts and adjusts the different strands of thought, and, in spite of accepting the fundamental tenets of Buddhism (at least in theory), comes to differ considerably from the latter in practice.

As we shall see in the sequel, detachment or renunciation is considered essential by the B.G. also for pursuing any of the holy paths prescribed by it.[1] But it is important to note that the B.G. modifies the meaning of the word 'renunciation' before absorbing it in its scheme. Unlike Buddhism according to which detachment or renunciation should be both inner and outer, the B.G. seems to lay an almost exclusive emphasis on inner detachment. Though in Buddhism also, mind is considered as more important on account of being the source of all actions, and greater emphasis is laid on its control and discipline, it is never forgotten that without the outer control of the body and speech, the control of mind is a psychological impossibility. So Buddhism prescribes an all-round inner and outer control in order to attain perfect detachment of renunciation. But the B.G. does not seem to care much for the outer action, and thinks that the true renunciation consists in giving up only the inner desire or attachment in its threefold form of passion, hatred and delusion. Defining a true renouncer (saṃnyāsī), the B.G. says: "He who does the work which he ought to do, without seeking its fruit, he is the saṃnyāsin, he is the yogin and not he who (simply) gives up lighting the fire and does no

1. Cf. Na hy asaṃnyastasaṅkalpo yogī bhavati kaścana, B. G. VI. 2.

work."[1] Similarly it is said: "The abandonment of the fruits of all works is called 'relinquishment' (tyāgam) by the learned."[2] "Having relinquished all attachment to the fruits of actions, ever content and free from any dependence, one even while engaged in action does nothing at all."[3] Thus, true renunciation, according to the B.G., consists not in the renunciation of action but in the renunciation of the desire underlying the action. Renunciation or detachment, having thus been defined, the B.G. conveniently puts forward its teaching of disinterested or desireless action (niṣkāma karma). One is asked to give up all desire or attachment appearing in the form of passion, hatred or delusion and remain actively engaged in all works, moving freely among all objects of the sense. Thus it is said: "A man of disciplined mind and self-control, being free from attachment and hatred (rāga dveṣa viyuktaiḥ) attains serenity (even) while letting his senses move among the objects (viṣayān indriyaiś caran),"[4] Again, Arjuna is told by Kṛṣṇa: "When thy intellect shall cross the mire of delusion (mohakalilam), then shall thou become indifferent to what has been heard and what is yet to be heard."[5] Arjuna is asked to shake off desire or attachment in all its forms and get ready for the battle with perfect indifference or equanimity. "Treating alike pleasure and pain, gain and loss, victory and defeat, get ready for battle. Thus thou shall not incur sin."[6] This explicit direction to fight with inner equanimity or detachment clearly indicates that the B.G. stands exclusively for the control of mind which having been done, bodily action becomes morally insignificant. The same is stated also in clear terms by the B.G.: "He who has no desires, who has controlled his mind and heart, who has given up all sense of possession, he incurs no sin while doing

1. Anāśritaḥ karmaphalaṃ kāryaṃ karma karoti yaḥ
sa saṃnyāsī ca yogī ca na niragnir na cā'kriyaḥ., B.G. VI. 1.
2. sarvakarmaphalatyāgaṃ prāhus tyāgaṃ vicakṣaṇāḥ., B.G.XVIII.2.
3. Tyaktvā karmaphalāsaṅgaṃ nityatṛpto nirāśrayaḥ
karmaṇy abhipravṛtto'pi nai'va kiñcit karoti saḥ., B.G. IV. 20.
4. B.G. II. 64
5. B.G. II. 52.
6. B. G. II. 38.

mere bodily action (śārīraṃ kevalaṃ karma kurvan nā'pnoti kilbiṣam)."[1] Śaṅkara seems to anticipate some difficulty in the above position and tries to change its real sense by interpreting 'śārīraṃ karma' (bodily action) in the sense of those actions which are performed "for the sake of bare maintenance of the body" (śarīrasthitimātraprayojanaṃ śārīraṃ karma iti, S.B.G. IV. 21). But Śaṅkara's interpretation is neither literal nor suited to the context. In fact, the teaching of the B.G. is so clear on this point and has been so often repeated in the text that it hardly leaves any room for doubt about the fact that according to the B.G. bodily action is considered simply undone, as it were, if the mind is under control. Of numerous verses[2] reiterating the very same idea, we may quote one: "The embodied self having renounced all actions by the mind (sarvakarmāṇi manasā saṃnyasya) dwells happily with self-control in the city of nine gates[3], without doing (as it were) or causing to do (naiva kurvan na kārayan.)"[4]

We may admit that it is theoretically possible to say that the mind being the spring of all right or wrong actions, absolute desirelessness on the part of the mind or its complete freedom from passion, hatred and delusion renders all actions ethically insignificant. This, indeed, is acceptable to Buddhism as well, and yet it is interesting to see how it differs significantly from the teachings of the B. G. It is admitted in Buddhism that "by desire one is bound in the world, and by the control of desire one is freed. By the destruction of desire all bondage is cut off."[5] So a desireless saint is said to live absolutely detached in the world just like a lotus leaf in the water (vāri pokkhara patteva, Dh. 401), the simile being exactly the same as one given by the B. G. (padmapattram ivā'mbhasā, V. 10) with regard to

1. B. G. IV. 21.

2. B.G. II. 50, 64, 71; III. 7, 9, 19, 30; IV. 20-23, 37; V. 7-10; XVIII. 56 and 57.

3. The nine gates are the two eyes, the two ears, the two nostrils, the organ of excretion, the organ of generation and the mouth; cf. Svetā., III. 18.

4. B.G. V. 13.

5. Icchāya bajjhatī loko, icchāvinayāya muccati;
icchāya vippahānena, sabbaṃ chindati bandhanan'ti., S.I. 40.

the man of disinterested action. We have already noted above that Buddha himself speaks of moving about in the world in a detached or uncontaminated manner like a lotus in the water (seyyathāpi, bhikkhave, uppalaṃ vā padumaṃ vā..ṭhāti anupalittaṃ udakena, evam eva..Tathāgato..vih-arati anupalitto lokenā'ti, S. III. 140). Whether in action or out of action, the Tathāgata is said to remain alike detached. Whether teaching or not teaching to the disciples, it is all the same for him (desento pi hi..Tathāgato sāvakānaṃ dhammaṃ tādiṣo va, adesento pi hi..tādiso va, M. I. 331). It is maintained in Buddhism that no potentiality, whether meritorious, demeritorious or impassible is incurred by the enlightened one (neva puññābhisaṅkhāraṃ ...na apuññābhisaṅkhāraṃ..na āneñjābhisaṅkhāraṃ abhisaṅkharoti, S. II. 82) just as in the B. G. it is said that a disinterested man or a renouncer remains free from the threefold consequences of actions (aniṣṭaṃ iṣṭaṃ miśraṃ ca trividhaṃ karmaṇaḥ phalam...na tu saṃnyāsināṃ kvacit, B. G. XVIII, 12). But despite this common ground, the differences can be clearly seen. According to Buddhism (i) the state of absolute desirelessness or perfect freedom from passion, hatred and delusion can be fully realised only on the attainment of the highest goal, viz., Nibbāna. It is only then that one can afford to move about freely in the world with utter detachment, transcending the normal experiences and emotions. (ii) It is possible to realise this state only after passing through the stage of moral discipline (sīla) pertaining to body and speech. (iii) The perfect saint having attained this infallible goal is said to become incapable of committing any evil deed. This shows that Buddhism does not accept the position that morally evil actions can produce no sin. On the other hand, it holds that to commit wrong action is an unmistakable indication of spiritual imperfection.

In the light of this Buddhist position, we can now see how the B. G., though theoretically accepting the Buddhist ideal, deviates in practice from it. The B. G. advocates the practice of disinterested action from the very beginning without first realising the infallible stage of perfection. We, of course, do not deny that the B. G. also prescribes bodily and verbal discipline as a necessary precondition for mental control and concentration[1], but it makes a great difference when without realising perfection in respect of the former, it prescribes indulgence in all actions. It holds the view that "even a little practice of this discipline (i. e. disinterested action) saves one from great fear" (svalpam apy asya dharmasya trāyate mahato bhayāt, B. G. II 40). One is, therefore, taught to practise disinterested action right from the very beginning (i. e. before acquiring perfection) and is advised to continue it unto the last (i. e. even after attaining perfection). One is assured that perfection is gradually realised in the course of practising disinterested action (tat svayaṃ yoga saṃsiddhaḥ kālenā'tmani vindati, B. G. IV. 38). Thus, the B. G. speaks of two stages of disinterested action: the one which is performed by the aspiring saint (āruruksa) with a view to reaching perfection, and the other which is performed by the perfect or accomplished saint (siddha or yogārūḍha) with a view to serving humanity with perfect equanimity. Thus, the active life is prescribed by the B. G. both before as well as after the attainment of perfection. In the former case, action is motivated by a desire to attain serenity and in the latter, the serenity itself leads to action. Thus, the B. G. says: "For the sage desiring to attain to yoga, action is said to be the means, and for the same person after he has attained to yoga, serenity (śamaḥ) is said to be the means."[2] The verse, thus, points out that so long as one is in the process of attaining the serenity of yoga (sādhanāvasthā), disinterested action serves as the means of serenity, but when one attains that goal (siddhāvasthā), the serenity itself becomes the means of disinterested action. In this way the B. G. teaches disinterested action at all stages of life in contradistinction to Buddhism which prescribes it only after the attainment of perfection.

---

1. B.G. II. 58, 61; III. 41; IV. 24; XVIII. 51, 52 (yata-vāk-kāya-mānasaḥ).

2. Ārurukṣor muner yogaṃ karma kāraṇam ucyate,
yogārūḍhasya tasyai'va śamaḥ kāraṇam ucyate., B.G. VI. 3.

Again in Buddhism the perfected saint. while actively engaged in detached or disinterested service to humanity, is said to be incapable of doing morally wrong action, whereas, according to the B. G., he may in face of certain exigencies perform even wrong actions and yet remain uncontaminated by sin.[1] According to Buddhism, wrong actions are irrevocably associated with evil consequences, of which there is no exception. Performance of wrong action is a sure sign of imperfection in holiness. But according to the B. G. there is a definite exception made in the case of an absolutely unconceited and disinterested man who "even when he slays all these people, neither slays nor is bound" (hatvā'pi sa imāṃllokān na hanti na nibadhyate, B. G. XVIII 17). Performance of wrong action on his part is no indication of imperfection.

Thus, we see that the very central teaching of the B. G. that action done without any desire for fruit is sterile (B. G. IV. 20, 21: II. 47, 50, 51), is not compatible with the teachings of Buddhism. According to Buddhism, it does not seem to be important whether the action is performed with or without the expectation of the fruit. What is important, according to it, is the fact as to whether the action is performed properly or improperly (yoniso or ayoniso). It is stated in the Bhūmija Sutta that "if they lead the holy life improperly (ayoniso), they are incapable of obtaining the fruit, whether they do it with an expectation, or without an expectation, or with and without an expectation, or neither with nor without an expectation."[2] Contrariwise, "if they lead the holy life properly (yoniso), they are capable of obtaining the fruit, whether they do it with an expectation, without an expectation, with and without an expectation, or neither with nor without an expectation of the fruit."[3] Thus, Buddha believes in the strict law of

1. B.G. II. 38; B.G. IV. 21; B.G. V. 10.

2. āsaṃ ce pi karitvā ayoniso brahmacariyaṃ caranti,...anāsaṃ ce pi karitvā,...āsaṃ ca anāsaṃ ce pi karitvā,...nevāsam nānāsaṃ ce pi karitvā..., abhabbā phalassa adhigamāya., M. III. 138.

3. M. III. 138-9.

causation according to whioh the action having been duly performed, its result is sure to follow. A truly perfect saint, therefore, is incapable of doing that action which would produce evil consequences. But the B. G. thinks that such an action may have to be performed by a perfected man in the course of discharging his worldly duties, and in that case the action is said to lose its potency to produce a consequence.[1]

(E) *The B.G.'s Preference for Active Worldy Life and the Consequent Slackening of the Rigour and Rigidity of Paths*:—

As a matter of fact, the attitude of the B.G. is largely determined in accordance with its pronounced leaning towards an active worldly life. It is perhaps in view of this consideration that it reduces the rigour and resoluteness of the holy life in relation to those who pursue the holy path while remaining actively engaged in their worldly duties. If we compare the general tone of the exhortation of the B.G. with that of early Buddhism, we can clearly see that the former is not as strict, resolute and rigorous as the latter. We have noticed that in Buddhism no relaxation or rest is sanctioned for a holy aspirant before the realisation of the highest goal.[2] No complacency is permitted so long as all defilements are not destroyed[3] and all fetters, great or small are not rent asunder.[4] Even a little defect or vice is to be feared.[5] The holy path which is sharp like the edge of a razor (khuradhārūpamo, Sn.133) is difficult to tread and "even as a Kusa grass cuts the hand itself, if wrongly grasped, so also the life of a recluse if wrongly pursued, drags one to hell.[6] Thus, early Buddhism constantly cautions one to pursue the holy path with the utmost care, strictness and seriousness. But the tone of the B.G. is quite different. In the second chapter

1. B.G. II. 38; IV. 20-23; V. 7-10; XVIII. 17.
2. M.I. 271 ff.
3. bhikkhū, vissāsa mā pādi appatto āsavakkhayaṃ, Dh. 272.
4. passasi...tam. saṃyojanaṃ aṇuṃ vā thūlaṃ vā yass'āhaṃ no pahānaṃ vadāmī'ti? M.I. 456.
5. aṇumattesu vajjesu bhayadassāvī, D.I. 63; II. 78.
6. Dh. 311.

itself where Kṛṣṇa starts his exhortation to Arjuna, he declares: "In this path, no effort is ever lost, no opposite result is ever produced. Even a little of this discipline saves one from great fear."[1] Arjuna is repeatedly encouraged and cheered: "Grieve not, O Arjuna, you are born with divine endowments."[2] "Casting aside all vacillating states of the mind come to me alone for shelter, I shall release you from all sins, do not grieve."[3] "Know it for certain, O Arjuna, that my devotee never perishes."[4] Even if one is of most vile conduct, if he worships me with unwavering devotion...he soon becomes a righteous man and attains eternal Peace."[5] "One should not abandon one's natural duty, even though it is defective,"[6] for "man attains perfection devoted each to one's own duty."[7] Though the B.G. also admits that "there is nothing pure like wisdom in this world" (na hi jñānena sadṛśaṃ pavitraṃ iha vidyate, B.G.IV.39), yet it shows no urgency to attain it: "He who acquires perfection in disinterested action, attains it (wisdom) of himself in course of time"[8] When Arjuna, referring to the highly difficult (suduṣkaram) process of yoga (B.G.VI.33,34), asks Kṛṣṇa about the fate of those who, though endowed with faith, fail to follow the yoga to perfection, and being careless fall from it,[9] Kṛṣṇa at once encourages him by saying: "There is no destruction (setback) for him, O Arjuna, either here or elsewhere. One who has done good can never, O Arjuna, tread the path of woe."[10] Then it is pointed out how after having spent a happy life in heaven for long, he is born in the family of those who are pure and prosperous, or in the family of glorious yogins

1. B.G. II. 40.
2. B.G. XVI. 5.
3. B.G. XVII. 66.
4. B.G. IX. 31.
5. B.G. IX. 30 and 31.
6. B.G. XVIII. 48.
7. B.G. XVIII. 45.
8. B.G. IV. 38.
9. Ayatiḥ śraddhayo'peto yogāc calitamānasaḥ,
aprāpya yogasaṃsiddhiṃ kāṃ gatiṃ Kṛṣṇa gacchati., B. G. VI. 37.
10. B.G. VI. 40.

themselves (B.G.VI.41-44) and ultimately "perfecting himself through many lives, he reaches the supreme goal."[1]

Thus, the general tone of the B.G. is one of encouragement and not of warning, and hence it seems to take things somewhat lightly. One is encouraged in carrying on one's worldly duties with a purity of purpose as far as possible. The aspirant following any of the holy paths is promised Security and Peace sooner or later. The serious atmosphere of Buddhism is hardly to be met with, and in place of warning and cautioning one of the danger of delay and complacency, the B.G. often encourages and cheers up by pointing to the merit accruing out of the holy pursuit, and assures success and security to the holy aspirant.

The above approach of the B.G. explains why, in spite of agreeing with Buddhism that the world is impermanent and sorrowful (anityam asukhaṃ lokam, BG. IX.33; cf. II.14; V.22), the B.G. refrains from giving a despicable picture of it and highlights, on the other hand, the importance of active indulgence in worldly affairs. Thus, neither is there an atmosphere of strictness with regard to the codes of discipline nor is there any rigidity with regard to the path of salvation. Let us now see how the B.G. tries to synthesise the divergent paths of salvation and advocates the efficacy of different paths in contradistinction to the validity of the one and only one path taught by Buddhism.

(*F*) *The Triple Path of the B.G. with Disinterested Action as Its Central Core*:-

Emphasising 'activism' (as professor Hiriyanna calls it[2]), as the key-note of its doctrine, the B.G. tries to establish it from the different standpoints of knowledge, devotion and action (without concern for the fruit). S. Radhakrishnan remarks: "The whole setting of the Gītā points out that it is an exhortation to action."[3] This action (pravṛtti), however, is sought to be compromised with renunciation

1. anekajanmasaṃsiddhas tato yāti parāṃ gatim., B.G. VI. 45.
2. Professor Hiriyanna concludes that in the Gītā "the central point of the teaching is activism."—Outlines of Indian Philosophy, p. 118.
3. Indian Philosophy, Vol. I. p. 568.

(nivṛtti) and in so doing, the latter, as we have indicated above, assumes a new meaning or connotation (B. G. V. 3; VI. 1, 2, XVIII. 2). Thus action as combined with renunciation constitutes the central message of the B. G. Renunciation is no longer a renunciation of action, but, as Professor Hiriyanna calls it, it is a "renunciation *in* action."[1] It is this 'renunciation in action' or what is known as disinterested or desireless action (niṣkāma karma), which is taught by the B.G. from the standpoints of knowledge (jñāna), devotion (bhakti) and action (karma) without concern for the fruit.

Knowledge, according to the B.G., consists in having an insight into the inner core of all things, realising what is perishable and what is imperishable. The deeper truth of both these perishable and imperishable elements is said to have been seen by the seers of truth (ubhayor api dṛṣṭo'ntas tv anayos tattvadarśibhiḥ, B.G. II. 16). Having known this truth, the knower rises above the vicissitudes of life and is no longer moved by the rise or fall (birth or death) of perishable things, no longer swayed by emotional weaknesses. Kṛṣṇa opens his exhortation to knowledge with disapproval of Arjuna's emotional weaknesses (hṛdayadaurbalyam B.G. II. 3). Arjuna, according to him, was grieving for those who were not worthy of grief, and so he is told: "Wise men do not grieve for the dead or for the living."[2] Introducing the knowledge of the imperishable metaphysical self, Kṛṣṇa exhorts him to remain firm and unperturbed in his duty and not to be perplexed by the consideration of the life and death of perishable beings. "The wise one is not perplexed by this" (dhīraḥ tatra na muhyati, B.G. II. 13.). This is how the metaphysical knowledge of the self is made the basis of imparting the teaching of action with equanimity (samatva) or detachment (saṃnyāsa). It is said: "The firm man, O Arjuna, who remains equal in pain and pleasure (samaduḥkhasukham) and who is not troubled by these (pairs of opposites), indeed, is fit for attaining

1. Op. cit. p. 121
2. B.G. II. 11.

immortality."[1] Emphasising the imperishable and immortal nature of the self at great length (B.G. II. 13-30), Arjuna is told again and again that he need not grieve[2], and is finally asked to get ready for his duty of fighting in a disinterested and detached spirit. "Treating alike pleasure and pain, gain and loss, victory and defeat, get ready for battle. Thus you shall not incur sin."[3] The same teaching is imparted by giving a symbolic interpretation of sacrifice as knowledge (jñānayajña, B.G. IV. 28, 33; IX. 15). In this sense sacrifice stands for detachment born of knowledge. Thus, it is said; "By action other than that which is performed as a sacrifice, the world is in the bondage of action"[4], but "one whose attachment has disappeared, who is freed, and whose mind is firmly set in knowledge. his action done as a sacrifice is entirely dissolved."[5] Considering knowledge as the best form of sacrifice, Kṛṣṇa says: "Knowledge as a sacrifice is greater than any material sacrifice, O Arjuna. All actions are entirely dissolved in knowledge."[6] "As the blazing fire reduces the fuel to ashes, even so, O' Arjuna, does the fire of wisdom turn all actions to ashes."[7] Again coming back to the metaphysical knowledge of Brahman and combining it with the symbolic meaning of sacrifice, the B.G. says: "His offering is Brahman, his oblation is Brahman. By Brahman is it offered into the fire of Brahman. Thus, by means of his action as absorption in Brahman, he attains to Brahman himself."[8] This mystic symbolism is expressed in plain language as follows: "He who having given up attachment performs actions by dedicating them to Brahman, is not contaminated by sin like a lotus leaf (untouched) by

1. B.G. II. 15.
2. nā'nuśocitum arhasi, B.G. II. 25; nai'naṃ śocitum arhasi, B.G. II. 26; na tvaṃ śocitum arhasi, B.G. II. 27; tatra kā paridevanā ?, B.G. II. 28; na tvaṃ śocitum arhasi, B.G. II. 30.
3. B.G. II. 38.
4. B.G. III. 9.
5. B.G. IV. 23.
6. B.G. IV. 33.
7. B.G. IV. 37.
8. B.G. VI. 24.

water."[1] Thus, it is clear that through all these metaphysical and symbolic modes of knowledge, the same detached or disinterested performance of action is taught.

Through the means of devotion also the same teaching is imparted. Devotion does not consist, according to the B.G., in escape from worldly duties but in dedication of all works to God It needs no abandonment of work but only the abandonment of the selfish desires. This is what the B.G. tries to convey through its teaching of complete self-surrender to God. By discharging his duties in the spirit of utter selflessness, the devotee is said to be free from all good or bad results of actions. Thus, Kṛṣṇa teaches: "Whatever you do, whatever you eat, whatever you offer, whatever you give, whatever penance you observe—dedicate all that to me O Arjuna. Thus, being possessed of the discipline of renunciation (saṃnyāsayogayuktātmā), you will be freed from all bonds of action, bearing good or bad results, and being freed, you will come to me."[2] It is important to note that Arjuna, as a devotee, is asked to do whatever is his duty and not to renounce action, and yet in so doing, he is said to be endowed with the discipline of renunciation (saṃnyāsayogayuktātmā). Thus, it is evident that through this method of devotion also, the B.G. intends to reinforce the same doctrine of 'renunciation in action' (the combination of nivṛtti and pravṛtti). Arjuna is exhorted to fight and yet is asked to remain a renouncer (saṃnyāsī), according to the B.G. definition of the term (B.G. V. 3; VI. 1). He is told : "Dedicating (saṃnyasya) all actions to me by your spiritualised mind and being free from desire and egoism, fight without the fever (of emotion)."[3] "Remember me, therefore, at all times and fight. With your mind and intellect given to me, you will undoubtedly come to me."[4] Thus, according to the B.G., renunciation and devotion are virtually the same and demand the same disinterested

1. B.G. V. 10.
2. B.G. IX. 27 and 28.
3. B.G. III. 30.
4. B.G. VIII. 7.

discharge of duty. Work alone is considered as worship to God through which men can attain perfection (svakarmaṇā tam abhyarcya siddhiṃ vindati mānavaḥ, B.G. XVIII, 46). Even while concluding with a devotional note (B.G. XVIII. 57, 65, 66), Kṛṣṇa teaches the true import of devotion as follows: "Doing continually all actions whatsoever, resigning unto me, one reaches the eternal and imperishable goal by my grace."[1]

The same teaching is contained in the gospel of karmayoga (duty for duty's sake). Yoga in this context is defined as equanimity (samatvaṃ yoga ucyate, B.G. II. 48), or skilfulness in action (yogaḥ karmasu kauśalam, B.G. II. 50). Action performed in the state of absolute equanimity or with utter detachment to the fruit is considered 'skilful', since in so doing one is said not to be contaminated by it. Arjuna is, therefore, asked not to be inclined towards inaction but to convert action itself into inaction by remaining utterly unattached to its fruit. Thus, the doctrine of 'skilful action' (karmayoga) is taught to him as follows: "Let action alone be thy concern and never its fruits. Let not the fruits of action be thy motive, nor let there be in thee any attachment to inaction."[2] Action without concern for the fruit is considered equivalent to inaction and can, therefore, cause no contamination to the doer. It is stated: "Having abandoned attachment to the fruit of action, ever content and free from dependence, one, even though engaged in action, does nothing at all."[3] "He is not contaminated even though he works" (kurvann api na lipyate, B.G. V. 7). "Man attains to the highest by performing action without attachment" (asakto hy ācaran karma param āpnoti pūruṣaḥ, B.G. III. 19). In this connection, the B.G. advocates the doctrine of 'specific duty' (svadharma) pertaining to each order of society and points out that one's own duty, even if defective, is better than the apparently good duty of another (śreyān svadharmo viguṇaḥ paradharmāt svanuṣṭhitāt, B.G.

1. B.G. XVIII. 56.
2. B.G. II. 47.
3. B.G. IV. 20.

III. 35, XVIII. 47), since man is said to attain perfection, devoted each to his own duty (sve-sve karmaṇy abhirataḥ saṃsiddhiṃ labhate naraḥ, XVIII. 45), if the duty is discharged with a detached intellect (asaktabuddhiḥ, XVIII. 49).

Thus, through the triple path of knowledge, devotion and action (jñāna, bhakti and karma), the B. G. seeks to establish the same doctrine of 'renunciation in action' (nivṛtti combined with pravṛtti). Desireless or disinterested action (niṣkāma karma) is thus made the central point in which all the paths are shown to converge. This is how the B. G. tries to establish an unity amidst diversity.

All through compromising as it is, it seems anxious to convey that all these different paths are in essence the same and not different. Devotion (bhakti) and knowledge (jñāna) are described as only two different approaches to the same reality, conceived by turn as personal and impersonal. The B. G., therefore, uses the same name, viz., 'adhyātma' for both of them.[1] Those who are engaged in unswerving contemplation or worship of a personal God (ye tu..ananyenai'va yogena māṃ dhyāyanta upāsate, B. G. XII. 6), attain the same goal which is reached by concentration on the impersonal Brahman (Brahmakarmasamādhinā, B. G. IV. 24). After having stated that "my devotee comes to me" (madbhaktaḥ....mām eti., B.G. XI. 55; cf. XII. 2), Kṛṣṇa at once adds that "those who meditate on the Imperishable, the Undefinable and the Unmanifest..,they also come to me indeed" (ye tv akṣaram anirdeśyam avyaktam paryupāsate.. te prāpnuvanti mām eva, B. G. XII. 3, 4). Thus, it is suggested that contemplation or worship (dhyāna or upāsanā) is only a devotional counterpart of the meditation (samādhi) on the Supreme. Similarly the paths of knowledge and action (jñanayoga and karmayoga) also are said to be essentially one, since the same spirit of renunciation constitutes the core of both. The B. G. explicitly declares: "(Only) fools speak of knowledge and action as different, and not the wise. He who is properly established even in one, obtains the fruit of both. The goal which is attained by men of knowledge,

1. B.G. XI. 1 (adhyātmasaṃjñitam).

is realised by men of action too. He who sees the paths of knowledge and action as one, (really) sees."[1] This is how the B. G. tries to remove the incompatibility between the two traditional paths of knowledge and action and puts forward its synthetic theory of knowledge and action (jñāna-karmasamuccayavāda).

(C) *The Controversy Regarding the Supremacy of One or the Other Path*:—

Notwithstanding persistent attempts on the part of the B. G. to indentify the divergent paths, the question as to which one of these paths is principal and which subordinate has, nevertheless, agitated the mind of traditional interpreters as well as modern exponents of the B. G , and different views have been expressed in relation to it. Traditional commentators take a partisan attitude and try to interpret the entire teaching of the B. G. in the light of the respective tenets of their own schools. Śaṅkara, the well-known champion of the path of knowledge, for example, makes an unambiguous declaration: 'Salvation is (to be attained) by knowledge alone—this, in deed,is the definite purport of the Gītā, as also of all the Ups."[2] He tries to show that other paths are taught as means to lower goals, like worldly prosperity (abhyudayārthaḥ)and the attainment of celestial abodes (devādisthānaprāptihetuḥ), and if performed disinterestedly they can lead utmost to the purification of the intellect (sattvaśuddhaye bhavati) and be ultimately subservient to the attainment of knowledge.[3] He tries to rule out the possibility of a combined path of knowledge and action (jñāna-karma-samuccaya) by saying that the two have been taught in the B. G. for people of different orders

1. B.G. V. 4 and 5.

2. Kevalād eva jñānād mokṣa iti eṣaḥ artho niścito gītāsu sarvopaniṣatsu ca S. B.G , Introduction to the IIIrd Chapter.

3. Abhyudayārthaḥ api yaḥ pravṛttilakṣaṇo dharmo varṇāśramān ca uddiśya vihitaḥ sa devāiṣṭdhānaprāptihetuḥ api san īśvarārpaṇabuddhyā anuṣṭhīyamāṇaḥ sattvaśuddhaye bhavati phalābhisandhivarjitaḥ. Śuddhasattvasya ca jñānaniṣṭhāyogyatāprāptidvāreṇa jñānotpattihetutvena ca niḥśreyasahetutvam api pratipadyate., S.B.G. Introduction.

aiming at different goals.[1] Rāmānuja, on the other hand, points out that "under the cover of encouraging the son of Pāṇḍu (Arjuna) for battle, the Lord, indeed, has propounded his own subject, the path of devotion, as the means of salvation, the highest goal of mankind, as embodied in the Vedānta—the path of knowledge and action being subservient to it."[2] The path of action is highlighted by B G. Tilak who says: "The Gītā has been composed to teach the method as to how the worldly duties are to be performed with a view to attaining salvation."[3] He further adds: "From this it is established that the doctrine of action (pravṛtti dharma) is the principal theme of the Gītā and all other things have been stated to support the same principal theme, in other words, they all are subsidiary."[4] The same view is voiced by Professor Deussen also.[5] But Garbe thinks that "the Bhagavadgītā is the song *par excellence* of Bhakti, the faithful and devout love to God. Devotion to God proceeding as much from the path of knowledge, as from selfless performance of duty, leads with unconditioned certitude to the goal. The whole poem is permeated by this sentiment—to preach this doctrine was the whole poem composed."[6] According to him "the characteristic feature of the Bhagavadgītā" is that "devotion to God is the climax of all knowledge."[7] K.N. Mitra also is inclined to think that in the B. G. "intellect is more or less an auxiliary of the emotion."[8] According to Professor Ranade also "the general upshot of the teaching of the B.G. in this respect

1. bhinnapuruṣā'nuṣṭheyatvena jñānakarmaniṣṭhayoḥ...jñānakarmaṇoḥ samuccayā'nupapattiḥ, S. B. G., Introduction to the IIIrd Chapter.

2. Pāṇḍutanaya-yuddhaprotsāhanavyājena paramapuruṣārthalakṣaṇamokṣasādhanatayā vedānto'ditaṃ svaviṣayaṃ jñānakarmānugṛhītaṃ bhaktiyogam avatārayāmāsa., R.B.G. Introduction.

3. Gītārahasya, preface, p. 16.

4. Ibid., Chapter I., p. 26.

5. Deussen points out that the B.G. makes "a demand for heroic action", though, he adds, that this is derived only "painfully and artificially" by the B.G. from its metaphysical premises., The Philosophy of the Upanishads, p. 362.

6. Indian Antiquary, Vol. 47, Supplement, p. 27.

7. Ibid, p. 21.

8. 'The Evolution of Vaiṣṇavism' in B. C. Law, Vol. I. p. 678.

seems to be that the Saguṇa-upāsanā might be regarded as even higher than the Avyakta-upāsanā."[1]

None of these verdicts, however, seems to be as clearly and consistently borne out by the text of the B.G. as a whole, as these scholars try to read into it. There are, no doubt, passages which, if taken in isolation, may seem to support any of the above views. But, if our judgment is to be based on the basis of the whole and not merely on the ground of some sections or dissections, the picture would appear to be different. None can doubt that the B.G. praises all the different paths almost in the same vein. Regarding 'knowledge', it says: "Nothing in this world is pure like wisdom" (IV. 38). "Even if you are the most sinful of all sinners, you shall cross over all sins by the boat of knowledge alone" (IV. 36). In a similar way, devotion also is applauded. Kṛṣṇa says: "Listen again to my supreme word, the most secret of all,..Fix your mind on me, be devoted to me; sacrifice to me; prostrate yourself before me. So shall you attain to me" (XVIII. 64 and 65). "Even if a man of the most vile conduct worships me with unwavering devotion, he soon becomes a righteous man and attains eternal Peace (IX. 30 and 31). Again, arguing the case for action without concern for the fruits, Kṛṣṇa says: "The wise men endowed with disinterested intellect, abandoning the fruit arising out of action, reach the blameless state being absolutely emancipated from the bondage of rebirth" (II. 51). "One who performs the prescribed work without depending on the fruit, is the renouncer (saṃnyāsī) or the yogī" (VI. 1).

The extolling of all these paths, almost in identical language naturally causes confusion, which the B.G. itself anticipates Arjuna is made to express this feeling of confusion, when he has listened to Kṛṣṇa speaking of knowledge and action almost in the same tone.[2] He plainly says: "You seem to perplex my intelligence with an apparently confused

1. The Bhagavadgītā as a Philosophy of God-Realisation, pp.230-231.

2. Cf. Eṣā te'bhihitā sāṅkhye buddhir yoge tv imāṃ śṛṇu, B. G. II. 39.

utterance."[1] "You praise, O Kṛṣṇa, the renunciation of actions (the path of knowledge) and again their disinterested performance (the path of action). Tell me for certain, which one is the better of these two."[2] Now, it is important to note that after having posed this question in a way quite natural to an inquisitive mind, the B.G. tries its best to show that it is wrong to see any intrinsic superiority or inferiority in these paths which are meant for people of different temperament to start with, but ultimately they all converge in one and lead to the same goal. They are said to be mutually complementary and essentially the same. Preferences for one or the other path are, of course. indicated by the B. G., as we shall see in the sequel, but it is done more on the ground of expediency than on the basis of any intrinsic superiority. To show a preference for one or the other path on the ground of its being easier and more expedient is one thing, and to speak of one having greater intrinsic worth is quite a different thing. Indeed, the compromising attitude of the B.G. is too strong to allow it to recognise a difference of value and to speak in terms of clear-cut superiority of one path over the other. The above-mentioned scholars, speaking in unequivocal terms of the superiority of one or the other path do not seem to do justice to the spirit of the B.G.

If we pay careful attention to what Kṛṣṇa says in reply to the aforesaid straightforward question of Arjuna, the attitude and intention of the B.G. would be quite evident. The reply of Kṛṣṇa is as follows:—"In this world, O Arjuna, the twofold way of life has been spoken of previously by me: the path of knowledge for men of contemplation, and that of works for men of action" (jñānayogena sāṅkhyānāṃ karmayogena yogınām).[3] After speaking of the suitability of the different paths for different types of men, it further points out that they lead to the same goal and are essentially one.

---

1. Vyāmiśreṇe'va vākyena buddhiṃ mohayasi'va me
tad ekaṃ vada niścitya yena śreyo'ham āpnuyām., B.G. III. 2.
2. Saṃnyāsaṃ karmaṇāṃ Kṛṣṇa punar yogaṃ ca śaṃsasi,
yac chreya etayor ekaṃ tan me brūhi suniścitam., B.G.V. 1.
3. B.G. III. 3.

"The goal which is obtained by men of knowledge is reached by men of action as well. He who sees the ways of knowledge and action as one, (really) sees,"[1] "(Only) fools and not the wise, speak of the paths of knowledge and action as different. He who is rightly established even in one, realises the fruit of both."[2] A similar reply is given when Arjuna enquires about the inferiority or superiority of the paths of devotion (worship of or contemplation on the personal God) and knowledge (meditation on the impersonal Absolute)[3] We have already noticed (supra, pp. 471-2) that contemplation or worship (dhyāna or upāsanā) to a personal God and meditation (samādhi) on the impersonal Absolute are considered by the B.G. as only two sides of the same spiritual (adhyâtma) discipline and are said to lead to the same goal (te prāpnuvanti mām eva, B.G. XII. 4).

The same is supported by an essentially similar description of the sthitaprajña or karmaniṣṭha (B.G.II 55-72), jñānin or Brahmaniṣṭha (B.G. IV. 9-33) and bhaktimān (B.G. XII. 13-19). The fact that these men perfected through the paths of action, knowledge and devotion are possessed of identical features cannot but indicate the essential unity of the paths adopted by them.

There are, of course, a few such verses wherein one particular path is spoken of as leading on to another and, on that basis, it may be possible for one to make out that the B. G. thereby suggests a relation of dominance and subservience with reference to these paths. But on a closer examination of the entire text, it is not difficult to see that all these paths are by turn said to pave the way for the others, which can only indicate that they are considered by the B.G. as mutually complementary. This explains why none of these paths is spoken of explicitly as principal or supreme. This conclusion alone can be in conformity with the avowed compromising stand of the B.G. according to which only "fools and not the wise speak of the paths of knowledge and

1. B.G. V. 5.
2. B.G V. 4.
3. B.G XIII. 1-4.

action as different" (V. 4). It alone can accord well with the open declaration of the B.G. that "one who is rightly established even in one, realises the fruit of both." (loc, cit). We may here refer to the verses in which the different paths are, by turn, spoken of as leading to one another:—

A. (i) *Karma leading to bhakti*:—Asaktabuddhiḥ sarvatra jitātmā vigataspṛhaḥ..
samaḥ sarveṣu bhūteṣu madbhaktiṃ labhate parām, XVIII. 49-54.

(ii) *Karma leading to jñāna* :—Na hi jñānena sadṛśaṃ pavitram iha vidyate, tat svayaṃ yogasaṃsiddhaḥ kālenā'tmani vindati, IV. 38.
Asaktabuddhiḥ sarvatra..naiṣkarmyasiddhiṃ paramāṃ saṃnyāsenā'dhigacchati.
Siddhiṃ prāpto yathā Brahma tathā'pnoti nibodha me
samāsenai'va kaunteya niṣṭhā jñānasya yā parā., XVIII. 49-50.

B. (i) *Bhakti leading to karma*:—Teṣāṃ..bhajatāṃ prītipūrvakam, dadāmi buddhiyogaṃ[1] taṃ yena mām upayānti te, X. 10.

(ii) *Bhakti leading to jñāna*:—Teṣām evā'nukampārtham aham ajñānajaṃ tamaḥ
nāśayāmy ātmabhāvastho jñānadīpena bhāsvatā., X. 11.
Bhaktyā tv ananyayā śakya aham evaṃvidho'rjuna
jñātuṃ draṣṭuṃ ca tattvena...XI. 54.
madbhakta etad vijñāya madbhāvāyo' papadyate, XIII. 18.
Bhaktyā mām abhijānāti, XVIII. 55

1. 'Buddhiyoga' is noting but a synonym of 'karmayoga' as indicated in B.G. II. 49. In the course of explaining 'karmayoga', Kṛṣṇa defines it as equanimity (samatvam, B.G. II. 48) of intellect, when one acts giving up all attachment (saṅgaṃ tyaktvā, loc. cit.) It is in this sense of the equanimity of intellect that the mere action (karma) is said to be far inferior to 'buddhiyoga' (or Karmayoga) in B.G. II. 49.

C. (i) *jñāna leading to karma* :— ... yo vetti tattvataḥ
so'vikampena yogena yujyate nā'tra saṃśayaḥ,
X. 7.
Tasmād ajñānasaṃbhūtaṃ hṛtsthaṃ jñānāsinā'
tmanaḥ
chittvai'naṃ saṃśayaṃ yogam
ātiṣṭho'ttiṣṭha bhārata, IV. 42.

(ii) *jñāna leading to bhakti* :—bhajanty ananyamanaso
jñātvā bhūtādim avyayam, IX. 13
iti matvā bhajante māṃ budhā bhāvasamanvitāḥ,
X. 8.
Yo māṃ evam asaṃmūḍho jānāti puruṣottamam
sa sarvavid bhajati māṃ sarvabhāvena bhārata,
XV. 19.

Thus, it appears that according to the B.G., these paths are interlinked and flow into one another. Though they look different to start with, they are ultimately and essentially not different. In keeping with its compromising nature, the B.G. shows no rigidity with regard to the path to be adopted and leaves the matter largely to the choice of the individual. As it says: "Some perceive the self in the self by the self through contemplation, others by the path of knowledge, and still others by the path of action."[1] In view of this attitude of the B.G., we cannot accept one-sided verdicts of the above-mentioned scholars.

However, it is interesting to notice how the B.G., despite its denial of the intrinsic superiority or inferiority of the different paths, tries to indicate its preference for one or the other paths. The primary purpose of the B.G. is to exhort the despondent Arjuna to adhere to his duty, which it does through various means. Thus, its preference for 'activism' (pravṛtti) is evident, but at the same time it combines it with the doctrine of renunciation (nivṛtti) which had hitherto been regarded as the special feature of the path of knowledge. In this combined form, the tenet of 'renunciation in action' is made the common feature of all the paths, as we have

1. B.G. XIII. 24.

already noticed (supra, pp.466-471). By so doing, the B.G. introduces activism into the very fibre of all the paths without making any open assertion about the intrinsic superiority of the path of action. Again, there are other ways through which it shows its preference for it, which we shall discuss separately under the next topic. Then again it indicates its preference for the path of devotion as compared to the path of knowledge without, of course, minimising the qualitative value of the latter. Thus, it represents the tenet of the Bhāgavata dharma in its true spirit (supra, pp.183-184), embodying a philosophy of action based on devotion and compromising it at the same time with the doctrine of knowledge or renunciation. Its preference in relation to these paths may be shown in the light of the following verses:—

In B.G.XII.2 Kṛṣṇa speaks of the preference of bhakti (devotion) to jñāna (knowledge). Arjuna asks him pointedly whether the one who is earnestly devoted to the worship of God, or the other who aspires to the knowledge of the Imperishable and the Unmanifest, is the better of the two.[1] In reply to this, Kṛṣṇa says: "those who fixing their minds on me, worship me, ever earnest and possessed of supreme faith—them do I consider as set in the best discipline."[2] The same is corroborated by B.G.XII.12 in which it is said that the contemplation of God is better than knowledge[3] Then speaking of the preference of disinterested action (Karmayoga) to knowledge or renunciation, Kṛṣṇa says: "The renunciation of actions and their disinterested performance both lead to salvation. But of the two, the disinterested performance of action (karmayoga) is better than the renunciation of actions."[4] In corroboration of this view B.G.VI.46 declares: "The performer of disinterested action (yogī) is better even

1. Evaṃ satatayuktā ye bhaktās tvāṃ paryupāsate,
ye cā'py akṣaram avyaktaṃ teṣām ke yogavittamāḥ, B.G. XII. 1.

2. Mayy āveśya mano ye māṃ nityayuktā upāsate.
śraddhayā parayo'petās te me yuktatamā matāḥ, B.G. XII. 2.

3. jñānād dhyānaṃ viśiṣyate, XII. 12. The word 'dhyāna' is used here as a synonym of devotion to personal God as it is indicated in an earlier verse (māṃ dyāyante upāsate, XII. 6).

4. B.G. V. 2.

than the man of knowledge (jñānibhyo)."[1] After having thus shown the preference of bhakti and karmayoga to jñāna, it is finally pointed out in B.G.XII. 12 that the path of renouncing the fruit of action (karmaphalatyāgaḥ) is better than devotion or the contemplation on God.[2]

On the basis of these utterances, one can reasonably arrive at the conclusion that according to the B.G. the paths of action, devotion and knowledge are preferred in a descending order. It is needless to remind that this preference depends not on the consideration of any qualitative value of these paths, but on the extent to which one path is considered easier and more expedient to practice than the other. This is clearly stated by the B.G. when showing its perference for bhakti over jñāna (XII. 2), it mentions the greater difficulty of the followers of the path of knowledge (kleśo'dhikataras teṣām...avyaktā hi gatir duḥkhaṃ dehavadbhir avāpyate XII. 5) and considers bhakti as easy to practise (susukhaṃ kartum, IX. 2) and bearing fruit immediately (nacirāt, XII. 7). Again in B.G. XII. 9-11, it advises an aspirant to take recourse to the practice of meditation, failing which it prescribes the dedication of all works to God and in case even that be found difficult, it advises one to do one's duty regardless of consequences. Summarising this position, it states in the next verse as follows: "Better (śreyo) than the practice of yogic disciplines is knowledge, better than knowledge is contemplation or devotion, better than contemplation is the renunciation of the fruit of action; renunciation is soon followed by Peace."[3] Thus, from the context it is clear that the word 'śreya' in the above verse is indicative of the preference given on the ground of expediency and not on the basis of intrinsic superiority.

But any kind of perference granted to the path of

---

1. yogī jñānibhyo'pi mato'dhikaḥ, VI. 46. Śaṅkara, however, in his attempt to maintain the supremacy of 'jñāna' tries to twist the direct meaning of it and says : "Knowledge here means the scriptural scholarship" (jñānam atra śāstrapāṇḍityam, S. B. G. VI. 46).

2. Śreyo hi...dhyānāt karmaphalatyāgaḥ, XII. 12.

3. Śreyo hi jñānam abhyāsāj jñānād dhyānaṃ viśiṣyate,
dhyānāt karmaphalatyāgas tyāgāc chāntir anantaram...,B.G.XII.12.

action is unpalatable to commentators like Śaṅkara and Rāmānuja who stand for the definite superiority of knowledge and devotion respectively. Naturally, therefore, they try to explain away the clear and unambiguous utterances mentioned above, by giving some ingenious explanations of their own. Śaṅkara comes out with the explanation that it is sheer praise or exaltation of the abandonment of the fruits of all actions with a view merely to coaxing Arjuna into action.[1] According to him, it is praised (stūyate), since it is worth practising by those who are incapable of adopting the perfect means.[2] Rāmānuja also makes the same plea and says that it is praised for those who are incapable of adopting the path of devotion (bhaktiyogā'bhyāsā' śaktasya, R.B.G. XII. 12). Thus, they try to suggest that Arjuna was not considered fit by Kṛṣṇa for practising the highest path to salvation. Śaṅkara tries to give a further twist by changing the meaning of the word 'jñāna' (knowledge). When in B.G. VI. 46, the man of disinterested action is said to be preferable to the man of knowledge (yogī jñānibhyo'pi mato'dhikaḥ), Śaṅkara tries to explain it away by saying that "knowledge here means the scriptural scholarship" (jñānam atra śāstrapāṇḍityam, S.B.G.VI.46). Similarly in B.G. XII. 12 where the contemplation of God is perferred to knowledge (jñānād dhyānaṃ viśiṣyate), Śaṅkara tries to make out that the term 'jñāna' here indicates only a non-discriminative knowledge (avivekapūrvakāt...jñānāt, S.B.G. XII. 12). But the contextual references as well as the literal meanings of the texts are so patent that one can see through the motive of these commentators who seem to be interested more in vindicating their own positions than in interpreting the exact sense of the text. It is difficult to accept, as Śaṅkara and Rāmānuja would have us believe, that Kṛṣṇa in the form of a blameless God speaks with guile in his heart, especially to Arjuna whom he addresses as his devotee and friend (bhakto' si me sakhā ce' ti, B.G. IV. 3). Moreover, it is repeatedly and explicitly told

1. sarvakarmaphalatyāgastutiḥ 'iyaṃ prarocanārthā, S.B.G. XII.12.
2. sarvakarmaphalatyāgaḥ stūyate sampannasādhanā'nuṣṭhānā' śaktau anuṣṭheyatvena, S.B.G. XII. 12.

by Kṛṣṇa that he is telling the supreme word, the most secret of all (sarvaguhyatamaṃ bhūyaḥ śṛṇu me paramaṃ vacaḥ, B.G. XVIII. 64 cf. IV. 3; IX. 1. X. 1; XI. 1); more secret than all secrets (guhyād guhyataram, B.G. XVIII. 63), the highest form of wisdom (jñānānāṃ jñānam uttamam, B.G. XIV. 1) by knowing which nothing else remains to be known (B.G. VII. 2), and the highest perfection is attained (B.G. XIV. 1). We, may therefore conclude that the B.G., in spite of its reluctance to recognise a relation of dominance and subordinance among the different paths, shows its preference for action, devotion and knowledge in a descending order. B.G. Tilak[1] has drawn attention to a verse of the Sūrya-Gītā in which the same view is very explicitly stated. The verse reads as follows : "Devotion is better than knowledge, and better than devotion is desireless action. He alone who knows this principle of Vedānta, is the best among men."[2]

From the above account it is evident that the B.G. advocates a diversity of paths as against the Buddhist teaching of the one single path to salvation. But the urge for compromise is so strong in the B.G. that it neither accepts the independence of the different paths nor does it recognise a relation of dominance and subordinance among them, despite the fact that it indicates its perferences in an indirect way. In view of the great stress laid by the B.G. on the essential unity or the oneness of the paths, it is possible that in doing so, it might be trying to indicate that its teaching of the diversity of paths is not incompatible with the unity of the path as taught in early Buddhism. The repeated attempt of the B.G. to unify action and renunciation (B.G. V. 4, 5; VI. 2) seems to suggest a conscious effort on its part to incorporate the essence of the Buddhist way of life. But there can be no doubt that the synthetic philosophy of the B.G. falls short of the true Buddhist ideal. The Buddhist way of life

---

1. Gītārahasya, p. 777; cf. Radhakrishnan—The Bhagavadgītā, p. 296.

2. Jñānād upāstir utkṛṣṭā karmotkṛṣṭam upāsanāt
iti yo veda vedāntaiḥ sa eva puruṣottamaḥ. —Sūrya Gītā IV. 77.

does not sanction disinterested action regardless of the nature of the work nor does it look upon it as a full-fledged means to be adopted right from the very beginning. Then again, it has little room for devotion. Even the path of knowledge is kept quite free from mystic or metaphysical elements. It must, however, be admitted that the B.G. has tried its best to assimilate the Buddhist tenet of renunciation in its diversified scheme of things so far as it could fit in with its exhortation to lead active worldly life.

The Path of Action Versus the Path of Renunciation :—

The foregoing discussion has made it clear that the attitude of the B.G. is largely guided by its pronounced leaning towards the active worldly life (pravṛtti) in contradistinction to the Buddhist preference for the life of renunciation (nivṛtti). It may, therefore, be interesting to see how they vindicate their respective positions.

It seems to be acknowledged both by the B.G. and Buddhism that the absolutely pure life is extremely difficult to live as a householder. Buddhism, therefore, in adherence to the life of strict purity prefers renunciation of the world to be able to practise the purest life, leading to Nibbāna here and now. The B.G., on the other hand, considers the defects of worldly life as a necessary evil and prefers the man who pursues the path of purity, while discharging his worldly duties as a householder. Some unavoidable defects of the worldly life are condoned perhaps because they are thought at times inescapable in fulfilling worldly obligations.

In the Pali Canon it is frequently stated: "Full of impediments is the household life, a dusty path (a path of defilements); whereas the life of renunciation is like the open sky (free from hindrances). It is not easy to lead this holy life in all its perfection and purity like a polished conch-shell by a person living the houshold life."[1] Raṭṭhapāla after having listened to the Master, says the same before him: "If I really understand the doctrine expounded by the Exalted One, it is not easy to lead this holy life in all its perfection and purity like a polished conch-shell by a person living the house-

1. D.I. 63, M.I. 179, 240, 267.

hold life."[1] Buddha himself is found pondering over the question as to whether it is possible to reign with dhamma, without killing or causing to kill, without conquering or causing to conquer, without grieving or causing to grieve (sakkā nu kho rajjaṃ kāretuṃ ahanaṃ aghātayaṃ ajinaṃ ajāpayaṃ asocaṃ asocāpayaṃ dhammenā' ti? S.I. 116). Māra at once, asserting its possibility, prompts him to take up the life of a king (kāretu, bhante, bhagavā rajjaṃ, kāretu sugato rajjaṃ ahanaṃ aghātayaṃ..,loc. cit.). But Buddha rebukes Māra and adds: "How can one be inclined towards worldly pleasures (kāmesu) which he has seen to be the source of suffering? Knowing that attachment to the world is an entanglement, a man should learn to surmount it."[2] It is not quite clear whether in disapproving of Māra's advice, Buddha precludes the possibility of ruling a kingdom altogether without killing or causing to kill etc., for he does not say anything direct on the subject, though he declines to reign on the ground that worldly pleasures are sources of suffering (dukkhaṃ) and attachment to them is an entanglement or a bondage (upadhiṃ). But on other occasions, we find references to kings meting out punishment to evil-doers (rājā ca daṇḍaṃ garukaṃ paṇeti. Dh. 310; ayaṃ te bhante coro āgucārī, imassa yaṃ icchasi taṃ daṇḍaṃ paṇehī'ti., D.II. 334). Only those are condemned who inflict punishment on innocent and guiltless.[3] Thus, it appears that Buddha also considers it very difficult for a king to avoid the duty of punishing criminals. In the Cakkavatti Sutta, however, we find reference to Cakkavatti kings conquering and ruling the entire world without punishment and without arms (imaṃ pathaviṃ sāgarapariyantaṃ adaṇḍena asatthena dhammena abhivijiya ajjhāvasi, D. III.

1. M. II. 56.
2. Yo dukkham addakkhi yato nidānaṃ,
kāmesu so jantu kathaṃ nameyya ?
upadhiṃ viditvā saṅgo ti loke,
tass'eva jantu vinayāya sikkhe ti., S. I. 117.
3. yo appaduṭṭhassa narassa dussati suddhassa posassa anaṅgaṇassa
tameva bālaṃ pacceti pāpaṃ sukhumo rajo paṭivātam'va khitto.,
Dh. 125; cf.
yo daṇḍena adaṇḍesu appaduṭṭhesu dussati
dasannam aññataraṃ ṭhānaṃ khippam eva nigacchati, Dh. 137.

59). This may be the Buddhist concept of an ideal king who rules the land righteously without waging war against others, though it seems to be acknowledged that this ideal is difficult of realisation. In any event, it is important to note that even this ideal (cakkavatti) king had to abandon his kingship and practise the holy life *as a recluse* in order to attain the highest goal.[1] Thus, the fact remains that according to Buddhism, the worldly life is an entanglement, and Nibbāna cannot be realised here and now without giving up the life of a householder. Naturally, therefore, the life of a householder is termed 'inferior' (hīna) in comparison to the pure life of a recluse, and it is considered preferable to go forth from home to homelessness and seek delight in seclusion (okā anokam āgamma viveke yattha dūramaṃ, tatrā' bhiratim iccheyya, S. V. 24; Dh. 87-88). To revert to the life of a householder from the life of a recluse is considered 'death' according to the Noble Discipline (maraṇaṃ h'etaṃ, bhikkhave, ariyassa vinaye yo sikkhaṃ paccakkhāya hināyā' vattati, S.II. 271). Buddha pictures the worldly objects of enjoyment as a huge heap of blazing fire[2], or as an all-round thorny forest[3] and says that a monk who has realised the true nature of worldly life is incapable of reverting to the life of a householder even when kings and councillors, friends and relatives may try to tempt him by saying: "Come along, O man, why do you put on the yellow robe, why do you move about shavenheaded with a begging bowl? Come along, revert to the low (household) life and enjoy worldly pleasures and do meritorious deeds as well."[4] It is as difficult to turn him back to the household life as it is difficult to change the course of the Ganges.[5] This shows that the idea of practising the virtuous life while enjoying the life of a householder (bhoge ca bhuñjituṃ puññāni ca kātuṃ M.I. 461) is not looked upon as an ideal in Buddhism. The household life is not considered quite conducive to the attain-

1. D. III. 76-77.
2. S. IV. 188-189.
3. S. IV. 189.
4. S. IV. 190; S. V. 53, 300-301.
5. S. IV. 191; V. 53, 300.

ment of the highest goal. It is impossible for a householder to attain Nibbāna here and now[1], though it is true that householders also are taught by Buddha to pursue the holy life while discharging honestly their family and social responsibilities[2] which can lead them to the state nearest to Nibbāna, known as 'anāgāmitā'. Realising this state one is no more liable to be born in the human world, but is to be born in the celestial region from where he would realise Nibbāna.[3]

Now, the B.G. does not deny the validity of the Buddhist ideal of renunciation and grants that it does lead to salvation here and now. But, unlike Buddhism, it holds the view that salvation is equally attainable by a householder who follows the path of disinterested action. Indeed, the latter is considered preferable to renunciation. We have already noticed how despite its constant attempt at reconciliation, the B G. tries to highlight the path of active worldly life and seeks to make 'activism' a common element of all paths, viz. the paths of knowledge, devotion and disinterested action. When Arjuna requests Kṛṣṇa not to confuse him by talking of different paths but to tell him decisively the one path leading to the highest goal (B.G. III. 2; V.1), Kṛṣṇa indicating his preference for the path of action advises him pointedly to follow the same. He says: "Do thou thy allotted work, for action is better than inaction."[4] "The renunciation of actions as well as their disinterested performance—both lead to the highest good. But of the two, the disinterested performance of action (karmayogaḥ) is better than the renunciation of action (karmasaṃnyāsāt)"[5] The same is emphasised by citing the example of the glorious king, Janaka (B.G. III. 20), by presenting the ideal of God himself (B.G. III.

1. Natthi kho...koci gihī gihisaṃyojanaṃ appahāya kāyassa bhedā dukkhass antaṃkaro'ti, M.I. 483.

2. Cf. Sigālovāda Sutta (D. III. 180 ff); Mānatthaddho Sutta (S.I.178); Mātuposaka Sutta (S.I. 181-182); Vatapada Sutta (S.I. 228); Veḷudvareyya Sutta (S.V. 353 ff).

3. M.I. 490.

4. Niyataṃ kuru karma tvaṃ karma jyāyo hy akarmaṇaḥ., B.G. III. 8.

5. B.G. V. 2.

22-44) and by tracing the long-continued ancient tradition of this discipline (B.G. IV. 1-3).

Justifying his stand for giving preference to the disinterested performance of actions (karmayoga), Kṛṣṇa points out that the complete abandonment or renunciation of actions is neither possible nor necessary for salvation. The root cause of bondage is not the action but the desire behind the action, and so what is necessary for salvation is to abandon the desire and not the action as such. It is thus pointed out: "A man does not attain the state of 'naiṣkarmya'[1] (the state beyond action i.e. the state in which one is unaffected by action) by merely not undertaking works; nor does he attain perfection by simply renouncing actions."[2] The root cause of bondage, the real spring of action being the inner desire of the mind, Kṛṣṇa says: "He, O Arjuna, who having controlled the senses by the mind performs disinterested actions without attachment with the organs of action, is better."[3] This indeed, is called the yoga, the skilfulness in action (yogaḥ karmasu kauśalam, B.G. II. 50). But on the other hand, "that deluded one who having restrained the organs of action, continues to brood over the objects of sense with the mind, is called a hypocrite."[4] "The learned ones call him the wise and whose undertakings are free from desire and selfish motive, and whose actions are burnt up in the fire of wisdom. Having abandoned attachment to the fruit of action, ever content and free from any dependence, he (really) does nothing, even though (apparently) engaged in action."[5] Such a man performing mere bodily action incurs no sin (śārīraṃ kevalaṃ karma kurvan nā'pnoti kilbiṣam, B.G. IV. 21), and thus even

1. Saṅkara and Rāmānuja take the word 'naiṣkarmyam' in the sense of absolute inaction or complete quietism. As Saṅkara puts it : "Naiṣkarmyaṃ—niṣkarmabhāvaṃ Karmaśūnyatāṃ jñānayogena niṣṭhām", S.B.G. III. 4. Rāmānuja also voices the same view when he says : naiṣkarmyaṃ, jñānaniṣṭām", R.B.G. III. 4. But in the very text of the B.G. 'naiṣkarmyasiddhi' is distinguished from 'jñānaniṣṭhā' (B.G. XVIII. 49-50).

2. B.G. III. 4.

3. B.G. III. 7.

4. B.G. III. 6.

5. B.G. IV. 19-20.

when he acts, he is said not to be bound or contaminated (kṛtvā'pi na nibadhyate, B.G. IV. 22; kurvann api na lipyate B.G. V.7). This is how the B.G. tries to show that the abandonment of action is not necessary for salvation.

Then it argues that it is not also possible to renounce all actions and remain completely inactive. Taking action in its broad sense (both physical and mental), it points out: "None can remain without doing action even for a moment."[1] So long as life remains, action is unavoidable. Thinking is an act; living is an act. All are compelled to engage in actions by the forces of nature (B.G. III. 5). Even the maintenance of physical life is not possible without action (śarīrayātrā'pi ca te na prasidhyed akarmaṇaḥ, B.G. III. 8).

Thus, after having shown that the renunciation of action is not necessary and actions in toto cannot be renounced, the B.G. further points out that the performance of action is necessary even for the maintenance of the world (lokasaṅgraham evā'pi sampaśyan kartum arhasi, B.G. III. 20.). It is in this connection that the example of king Janaka attaining to perfection by disinterested action is adduced (B.G. III. 20), and God himself is cited as an ideal who without any interest of his own is engaged in the work of maintaining the world-order (B.G. III. 22-24). As the origin of the world is traced to God, it becomes the duty of man to live in the world and promote its welfare. The wheel of the world, according to the B.G., goes on by means of sacrifice or renunciation, and one who does not discharge his selfless service to the world lives only in vain. As the B.G. puts it: "He who does not, in this world, help to turn the wheel, thus set in motion, is indeed a sinful man, sensual in delight and he, O Arjuna, lives in vain."[2] Thus by pointing out the divine origin of the world, the B.G. tries to establish that the selfless or disinterested service to the world is the essential duty of man.

Pursuing further the same line of argument, the B.G. refers to the divine-origin theory of the different social orders (varṇa-vyavasthā)[3] and the divinely ordained duty (svadharma)

1. Na hi kaścit kṣaṇam api jātu tiṣṭhaty akarmakṛt, B.G. III. 5.
2. B.G. III. 16.
3. B.G. IV. 13 (cāturvarṇyam mayā sṛṣṭam)

of men belonging to these orders.[1] It is pointed out that those who are disinterestedly engaged in the relentless discharge of their divinely ordained social duty (svadharma), can attain perfection, despite inherent defects in their profession. The B.G. clearly says: "Devoted each to one's own duty, man attains perfection...He from whom all beings arise and by whom all this is pervaded—by worshipping Him through the performance of his own duty, man attains perfection."[2] Thus, to use the expression of Radhakrishnan, "Work is worship of the Supreme, man's homage to God."[3] Works being ordained by God, their defects, if any, are immaterial and one must not give up one's own allotted work. The B.G. says: "One's own duty (svadharma), even though defective is better than the well-executed duty of another (paradharmāt). One does not incur sin when he performs the duty ordained in accordance with his own nature."[4] The B.G. makes the plea that the duties of men belonging to different social-orders are divided in accordance with their inherent aptitudes (karmāṇi pravibhaktāni svabhāvaprabhavair guṇaiḥ, B.G. XVIII. 41). Following this plea it finally declares: "One should not abandon one's own natural duty even if it be defective (sadoṣam api), since all works are associated with defects as fire is associated with smoke. He whose intellect is unattached everywhere, who is self-restrained and who is free from desire, attains the supreme state of the transcendence of actions (naiṣkarmyasiddhiṃ paramām) by means of disinterested actions."[5] Thus, the B.G. condones the defects associated with some worldly duties, if they are performed disinterestedly and desirelessly in a spirit of divine service.

Then again, the B.G. points out that the path of the renunciation of action is difficult and cannot be practised without cultivating the attitude of disinterestedness. But the

1. B.G. XVIII. 41-44.
2. B.G. XVIII. 45 and 46.
3. The Bhagvadgītā, p. 368.
4. B.G. XVIII. 47.
5. B.G. XVII. 48 and 49.

path of disinterested action is easy and leads to perfection within a short time. Kṛṣṇa says: "Renunciation is difficult to attain, O Arjuna, without disinterested action (yoga). But the sage endowed with yoga (following the path of disinterested action) attains to Brahman in no time."[1] Thus, the path of disinterested action (karmayoga) has the advantage of being easier and yet it leads to the same goal which is arrived at by the difficult path of renunciation. The *raison d'être* of it, according to the B.G., is that the essential factor responsible for Nirvāṇa, viz., desirelessness or detachment is wholly contained in the disinterested action. As the B.G. says: "He who neither hates nor desires should be known always as a renouncer (saṃnyāsi), for, O Arjuna, he being free from the pairs of opposites, is easily released from bondage."[2] This is how the B.G. tries to show its preference for the path of action (pravṛtti mārga), notwithstanding its compromise with the path of renunciation (nivṛtti mārga), championed by Buddhism. We have already referred to the compromising declaration of the B.G. according to which "the goal which is attained by men of renunciation, is attained by men of action as well and he who sees the path of renunciation as one with the path of action, really sees."[3]

Now it may be noticed that the difficulties referred to by the B.G. in the path of renunciation are not unknown to early Buddhism and so when the latter declares renunciation as the sole means to salvation here and now, it does so after duly considering all the pros and cons of the problem.

As regards the contention of the the B.G. that the renunciation of outer activities is not necessary and one should only try to shake off the inner desire of the mind, we have seen that Buddhism is well aware of the theoretical truth that the mind is the spring of all actions, but, unlike the B.G., it recognises the psychological impossibility of a thorough mental control without perfect bodily control. So it does not consider it advisable that a beginner should indulge freely

1. B.G. V. 6.

2. B.G. V. 3.

3. B.G. V. 5; cf. VI. 2 (yaṃ saṃnyāsam iti prāhur yogaṃ taṃ viddhi pāṇḍava); XVIII. 1 and 2.

in all worldly activities on the pretext of a theoretical mental control. But when the purpose of non-indulgence in worldly activities is achieved and one attains perfect mental control or absolute detachment, Buddhism does grant full liberty to move about in the world for the welfare and happiness of many (bahujanahitāya bahujanasukhāya, Vin. I.21). This, however, does not imply, according to Buddhism, that such a perfected saint can commit wrong deeds without incurring any sin, as the B.G. would have us believe. According to Buddhism, the perfected saint is simply incapable of doing any wrong action.

So far as the B.G. objection against the pseudo-renouncers is concerned, Buddhism is in perfect accord with it. In fact, we find Buddha denouncing more strongly the behaviour of such monks who only renounce the world, but do not duly practise the holy life. He clearly points out that mere outer forms of reclusehood, such as shaving the head, putting on the yellow robe, going about with the begging bowl etc. are not the real marks of reclusehood. The real purpose of reclusehood lies in giving up defilements and in realising the true enlightenment. Thus, he says : "One does not become a recluse (samaṇa) by shaving the head if one is undisciplined and utters falsehood. How will one be a recluse when one is full of desire and greed ? He who wholly subdues evil-both small and great, is called a recluse by virtue of subduing evils. One does not become a monk (bhikkhu) by begging from others. By adopting evil ways, one cannot become a monk. He, who having abandoned virtue and vice, and being possessed of holiness, moves about with enlightenment in the world, indeed, is called a monk."[1] He further points out: "Having yellow robes on, there are many who are uncontrolled and of evil conduct. Such wicked ones on account of their evil deeds are born in hell."[2] Referring to such a pseudo-renouncer, Buddha says : "Just as, O monks, there were a double-edged Maṭaja weapon, sharp and poisoned, covered and wrapped by the outer robe. Like unto this do I declare

1. Dh. 264-267.
2. Dh. 307; cf. Dh. 9.

the reclusehood of such a monk."[1] Therefore, monks are taught by Buddha to live up to their ideal and fulfil the purpose of their renunciation, bringing about purification to themselves and merit to the alms-giver. Thus, he says : "You, O monks, are reckoned by people, as 'recluses' (samaṇā); and you too on being asked as to who you are, acknowledge that you are 'recluses'. Having thus been reckoned by them and acknowledged by you, you should train yourselves thus : 'we shall tread the path of reclusehood in such a way that their reckoning would be true and our acknowledgment would be valid. Of whomsoever requisites like robes, food, lodgings and medicaments, we make use of, to them their offerings to us would be of great fruit and benefit and our reclusehood also would not be vain but be fruitful and accomplishing'."[2]

As regards the objection of the B.G. that absolute inaction is an impossibility and that one has to take recourse to action at least for the maintenance of one's physical existence, Buddhism seems to have anticipated it. This objection evidently hints at the monk's activity of going about for alms. Buddha accepts the fact that begging is the meanest profession, but points out that it is to be adopted, since it alone is the most conducive to the attainment of the highest goal. He, however, warns at the same time that those who fail to justify their life as a recluse are worse than householders and are really good for nothing. He says : "This begging, O monks, is the meanest of all livelihoods. It is a curse, O monks, in the world to hear, 'you scrap-gatherer ! with bowl in hand you roam about'. But this, O monks, the clansmen resort to with a purpose in view...so that they may realise the end of this entire mass of suffering. Thus, O monks, a clansman takes to reclusehood. But if he turns out to be covetous, acutely given to sensuous pleasures, malevolent in mind, evil in resolve, corrupt in mindfulness, thoughtless, uncomposed, distracted in mind and unsubdued in senses, then I deem him like unto a firebrand from a funeral pyre which is lit at both ends and smeared with filth in the middle,

1. M.I. 281.
2. M.I. 271, 281.

serving no purpose as fuel either in the village or in the forest, for he is devoid of household pleasures and yet does not fulfil the purpose of the life of a recluse."[1] He, therefore, declares, "It is better to eat a red-hot iron-ball like a flame of fire than to eat the food of the country while remaining immoral and uncontrolled."[2] Moreover, the food and robe etc. permitted by Buddha are only the bare necessities of life implying no luxury and sensuous pleasures. He clearly says : "The noble disciple takes food reflecting carefully, not for enjoyment, nor for adornment nor for beautification, but only for the sake of maintaining this body and keeping it going, for keeping it unharmed and for the promotion of the holy life."[3] The same does he say with regard to the robe, lodging and medicaments. "Whatever robe has been prescribed by me, that is just for the sake of guarding against cold, heat, wasps, mosquitoes, wind, sunstroke, reptiles and to cover the nakedness."[4] Similarly, lodgings and medicaments are also recommended only to meet the bare needs of the daily life.[5] Thus, a monk is contented with a robe just enough to cover his body and with food just enough to satisfy his hunger (bhikkhu santuṭṭho hoti kāyaparihārikena cīvarena, kucchi parihārikena piṇḍapātena, M.I. 180). Even this bare food has to be taken without seeking any delight.[6]

It is further pointed out by Buddha that it is wrong to think that a monk eats food of the country without rendering any service to it. Seeing Buddha standing for alms, Kasi Bhāradvāja, the agriculturist, tells him to eat after taking the trouble of tilling the land just as the latter does.[7] Buddha in reply tells that he (Buddha) too is engaged in 'agriculture'[8]

1. S. III. 93.
2. Dh. 308.
3. M.I. 355; cf. D. III. 130; M.I. 273.
4. D. III. 130.
5. D. III. 130.
6. S. II. 98.
7. S.I. 172.
8. S.I. 172.

and explains how his spiritual agriculture is the best form of agriculture yielding the fruit of immortality and leading the agriculturist to the cessation of all suffering.[1]

In fact, a true monk contributes to the good of the country more than any other man, though the nature of his contribution is different. At least, his work is as important and useful for society as any other. Professor Jayatilleke rightly points out : "He is one who is expected to specialize in his field of inquiry as much as the physicist specializes in his. The development of the mind is a full-time job and the findings of these explorations are of no less interest and value to society than the findings of the natural scientist working in his laboratory. Both have something to offer to society; and monasticism, if understood rightly, has a big part as yet to play in the moral and spiritual regeneration of mankind."[2]

This shows that Buddha also like the B.G. accepts the legitimacy of service to the world. Besides himself serving humanity for the whole of his life, he ordains the accomplished monks to go about preaching in the world for the welfare and happiness of many (Vin. I. 21). But unlike the B.G., his conception of true service to humanity does not lie in mere performance of worldly duties (which more often than not strengthen attachment to the world and prolong the chain of suffering) but in preaching the Noble Doctrine and promoting the mankind to seek release from the bond of worldly existence as far as possible.

So far as the divine-origin theory of social orders and the divinely ordained duties of men are concerned, Buddhism repudiates them in toto—thus cutting at the very root of the B.G. doctrine that perfection can be attained through disinterested discharge of prescribed duties (B.G. XVIII. 45). We have already discussed in the preceding chapter (supra, pp. 401-405) how the theory of the divine origin of the world is repudiated in Buddhism. Thus, the B.G. theories of the divine origin of social orders (B.G. IV. 13) and of their divinely

1. S. I. 172-173.

2. Buddhism and Peace, The Wheel Publication. No. 41. pp. 22-23.

ordained duties fall to the ground. Repudiating the concept of prescribed duties based on caste, Buddha points out that Brahmins have acted unwarrantedly in laying down specified duties for different castes. Addressing Esukāri Brahmin, he says: "Just as, O Brahmin, they might separate a morsel (of meat) for a poor needy destitute man without his desire, saying: 'you must eat this meat, my good man and must also pay a price for it'—even so do the Brahmins lay down the fourfold virtue or conduct without the assent of recluses and true Brahmins."[1]

Again unlike the B.G. which approves of all professions including even the defective ones (B.G. XVIII. 47, 48), early Buddhism recommends only the righteous professions (sammā ājīva). The following five trades are forbidden as unrighteous forms of livelihood (micchā ājīva):—The trade of (i) selling arms (sattha vaṇijjā), (ii) selling human beings or animals (satta vaṇijjā), (iii) selling flesh (maṃsa vaṇijjā), (iv) selling intoxicating drinks (majja vaṇijjā) and (v) selling poison (visavaṇijjā).[2] Thus, Buddhism neither accepts the validity of hereditary caste-professions nor does it approve of all professions.

As regards the last objection of the B.G. that the path of renunciation is a difficult one, Buddhism does not deny it, but points out at the same time the extremely difficult task of getting rid of all suffering. If one sincerely aims at realising the most difficult goal, he must adopt a means adequate to its realisation. But if one intends, on the one hand, to realise the highest goal, and, on the other, takes a lenient attitude and looks for an easier means, he cannot but fall short of realising the true ideal. Acknowledging the difficulty of the path of renunciation, it is said: "Taking to reclusehood is, indeed, difficult, brethren, in this order of the Dhamma..... Those who have taken to reclusehood. for them it is again difficult to take delight in reclusehood...Even for those who take delight, difficult it is to follow the directions of the

1. M. II. 181.
2. A. III. 208.

Dhamma point by point."[1] But it is added that one who follows the directions of the Dhamma point by point, attains to arahatship (perfection) in no time (na ciram).[2] Thus, the path of renunciation which is admitted to be difficult like the sharp edge of a razor (khuradhārūpamo, Sn. 133) is resorted to for the sake of realising the most difficult goal. The extreme difficulty of the task is indicated by Buddha when he speaks of the feat of a holy aspirant as much more difficult than that of a skilled archer. When Ānanda reports to Buddha about the difficult feat of Licchavi youths who were shooting with their arrows a very minute key-hole from a distance, Buddha asks: "What do you think, Ānanda, which is more difficult and harder to accomplish: to splinter an arrow from a distance through a very minute keyhole, shot after shot, without ever a miss, or to pierce one strand of a hair, a hundred times divided, with another strand?"[3] Ānanda replies that the latter is, of course, much more difficult. Then Buddha remarks: "Just so, O Ānanda, those who properly penetrate the truth that 'this is suffering' pierce through something which is still more difficult and harder to accomplish."[4] Thus, Buddha realising full well the extreme difficulty of attaining the true goal, does not favour any half-hearted measures and enjoins a holy life pure and perfect.

This, however, does not mean that Buddha expected everyone to be a recluse. He only sets it as an ideal condition for pursuing the holy goal in all its purity and perfection. But he knows that there are many who are too deeply engrossed in worldly objects to give them up and tread the Noble Path to its end.[5] So he shows the way and prescribes codes of virtue and discipline to them also[6], by practising which,

---

1. S· IV. 260, 262.
2. Ibid. 260, 262.
3. S.V. 454.
4. S.V. 454.
5. Appekacce kho...mama sāvakā evaṃ ovadīyamānā evaṃ anusāsīyamānā accantaṃ niṭṭhaṃ nibbānaṃ ārādhenti, ekacce nā'rādhentī'-ti., M.III. 4.
6. Cf. sigālovāda Sutta (D. III. 180 ff); Parābhava Sutta (Sn. 17-20); Mahāmaṅgala Sutta (Sn. 45-47); Mānatthaddho Sutta (S.I. 178); Mātuposaka (Sutta (S.I. 181-2); Vatapada Sutta (S.I. 228); Veḷudvareyya Sutta (S.V. 353 ff).

according to their capacity, they may try to advance towards the highest goal. Again, we have seen that the mere going forth from home to homelessness is not sufficient. It only provides a better opportunity for the holy pursuit. But Buddha envisages the possibility of a householder making greater progress than a slack recluse by being rightly set in the Path. The Brahmin student, Subha, asks Buddha: "The Brahmins, O Gotama, speak thus: 'A householder is the obtainer of the wholesome state of knowledge and not a recluse. Now, what does Venerable Gotama think about this?'"[1] Buddha says: "In this respect, O Brahmin, I reply after analysis; I do not make a categorical (ekaṃsa) assertion. Whether one lives the life of a householder or of a recluse, I do not praise him, O Brahmin, if he is set in a wrong way. Whether one is a householder or a recluse, if he conducts himself in a wrong way, he, O Brahmin, on account of his wrong living cannot obtain a wholesome state of knowledge. Whether one lives a household life or the life of a recluse, I praise him, if he conducts himself in a right way. Whether he be a householder or a recluse, if he conducts himself rightly, he, on account of his right living can obtain a wholesome state of knowledge."[2] In the light of this statement, Buddha's preference for the life of the recluse can only mean that, other conditions being the same a recluse can make an easier and a quicker progress than a householder. This position, as we have seen, is precisely the reverse of what the B.G. advocates. However, according to the B.G., with greater or lesser difficulty, both the path of renunciation as well as that of action can lead to the highest goal here and now.[3] But according to Buddhism, the household life, howsoever favourable for the holy life, can never be of such a kind as to enable one to realise the complete deliverance in this very life.[4]

The above discussion makes it quite clear that the B.G.,

1. M.II. 197.

2. Ibid.

3. B.G. V. 2 (Saṃnyāsaḥ karmayogaś ca niḥśreyasakarāv ubhau); V. 19 (ihai'va tair jitaḥ sargaḥ); V. 26 (abhito Brahmanirvāṇaṃ vartate viditātmanām).

4. M.I. 483.

notwithstanding its compromising attitude, enthusiastically supports worldly life. Naturally, in so doing, it propounds a theory which seems somewhat to moderate its ethical position. This point may be well illustrated by considering the views of the B.G. on the problems of the classification of society and war, and comparing them with those of early Buddhism.

The Problem of Caste[1]

We have noticed that the B.G. from its different standpoints of knowledge, devotion and disinterested action harps on the same note of activism. Duty and duty alone is said to be the concern of man (karmaṇy evā'dhikāras te, B.G. II. 47); he is supposed to attain perfection in the course of discharging his own duty (sve-sve karmaṇy abhirataḥ saṃsiddhiṃ labhate naraḥ, B.G. XVIII. 45) and through duty alone he is said to serve God and secure salvation (svakarmaṇā tam abhyarcya siddhiṃ vindati mānavaḥ., B.G. XVIII. 46). But what exactly is the concept of duty? This is a crucial point and it is here that the B.G. brings in the question of social divisions and their prescribed duties.

The B.G. puts forward the view that the social classification has a divine origin and each social order has some divinely sanctioned duties, by performing which one fulfils the mission of one's life. The duty of a man, thus, consists in pursuing the profession of his own social order. Adopting this line of thought, the B.G. not only upholds the validity of social divisions but also tries to justify them on religio-theological grounds. It would be convenient if we consider the position of the B.G. from the biological, sociological and religious standpoints, and see how the Buddhist attitude in all these respects is basically opposed to that of the B.G.

(A) *The Biological Point of View*:—

The B.G. holds the view that the human society with its inherent fourfold division was created by God. Each individual as belonging to a particular division has natural

1. The word, 'caste' is used here in a broad sense indicating the fourfold social order.

qualities and an aptitude for performing certain types of work and, accordingly, it is his duty to seek fulfilment of his life by performing this kind of work alone. Individuals are thus said to be born in a particular division of society, because they were thought fit by God, by virtue of their specific dispositions and potentialities for the profession of a particular class. Thus, Kṛṣṇa, the incarnate God, declares: "The fourfold class was created by me according to the divisions of aptitude and action" (Cāturvarṇyaṃ mayā sṛṣṭam guṇakarmavibhāgaśaḥ, B.G. IV. 13). Enumerating the specific duties of the four classes, Kṛṣṇa again says: "The duties of Brahmins, Kṣatriyas, Vaiśyas as well as of Śūdras are well divided according to the qualities born of their nature."[1] Thus, there appears to be no doubt about the fact that the B.G. upholds the theories of the divine origin of society and divinely ordained duties of men.

Most of the Indian scholars, however, feel embarrassed to face this truism. Even scholars like K.T. Telang, S. Radhakrishnan and D.M. Datta try to interpret the above view of the B.G. in the light of modern Indian trend of a classless and casteless society. Referring to the first of the above quoted verses, Telang observes that "there is nothing in the Gītā to indicate whether caste was hereditary",[2] and similarly in relation to the second verse he remarks that "there is nothing in that list of duties which has any necessary or natural connexion with any privilege as belonging to the caste."[3] Radhakrishnan commenting on the first verse says: "The emphasis is on guṇa (aptitude) and karma (function) and not jāti (birth). The varṇa or the order to which we belong is independent of sex, birth or breeding. A class determined by temperament and vocation is not a caste determined by birth and heredity."[4] He tries to see in this fourfold division a

1. Brāhmaṇakṣatriyaviśāṃ śūdrāṇāṃ ca paraṃtapa,
karmāṇi pravibhaktāni svabhāvaprabhavair guṇaiḥ.,
B.G. XVIII. 41

2. S.B.E., Vol VIII. p. 21.

3. Ibid. p. 22.

4. The Bhagavadgītā, pp. 160-161.

natural gradation of men based on psychological characteristics and not on birth or heredity. Thus, commenting on the second verse he remarks: "There are four broad types of nature and answering to them are four kinds of social living. The four classes are not determined by birth or colour but by psychological characteristics which fit us for definite functions in society."[1] Similarly, Professor Datta observes: "There are natural divisions among men in accordance with their intrinsic qualities and actions; their capacities and duties vary accordingly."[2]

A little reflection, however, would show that such interpretations are fair neither to the text nor to the spirit of the B.G. They merely appear to be conscious efforts on the part of these scholars to rationalise the teaching of the B.G. according to the modern trends of Indian thought. The text, evidently, refers to the fourfold social order (cāturvarṇyam) and not to fourfold psychological types, as Radhakrishnan suggests. In a quite unambiguous manner, B.G. XVIII. 41 enumerates the well-known fourfold division of society, viz., the Brahmin, the Kṣatriya, the Vaiśya and the Śūdra, and points out that the duties of people belonging to each class are based on their inborn natural qualities. In view of the statement that the social distinction or division is created by God (B.G. IV. 13), this verse (B.G. XVIII. 41) can only mean that God causes an individual to be born in that particular social order for which his qualities and aptitudes are suited. In other words, the very event of birth in a particular social order is indicative of the child's qualities and aptitudes for the profession of that social order. Evidently, it is nothing but a theological and religious justification for a hereditary division of society. To think that the four divisions, viz. the Brahmin, the Kṣatriya, the Vaiśya and the Śūdra are not the names of hereditary classes but merely of psychological types is to give these names meanings, completely unknown to tradition. Even today, we know of no psychological divisions under these names. In fact, no recognised division of society based on psychological characteristics, under whatsoever name, was ever

1. Ibid. p. 365.
2. The Chief Currents of Contemporary Philosophy, p. 566.

existent referring to which Kṛṣṇa could speak of having created or organised it. Therefore, the word 'cāturvarṇyam' has to be accepted as it stands, i. e. in the sense of the fourfold hereditary division of society. Moreover, if we accept the interpretation of the above-mentioned scholars and take the fourfold social order (cāturvarṇyam) in the sense of a fourfold psychological type, independent of birth and heredity, then the entire concept of svadharma (specific duty) falls to the ground, and Kṛṣṇa's exhortation to Arjuna to fight on the ground of being a Kṣatriya[1] becomes meaningless. How is one to know whether he is a Brahmin, a Kṣatriya, a Vaiśya or a Śūdra and how is he to determine his specific duty (svadharma), if not by hereditary social order ? Again, as Professor K. N. Jayatilleke has pertinently pointed out: "If the individual types were created in accordance with their guṇas or aptitudes and karmas or social functions, it is difficult to see why the number of types should be four and not less or more, for if the types represented the guṇas there would have been three types corresponding to the guṇas of sattva, rajas and tamas, while if they represented the karmas or social duties, surely many more."[2]

In fact, in the very first chapter of the B.G. its concept of social classification by birth and heredity is very clearly borne out. Arjuna speaking of the dreadful consequences of war refers to the destruction of caste-laws (utsādyante jātidharmāḥ, B.G. I. 43) and the emergence of the intermixture of castes (jāyate varṇasaṅkaraḥ, B.G. I. 41). This is considered as a disastrous consequence, for "the offspring of mixed blood cannot but lead to hell" (saṅkaro narakāyai'va., B.G. I. 42), and cause the fall of the deceased ancestors from the celestial region on account of their being deprived of rice-balls and libation.[3] Evidently, the B.G. upholds the traditional view according to which the deceased ancestors are said to receive

1. Svadharmam api cā'vekṣya na vikampitum arhasi; dharmyād dhi yuddhāc chreyo'nyad kṣatriyasya na vidyate...sukhinaḥ kṣatriyāḥ pārtha labhante yuddham īdṛśam., B.G. II. 31 & 32.

2. Some Aspects of Gītā and Buddhist Ethics., U.C.R., Vol. XIII, Nos. 2 & 3, p. 150.

3. patanti pitaro hy eṣāṃ luptapiṇḍodakakriyāḥ., B.G. I. 42.

rice-balls and libations only from the offspring of their own pure (unmixed) blood.[1] The B.G., thus, stands for the purity of hereditary social orders, and declares that the intermixture of blood leads definitely to hell(narake niyataṃ vāso bhavatī'ti., B.G. 1. 44). This amounts to saying that each of the four classes is biologically different, having well-marked nature, aptitude and function, and the intermixture of blood is fraught with disastrous consequences. It would, thus, appear that the B.G. through its theory of the divine origin of social orders and the doctrine of divinely ordained duties of men (presumably based on the natural qualities and aptitudes of people) tries to provide a religious and moral justification for the traditional belief in a hereditary division of society.

It is not difficult to see that the approach of Buddhism in this respect is basically opposed to that of the B.G. Buddha in unmistakable language asserts the biological unity of mankind and makes a radical departure from the traditional concept of hereditary division of society. In the Vāseṭṭha Sutta (M. II. 196; Sn. 112-121) Buddha explains at great length that there are no distinguishing characteristics of genus and species among men as are found in the case of grass, trees, insects, moths, fish, reptiles, birds, beasts etc. The apparent divisions made among people are but nominal or conventional (samaññā). To quote a few verses of the above Sutta: "Not as regards their hair, head, ears, eyes, mouth, nose, lips, brows..nor as regards their hands, feet, fingers, nails, calves, thighs, colour or voice are there marks constituting species, as in the case of other species. Difference there is among other embodied beings, but amongst men, this is not the case; the difference amongst men is merely nominal."[2] Then it is finally concluded in clear terms: "Not by birth does one become a Brahmin, nor by birth does one become a non-Brahmin. By work one becomes a Brahmin and by work does one become a non-Brahmin. By work one becomes a peasant and by work does one become an artisan. By work one becomes a merchant and by work does one become a messenger."[3]

1. Manusmṛti III. 18, 82.
2. Sn. 115.
3. Sn. 120.

In view of such clear statements, the remark of Chalmers cannot but be considered apposite when he says: "Herein, Gotama was in accord with the conclusion of modern biologists that '*The Anthropidae*' are represented by the single genus and species, 'Man'—a conclusion which was the more remarkable inasmuch as the accident of colour did not mislead Gotama."[1] Likewise Professor Malalasekera and Professor Jayatilleke observe: "Buddhism is in accord with the findings of the modern biologists who exploded the doctrines of racism and would urge the biological unity of mankind in support of the concept of a common humanity."[2] Buddhism, thus, cuts at the very root of the so-called fundamental distinctions based on inborn aptitudes and abilities of men. Men are not divided inherently by birth but are distinguished on the basis of the profession they choose, and this distinction also is by no means fundamental or divine but merely nominal or conventional (samaññā).

As regards the statements about the purity of caste and disastrous consequences of the intermixture of blood, Buddha not only questions the validity of caste-purity but also cites historical examples of the intermixture of blood having no disastrous consequences whatsoever. It is pointed out that one cannot be certain whether caste-purity was strictly observed by one's parents and grandparents even up to the seventh generation.[3] Devala, the Dark, having come to know about the false and evil view (pāpakaṃ diṭṭhigataṃ) of the seven Brahmin sages about the superiority of the Brahmins, approaches them and asks whether they know for certain that their parents and grandparents remained strictly confined, in matters of sexual relation, to their own caste even up to the seventh generation, to which they answer in the negative.[4] Thus the boast of caste-purity is shown to be based on ignorance.

---

1. 'The Madhura Sutta concerning Caste' in J. R. A. S., 1894, p. 346.
2. Buddhism and the Race Question, p. 37.
3. M. II. 156.
4. M. II. 155-156.

Buddha in repudiating caste-distinction draws attention to the prenatal growth of a child and shows that those who indulge in vain talks about caste-distinctions ignore the important consideration that the psychic factor or the spirit (gandhabba)[1] seeking rebirth in conjunction with the genetic factors derived from the parents cannot be said to have any caste.[2] The birth of a child according to Buddhism is due to the combination of the psychic factor resulting from the impressions of previous lives and the genetic factors derived from both parents. Obviously then, it is futile to speak of the class or caste of an individual on the basis of the parental factors leaving aside the essential factor of his personality, which indeed is beyond class or caste.

Buddha further cites cases of the intermixture of blood which, on the one hand, expose the falsity of caste-purity and, on the other, explode the myth of the disastrous consequences of the intermixture of castes. Ambaṭṭha, a Brahmin youth, conceited because of his high Brahmin lineage, does not observe the usual courtesies while talking to Buddha, since he considers himself as belonging to a class superior to that of the latter. But Buddha points out to him in the course of the conversation: ' If one were to follow up your ancient name and lineage on the father's and the mother's side, it would appear that one of your ancestors was the son of one of the slave-girls of the Śākyas."[3] It is, however, important to note that Buddha adds at the same time that the said son of the slave-girl, namely, Kaṇha was a great sage (uḷāro so Kaṇho isi, D. I. 96). The intermixture of blood is thus shown to have produced no disastrous consequence. Ambaṭṭha himself is described as a highly accomplished scholar, expert in all the different branches of Brahminical learning and equal in scholarship to his teacher, Pokkharasāti.[4]

As regards the divine origin of social order, Buddha

1. For a discussion on the Buddhist concept of 'gandhabba' see Professor Wijesekera's 'Vedic Gandharva and Pali Gandhabba' in U.C.R. Vol. III. No. 1,1945, pp. 73-107.

2. M. II. 157.

3. D.I. 92.

4. D.I. 87.

explains to the Brahmin student, Assalāyana (Skr. Āśvalāyana) that men of all classes including those of the Brahmin are alike born of human parents, and it is ridiculous to associate the birth of anyone with the divinity.[1] Referring further to the possibility of the intermixture of castes, Buddha points out that there would be no mark or characteristic to indicate a caste-distinction in the event of a progeny born of an intercaste relation.[2]

Thus, by referring to the intermixture of blood not only as a possibility but also as an historical fact, Buddha shows that the claim of caste-purity is not a fact but a fiction. The superstition of the disastrous consequences of the intermixture of blood is also shown to be baseless on grounds of factual evidence, and it is established that there is a fundamental biological unity in the entire human race, and all distinctions of class or caste are merely conventional or nominal (samaññā).

(*B*) *The Sociological Point of View*:—

The B.G. conception of society is a static one with four fundamental and absolute divisions in it. The duties of each of the four classes are fixed and the origin, order and arrangement of society are explained in terms of divinity. In all these respects the Buddhist approach is quite different.

As against the creationist and static conception of society, Buddhism puts forward a dynamic and evolutionary view of it. The fourfold division of society is by no means absolute and fundamental according to Buddhism. Buddha by drawing attention to the existing social order in other places says: "Among the Yonas and Kāmbojas and others living in the bordering territories there are only two classes (dveva vaṇṇā), namely, the masters and the slaves,"[3] and even this distinction is not rigid, for "one who is a master may become a slave and one who is a slave may become a master" (ayyo hutvā dāso hoti dāso hutvā ayyo hotī'ti., M. II. 149).

1. M.II. 148.
2. M.II. 153-154.
3. M.II. 149.

The theory of the divine origin of the social order is also discarded and in place of it we find an evolutionary account of society[1] (though presented in a mythological garb), which explains the development of occupational groups at a certain stage of social evolution. It is not possible here to give this long narrative (D. III. 80—98), but those who are conversant with it cannot fail to note that despite its mythological form, it contains a kernel of historical truth and makes an attempt to offer an evolutionary account of the growth of society and its functional groups. Professor Rhys Davids referring to this account observes: "We may not accept the historical accuracy of this legend. Indeed a continual note of good-humoured irony runs through the whole story. But it reveals a sound and healthy insight and is much nearer to the actual facts than the Brahmin legend it was intended to replace."[2]

The divine origin of the social order being rejected, the B.G. theory of a divinely ordained specific duty (svadharma) for each class (B.G. XVIII, 41-49) also falls to the ground. We have already noticed (supra, pp. 494-5) how Buddha criticises this concept of prescribed duties and considers such an imposition of specific duties on people as an unwarranted act of the Brahmin priesthood. This act according to him is as uncalled for as the imposition of a share of meat on a poor destitute person without his desire and yet with the command that he must eat it and pay for the same.[3] Thus, as against the B.G., which on the plea of men being born with special aptitudes for their hereditary professions, makes it obligatory for them to follow the professions of their own social orders even if the professions be morally defective (sadoṣam api B.G. XVIII. 48), Buddhism neither considers the hereditary profession as obligatory nor does it sanction the practice of all professions irrespective of moral considerations. We have seen (supra, p. 495) that certain professions which are considered morally wrong are forbidden and people are

1. D.III. 84-97.
2. Dialogues of the Buddha, Part I, S.B.B. Vol. II., p. 106.
3. M. II. 181.

advised to adopt only a rightful means of livelihood (sammā ājīva).

It may again be noticed that the B.G. in keeping with its conservative character adheres to the traditional view[1] that menial service is the natural obligatory duty of a Śūdra (paricaryātmakaṃ karma śūdrasyā'pi svabhāvajam, B.G. XVIII. 44). But Buddhism disregarding the traditional division of society and recognising full well the importance of the economic factor clearly points out that the ability to command the service and labour of others depends not on the birth in a so-called superior social order but on the possession of sufficient wealth. An individual of whatsoever class can solicit service from all classes, if he commands enough wealth. Even a Śūdra can, thus, keep a Brahmin servant and engage him in menial work.[2] None is superior or inferior by virtue of mere birth. It is concluded in clear terms: "This being so, all these *four classes are equal*, there is no distinction whatsoever among them in this respect" (evaṃ sante ime *cattāro vaṇṇā samasamā* honti. Nesaṃ ettha kiñci nānākaraṇam samanupassāmī'ti., M.M. II. 89).

(*C*) *The Religious Point of View*:—

Notwithstanding its conservatism, the B.G. in religious matters seems to adjust itself to the growing influence of new thought movements like Buddhism and Jainism. Like them it also opens the door of salvation to all people ignoring the distinctions of class, creed and sex. Kṛṣṇa says: "Those who take refuge in me, O Arjuna, though they are lowly born, women, Vaiśyas as well as Śūdras, they also attain to the highest goal."[3] In fact, according to the Bhāgavata Purāṇa, it is out of special consideration for women, Śūdras and nominal Brahmins, who had no access to the three Vedas, that the composition of the entire MB. (including the B.G.) was undertaken.[4] Whatever the case may be, it

1. Ait. Brāhmaṇa VII. 29; Manusmṛti VIII. 413 and 414.
2. M. II. 84-85.
3. B.G. IX. 32.
4. strīśūdradvijabandhūnāṃ trayī na śrutigocarā...
iti bhāratam ākhyānaṃ kṛpayā muninā kṛtam., Bhāg. Purāṇa, I. 4. 25.

is evident that the B.G. relaxes the rigour of caste with regard to the practice of religion.

It may also be worth noticing that despite its advocacy of hereditary professions, it makes no mention of the intrinsic superiority or inferiority of any profession. It rather emphasises that "man attains perfection devoted each to his own duty" (B.G. XVIII. 45). It is further said that "all actions are associated with (more or less) defects as fire by smoke" (B.G. XVIII. 48) and so what is important is the intellect with which the work is done rather than the mere outer action.[1] This idea is conveyed more explicitly in the MB. in the course of the dialogue between the Brahmin and the meat-seller (MB., Vanaparva, 206-215) wherein the latter, who discharges his duty devotedly for the good of others, is not only defended but is considered superior to the Brahmin practising penance for his own selfish purpose. Similarly in the dialogue between the pedlar and Jājali (MB., Śāntiparva 260-263), the former is found to justify his own profession of pedlary. This line of thought is, no doubt, primarily aimed at justifying the validity of hereditary professions; it nevertheless undermines the intrinsic superiority and inferiority attached to different professions. In any case, there appears to be no doubt about the fact that the B.G. is trying to adjust itself to the new trends of thought heralded specially by Buddhism and Jainism, though without making a basic departure from the orthodox position.

The relaxation exhibited by the B.G. is by no means unimportant in view of the strict rigidity preached by the Brahmanical priesthood in this respect. We may, for illustration, briefly refer to some of the views of the latter about the status of the Śūdra which would indicate the extent to which the B.G. has reduced the rigidity and rigour of social order. According to the Aitareya Brāhmaṇa[2] as

---

1. Dūreṇa hy avaraṃ karma buddhiyogād dhanañjaya., B.G. II. 49.

2. (Śūdraḥ) anyasya preṣyaḥ kāmotthāpyo yathākāmavadhyḥ, Ait. Brāh. VII. 29.

well as the Manusmṛti[1], the Śūdra is said to be created by God for the sake of serving others—a belief shared by the B.G. as well.[2] But the Brahmanical orthodoxy goes further and deprives the Śūdra of religious freedom as well. Manusmṛti quite explicitly says that a Brahmin "who imparts religious instruction to him (a Śūdra) or dictates to him a religious observance sinks along with him into a hell called Asaṃvṛta."[3] Brahmins should not even recite the sacred texts in the presence of Śūdras (Śūdrajanasaṃnidhau).[4] A Brahmin teacher is to be condemned if he has a Śūdra as his 'pupil (śūdraśiṣyo guruḥ)[5] Unlike other castes, a Śūdra has no right to be initiated[6] nor to have religious ceremonies performed for himself.[7] Naturally, therefore, the door of salvation is altogether closed for him. The Śatapatha Brāhmaṇa goes to the extent of saying that a Śūdra is untruth itself.[8] Ghurye rightly observes referring to the Manusmṛti: "Manu declares roundly that a Śūdra cannot commit an offence causing loss of his caste, so degraded was he. Where some kinds of spirituous liquors are forbidden to the members of the twice-born castes, the Śūdra is left to himself. Evidently, the Śūdra was regarded beyond the pale of moral influence. The Brahmin did not even condescend to expect of him an adherence to his high moral precepts."[9] Now, in the light of all these strict laws debarring the Śūdra from all religious instruction and precluding the very possibility of his salvation, the laxity of the B.G. in opening the door of salvation to him and granting him the possibility of

---

1. Śūdraṃ tu kārayed dāsyaṃ...dāsyāyai'va hi sṛṣṭo'sau...
   Na...śūdro dāsyād vimucyate, nisargajaṃ hi tat tasya...
   Manusmṛti VIII 413 & 414.
2. paricaryātmakaṃ karma śūdrasyā'pi svabhāvajam.,
   B.G. XVIII. 44.
3. Yo hy asya dharmam ācaṣṭe yaś cai'vā'diśati vratam;
   so'saṃvṛtaṃ nāma tamaḥ saha tenai'va majjati, Manusmṛti IV. 81.
4. Ibid. IV. 99.
5. Ibid. III. 156.
6. Ibid. X. 4.
7. Ibid. III. 178 and 179.
8. Eggeling's translation, Part V, p. 446.
9. Caste and Race in India, p. 84.

final release, is by no means insignificant. It appears that the B.G. in so doing tries to compromise with the changing tide of the time, though still holding fast to the traditional view that the inborn natural duty of a Śūdra is to serve others.

The case, however, is quite different with regard to Buddhism which openly challenges the prevalent dogmas of the Brahmanical religion. It seeks no compromise but complete freedom from the shackles of tradition. Not only does it open the door of salvation to all, regardless of class and creed, but it also emphasises their inherent equality, and considers caste-prejudice as an obstacle in the path of salvation. It was, indeed, a great venture on the part of Buddha to challenge the Brahmanical orthodoxy during those days. Brahmin priests were greatly perturbed to learn that "the recluse Gotama proclaims the purity of all the four castes" (samaṇo Gotamo cātuvanniṃ suddhiṃ paññāpeti, M. II. 147), and came in a body for disputation.[1] It is interesting to see how, with an element of irony and sarcasm, Buddha in his disputation with the Brahmins establishes the equality of all castes. He asks: "What do you think, O Brahmin, can only a Brahmin by taking soap and going to the river wash his dirt but not a Kṣatriya, a Vaiśya or a Śūdra?"[2] The Brahmin naturally replies that it is not so. Buddha then adds: "Similarly, O Brahmin, a man from the Kṣatriya family, Brahmin family, Vaiśya family as well as Śūdra family having adopted the Doctrine and Discipline preached by the Tathāgata obtains the knowledge of the Noble Doctrine" (M. II. 183). Similarly he points out that the fire kindled by all the four castes will be alike in flame, hue and brilliance (accimā ceva vaṇṇavā ca pabhassaro ca, *loc. cit.*). This simile of kindling fire of the same nature by different people and with different woods is commonly used by him.[3] The king of Kosala once pointedly questioned him with regard to his teaching of the equality of castes: "There are

1. M. II. 147-148.
2. M. II. 182.
3. M. II. 129-130, 152, 183

these four castes, Sir, the Kṣatriya, the Brahmin, the Vaiśya and the Śūdra. Let us suppose them to be imbued with the five forms of strenuous exertion to attain salvation. In this case, would there be any distinction, Sir, any difference among them?"[1] Buddha using his usual simile of a fire says: "Here also, Sire, I do not admit any difference whatsoever in regard to the nature of their salvation. Just as if, Sire, a man were to kindle a fire with dry herbs, and another with dry Sal wood, and a third with dry mango wood, and a fourth with dry fig wood—what think you, Sire, would these diverse fires kindle with diverse woods show any difference whatsoever in respect of their flame, hue and brilliance?" (*loc. cit.*). The King naturally says: "No difference at all, Sir." (*loc. cit.*) Buddha then adds: "Even so, Sire, is the inward illumination which is kindled by effort and nursed by strenuous exertion. I declare that there is no difference whatsoever herein with regard to their salvation."[2]

It is, moreover, pointed out by Buddha that any prejudice of caste or clan is an obstacle in the way of salvation. It is clearly regarded as a bondage. Buddha addressing Ambaṭṭha says: "Whosoever, Ambaṭṭha, is bound by caste-prejudices or clan-prejudices...is far removed from the way of the highest salvation. By casting aside the bond of caste-prejudices or clan-prejudices, Ambaṭṭha, the highest salvation is realised"[3]

All men irrespective of caste stand alike before the moral law. The moral reward or punishment is meted out in accordance with the good or evil conduct of the man and not according to his caste-status. People are born in heaven or hell after death according as they perform meritorious or demeritorious deeds, regardless of their castes.[4] Everyone with-

1. M. II. 129.

2. M. II. 130.

3. Ye hi keci, Ambaṭṭha, jātivādavinibaddhā vā gottavādavinibaddhā vā...ārakā te anuttarāya vijjācaranasampadāya. Pahāya kho, Ambaṭṭha, jātivādavinibaddhaṃ ca gottavādavinibaddhaṃ ca...anuttarāya, vijjācaraṇasampadāya sacchikiriyā hotī'ti., D.I. 99-100.

4. M. II.149-150.

out any consideration of caste is capable of moral and spiritual development. Everyone "can develop within him loving thoughts towards all beings free from hatred and ill-will."[1] Thus, there is only one criterion of deciding the inferiority or superiority of man and that is the criterion of moral and spiritual progress. But, since moral and spiritual progress is equally open to all, there can be no fixity or rigidity in this classification. Men are always changing and are capable of change.

(*D*) *Conclusion*:-

All this indicates that the entire attitude of Buddhism in respect of caste is radically opposed to the traditional view of the Brahmanical orthodoxy, whereas the B.G., in spite of granting certain concessions, is too conservative in its tone and spirit to break away radically from the traditional belief in the hereditary and hierarchical caste-system. Buddhism, as Professor Rhys Davids rightly points out, "ignores completely and absolutely all advantages and disadvantages arising from birth, occupation or social status and sweeps away all barriers and disabilities arising from the arbitrary rules of mere ceremonial or social impurity."[2] It would not, therefore, be fair to place Buddhism and the B.G. on the same footing merely on the ground that the latter, as compared to the strict Brahmanical orthodoxy, makes certain relaxations. It is difficult to agree with Professor S. Radhakrishnan who by giving a different twist to the hereditary account of caste in the B.G. on the one hand, and by underrating the significance of the open Buddhistic repudiation of it, on the other, tries to measure both the B.G. and Buddhism with the same scale. He says: Both attempt to relax the rigours of caste by basing it on a less untenable foundation."[3] He seems to have ignored or, at least, underrated the repeated teaching of Buddha about the equality of men born low and high, when he pronounces the view that

1. M.II. 151.
2. Dialogues of the Buddha, Part I, S.B.B. Vol. I, p. 100.
3. Indian Philosophy, Vol. I, p. 526.

"the religion of Buddha is an aristocratic one"[1], We, on the basis of the discussion set forth in the preceding pages, cannot but come to the conclusion that the B.G., despite its effort to adjust itself with the new movements of thought, does not give up its orthodoxy and remains by and large conservative in its outlook, whereas Buddhism departs radically from tradition challenging the views of the Brahmanical orthodoxy and propounds in unmistakable language the equality of all men.

The Problem of War :—

(*A*) *The War Looked from the Moral Point of View*:—

The B.G., evidently, is presented as an exhortation to prepare the despondent Arjuna to fight. It naturally seeks to establish the *righteousness* of war in many and varied ways.

It is important to note at the very outset that the despondency of Arjuna was purely on moral grounds. He was afraid not of his enemies but only of moral sins. Being touched with utter compassion (kṛpayā parayā'viṣṭo, B.G.I.28) at the sight of his kinsmen (svajanam, *loc. cit.*), he utters with sadness: "Alas, what a great sin (mahat pāpam) are we resolved to commit in being prepared to slay our own kinsmen out of greed for the enjoyment of kingdom."[2] "Though they (the kinsmen standing as enemies) do not see the evil (doṣam) resulting from the destruction of the family and the sin (pātakam) accruing from treachery to friends, why should we not have the wisdom to turn away from this sin (pāpad asmān nivartitum) ?"[3] "Only sin (pāpam eva) shall we incur by killing these evil-doers (ātatāyinaḥ)."[4] Thus, over and over again Arjuna expresses his concern for the same moral sin and wants to know for certain wherein lies the moral good (śreyaḥ). He says: "I do not see any good (śreyo) in killing kinsmen in the fight."[5] "Tell me for

1. Ibid., 438.
2. B.G. I. 45.
3. B.G. I. 38 and 39.
4. B.G. I. 36.
5. B.G. I. 31.

certain whatever be the good (śreyaḥ)."[1] "Tell me then decisively the one thing whereby I may attain to the good (śreyo)."[2] Kṛṣṇa, therefore, has to convince him on moral grounds that his fighting against evil-doers involves no sin. So he tells Arjuna in clear terms: "You shall not thus incur sin" (nai'vaṃ pāpam avāpsyasi, B.G.II.38). "You shall cross over all sins by the boat of wisdom alone" (sarvaṃ jñānaplavenai'va vṛjinaṃ saṃtariṣyasi, B.G.IV.36). "He who works having given up attachment...is not touched by sin" (lipyate na sa pāpena, B.G.V.10). On the contrary, "If you do not fight this righteous battle, then having fallen from your duty, and glory you shall incur sin" (pāpam avāpsyasi B.G. II.38). Kṛṣṇa claims to teach Arjuna the way whereby the latter would really attain the supreme good (śreyaḥ param avāpsyatha, B.G.III.11). Thus there is no doubt that the issue involved here is a moral one and the solution offered is also on moral considerations. In other words, the B.G. intends to show that war is compatible with morality.

(*B*) *Is the B.G. Reference to War Allegorical?*

Some admirers and followers of the B.G. seem to apprehend some difficulty in the above position and try to obscure and mystify this plain teaching of the B.G. by suggesting that war is not intended to be taken literally but only allegorically. M.K. Gandhi, the well-known champion of non-violence and a noted admirer and devoted follower of the B.G. puts forth his comment as follows: "I felt that it (the B.G.) was not a historical work but that under the guise of physical warfare it described the dual that perpetually went on in the hearts of mankind, and that physical warfare was brought in merely to make the description of the internal duel more alluring."[3] S. Radhakrishnan attempting a further amplification of the same view observes: "The life of the soul is symbolised by the battlefield of Kurukṣetra and the Kauravas are the enemies who impede the progress of the soul. Arjuna attempts

1. B.G. II. 7.
2. B.G. III. 2; cf. V. 1.
3. Gitā, the Mother, Edited by Jag Parvesh Chander, p. 4.

to recapture the kingdom of man by resisting the temptations and controlling the passions. The path of progress is through suffering and self abnegation. Arjuna tries to evade the rigorous ordeal by subtle arguments and spacious excuses. Kṛṣṇa stands for the voice of God, delivering his message in thrilling notes, warning Arjuna against dejection of spirit."[1] According to this allegorical interpretation of his the word 'dharmakṣetre' used in the opening verse of the B.G. symbolises "the world,...the battleground for a moral struggle,"[2] though, literally, it is evident that it is used as an epithet of the battle-field, Kurukṣetra, the well-known abode of Vedic religion. Similarly when the narrative proceeds and the fact of Kṛṣṇa and Arjuna blowing their conches, seated in the chariot, is mentioned (B.G.I.14), Radhakrishnan is tempted to see an allegorical significance in it. He says: "Throughout the Hindu and the Buddhist literatures, the chariot stands for the psychophysical vehicle. The steeds are the senses, the reins their controls, but the charioteer, the guide is the spirit or real self, ātman. Kṛṣṇa the charioteer, is the spirit in us."[3]

These attempts at allegorical explanation may be quite ingenious but are not satisfactory, since it is almost impossible to provide similar explanations for all the different warriors of the two parties mentioned by name, for the various paraphernalia of war referred to in a realistic way and for the entire sequence of events described in the course of the narrative. In fact, if the allegorical or metaphorical interpretation is accepted, the B.G. loses all its relevance to the context in which it is fitted in the MB. and which it itself presupposes and reflects throughout the text. Professor Jayatilleke criticising this metaphorical interpretation of Radhakrishnan has rightly pointed out that "the greater majority of the passages containing references to war, far from admitting of a metaphorical interpretation have sense only when taken literally. On the other hand, the few passages which may possibly be in-

1. Indian Philosophy, Vol. I. pp. 520-521.
2. The Bhagavadgītā, p. 79.
3. Ibid. p. 85.

terpreted metaphorically are so interpreted only at the cost of obscuring their meaning especially when we consider their contexts."[1]

At one place Radhakrishan points out a difficulty in the literal interpretation of war (yuddha) and tries to show that metaphorical meaning alone can resolve the difficulty. Commenting on the line 'tasmāt sarveṣu kāleṣu mām anusmara yudhya ca' (therefore, at all times remember me and fight, B.G. VIII. 7), he says : "It is not fight on the material plane that is intended here for it cannot be done at all times. It is the fight with the powers of darkness that we have to carry on perpetually."[2] Now this difficulty is an imaginary one. The phrase 'sarveṣu kāleṣu' which qualifies the nearest verb, 'anusmara' has unnecessarily been imagined to qualify the other verb 'yudhya'. The purport of the verse is to emphasise the remembrance of God at all times, signifying utter resignation of the mind and intellect to God, as the subsequent expression, 'mayy arpitamanobuddhiḥ' makes it evident. Moreover, even if the phrase 'sarveṣu kāleṣu' is admitted to qualify the verb 'yudhya', it may not mean anything more than a usual figure of speech implying remembrance of God whenever Arjuna has to fight, just as the phrase 'always speak the truth' implies that one should speak truthfully *whenever* one has to speak (and not that one should go on speaking perpetually without a pause).

Another effort to extricate the B.G. from the aforesaid difficulty is made by Nataraja Guru who, though accepting the fact of actual war, makes the plea that the background of war should not be taken to impair 'the wisdom teaching' of the B.G. He urges "that in the study of the Gītā the blemish of the canvas should not be attributed to the picture in the mind of the painter. The canvas here was the historical setting of the Mahābhārata war as described in the epic poem, and the painting was the wisdom teaching that Yyāsa wanted to transmit to future generations through this

1. Some Aspects of Gītā and Buddhist Ethics in U.C.R., Vol. XIII, Nos. 2 & 3, pp. 144-45.

2. The Bhagavadgītā, p. 229.

medium."[1] This observation of Nataraja Guru amounts to saying that Vyāsa, the author of 'the wisdom teaching' (the B.G.) has not displayed his wisdom in selecting the appropriate background for this teaching and that the background or the context is ill-chosen. We, however, have shown (supra. pp. 6-7) by citing many other instances from the MB. that its author was really anxious to bring out as prominently as possible his commendation for the relentless discharge of one's own duty (svadharma) at all costs and in all situations and that the background for this teaching (which the B.G. represents) is well-chosen, since by weaving it with the central theme of the epic, viz. the war itself, the author secures for it the desired prominence. Moreover, by placing Arjuna against his own kinsmen, relatives, friends and the teacher, the author adds further to the poignancy of the occasion and thereby establishes the importance of the relentless performance of one's duty all the more. Nataraja Guru perhaps by referring to 'the wisdom teaching' intends to emphasise the elements of knowledge and renunciation and the descriptions of ideal seers and yogins found in the B.G. But we have already shown that these elements are there in the B.G. in view of its compromising character, and amidst all other elements, its activistic note comes out most prominently. In the words of the MB. itself it is said to be characteristically activistic (pravṛttilakṣaṇaś caiva dharmo nārāyaṇātmakaḥ, MB., Śānti. 347. 80-81), though embodying briefly the tenet of renunciation as well.[2]

Thus there is hardly any doubt that the B.G. speaks of war in the literal sense as being compatible with morality. We may now see how the B.G. argues its case and how it stands in comparison with the Buddhist attitude to war.

(C) *The Line of Argument Adopted by the B.G.*:—

We have noticed that activism is the keynote of the B.G. and in the course of highlighting this teaching the B.G.

---

1. The Bhagavadgītā, preface, p. ix.
2. Yatīnāṃ cā'pi yo dharmaḥ sa te pūrvaṃ nṛpottama
kathito hari-gītāsu samāsavidhikalpitaḥ., M.B., Śānti. 348. 53.

puts forward the doctrine of prescribed duty (svadharma) for each class in society. Every individual is required to perform his own duty relentlessly and dispassionately irrespective of the consequences, for man is to attain perfection by discharging his own duty (sve-sve karmaṇy abhirataḥ saṃsiddhiṃ labhate naraḥ, B.G. XVIII. 45) with a detached view (asaktabuddhiḥ, B.G. XVIII. 49). Now to fight gallantly in the battle and not to run away from it is one of the prescribed duties of a Kṣatriya. The B.G. enumerates the duties of a Kṣatriya as follows : "Heroism, valour, fortitude, skilfulness, not running away even from the battle (yuddhe cā'py apalāyanam), charity and lordship—are the natural duties of a Kṣatriya."[1]

We have noted already that from its different standpoints of knowledge, devotion and action (without concern for the fruit), the B.G. reinforces the same teaching of the disinterested discharge of one's own duty. Thus from all these standpoints Arjuna is exhorted to remain firm to his duty of fighting. From a metaphysical point of view, he is reminded of the eternal and indestructible nature of the self and asked not to be perturbed by the physical destruction of the destructible body.[2] The true self is not slain when the body is slain (na hanyate hanyamāne śarīre, B.G. II. 20). "Weapons do not cut this (self), nor does the fire burn it,... it is uncleavable, incombustible...eternal, all-pervading, firm, immovable and everlasting."[3] Thus by pointing out the inevitability of the destruction of the physical body, on the one hand and the impossibility of the destruction of the eternal metaphysical self, on the other, Arjuna is asked to remain firm and unflinching in his duty of fighting. Kṛṣṇa says : "These bodies of eternal, imperishable and incomprehensible soul are said to be perishable. Therefore, fight, O Arjuna (tasmād yudhyasva bhārata)."[4] Again from the devotional

---

1. Śauryaṃ tejo dhṛtir dākṣyaṃ yuddhe cā'py apalayanam
   dānam īśvarabhāvaś ca kṣātraṃ karma svabhāvajam.,
   B.G. XVIII. 43.
2. B.G. II. 11-30.
3. B.G. II. 23 & 24.
4. B.G. II. 18.

point of view it is said : "Man attains perfection by worshipping him (God) through his own duty."[1] Disinterested work is considered as the best worship, for in so doing man resigns or offers his whole being to God. In that case, he is said to remain absolutely free from the bonds of action bearing good and bad results.[2] It is said : "He who works having given up attachment, resigning his actions to God, is not contaminated by sin even as a lotus leaf (is untouched) by water."[3] Arjuna is therefore, advised : "Dedicating all actions to me through your spiritualised mind, being disinterested and free from egoism, fight dispassionately (yuddhyasva vigatajvaraḥ)."[4] From the point of view of desireless action (niṣkāma karma) also the same is reiterated. The famous teaching of the B.G. is : "Action alone is thy concern and never its fruits". (karmaṇy evā'dhikāras te, mā phaleṣu kadācana).[5] "Having abandoned attachment to the fruit of action, ever content and free from dependence, one does nothing at all even though he is engaged in action."[6] It is said : "He who is not self-conceited, whose intellect is not attached though he slays these worlds, he (really) neither slays nor is he bound." (hatvā'pi sa imāṃl lokān na hanti na nibadhyate., B.G. XVIII. 17). In the light of this attitude, Arjuna is given the following explicit advice : "Treating alike pleasure and pain, gain and loss, victory and defeat—get ready for battle (yuddhāya yujyasva). Thus you shall not incur sin."[7]

Lest Arjuna may still desist from fighting on the ground that the ideal state of mind, viz. the utter detachment, required for going unsullied in the battle, is not possible for him to attain, Kṛṣṇa further adds that "even a little of this discipline saves one from great fear."[8] He justifies the former's

1. B.G. XVIII. 46.
2. B.G. IX 28.
3. B.G. V. 10.
4. B.G. III. 30.
5. B.G. II. 47.
6. B.G. IV. 20.
7. B.G. II. 38.
8. svalpam apy asya dharmasya trāyate mahato bhayāt, B.G., II. 40.

duty of fighting on other grounds as well. He points out that to follow the prescribed duty (svadharma) of fighting is firstly, in keeping with the noble traditions of the royal sages; secondly, virtuous, enough to lead to heaven and thirdly, glorious enough to establish fame on the earth. Thus it is emphasised that this line of action has come down through tradition (paramparāprāptam, B.G.IV.2) of the royal sages rājarṣayaḥ, *loc. cit.*). It is said that "for a Kṣatriya there is no good higher than a righteous fight",[1] and for him it is like "an open door to heaven "(svargadvāram, apāvṛam B.G. II. 32). The B.G., as also the MB., in keeping with the teaching of the prescribed duty (svadharma) hold that a warrior following his royal duty (rājadharma) and a contemplative seer following the duty of a recluse (yatidharma) reach the same goal. We have already referred to the declaration of the B.G. that both these paths lead to the same goal (niḥśreyasakarāv ubhau, B.G.V.2; yat sāṅkhyaiḥ prāpyate sthānaṃ tad yogair api gamyate, B.G.V.5). The MB. also proclaims in the same vein: "O thou best of men, there are only these two who pierce the constellation of the sun (reach the sphere of Brahman); the one is the recluse who is endowed with yoga and the other is the warrior who falls fighting in the battle-field."[2] They should, therefore, confine themselves to their respective duties. "The duty of a Kṣatriya is to take the rod and not to shave the head," (daṇḍa eva hi rājendra kṣatradharmo na muṇḍanam, MB., Śānti.23.46). "He is called a Kṣatriya because he protects from destruction" (kṣatād yo vai trāyatī'ti sa tasmāt kṣatriyaḥ smṛtaḥ MB.XII.29.138). To fall from this duty is to incur ill-fame or dishonour for ever and "for a man of repute, ill-fame is worse than death" (sambhāvitasya cākīrtir maraṇād atiricyate, B.G. II.34). In short, desisting from fighting "is neither trodden by noble ones, nor is it conducive to heaven nor can it give rise to

---

1. dharmyād dhi yuddhāc chreyo'nyat kṣatriyasya na vidyate., B.G., II. 31.

2. Dvāv imau puruṣavyāghra sūryamaṇḍalabhedinau;
parivrāḍ yogayuktas ca raṇe cā'bhimukho hataḥ.,
32. 65. MB. Udyoga.

fame."[1] Arjuna is therefore clearly told: "If you do not fight this righteous battle you shall fall from duty and fame and incur sin."[2] On the other hand, the participation in war would do good in any case: "If slain, you shall go to heaven and if victorious, you shall enjoy the earth" (hato vā prāpsyasi svargaṃ jitvā vā bhokṣyase mahīm, B.G.II.37).

In his further attempt to encourage and persuade Arjuna to fight, Kṛṣṇa in his capacity of the all-knowing supreme Lord[3] reveals before him the destiny of the people assembled there for the battle and points out that it is futile on his part to think that merely on account of his desisting from fighting, the battle would be avoided and the lives of these people would be saved. In keeping with the line of argument that the evil-doers (ātatāyinaḥ) are killed by their own outrageous conduct and the man who is merely instrumental in their killing is not guilty of the sin (infra, pp. 526-528), Kṛṣṇa exhorts him to follow his duty and earn the glory of a true warrior. He says: "Even without you, all the warriors standing arrayed in the opposing armies shall cease to be. Therefore, stand up, and obtain fame by conquering your foes and enjoy a prosperous kingdom. They are already killed by me alone be merely instrumental (nimittamātram), O Arjuna in their death."[4] Arjuna is told to be wise enough to realise the true duty of a Ksatriya, with the natural endowment of which he is born and not to allow his egotism and emotion to get better of him (nirmamo bhūtvā yudhyasva vigatajvaraḥ, B.G. III. 30). But if on the other hand he, on account of his vision being blurred with egotism (ahaṅkāra), fails to exercise his wisdom and desists from following his natural duty, it is pointed out, that it may

---

1. anāryajuṣṭam asvargyam akīrtikaram Arjuna.. B.G. II. 2.

2. Atha cet tvaṃ imaṃ dharmyaṃ saṅgrāma naṃ kariṣyasi;
tataḥ svadharmaṃ kīrtiṃ ca hitvā pāpam avāpsyasi.,
B.G. II. 33.

3. Vedā'haṃ samatītāni vartamānāni cā'rjuna bhaviṣyāṇi ca bhūtāni..., B.G. VII. 26.

4. ṛte'pi tvāṃ na bhaviṣyanti sarve ye'vasthitāḥ pratyanīkeṣu yodhāḥ
Tasmāt tvaṁ uttiṣṭha yaśo labhasva jitvā śatrūn bhuṅkṣva rājyaṃ samṛddham,
mayai'vai''te nihatāḥ pūrvam eva nimittamātraṃ bhava savyasācin,
B.G. XI. 32-33.

not be possible for him in that egoistic state to keep control over his natural urge for long and ultimately he will be compelled by his nature to fight —the only difference being that in the latter case he will fight with a fever of emotion and egotism and not dispassionately with the wisdom of his rightful duty, as Kṛṣṇa wants him to do. Thus he is clearly told: "If indulging in egotism (ahaṅkāram āśritya) you think 'I will not fight', vain is this conceited resolve of yours, since nature will impel you."[1]

(*D*) *The Problem of Freedom and Predestination*:—

The last argument stated above has given rise to a feeling that the B.G., in contradiction to its entire ethical teaching, sounds a note of determinism or predestination. Scholars have expressed opposite views in this respect. S. Radhakrishnan commenting on B.G. III. 33 (prakṛtiṃ yānti bhūtāni nigrahaḥ kiṃ kariṣyati) observes: "This verse seems to suggest the omnipotence of nature over the soul and requires us to act according to our nature."[2] Similarly in his comment on B.G. XI.33, he adds: "The writer seems to uphold the doctrine of Divine predestination and to indicate the utter helplessness and insignificance of the individual and the futility of his will and effort."[3] He, however, seems to contradict himself when, commenting on B.G. XVI. 20, he speaks of the power of 'the Indwelling Spirit' and roundly denies the doctrine of predestination. He remarks: "We are advised to shake off this demoniac nature. This does not mean predestination, for it is said that it is always open to us to turn godward and achieve perfection. It is not impossible at any stage. The Indwelling Spirit is in each soul and that means the hope of immortality is always there."[4] Professor Jayatilleke, unlike Radhakrishnan, argues consistently in support of determinism and concludes: "Man is thus impotent in the Gītā, since,

1. Yad ahaṅkāram āśritya na yotsya iti manyase
mithyai'ṣa vyavasāyas te prakṛtis tvāṃ niyokṣyati.,
B.G. XVIII. 59.
2. The Bhagavadgītā, p. 146.
3. Ibid. p. 280.
4. The Bhagavadgītā, p. 340.

he is subject to the power of *prakṛti* or svabhāva."[1] Garbe, on the other hand, expresses an opposite view. According to him "when it is said (III. 33) that 'beings follow (their) nature' and when at XVI. 1 and ff. there is a distinction made between men as those who are born to a divine (inheritance of) nature, and those to a demoniac one, this predestination is to be regarded as a working of the former karman. There is no word in the Gītā of predestination as such; on the other hand, the presupposition of moral freedom can be recognised as pervading the work quite through. One is entirely at liberty whether he would strive after a lower or after a higher ideal,"[2]

We do not intend to enter into a digression by discussing this much vexed question at any length. But in view of the issue involved being a vital one, we only wish to make it clear very briefly that the B.G. despite some apparently conflicting statements tending to indicate deterministic ideas, does not on the whole seem to subscribe to a deterministic view. None can doubt the truism that 'either free-will is a fact or morality is a fiction'. It is difficult, to accept therefore, that the B.G.which discusses moral problems at great length, emphasises the need for self-control and moral discipline, and prescribes different means of salvation, has left no room for the freedom of will. It is chiefly on account of the loose uses of certain terms and a non-methodical treatment of the subject that confusion is created and obscurity creeps in. But the difficulty can be resolved if we bear in mind the following facts.

The word 'prakṛti', which is one of the chief causes of confusion, is used by the B.G. in more than one sense. Besides being regarded metaphysically as the lower nature of the supreme reality (in contradistinction to the higher nature, viz. puruṣa)[3], it is used in the sense of the sum-total of the impressions or dispositions of previous lives expressing itself in the form of inborn urges and tendencies. There is no doubt

---

1. Some Aspects of Gītā and Buddhist Ethics, in U.C.R. Vol. XIII. No. 2 & 3, p. 141.

2. I.A. Vol. 47, Supplement, p. 26.

3. B.G. VII. 4 & 5.

that according to the B.G. impressions of Karmas are preserved and carried on to the next life.[1] They partly in the form of the fruition of past karmas constitute the pre-determined destiny (daiva) of man and partly in the form of inborn dispositions express themselves as urges and tendencies in man[2]. It is mainly in this sense that the word 'avaśaḥ' is used in the B.G.[3]. If this meaning of the word prakṛti is borne in mind, then one can easily understand the correct position of the B.G. The purport of B.G. III. 33 is only to indicate that the self-mortification or the repression of natural urges and impulses is ultimately of no avail. This, however, does not imply that the B.G. rules out the possibility of sense-control and discipline, since both in the preceding as well as the succeeding verses, it explains the method of acquiring self-control. By speaking of the forceful character of the urges and tendencies of man, the B.G. only seeks to emphasise the need for great care in curbing the senses, as also the futility of undue repression and self-mortification. In II. 60, for example the B.G. referring to the forceful nature of the senses cautions us as follows: "The impetuous senses, O Arjuna, forcibly carry away the mind of even a striving wise man."[4] But at once it adds: "Having brought all of them under control, one should remain firm in yoga intent on me, for only he whose senses are under control can have his intellect firmly settled."[5] Thereafter the B.G. proceeds to explain the stages through which one gradually controls his senses and the mind and reaffirms: "Therefore, the intellect of him, O Arjuna, whose senses are all withdrawn from their objects, is firmly

1. Tatra taṃ buddhisaṃyogaṃ labhate paurvadehikam, B.G. VI. 43.

2. B.G. VI. 40-45.

3. Purvābhyāsena tenaiva hriyate hy avaśo 'pi saḥ., B.G. VI. 44; cf. B.G. VIII. 19 and IX. 8. The fact that beings are born again and again being impelled by their own actions and not only by the fiat of a capricious God is indicated by B.G. IX. 9 where God is said to operate the process of evolution and dissolution in an indifferent and detached way (udāsīnavad āsīnam asaktaṃ teṣu karmasu).

4. Yatato hy api kaunteya puruṣasya vipaścitaḥ,
indriyāṇi pramāthīni haranti prasabhaṃ manaḥ., B.G. II. 60.

5. Tāni sarvāṇi saṃyamya yukta āsīta matparaḥ,
vaśe hi yasye'ndriyāṇi tasya prajñā pratiṣṭhitā, B.G. II. 61

settled."[1] In like manner after having referred to the futility of repression (B.G. III. 33), the B.G. in subsequent verses (B.G. III. 34-43) explains how one should gradually control the senses (so hard to control) by the next higher faculty, the mind and the latter by the still higher faculty, the intellect so that ultimately one should be possessed of the inmost light of the self, the highest of all faculties. Thus it is pointed out that though the evil tendencies of desire and anger (kāma, krodha) appear to impel one to commit sin, *as it were* by force (balād *iva*), they can, nevertheless be controlled and one must control them (B.G.III. 36-37). This shows that prakṛti according to the B.G., is considered only as an impelling force and not a compelling one. Morever, this impelling force, as both Śaṅkara[2] and Rāmānuja[3] point out, is the cumulative effect of one's own past deeds. In any case man is conceived by the B.G. as a composite of prakṛti, and puruṣa and accordingly, he is supposed to have the freedom to curb the influence of prakṛti by the due exercise of his higher nature.

The fact that the B.G. stands for partial determinism and partial indeterminism is conveyed in its enumeration of the five factors responsible for the execution of an act. It is said: "Whatever action a man undertakes by his body, speech or mind, whether it is right or wrong, these five factors are involved in it: the seat of action (adhiṣṭhāna), as also the doer (kartā), the different kinds of instruments (karaṇaṃ ca pṛthagvidham), the diverse efforts of different types (vividhāś ca pṛthakceṣṭā) with destiny (daivaṃ) as the fifth."[4] It can be noticed here that destiny (daiva) is only one among the five factors and effort or endeavour (ceṣṭā) also is said to be essential for the accomplishment of an act.

In the B.G. XI. 32-34 also where Kṛṣṇa discloses the inevitable destiny of the warriors assembled for the battle, it is important to note that only the death of the warriors said to

1. B.G. II. 68.

2. prakṛtir nāma pūrvakṛtadharmādharmādisaṃskāro vartamānajanmādau abhivyaktaḥ., S.B.G. III. 33.

3. svasyāḥ prakṛteḥ: prācīnavāsanāyāḥ sadṛśam., R.B.G. III. 33.

4. B.G. XVIII. 14 and 15.

be determined and not the instruments (nimitta) thereof. Arjuna is advised to be instrumental in the execution of a predetermined act (nimittamātraṃ bhava savyasācin, B.G. XI. 33), though it is added that even without him the inevitable would be accomplished (ṛte'pi tvāṃ na bhaviṣyanti sarve, B.G. XI, 32).

Again it is not without significance that Arjuna is said to be impelled to take up arms by nature only when he were to allow himself to be swayed by egotism (ahaṅkāram āśritya, B.G. XVIII. 59). This may be an indication of the fact that according to the B.G. man is supposed to lose control over himself only under the influence of weaker emotions.

In the light of these considerations, we are inclined to think that the B.G., notwithstanding its use of somewhat deterministic expressions, does not on the whole deny the value of human effort and free-will. We may, however, concede the fact that unlike Early Buddhism[1], it emphasises the inherent nature and aptitude of man as also his destiny, born of his past deeds.

(*E*) *The Concept of Righteous war*:—

Reverting to our original point, it is important to note that the war which Arjuna is exhorted to plunge in is not reckless aggression but a righteous war (dharmya yuddha, B.G.II.81; dharmya saṅgrāma B.G. II. 33) aimed at fighting against evil-doers (ātatāyinaḥ, B.G. I.36). Śaṅkara means by it a war which is fought in defence of people (prajārakṣaṇārtham, S.B.G. II. 31), and Rāmānuja takes it in the sense of a war which is in keeping with justice (nyāyataḥ pravṛttāt yuddhāt, R.B.G. II.31). Though the B.G. does not elaborate this concept of a righteous war, yet it contains a clue whereby its view may be ascertained with reasonable plausibility. We have stated that Arjuna's despondency was on moral grounds and he takes the stand that killing even of evil-doers (ātatāyinaḥ) is sinful. He clearly says: "Only sin shall we incur by killing these evil-doers"

1. For a discussion about the Buddhist approach to the problem of free-will and its criticisms of different forms of determinism see Professor Jayatilleke's 'Some Aspects of Gītā and Buddhist Ethics' in U.C.R. Vol. XIII. Nos. 2 and 3, p. 141ff.

(pāpam evā'śrayed asmān hatvai'tān ātatāyinaḥ R.B.G. I.36). Kṛṣṇa dissuades him from this thought and tries to convince him of the traditional ideal practised by the royal sages. According to this ideal "there is no sin in killing an evil-doer (nā'tatāyivadhe doṣo),[1] rather it is the righteous duty of a Kṣatriya to fight against such an offender. The word 'ātatāyi' is a significant one. It is said: "One who sets fire, gives poison, attacks with weapon in hand, plunders property, and dispossesses people of territory as well of women—these six are evil-doers (ātatāyinaḥ)."[2] With regard to such a heinous criminal, the Manusmṛti says: "Whether he be a teacher, an infant, an old man or a much learned brahmin, if he comes as a criminal (ātatāyi) one should kill him without any consideration. There is no sin in killing a criminal(ātatāyi)."[3] He is said to be killed by his own outrageous conduct.[4] Now, in the light of the story of the MB. (which the B.G. presupposes), it is not difficult to see that the Kauravas against whom Arjuna is asked to fight, had committed not one but all the six heinous crimes.[5] They had further thwarted all attempts made by Kṛṣṇa for a peaceful settlement of the dispute by refusing to accept the request of giving even five hamlets, the bare minimum for the five Pāṇḍavas, the exiled princes. Duryodhana bluntly tells Kṛṣṇa: "Even that much of our land which may be covered by the tip of a sharp needle shall not, O Keśava, be given unto the Pāṇḍavas."[6] Arjuna is thus justified in calling the Kauravas

1. Manusmṛti, VIII. 351
2. Agnido garadaś cai'va śastrapāṇir dhanāpahaḥ,
kṣetradāraharaś cai'va ṣaḍ ete ātatāyinaḥ., Vaśiṣṭhasmṛti III.16.
3. Gurum vā bālavṛddhau vā brāhmaṇam vā bahuśrutam;
ātatāyinam āyāntam hanyād evā'vicārayan,
nātatāyivadhe doṣo..., Manusmṛti VIII. 350-351.
4. Ibid. 351.
5. We are told by the epic narrative that the Kauravas had set fire to the house of the Pāṇḍavas, given poison to Bhīma, deprived them of their property and kingdom, insulted their wife in open royal court and were ultimately planning to launch an armed attack on them.
6. Yāvad dhi tīkṣṇayā sūcyā vidhyed agreṇa Keśava,
tāvad apy aparityājyam bhūmer naḥ pāṇḍavān prati.,
M.B. Udyogaparva. 126. 25.

'criminals' (ātatāyinaḥ, B.G.I. 36), though he still considers it sinful to kill them (*loc. cit.*). It is against this attitude of Arjuna that Kṛṣṇa imparts the teaching of the righteous fight (dharmyaṃ saṅgrāmam, B.G. II. 33). Kṛṣṇa (the incarnate God) himself is said to "assume birth for the protection of the righteous ones, destruction of the evil-doers and the establishment of righteousness."[1] It is important to bear in mind that the establishment of righteousness (dharma) is said to be brought about by killing the evil-doers. It is no wonder, therefore, that war against evil-doers is called by the B.G. a righteous war (dharmyaṃ saṅgrāmam). This is how the B.G. tries to vindicate the righteousness of war.

In view of this attitude of the B.G. to war, we may now see how the entire approach of Buddhism in this respect is basically different from that of the former.

(F) Buddhist Attitude Diametrically opposed to that of the B.G.:—

Neither does Buddhism accept the validity of the concept of prescribed duty (svadharma) nor does it believe in the possibility of disinterested warfare. Referring to the concept of prescribed duty taught by the Brahminical priesthood (and upheld by the B.G.) Buddha points out that he, in contradistinction to brahmins who teach the fourfold duty(cattāri dhanāni paññāpenti, M. II. 180) teaches the supramundane Noble Doctrine as the only duty of man (ariya kho ahaṃ.. lokuttaraṃ dhammaṃ purisassa sandhanaṃ paññāpemi, M. II. 181). This practice of holy life is alike meant for all without distinction. He does not lend countenance to the idea of adopting an unrighteous profession or means of livelihood under the guise of prescribed duty. We have already seen (supra. pp. 494-5, 506-7) how he rejects the concept of divinely ordained or prescribed natural duties.

Moreover he considers it impossible for a disinterested and enlightened man to commit moral sins. According to him in no circumstance can a truly detached and disinterested

---

1. Paritrāṇāya sādhūnāṃ vināśāya ca duṣkṛtām, dharmasaṁsthāpanārthāya sambhavāmi yuge-yuge., B.G. IV. 8.

man resort to violence. Of the nine moral vices which a truly detached person is considered incapable of doing (abhabbo so nava ṭhānāni ajjhācaritum̥, D. III. 133), the deliberate destruction of the life of a living creature (sañcicca pāṇam jīvitā voropetum̥, *loc. cit.*) is reckoned as the first. The enlightened one is said to be incapable of doing such a bodily, verbal or mental action, which is morally wrong or deprecated by recluses, brahmins and the wise.[1] Buddha altogether precludes the possibility of war without attachment, passion or desire. He makes it clear that people resort to violence and war on account of their selfish desire or passion and reap the consequences of their evil deeds both here as well as hereafter. Thus he observes: "It is on account of passion or desire that kings dispute with kings, Kṣatriyas dispute with Kṣatriyas... They entering into quarrel, conflict and dispute, attack one another with hands, stones, rods and weapons... It is on account of passion or desire that they wage war having taken sword and shield, having girded on bow and quiver and being drawn out in battle-array on both sides. Hurling arrows, hurling daggers, flashing swords, they pierce with arrows, pierce with daggers and cut off heads with swords. They thereby suffer death or death-like pain. This, monks, is the visible (sandiṭṭhiko) worldly consequence of passion or desire. Having performed evil deeds by body, speech and mind they at the destruction of body after death are born in a lowly and evil state of downward hell. This, monks, is the otherworldly (samparāyiko) consequence of passion or desire."[2] Thus Buddha discards not only the traditional view of war being the prescribed duty of a Kṣatriya and the possibility of its being fought dispassionately or disinterestedly, but he also speaks of its dreadful consequences both from a worldly as well as an otherworldly point of view—a position diametrically opposed to that of the B.G.[3]

1. Na kho...so bhagavā tathārūpam̥ kāyasamācāram̥...vacīsamācāram̥ ...manosamācāram̥ samācareyya, yvāssa...opārambho samaṇehi brāhmaṇehi viññūhi'ti., M. II. 113-114.

2. M. I. 86-87.

3. Contrast the B.G. view: 'hato vā prāpsyasi svargam̥ jitvā vā bhokṣyase mahīm'.—B.G. II. 37.

None of the arguments adduced by the B.G. in support of disinterested warfare appears to be tenable from the Buddhist point of view. From the metaphysical standpoint the B.G. argues on the basis of the indestructibility and eternity of the self. But the very existence of it is denied by Buddha. Even if the existence of the supramundane or transcendental self is admitted for argument's sake, it cannot be said to have bearing on mundane acts prompted by passion and emotion. How then, can it be invoked for either justifying or condemning a mundane act? Indeed, in so doing one is led to an absurd position of moral anarchism. Professors Ranade and Belvalkar have noticed the absurdity involved in this absolutistic concept of the self. They observe: "To say that Ātman dies not is legitimate. To say that weapons cannot cut Him nor fire burn Him is also a legitimate varying of the phrase. But to argue that therefore the murderer is no murderer and there is nobody really responsible for his action is to carry this 'śāśvata' or 'Akriyā' doctrine to a point, which if seriously preached would be subversive of all established social institutions and religious sacraments."[1] The theological argument also fares no better in the Buddhist context than the metaphysical one. The existence of God being unacceptable and the theory of the divine origin of society as well as the doctrine of the divinely ordained duties of men being rejected, the question of serving God through the disinterested discharge of one's divinely ordained duty loses its meaning. Again, the doctrine of action without concern for the fruit also seems to find no favour with Buddhism. We have already pointed out that according to Buddhism it is immaterial whether an action is performed with an expectation, without an expectation, with and without an expectation or neither with nor without an expectation (āsaṃ ce pi karitvā,..anāsaṃ ce pi karitvā..āsaṃ ca anāsaṃ ce pi karitvā,...nevāsaṃ nānāsaṃ ce pi karitvā, M. III. 138, 139). What matters is the fact whether the action is performed properly (yoniso) or improperly (ayoniso). If one makes due efforts, the fire is bound

1. History of Indian Philosophy, Vol. II. p. 399.

to be kindled out of the dry wood whether one does or does not desire it.[1]

In fact the incompatibility of the B.G. ideal with that of the Buddhist is evident from the very fact that Buddha, in spite of being born as a Kṣatriya, renounces his royal duties and goes about shaven-headed. Not only does he himself lead the life of a recluse but he also ordains many other Kṣatriyas and royal princes to the Order. He does not entertain the theory of prescribed duty as a cloak for covering the immorality of certain professions. Wrong means of livelihood must be abandoned and immoral acts must not be performed even though it is deemed as part of one's duty to the king (rañño ceva rājakaraṇīyaṃ kātuṃ, M. II. 191).

As regards the considerations of the noble tradition, the attainment of heaven and the establishment of fame[2] also Buddhism takes an opposite stand. We have seen in the course of our epistemological discussions that tradition (paramparā) is one of the ten kinds of knowledge criticised and rejected by Buddha (A. I. 189; II. 191-193). The traditional view that the warrior killed in battle goes to heaven is expressly placed before Buddha for his comment. A warrior chief (yodhājīvo gāmaṇi) telling Buddha that he has heard from his ancestral teachers in the martial arts that the spirited soldier who fights energetically and kills his enemies in the battle is born in heaven, wants to know whether it is correct.[3] Buddha, to the utter disappoinment and dismay of the warrior chief says that such a soldier "at the dissolution of body after death is born in a hell named, Parajita" (so kāyassa bhedā paraṃ maraṇā parajito nāma nirayo tattha upapajjatī'ti, S IV. 309). So far as the question of fame about gallantry and bravery is concerned, it is pointed out that the real gallantry consists in achieving victory over one's own passions and in meting out love or non-anger to the angry. The display of brutal

1. M. III. 143-144.
2. anāryajuṣṭam asvargyam akīrtikaram Arjuna. B.G. II. 2.
3. S. IV. 308-309.

force is considered merely foolish and this can win applause and fame only from fools. The truly enlightened one should not care for such fame and try to acquire true virtue and real fame. Thus Buddha observes: "One may conquer a thousand of a thousand men in the battlefield, yet he, indeed is the noblest victor (saṅgāmajuttamo) who conquers his own single self."[1] It is again stated: "One expressing no anger to the angry (really) wins a war difficult to win" (kuddhaṃ appaṭikujjhanto saṅgāmaṃ jeti dujjayaṃ, S. I. 222). To resist force with force is only brutal and foolish and is, indeed, an indication of weakness. It is said: "That strength is really weakness which is the strength of fools. There is none to counter the power of one protected by righteousness,"[2] To keep oneself to righteousness in the face of provocation is really the highest feat and nothing is higher than forgiveness.[3] Thus the entire approach of Buddhism seems to be radically different from that of the B.G.

The B.G. concept of righteous war (dharmyaṃ saṅgrāmam), according to which it is deemed morally right to fight against evil-doers, is also incompatible with the Buddhist ideal. In fact, according to the true Buddhist ideal, the phrase 'righteous war' cannot but be a contradiction in terms, since righteousness and war can hardly go hand in hand. In no circumstance is a true Buddhist to resort to violence. In the Kakacūpama Sutta, Buddha says: "Though, monks, thieves and brigands were to cut limb by limb with a double-edged saw, even then one who defiles his mind (feels angry about it), is not then the follower of my instructions."[4] With the same attitude of loving kindness the monk Puṇṇa goes to the place known as Sunāparanta,notorious for its cruel and callous people.[5] The bidding of Buddha is to meet anger with love and not with anger; evil with good and not with

1. Dh. 103.
2. Abalaṃ taṃ balaṃ āhu yassa bālabalaṃ balaṃ,
   balassa dhammaguttassa paṭivattā na vijjati, S.I. 222.
3. sadattha paramā atthā khantyā bhiyyo na vijjati., S.I. 222.
4. M. I. 129.
5. M. III. 268-269.

evil. He says: "Conquer anger with non-anger (love), evil with good; conquer the miser with generosity and the liar with truth."[1] This is the Buddhist ideal. In so far as one compromises with or deviates from this ideal he deviates from the true goal, whether he is a monk or a honseholder. The ideal of morality, if it is a true ideal, must remain one and the same for all men, since it is always within one's own power to decide whether to go forth from home to homelessness in pursuit of the purest holy life or to continue as a householder enjoying worldly pleasure and following the holy path in a partial way with some compromises. Unlike the B.G. which speaks of two separate codes of morality, one for the recluse and the other for the householder, both equally efficacious in leading to the highest goal[2], Buddhism speaks of the one and the only path leading to the true goal so that the deflection from the right path cannot but take one astray Thus Buddha seeking no compromise with immoral acts and professions sets the same noblest ideal for all.

The Buddhist attitude to war is well indicated in the Mahāsīlava jātaka where Buddha narrating the story of his own previous life describes how he, as a king of Benares, was attacked by the then King of Kosala and how he even amidst the most provocative situation remained firmly established in non-violence and peace, and ultimately succeeded in changing the heart of the enemy by sheer force of love.[3]

We have already shown (supra.pp.131-133) by comparing the dialogue of Mātali and Sakka mentioned in the Pali Canon with that of Arjuna and Kṛṣṇa occurring in the B.G. that the Buddhist ideal of meeting anger with love and evil with good is represented by Sakka in the Pali Canon and by Arjuna in the B.G., whereas the opposite ideal of meting out punishment to the evil-doer is represented by Mātali in the Pali Conon and by Kṛṣṇa in the B.G. In both the Pali Canon and the B.G. similar arguments referring to fear, weakness and ill-fame are invoked against the Buddhist ideal. But in

1. Dh. 223.
2. B.G. V. 2, 5.
3. Jātaka, I. 261-267.

the Pali Canon Mātali is silenced when it is pointed out to him by Sakka that man by meeting anger with anger only incurs sin (tass'eva tena pāpiyo yo kuddhaṃ paṭikujjhati, S I.222), whereas in the B.G.,it is Arjuna who is silenced when he is told by Kṛṣṇa that he (Arjuna) would incur sin if he gives up his duty of righteous battle.[1] Thus it appears that by utilising fully the arguments of Mātali Kṛṣṇa wins over Arjuna and what is held inferior in Buddhism is given a superior status in the B.G.

From what has been said above, it is evident that the Buddhist ideal of morality has no room for war. Evidences are many where we find Buddha indicating either directly or indirectly his abhorrence of war. He conveys his views firstly by showing the futility, harmfulness and inconclusiveness of war, secondly by contrasting the use of physical force with the exercise of righteousness and thirdly by actual demonstration of the life of loving-kindness within the community of monks. We may briefly illustrate these varied ways of expressing his views.

On one occasion a dispute had arisen between the Sākyas and their blood brothers, the Koliyas over the waters of the river Rohiṇī, which flowed between their territory. From both sides soldiers had assembled and a battle was to begin when Buddha personally intervened and stopped them by pointing out how foolish it was for them to destroy invaluable lives for a matter so trivial. Having been told on his inquiry that the sole cause of the dispute is the waters of the river, he says: Why on account of some water of little worth would you destroy invaluable lives of these soldiers?"[2] This episode indicates how Buddha by pointing out the utter triviality of the causes of war and its dreadful consequences expresses his abhorrence of war. We have already referred to his view according to which war is said to be rooted in man's selfish desire or passion, producing dreadful consequences both here as well as hereafter.[3]

---

1. Atha cet tvam imaṃ dharmyaṃ saṅgrāmaṃ na kariṣyasi, tataḥ svadharmaṃ kīrtiṃ ca hitvā pāpam avāpsyasi., B.G. II.33.
2. J. V. 412-414.
3. M.I. 86-87.

In contradistinction to the B.G. Buddhism considers war to be harmful both for the victor as well as for the vanquished. Commenting on the war between the Kings Ajātasattu and Pasenadi, Buddha says: "Victory begets enmity and the vanquished lives in sorrow."[1] Moreover, as the victor has aroused enmity, war can never end in peace or be conclusive but would give rise to further wars. It is said: "The victor gets one who vanquishes him,...he who spoils is spoiled in his turn."[2] Buddha, therefore, declares: "Hatreds never cease by hatred in this world. By love alone they cease. This is an eternal law."[3]

We have already quoted some verses wherein Buddha shows the inferiority of physical force in comparison with the strength of righteousness. One is called the noblest victor (saṅgāmajuttamo) by one's perfect selfcontuol and not by fighting a thousand enemies in the battlefield.[4] To take recourse to physical force is considered mere foolishness and an indication of weakness. No strength is greater than the strengh of righteousness and forgiveness.[5] At the ordination of the notorious robber, Aṅgulimāla, King Pasenadi exclaims with utter surprise: "Wonderful, Sir! marvellous, Sir! One whom I could not control, Sir, with rod or weapon, the same has been controlled by the Lord without rod or weapon."[6]

The order of monks established by Buddha was a perfect symbol of peace, harmony and loving-kindness. To desist from destroying life (pāṇātipātā verāmaṇī, M.I.47) was the first and the most primary lesson of moral conduct. In Buddhism it is not merely a negative virtue confined to mere desistance from killing but is a definitely positive virtue implying loving-kindness to all creatures. The value attached to it is well indicated from the following remark of Buddha: "None of the good works employed to acquire religious merit

1. S. I. 83; Dh. 201.
2. S.I. 85.
3. Dh. 5.
4. Dh. 103.
5. S. I. 222.
6. M· II. 102.

is worth a fraction of the value of loving-kindness."[1] According to the Buddhist concept of 'Brahma-vihāra' one is required to radiate all directions with boundless love or friendliness (mettā) towards all creatures, compassion (karuṇā) for those in distress, rejoicing (muditā) with those who are justly happy and acting with equanimity and impartiality (upekkhā) towards all beings.[2] Those who were to go about preaching the Noble Doctrine were to train themselves in such a way as not to feel angry or agitated even in the face of the strongest provocation or torture.[3] Even indulgence in talk concerning the army or war (senākathaṃ, yuddhakathaṃ) is forbidden to Buddhist monks, for it is considered low, inferior and unconnected with the holy goal.[4] Such talk is included in the twenty-seven topics collectively known as 'tiracchānakathaṃ' which other sects were prone to discuss.[5] Similarly trading in weapons (sattha vaṇijjā) is also included in the forbidden trades.[6]

All this is ample evidence of the fact that war was considered wholly incompatible with the true Buddhist ideal of morality. It must, however, be admitted that the true Buddhist ideal of absolute non-resistance in face of any provocation is extremely difficult to practise for the average ruler or householder. Even Sakka who is portrayed as a great admirer and worshipper of Buddha (S.I. 233-235) and who is found to be so compassionate as to welcome death at the hands of his enemies rather than to save his life by destroying the nests of birds (S. I. 224) is found fighting against demons in defence of peace-loving and righteous gods (S.I. 216-224). The King Pasenadi also who is described by Buddha himself as a friend, helper and companion of goodness (kalyāṇamitto, kalyāṇasahāyo, kalyāṇasampavaṅko, S.I. 83) has to defend himself against the attack of King Ajātasattu who is described as a friend, helper and compan-

1. It. 19-21.
2. M.I. 38.
3. M.I. 129.
4. S.V. 419-420.
5. D.I. 7, 178; III. 54; M.I. 513; II. 1, 23.
6. A. III. 208.

ion of evil (pāpamitto, pāpasahāyo, pāpasampavaṅko, *loc. cit.*). This indicates that a peace-loving defender is considered moderately good, though he still falls short of moral perfection in so far as he wavers from the true Buddhist ideal. That is why Sakka is portrayed as not yet free from lust (A. I. 143) and referring to the war between Pasenadi and Ajātasattu, disapproval and dissatisfaction has been shown by uttering words of censure both for the victor as well as for the vanquished (S.I. 83). In fact, we find no occasion whatsoever when war is approved, appreciated or justified by Buddha. On the contrary he takes every opportunity to express his disapproval and depreciation of war in any shape or form. Miss I.B. Horner, however, feels "surprise...that not more opportunities were taken roundly to condemn fighting," as it was done "to abolish blood sacrifices."[1] But one would do well to remember that there were some important reasons on account of which it was perhaps not possible to do anything more than what was done by Buddha for the condemnation of war. Firstly, as pointed out above, it was very difficult for average kings and people to do without it in the face of attack from other ambitious rulers; secondly, Buddha as an embodiment of peace and love could not but adopt a method of gentle rational persuasion avoiding all situations of strife or conflict with temporal rulers;[2] thirdly, unlike temporal monarchs, he could not pass strictures or impose penalties on the laity for violating the righteous law as he could do in relation to his monastic followers; and fourthly, war was mainly a matter of mundane concern and did not directly affect the man engaged in holy pursuits or religious practices, as blood sacrifices perpetrated in the very name of religion, did.

(*G*) *Conclusion* :—

In the light of what has been said above it is clear that

1. 'Early Buddhism and the Taking of Life' in B.C. Law Vol. Part I. P. 455.

2. It is with a view to avoid such strife and conflict that on the request of King Pasenadi, Buddha asks monks not to ordain soldiers (Vin. I. 73-74). A similar attitude was adopted with regard to the ordination of thieves and robbers (Vin. I. 74).

in the Buddhist ideal of morality there is no room for war and the attitude of Buddhism in this respect is basically different from that of the B.G. The fact that the true Buddhist ideal is difficult to practise in an average society of aggressors and evil-doers, is no excuse for violating the moral ideal which in itself is pure and perfect. If we admit that moral and spiritual truths are valid in their own right, then it is not difficult to decide whether morality should be toned down to suit the corrupt world or the latter should be raised to a more lofty ideal of morality at all costs. Buddha himself is conscious of the fact that "a holy life in all its purity and perfection is not easy to practise while one is leading the life of a householder"[1] and seeking delight in the pleasures of transitory mundane objects.[2] But he does not on that ground shrink from following the right path and realising the highest goal. Indeed, one has to change one's mundane outlook and mend one's misguided ways if one seeks to realise the supramundane ideal, not that the ideal itself should be modified to suit the debased state of man. But the B.G. seems to exhibit somewhat the latter tendency when it advocates the view that a warrior engaged in violent war reaches the same ideal state which is attained by a contemplative seer, practising the life of loving-kindness[3]. It seems patent that the B.G. in its attempt to highlight the worth and importance of worldly duties makes some concessions in the lofty ideals of morality. Without so doing it is perhaps impossible to make violence or war compatible with pure and perfect morality.

It is interesting to see that the incompatibility of violence or war with the pure and perfect life of holiness and renunciation is acknowledged by Gandhi himself, the well-known admirer and follower of the B.G. ideal. After a long and arduous attempt to live up to the ideal of the B.G. he

1. M. I. 179, 240, 267; II. 56.
2. M. II. 62ff; S.I. 117.
3. B.G. V. 2, 5.

expresses his personal experience as follows: "Let it be granted[1] that according to the letter of the Gītā it is possible to say that warfare is consistent with renunciation of fruit. But after forty years' unremitting endeavour full to enforce the teaching of the Gītā in my own life, I have in all humility felt that perfect renunciation is impossible without perfect observance of Ahiṃsā in every shape and form."[2] This frank expression on the part of Gandhi only supports the Buddhist view according to which war is altogether incompatible with the true ideal of morality.

In the light of this it may not be unreasonable to say that early Buddhism endeavours to lift up the mundane man to the supramundane level, whereas the B.G. tries to meet the supramundane on the mundane plane; in the one we have the unwavering allegiance to the ideal, pure and perfect, whereas the other seeks a compromise with the average world. In other words, the former embodies the purest ideal of the recluse life, whereas the latter represents the ideal of the household life at its best.

1. Since Gandhi is personally disinclined to grant the position that the B.G. sanctions actual warfare, he can grant it only hypothetically. We have already shown that he prefers symbolic interpretation of war, mentioned in the B.G.

2. Gītā the Mother, Edited by Jag Parvesh Chander, p. 12.

BIBLIOGRAPHY

1. Original Sources:—

A. Sanskrit Texts and Translations

Aitareya Āraṇyaka : Ed. A.B. Keith, Oxford 1909.
Tr. F. Max Muller, The Upaniṣads, Part I S.B.E. Volume I, Oxford 1879.

Aitareya Brāhmaṇa : Ed. B.G. Apte, A.A.S., Poona 1931.

Aṣṭādhyāyī of Pāṇini : Chaukhambhā Sanskrit Series.

Atharvaveda Saṃhitā : Ed. R. Roth and W.D. Whitney, Berlin, 1924.

Atharvaveda : Tr. Griffith Vol. I & II, 2nd Edition, Benares, 1916-17.

Bhagavadgītā : Gītā Press, Gorakhapur 1926.
Tr. Radhakrishnan, Allen & Unwin, London, 6th Impression 1960.
With Comy. of Śaṅkara, Gītā Press, Gorakhapur, 10th Impression 1961.
With Comy. of Rāmānuja, Gītā Press Gorakhapur. 3rd Impression 1960.

Bhāgavat Purāṇa : Gopal Narain Company, Bombay 1898.

Brahma Sūtra : With Comy. of Śaṅkara, Ed. Narayana Ram Acārya, 3rd Edition, Bombay, 1948.
Tr. G. Thibaut, The Vedānta Sūtras, 2 Vols., S.B.E. Vol. 34 & 38, Oxford 1890 and 1896.
Tr. V.M. Āpte, Bombay 1940.
With Comy. of Rāmānuja, Ed.

and Tr. by R.D. Karmarkar Poona 1959.
As read by different commentators, Ed. N. Goswami, Calcutta 1932.

Bṛhadāraṇyaka Upaniṣad : v. PU.; Comy. of Śaṅkara, V. Śaṅkara's Works.

Buddhacarita : Ed. E.H. Johnston, Part I, Calcutta, 1935.
Tr. E.B. Cowell, S.B.E. Vol. 49, 1894.

Caraka Saṃhitā : With Āyurvedadīpikā, of Cakrapāṇidatta, Ed. N.N. Sastri, 2 Vols., Lahore, 1929.

Chāndogya Upaniṣad : v. PU.; Comy. of Śaṅkara, v. Śaṅkara's Works.

Gopath-Brāhmaṇa : Ed. R. Mitra and H. Vidyabhushana, Bibliotheca Indica, New Series Nos. 251, 252 Calcutta 1872.

Gṛhya-Sūtra of Āśvalāyana : Ed. J.V. Bhaṭṭācārya, Calcutta 1893.
Tr. H. Oldenberg, The Gṛihya Sūtras, S.B.E. 29., Oxford, 1886.

Harivaṃśaparvam : Ed. R. Kinjawadekar, Poona, 1936.

Iśāvāsya Upaniṣad : v. PU.

Jābāla Upaniṣad : v. PU.

Kādambarī of Bāṇabhaṭṭa : Ed. Taranath Tarkavacaspati, Calcutta 1893.

Karṇabhāra, of Bhāsa : Ed. C.R. Devadhara, Poona 1957.

Kaṭha Upaniṣad : v. PU. Ed. and Tr. J.N. Rawson, Oxford University Press 1934.

Kathāsaritasāgara : Ed. Jibananda Vidyasagara, Calcutta, 1883.

Kauṣītakī Brāhmaṇa : Ed. G.R.V. Chaya, A.A.S. No. 65 Rajkot, 1911.

Tr. A.B. Keith, Ṛgveda Brāhmaṇas Translated H.O.S. Vol. 25.

Kauṣītakī Upaniṣad : v. PU.

Kena Upaniṣad : v. PU.

Kumārasambhavam of Kālidāsa : Ed. Rev. K.M. Banerjea, Calcutta, 1867.

Mahābhāratam : 18 Parvas in 4 vols., Gītā Press, Gorakhapur, 1956-58.

Tr. Pratap Chandra Roy, 12 vols. Calcutta, 1955-61.

(Southern Recension), Ed. PPS. Sastri 18 vols. Madras, 1931.

Maitrī Upaniṣad : v. PU.

Māṇḍūkya Upaniṣad : v. PU.

Manusmṛti : With Comy. of Kullūkabhaṭṭa, Ed. Kṣemarāja Śrīkṛṣnadās Śreṣthī

Tr. M.N. Dutta, Calcutta 1909.

Mīmāṃsā Sūtra : With Comy. of Śabarasvāmin, Ed. Pandit Mahesacandra Nyāyaratna, 2 Vols. Bibliotheca Indica, Calcutta, 1873-89.

Tr. G. Jha, SBH, vol. 10 Allahabad 1916.

Tr. M.L. Sandal SBH. Vol. 27 Part I, Allahabad 1923-25.

Muṇḍaka Upaniṣad : v. PU.

Nārada Pāñcarātra :

Nārada Sūtra

Nyāya Sūtra With Nyāyabhāṣya Vātsyāyana, Ed. D.N. Josi, A.A.S No. 91, 1922.

Nyāya Sūtras of Gotama : Ed. and Tr. S.C. Vidyābhūṣaṇa, S B H, Vol. 8, Allahabad, 1913.

Nyāyavārtika Tātparyaṭīkā of Vachaspati Misra : Ed. R. Sastri, Benares, 1925.

Pitṛmedha-Sūtra of Baudhāyana etc. : Ed. W. Caland, Leipzig, Brockhaus, 1896.

Praśna Upaniṣad : v. PU.

Raghuvaṃśa of Kālidāsa : With Mallinātha's Comy. Ed. M. R. Kale, 4th Edition, Bombay 1925.

Ṛgvedasaṃhitā : With Comy. of Sāyaṇa. Ed. F. Max Muller, 6 Vols., London, 1849-74.
Tr. R.T.H. Griffith, The Hymns of the Ṛgveda 4 Vols. Benares, 1889-92.

Saddharmapuṇḍarīka : Ed. P. L. Vaidya, Darbhanga, 1960.

Śāṇḍilya Sūtra : Tr. E. B. Cowell, Bibliotheca Indica, Calcutta, 1878

Śaṅkara's Works : 20 vols. Śri Vani Vilas Edition, Srirangam 1910.

Sāṅkhya-Karikā of Iśvarakṛṣṇa : Ed. S. N. Shastri, University of Madras 1948.

Sarvadarśanasaṅgraha : Ed. V.S. Abhyaṅkara, 3rd Edition, Poona 1951.
Tr. E.B. Cowell, London, 188 .

Sarvārthasiddhi of Pujyapāda : Ed. Vanshidhar Pandit, Merath, 1938.

Śatapatha Brāhmaṇa : 2 Vols. Acyutagranthamālā Kāryālaya, Kāśī, 1937-40.
Tr. J. Eggeling, 5 parts, S.B.E. Vols. 12, 26, 41, 43, 44, 1882-1900.

Saundarananda of Aśvaghoṣa : Ed. E. H. Johnston, Oxford University Press, London, 1928.

Ślokavārtika of Kumārila Bhaṭṭa : With Comy. (Nyāyaratnākara)Ed. R.S. Tailaṅga, Benares, 1898.

Śvetāśvatara Upaniṣad : v. PU.

Taittirīya Āraṇyaka : Ed. B.S. Phaḍake, IInd Edition, 2 Vols., A.A.S. No. 36, 1926-7.

Taittirīya Brāhmaṇa : Ed. Narāyaṇa Śāstrī, 3 Vols. A.A.S. No. 37, 1934-38.

Taittirīya Upaniṣad : v. PU.

Tarkasaṅgraha of Annambhaṭṭa : Ed. Y. V. Athalya, Bombay Sanskrit Series, No. 55, Bombay, 1930.

Tattvārthādhigama Sutta : Ed. and Tr. J. L. Jaini, Jain Publishing House, Arrah,

Tattvasaṅgraha with Tattvasaṅgrahapañjikā of Kamalaśīla : Ed. E. Krshnamacarya, 2 Vols., Gaekwad's Oriental Series, Nos. 30 and 31, Baroda, 1926.
Tr. Ganganath Jha, 2 Vols. Gaekwad's Oriental Series, Nos. 80 and 83, Baroda, 1937-39.

Upaniṣads : Ed. and Tr. S. Radhakrishnan, The Principal Upaniṣads, London, 1953.
Tr. F. Max Muller, The Upaniṣads Part I, S.B.E. Vol. I., Oxford, 1879.
Tr. R.E. Hume, The Thirteen Principal Upaniṣads, 2nd. Edition, Oxford University Press, 1934.
with Comy. of Śaṅkara, V. Śaṅkara's Works.

Yajur Veda Tr. R. T. H. Griffith, Benares, 1899.

Yoga Sūtras : Ed. and Tr. R. Prasad, 3rd Edition, SBH, Vol. 4., Allahabad, 1924.

Vedānta Sāra of Sadānand : Tr. Nikhilanand Swami, Advaita Ashram, Mayavati, 1949.

Viṣṇu Purāṇa : Ed. Jivanand Vidyasagar Bhaṭṭacharya, Calcutta, 1882.

B. Pali Texts and Translations

Aṅguttara Nikāya : Ed. R. Morris and E. Hardy, 5 Vols. PTS., London, 1885-1900.
Tr. F. L. Woodward and E. M. Hare. The Book of the

Gradual Sayings 5, Vols. P. T.S. London, 1932-36.

Dhammapada : Ed. S. Sumangala Thera, P.T.S., London, 1914.

Dhammasaṅgaṇi : Ed. E. Muller, London, 1885.

Dīgha Nikāya : Ed. T.W. Rhys Davids and J.E. Carpenter, 3 Vols., P.T.S., London, 1890-1911.

Tr. T.W. Rhys Davids and C.A.F. Rhys Davids, Dialogues of the Buddha, S.B.B., Vols. 2, 3 and 4, Oxford University Press. 1899-1921.

Dīpavaṃsa : Ed. and Tr. H. Oldenberg, William and Norgate, Edinburgh, 1879.

Itivuttaka : Ed. E. Windisch, P.T.S., London, 1889.

Jātaka : Ed. V. Fausboll, 6 Vols. and Index, London, 1895-1907.

Kathāvatthu : Ed. A.C. Taylor, 2 Vols. P.T.S., London, 1894-97.

Tr. S.Z. Aung and C.A.F. Rhys Davids 'Points of Controversy', P.T.S., London, 1915.

Khuddakapāṭha : Ed. H. Smith, P.T.S., London, 1915.

Mahābodhivaṃsa : Ed. S.A. Strong, P.T.S., London, 1891.

Mahāvaṃsa : Ed. W. Geiger, P.T.S., London, 1958.

Majjhima Nikāya : Ed. V. Trenkner and R. Chalmers, 3 Vols. P.T.S. London, 1948-51.

Tr. I.B. Horner, Middle Length Sayings, 3 Vols. P.T.S, London, 1954-9.

Tr. R. Chalmers, Further Dialogues of the Buddha, 2 Vols. P.T.S., London, 1888.

Manorathapūraṇī : Comy. to Aṅguttara Nikāya, Ed. M. Walleser and H. Kopp, 5 Vols. P.T.S., London, 1924-56.

Milindapañha : Ed. V. Trenkner, Londo ı, 1928.

Nettippakaraṇa : Ed. E. Hardy, P.T.S., London, 1902.

Niddesa I—Mahāniddesa, : Ed. L. de La. Vallee Poussin and E.J. Thomas, 2 Vols.;

II—Cullaniddesa, Ed. W. Stede, P.T.S., London, 1916-18.

Papañcasūdanī : Comy. to Majjhima, Nikāya, Ed. J.H. Woods, D. Kosambi and I.B. Horner, 5 Vols., P.T.S., London, 1922-38.

Paramatthadīpanī : Comy. to Khuddaka Nikāya, Part III (to Petavatthu) Ed. E. Hardy, P.T.S., London, 1894.

Comy. to Udāna (part not mentioned), Ed. F.L. Woodward, P.T.S., London, 1926.

Paramatthajotikā II : Comy. to Suttanipāta, Ed. H. Smith, 3 Vols., P.T.S., London, 1916-18.

Paṭisambhidāmagga : Ed. A.C. Taylor, 2 Vols. P.T.S., London, 1905-7.

Puggalapaññatti : Ed. R. Morris, London, 1883.

Samantapāsādikā : Ed. J. Taka Kusu, P.T.S., London, 1924.

Sammohavinodanī : Comy. to Vibhaṅga, Ed. A.P. Buddhadatta Thera, P.T.S., London, 1923.

Saṃyutta Nikāya : Ed. L. Feer, 6 Vols., P.T.S., London, 1884-1904.

Tr. C.A.F. Rhys Davids and F.L. Woodward, The Book of the Kindred Sayings, 5 Vols., P.T.S. London, 1917-30.

Sāratthappakāsinī : Comy. to Saṃyutta Nikāya, Ed. F.L. Woodward, 3 Vols., P.T.S., London, 1929-37.

Sāsanavaṃsa : Ed. M. Bode, P.T.S., London, 1897.

Sumaṅgalavilāsinī : Comy. to Dīgha Nikāya, Ed. T.W. Rhys Davids, J.E. Carpenter and W. Stede 3 Vols., P.T.S., London, 1886-1932.

Suttanipāta : Ed. D. Anderson and H. Smith, P.T.S., London 1948.
Tr. V. Fausboll, S. B. E. Vol. 10, Part 2, Oxford, 1881.

Thera-and Therīgāthā : Ed. H. Oldenberg and R. Pischel, P.T.S., London, 1883.
Tr. C.A.F. Rhys Davids, Psalms of the Early Buddhists, 2 Vols., P.T.S., London, 1903-1913.

Udāna : Ed. P. Steinthal, P.T.S. London, 1948.

Vibhaṅga : Ed. C.A.F., Rhys Davids, P.T.S., London, 1904.

Vinaya Piṭaka ; Ed. H. Oldenberg, 5 Vols., London, 1879-83.
Tr. T. W. Rhys Davids and H. Oldenberg, S.B.E., Vols. 13, 17, 20, Oxford 1881-1885.

Visuddhimagga of Buddhaghosa : Ed. C.A.F. Rhys Davids, 2 Vols., London, 1920-21.

Yamaka : Ed. C.A.F. Rhys Davids, M. C. Foley, M. Hunt and M. Smith, 2 Vols., P. T. S., London, 1911-13.

C. Prakrit Texts and Translations.

Āyāraṅga Sutta : Ed. H. Jacobi, Part I (Text), London, 1882. Tr. H. Jacobi, Jain Sūtras, Part I (Ācāraṅga and Kalpa), S.B.E. Vol. 22, Oxford, 1884.

Bhagavatī Sūtra : with the Comy. (vṛtti) of Abhayadeva. Ed. S. C. P. Jhaveri and S. Keśarīmalajī, 2 Vols.; Vol. I, Surat, 1937; Vol. II Jamnagar, 1940.

Samavāyāṅga Sūtra : with the Comy. (Vivaraṇa) of Abhayadeva, Ed. N. Nemachandra, Ahmedabad, 1938.

Sthānāṅga Sūtra : Ed. V. Surachandra, 2 Vols., Bombay, 1918-20.

Sūtrakṛtaṅga : with the Comy. (Vivaraṇa) of Śilāṅka, Ed. A. S. Sūri and C. Gaṇīndra, 2 Vols., Bhāvanagar, 1950-53.
Tr. H. Jacobi, Jain Sūtras, Part II (Uttarādhyayana and Sūtrakṛtāṅga) S.B.E. Vol. 45, Oxford, 1895.

Uttarādhyayana Sūtra : Ed. R.D. Vadekar and N. V. Vaidya, Poona 1954.
Tr. H.Jacobi, V. Jain Sūtras; Part II, S. B. E. Vol. 45 Oxford, 1895.

II. Secondary Authorities :—

A. Reference Books

Buddhist Hybrid Sanskrit Dictionary, Ed. F. Edgerton, New Haven and London, 1953.

Concise Oxford Dictionary, Ed. H.W. Fowler and F.G. Fowler, 4th Edition revised by E. McIntosh, Oxford, 1959.

Concordance to the Principal Upanishads and Bhagavadgītā, by G A. Jacob, Bombay, 1891.

Critical Pali Dictionary, Ed. V Trenckner, D. Anderson, H. Smith and H. Hendriksen, Vol. I, Copenhagen, 1924-48.

Critical Word-Index to the Bhagavadgītā, by R. B. Prahlad, C. Divanji, Bombay, 1946.

Dictionary of Pali Proper Names, Ed. G. P. Malalasekera, 2 Vols. London, 1937-8.

Dictionary of Philosophy, Ed. D. Runes, London, 1945.

Dictionary of Philosophy and Psychology, Ed. J. H. Baldwin, 3 Vols., New York, 1940-9.

Encyclopaedia of Religion and Ethics, Ed. J. Hastings, 12 Vols., Edinburgh, 1908-1926.

Index to the Names in the Mahābhārata With Concordance, Ed. S. Soresen, London, 1904.

Pali Text Society's Pali-English Dictionary, Ed. T. W. Rhys Davids and W. Stede, London, reprinted, 1959.

Sanskrit-English Dictionary, Ed. M. Monier—Williams. Oxford, 1899.

Vedic Concordance, by M. Bloomfield, Cambridge, Massachusetts, 1906.

Vedic Index of Names and Subjects, by A. A. Macdonell and A. B. Keith, 2 Vols., London, 1912.

B. Monographs

Bahm, A. J., *Philosophy of the Buddha*, London, 1958,

Bapat, P. B., *2500 years of Buddhism*, New Delhi, 1956.

Barth, *Religions of India*, Tr. by Rev. J. Wood, 3rd Edition, London, 1891.

Basham, A. L., *History and Doctrines of the Ājīvikas*, London, 1951.

Barua, B. M., *Bharhut Inscriptions*, University of Calcutta, 1926; *A History of Pre-Buddhistic Indian Philosophy*, Calcutta, 1921.

Beal, Samuel, *Buddhist Records of the Western World*, Kegan Paul, Date ?

Beckh, H., *Buddhismus*, Vol. I, Berlin und Leipzig, 1919.

Belvalkar, S. K. and Ranade, R. D., *History of Indian Philosophy*, Vol. II, Poona, 1927.

Bhandarkar, D. R., *Aśoka, Carmichael Lectures*, University of Calcutta, 1925, 1955.

Bhandarkar, R. G., *Collected Works of R. G. Bhandarkar*, Vol IV. Ed. N. B. Utgikar, Poona, 1929.
Vaiṣṇavism, Śaivism and Minor Religious System, Strassburg, 1913.

Bhattacharya, V., *The Basic Conception of Buddhism*, Calcutta, 1934.

Buhler, George, *Dharma Sūtras*, S. B. E. Vol. II and XIV, Oxford 1879 and 1882.

Burnell, A. C., *Sāmavidhāna Brāhmaṇa* (with Text and Comy. of Sāyaṇa), London, 1873.

Chatterjee, S. C.; *The Nyāya Theory of Knowledge*, Calcutta, 1939.

Chatterjee, S. C. and Datta, D. M., *An Introduction to Indian Philosophy*, 4th Edition, Calcutta, 1950.

Colebrook, H. T., *Miscellaneous Essays*, Vol. I, London, 1873.

Coomaraswamy, A. K. and Horner, I. B., *The living Thoughts of Gotama, the Buddha*, London, 1949.

Copleston, R. S., *Buddhism, Primitive and Present*, 2nd Edition, London, 1908.

Dasgupta, S. N., *A History of Indian Philosophy*, Vol. I and II reprint, Cambridge University Press, 1957 and 1961.

Datta, D. M. *The Chief Currents of Contemporary Philosophy*, 2nd Edition, Calcutta, 1961. *An Introduction of Indian Philosophy*, V. S. C. Chatterjee.

Deussen, P., *The Philosophy of the Upaniṣads*, Tr. A. S. Gedden, Edinburgh, 1906.

Dutt, N., *Early Monastic Buddhism*, Vol. I and II, Calcutta, 1941. *Early History of the Spread of Buddhism and the Buddhist School*, London, 1925.

Dutta, S. K., *Early Buddhist Monachism*, London, 1924.

Edgerton, F., *The Bhagavadgītā or Song of the Blessed One*, Chicago, 1925. *The Bhagavadgītā Parts I and II*, H. O. S. Vols. 38 and 39, London, 1944.

Eliot, Sir Charles, *Hinduism and Buddhism*, Vol. I, London, 1921.

Farquhar, J. N., *An Outline of the Religious Literature of India*, Oxford University Press, 1920.

Fick, R., *The Social Organisation in North-East India in Buddha's Time.*

Fleet, J. F., *Corpus Inscriptinum Indicarum*, Vol. III, Calcutta, 1888. Tr. by S. Maitra, Calcutta, 1920.

Gandhi, M. K., *Gītā, the Mother*, Ed. Jag Parvesh Chander, Lahore, 1931.

Garbe, R., *Die Bhagavadgītā* (Introduction),
Tr. N. B. Utgikar in I. A. Vol. 47, Supplement, Bombay, 1918.
Die Sāṅkhya Philosophie, Leipzig Haessel, 1894.

Geiger, W., *The Mahāvaṃsa*, Tr. Oxford University Press, London, 1934.

Ghurye, G. S. *Caste and Race in India*, London, 1932.

Glasenapp, H. von., *Vedānta and Buddhism, Kandy*, 1958.

Grimm, George, *The Doctrine of the Buddha*, 2nd revised Edition, Berlin, 1958.

Hall, Fitz-Edward, *Sāṅkhyasāra, Asiatic Society of Bengal*, Calcutta, 1862.
Vāsavadattā, Calcutta, 1859.

Hill, W. D. P., *The Bhagavadgītā*, London, 1928.

Hiriyanna M., *Outlines of Indian Philosophy*, 4th Impression, London, 1958.

Hultzsch, E., *Inscriptions of Aśoka*, Corpus Inscription Indicarum, Vol. I, Oxford, 1925.

Hume, David, *Inquiries concerning Human Understanding*, Part II, The World Library Edition.

Hume, R. E., *The Thirteen Principal Upaniṣads*, London, 1934.

Hopkins, E. W., *Religions of India*, Boston, 1895. *The Great Epic of India*, New Haven, Reprinted 1920.

Jayatilleke, K. N. *Early Buddhist Theory of Knowledge*, Allen and Unwin, London, 1963. *Buddhism and Peace*, Kandy, 1962. (with Malalasekera G. P.) Buddhism and the Race Question, Unesco, Paris, 1958.

Jennings, J. G., *The Vedantic Buddhism of the Buddha*, London, 1947.

Keith, A. B., *Indian Logic and Atomism*, Oxford, 1921. *A History of Sanskrit Literature* Oxford 1928. *Religion and Philosophy of the Veda and Upaniṣads* H. O. S.

Vol. 31 and 32, Oxford University Press, London 1925. *Buddhist Philosophy in India and Ceylon*, Oxford, 1923.

Kern, H., *Manual of Indian Buddhism*, Strassburg, 1896.

Law, B. C., *Buddhistic Studies*, Calcutta, 1931.

Legge, James, *A Record of Buddhistic Kingdoms*, Oxford, 1886.

Lindquist, S., *Siddhi und Abhiññā*, Lund, 1935.

Lovell, A. C. B., *The Individual and the Universe*, London, 1959.

Lorinser, *Die Bhagavadgītā*, *Tr.* in I. A., Vol. II, Bombay 1873.

Macdonell, A. A., *A History of Sanskrit Literature*, London, 1917. *Vedic Mythology*, Strassburg, 1897.

Maclay, E. J. H., *The Indus Civilization*, London, 1935.

Maisey, F. C., *Sāñchi and its Remains*, London, 1892.

Majumdar, R. C., and Pusalker, A. D., *The Vedic Age*, London, 1951.

Malalasekera, G. P., *The Pali Literature of Ceylon*, London, 1928. v. K. N. Jayatilleke, '*Buddhism and the Race Question*'.

Marshall, John, *A Guide to Sānchi*, Calcutta 1918. *Mohenjodaro and the Indus Civilization*, Probsthain, 1931.

Martineau James, *Types of Ethical Theory*, Vols. I and II. 2nd Edition, Oxford, 1886.

Max Muller, F. *Sacred Books of the East*, Vol. 10 2nd Edition, London, 1924. *Hilbert Lectures on the Origin and Growth of Religion*, 2nd Edition, Longmanns, Green, 1878. *A History of Ancient Sanskrit Literature*, 2nd Edition, London, 1860.

M'Crindle, J. W., *Ancient India*; Its Invasion by Alexander, the Great, Westminster, 1862.

Mill, J. S., *A System of Logic*, London, 1884.

Minayeff, J. P., *Recherches sur le Buddhisme*, Paris, 1894.

Muller, E., *Ancient Inscriptions in Ceylon*, London, 1883.

Murti. T. R. V., *The Central Philosophy of Buddhism*, London, 1955.

Nanjio, A., Bunyiu, *Catalogue of the Chinese Translation of the Buddhist Tipiṭaka*, Oxford, 1883.

Nārada Thera, *Buddhism in a Nutshell*, New York, 1959.

Nyānaponika Thera, *Anattā and Nibbāna*, Kandy, 1959.
Advice to Rahula (Introduction), Kandy, 1961.

Nataraja Guru, *The Bhagavadgītā*, Asia Publishing House, Bombay, 1961.

Oldenberg, Buddha, Tr. William Hoey, Calcutta, 1927. *Die Lehre der Upanishaden und die Anfange des Buddhismus*, Gottingen, 1915. *Die Religion des Veda*, 7th Edition, Stuttgart J. G. Cotta'sche, Buch, 1950.

Opik, E. J., *The Oscillating Universe*, New York, 1960.

Omam, J. C., *Brahman Theists and Muslims of India*, London, 1907.

Pande, G. C., *Studies in the Origins of Buddhism*, Allahabad, 1957.

Piggott, S., *Pre-Historic India*, Harmondsworth, 1950.

Poussin, L dela V., *Buddhisme*, Gabriel Beauchesne, 1925.
The Way to Nirvāṇa, Cambridge University Press, 1917.

Pratt, J. B. *Pilgrimage of Buddhism and a Buddhist Pilgrimage*, London, 1920.

Pusalker, A.D. and Majumdar R.C., *The Vedic Age*, London, 1951.

Radhakrishnan, S., *Indian Philosophy*, Vols. I and II, 8th Impression, London, 1958.
The Bhagavadgītā, 6th Impression, London, 1960.
The Dhammapada, reprinted, London, 1958.

Ranade, R.D. *The Bhagavadgītā as a Philosophy of God-Realisation*, Nagpur University, 1959.
Constructive Survey of the Upaniṣadic Philosophy, Poona, 1926.
History of Indian Philosophy, Vol. II, V. S. K. Belvalkar.

Rapson, J. P., *The Cambridge History of India*, Vols. I and II, Delhi, 1925.

Ray Chaudhury, H.C., *The Political History of Ancient India*, Calcutta, 1955.

Rhys Davids C.A.F., *Buddhism*, London, 1912.
Wayfarer's Words, 3 Vols. London, 1940-42.
Buddhism; its Birth and Dispersal.,
The Home University Library of Modern Knowledge, 4th revised Edition, London, 1934.

Outlines of Buddhism, London 1934.
Śākya or Buddhist Origins, London, 1931.

Rhys Davids, T.W., *Origin and Growth of Religion*, London, 1881. *Buddhist Suttas*, S.B.E. Vol. 11, Oxford, 1900. *Buddhist India*, London, 1903.

Rockhill, W.W., *The life of the Buddha and Early History of His Order*, Trubner's Oriental Series, 1884.

Rudolf Otto, *The Original Gītā*, Tr. J.E. Turner, London, 1939.

Russell, B.A.W., *A History of Western Philosophy*, 3rd Impression, London, 1958.

Ryle, G. *The Concept of Mind*, London, 1950.

Sarathchandra, E.R., *Buddhist Psychology of perception*, Colombo, 1958.

Schweitzer, A. *Indian Thought and Its Development*, London, 1951.

Senart, *Mahāvastu Avadāna*, Paris, 1924.

Sharma, C.D., *Indian Philosophy*, Banaras, 1952.

Smith, V.A., *A History of Fine Arts in India and Ceylon. The Early History of India*, 4th Edition, Oxford, 1924.

Stcherbatsky, Th., *The Conception of Buddhist Nirvāṇa.*, Leningrad, 1927.

Stebbing, L.S., *A Modern Introduction to Logic*, London, 1945.

Tachibana, S., *The Ethics of Buddhism*, Colombo, 1943.

Tatia, N., *Studies in Jain Philosophy*, Banaras, 1951.

Telang, K.T., *The Bhagavadgītā with Sanatsugatiya and the Anugītā*, S.B.E., Vol. VIII, 2nd Edition, Oxford, 1908.

Thibaut, *The Vedānta Sūtras with Comy. of Śaṅkara*, S.B.E. Vol. 34, Oxford, 1890.

Thomas, E.J., *The History of Buddhist Thought*, London, 1959. *The Life of the Buddha*, 3rd Edition, reprinted, London, 1956.

Tilak, B.G., *Śrimad Bhagavadgītā Rahasya* (Karmayoga Śāstra) 5th Hindi Impression, Poona, 1925.

Vidyabhusana, S.C., *A History of Indian Logic*, Calcutta, 1921.

Vireswarananda Swami, *Brahma Sūtras*, Almora, 1936.

Weber, A., *The History of Indian Literature*, 44th Edition, Popular re-issue, Trubner's Oriental Series, London. 1914.

Wheeler, J. Talboys, *The History of India*, Vol. I, London, 1869.

Wheeler, M., *The Indus Civilization*, London, 1953.

Whitehead, A.N., *Process and Reality*, Cambridge University Press, 1929.

Wickremasinghe, M. de Z. Ed. and Tr. *Epigraphia Zeylanica*, Vol. I, Oxford University Press, London, 1912.

Wijesekera, O.H., de A., *The Three Signata*, Kandy, 1960.

Winternitz, M., *A History of Indian Literature*, Vols. I and II Tr. Mrs. S. Ketkar and Miss H. Kohn, Calcutta, 1927 and 1933.

Wittgenstein, L., *The Blue and Brown Books*, Oxford, 1958. Tractatus Logico-Philosophicus, London, 1933.

Wundt, W., *Ethical Systems*, Tr. Margaret Floey, Washburn, London, 1917.

C. Articles

Aiyar, K.G. Śaṅkara, '*The Hathigumpha Cave Inscription on Khāravela*' in I.A. Vol. 49, Bombay, 1920.

Aiyer, V.G., "*The Date of the Buddha*" in I.A. Vol. 37, Bombay, 1908.

Barnett, L.D., '*The Plays Ascribed to Bhāsa and the Matta Vilāsa*' in J.R.A.S., London. 1919.

Barua, B.M., '*Faith in Buddhism*' in *Buddhistic Studies*, Ed. B.C. Law Calcutta, 1931.

Bhandarkar, R.G., '*A Peep into the Early History of India*' in J.B.B.R.A.S. (Bombay Branch of the Royal Asiatic Society), Vol. II.

Buhler, G., '*Asoka—Inschriften*' in Z.D.M.G., Vol. 48, Leipzig. 1894. *Note on Professor Jacobi's Age of the Veda and on Professor Tilak's Orion*' in I.A. Vol. 23, Bombay, 1898.

Chalmers, R. '*The Madhura Sutta Concerning Caste*' in J.R.A.S. 1894.

Chanda, R.P., '*Date of Khāravela*', in I.A. Vol. 48, Bombay. 1919.

Charpentier, J., '*The Date of Mahāvīra*' in I.A. Vol. 43, Bombay, 1914.

Chatterji, S.K. '*Race Movements and Pre-Historic Culture*' *in the*

Vedic Age, Ed. Majumdar, R.C. and Pusalker, A.D., London, 1951.

Chattopadhyaya, K., *Presidential Address in the Vedic Section*; in 'Proceedings and Transactions of the 9th A.I.O.C. (All India Oriental Congress)', Trivandrum, 1937.
'*Dāsa and Dasyu in Ṛgveda Saṃhitā*' in Proceedings of the 29th International Congress of Orientalists, held at Rome, 1935.

Dasgupta, Miss Mrinal, '*Śraddhā and Bhakti in Vedic Literature*' in I.H.Q. Vol. 6, Calcutta, 1930.

Dutt, N. '*Place of Faith in Buddhism*' in I.H.Q., Vol. 16.

Edgerton, F., '*The Kashmir Recension of the Bhagavadgītā*' in J.A.O.S. Vol. 52, New Haven, 1932.

Fleet, J. F., '*The Day on which Buddha Died*' in J.R.A.S., London, 1909.
'*Sanskrit and Old Canarese Inscriptions*' in I.A. Vol. 5, Bombay, 1876.
'*The Origin of the Buddhavarsha*', in J.R.A.S., London, 1909.
'*The Last Words of Ashoka*' *in* J.R.A.S., London, 1909.

Flew, A., '*Divine Omnipotence and Human Freedom*' in 'New Essays in Philosophical Theology' Ed. Antony Flew and Alasdair Macintyre, 2nd Edition, London, 1958.

Franke, R.O., '*The Buddhist Councils at Rajagaha and Vesali*' in J.P.T.S. London, 1908. *Die Buddhalehre in ihrer erreichliar altesten*, Gestalt, Z.D.M.G. Vol. 69. 1915.

Gyomroi-Ludowyk, E., '*The Valuation of Saddha in the Early Buddhist Texts*' in U.C.R. Vol 5.

Hardy, E. '*On a Passage in the Bhabra Edict*' in J.R.A.S. Vol. 22, London, 1901.

Horner, I.B., '*Early Buddhism and the Taking of Life*' in B.C. Law Volume, Part I, Calcutta, 1945.

Hultzsch, E., '*Ueber eine Sammlung indischer Handschriften und Inschriften*' in Z.D.M.G. Vol. 40, Leipzig, 1886.
'*Contribution to Sinhalese Chronology*' in J.R.A.S. 1913.

Hume, R.E., '*Miracles in the Canonical Scriptures in Buddhism*' in J.A.O.S., Vol. 44.

Jayaswal, K.P., '*Vaiṣṇava Worship and Buddhism*' in I.A., Vol. 47, Bombay, 1918 '*The Śaiśunaka and Maurya Chronology and the Date of the Buddha's Nirvāṇa*' in J.B.O.R.S., Vol. I, Patna 1915., *Hāthīgumphā Inscription Revised from the Rock*' in J.B.O.R.S. Vol. IV, Patna, 1918.

Jayatilleke, K.N., '*Some Aspects of Gītā and Buddhist Ethics*' in U.C.R., Vol. XIII, Nos. 2 and 3, 1955. '*The Buddhist Concept of Truth*' *in Knowledge and Conduct*, Kandy 1963.

Keith, A.B., '*The Śaubhikas and Indian Drama*' in B.S.O.S., London, 1920.

Majumdar, R.C., '*Hāthīgumphā Inscription*' in I.A., Vol. 47, Bombay, 1918.

'*Second Note on the Hāthīgumphā Inscription of Khāravela*' in I.A., Vol. 48, Bombay 1919.

Mitra, K.N., '*The Evolution of Vaiṣṇavism*' in B.C. Law, Vol. I, Calcutta, 1945.

Normal, H.C., '*A Defence of the Chronicles of the Southern Buddhists*' in J.R.A.S., 1908.

Oldenberg, '*Buddhistische Studien*' in Z.D.M.G., Vol. 52, Leipzig, 1898.

Paranavitana, S., '*The Buddhist Era in Ceylon*' in U.C.R. Vol. XVIII, Nos. 3 and 4, Colombo, 1960.

Poussin, L. de la V., '*The Buddhist*' in I.A. Vol. 37, Bombay, 1908 '*Faith and Reason in Buddhism*' in Transaction of the Third International Congress for the History of Religions, Vol.2, 1908.

Ray Chaudhury, H.C., '*Some Problems of Early Maurya History and Chronology*' in Indian Culture, Vol. 2, Calcutta, 1935-6.

Rhys Davids, '*The Sects of the Buddhists*' in J.R.A.S. London, 1891.

Sarup, L., '*The Ṛgveda and Mohenjodaro*' in Indian Culture, Vol. 4, Calcutta, 1937-38.

Senart. E., '*Origines Bouddhiques*' Tr. Manoranjan Roy in I.H.Q. Vol. 6. Calcutta, 1931.

Seneviratne, M., '*Translation of Sylvain Levi's Paper*' in Journal of the Ceylon Branch of the Royal Asiatic Society, Vol. 24 (No. 68) 1935-6.

Shastri, Nilakantha, '*A Historical Sketch of Śaivism*' *in Cultural Heritage of India*, Vol. II, Calcutta, 1935.

Shastri, Mahamahopadhyaya Haraprasad, '*History of Nyāya Śāstra from Japanese Sources*' in J.A.S. of Bengal, 1905.

Smith, V.A., '*The Identity of Piyadassi with Aśoka Maurya and Some Connected Problems*' in J.R.A.S., 1901. '*New Light on Ancient India*' in J.R.A.S. 1918.

Takakusu, J., '*Pali Elements in Chinese Buddhism*' in J.R.A.S., London, 1896. '*The Abhidhamma Literature: Pali and Chinese* in J.R.A.S. London, 1905.

Thomas, F.W. '*Verse Quotation by Aśoka* in J.R.A.S. London, 1903.

Waddell, L.A., '*Date of Bharahut Stupa Cultures*' in J.R.A.S. London, 1941.

Wijesekera, O.H. de A., '*Buddhist Ethics*' *in Knowledge and Conduct*', Kandy, 1963.
'*Vedic Gandharva and Pali Gandhabba*' in U C.R., Vol. III, No. 1, Colombo. 1945.

INDEX